The Politics of Innovation

The Politics of Innovation

Why Some Countries Are Better Than Others at Science and Technology

MARK ZACHARY TAYLOR

OXFORD
UNIVERSITY PRESS

OXFORD
UNIVERSITY PRESS

Oxford University Press is a department of the University of Oxford. It furthers the University's objective of excellence in research, scholarship, and education by publishing worldwide. Oxford is a registered trade mark of Oxford University Press in the UK and certain other countries.

Published in the United States of America by Oxford University Press
198 Madison Avenue, New York, NY 10016, United States of America.

Library of Congress Cataloging-in-Publication Data
Names: Taylor, Mark Zachary.
Title: The politics of innovation: why some countries are better than others
at science and technology / Mark Zachary Taylor.
Description: New York, NY: Oxford University Press, [2016]
| Includes bibliographical references and index.
Identifiers: LCCN 2015043791 (print) | LCCN 2015045387 (ebook)
| ISBN 978–0–19–046412–7 (hardcover: alk. paper) | ISBN 978–0–19–046413–4 (pbk.: alk. paper)
| ISBN 978–0–19–046414–1 (E-book) | ISBN 978–0–19–046415–8 (E-book)
| ISBN 978–0–19–060925–2 (Online Component)
Subjects: LCSH: Science and state. | Technology and state.
Classification: LCC Q125 .T34 2016 (print) | LCC Q125 (ebook)
| DDC 338.9/26—dc23
LC record available at http://lccn.loc.gov/2015043791

This book is dedicated to D. Allan Bromley, who dared to take a risk on me when I was young and overly ambitious; and to James Burke, Joel Mokyr, and Richard R. Nelson, who have for years inspired me with fascinating scholarship and wonderful prose.

CONTENTS

ACKNOWLEDGMENTS

First and foremost, thanks to Dan Winship, my friends, and my family, who supported (and tolerated) me during the tumultuous years of writing this book. Without them, it simply could not have been written.

To my mentors who have supported me throughout the very tough process of building my research program which led to this book, I wish to thank: Dan Breznitz, Richard Doner, David Hart, Julia Lane, Michael Piore, and J. P. Singh.

An enormous debt is also owed to those leading scholars who took the time to give me guidance and advice over the years: Alice Amsden, Sheila Jasanoff, Loet Leydesdorff, Robert Litan, Ben Martin, Joel Mokyr, Richard R. Nelson, Daniel Sarewitz, Phil Shapira, Merritt Roe Smith, Robert Solow, and Paula Stephan.

People who thoughtfully read and critique entire drafts of manuscripts deserve a special place in the afterlife. I give my nominations to Roselyn Hsueh, David McBride, Michael Murphree, Abe Newman, Darius Ornston, and Dan Winship.

Each individual chapter has its own specialty and focus. To those experts who read and advised me in their particular subject area, I give thanks to: Dan Breznitz, Chappell Lawson, Austin Long, Sean O'Riain, Michael Piore, Jeremy Pressman, Jonathan Rodden, Lawrence Rubin, Andrew Schrank, James Snyder, and Adam Stulberg. For their advice on the introduction, I also thank Mia Bloom, Jenna Jordan, and Scott Winship. Much appreciation also goes to Chad Stolper who assisted in bringing my tables and figures up to professional quality.

To those who pointed me toward important resources or provided valuable advice over the years, I thank: Jonathan D. Aronson, David Art, Paul Baker, Suzanne Berger, Chris Bosso, Shiri Breznitz, David Burbach, Clayton Christensen, Diego Comin, Peter F. Cowhey, Susan Cozzens, Mary Daly, Steven Epstein, Miki Fabry, Kaye Husbands Fealing, Harvey B. Feigenbaum, Maryann Feldman, Kenneth Flamm, Erica Fuchs, Jeffrey L. Furman, James K. Galbraith, John Garver, Eugene Gholz, Benoit Godin, Christopher Gore, Peter Gourevitch,

Frederick Gregory, David Guston, Daniel Gutierrez-Sandoval, Stephan Haggard, Peter A. Hall, Patrick Hamlett, Robert Hancké, Justin Hastings, Diana Hicks, Robert Higgens, Hugo Hollanders, Patrick Honohan, Michael Horowitz, Adam Jaffe, Martin Kenney, So Young Kim, David Knoke, Kei Koizumi, Frank Laird, Josh Lerner, Loet Leydesdorff, Lars Magnusson, Cathie Jo Martin, Ron Martin, Kathleen McNamara, Helen Milner, Gautam Mukunda, Dan Nexon, Cormac ÓGráda, Kenneth Oye, Roger Pielke Jr., Gordon Reikard, Paul Rich, Dani Rodrik, Petri Rouvinen, Neil Ruiz, Richard Samuels, Harvey Sapolsky, Henry Sauermann, Stuart Schulman, Susan Sell, Kenneth Sherrill, Eugene Skolnikoff, David Soskice, Erik Stam, Cassandra M. Sweet, Jeremy and Marie Thursby, Sean Twombly, Steven Usselman, Stacy van Deveer, Chris van Egeraat, Eric von Hippel, James Vreeland, Caroline Wagner, Anne and John Walsh, Catherine Weaver, Josh Whitford, Joseph Wong, Jan Youtie, Amos Zehavi, Rosemarie Ziedonis, and John Zysman. And to the countless others who helped along the way but whom I failed to recognize, my thanks and apologies.

I would also like to thank for their material support Yale University, the Massachusetts Institute of Technology, the National Science Foundation, the Kauffman Foundation, the European Union Centers of Excellence, the Georgia Institute of Technology, the Policy Studies Organization, and Ed and Jane Greenberg.

Finally, in 2001, I first proposed the basic thesis of this book separately to Daron Acemoglu and Scott Stern while I was a graduate student at MIT. Each politely told me that he doubted it could work and that it was probably the wrong direction for a research career. Yet they encouraged me to explore. It may have taken thirteen years to report the results of my voyage, but I hope this book makes them proud of their reluctant advice!

COUNTRY CODES

Country	Code
Angola	ANG
Argentina	ARG
Australia	AUS
Austria	AUT
Bangladesh	BGL
Belarus	BLR
Belgium	BEL
Botswana	BWA
Brazil	BRA
Bulgaria	BGR
Canada	CAN
Chile	CHL
China	CHN
Colombia	COL
Costa Rica	CRI
Croatia	CRT
Czech Rep.	CZE
Denmark	DNK
Dominican Rep.	DRP
Ecuador	ECU
Egypt	EGY
El Salvador	ESV
Finland	FIN
France	FRA
Germany	GER
Ghana	GHA
Greece	GRC

Hong Kong	HKG
Hungary	HUN
India	IND
Indonesia	IDN
Iran	IRN
Ireland	IRL
Israel	ISR
Italy	ITA
Japan	JPN
Jordan	JOR
Kenya	KYA
Korea, Rep.	KOR
Lebanon	LBN
Liberia	LBR
Malaysia	MYS
Mexico	MEX
Morocco	MAR
Netherlands	NLD
New Zealand	NZL
Nicaragua	NIC
Nigeria	NGA
Norway	NOR
Pakistan	PAK
Paraguay	PGY
Peru	PER
Philippines	PHL
Poland	POL
Portugal	PRT
Romania	ROM
Russia	RUS
Saudi Arabia	SAU
Senegal	SGL
Serbia	SRB
Singapore	SGP
Slovak Rep.	SVK
Slovenia	SVN
South Africa	ZAF
Spain	ESP
Sri Lanka	SRI
Sweden	SWE
Switzerland	SWZ

Taiwan	TWN
Thailand	THA
Tunisia	TUN
Turkey	TUR
Ukraine	UKR
United Arab Em.	UAE
United Kingdom	GBR
United States	USA
Venezuela	VEZ
Vietnam	VTN
Zimbabwe	ZWE

PART ONE

CARDWELL'S LAW

1

Introduction

The Puzzle of Cardwell's Law

This book attempts to answer the question: *why are some countries better than others at science and technology*? This is the question posed to us by a phenomenon known as Cardwell's Law. During the early 1970s, British historian Donald Cardwell set out to identify the main turning points in the history of Western technology. He surveyed over a thousand years of developments in science and technology (S&T), cataloging what many consider to be the most important discoveries and inventions in human history, from the medieval horse stirrup to nuclear power. Cardwell offered strong opinions on the relative importance of different technologies, but he purposely ignored the nationality of the scientists or inventors who created them. Explaining this omission at the end of his survey, he made a simple observation that has since been christened Cardwell's Law. Nationality should *not* matter, he wrote, because:

> no nation has been very creative for more than an historically short period. Fortunately as each leader has flagged there has always been, up to now, a nation or nations to take over the torch.[1]

Of course, Cardwell was writing about the innovativeness of different societies across the grand sweep of history. This book is more tightly focused. It recognizes that something like Cardwell's Law continues to describe nations during our own lifetimes. For example, currently, a small handful of nations dominate the global creation and production of S&T. This elite club includes the United States, Japan, Germany, Taiwan, Sweden, Korea, Israel, and less than a dozen others. Yet, several of these countries did not innovate much back in 1945; some did not even exist. Meanwhile, there are many countries that have enjoyed long histories of wealth, democracy, industrialization, and S&T production but today innovate only very modestly. Examples include nations such as Spain, Italy, and Austria. Then there are the dozens of countries that, inexplicably, do not innovate much at all despite their favorable characteristics. These are countries like Argentina, Chile, the Philippines, South Africa, Thailand, and Turkey. Many of them are fairly democratic, are relatively capitalist, and possess well-educated citizens, and none are impoverished. But they produce relatively little indigenous S&T compared to the world's leading innovators.

These national disparities in innovation rates pose a crucial puzzle. In the twenty-first century, national borders and distance should *not* matter much for innovation. Scientific knowledge and technical information are easier than ever to copy and transmit internationally, allowing inventors anywhere to tap into global stores of S&T know-how. So too can capital, equipment, and people move rapidly around the world at historically low costs. Also, most people now well understand the advantages that S&T brings to a nation, which was not always the case.[2] Therefore, most countries today should have similar S&T capabilities. Yet, despite our heightened respect for innovation and an incredible surge in the supply and demand of everything S&T related, vast differences in national S&T performance abound, even among wealthy, industrialized democracies.

This simple observation, that national leadership in science and technology remains fickle and irregular, has evolved into one of the greatest enigmas in the history of social science and public policy. While Cardwell recognized the inevitable rise and fall of nations in S&T performance across time and space, neither he nor anyone else has yet been able to fully explain these differences in national capabilities. This void in our understanding is so important that it bears repeating: *no one has yet been able to explain why some countries succeed at S&T while others fail, or why national S&T success tends not to last long.* Certainly there have been many attempts at an explanation. Some of them have been quite compelling, and we will investigate several of these explanations in the following chapters. However, despite years of theory and research, the explanation for why some countries are better than others at S&T remains a stubborn mystery. The goal of this book is to solve it.

To do so, this book will tackle several tasks. First, it clarifies the often confusing and overlapping terms and data used in the innovation debate. Second, current explanations of Cardwell's Law tend to conflate *how* nations innovate with *why* they do so. In contrast, this book separates the *how* from the *why*. That is, most theories argue that a specific domestic institution or policy (or a combination of them) determines national innovation rates. These explanations of Cardwell's Law emphasize factors such as research and development (R&D) spending, education, universities, patent systems, democracy, political decentralization, different varieties of capitalism, and so forth. This book carefully investigates and tests each of these "institutions rule!" theories. It will argue that domestic institutions and policies only partly explain *how* nations innovate and mostly fail to explain *why*. Third, this book finds that, although institutions and policies do matter, there is no single "best" institution or policy design upon which all countries must converge. This book further argues that what's missing on the *how* side of the explanation is social networks. Social networks provide vital information that neither free markets nor government institutions easily capture, but networks are often ignored due to our preoccupation with domestic institutions and policies. Also, because foreign information is often the most difficult knowledge to capture, *international* networks play important roles in national S&T performance. Explaining Cardwell's Law is not just a domestic story; it also has an international side.

Of course, understanding *how* nations innovate does not explain *why* some countries create and use their institutions, policies, and networks to foster innovation while others choose not to. To answer the *why* question, this book offers a novel theory called "creative insecurity." This is the idea that each nation's balance of domestic versus external security concerns influences its innovation rate. Specifically, security concerns affect the willingness of people to accept the heavy costs, risks, and sacrifices necessary to create competitive, national S&T capabilities. In sum, institutions, policies, and networks (both domestic and international) together help to explain *how* nations innovate, while a country's net balance of security concerns helps to explain *why* countries innovate (or not).

Some Cardwellian Riddles

Japan is the classic example of Cardwell's Law in action. During the 1950s, the Japanese economy was widely dismissed as technologically backward and noncompetitive. One anecdote maintains that Japanese products were so shoddy and poorly regarded in international markets that a small town renamed itself "Usa" so that its exports might bear the label "Made in USA."[3] Japan's technological base was so meager back then that the country's primary exports were all decidedly low tech: textiles, clothing, and toys.

Only twenty years later, Japan had transformed itself. By 1970, Japan's top industries had advanced to include steel, ships, automobiles, and transistor radios, and "Made in Japan" was fast becoming the mark of highest quality.[4] Still, skeptics protested that Japan could never compete in that decade's truly advanced technologies: computers and semiconductor chips.[5] But it took less than a decade for Japan to prove these skeptics wrong. By 1978, Japan's Hitachi, NEC, and Toshiba had joined the list of top ten advanced memory-chip producers, and by 1987, Texas Instruments was the only major *non*-Japanese producer of the leading memory chips.[6] By 1989, Japan was producing over half of the world's semiconductors and half of the world's semiconductor fabrication equipment, and was responsible for over 70% of total semiconductor materials production.[7]

In fact, by the 1980s, Japan had advanced to dominate high-tech innovation and production throughout much of the global economy.[8] Japan became the lead innovator in automobiles, computers and computer equipment, electronic components, office equipment, and audio, video, and communications technologies.[9] In each of these high-technology sectors, formerly invincible American firms quickly lost profits and market share to Japanese manufacturers. Perhaps most ironically, US firms fell behind in technologies and product lines that had *originated* in the United States. Japan soon also became a top producer of science and engineering publications, a top recipient of science prizes, and a major participant in international S&T research conferences.

What makes Japan's tale of success so surprising is not merely its Cinderella-like aspect, but that it was Japan, and *not* its more likely rivals, that performed so well. For example, why on earth was Japan, and not France, the technological success story of the 1960s to 1990s? After all, Japan had come out of World War II a physically devastated, occupied, late industrializer with a relatively brief and arguably shallow history of indigenous S&T. Meanwhile, France benefited from two hundred years of experience at the forefront of science and technology. France had once led the world in chemistry, electricity, advanced weapons, and many high-tech manufacturing sectors. Nor was France short on capital as, after the war, Paris was showered with billions of dollars in Marshall Plan and reconstruction benefits.[10] France then became a member of the European customs union, giving it access to customers and investors far beyond its own market. France was also physically safe, buffered securely by weak states on all sides, and relatively far from the Cold War violence then being perpetrated by both Moscow and Washington. Hence, France had well-established S&T foundations, had growing economic resources, and was surrounded by supportive allies with strong, increasingly open economies. And, just like Japan, France also sought to develop a lead in advanced electronics, automobiles, and other high-technology industries after World War II.[11] Yet, France's technologies generally failed to compete well on world markets, whereas Japan's technologies flourished. France had all the advantages; Japan had nothing but obstacles. So why did Japan "out-innovate" France?

Similar puzzles can be posed regarding the Nordic countries of Sweden, Finland, Denmark, and Norway. These four countries are so close that they have similar or shared geographies, climates, histories, cultures, and ethnic constituencies.[12] They even have roughly equivalent sized populations and economies. Given these similarities, one would expect comparable outcomes in national S&T performance. But instead, we see drastic differences in Nordic innovation rates. Sweden has been quietly operating at the scientific and technological frontier for generations, stretching the temporal limits of Cardwell's Law. Since the last decades of the nineteenth century, Swedish technologies have been fierce competitors in international markets.[13] They have included some of the world's most advanced industrial and electric power systems, automobiles, military weapons, telecommunications hardware, and industrial robots.[14] At the other extreme, Finland was technologically backward for much of its history. Its economy was dominated by fishing, agriculture, and light industry throughout most of the twentieth century. Then, suddenly, during the mid-1980s, Finland began a sustained rise in S&T output that has since brought it into the ranks of the world's most innovative nations. Finland now hosts myriad high-tech firms such as Nokia (telecom), Ahlstrom (high-performance materials), Nexstim (medical instruments), and Tieto (information technology). Meanwhile, for decades, Denmark has been humming along contentedly as a midranked innovator, with strengths in machinery, instruments, chemicals, and, more recently, health sciences. Denmark has been neither a world leader nor laggard in innovation; there are no drastic build-ups or declines in Denmark's S&T history, just decades of steady midlevel performance.[15] Then there is Norway. Peacefully separated from Sweden over a century ago, democratic long before then, Norway is a modern, wealthy, but relatively *un*-innovative nation. Norway began the previous century as a scientific and technological straggler and remains so today. Norway is certainly not backward, but it does not produce S&T in the same league as its Nordic neighbors. In high-tech industries, technology patents, science prizes, S&T research conferences, and research publications, Norway reliably ranks below the other Viking states.[16]

Perhaps more disturbing are the Cardwell's Law puzzles of unexpected decline. One of the most baffling is Great Britain, which once dominated the world in science and technology but is now merely a midlevel innovator. For centuries, England had been an impoverished S&T backwater at the periphery of medieval and Renaissance Europe. Then it abruptly leapt to the S&T frontier in a very short time frame. During the seventeenth century, Englishmen led the scientific revolution, with geniuses like Isaac Newton, Robert Boyle, Robert Hooke, Joseph Priestley, Henry Cavendish, and Richard Bright transforming and modernizing the entire scientific endeavor. A century later, during the eighteenth and early nineteenth centuries, Great Britain became the birthplace and leader of the first industrial revolution. British engineers and entrepreneurs linked steam and water power with mechanical production technologies to mass-produce fabrics and textiles, wrought iron, steel, and chemical compounds. These high-tech products were all made in modern factories connected to distribution points by a complicated system of modern river canals and "macadamized" roads. Countries throughout Europe scrambled to catch up with British science and technology. But they rarely succeeded, and often only by copying or stealing British technology. The suddenly, within a generation, the United Kingdom lost its technological edge. It surrendered leadership to Germany and the United States in the second industrial revolution, which was based on chemicals, advanced metallurgy, electricity, and petroleum fuels and engines. Most relevant to this book, Great Britain has not been the forerunner in the aerospace, information technology, telecommunications, biotechnology, or other major S&T revolutions of the last seventy years. The modern United Kingdom is certainly *not* a "do nothing" in S&T, and the British contribute significantly to twenty-first-century innovation. However, they are no longer the unchallengeable envy of the world that they once were.[17]

Most recently, the case of the USSR haunts us. For decades after World War II, the Soviets were fierce competitors in many fields of science, technology, engineering, and mathematics (STEM). Russian leaders promised to "bury" the West with Soviet progress. This was a credible threat given that the USSR was first into space, produced atomic weapons with the world's largest yields, and won a flurry of Nobel Prizes in chemistry and physics. By the 1980s, the Soviets employed more scientists and engineers than any other country in history.[18] Soviet airplanes, ships, submarines, computers, nuclear power stations, satellites, and spacecraft were widely perceived as the leading challengers to, if not surpassing, their Western counterparts. Yet after a few short decades at the S&T frontier, Soviet technology fell into rapid decline, which was followed soon after by the deterioration of much of its science and engineering. Today, nobody fears being buried by Russian S&T; indeed, few consumers even seek it out.

The American Imperative

Lurking in the background of this discussion is the question: can the United States break Cardwell's Law? This is a key concern for us to tackle in the following chapters. The United States has been the world's S&T leader for around a century. Therefore, if Cardwell is correct, then our "historically short period" may soon be coming to an end. However, if we can explain how Cardwell's Law works, then we may be able to postpone the day when the United States falls into technological stagnation and scientific irrelevance.

The United States is in fact a choice example of a Cardwell's Law miracle. The United States was originally a technologically backward, agricultural state. For decades, it had little S&T infrastructure other than a poorly enforced patent system and a handful of colleges, most of which prioritized the study of theology and the classics. Colonial and antebellum American S&T were therefore regularly snubbed by Europeans and ridiculed at home. In fact, many of America's early leaders, exemplified by Thomas Jefferson, actually *opposed* industrialization and the technological progress that accompanied it. They believed that the mechanization and factory production sweeping England led to industrial slavery, reckless urbanization, and moral decay. The English inventions of spinning jennies, power looms, and cotton gins were frequently demonized in America as sources of destructive social and economic tensions. As for science, early Americans praised it as a fine personal hobby, but it was generally seen as peripheral to the nation's interests and not a legitimate government pursuit. Plans for a national S&T university were repeatedly voted down by Congress, popularly decried as either a useless expenditure or a subsidy for the wealthy. So too were other federal appropriations for research or development.[19] The result was decades of low-quality US science. Top American scientists, including Joseph Henry and Alexander Dallas Bache, frequently complained about the "charlatanism" and "quackery" that plagued antebellum US science.[20] Even pro-America enthusiast Alexis de Tocqueville, after his 1831–1832 tour across the United States, reported dimly that "in few of the civilized nations of our time have the higher sciences made less progress than in the United States."[21] Three decades later, in 1860, the *New York Times* was still asking: "*American* science: is there such a thing?"[22]

Yet only a generation later, the United States was at the forefront of the second industrial revolution, and this was just the beginning. By 1890, the United States had grasped the technological lead in steel, electricity, railroads, chemicals, mining, and processed foods. Soon American research universities and corporate laboratories were pumping out new discoveries and inventions that rivaled those produced in Europe. By 1910, its modern navy had transformed the United States into a global military power. Meanwhile, America's advanced medicine, manufacturing, automobile, and aircraft industries were fast becoming world leaders. But it was World War II and the Cold War that launched US leadership in S&T to spectacular heights. For decades after 1940, American S&T was no longer simply *primus inter pares*, but globally dominant. The world's top students streamed into American research universities, Nobel Prizes piled up, new industries bloomed like wildflowers (e.g., computing, telecommunications, software, aerospace, composite materials, genetically modified organisms, biotech), and US technology dominated world markets.

Then, during the 1970s, Cardwell's inexorable logic appeared to take hold yet again. Not only did the United States lose rank and market share in many technologies originally invented in America, but also US industries stopped producing some of these technologies altogether. First Japan and Germany, then Taiwan, South Korea, and others rose to challenge American dominance in steel, ships, automobiles, consumer electronics, computing, semiconductors, aerospace, and even the budding biotechnology industry.[23] By the 1980s and early 1990s, American manufacturing technologies were regularly blasted as inefficient, obsolete, and costly.[24] In scientific research, the United States also appeared to be losing out. American university students increasingly opted for less rigorous, or more glamorous, majors, while US politicians derided many of the newest STEM fields and research as either heretical or wasteful.[25] European and Asian scientists began to win science prize competitions once dominated by Americans. Foreign research publications at first trickled but then flooded into the top scientific journals. Economists struggled to explain a lull in American R&D productivity, as well as the large and growing trade deficits in high technology.[26]

Although the Internet bubble provided a brief hiatus, the US deterioration in S&T appears to have accelerated in the early twenty-first century.[27] The relative downturn has now become so severe that even an infamously gridlocked Congress has begun to act. In response to thirty years of perceived decline in American S&T, in 2005, US Congress commissioned *Rising Above the Gathering Storm.* This five-hundred-page study of American competitiveness in S&T, authored by the nation's top S&T academies, concluded grimly that "the scientific and technological building blocks critical to our economic leadership are eroding at a time when many other nations are gathering strength."[28] Five years later, a 2010 update to that study warned that "our nation's outlook has worsened."[29] It pointed out that the majority of US patents are now awarded to non-US firms, far more foreign students now study the physical sciences and engineering in US graduate schools than do Americans, and the United States continues to rank low across a legion of measures of S&T competitiveness (e.g., STEM education, high-tech manufacturing, Internet penetration, advanced auto and energy research).[30] Much of this decline is associated with ever fewer resources allocated to S&T research or to train high-quality STEM workers. Now China, and perhaps soon India, is widely heralded as the world's next technological superpower.[31] Concurrent with America's relative decline in S&T have come a decline in the US dollar, bloated federal deficits, recurring energy crises, rising inequality, and a hollowing out of manufacturing. The "American Century" in S&T now seems over, another victim of Cardwell's mysterious law.

Thus, one goal of this book is to change our fate. If we can understand the forces that drive Cardwell's Law, then perhaps we can reverse this decline.

"Why Nations Fail": The Wrong Explanation for Cardwell's Law

The vast majority of observers have concluded that the solution to the S&T puzzle posed by Cardwell's Law is as follows: nations must get their domestic institutions and policies right! The reason for such certainty is their diagnosis of failure. Everyone agrees that progress in S&T is routinely blocked by status quo interest groups or slowed by troubles known as "market failures." Domestic institutions and policies can solve both of these problems. Therefore, domestic institutions and policies must determine national innovation rates. In sum, conventional wisdom tells us that bad policies and missing institutions explain "why nations fail" at innovation, end of story![32]

Empirically, this certainly makes sense, at least at first. Domestic institutions and policies are what governments use to promote innovation. Also, different countries use different sets of institutions and policies. Therefore, it must be the differences in these national institutions and policies that explain why some countries are better at S&T. To support this belief, scholars have produced a bounty of anecdotes about how missing, broken, or corrupt institutions and policies have hurt progress in S&T. Meanwhile, most national success stories involve government institutions and policies acting to either solve market failures or counteract status quo interest groups.

In particular, most of the domestic *policy* explanations for Cardwell's Law tested in this book address different types of market failures that obstruct innovation. For example, because new S&T is often easy to copy and share, some argue that the strength of a country's intellectual property rights is the key to explaining S&T performance. Other scholars instead prioritize national differences in R&D subsidies, spending on STEM education, or public research programs. Each of these domestic policies attempts to compensate for the problem of spillovers of knowledge and expertise: the fact that private actors will tend to underinvest in S&T because they often cannot capture all the returns on their investment. Still other policy arguments highlight the usefulness of infant industry protection, even for wealthy countries, as an essential tool for entering and dominating new S&T sectors. We will explore each of these arguments.

In contrast, many of the most prominent *institutional* arguments take a more holist view of innovation. Some are admittedly more aggregations of various policy solutions. For example, the first systematic cross-national approach to studying innovation rates held that multiple national policies and institutions work in concert to foster innovation. This "National Innovation Systems" (NIS) approach has become one of the dominant paradigms within innovation research. But most holistic institutional explanations for Cardwell's Law focus instead on the domestic incentives to innovate. For example, "Varieties of Capitalism" scholars have argued that the S&T goals of NIS institutions and policies, and their efficiency in achieving these goals, are determined by the degree to which free markets are allowed to structure the incentives of national actors. Democracy offers another institutional route to explaining Cardwell's Law in that democracy creates the political competition necessary for free market capitalism to function. Hence, many scholars argue that democracy is the sine qua non for achieving a more innovative economy. Of course, sometimes even democracies can become centralized and stagnant. Therefore, political decentralization has become yet another popular institutional explanation for national S&T success. Decentralized governments are widely seen as agile, competitive, and well structured to adapt to innovation's gale of creative destruction. Meanwhile, centralized organizations of all sizes, from firms to nation-states, have come to be viewed as rigid and hostile to the risks, costs, and changes associated with new S&T.

This book will explain how each of these types of domestic institutions and policies works to lower the risks and costs of innovation or increase the penalties for stagnation. It will also test how well any of them alone, or several together, can explain Cardwell's Law. It will present substantial evidence showing that domestic institutions and policies do *not* explain national innovation rates well. There are simply too many countries with "good" institutions and policies that fail to innovate much (e.g., Norway, Austria, Italy). Also, there are many countries with "bad" or missing institutions and policies that innovate surprisingly well (e.g., Taiwan, Israel, South Korea). And no one has yet identified precisely *which* set of institutions and policies are the "right" ones. Yes, there are plenty of theories that emphasize the vital importance of this or that institution or policy (e.g., patent rights, science education, R&D subsidies, research universities, etc.). But although institution or policy X may explain success in country Y at a particular point in time, it fails to do so in other countries or even in the same country during a different time period. Also, the evidence for these theories often consists of anecdotal observations or stylized case studies, or they are based on the experiences of only one or two countries, usually success stories, with no comparison with cases of failure. Nor do the long-run, cross-national data on S&T support the conclusion that any particular domestic institution or policy causes nations to succeed.

This book will further show that there exist additional tools, often ignored, that governments can use to improve S&T competitiveness: social networks. Social networks help to explain why institutions and policies alone are not sufficient for achieving national success in S&T. That is, success at S&T is not simply a matter of governments solving market failures, but also of dealing with network failures. States that seek innovative economies must first knit together domestic networks of STEM labor with local entrepreneurs and investors. Then, the government must help create several types of international networks, especially linkages between domestic innovators and foreign markets for exports, investment capital, and sources of technical skills and knowledge. Nations must also be strategic about decisions to create and internationalize technology standards, and whether to accept foreign ones.

This explains why a focus on *domestic* factors alone cannot explain national innovation rates. Successful S&T states are typified by *international* networks of trade, finance, production, knowledge, and human capital flows that play important roles in determining national innovation rates. Also, like institutions, networks are not causal forces; they are a means to a national technological end. Indeed, these three tools (institutions, policies, and networks) must build upon one another. In other words, institutions, policies, and networks together help us to better explain *how* nations can innovate, but not *why* they are willing to do so.

This book therefore develops an alternate theory called "creative insecurity" that more fully explains Cardwell's Law, especially during the last seventy years. It answers the question of *why* some countries are better than others at S&T over the long run. Instead of institutions and policies, it emphasizes politics.[33] Institutions and policies are merely the tools that nations use to improve their S&T capabilities. But neither institutions nor policies *cause* nations to innovate. In making this assertion, this book recognizes that even the right tools will fail to produce results when placed into the wrong hands, or into hands not motivated to use them properly. Therefore, to explain Cardwell's Law, we need to explain why some countries adopt the "right" institutions and policies and then use them properly over time, while others do not.

Creative Insecurity: The Driver of National Innovation Rates

This book contends that, to lead in S&T, often a nation must enjoy a state of ***creative insecurity***.[34] Creative insecurity is the condition of feeling more threatened by external hazards than by domestic rivals. *It is the positive difference between the threats of economic or military competition from abroad and the dangers of political-economic rivalries at home.* One major finding drawn from the evidence presented in this book is that creative insecurity generally motivates broad and sustained support for S&T. The greater the creative insecurity is, and the longer a nation is faced with it, the more its people are willing to risk their political capital and economic resources on rapid S&T progress. This relationship holds true regardless of a nation's institutions or policies. The bottom line is that *countries for which external threats are relatively greater than domestic tensions should have higher national innovation rates than countries for which domestic tensions outweigh external threats.*

It is important to recognize that creative insecurity emphasizes the *balance* between external threats and domestic tensions. One is not more important than the other. Each affects a nation's S&T capabilities. Countries do not fail at S&T because their external threats disappear. Rather, countries fail at S&T when domestic rivalries rise to exceed the level of external threats, because these domestic rivalries erode political support for S&T progress. Conversely, nations do not succeed at S&T just because an external threat exists. All countries face external threats. It is only when external threats rise to exceed the level of domestic tensions that a modern society will increase its political support, and economic resources, for S&T. Therefore, creative insecurity tells us to look at *both* external threats and domestic tensions.

In other words, there is a politics of Cardwell's Law. At its core, the creative insecurity argument gives priority to two types of politics: domestic distributional politics versus security politics. They act as opposing forces to affect national S&T performance. Distributional politics tend to slow innovation; security politics tend to accelerate innovation. Both are always operating. It is the balance between them that helps to determine national innovation rates over the long run. The next two sections briefly summarize how these politics work.

Domestic Distributional Politics: The Enemy of Science and Technology

The domestic distributional politics of S&T act to *slow* innovation through various mechanisms. For example, different actors and interest groups often fight over the *inputs* to S&T progress. Innovation is very expensive. Also, every dollar the government allocates toward expensive S&T progress is a dollar not available for welfare provision, natural resource development, consumption, or the lining of elite pockets.[35] No one wants their favorite government program cut or taxes raised; therefore, political battles erupt to shift the burden to someone else. Worse yet, some taxpayers may seek to eliminate their S&T fiscal burden altogether. Alternately, domestic battles can also erupt over the *effects* of S&T progress, which then slow innovation. Progress in S&T may increase the wealth and well-being of society as a whole, but it has its victims, and these victims fight back. They often resort to politics by lobbying for regulations, taxes, government spending, and other policies which slow or obstruct technological changes that threaten the value of their assets.[36] Similarly, even when people support S&T, domestic political resistance can arise to oppose the institutions and policies that promote innovation. This resistance can take the form of fights over patent laws, trade policies, antitrust regimes, and so forth, all of which are important for S&T progress but also create winners and losers within society.

Government is never the neutral observer in these upheavals but, rather, is pursued by both supporters and opponents of S&T in the hope of gaining policy advantages in their mortal conflict.[37] These politics are often neglected by innovation researchers, who tend to assume widespread support for progress in science and technology and then ask which types of institutions and policies will achieve the best results. Yet political resistance to technological change can obstruct or warp otherwise "good" S&T institutions and policies.[38] Well-known specialized examples in the United States include resistance to nuclear power,[39] stem cell research,[40] alternative energy,[41] HIV-safe blood products,[42] and even new weapons systems.[43] In each of these cases, the losing interest groups created by scientific or technological change were able to convince politicians to block, slow, or alter government support for scientific and technological progress. This book will present evidence that political resistance is a general phenomenon that slows national innovation rates around the world.

In sum, S&T progress, and the institutions and policies that support it, can sometimes cause new domestic conflicts or excite traditional ones. When this happens, political leaders will tend to endorse policies that slow such change. This is especially true of political leaders who seek to quiet domestic tensions, directly represent resistor interests, or strongly support the status quo. Each of these priorities should cause elites to show limited policy support for S&T progress, and perhaps even oppose it, often with strong support from their constituents. The net effect is that a nation's domestic tensions should act as a force to obstruct support for S&T.

Security Politics: The Ally of Science and Technology

The second type of politics that affects Cardwell's Law is the politics of security, which act to *accelerate* S&T progress. The main premise is that domestic S&T capabilities enhance a nation's ability to provide both military and economic security. Therefore, threats to a nation's military or economic security will tend to increase and broaden support for S&T progress.

External threats to a nation's military or economic security increase the relative benefits of technological change, while raising the relative costs of technological stagnation. For example, technological innovation can create an economy that is more competitive in international markets. As a result, innovation can boost exports, thus earning the foreign exchange necessary to purchase strategic imports, such as energy, food, raw materials, or military equipment. Also, a globally competitive high-technology sector can provide the foundation for a domestic defense industry. This can ease a nation's reliance on imports of foreign weaponry. In civilian sectors, the development of indigenous high-tech capabilities can enable domestic industry to produce those strategic goods that either are expensive to purchase abroad, have unreliable foreign suppliers, or are vulnerable to hostile interdiction. Competitive S&T-based industries can also generate capital by satisfying investors at home and luring investment from abroad. High-tech sectors also provide jobs for skilled workers and an attractive career path for youths, while pulling up the aggregate skill level.[44] Therefore, higher levels of external threats to a nation's military or economic security should cause political-economic elites to reverse their calculus regarding the relative costs and risks of technological change.

It is the difference between these two forces, then, domestic rivalries versus external threats, that drives national innovation rates. S&T progress creates winners and losers, and the losers resort to politics to slow innovation. However, external threats increase political support for S&T and thereby counteract domestic political resistance to innovation. Indeed, as the threat balance shifts more and more toward the external, even many domestic technological losers may recognize that their interests are better served by accepting the costs of technological change, and government actions that support it. Thus, a nation's elites, and the people they represent, often must enter into a state of creative insecurity before they are willing to accept the risks, costs, and distributional consequences of S&T. They must feel enough military and economic threats from external sources to overcome their domestic fears and jealousies.

"Is This the Right Room for an Argument?"

Since this book takes a somewhat novel approach to both innovation and security, it is important to clarify what this book does *not* argue.[45] Its thesis is not that defense spending is the key policy variable or that external security concerns alone drive technological. Nor does this book argue that war or crisis is necessary for S&T progress.[46] While wars and crises may catalyze innovation in some instances, this book recognizes that there have been plenty of wars and crises that did *not* result in much S&T progress. Rather, the original argument made in this book is that there is a politics to Cardwell's Law. External hazards must threaten a society *more* than domestic rivalries for a nation to sustain the risks and costs of innovation over the long run. And these external threats can include economic, demographic, or other factors. We do not require war for science and technology to progress.

Certainly a handful of observers have recognized that S&T progress creates winners and losers, and that the losers will resort to political resistance to slow innovation.[47] But this book is not a repackaging of classic Olsonian arguments about the political-economic power of status quo interest groups. Rather, keep in mind that these other scholars almost universally prescribe "good" institutions and policies as their solutions to the innovation problem. These institutional solutions usually take the form of property rights, free markets, and decentralized democracy. Their argument is that the less an economy is controlled by government, or the more diffusely power is institutionalized within the polity and economy, the less vulnerable it will be to capture by status quo interest groups. However, this ignores the fact that progress in S&T suffers from a variety of major market failures and network failures, and therefore often *requires* government intervention. It also ignores the fact that institutions and policies are themselves vulnerable to capture by status quo interest groups. In fact, often the *same* institutions and policies can be used to either foster *or* fight S&T progress.

Connoisseurs of the innovation debate should also note that this book is *not* making an argument about "systemic vulnerability" (SV) theory.[48] SV theory also concerns itself with external versus domestic threats. However, SV theory attempts to explain national differences in *upgrading*, where *upgrading* is defined as moving up the value chain, producing at high levels of efficiency, and doing so with local inputs. Therefore, SV theory generally focuses attention on the diffusion of technology, often invented elsewhere, throughout an economy. Cardwell's Law is more concerned with indigenous innovation than with diffusion. Also, SV theory is tightly restricted to developing, middle-income economies (e.g., Thailand, Brazil, Indonesia, the Philippines); creative insecurity seeks to explain national innovation rates in *all* economies, even wealthy, fully industrialized countries. Most important, SV theory's main argument is that institutions determine upgrading. Specifically, SV theory holds that the number of veto players in a nation's political system determines the ability of the state to decide on and commit to upgrading. This book's argument is that institutions determine nothing; they are tools, not causal forces.

How do institutions and policies fit into creative insecurity theory? Again, it is important to be clear about what this book does *not* argue. This book is *not* suggesting that domestic institutions and policies do not matter or never matter. Rather, it makes three specific claims about the roles of institutions and policies.

First, institutions and policies are influential, but they are not causal. Institutions and policies are the tools that modern societies use to achieve their technological goals, but like any other tool, institutions can be ignored, underfunded, misused, or allowed to fail. The intent of the tools' users matters. The same institutions that can be used to foster technological innovation can also be directed toward entirely tangential goals or be neglected altogether. To advance S&T, institutions require skilled practitioners (bureaucrats, politicians, innovators, and entrepreneurs) to use them with the intent of producing innovative outcomes. When these conditions are met, institutions do indeed improve national innovation rates. They allow individuals, organizations, and nations to achieve better science and technology than without them. This can create the appearance of institutional causality. But the idea that institutions cause innovation assumes that all nations pursue S&T with equal enthusiasm. The evidence in this book strongly contradicts both of these allegations. It argues that the more a society is put into a state of creative insecurity, the more it will seek to improve its S&T capabilities, and hence the more it will use its tools (institutions and policies) to achieve this goal.

Second, there is no "secret sauce" of institutions and policies that is the key to S&T success. The evidence reviewed in the following pages shows that, as long as institutions and policies solve the basic market failures and network problems that impede innovation, then which particular institutions a government selects may not be so important. Therefore, the search for a "best" S&T institution or policy design may be unproductive, or at least secondary, because different designs can achieve the same basic goals. This also means that different nations can customize their approach to innovation; governments have choices about which institutions and policy designs they can use.

Third, most S&T institutions and policies are supposed to solve the classic market failures that impede innovation, but this alone is not enough. Social networks also play a major role in explaining success and failure. Therefore, S&T institutions and policies must address a nation's network failures as well. Specifically, states that seek to create innovative economies must first knit together domestic networks of STEM labor with local entrepreneurs and investors. Then, the state must support different types of international networks, especially linkages between domestic innovators and foreign markets for exports, investment capital, and sources of technical skills and knowledge.

Finally, this book does not present a mono-causal or determinist relationship. Creative insecurity is an important and often ignored causal factor. Adding it to the innovation debate takes us a considerable way toward explaining Cardwell's Law, especially during the past seventy years. But admittedly, it is not the only driver of national innovation rates, nor does it explain the entire universe of innovation. Ideas, culture, individuals, and plain luck may also play important roles, especially in some cases.[49] We innovation scholars still have much work to do.

Who Should Read This Book?

First and foremost, this book serves as a comprehensive introduction to the debate over national S&T competitiveness. In its search for an explanation of Cardwell's Law, this book synthesizes over fifty years of theory and research on national innovation rates. It brings together the current political and economic wisdom, and latest findings, about how nations become S&T leaders. My own contribution consists of research and findings made over twenty-five years, including work done at University of California, Berkeley; Kansai University of Foreign Studies (Japan); Yale; MIT; and Georgia Institute of Technology, as well as observations made while working as a technology strategy consultant in the private sector. All told, this book draws on statistical analysis, comparative case studies, interviews, site visits, and survey research done by myself and others in Japan, South Korea, China, Taiwan, Thailand, the Philippines, Argentina, Brazil, Mexico, Canada, Turkey, Israel, Russia, and roughly a dozen countries across Western Europe.

Most urgently, this book is directed at all readers who want a better understanding of innovation and what governments can do to help or harm it. It is therefore written in a straightforward, even colloquial, style to maximize accessibility. In particular, this book focuses attention on the question: what is the appropriate role of the state in promoting S&T? It therefore tours competing theories that attempt to explain differences in national innovation rates, exploring both long-held beliefs and new hypotheses. In the process, it also delves into important issues of definitions, data, measurement, policy, and the key tensions between contending viewpoints.

Clearly policy scholars and economists who focus on science, technology, and innovation are another primary audience for this book. For them, this book's warning—that science and technology are a function of politics—is urgent. Most innovation scholars and economists tend to ignore politics. For them, politics and government are annoyances. Politics represent irrational inefficiencies that are to be assumed away, or random "exogenous" factors that cannot be modeled. This book shows that politics are the sine qua non for successful explanations of national innovation rates. I argue that innovation scholars will operate at a handicap until they more fully incorporate politics and security into their research. Again, the main lesson here is that just having "good" institutions and policies is not enough; you have to get the politics right.

International development scholars and practitioners can learn much from this volume. They have long been concerned with innovation because S&T plays such a vital role in poverty alleviation, rural development, and sustainable economic growth. The transition from importing foreign S&T, to local improvement and imitation, and eventually to indigenous S&T production is key to moving impoverished countries up the value chain. Innovation is often the best vehicle for delivering developing economies out of subsistence agriculture, natural resource exploitation, and dependence on foreign aid. The creation of indigenous capabilities for innovation also has important ramifications for women, indigenous peoples, small farmers, poor urban residents, and landscapes and ecosystems in the countries of the global south. For these reasons, in perhaps no other field does understanding why some countries succeed or fail at S&T matter so much for so many lives.

Business and management experts have also recently created a cottage industry of innovation studies. This is because firms are responsible for a large share of the S&T produced around the world. But most business professors, and their students, ignore the fact that private firms operate within a web of powerful state institutions, national political-economic battles, and international security agendas. This book will show that these political factors powerfully affect the incentives for private corporations to invest in, and succeed at, innovative activity. Business scholars also need to recognize that the firms, universities, and individuals that are the focus of their research do not operate in a vacuum. Rather, the political environment can have a major impact on high-tech business strategies, networks, and performance.

Ironically, political scientists are perhaps the toughest crowd to reach. In discussions with colleagues within my own field, I am consistently struck by how enthusiastically they perceive politics in all aspects of social life *except* for science and technology. Rather, most of my colleagues tend to view S&T progress as immune from politics. S&T is assumed to be a "black box" proceeding according to its own internal scientific dynamics in a drive toward greater and greater technical efficiency, and in a manner determined by the physical laws of nature.[50] This book shows that this assumption is false, that politics play a major role in determining the rate and direction of inventive activity. Since much of the discussion revolves around the design and maintenance of state institutions, this book also contributes to the "endogenous institutions" debate, which investigates how institutions form and evolve.[51]

The puzzle of Cardwell's Law should be especially important to the study of international relations. Progress in S&T affects almost every aspect of that subfield: war, alliances, terrorism, trade, and the balance of power. Yet to date, while most major international relations theorists note the importance of technology to international political behavior, few make any attempt to explain the underlying variance of national innovation rates. Rather, this area has largely become the purview of a small number of economists and sociologists who often ignore or misconjecture important international political variables in their analysis. As if in retaliation, most international relations scholars who discuss technological variables often neglect the enormous body of innovation research that has developed over the past twenty years in the other social sciences.

This book reveals that a political science approach to S&T can improve our understanding of national innovation rates. Specifically, theory and research in security studies and political economy can complement one another, with insight and advances in one field acting to fill in the gaps in the others. Unfortunately, these complementarities often go unrealized. This work attempts to demonstrate the value of bringing together diverse theories, methods, and data for explaining national innovation rates and pointing toward the policy implications of these findings. Hence, this book can be interpreted as a call for greater integration of science and technology politics within the fields that study it. We need to combine dispersed problem-specific and country-specific approaches into a more generalizable theoretical and policy-relevant cross-field debate about the politics of innovation. Thus, this book serves as a call for greater cooperation and common focus among fragmented S&T scholars within political science and across the social sciences.

Finally, one rather frightening implication of this book is that nations should forever create foreign enemies to fear. With external threats serving as a constant menace, the risks and expense of innovation can be justified indefinitely. This has been the unintended course followed by the United States since World War II. At first, defense research in the United States meant weapons and perhaps battlefield medicine. But over time, it has come to include research on information technology, telecommunications, infrastructure, and education policy, and, more recently, investment in energy and general health care advances.[52]

However, in a world typified by freedom of information and debate, this innovation strategy is unsustainable. In open societies, false alarms about manufactured enemies soon become transparent. Also, without a real competitive threat, S&T institutions and policies become corrupt and mismanaged. Worse yet, in nations typified by restricted information and debate, such a strategy is highly destructive. Imaginary enemies can become real ones, risking unnecessary and destructive conflicts. In either case, it leads to a bloated defense sector and a militarized society in which all spending is questioned except that which goes toward defense. A far smarter strategy is to identify the real long-run competitive and security threats, such as energy efficiency, climate change, aging, and disease. This book will argue that war and the garrison state are not necessary for S&T leadership.

Tour of the Book

The next chapter establishes some working definitions and boundaries, and briefly explains the innovation measures and data used in this book. For example, what exactly do we mean by *innovation*? How do we recognize innovation when we see it? How do we distinguish innovation from *non*innovation? The answers are not obvious. Then, once we define innovation, how do we measure it? How does one rank one innovation against another? If we want to test different explanations of Cardwell's Law, then we have to figure out how to do this at the national level for dozens of countries, over several decades. These are not trivial tasks. This chapter also explains how this book distinguishes (and sometimes why it does not distinguish) between *institutions* and *policies*.

Chapter 3 presents evidence for Cardwell's Law acting in our own time. It examines some initial innovation data for dozens of nations over the past several decades to identify which countries are the current global leaders and laggards in S&T, and how these positions have recently changed. It is these differences in national innovation rates that the rest of the book seeks to explain. This chapter also briefly investigates some of the most seemingly obvious and apolitical explanations for why some countries excel at S&T (e.g., random chance, size, culture).

The rest of the book attempts to answer two separate but related questions. Chapters 4 through 6 explain and test existing theories about *how* nations achieve S&T competitiveness. These chapters investigate some long-held, popular beliefs about domestic institutions and policies, followed by a survey of more recent insights into the powerful roles of networks, both domestic and international. Chapters 7 through 9 then tackle *why* some countries innovate and others do not. That is, if institutions, policies, and networks constitute tools that states can use to aid innovation, then why don't all nations create and use them to improve their S&T competitiveness?

Chapter 4 begins the investigation by asking the question: why government? That is, does progress in S&T truly require support and interference from this entity we call "the state"? After all, free markets are celebrated for their ability to foster and maintain innovation. The goal of this chapter is to show that, while markets may excel at producing S&T, they can also malfunction, and this creates a role for government. It therefore delves into the phenomenon of S&T market failures and their effects on national S&T competitiveness. If market failures strike often, then the explanation for Cardwell's Law may lie in the presence (or absence) of national institutions and policies that can correct them. This chapter therefore examines the five most popular institutions and polices that governments have traditionally used to correct the classic market failures that plague innovation. These institutions and polices constitute what I call the "Five Pillars" of innovation: intellectual property rights, research subsidies, public education, research universities, and trade policy. How do these five institutions and policies aid innovation? Perhaps more important, how far do they go toward explaining why some countries are better at S&T than others? The evidence presented in this chapter suggests that government policies, such as the Five Pillars, *do* take us part of the way to understanding Cardwell's Law, but they also leave an enormous amount of unexplained success and failure.

Chapter 5 adds more domestic institutions and policies to our investigation, but takes a broader, "macro" approach. It first asks whether there exists some special combination of institutions and policies that is the silver bullet for explaining Cardwell's Law. It therefore examines research on how a country's institutions and policies fit together to form a National Innovation System. Can we identify any specific characteristics of these complex systems that cause some nations to innovate better? This chapter also takes a look at the "why nations fail" argument, and its variants, that currently dominates both academic and popular theories of economic success, and hence successful innovation.

It therefore explores institutional theories of democracy, political decentralization, and "Varieties of Capitalism." These investigations show that, regardless of which data one considers, *none* of these theories adequately explains success in S&T across time and space. It is important to restate here that I am *not* arguing that national innovation systems, democracy, decentralization, and free markets have *no* effect on national innovation rates. Rather, I am contending that theories that put specific institutions or policies at their core, as the causal forces of sustained S&T progress, have been overstated and oversimplified, and need to be re-examined. In other words, we are missing something. To find that missing something, we need to abandon our preconceived notions of what motivates societies to innovate. We therefore need to go beyond the vague platitude that "institutions and policies matter!"

Chapter 6 lets the data do the talking. That is, perhaps the best way to solve the puzzle of Cardwell's Law is to look at recent cases of success and failure and then ask: what did *successful* governments do (or avoid doing) that the cases of *failure* did not? To this end, this chapter examines some recent S&T success stories (e.g., Israel, Taiwan) to see what characteristics they shared. It then compares them against a case of more moderate success (Ireland) and a case of relative failure (Mexico). Two surprises come out of this investigation. First, there is no single "best" institution or policy that the world's policymakers need converge upon to achieve national S&T competitiveness. Different countries have achieved S&T success using very different sets of institutions and policies. Governments therefore have considerable freedom to choose and customize national strategies for improving their nation's innovation rate. Second, solving market failures alone is not enough. Most national success stories in S&T also involve the use of social networks to take shortcuts around markets for access to high-quality STEM labor, technical knowledge, investment capital, and even marketing expertise. Recent research on variants of networks, such as R&D clusters and technology standards, is also examined.

Chapter 7 asks the next question in the causal chain: if solving market failures and setting up social networks are the keys to national success in S&T, then *why* do some countries perform these tasks so well while others fail? The answers usher us into the distributive nature of both technological change and the institutions and policies that support S&T. This chapter examines how S&T progress, and even S&T institutions and policies, can create winners and losers within society. They can therefore cause new domestic conflicts or excite traditional ones. When these domestic conflicts arise, public support for S&T will wane and political elites will seek to slow it down. The net effect is that a nation's domestic tensions should act as a force to slow and obstruct political support for technological change.

Chapters 8 and 9 continue our discussion about *why* nations innovate, using several different approaches to show that external security concerns can counteract domestic political resistance to innovation. External security concerns raise the benefits of technological change and the costs of technological stagnation. Therefore, higher levels of external threats should cause a society to alter its calculus regarding the relative costs and risks of technological change. Chapter 8 explains how this works and presents cross-national statistical data to support it. Then, because quantitative data alone may not convince some readers, Chapter 9 revisits the cases of Israel, Taiwan, Ireland, and Mexico to show how the balance of external threats versus domestic tensions explains S&T success and failure in these countries.

Chapter 10 summarizes and discusses the implications of this book's findings for research and policy. One implication is that nations should forever create foreign enemies to fear. As long as an armed external menace threatens society, the risks and costs of S&T progress can be justified in perpetuity. However, this strategy is untenable in twenty-first-century democracies. This chapter will show that war and militarization are not necessary for S&T leadership. It argues that a superior innovation strategy would instead emphasize the actual emerging threats to societies around the world, such as the skyrocketing demand for energy, global climate shifts and environmental degradation, and the debilitations of age and disease.

Three appendices round out this book's discussion of national innovation rates. The debate over innovation is often hindered by confusion over key terms, definitions, and measures. Appendix 1 therefore serves as a "Beware!" sign. It alerts readers to the confusing and constantly changing jargon in innovation research. It reveals how the basic vocabulary of Cardwell's Law has been chaotic and varied over time and across different subfields. Appendix 2 then takes up the perennial problem of how to observe and measure innovation. Using a historical approach, it explains the major attempts to measure national innovation rates during the past century, as well as their advantages and pitfalls. Appendix 3 surveys of the current state of the debate over national innovation measures and data. It more thoroughly justifies this book's choices. It also provides an overview of the major types of S&T data and indicators used today, examines their strengths and weaknesses, identifies some of the major data sources and research centers, and cites some of the prominent scholars who are central to this area of research.

2

Measuring the Black Box

This chapter tackles the fascinating and necessary work of boundaries, definitions, measurement, and data. It thereby performs some basic housekeeping that must get done before we can wrestle seriously with national innovation rates. These topics are fascinating because they get at the heart of what innovation is. The simple question of "What is *innovation* and how do we know it when we see it?" sounds straightforward. However, serious attempts to define, observe, measure, and then gather empirical data on innovation can force us into some very subtle and complicated discussions. After all, innovation has both visible and unobservable aspects. Also, an evaluation of just how innovative a particular technology is involves both objective and subjective judgments. Resolving these issues can get very messy.

Take, for example, the modern shipping container, which has radically transformed the global economy.[1] Shipping containers incorporate a combination of marvelous twentieth- and twenty-first-century technological advances that required substantial research and development (R&D) in construction, metals fabrication, and computer software. Simply figuring out the container's optimum geometry and setting the technical standards consumed millions of dollars in research. But to most of us, shipping containers appear to be plain metal boxes that have not changed in generations.

This irony is not unique to containers. In many cases, even among technology experts, what is considered a revolutionary innovation to some may seem merely incremental to others. Sometimes a major innovation can go unrecognized for years, even by its creator. For example, penicillin, the automated loom, and rocket propulsion were each dismissed by their own inventors only to be rediscovered by others, sometimes decades later. Other innovations are immediately heralded as revolutionary but then gradually fizzle out over the years, such as superconductors, magnetic bubble memory, supersonic air travel, and the Segway personal transport. Recognizing and judging innovation is neither simple nor clear-cut.

Finally, we know that *innovation* has something to do with *scientific progress* and *technological change*. They are the focus of this book. But this realization just moves the question down the causal chain. That is, if science and technology (S&T) progress is the main element of innovation, then what exactly counts as science and technology, and how do we recognize or measure *their* progress? Answering these questions is equally problematic because progress in *science* and progress in *technology* overlap and interact. Hence, it can be difficult to distinguish one from the other to figure out which is cause or effect. So too is it difficult to separate out *innovation* from *diffusion*.

To further complicate matters, there is no consensus on any of these issues. Research on how progress occurs in science, technology, and innovation is now conducted throughout the social sciences, with thousands of articles and books published yearly. However, the basic concepts are treated very differently across these fields and sometimes even across individual scholars within the same field. For newcomers to the innovation debate, and even for many old hands, it is important to recognize how chaotically this debate has evolved. Even more important, readers should recognize that scholars from different parts of the innovation debate often mean strikingly different things when using terms like *technology* or *innovation*. Even where definitions concur, researchers often use different variables and data to measure them. This confusion muddies the debate and retards progress in understanding Cardwell's Law. For these reasons, this chapter summarizes this book's approach to boundaries, definitions, measurement, and data; more in-depth explanations can be found in the appendices.

Boundaries

Let's start by setting some useful boundaries for the chapters that follow. First, this book's goal is to understand why some countries are better than others at S&T. The short-hand term for this is ***Cardwell's Law***.[2] Specifically, we are concerned with explaining national differences in S&T performance both over time and across different countries within the same time period.

Second, this book mostly concerns itself with explaining differences in national innovation rates since World War II. Prior to this, there is much less data with which we can judge or compare national S&T capabilities.[3] Also, one purpose of this book is to examine the role of government institutions and policies in promoting innovation. Before World War II, most modern S&T institutions or policies were notoriously absent, weak, or used for tangential purposes. Many governments believed they could, or should, do little to support innovation before the twentieth century. Therefore, if we want to test the effectiveness of government at promoting S&T, then we need to focus on the past seventy years. Finally, the benefits of globalization for S&T progress rose exponentially after World War II. This does not mean that this book's conclusions do not apply to earlier time periods. Nor will it omit entirely all discussion of deeper history. But it will tend to stick with recent decades because the evidence and action are richest then.

Third, this book takes the *nation-state* as its unit of analysis. It therefore does *not* center its attention on the individual, firm, or laboratory. This is because *national* politics, institutions, and policies create the environment within which innovation occurs. That is, even though individuals and firms are the direct producers of innovation, their productivity is strongly affected by characteristics of the nation-state in which they operate. The *national* environment helps to explain why the best and brightest direct their energies toward S&T rather than religion, war, the arts, or illegal activities. The *national* environment also helps to explain the results of these innovative energies. These are precisely the kinds of relationships that this book seeks to explore. Therefore, a focus on the nation-state makes sense.

Fourth, this book attempts to cover as many nations as possible, but it highlights the most paradoxical country cases because they can provide the deepest insights into why countries innovate (or fail to). For example, it is interesting, but probably not surprising, that Germany is more innovative than Tanzania, Cambodia, or Moldova. Poverty, level of development, and bad government clearly stand out as the prime suspects in those countries. But it is far more difficult, and interesting, to explain why Germany is so much more innovative than France, Australia, or Norway. That is, why are there such major differences in innovation rates among the many wealthy, developed, and relatively well-run democracies? It is more challenging still to explain the rapid rise of formerly undeveloped or nondemocratic countries like Israel, Ireland, Taiwan, and Singapore. These countries each suffered from histories of poor, backward economies, and some were further burdened with autocratic or corrupt governments, yet each has become successful at S&T. It is the experiences of those countries that contradict our expectations that should give us the most leverage for explaining national innovation rates.

This book also tends to omit very small states from its analyses.[4] For example, some tiny countries like Liechtenstein, Monaco, and Barbados have disproportionally large footprints in the S&T data. This is because foreign corporations and individuals use these nations as tax and tariff havens or export hubs, but there is little indigenous innovation going on there. More important, one of this book's arguments is that international social networks are vital for innovation. These small countries skew the statistical data in favor of this argument. Therefore, omitting them creates a stronger test of that hypothesis. For similar reasons, very small economies are omitted. For example, it could be argued that countries like Burundi, Nepal, and Fiji simply lack the economic resources, scope, or scale to become innovative and are therefore forced to either network internationally or stagnate. Therefore, as a rule of thumb, this book often uses as its lower boundary a population of four million people and/or $10 billion in annual gross domestic product in 2010.[5]

Fifth, *science* and *technology* often overlap. However, where possible, attention here is paid mainly to technology, less so to science. Why? Scientific progress can be purely theoretical. It must usually be embodied in new products or processes for it to result in the economic growth, industrial competitiveness, or military might that this book cares most about. Therefore, a greater emphasis on technological change is rational.

Sixth, the primary concern of this book is more with *innovation* than *diffusion*. Again, these two phenomena are sometimes so interdependent that they are difficult to distinguish. This book makes no claim to have solved this perennial problem. But where possible, I focus more on why some countries are better at inventing new technologies, developing them from prototype to mass production, improving them, or adapting them to new uses. I am somewhat less concerned with the spread of new technology throughout society.

Definitions

Key terms like *science, technology,* and *innovation* get tossed around carelessly in the debate over national innovation rates. They are often left undefined. This has led to considerable confusion and unproductive debate as scholars compare, sometimes angrily, technological "apples" with innovation "oranges." So it is important to clarify how these major concepts are used in this book. The following are proposed as working definitions for use in subsequent chapters.[6]

For the purposes of this book, ***technology*** *is defined as a physical product, or a process for physically altering materials, that is used as an aid in problem solving.*[7] More precisely, technology is a product or process that allows people to perform entirely new activities or to perform established activities with increased efficiency. For example, the transistor and Bessemer process both count as technologies by this definition, but the corporation, just-in-time production, patent systems, and democratic federalism do not. Some aficionados of the innovation debate insist on distinguishing between high, rapid, revolutionary technology and low, slow, incremental technology, in which case this book focuses more on the former because it is inseparable from the cutting-edge innovation with which this book is most concerned.

Science is concerned with additions to the stock of public knowledge. *It is defined as the public and reproducible application of methodology to explain, predict,* *or control cause-and-effect relationships in the natural world (physical or social) or the gathering and classification of data to that end.* Science evolves via debate. Therefore, scientific progress often occurs through a series of conflicts and consensus among practitioners about research questions, definitions, theories, data, methods, and the interpretations of findings.[8]

Innovation *is defined as the discovery, introduction, and/or development of new technology, or the adaptation of established technology to a new use or to a new physical or social environment.* Innovation occurs throughout the technical evolution of an invention. It includes any technological changes introduced, from first prototype to the establishment of a globally competitive industry.[9] It therefore takes place both inside and outside of the research laboratory. Note that since technology is defined as a product or process, innovation can refer to advances in either. Students of military innovation should also observe that, for the purposes of this book, *innovation* is limited to improvements in technology; it does *not* include changes or improvements in doctrines, organizations, policies, or institutions. These are the causal variables I seek to test, so it would not make sense to include them as both cause and effect. Nor do I include creativity in food, fashion, entertainment, or cultural products in my definition. These are not the types of innovation I wish to capture. Rather, I am specifically interested in technological innovation because it brings with it the increasing returns upon which endogenous growth, military and industrial competitiveness, and considerable national wealth are based. For example, both the transistor and the bikini are inventions that changed the world.[10] But the bikini is not much different today than when it was introduced in 1946, whereas the transistor has led to near-exponential growth in computing and communication efficiency, power, and speed, at ever lower prices.

The term ***national innovation rate*** *refers to a country's indigenously produced technological change over a given period of time.* It is a measure of output or performance. Therefore, in the context of an international system of rival states, one might interpret relative national innovation rates as an indicator of ***technological competitiveness***—*the relative quantity and quality of states' outputs of new technology.* National innovation rates are a function of a country's ***technological capability***: *the aggregate ability of a nation's science, technology, engineering, and mathematics (STEM) labor, often working together with its businesspeople and entrepreneurs, to innovate.* This distinction is necessary because, although innovation requires technological capability, merely possessing the capability to innovate does not compel a nation to do so. Note also that no distinction is made in this book between invention and development, or between military and civilian innovation. These often overlapping phenomena can be "black boxed" without affecting this book's argument. Future research might consider distinguishing between these different kinds of technological change; however, the purpose of this book is to develop theory fundamental to overall innovation.

As mentioned earlier, the overlapping realms of *science* and *technology* are often left alloyed in this book. However, where possible, attention is paid mainly to technology. Nations with highly competitive science programs but less remarkable high-technology industries (e.g., Australia, Denmark) are not as relevant to this discussion as those states with the opposite characteristics (e.g., Singapore, Taiwan). Critics may argue that science and technology are distinct, but they are often difficult to distinguish in practice. One stereotype asserts that technological change mostly comes from new developments in science. This has become known as the "linear model" in which developments in the lab get taken up by firms, which then turn them into final products and processes. However, technology often precedes the science that explains it. For example, many major advances in semiconductors, medicine, metallurgy, and telecommunications occurred as a result of trial and error rather than by directed scientific inquiry. Only later did scientists produce theories that explained the technological breakthroughs. And in some labs, innovation can entail an iterative process, with improvements in science and technology occurring on top of one another or in a complementary way. I do not mean to dismiss the distinctions between science and technology. They *are* important. However, I leave these refinements for future research, for one cannot resolve everything in a single book. Most important, lumping *science* and *technology* together for now will not affect the argument made in this volume, which can serve as a basis for investigating precisely these more nuanced questions.

Finally, this book limits its discussion of *institutions* to those that adhere closest to economist Douglass North's description of them as "the rules of the game in a society."[11] ***Institutions*** are defined here as *sets of formally established practices, rules, or laws that regulate the relations between individuals, groups, and organizations*. Of course, public policy also plays a major role in competing explanations of national innovation rates. Therefore, following Richard Wilson, ***policies*** are defined here as *the actions, objectives, and pronouncements of governments on particular matters; the steps they take (or fail to take) to implement them; and the explanations they give for what happens (or does not happen).*[12] It is important to recognize that the definitional debate over *institutions* and *policies* is ongoing, rich, varied, and better summarized elsewhere.[13] The interpretations suggested previously are merely working definitions for use in this volume.

Also, in practice, the terms *institutions* and *policies* are often used interchangeably in debates over national innovation rates. That is, they are often treated as different degrees of the same concept, or as overlapping concepts, with *institutions* being greater in scope, depth, and/or longevity than *policies*. Where necessary, this book follows this custom. Specifically, the overlap between *institutions* and *policies* is retained in those cases where either common parlance demands it or where the boundary between them is obscure. For example, it is not entirely clear where the specific *policies* of a nation's patent system (e.g., duration, filing requirements, scope) become the *institution* of property rights. Alternately, is free market capitalism an *institution,* a collection of *policies,* or some combination thereof? In a related issue, the causal relationships between *institutions* and *policies* are mostly ignored in this volume. Thankfully, each of these issues has limited impact on this book's primary arguments and findings. That is, it matters little if an *institution* is occasionally mislabeled as a *policy* or vice versa; also, the specific details of how *institutions* and *policies* affect one another need not presently concern us. These issues may be important for subsequent stages of research, but they are largely immaterial here.

Beware—*Hic Sunt Dracones*

The previous S&T definitions may sound simple, straightforward, and noncontroversial, but they are nothing of the sort. For example, it is important to recognize that the words *science, technology,* and *innovation* each have relatively new meanings, arrived at only during the mid-twentieth century.[14] Since then, definitions of key terms have remained sloppy, vague, and highly contested. In economics and political science, only a handful of scholars strictly define *technology* and *innovation* in their writings. Everyone agrees that they have something to do with knowledge, research, education, and applying all of that to economic production. But beyond this, they are often not terribly specific. *Technology* is more often a "sort of measure of our ignorance."[15] For decades, *innovation* has been an undefined mix of invention and technological diffusion, more often the latter. A few economists prefer to emphasize *science* and its inputs to *invention,* where the former is the advancement of knowledge and the latter is the creation of new and improved products and processes.[16] However, others describe *invention* as the production of knowledge or information, a definition that has since become a mainstay of economic growth theory. Yet *invent* and *innovate* are often used interchangeably by some economists, while *inventive activities* and *research activities* are sometimes oddly separated. Also, *innovation* might be used to refer to either outputs (new technology) or the process of inventing and developing them.[17] In other theories, *innovation* is treated more like *technology,* other times like *invention,* and still other times like *entrepreneurialism.* More recently, *science, technology,* and *innovation* have been almost indistinguishably mixed into discussions of development, modernization, industrialization, economic growth, upgrading, productivity, standards of living, and competitive advantage.[18]

Appendix 1 explores this mayhem over definitions more deeply. The point of introducing it here is to emphasize how chaotic and disorderly the innovation debate is. Innovation research is currently full of inconsistencies, overlaps, and vagaries. Readers need to be aware of this chaos or risk utter confusion. For decades, scholars and policymakers have either used the same terms to discuss different concepts or used different terms to reference the same phenomenon. Worse yet, authors sometimes mix or change word meanings within the same discussion! Yet this problem generally goes unacknowledged within the innovation debate.

Both experts and general readers should care about this mess. It means that data and evidence relevant to one definition are often used inconsistently to prove theories based on entirely different definitions. Then, when subsequent research or policy is built upon these assertions, it often fails, further confusing the debate. This is one reason that the debate over national innovation rates does not progress as purposefully as it should. Imagine, for example, if different chemists mixed up their usage of terms like *hydrogen* with *oxygen*, or *catalyst* with *reactant*. No progress would occur. Chemists would constantly be confused as to why one researcher's successful formula was another's failure. In short, innovation scholars and S&T policymakers need to be more specific and consistent with their terms, while readers need to pay better attention to them and cry foul when necessary. The working definitions and boundaries used in this book are not perfect. There remain overlaps and vagaries that need to be worked out. But at least the definitions used here, and their faults, are specific and explicit.

The working definitions used in this volume also establish a vitally important premise: that progress in S&T is intimately bound with a nation's performance in economic growth, development, industrialization, entrepreneurialism, manufacturing, upgrading, and modernization. S&T is also necessary for modern defense. These debates are often treated separately. I argue that they must be joined together.

American anxieties over China underscore why this matters. China today is seen as the primary challenger to US economic and military power. But we do not fear China simply because it is large, undemocratic, or culturally and historically distinct. Many countries fit that description. Indeed, prior to 2000, the United States did not fear China much at all because the Chinese did not have the ability to compete economically or to project military force beyond their own borders. Rather, it is China's industrialization and modernization that make its size, political ideology, and cultural distinctions so potentially threatening to Americans. And progress in indigenous S&T capability is indispensable for China's rise to power. Without S&T, China would remain a curious and recalcitrant annoyance, a malcontent at the periphery of our attention.

It is also impossible to debate why nations succeed or fail at industrialization, manufacturing, modernization, and so forth without implicitly discussing innovation. Therefore, findings about why some countries are better at S&T have enormous implications for these other debates. Unfortunately, these complementarities often go unrealized. In many ways, the scattered approaches to studying S&T resemble the proverbial men in a dark room who examine different parts of an elephant and then disagree on what animal is before them. In fact, despite similar findings on questions of common interest, few of these scholars cite one another, and many seem unaware of the contributions each may have for the other. Collectively, however, there is tremendous value in bringing together diverse theories, methods, and data for explaining national innovation rates and pointing toward the policy implications of these findings. Hence, this book can be interpreted as a call for greater integration of science and technology politics within the major debates over innovation.

Measuring the Black Box

If defining innovation is problematic, then observing and measuring it can be downright controversial.[19] This is because innovation is very difficult—some might argue impossible—to observe directly. Scholars therefore often describe innovation as a "black box,"[20] a moniker borrowed from science and engineering, where a "black box" indicates an unobservable process, like a computer program whose code is hidden, or a sealed electronic circuit with wires running to and from it. Most of us feel surrounded by black boxes, such as our televisions, cars, mobile phones, and even our refrigerators. We can see the inputs and dials going in and experience the results coming out, but what happens inside the black box is opaque to most of us.

This is precisely the problem that bedevils the measurement of innovation. We can track the inputs and outputs (Figure 2.1), but innovation itself takes place out of public view: on the factory floor, in laboratories, even on the battlefield. To further complicate matters, measuring *national* success in S&T over time requires us to gather and combine all the observations of individual innovations as they occur, few of which are formally tracked or recorded by government or business. Worse yet, even experts can fail to recognize an innovation until long after it has been adopted and diffused. Indeed, some of the most life-changing, society-altering technologies in history were not perceived as being especially innovative when they first appeared. Also, decisions about what is *revolutionary* versus *incremental* S&T progress are a combination of objective and subjective judgments, which themselves can change drastically over time.

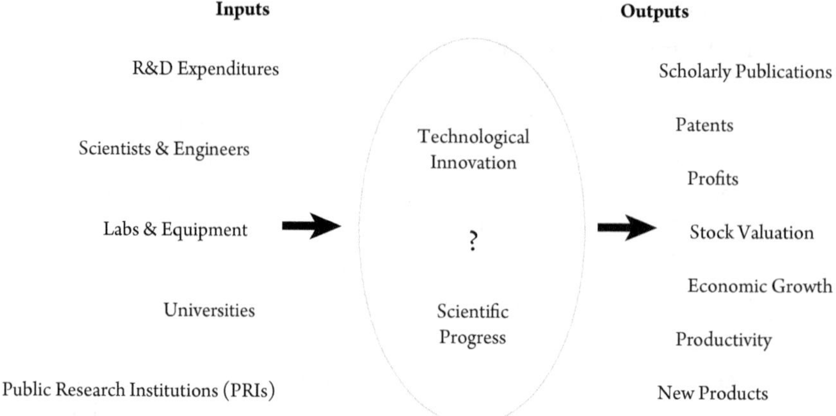

Figure 2.1 The black box of innovation.

Take, for example, the transistor (Figure 2.2). The transistor is often heralded as the greatest invention of the twentieth century, perhaps of all time. It has revolutionized almost every realm of human activity by simply allowing us to amplify electric currents or to quickly switch them on/off. These two properties make the transistor the fundamental building block of all the modern computers, telecommunications equipment, and electronic devices that pervade our daily lives.[21] But it is not clear when exactly this technology was invented *or* when it became revolutionary.

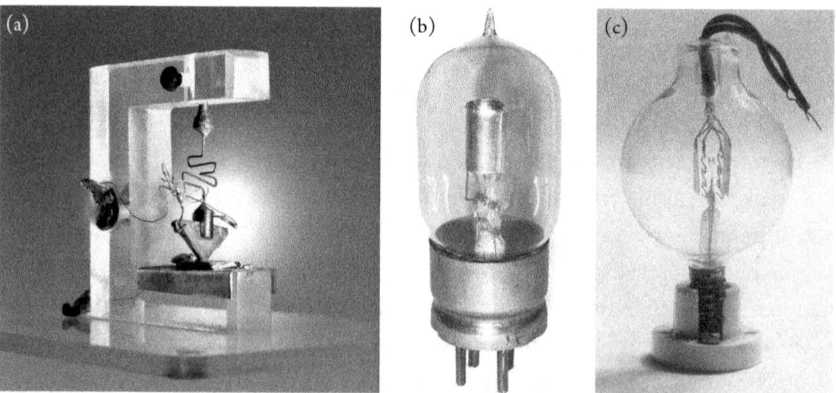

Figure 2.2 Which is the "revolutionary" technological innovation?

a) The world's first transistor, developed in 1947 by John Bardeen, Walter Brattain, and William Shockley at Bell Laboratories. Photo courtesy Alcatel-Lucent.
b) An early high-vacuum thermionic tube, the type used by the millions from 1913 until the 1970s. Photo Courtesy, Ian Poole, Electronics+Radio Ezine www.electronics-radio.com
c) Lee de Forest's audion invented around 1907. Photo courtesy, History San Jose.

The usual date given for the invention of the transistor is sometime during December 1947. This is when the team of John Bardeen, Walter Brattain, and William Shockley, working together at Bell Labs, successfully tested a solid-state amplifier made of germanium, plastic, and a strip of gold foil. A colleague called their bizarre-looking, palm-sized prototype a "transfer resistor" or *transistor*. They soon patented their device. But interestingly, Shockley's team did not publish or announce their great discovery for several months. Even when they did, few people cared about it. When the transistor was finally showcased for the press in July 1948, the *New York Times* buried the story on page forty-six and gave it only three short paragraphs in the "News of Radio" column, the last of nine stories on the radio industry.[22] This is an oddly subdued reaction to the most revolutionary invention of the century.

One reason for the lack of excitement over the first transistor was that vacuum tubes had already been doing its job for decades. The first device to act like a transistor was the *audion*, a basic three-electrode vacuum tube created around 1907 by the independent American inventor Lee de Forest. The audion was the first electronic amplifier. It allowed a small electrical signal coming into it to control a larger current flowing out. But the audion was a technical curiosity until scientists at AT&T improved upon it a few years later. Renaming the technology a *high-vacuum thermionic tube*, AT&T began installing them on phone lines in 1913 and they assisted in long-distance telephony. A German physics professor, Julius Lilienfield, then figured how to construct an electronic amplifier out of solid blocks of copper sulfide. This innovation promised to get rid of the bulky vacuum tube, which was slow, often overheated, and used much power. Lilienfield patented his ideas in 1930, but he never put them into production, and they quickly faded from the scientific debate.[23] It was only when Shockley tried to patent his own contributions to the 1947 transistor at Bell Labs that he discovered that he had mostly just replicated Lilienfield's work.[24]

As for the transistor "revolution," that was far in the future. For years after its 1947 "invention," it was not clear whether the transistor was technologically innovative. The big improvement made by Bell Labs' device over either vacuum tubes or Lilienfield's amplifier was in the way that the transistor amplified currents by introducing electric charges. It was scientifically brilliant! It helped physicists understand atomic behavior, eventually winning Shockley's team the Nobel Prize. But the actual transistor was too large and too fragile to use in business or military applications. Worse yet, the first transistors suffered from terrible performance characteristics. No two behaved alike. The head of Bell Labs' development group joked that "In the very early days, the performance of a transistor was apt to change if someone slammed a door."[25] So while it was scientifically fascinating, there were no practical uses for it. The transistor's first commercial applications wouldn't come until years later, in 1953, when it appeared in the

Sonotone 1010 hearing aid. Yet even this was far from a revolutionary technology. The Sonotone used a single transistor to conserve power, but the heavy lifting of amplification was more reliably performed by two small vacuum tubes. So anyone measuring technological innovation during the early 1950s would not have considered the transistor to be big news.[26] Its impact was potential, not realized. Practical uses for the transistor appeared only slowly thereafter. The milestones include their spread to handheld radios (1954), basic military applications (1955), satellites (1958), mini-computers (1964), and handheld calculators (1967). But it was only during the 1970s, when the transistor-based computer industry boomed, that "revolutionary" became a popular accolade to describe the transistor.

The point is that identifying and measuring innovation is much more difficult than it sounds. Innovation does deliver *objective*, physical improvements. But evaluating these improvements can depend on *subjective* human judgments and time-sensitive actions. And these judgments can change drastically over time and place. There are likely many inventions that exist today that we dismiss or ignore but that our grandchildren may one day trumpet as among the greatest innovations of the twenty-first century.

This Book's Approach to Measurement and Data

The issues discussed previously make gathering data on national innovation rates an area of intense disagreement. How does one measure what cannot be seen? And how can we compare innovation rates across countries? To date, no ideal "catch-all" indicator has been developed. Instead, each policymaker, think tank, and scholar tends to use a particular measure that is his or her favorite. A brief history of the attempts to measure national innovation rates can be found in appendix 2.

To simplify, there are four major types of innovation measures to consider. First, S&T *input measures* attempt to gauge innovation by quantifying the resources dedicated to producing scientific progress and technological change. Usually this involves measuring proximate inputs to the R&D process such as spending, STEM labor, and different types of research equipment or facilities. Second, S&T *output measures* track the products of the R&D process, ranging from proximate measures (technology patents, research publications, new products and processes) to more distant calculations (the performance of high-tech corporations or of the general economy). Third, *surveys* ask for the judgment of experts, businesses, or scientists regarding the value and sophistication of science and technology in their sector or country. Finally, innovation *indices* aggregate input and output measures into a single figure using some sort of weighted average decided upon by the index author(s). Some indices also often include survey data and measures of political-economic institutions (e.g., property rights, education systems, financial institutions) and technological diffusion.

In this book, output measures are usually preferred over input measures. There are four reasons for this preference. First, inputs do not necessarily lead to high-quality or high-quantity outputs. R&D funding can be misspent or misappropriated. STEM workers may not be used for much R&D or may not be well qualified. Equipment may sit unused because of a lack of trained personnel, it is not suited to the necessary R&D task, or it may be obsolete or dysfunctional. Second, the effectiveness of S&T inputs on innovation often depends on the sector or industry in which they are employed. For example, R&D spending is heaviest in manufacturing industries; therefore, countries with large service sectors would see their innovation rate underreported relative to countries with large indigenous manufacturing sectors. Third, there is often a time lag between the application of inputs to R&D activity and the delivery of new science or technology, often stretching across several years. Hence, it is sometimes unclear how to match the dates of the inputs with the resulting innovations. Fourth, and perhaps most important, this book seeks to test the effects of different institutions and policies on national innovation rates. They are inputs. So it would be tautological to use both input measures of innovation *and* data on institutions and policies in the same test. For example, if government creates a policy to increase R&D spending (a policy variable), then obviously we expect that R&D will rise (an input measure of innovation). But to claim this as proof that policy increases innovation is dishonest. It shows a tautology, not causality. It makes little sense to use inputs as measures of the very outputs we seek to explain. In sum, this book does use some input measures where appropriate, but it prefers output measures where possible.

By far, the most frequently used output measure of innovation is technology patents. They have been used to assess national innovation rates since at least the 1920s. Patents are by no means a perfect index of innovation, but they are among the best studied, most clear-cut, and well understood of all the innovation data. The debate over the proper use of patent data has proceeded vigorously and with increasing sophistication over the past several decades. The current consensus holds that patent data is a good measure of innovation when used in the aggregate (e.g., as a rough measure of national levels of innovation across long periods of time) but is less appropriate when used as a measure of micro-level innovation (e.g., to compare the innovativeness of individual firms or specific industries from year to year). Researchers have also found that patent data works best to measure national innovation rates when patents are weighted by forward citations[27] and per capitized.[28] In this form, patent data has been found to correlate strongly with other phenomena that we generally associate with aggregate innovation rates (e.g., science prizes, capital goods production, productivity). Patents may be imprecise measures of innovation, but they offer considerable advantages over rival measures. Therefore, for statistical data on innovation, in this book, *national innovation rates are often measured using technology patents, per capita, weighted by forward citations, granted during a specified time period.* For readers who remain skeptical of patent measures, appendix 3 offers a more thorough discussion of their strengths and weaknesses.

Of course, not everybody will be convinced by patent data, especially since this data may favor more developed countries. Therefore, this book also considers case studies of, and statistical data on, STEM research, industrialization, modernization, manufacturing, productivity, and export composition.

Data for other factors (e.g., institutions, external threats, domestic tensions) will be discussed as they arise in subsequent chapters. Innovation deserves its own separate discussion here because measuring it is so poorly understood, difficult, and controversial. Most people assume that quantifying social factors like institutions and security are highly problematic and contentious, whereas gathering data on S&T is straightforward. But among experts, the opposite often holds true.

Another methodological strategy employed in this book is to triangulate wherever possible. This means using multiple, independent datasets of the same phenomenon, perhaps together with case studies, to test hypotheses. The idea here is that the random noise in any single dataset gets cancelled out by the randomness in others, allowing the common signal to come through. Also, if multiple, independent measures each produce the same result, then we can be more confident of the result than when using a single dataset.

A complementary solution is to remind ourselves that *all* data have errors, noise, and perhaps bias. This is true even in physics, chemistry, and engineering. In fact, in the physical sciences, many important properties could not be well measured for centuries, including velocity, heat, pressure, brightness, and magnetism. Yet these fields still progressed, providing us with a steady stream of valuable insights. So we should not let our quest for "perfect" innovation data prevent us from using the much "good" data that we have available. We just need to be aware of its limitations.

In sum, innovation measures are often imprecise, indirect, and fraught with errors and potential biases. This might sound like a damning set of problems, but it just makes them like any other measure in economics or politics, and even many in the physical sciences. All empirical measures come with flaws. The solution is *not* to dismiss these data out of hand. It would be unscientific to throw out the statistical baby with the error-prone and biased bathwater. Rather, good scientists take the best data they can get. They then try to extract the signal from the noise by using multiple independent datasets and methodologies. This is the strategy used in this book. But innovation scholars and policymakers also need to be honest and explicit about the potential problems with the data. Too many theories and policies are sold to the public without much discussion of how messy the data might be. If the arguments made in this book stand the test of time, it is because they have been based on the most honest and scientific assessments of as much data as possible.

Some readers who believe the issues of definitions, measures, and data to be essential may remain unsatisfied by the brief discussion given previously. I again refer them to the appendices at the end of this book. Appendix 1 surveys the definitions debate over time and across different subfields. It provides evidence of how chaotic, varied, and nuanced this debate is, and has always been. Appendix 2 describes various attempts to measure national innovation rates during the past century. It discusses the evolution of innovation measurement over time, as well as the technical and political factors driving this endeavor. Appendix 3 offers an in-depth discussion of national innovation measures and data. It more thoroughly justifies this book's choices. It also provides an overview of the major types of S&T data and indicators, examines their strengths and weaknesses, identifies some of the major data sources and research centers, and cites some of the prominent scholars who are central to this area of research.

3

Cardwell's Law in Action

Looking across several millennia of human history, one finds that the torch of global leadership in science and technology has passed, seemingly at random, between disparate societies over the past five thousand years. Several in-depth historical surveys of technological change[1] reveal that the shortlist of global innovation leaders has included such diverse nations[2] as the ancient Egyptians, Greeks, Romans, early Muslim Sultanates, China's Yuan Dynasty, the Italian city-states, the Dutch Republic during its "golden age," and Britain in the first industrial revolution, just to name a few.[3] These societies usually appeared at the science and technology (S&T) frontier with little warning. Then they faded or disappeared almost as inexplicably. This constantly changing leadership was also accompanied by tremendous differences in S&T performance across countries and regions. Individual states rose and fell over time, but diversity in national innovation rates remained strong and persistent.

However, it is not so obvious that such enormous shifts and disparities in national innovation rates still occur in our own time. After all, both science and technology were fairly low priorities throughout most of human history. Societies were simply not trying to innovate much. Instead, for millennia, technological change occurred more through accident, trial and error, and tinkering than as a result of systematic research and development (R&D) or the application of scientific knowledge.[4] In fact, the connection between science and technology was not broadly recognized before the late nineteenth century. Before then, scientific research was more of a quirky hobby than a useful occupation.[5] In many circles, it was also widely believed that technological change was unnecessary, effete, and perhaps even dangerous to society.[6] Thus, for most of history, S&T was more often a curiosity than a national goal. As a result, S&T proceeded glacially.

In contrast, the past seventy years have witnessed the rise of an entirely new social paradigm regarding innovation.[7] Modern economic thought is now practically defined by the quest for new science and technology. Most societies also now realize that S&T can vastly improve their standards of living, economic competitiveness, and physical security. In fact, S&T progress has become so idolized that it is even prescribed as the solution to problems caused by S&T itself, such as air pollution, industrial poisons, automobile deaths, or climate change. As a result, almost all countries now dedicate at least some resources toward the pursuit of S&T. This dramatic change may have nullified anything like Cardwell's Law.

Similarly, attitudes toward government have also been transformed.[8] As recently as seventy years ago, most governments felt that they had little duty or ability to promote innovation. S&T progress was long believed to be a random occurrence—a product of luck, not policy. Many states also viewed S&T as peripheral, even inimical, to national interest. Therefore, governments should stay out of it. This was the historic norm for most governments throughout human history. Since World War II, however, governments around the world have come to believe that they can, and should, do something positive about national innovation rates.

Yet another factor that makes our current time period unique is how easy it has become to innovate. Since World War II, globalization has eliminated many of the historic barriers to innovation around the world. For example, transportation and communications costs have dropped to a fraction of their historic levels. Education and literacy rates are today higher than ever, and by a substantial margin. This means that scientific and technical knowledge, investment capital, equipment and supplies, and science, technology, engineering, and mathematics (STEM) workers can now diffuse globally with relative ease. The inputs to innovation can travel cheaply. Therefore, location should not matter. Nations of all types should be rapidly converging toward the S&T frontier. These conditions are drastically different than during most of the periods studied by historians.

The purpose of this chapter is to investigate whether stark national differences in S&T performance still persist. That is, is there anything left to explain? Does something like Cardwell's Law still apply today? To answer these questions, this chapter presents some initial innovation data for dozens of nations over the past several decades. It also identifies which countries are the current global leaders and laggards in S&T, and how these positions have recently changed.

What Needs Explaining?

At first appearances, the ability of nations to produce science and technology seems evenly spread throughout the world. For example, a person traveling through most countries in North America, Europe, Asia, and Latin America can encounter similarly modern transportation systems, advanced telecommunications, computers, nuclear power stations, modern supermarkets, and even imposing military hardware. Certainly one can still find stereotypically "backward" villages in large parts of Africa, Eastern Europe, South Asia, and the Middle East. But then, some mountain towns, desert settlements, and farming communities in the United States, Germany, and Japan also fit that same stereotype. There appears to be more technological disparity within countries than across countries. Thanks to globalization, it seems that many of the world's nations are rapidly converging on the S&T frontier.

However, such a conclusion would be superficial, one based more on S&T consumption than production. Many countries can now afford to buy cutting-edge S&T, but they cannot create it. For example, Saudi Arabia now boasts of one of the most technologically advanced militaries in the world, replete with modern fighter jets, tactical radar, battle tanks, and cruise missiles. Of course, all of these technologies were produced by American or European defense firms.[9] Wealthy Argentines proudly sport the latest smart phones, luxury cars, and laptop computers. All are imported. Even the Buenos Aires subway system was designed, built, and supplied by British and Belgian firms. Countries throughout Eastern Europe are increasingly exporters of high technology,[10] but few of Eastern Europe's high-tech exports were invented, designed, or developed locally. They are mostly a result of offshoring by Western European firms. Even the factories in Eastern Europe, like those in Hungary and the Czech Republic, that produce these exports are often set up and run by foreigners; the host countries merely supply cheap labor and strategic locations for shipment.[11]

To confirm whether national innovation rates still vary, we need to look at S&T creation instead of consumption. This focuses our attention on a particular set of countries. That is, it is important to recognize just how lopsided global S&T activities are. There are roughly two hundred nation-states in the world today.[12] The vast majority of these countries produce little or no S&T whatsoever. For example, the bottom-most 146 countries together have produced only 1% of the world's technology patents over the past four decades, while the bottom-most 166 countries together published only 1% of the world's STEM research publications.[13] In R&D, the situation is equally askew. A mere thirty nations spent 95% of the world's R&D budget during 2014. As a result, as Table 3.1 shows, fewer than ten countries are responsible for the lion's share of global S&T production, at least according to these measures. Even being generous with the data, only a few dozen countries can be said to have much innovative footprint at all. Put simply, the club of innovative nations is very elite.

These disparities continue even *within* the small club of innovative nations. One way to observe this variation is through national patent data. Figures 3.1a–c graph the citations-weighted patent rates (per capita) of twenty-five of the world's wealthiest, most industrialized democracies over the 1970–2012 period, the longest time period that current data will allow us to analyze with such a high

Table 3.1 **Few Countries Produce Most of the World's S&T**[†]

75% of the World's STEM Research Pubs[*] *(1981–2011)*	*95% of the World's STEM Research Pubs*[*] *(1981–2011)*	*75% of the World's Tech Patents*[*] *(1976–2006)*	*95% of the World's Tech Patents*[*] *(1976–2006)*	*75% of the World's R&D Spending (2014)*	*95% of the World's R&D Spending (2014)*
USA	USA	USA	USA	USA	USA
Germany	Germany	Japan	Japan	China	China
Japan	Japan		Germany	Japan	Japan
UK	UK		France	Germany	Germany
France	France		UK	S. Korea	S. Korea
Canada	Canada		Canada	France	France
Italy	Italy		Switzerland	UK	UK
Netherlands	Netherlands		S. Korea	India	India
	Australia				Russia
	Switzerland				Brazil
	Sweden				Canada
	Spain				Australia
	China				Taiwan
	Belgium				Italy
	Denmark				Spain
	Israel				Netherlands
	Russia				Sweden
	India				Israel
	Finland				Switzerland
	S. Korea				Turkey
	Austria				Austria
	Brazil				Singapore
	Norway				Belgium
	Poland				Iran
	Taiwan				Mexico
	N. Zealand				Finland
	Hong Kong				Poland
	Greece				Denmark
					South Africa
					Qatar
n = 8	*n* = 30	*n* = 2	*n* = 8	*n* = 8	*n* = 30

[†] Countries listed in descending order; not adjusted for population size.

[*] Weighted by forward citations.

Sources: National Bureau of Economic Research (2006); Thomson-ISI (2013); *R&D Magazine* (2014).

level of precision. Since the United States is by far the most innovative country in the world during this time period, the data in Figures 3.1a–c have been normalized to show each country's innovation rate relative to that of the United States (US = 1.0). Figure 3.1a presents data on those countries that are consistently the world's most innovative nations, Figure 3.1b shows the midlevel innovators, and Figure 3.1c highlights those countries that have had the most significant increases in innovation rates during the forty-two-year period. Note that all of the graphs use the same vertical scale and therefore can be compared against one another. With this aggregate data in hand, we can begin to make some initial judgments about national innovation rates.

According to Figures 3.1a–c, Cardwell's Law is alive and well. The topmost panel (Figure 3.1a) shows the world's "most innovative" countries for the past four decades. Japan's legendary miracle leap to the technological frontier is clearly visible in these patent data, with Japan even outperforming the United States in recent years. Sweden also appears to be experiencing a slow but steady climb since the early 1990s. Conversely, Switzerland has experienced some rapid relative decline, but it still remains a top innovator. Meanwhile, decade after decade, the United States, Canada, and Germany have produced new technology at a steady rate that consistently eclipses that of most other nations in the world.

The second panel shows the set of "midlevel" innovators (Figure 3.1b). These countries do add significantly to the world's stock of new S&T, just not at the high innovation rates of the world's most innovative nations. This pack of midlevel countries is also relatively stable over time.[14] We can see in these data some occasional jockeying for relative position, but there are few dramatic leaps or dips. The only exceptions are the recent upsurge by the Netherlands and perhaps the gentle climb of Denmark.

Then there are the "rapid innovators," shown in the bottom panel (Figure 3.1c): Finland, Taiwan, Israel, Singapore, and South Korea. In 1970, each of these countries was either a low ranking midlevel innovator or worse. Nevertheless, by 2000, after years of steady improvement, each of these nations had entered the ranks of the world's most innovative nations. It is precisely these disparities that this book seeks to explain: why did the countries in Figure 3.1c become so innovative, while the midlevel nations in Figure 3.1b did not?

Of course, patents can be selective measures of innovation. For several countries, it is reasonable to ask whether patents really reflect *national* innovation rates or just those of particular industries. For example, does the impressive patenting performance of Finland or Sweden truly represent that entire nation's ability to innovate, or just the unprecedented technological change created by a few telecom firms like Nokia (Finland) and Ericsson (Sweden)? Table 3.2 answers this question by breaking down the patent data by industry for several countries.

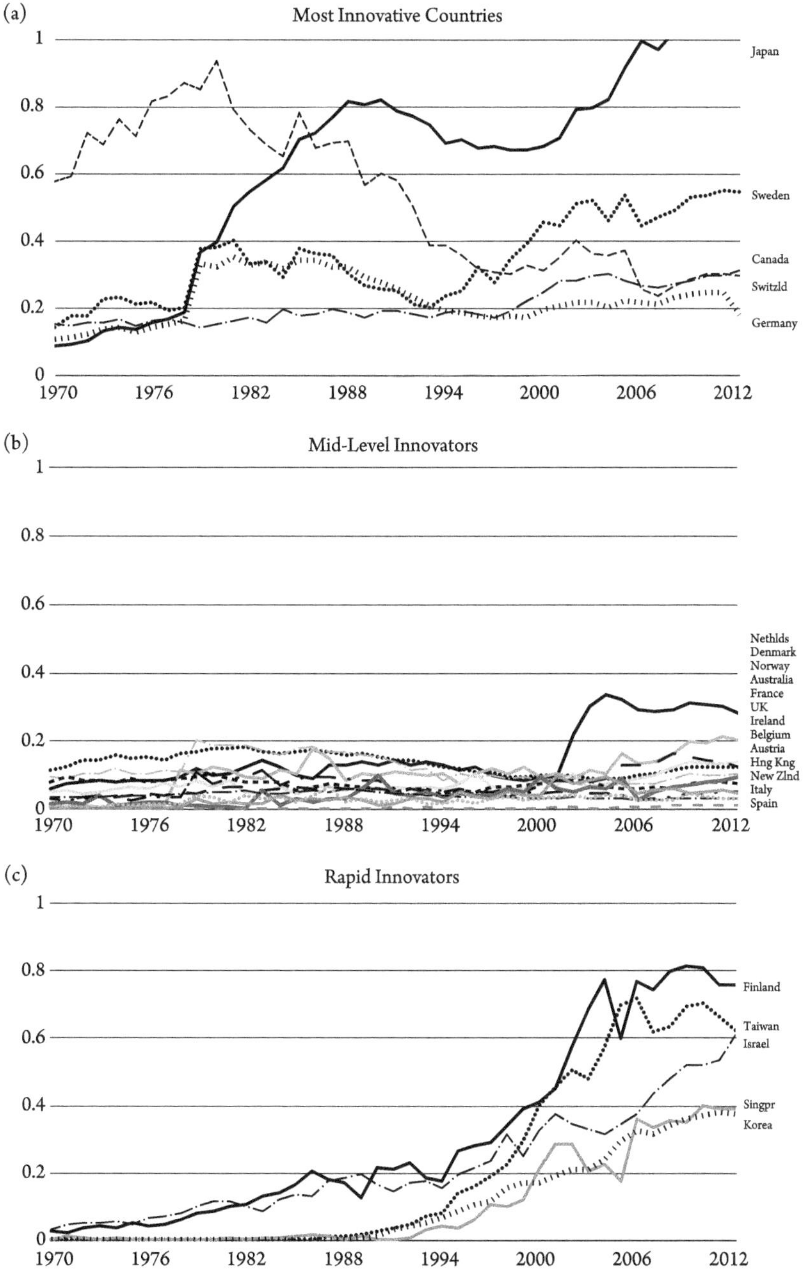

Figure 3.1a–c Total citations-weighted technology patents per capita (US = 1.00).

This deeper inspection of patenting in Finland and Sweden reveals that innovation there is indeed economy-wide. As expected, Finland is overweight in information technologies (IT) and telecommunications patents, but it is also strong in chemicals and mechanical patents. Sweden is surprisingly underweight in IT

Table 3.2 **Percentage of Total Patents, by Industry (1963–2006)**

Grey cells indicate overweight/underweight relative to the world average; Bold = overweight; Italic = underweight.

	World	*USA*	*JPN*	*SWE*	*SWZ*	*GER*	*CAN*	*KOR*	*TWN*	*FIN*	*ISR*	*CHN*
Chemical	18.9%	19.7%	16.9%	**26.5%**	19.5%	**26.7%**	16.7%	*9.7%*	*7.1%*	21.9%	15.1%	**26.9%**
IT-Telecom	13.5%	13.7%	**21.6%**	*4.0%*	*5.2%*	*6.0%*	12.9%	**31.3%**	14.2%	**25.6%**	**19.2%**	10.3%
Medical-Drugs	8.2%	9.1%	*4.3%*	9.5%	11.1%	7.0%	8.4%	*2.3%*	*1.9%*	5.9%	**21.0%**	**13.3%**
Electrical	18.4%	17.8%	**24.7%**	14.1%	15.2%	16.1%	*13.5%*	**37.6%**	**43.5%**	*13.0%*	16.7%	19.9%
Mechanical	20.9%	19.1%	21.5%	22.2%	23.9%	**27.3%**	22.5%	*11.1%*	*15.0%*	20.8%	*13.0%*	*14.5%*
Other	20.1%	20.6%	**11.1%**	23.7%	**25.1%**	16.8%	**25.9%**	*8.0%*	18.4%	*12.6%*	*15.1%*	*15.0%*

Source: National Bureau of Economic Research (2006).

and telecom patents while overweight in chemicals. However, neither of these Nordic countries is a single-company, or even a single-industry, innovator. Other countries' patent specializations match their individual reputations: Germany is overweight in chemicals and mechanical patents; Japan and Korea are strongest in IT, telecom, and electrical; Taiwan patents heavily in electrical industries and lightest in medical and pharmaceuticals; and the distribution of US innovation roughly matches the global distribution.

What about the data on science? This book is admittedly more concerned with technological change, but new scientific knowledge is regularly used as an input to the innovation process. Also, performance in science often correlates strongly with a nation's ability to innovate. Figures 3.2a–d attempt to get at the science aspect of innovation. They graph the citations-weighted STEM research publication rates (per capita) of the world's top science producers over the 1981–2011 period, the longest time period covered by existing datasets. Again, the data have been normalized to show each country's innovation rate relative to that of the United States (US = 1.0).

The STEM publications data in Figures 3.2a–d likewise confirm that enormous differences in national innovation rates persist in our own time. The publication data suggest that the world's "top" science nations (Figure 3.2a) include Switzerland, the Netherlands, and the Nordic countries. Here Switzerland clearly outpaces all other nations, with Denmark in second, while Norway generally trails the pack.

The second panel (Figure 3.2b) shows the "strong" science nations. These are the half-dozen countries, including the United States, that rank as reliable, regular producers of large amounts of scientific knowledge. Among them, Australia and Hong Kong are notable for their surge in productivity since the early 1990s.

The third panel (Figure 3.2c) charts the "midlevel" science nations. These countries are an interesting mix, especially when compared with their patent performance data (Figure 3.1). Each midlevel nation consistently produces scientific knowledge at a rate below that of the dozen top and strong science nations. However, three midlevel publications (science) nations are also top patenting (technology) countries (Taiwan, Japan, and South Korea), while another three fail to rank at all in the patent measures (Portugal, Greece, and Hungary), and two are equally midlevel innovators in both science and technology (Figure 3.1b), which is what one might expect.

The differences between national science and technology performance provide evidence of a divide recognized earlier in this book: that scientific progress and technological innovation overlap, but the former does not necessarily lead to the latter. Countries can be better at one or the other. Figure 3.3 shows this more clearly. The regression line in Figure 3.3 represents the global average balance of science versus technology productivity (publications vs. patents). The United States

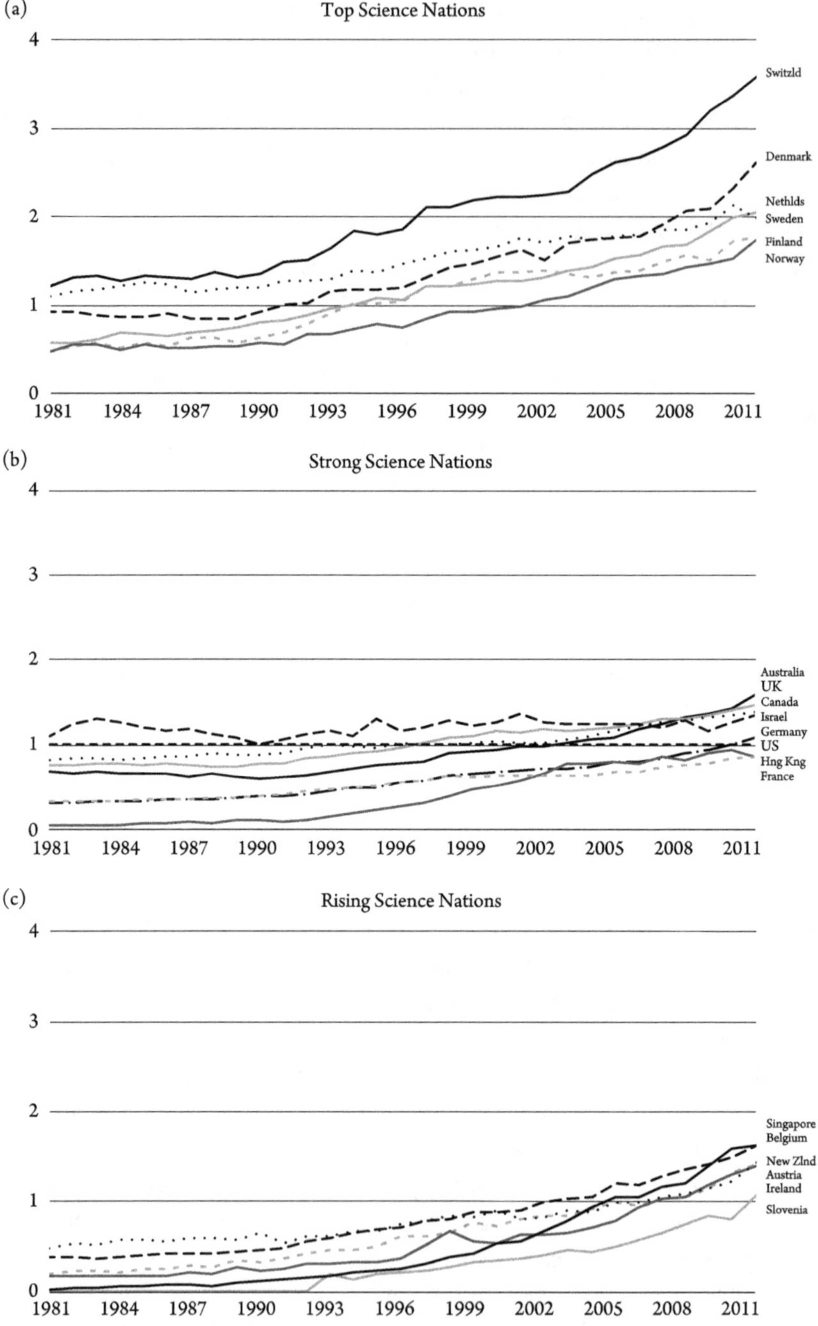

Figure 3.2a–d Total citations-weighted STEM research publications per capita (US = 1.00).

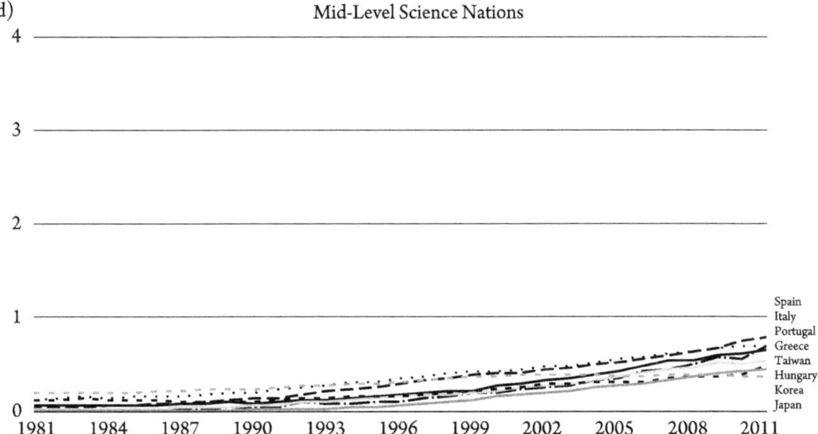

Figure 3.2a–d Continued

and Japan clearly stand out as marked outliers, far better at producing new technology than new science, at least relatively speaking. Germany, Taiwan, and South Korea also appear to be relatively more technology oriented than science oriented. On the other hand, several countries appear to be far more focused on scientific research than on technological innovation, including Denmark, the Netherlands, Great Britain, Norway, Australia, New Zealand, Belgium, and Austria.

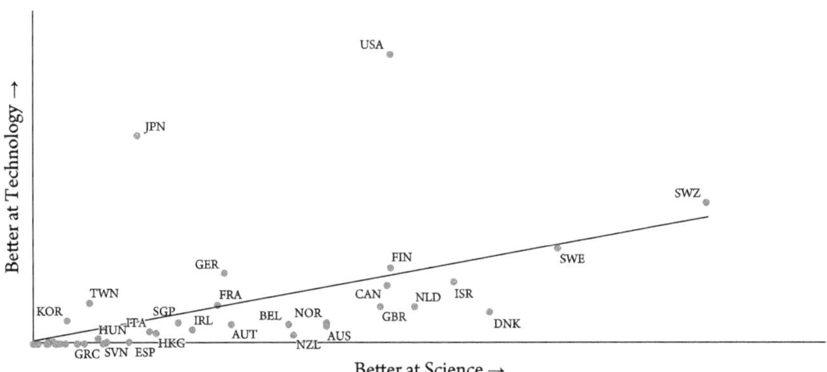

Figure 3.3 Technology patents versus research publications for the top 40 innovators (1981–2011). Aggregate number of patents per capita (weighted by forward citations) vs. aggregate number of STEM research publications per capita (weighted by forward citations) for the 1981-2011 period. Sources: NBER Patent Database, Thomspon-ISI Web of Science, US Patent and Trademark Office. Countries included: Australia, Austria, Belgium, Bulgaria, Canada, Chile, China, Croatia, Czech Republic, Denmark, Finland, France, Germany, Greece, Hong Kong, Hungary, India, Ireland, Israel, Italy, Japan, Mexico, Netherlands, New Zealand, Norway, Poland, Portugal, Russia, Singapore, Slovakia,

Interestingly, the United States does *not* rate as the global leader in science according the STEM publications data. The United States rapidly loses position after the mid-1990s and currently ranks only eighteenth by this measure. In other words, the upward slope experienced by most countries shown in Figures 3.2a–d

Table 3.3 **Nobel Prize Laureates by Nation**

	1950s	*1960s*	*1970s*	*1980s*	*1990s*	*2000s*	*2010s*[*]	*Total*
USA	32	28	36	39	43	57	29	264
UK	8	12	14	5	2	8	7	56
Germany	7	5	3	5	5	5	1	31
France	0	4	1	3	4	5	4	21
Switzld	1	0	2	9	3	1	0	16
Japan	0	1	0	1	0	7	5	14
Russia	6	3	1	0	0	2	0	12
Sweden	1	1	2	3	0	1	0	8
Canada	0	0	1	1	2	0	1	5
Israel	0	0	0	0	0	3	1	4
Australia	0	1	0	0	0	2	1	4
Belgium	0	0	3	0	0	0	1	4
Italy	1	1	1	1	0	0	0	4
Norway	0	1	0	0	0	0	2	3
Denmark	0	0	2	0	1	0	0	3
Argentina	0	1	1	0	0	0	0	2
Nethrlds	1	0	0	0	1	0	0	2
Hng Kng	0	0	0	0	0	1	0	1
Austria	0	0	1	0	0	0	0	1
Czech	1	0	0	0	0	0	0	1
Ireland	1	0	0	0	0	0	0	1
China	0	0	0	0	0	0	1	1

Nationality according to the university, research institution, or company with which the Laureate was affiliated at the time of the Prize announcement. Includes only Nobel Laureates in physics, chemistry, and physiology or medicine. Data not weighted by size of population or GDP.

[*]2010-2015.

Source: Nobelprize.org.

represents a relative decline by the flat United States (US = 1.0). Of course, this might simply reflect the fact that the United States excels more at revolutionary, cutting-edge, or "big" science than other countries, which is suggested by the list of Nobel Prize laureates that remains dominated by American winners (Table 3.3). Alternately, the relatively poor performance in science by the United States, as well as by Japan, Germany, Taiwan, and other top technology nations, could also be the result of industrial research. That is, private firms often do not publish their scientific research. Therefore, this scientific output would not show up in the data that tracks research published in peer-reviewed scientific journals. Instead, much corporate science is kept in-house, either as trade secrets, distributed internally, or sold on private markets. Classified research by the military and defense contractors would also tend to remain unpublished. As discussed in chapter 2 and the appendices, these types of signal versus noise issues are typical of all innovation data. One solution is to compare several different innovation measures and look for correlations among them, which is attempted the next section.

Which Are the World's Most Innovative Nations?

What about other measures of S&T performance? It may be tempting to attribute the patterns shown in Figures 3.1 and 3.2 to the idiosyncrasies of national patent laws or publishing behavior. However, other national S&T measures strongly corroborate the patent and publications data. For example, at the national level, the patent data correlate highly with other phenomena generally associated with innovation, including per capita gross domestic product (GDP) growth, manufacturing growth, exports of capital goods, R&D spending, and capital formation.[15] Also, as subsequent chapters will show, qualitative case studies tend to confirm the patent findings. Perhaps a simple litmus test of the credibility of the patent and publications data is that one cannot find an innovative country that is not relatively well represented by its aggregate patent or publications data. Even the Soviet Union regularly applied for patents during the Cold War and innovated at roughly the rate and quality represented by their citations-weighted patents per capita. Also, there is no counterfactual. That is, there is no hidden computer industry in Tanzania or high-performing biotech sector in Bulgaria that the patent and publication data are somehow missing. Nor are these patterns necessarily limited to 1970–2012. If historical case studies were included in this analysis, then many of the trends observed in Figures 3.1 and 3.2 would stretch back another fifty, and possibly one hundred, years.

If patent and publication data are not sufficient, then Table 3.4 brings together several innovation measures in one place. To construct this table, data in six

Table 3.4 **Top 50 Most Innovative Nations Across Multiple Measures**

	Patents	*Pubs*	*TFP*	*Tech Exports*	*Florida Index (2011)*	*INSEAD Index (2013)*	*WEF 2013*	*Composite Score*
Switzrlnd	2	1	1	1	2	1	1	68
Sweden	2	1	2	2	1	1	1	67
Nethrlds	3	1	1	1	4	2	2	63
USA	1	2	1	5	1	2	2	63
Finland	3	2	4	2	1	2	1	62
Germany	1	3	3	3	2	2	1	62
Israel	3	1	3	4	1	1	2	62
Denmark	4	1	2	2	2	4	3	59
UK	2	2	3	3	4	2	2	59
Japan	1	5	4	4	1	3	1	58
Belgium	4	3	1	2	4	4	3	56
Canada	2	2	2	4	3	3	5	56
Singapore	4	4	5	1	2	3	3	55
France	2	4	2	3	3	4	4	55
Ireland	5	4	4	1	4	1	4	54
Austria	4	3	3	3	3	5	3	53
Norway	4	3	1	5	3	6	3	52
S. Korea	1	6	7	3	2	3	4	51
Australia	3	2	2	7	3	7	5	48
Italy	3	4	3	5	5	4	6	47
New Zlnd	5	3	4	7	4	5	5	44
Hng Kng	5	4	5	5	5	6	4	43
Taiwan*	1	5	6	1	unranked	unranked	2	40
Spain	5	5	4	6	5	6	6	40
Czech Rep	8	6	5	4	5	5	7	37
Hungary	6	5	6	4	6	3	10	37
Malaysia	7	10	—	2	10	5	4	29
China	6	—	—	7	6	1	6	29
Portugal	8	6	6	7	6	9	7	28

Table 3.4 **Continued**

	Patents	*Pubs*	*TFP*	*Tech Exports*	*Florida Index (2011)*	*INSEAD Index (2013)*	*WEF 2013*	*Composite Score*
Costa Ric	10	8	—	5	8	4	6	27
Slovakia	8	6	5	6	7	7	—	27
Poland	7	6	6	7	7	9	9	26
Greece	9	5	5	8	7	—	—	21
Russia	7	8	—	9	5	8	10	21
S. Africa	6	7	—	9	9	—	7	20
Bulgaria	—	7	7	8	8	6	—	19
Brazil	6	9	8	9	8	10	8	19
Turkey	7	8	8	10	9	8	8	19
India	5	—	—	—	8	6	7	19
Chile	9	7	7	10	9	10	8	17
Mexico	7	10	7	6	—	—	9	16
Romania	—	9	8	8	9	5	—	16
Croatia	10	7	—	—	6	7	—	16
Argentina	8	7	7	9	10	—	—	14
Ukraine	9	10	—	9	7	7	—	14
Saudi	6	9	—	—	—	—	5	14
Thailand	10	—	—	6	—	8	8	12
Philppns	10	—	—	6	10	9	9	11
UAE	—	8	—	—	—	—	5	11
Belarus	—	9	—	8	—	8	—	9

* Taiwan suffers from a low composite score in because it is not included in two of the indices. Columns: patents per capita, weighted by forward citations (1976–2006 average, National Bureau of Economic Research [2006]); STEM research publications per capita, weighted by forward citations (1981–2011 average, Thomson-ISI Web of Science); total factor productivity (1970–2012 average, Conference Board); high-tech exports per GDP (1988–2012 average), Richard Florida's Technology Index (2011, most recent year available); INSEAD Global Innovation Index: "Knowledge & Tech Outputs" (2013, most recent year available), World Economic Forum: Innovation & Sophistication subindex (2013–2014, most recent year available). The "composite score" in the rightmost column is calculated by awarding 1 point for each decile in each category (e.g. each top ranked country in a category gets 10 points, bottom ranked countries get 1 point), then these points are summed for each country across categories to produce the composite.

categories of S&T outputs were gathered for roughly two hundred nation-states. The top fifty countries in each category are listed in Table 3.4. The numbers 1 through 10 indicate the decile within which each country falls for a particular category. A "1" indicates a nation ranking among the top five nations in that category; "10" indicates a nation ranking among the bottom five nations. A simple composite score was then calculated to aggregate ranks across all categories.[16]

One confirming message in Table 3.4 is the strong correlation between the category rankings. Despite the wide variety of sources and the differences in time periods covered, there is remarkable cohesion among the rankings. Countries that score well in one category tend to rank highly in the others. The correlations are not perfect, and there are some odd exceptions (e.g., South Korea's low total factor productivity [TFP], Malaysia's high exports of tech, China's high INSEAD index). Nevertheless, the country rankings are generally in the same vicinity of one another across multiple categories. What we are seeing in this table is the combination of signal and noise typical of innovation data. Each category captures some objective aspects of S&T output mixed together with random or unrelated aspects. These unrelated aspects might be institutions, historical factors, or other country fixed effects (e.g., Malaysia is a major base for Japanese high-tech production but does not produce much indigenous S&T).

Of course, it is important not to misuse or abuse Table 3.4. It presents the results of an admittedly simple ranking exercise that suffers from a few weaknesses. For example, it comingles technological change with scientific progress. Also, a country's TFP rank can be a result of factor endowments, institutions, or policies rather than S&T. The World Economic Forum (WEF) index is produced from survey data, and hence comes with much subjectivity. Due to changing questions and their recentness, the three innovation indices (Florida, INSEAD, and WEF) can offer only snapshots of a single recent year rather than an average across decades. But it is precisely these problems that make the high correlation between different categories so surprising! They suggest that there is a real, strong, and persistent innovation "signal" coming through all the "noise" in the data. Of course, one should *not* conclude from Table 3.4 something like "Switzerland is clearly a better innovator than Sweden" because of the former's one-point advantage in the composite score. However, we can say with more confidence that countries with composite scores in the sixties are better innovators than those in the fifties. We can be more confident still of the significance of even larger differences between country scores.

What About China?

Where's China in the innovation data? China has been widely hyped as the new lead rival to the United States in S&T. The media report daily on China's fantastic economic growth, its exports of S&T products, and the rise of its S&T-based industries and infrastructure. For over a decade, foreign high-tech firms have invested billions of dollars there, resulting in the transfer of millions of American and European jobs, especially in manufacturing.[17] Thus, most Americans now believe that China will soon surpass the United States in S&T, if it has not already done so.[18] Figures 3.4a–d present data on the seemingly explosive growth of Chinese technology patents, STEM research publications, engineering degrees, and exports of high-technology. These are the types of shocking graphs that are regularly offered as supporting evidence of the rising Chinese S&T dragon. However, China is missing from many of the figures and tables of top innovators presented here. How can this be reconciled?

The answer is that, while China has dramatically improved its S&T capabilities in an absolute sense, it still remains a minor player relative to the world's most innovative nations. Figures 3.5a–d reveal this by putting Chinese innovation into better context. While Chinese patents have grown in number, the quality of Chinese innovation has grown less rapidly, especially on a per capita basis (Figure 3.5a). For example, most of the patent filings by China have been for utility models[19] and industrial designs. These types of patents are faster, are less expensive, and are required to meet lower standards than patents for new products or processes. Some critics further describe these utility and design patents as being of particularly low quality.[20] Likewise, the citations-weighted data on STEM publications put Chinese science in the same league as Thailand's, and far below that of Bulgaria or Poland (Figure 3.5b). In R&D, the Chinese workforce employs only around one-fifth the proportion of STEM workers as found in Japan, Germany, or the United States, and only one-tenth that found in Finland (Figure 3.5c). And while Chinese universities grant millions of STEM degrees every year, the vast majority of these students receive educations of dubious quality.[21] China's STEM workers also have far less funding and equipment with which to do research than their counterparts elsewhere. Prior to 2013, Chinese R&D spending ran at less than 2% of GDP, while some of the world's top and rapid innovators regularly spent upward of 4% of GDP on research.[22] As a result of these combined factors, China generally lacks the ability to do "big science" or organize large-scale research projects.[23] Chinese science therefore trails far behind even that of the world's midlevel innovators.

The stereotype of a Chinese S&T dragon is also contradicted by reports from inside the "Middle Kingdom," especially outside of Beijing or Shanghai. Studies of Chinese industry repeatedly show that the Chinese do not invent breakthrough technologies themselves. Instead, they create highly efficient workshops for manufacturing *other* countries' innovations.[24] The Chinese have certainly become skilled at developing low-cost knock-offs of foreign products for their domestic marketplace. But much of the high technology *exported* from China was invented or designed elsewhere, including the products of Motorola, Sony, and Siemens.

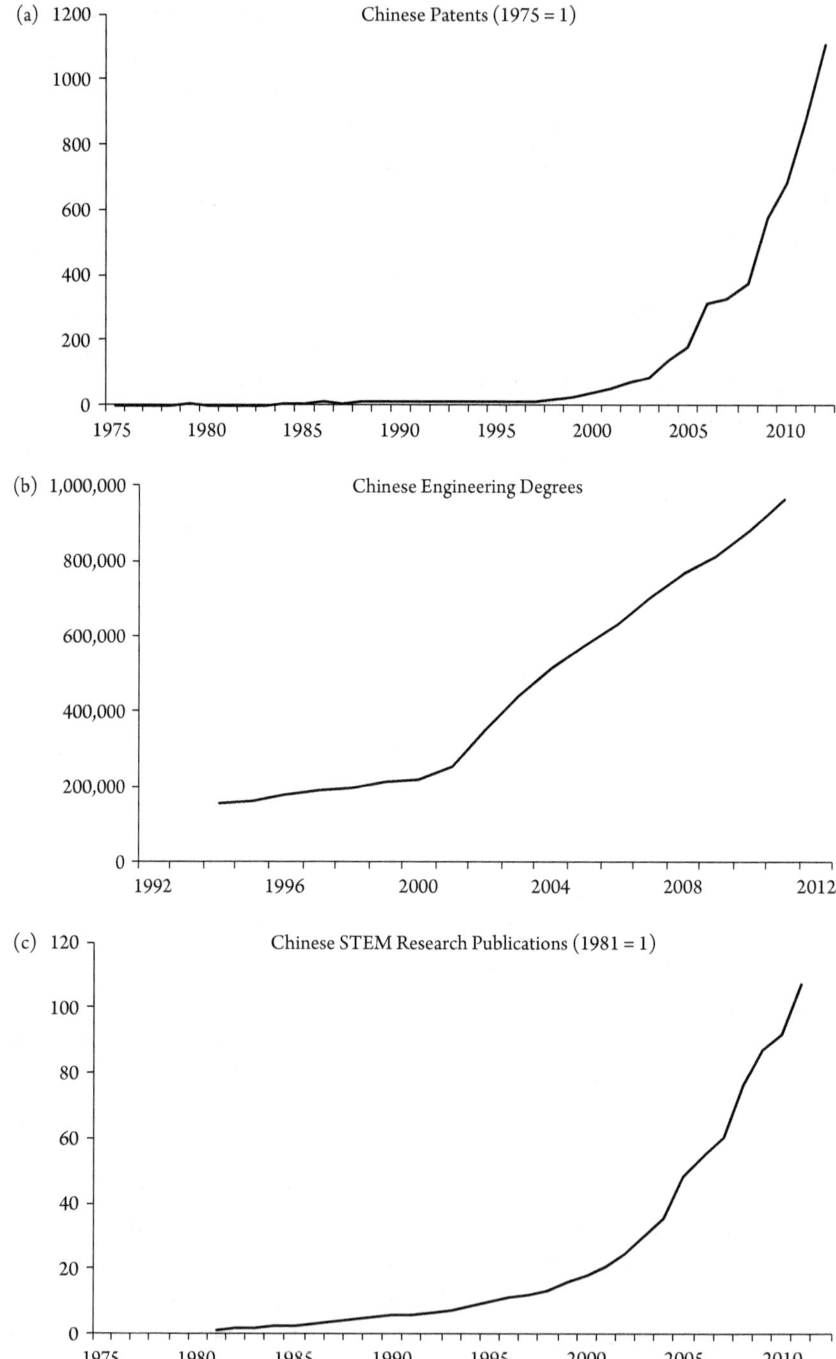

Figure 3.4a–d Is China an S&T dragon? Sources: NBER Patent Database; US Patent and Trademark Office; Thomson-ISI; China Statistical Yearbook, National Bureau of Statistics of China; World Bank.

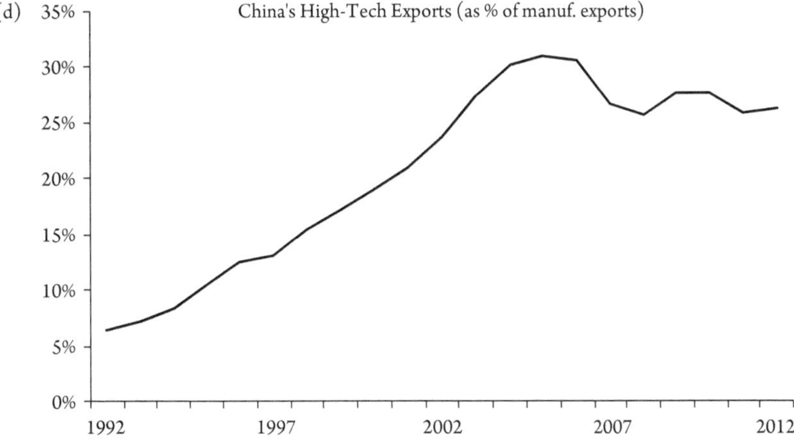

Figure 3.4a–d Continued

To take a now-famous example, during the past decade, many of Apple's most innovative products have been manufactured in China. This has resulted in ominous headlines and political backlash in the United States against outsourcing, risky technology transfers, and ballooning trade deficits with China.[25] However, a closer examination finds that the Chinese contribute only 1.8% of the value of an Apple iPhone and 2% of an iPad. In 2010, that equated to around $10 and $8 per unit, which sold in the United States for $549 and $499, respectively.[26] A recent analysis of the 2014 iPhone 6Plus suggests that China still accounts for only around $10 for each $242 phone.[27] More precise estimates for the 2008 iPhone are shown in Table 3.5. They reveal that most of the important technologies for these Apple products (the electronics, chips, and software) are designed elsewhere. China mostly serves as a low-cost production and assembly hub, at least for now.

This situation is not limited to a few individual companies or products. One can clearly see the relative weakness of Chinese innovation in the data on domestic versus foreign value added to the entire Chinese export sector (Figure 3.5d). Across all types of merchandize exports, China contributes just over half of the value added. In the tech-heavy processing sectors, Chinese value added drops to only around 25%. In exports of electronics and IT, China's domestic value added drops further, to only 15% of the total values.[28]

In sum, Chinese innovation is currently typified by short-term, low-risk improvements to production or distribution processes, or incremental improvements to foreign products. This has resulted in fantastic economic growth, but the Chinese do not yet create much cutting-edge S&T. Similar arguments and evidence can be presented for a handful of other nations (e.g., Russia, India, Brazil, South Africa) that also occasionally win attention from the media as the

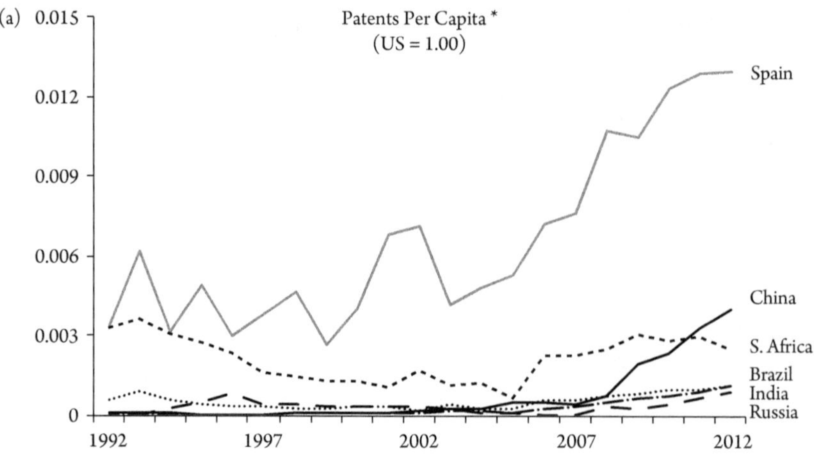

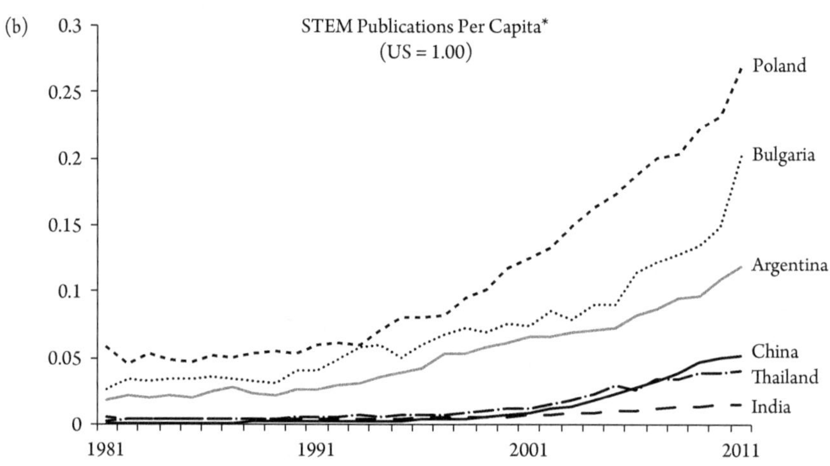

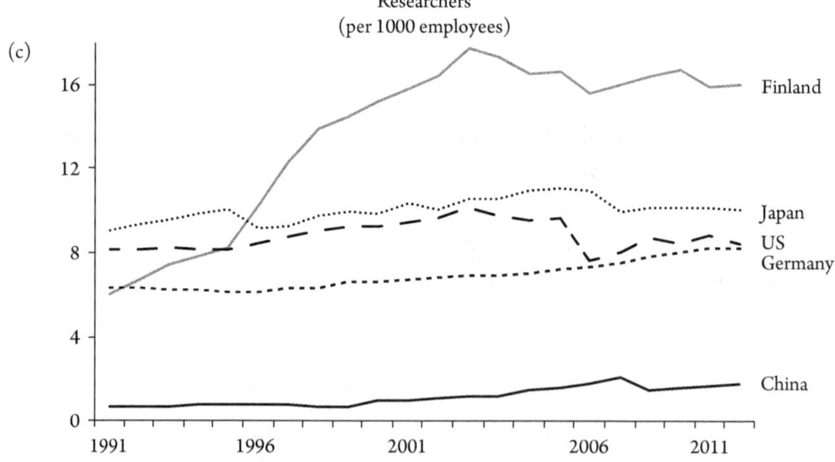

Figure 3.5a–d Or is China an S&T mouse that roars?.

Sources: NBER Patent Database; US Patent and Trademark Office; Thomson-ISI; China Statistical Yearbook. National Bureau of Statistics of China; World Bank; OECD Main Science & Technology Indicators; US International Trade Commission.

*Weighted by forward citations

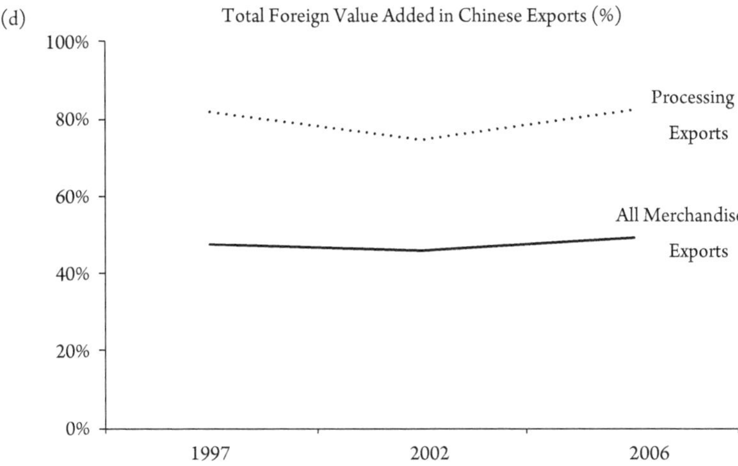

Figure 3.5a–d Continued

next "miracle economy" but actually produce little in S&T relative to the top two dozen innovators. This does not mean that we can safely ignore these countries. China and its brethren are certainly laying the groundwork for a place at the S&T frontier, but they still have much work to do.

Popular Explanations of National Innovation Rates

The data presented previously allow us to challenge some of the seemingly obvious apolitical explanations for Cardwell's Law. For example, many observers assume that the rate and direction of scientific progress and technological change are the products of random chance. This has become known as the "Easter egg" or "heroic" model of innovation. This model is rarely stated explicitly, but it is implicit in many innovation theories and polices. The "Easter egg" model assumes that new technology lies hidden like so many individual Easter eggs. Innovators are like Easter egg hunters. They are more or less loners, or very small teams, who forage into the darkness of the unknown. Through experimental struggle, mental acuity, and a lot of plain luck, the innovator eventually reaches a "Eureka! I have found it!" moment and, like a hero, discovers a new innovation. Then, the search begins anew for other eggs hidden elsewhere. Unfortunately, there is no means by which to predict success or failure of finding an Easter egg. Even dumping money into R&D can be fruitless if STEM workers "dig" in the wrong place, as they often do. Innovation is a random search. Importantly, this means that innovation is exogenous to politics because randomness is outside of political causality.

Table 3.5 **Apple 2008 iPhone 3G Major Components and Cost Drivers ($US)** Data is for the 16Gbyte version of the Apple iPhone 3G S which retailed for $199; however, the actual price paid by the wireless service provider was considerably higher, reflecting the common practice of subsidizing a mobile phone's upfront cost and then profiting from usage subscriptions.

Manufacturer	*Component*	*Cost*
Toshiba (Japan)	16GB Flash Memory Color TFT Display Module Touch Screen	$59.25
Samsung (Korea)	Application Processor SDRAM Mobile DDR	$22.96
Infineon (Germany)	Baseband 3M Camera Module RF Transceiver GPS Receiver Power IC RF Function	$28.85
Broadcom (US)	Bluetooth/FM/WLAN	$5.95
Numonyx (US)	Memory MCP	$3.65
Murata (Japan)	FEM	$1.35
Dialog Semiconductor (Germany)	Power IC Application Processor Function	$1.30
Cirrus Logic (USA)	Audio Codec	$1.15
Rest of Materials		$48.00
Manufacturing Costs		$6.50
Grand Total		**$178.96**

Source: Rassweiler, Andrew. 2009. "iPhone 3G S Carries $178.96 BOM and Manufacturing Cost, iSuppli Teardown Reveals". *iSuppli*, 24 June 2009.

However, one lesson we learn from the previous data (Figures 3.1 and 3.2) is that national innovation rates are *not* dominated by random chance, at least not on the time scale shown. That is, if innovation was mostly a random phenomenon, then we would expect to see very different sets of rankings each year. No nation should remain among the world's technological leaders for very long, and newly innovative nations should frequently rise up. But we do not see this kind of randomness in the innovation data, even from decade to decade. Only a few countries have experienced drastic changes in their S&T performance over the past seventy years. Those nations that do transform themselves usually incline or decline continuously for decades. Therefore, either there is some causal force keeping nations locked into established trends during this long period or there is a lack of forces strong enough to knock countries out of their inertia.

Of course, a common-sense corollary to the Easter egg model is that the size of a country's population or economy will determine its national innovation rate. If innovation is an Easter egg hunt, then society must get as many well-trained hunters out into the field as possible and give them plenty of resources with which to pursue their search. It follows, then, that nations with larger populations can provide more STEM workers and entrepreneurs, and hence more innovation. Also, larger economies have more resources to dedicate toward S&T, as well as grander economies of scale to exploit for profits and world market share. Therefore, size should strongly determine national S&T performance. Certainly the United States, Japan, and Germany fit this description: they are among the largest and most innovative economies on the planet. But otherwise, size does not correlate well with national innovation rates at all (Figures 3.6a,b). It certainly does not apply to the many highly innovative but small states like Singapore, Israel, Hong Kong, Finland, Taiwan, and Denmark. At the extremes, Switzerland and Sweden both innovate at the S&T frontier, but each has only very small populations (ranked number ninety-six and ninety-three globally in population size) and economies (ranked number thirty-seven and thirty-five globally in GDP).[29] Canada is only a midsized nation in both population (ranked thirty-eight) and economy (ranked fourteen) but still competes well globally in S&T. Finally, if size determines performance, then very large countries such as China, India, Indonesia, Russia, Pakistan, and Mexico should be among the world's best innovators, but they are curiously missing from the top ranks of S&T producers.

Another popular explanation for differences in national innovation rates is military spending. Military capability has long been associated with technological change. Prominent historians, sociologists, and economists have argued for decades that the development of military technical ability, either weapons systems or their production processes, largely determines national innovation rates.[30] However, even a cursory look at the previous data tends to contradict this thesis. The military explanation certainly applies to the United States, where defense-related innovation consistently spills over into the civilian economy.[31] Otherwise, the military thesis fails to explain the high rates of innovation in the other countries, especially during the Cold War (Figure 3.7). Not one of Sweden, Switzerland, Germany, Canada, or Japan could be considered a great juggernaut of military research during the past seventy years. Indeed, many observers argue that S&T progress has flowed in reverse, from civilian to military, in several of these countries during this period.[32] Meanwhile, many of the world's top military weapons producers are not on the list of top innovators. According to the Stockholm International

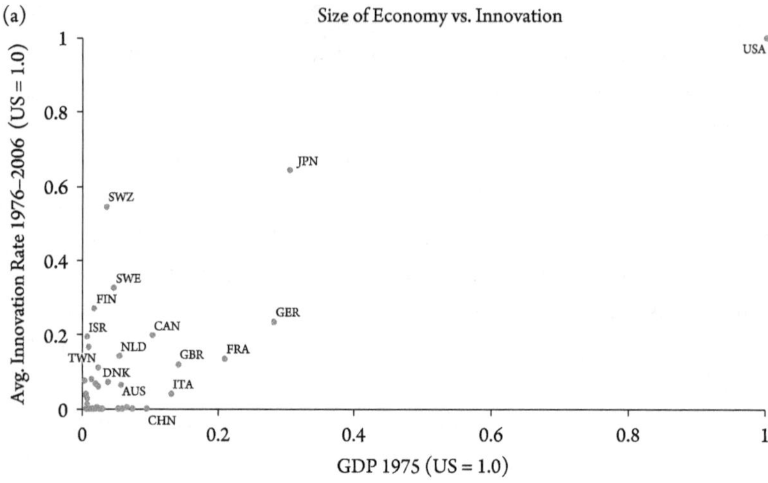

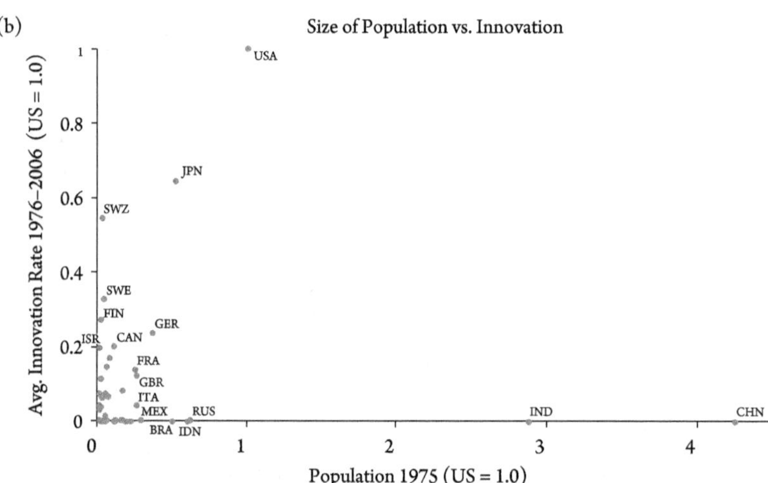

Figure 3.6a–b Innovation and country size. Sources: NBER Patents Dataset, World Bank Development Indicators; US, Japan, Germany de-emphasized to show weakness of general relationship.

Peace Research Institute, the world's largest arms-producing and military services companies reside in the United States, Italy, France, the United Kingdom, and Russia.[33] Some of these are highly innovative nations, others less so. Overall, neither military spending nor weapons production correlates well with national innovation rates.

Still another popular explanation holds that first-mover advantages give some countries a historical head start in S&T while locking others out of competition. That is, innovation is typified by high barriers to entry. It is very expensive and time-consuming to establish cutting-edge research and production capabilities in S&T. But once a country has set up an education system,

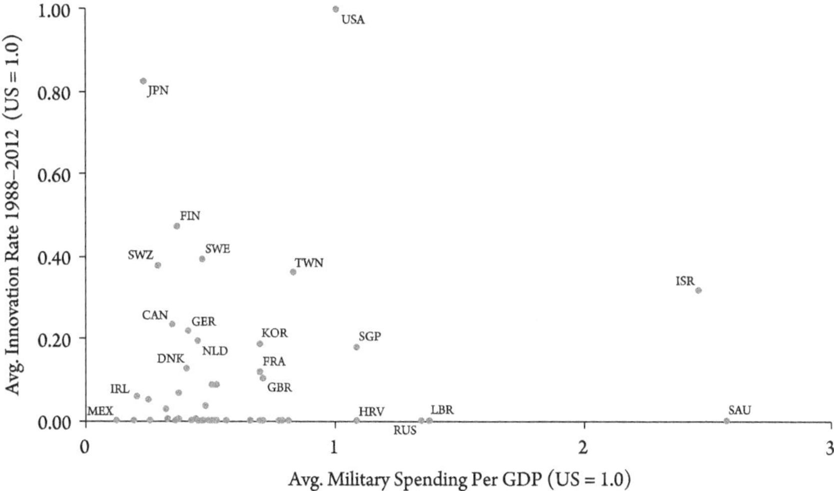

Figure 3.7 Innovation and military spending. Sources: SIPRI Military Expenditure Database, NBER Patents Database.

trained a large STEM workforce, built laboratories and research facilities, and created S&T based industries, it is much easier to maintain one's place at the technological frontier. It is also difficult for newcomers to compete with established S&T players because these fixed costs only increase as technology advances. For example, conducting aeronautical research and starting an airplane industry was far more costly in 2010 than it was in 1910. It follows that early developers should have an innovative advantage. Once a country achieves high rates of innovation, it should tend to maintain them. However, this theory is clearly violated by late innovators such as Japan, Israel, Taiwan, and others. It is also contradicted by the relative decline of Great Britain, which led the first industrial revolution during the eighteenth and nineteenth centuries, and was the source of much primary research upon which the second industrial revolution and computer and Internet revolutions were based. Perhaps more striking is the often ignored case of China, which became so advanced in S&T during the fourteenth century that it nearly industrialized, three hundred years ahead of Europe. Yet, instead of holding its global lead in S&T, China soon slipped into an innovative atrophy so grave that by the eighteenth century, the Chinese had to relearn from Europeans many of their own indigenous inventions.[34]

A fifth theory comes from students of economic historian Alexander Gershenkron. They reverse the "first-mover advantage" argument by hypothesizing that late industrialization explains national innovation rates.[35] This theory is motivated by success stories like Japan, Korea, Israel, and Taiwan. Each had an impoverished, backward economy based almost entirely on agriculture. Each society also came late to innovation, deciding to create S&T-based economies only during the mid-twentieth century.[36] But they then quickly surged ahead of many wealthier, more advanced S&T nations. The thesis here is that, due to their relative poverty, underdeveloped late-comers have the strongest incentives to leap ahead to the technological frontier. These lesser developed countries also have the advantage of free-riding on the scientific achievements of the advanced S&T countries. They need only a strong, interventionist government to allocate resources properly and follow the path to the technological frontier already blazed by earlier industrializers. These catch-up countries also need not reinvent costly established S&T. They can instead beg, buy, copy, or steal S&T from the advanced innovators at a fraction of the cost that it took the originators to create. Certainly this explanation seems to describe a handful of countries. The problem with this argument is the persistence of the United States as a lead innovator for almost a century, still today outperforming most powerful newcomers. Also, nineteenth-century industrializers like Germany, Sweden, and Switzerland continue to innovate better than newcomers like Taiwan, South Korea, and Israel in many sectors. These important exceptions severely hurt the "free-riding" thesis, at least as a general theory.

Still another theory emphasizes the role of national culture in fostering innovation.[37] Culture matters to innovation because it establishes, at the macro level, fundamental expectations about the risks, rewards, and opportunities that guide economic activity.[38] Culture also helps to determine the level of trust in a society, which affects entrepreneurship, investment, and the breadth and depth of economic transactions upon which successful innovation depends.[39] As one historian of innovation has written, "All societies have to eat, but cultural factors determine whether the best and brightest in each society will tinker with machines or chemicals, or whether they will perfect their swordplay or study the Talmud."[40] However, history has yet to produce a major cultural group that does not innovate. The Greeks, Romans, Incans, Mayans, Aztecs, Chinese, Muslim caliphates, French, Belgians, Dutch, British, Russians, Japanese, and Israelis have each, at one time or another, made major contributions to S&T. Yet these societies have widely different cultural values. Finally, there is no consensus yet on which are the "right" cultural values that promote long-run national innovation rates.[41]

The point here is not to argue that none of the causal factors described earlier have any effect on national innovation rates, but rather to defuse some older, unsubstantiated generalizations about the sources of relative technological power. The explanations given previously are sometimes paraded as "accepted wisdom" during discussions of national innovation rates. Certainly some of them might make sense when used to explain a particular country's innovation rate at a specific point in time. Yet on closer consideration, not one of these popular theories can be consistently applied across time and space to explain the world's most (or least) innovative countries. Statistical analysis tends to confirm these nonfindings. Therefore, it is reasonable to suspect that none of these variables alone, especially those that contradict each other, has any overall systematic or deterministic explanatory power, and that a better explanation is needed.

Conclusion

The previous data suggests that Cardwell's Law still holds strong. Despite globalization and the widely accepted importance of S&T, there remains significant variation in national S&T outputs across time and country. Even just during the past seventy years, a handful of countries have experienced dramatic improvements in their S&T capabilities. These rapid innovators include countries such as Japan, Finland, Israel, Taiwan, Korea, Singapore, and Ireland. Also, among the world's top innovators, we can find substantial variation in S&T outputs. For example, the United States, Switzerland, Germany, and Sweden have been strong, stable, leading S&T nations for decades. A dozen other nations have remained equally reliable midlevel innovators, such as France, Great Britain, Denmark, and Belgium. There has been some jockeying for relative position within this group of midlevel innovators (e.g., Denmark), but some of these nations consistently hug the bottom of their midlevel class (e.g., Australia, Italy, New Zealand, and Spain), while others hug the top (e.g., the Netherlands, the United Kingdom, and France). Then there are the many low-level innovators, such as Hungary, Malaysia, Portugal, Poland, South Africa, Turkey, Argentina, the Philippines, Costa Rica, and Mexico. These countries have ample economic resources with which to innovate. In fact, many less innovative nations are wealthier than some of the top or rapid innovators. A few even have better governments and freer markets. Yet they consistently fail to produce S&T at anywhere near the rate and quality of even the midlevel innovators.

The mix of national variation and stability revealed in the figures and tables presented in this chapter is puzzling. Almost every industrialized nation expends a considerable share of its resources on the pursuit of technological progress. Yet, despite the seemingly clear policy and fiscal requirements for promoting innovative behavior, some countries are consistently more successful than others at innovation, even among the wealthy democracies. The regularities in the data need explaining, as do the countries that violate them. For the past several decades, that explanation has been government. The next chapter asks "why?"

PART TWO

HOW DO NATIONS INNOVATE?

Policies and Institutions

4

Does Technology Need Government?

The Five Pillars of Innovation

When experts now attempt to explain Cardwell's Law, they rarely rely on factors like random chance or country size. Instead, they tend to emphasize the importance of domestic institutions and policies. In particular, two leading schools of thought have emerged to explain the differences in national science and technology (S&T) performance observed in the previous chapter.

The first school of thought argues that government plays a vital role in innovation. When looking at the data, this certainly makes sense, at least at first. Domestic institutions and policies are what governments use to promote innovation. Also, different countries use different sets of institutions and policies. Therefore, it must be the differences in these national institutions and policies that explain why some countries are better than others at S&T. To support this belief, scholars have produced a bounty of anecdotes about how missing, broken, or corrupt institutions and policies have hurt progress in S&T. Meanwhile, most national success stories involve government institutions and policies acting to foster innovation.

However, a second school takes the exact opposite view: that the absence of government interference fosters innovation. This is the classic free market hypothesis. It runs especially strong among those American and British thinkers who have long held that the solution to most economic problems is markets. Innovation is not their only concern here. Generally, free market supporters extol markets for three main benefits they provide: *innovation, efficiency*, and *autonomy*. More to the point, markets tend to be *better* than governments at providing these things. In a free market, consumers freely demand a particular good or service and are willing to pay for it. In response, producers rise to fill that demand at a price that should create an equilibrium where, ideally, everyone is content. Competition between all these buyers and sellers results in ever-increasing improvements in quality and price, as well as innovations in new goods and services. And according to free market purists, the miracle of free markets is that no politician or government agency coordinates or orders any of this. Innovation and efficiency happen naturally as a result of market forces. Dictators and social planners need not apply. Therefore, modern "neo-classical" economists, and their followers, tend to adore markets and disdain state-run economies.

The twentieth-century contest between communism and capitalism appears to provide an abundance of evidence in support of the free market school. Around the world, state-run systems, such as those created in the Soviet Union, in Mao Zedong's China, and throughout Eastern Europe, concentrated economic decision making within the state, with bureaucrats trained in Marxist philosophy. Instead of individuals and corporations acting on their own, these governments created professional bureaucracies that studied the economy and then "scientifically" decided national production, consumption, prices, and distribution.[1] In the beginning, the results seemed to be fairly impressive. Modernization and industrialization occurred rapidly in many communist states as agriculture was centralized and workers were forced into new industries. However, each of these systems then slowly fell into complete and utter stagnation.[2]

Take, for example, the USSR. After several decades of seemingly miraculous innovation, technological backwardness had set into the Soviet system fairly deeply by the 1980s.[3] During that decade, American computer production was estimated to be ten times higher than the USSR's, while the lag in advanced information technology research was upward of twelve years. Russia was attempting to enter the information technology era with telephone systems equivalent to those found in the United States during the 1930s. For every long-distance call made within the Soviet Union, Americans made 25; for every one Soviet international call, Americans made 150. In 1988, over one hundred nations had more telephones per capita than the USSR, while eighty-eight nations had greater car ownership. A Russian was twelve times less likely to own a car than an American, and the car he or she eventually purchased would break down more often, and when it did, it would spend more time waiting for spare parts. In fact, Russian cars were considered so horrendous that the few foreigners who imported them usually opted to rip out the Russian electrical system and replace it with a Western one. In the living rooms of Moscow, thousands of faulty Soviet televisions exploded yearly, causing house fires. And Russian shoppers lined up for imported shoes despite the fact that close to a billion pairs were produced domestically every year. By these measures, the Soviet standard of living ranked near third world nations such as Jordan or Mauritius. Meanwhile, her vanquished rivals from World War II, Japan and West Germany, had risen to challenge even the United States in terms of economic growth, living standards, and technological capabilities.

In Soviet industrial production, the declines were equally spectacular. Russia was producing almost twice as much steel as America during the late 1980s, but the Russian manufacturers that used this steel only put out 75% as many goods as their American counterparts. On the shop floor, the percentage of metal-working machinery that was over twenty years old increased from 16% in 1980 to 21% in 1985. In other words, while American capital equipment was being replaced at 5% per year, and Japanese equipment at upward of 10%, the Soviet proportion was under 2%, bringing the average age of Soviet factory equipment to over twenty-five years. Tales of inefficiency and technological blunders abounded throughout the Soviet empire. For example, in the rush to meet production targets and qualify for bonuses, Lithuanian workers later admitted, "We never use a screwdriver in the last week. We hammer the screws in."[4] Meanwhile, factories in Leningrad produced welding robots that did the job of a single human while taking the space of a welding team and breaking down more frequently "than the heaviest vodka-drinker."[5]

To many observers, the economic contest between the United States and USSR during the Cold War serves as an unambiguous historical demonstration of why markets work and how governments fail. To them, it clearly shows that markets are more innovative than governments. It also implies that *innovation* is intimately bound up with *efficiency* and *autonomy*, and that all three factors are essential for both national economic performance and personal fulfillment. If a system is *autonomous*, then no one person or organization is required to, or has the power to, arbitrarily determine supply, demand, prices, distribution, or production. Individuals can act freely according to their own judgments of what is right for them. *Efficient* economies make the maximum use of existing resources, with little or no waste; supply meets demand, ideally with neither surplus nor shortage.[6] *Innovative* economies produce new goods and services over time, often taking the form of new technology based on, or leading to, new scientific and engineering knowledge.[7] Furthermore, new science and technology increase efficiency and provide individuals and firms with greater ability to make independent decisions. Meanwhile, the freedom of choice implied by autonomy often creates competition, which then drives efficiency and innovation. Therefore, if markets provide *innovation, efficiency,* and *autonomy* better than governments, then free markets likely play an important role in explaining national S&T performance.

Do Markets Need Government?

If our historical experience with free markets is so compelling, then the challenge for the first school of thought is to explain: why government? That is, does progress in science and technology truly require support and interference from this entity we call "the state"? Why not just let free markets reign?

To resolve this apparent contradiction, we need a better idea of exactly what a "market" is and how it causes actors to innovate. The conventional definition we learn in school holds that a market is created whenever potential sellers of a good or service are brought into contact with potential buyers and a means of exchange is available. Unfortunately, this vague description is not terribly useful for explaining Cardwell's Law; it does not help us to identify a proper role for government (if any) in creating and sustaining free markets.

This book therefore employs a far more useful description of markets: a *market is characterized by a large number of informed, rational individuals involved in the free exchange of goods, services, and capital, resulting in economic efficiency and innovation.* This definition forces us to focus on the essential working parts of markets: individuals who are informed, rational, and free, and who have secure property rights (in their goods, services, and capital). These characteristics make the market a competitive environment because wherever individuals can freely choose to contract (buy/sell) from one another, they must compete. Business firms act just like large individuals in this formulation. Those not offering quality goods and services at a good price must either improve their wares or exit the market, while new buyers and sellers can easily enter the market to replace them. Therefore, if I want to get rich, impress my peers, and achieve my dreams, then I am forced by competition to innovate, to make sure that what I am selling meets demand. Our more useful definition of markets also identifies the warning signs for when markets are failing: real prices rise, quality worsens, innovation slows, and freedom of choice declines, at least over the long run.

This more useful definition of markets also identifies for us two primary ways that markets can fail. The first, and most curious, is where all the essential parts of a market are present and working correctly, yet they perversely produce bad outcomes (Figure 4.1). That is, the first type of market failure consists of those bizarre cases in which informed, rational individuals involved in the free exchange of goods, services, and capital do *not* result in innovation, efficiency, or autonomy. A classic example is a bank run. Imagine that you keep your money in a perfectly healthy bank with plenty of deposits on hand. One morning, you see your neighbor withdrawing all of his money from that bank. You do not know why. Maybe he discovered something wrong with the bank, or perhaps it's money for a major purchase or family vacation. Who knows? In the end, it does not matter, because you realize that if other depositors find out, then they might become concerned and withdraw their money too. If enough people pull their money out of that bank, then the bank will collapse, taking your savings with it. So you freely, rationally decide to withdraw your money to protect yourself. If other bank customers act in a similarly informed, rational, and free manner, then that perfectly healthy bank will fail. It does not matter if you trust the bank, because once a bank run starts, the first people out the door will rescue their deposits, and the stragglers will lose. And that bank will no longer exist to invest in innovative businesses or individuals. This is clearly an inefficient result.[8]

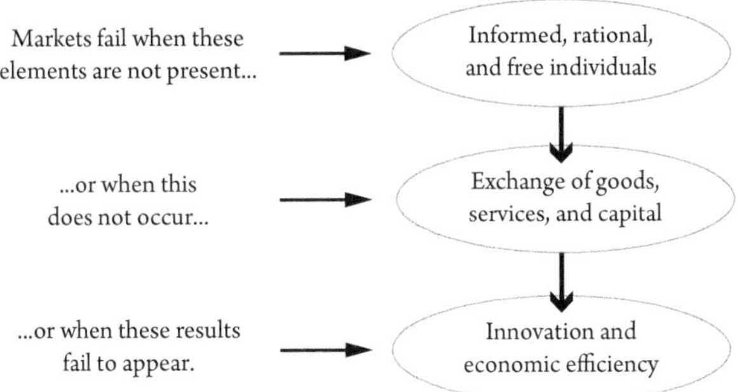

Figure 4.1 Markets and market failures.

The second type of market failure occurs when the essential inputs for markets (i.e., informed, rational individuals involved in the free exchange of goods, services, and capital) are *not* present or working properly (Figure 4.1). For example, this can occur when people do not have well-defined and strongly enforced property rights. If I cannot be certain that a particular property is mine to use or exchange exclusively, then I will not invest much to improve it due to the possibility that my investment may get appropriated or ripped out by others. A similar type of market failure is called "spillovers" or "externalities." In these cases, the benefits or costs of providing a particular good or service spill over to outsiders. When outsiders are forced to bear costs or allowed to enjoy benefits, which they did not agree to beforehand, then inefficiencies and stagnation can result. Another example of a market failure occurs when people have information that is incorrect or limited, or when some actors have more information than others. In these cases, people can abandon the market because they are not sure what they are buying or selling, or what the appropriate price is. Yet another example of a market failure is when an individual buyer or seller becomes so powerful that he or she drives out the competition, reducing freedom of choice, and thereby wrecking the very mechanism that motivates actors to be efficient or innovative.

The takeaway point is that, by describing how markets can fail, we answer the question of "why government?" It neatly identifies specific roles that governments can play to construct and support markets, and thereby foster an innovative economy. Even among economic conservatives who despise government intervention, many admit that we do need government action to prevent or solve market failures. Of course, conservatives and liberals will disagree on precisely which problems constitute market failures and what exactly the responses should be. Nevertheless, generally, our definition of markets suggests that governments act to best aid innovation when they perform the following tasks:[9]

- Define and enforce property rights
- Maximize freedom of exchange, consumption, and production
- Improve the quality and quantity of information available to market actors
- Prevent a small number of actors from eliminating competition
- Provide those goods and services that private markets do not provide more efficiently (also known as "public goods")
- Ensure that investors, producers, and consumers each bear the costs, and capture the benefits, of their own activities
- Reduce the costs of market participation (e.g., lower transaction costs, solve coordination dilemmas)

We can now answer the question that began this section: does innovation need the state? The premise established here is that, if market failures obstruct or slow innovation, then actions by government to solve these market failures may explain the rise and fall of the world's technological powers. When government institutions and policies act properly, then innovation should flourish. When government fails to act or misfires, then so too should innovation. Thus, the explanation for different national innovation rates may lie in state action.

Accordingly, the remainder this chapter serves as a basic primer on S&T market failures. It surveys the strengths and weaknesses of the five most prominent institutions and polices that governments use to correct the market failures that plague innovation. They constitute what I call here the "Five Pillars" of innovation: intellectual property rights, research subsidies, education, research universities, and trade policy. The main question to keep in mind throughout this discussion is, why do these institutions and policies aid innovation? Perhaps more important, do they really explain why some countries are better at S&T than others? The evidence that follows suggests that these Five Pillars do take us part of the way to understanding why some countries are better at S&T, but they also leave an enormous amount of unexplained success and failure.

Pillar One: Property Rights

Perhaps the most obvious task for a government seeking to improve the nation's rate of innovation is to create and enforce property rights in new science and technology. To understand why, let's revisit the case of the USSR. The "parade of horribles" of Soviet stagnation recounted earlier might seem obvious to us now, but from the 1950s through the 1970s, the USSR appeared to all as a rising technological juggernaut. When the Bolsheviks took over in 1917, Russia was a backward, agricultural state only decades out of feudalism. Its economy mostly consisted of tens of millions of inefficient peasant farmers with little industry or indigenous technology to offer. Vladimir Lenin (1870–1924) moved to centralize economic control within the Soviet state and attempted to eliminate private enterprise. His successor, Joseph Stalin (1878–1953), then used the totalitarian power of the new Soviet government to force industrialization and modernization onto this society, sometimes with great violence. Despite its enormous losses during World War II and Stalin's bloody purges and forced relocations, the USSR soon loomed as the lone superpower challenger to the postwar United States.[10] After 1945, the Red army, navy, and air forces appeared to steadily advance every year with ever greater firepower, speed, and throw-weights. In 1949, Moscow developed a Soviet atomic fission bomb and, by 1955, tested a far more powerful hydrogen fusion bomb. The Russians then beat Americans into space by launching Sputnik, the world's first artificial satellite, into Earth's orbit in 1957. In 1961, Yuri Gagarin, a Soviet cosmonaut, became the first human to journey into space and orbit the planet. Meanwhile, American rockets regularly failed, exploded, or veered off course.[11] Analysts spoke regularly of US industry being outpaced by Soviet competitors, especially in military technologies. Fears grew first of a bomber gap, then of a missile gap, between the United States and the USSR.[12]

Soviet science was equally impressive. Soviet chemists won their country's first science Nobel Prize in 1956, quickly followed by Nobel Prizes for six Soviet physicists during the 1950s and 1960s.[13] Soon, it seemed to many that the Soviets were performing at the scientific frontier of numerous fields, including mathematics, computing, metallurgy, synthetics, theoretical physics, astronomy, and several areas of engineering (including aeronautic, petroleum, and nuclear).[14]

Americans therefore faced an ideological dilemma. They believed deeply in free market capitalism, but their greatest rivals during the twentieth century seemed to be succeeding in S&T, even beating the United States, by using heavy government intervention. For alongside the USSR's advancement, the world had also witnessed Japan's state-assisted industrialization miracle from the 1890s through the 1930s, and Germany's S&T recovery under Hitler. Then came World War II's swath of highly successful government research and development (R&D) programs, both Allied and Axis, which produced jet aircraft, radar, penicillin, atomic weaponry, rocketry, electronic computing, and a host of other major scientific and technological advances. Science had long been viewed as somewhat separate and distinct from technological change.[15] Now people came to accept that science could drive technological innovation[16] and that government *could* play a useful role in that process. However, living in a society dominated by free market ideology and facing an existential threat from totalitarian communists, Americans were confronted with the question of whether markets alone were necessarily the best mechanism by which to produce scientific progress and technological change.

In 1962, economist Kenneth Arrow formalized the answer.[17] Arrow argued that inventive activity is, at its core, the production of new knowledge. But this is not just any knowledge. Inventive activity requires the production of very high-risk and very high-cost scientific and technical knowledge. The problem, Arrow explained, is that all knowledge is "nonrival" and "nonexcludable." That is, knowledge is very easy to share with large numbers of people (nonrival) and it is nearly impossible to prevent people from sharing it (nonexcludable). Therefore, once highly risky, expensive S&T knowledge is produced, it can be easily copied and transmitted at low cost and low risk by onlookers. Thus, Arrow concluded that free market economies will always *under*invest in invention and research. After all, why bear all the risk and expense of discovering new S&T if observers can simply waltz in and copy it? Indeed, it makes far more economic sense for a business to let others develop new S&T and then just duplicate it. This is a typical market failure: people acting in an economically rational manner (duplicating another firm's technology) but producing inefficient, noninnovative outcomes overall (a decline in R&D investment).

Arrow's solution was simple. First, government must create property rights in S&T knowledge; then, government must support markets for trading these property rights. In other words, to fix the market failure in inventive activity, government needs to make this vital S&T knowledge hard to copy and difficult to share *without* the owner's permission. Just as important, S&T property rights must themselves be transferable. If knowledge can be sold or licensed for a profit, then it creates incentives for individuals and businesses to invest in R&D. Fines and bans must be enforced to punish violators who abuse, or refuse to purchase, that permission. Of course, this is all just economics speak for intellectual property rights (patents, trademarks, copyrights, and trade secrecy laws).

Patents and other intellectual property rights (IPRs) constitute an important bargain between society and inventors: if inventors share their new knowledge and discoveries with society, then society will grant them a short-run monopoly—often twenty years for technology patents[18]—to manufacture products based on that knowledge so that inventors can recoup their investment and make a profit. In the United States, this bargain was enshrined in the patent system established in 1790.[19] Since then, patents have been used as a primary policy tool for driving progress in American science and technology.

The Problems with Patents

While patents have historically improved the incentives for innovation, since the mid-1990s, problems have developed in the patent system that may severely handicap the ability of patents to foster future innovation, especially in new high-tech industries.[20] One problem is that patents are increasingly granted with ever broader scope and vaguer claims, while the public sometimes has limited access to the scientific claims listed on the patent. This means that the knowledge disclosure aspects of patents may no longer be of much value.[21] Also, in some industries, patents are granted for frivolous inventions ("everything under the sun") and then used to block legitimate innovations or to sue for exorbitant licensing fees and legal settlements.[22] As a result, patent litigation has skyrocketed in many sectors, driving up the costs of innovation and driving away some investors altogether. This acts like a stranglehold on innovation because patents are often necessary for doing business in high-tech industries, but their litigation costs can now outweigh the profits of the very innovations that patents are meant to foster.

Stories of legal patent abuse abound. The most outlandish anecdotes regularly make headlines, such as the case of J. M. Smucker Company, which, in 1999, acquired a patent for a peanut butter and jelly sandwich with the crusts cut off and then used this patent to sue small grocers for selling crustless sandwiches without a license.[23] Far more serious threats to innovation involve patents on software and the computerization of business processes. For example, Amazon patented its "one-click" ordering procedure and threatened to sue all websites that used a similar process. Amazon then followed through on that threat by filing suit against Barnes & Noble for its rival website.[24] Priceline.com did the same with its "name your own price" auction patent, which it then used either to sue or to threaten Microsoft, Expedia, and dozens of other competitors both at home and abroad.[25] The popular music distributor Spotify is currently being sued for its music streaming technology, while the maker of the best-selling "Angry Birds" video game is being sued for the method by which players purchase new levels in the game.[26] Little of this patent or lawsuit activity acts to spur innovation. Rather, its goal is to prevent competitors from innovating and to charge rents for obvious, overlapping, or previously invented technologies.

In the early 2000s, this new breed of patents on business methods was extended to health and medical processes. In 2002, two researchers in Montreal acquired a patent on a method for treating autoimmune disorders such as Crohn's disease. They had not invented a new drug, only identified specific ranges of blood metabolite levels that indicate a need to raise or lower drug dosages. Their patent was soon bought by Prometheus Laboratories, which, in 2011, used it to sue the Mayo Clinic for coming up with its own method of linking metabolite levels with drug dosage prescriptions.[27] This "indicate a need" patent had the implication of allowing patents not just on medical decision making (e.g., doctors making diagnoses), but for all sorts of formalized technical advice: financial advisers giving stock recommendations to clients, cooks writing or using recipes, and architects and engineers providing structural analysis of building safety.[28]

The US Patent and Trademark Office (USPTO) is sometimes a source of these problems with modern patents. Prodded by a well-meaning Congress, the USPTO became fairly zealous in its granting of intellectual property during the 1990s. Critics also argue that, due to the declining resources allocated to it, the USPTO has become unable to properly gauge quality or identify prior art. As a result, the USPTO has increasingly granted patents to quite broad, sometimes obvious claims, such as Amazon's "one-click" or Prometheus's "indicate a need" technologies. These vague or overly broad patents can hurt innovation. An overly generous patent claim can create a situation in which innocent investors may not understand when it is legal for them to create new products based on a given piece of knowledge. Some investors will accidentally become buried in costly, frequent, and lengthy litigation, which diverts resources away from innovation. Others will forgo the trouble and desist from innovating altogether.

In the worst cases of abuse, some businesses are created solely to exploit these flaws in the patent system and contribute little or no innovation whatsoever. For example, a business might seek the most fuzzy and flexible claims possible on its invention to scare off potential competitors. Firms can also use legal techniques to keep claims hidden or to addend them over time, thus further obfuscating and confusing the boundaries on intellectual property. At the extreme, firms known as "patent trolls" acquire patents with no intention of bringing the protected invention to market, only to use the patent to threaten litigation and exact fees from legitimate innovators.[29]

For example, in 2010, the Texas-based firm Geotag sued some four hundred companies for violating its patent on a "find a retailer" feature that allow users to provide a zip code to a company's website to see nearby stores.[30] Geotag did *not* invent the technology but simply bought the patent the previous year for the sole purpose of filing predatory lawsuits. In a more wide-reaching set of lawsuits, a flailing software company, the SCO Group, decided in 2002 to stop making or selling new products altogether. Instead, it chose to use the UNIX copyrights it had recently purchased to extort fees and settlements from *all* users of the open-source Linux operating system, especially targeting 1,500 of the world's largest and wealthiest corporations. The strategy failed, but only after untold millions of dollars in litigation costs were incurred by legitimate innovators such as IBM, Red Hat, Novell, AutoZone, and DaimlerChrysler.[31]

Problems with patents also arise when patented knowledge overlaps new knowledge. Specifically, it is not clear if patents help or hurt innovation when the knowledge they protect is cumulative.[32] For example, just how much should the single 1948 patent on the transistor have limited successors from inventing all the computer, radio, television, automobile, airplane, satellite, weapons, and medical technologies that were based on, or composed of, transistors? These issues are complicated by the fact that a high percentage of twenty-first-century innovations are based on S&T knowledge protected by multiple patents held by different owners. For example, Steven Jobs warned in 2007 that Apple had "filed for over 200 patents for all the inventions in iPhone and we intend to protect them."[33] And this did not even include the dozens of patents that Apple had licensed or acquired from other firms to improve the iPhone without diverting resources away from Apple's other R&D efforts.[34]

These webs of overlapping IPRs are known as "patent thickets." They are defined as a myriad collection of basic patents spread across multiple owners upon which a single, new, complex technology might infringe. Due to their diversity and scope, patent thickets drive up the costs of coordinating, negotiating, licensing, and permissions, and can result in conflicting and unclear claims to ownership. They have created a situation where it is nearly impossible to, say, develop new software or produce a new telecommunications device *without* violating some patent somewhere, and probably dozens of patents divided among multiple owners.[35] To take just one example, by the mid-2000s, a typical inventor seeking to introduce new technology into the 3G communications market had to negotiate a thicket of some eight thousand patents held by over forty different firms.[36]

Perhaps the most revealing question is: why did patents work so well to motivate innovation for centuries but then suddenly seemed to break down toward the end of the twentieth century? In general, a patent works best when it acts like a physical fence around an empty sandlot. That is, a fence need not be impenetrable to protect an empty lot, but it does need to be easy to see. While the occasional trespasser is an annoyance, the real threat to private property is that of someone else using it or building upon it without permission. A good fence defines the borders of privately held land, clearly communicating to outsiders where they can and cannot build. Without fences, even innocent investors might inadvertently build on someone else's property and then be forced to pay stiff fines while also losing their investment.

Patents must act like good fences to foster innovation properly.[37] They must restrict production on a fertile plot of new S&T knowledge by clearly defining the "borders" of that knowledge. Outsiders must be able to easily discern which knowledge is public, and therefore legal to build upon, versus which knowledge is private and therefore off-limits to investment without permission. This means that patents should work well to spur innovation when new inventions and discoveries are clearly definable and easily "fenced in." This helps to explain why patents worked so well to foster innovation before the 1990s but have suffered problems since then. Patents often do act like good fences when they define and protect mechanical, chemical, and basic electrical inventions. These sorts of technologies are based on knowledge that has clearly defined borders. They are also the sectors in which most nineteenth- and twentieth-century innovation occurred. Patents also seem to motivate innovation in the modern pharmaceutical and chemical industries, where very specific molecules or production techniques can be precisely detailed in the patent.

However, critics now warn that Arrow's simplistic model of patents may no longer apply in certain twenty-first-century high-tech sectors. This warning applies to less patentable inventions made in software and biotechnology, and to the even more abstract innovations that now typify computerized business practices, clinical medicine, and mathematical and statistical analyses. These areas of knowledge are often too abstract to clearly define. As a result, patents in these sectors have become so vague that they fail to provide predictable, legal boundaries and might actually harm innovation.

Patents may also spur innovation more effectively in wealthy developed countries than in poor, developing countries. [38] Poor countries have few resources and a small S&T base upon which to build, yet they are still forced to compete with products coming from technological behemoths such as the United States, Europe, and Japan. For example, patents are great for helping the likes of Boeing compete with Airbus, Ford with Nissan, and Apple with Nokia. In contrast, imagine a small start-up firm in, say, Chile or Vietnam attempting to introduce a new computer, automobile, or aircraft that could compete on global markets, or even locally, with the products of Apple, Ford, or Boeing. Such a new firm could never generate enough indigenous innovation at a low enough cost to be competitive. If that same firm could copy (some might say "steal") existing technical knowledge, then it might be able to build upon (some might say "free-ride upon") those investments and come up a viable product. Hence, patents and other IPRs in wealthy nations might act like a wall that keeps private firms in poor countries locked out of high-tech industries. This helps to explain why lesser developed countries often disrespect IPRs until they have achieved enough innovative capacity to benefit from them.[39]

Yet, despite these problems, patents have remained a classic "pillar" of innovation policy throughout the world. Partly due to pressure from high-tech firms in advanced nations, international treaties to bolster and extend IPRs have now become a centerpiece of world trade negotiations. Where multilateral treaties do not suffice, diplomatic pressure and corporate intimidation have proven effective in toughening IPRs.[40] As a result, out of the 122 countries tracked by economist Walter Park, 82 of them have significantly strengthened their IPRs during the past decade, while only 5 countries have weakened them (Bangladesh,

Bolivia, Cyprus, Turkey, and Venezuela).[41] Here in the United States, efforts also are underway to improve the patent system. During the early 2000s, the Supreme Court began to reign in the patentability of "methods," while the recent American Invents Act of 2012 attempted to reduce costly litigation and uncertainty by switching the United States to a first-to-file rather than the more difficult-to-establish first-to-invent system.[42]

Nonetheless, many critics argue that far more needs to be done to modernize the world's patent systems.[43] It is not yet clear what is the best design for each nation's patent system, if there is one. Patents systems can vary widely according to the length of monopoly granted, the scope of knowledge covered, the specificity of knowledge claims to be protected, and the fees for filing, grants, and renewals. Recent decades have also revealed that even minor, seemingly innocuous changes in these characteristics can have a major effect on innovation rates. Some analysts even argue that patents are either unnecessary or too susceptible to abuse, and therefore should be minimized or eliminated altogether.[44]

Given the mixed effects of IPRs on innovation, how much success versus failure in national innovation rates can be explained by patent rights? Figure 4.2 shows national performance in science plotted against a popular measure of intellectual property rights protection for the fifty most productive S&T countries, those responsible for roughly 99% of the world's output. Granted, IPRs tend to protect technology, not science; therefore, they have only an indirect role in motivating scientific research. But science and engineering publications, per capitized and weighted by forward citations, have a high correlation with

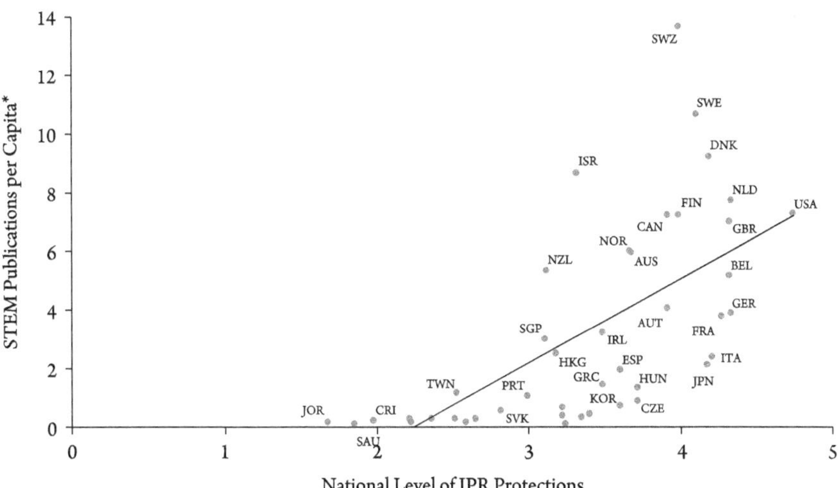

Figure 4.2 IPR protections versus national science performance (1981–2011).
Sources: Thomson-ISI National Science Indicators database; Ginarte and Park (1997); Park (2008), most recent update at: http://nw08.american.edu/~wgp/
*Per million people, weighted by forward citations.

national technological capabilities. Also, science is often a precursor to technological innovation. Therefore, science is used here as a proxy for overall national innovation rates to avoid the tautology of measuring technological property rights versus technological performance, which is itself often measured using property rights.

As both theory and history predict, Figure 4.2 shows that there is a strong correlation between national IPR protection and innovation rates. This relationship holds throughout the entire time period covered by the available data. This includes the period before the mid-1990s, which is before the time when critics argue that IPR abuses became more systematic than incidental. However, statistical analysis also reveals that differences in national IPR regimes explain just under 40% of the differences in national innovation rates.[45] This seems low for such a powerful policy tool. In fact, if we cheat and regress a patent-based measure of national innovation rates against IPRs, then the latter still only explains about half the variation in the former. This somewhat tautological approach should heavily stack the results in favor of IPRs, but even this advantage leaves a considerable amount of unexplained variation in national innovation rates. In sum, IPRs may be important for innovation, but they only get us halfway toward an explanation of national differences in innovation rates. Perhaps the remainder can be explained by another pillar: R&D subsidies.

Pillar Two: Research and Development Subsidies

Innovation is expensive. The development of new science and technology often involves a lengthy trial-and-error process and the endurance of many dead ends. It also requires the employment of workers highly skilled and well trained in science, technology, engineering, and mathematics (STEM), who are often in high demand but short supply, and therefore costly. Physical capital, such as laboratories and testing facilities equipped with scientific equipment, adds further to the innovation bill. Therefore, if policymakers were to support only one form of government action to help a nation's innovation rate, then increasing R&D spending might be it. Thus, R&D subsidies have traditionally formed a second pillar of the classic forms of government actions to aid innovation.

The importance of public investment in R&D has been common sense since ancient times when natural philosophers sought the support of the state, wealthy patrons, or religious institutions. The major science and engineering accomplishments of the ancient Greeks and Romans were the combined result of both government and private investment.[46] In the medieval period, the Catholic Church took over as the main, often only, source of support for science and technology.[47] During the renaissance and early modern period, monarchs and aristocrats became the primary funders of S&T.[48] Although history warns us that generous funding does not guarantee success, most cases of scientific progress and technological change do share it in common. Meanwhile, examples of poorly funded successful innovation are rare and limited.

But why should the state, rather than the private market, invest in R&D? Once again, the most compelling reason for government support of R&D expenditures involves Arrow's insights into S&T market failures.[49] Specifically, R&D suffers from a problem known as "positive externalities." The market failure here is similar to that addressed by IPRs. S&T knowledge is just so easy to copy or take (nonexcludable) and so easy to share (nonrival) that even with quite strong property rights, some benefits from R&D can still spill over into the public domain. That is, IPRs can provide some protection, but not perfect protection. And, as the previous section showed, if you cannot force people to pay for S&T knowledge, then there is very little incentive to invest in its production. Add to this the high risks, uncertainties, and long development times that typify innovation, and you wind up with extremely timid private investors. Under such conditions, those actors who bear the enormous risks and costs involved in innovation are often unable to capture benefits large enough, or fast enough, to justify their initial investment. This is especially true in the case of basic research, which has even higher costs and risks than applied research or development.[50]

Measuring S&T knowledge spillovers is notoriously difficult; however, studies repeatedly show that their effects are likely large and widespread, affecting sectors throughout the economy.[51] For example, recent analysis of innovation in a sample of Fortune 500 corporations found that spillovers affected private firms of all types and all levels of technology.[52] Precisely how much money is lost to spillovers is hard to say and may differ by industry or geographic proximity. A recent study of thermonuclear energy research showed that spillovers there take with them nearly 20% of the initial R&D investment.[53] Analysis of innovation in the semiconductor industry during its "golden age" in the 1980s and 1990s found that the total value of knowledge spillovers appropriated by private corporations totaled as much as 50% of their in-house R&D spending. And while the losses (or gains, depending on one's vantage point) from spillovers appear to decrease with physical distance, their reach has gone global as the costs of international trade, knowledge flows, and personnel transfers get cheaper every decade.[54]

A more concrete illustration of the damage done by positive externalities can be found in drug development within the pharmaceuticals industry. R&D spending, as a percentage of sales revenue, is far higher in pharmaceuticals than in almost any other industry: 30% more than communications equipment, 300% more than computers, and over 600% more than in manufacturing.[55] In raw dollar amounts, an early analysis of drug development during the 1970s and early 1980s found that new drugs tend to take a dozen years to develop, while incurring an average pretax cost of roughly $443 million.[56] During the following decade, those average R&D costs grew to $1 billion.[57] By the 2000s, they had surpassed $1.8 billion, while drug development times were shown to extend as long as thirty years.[58]

This valuable S&T knowledge can costlessly spill over to competitors through a variety of mechanisms. R&D personnel switch firms, or start their own firms, bringing their experience and training with them. The results of scientific research are published and circulated effortlessly. In the worst case, once discovered, a drug formula can be cheaply copied and produced by competitors. Each of these spillovers can potentially wipe out the returns on the original innovators' investment.[59] For example, the antianxiety drug Ativan was first marketed by Wyeth Pharmaceuticals in 1971 and earned its producer $9.1 million in sales during its first years of production. Then, in late 1985, Ativan was copied and generically produced as lorazepam, bringing its imitators a predicted $4.6 million in rents.[60]

A second difficulty that tends to reduce free market investment in R&D is the unpredictability of the results. If research results are unpredictable, then neither investors nor innovators can properly evaluate how many resources to dedicate to a particular R&D program or for how long. In pharmaceuticals, 70% to 80% of the new drugs that enter phase I trials fail to make it to US Food and Drug Administration (FDA) approval. Those few that do get approved must still compete on the commercial market before they can earn any profit for investors.[61]

Worse yet, the products of a particular R&D project may turn out *not* to be applicable to a firm's existing business model and then get written off as a waste of investment. Several examples can be found in the personal computing revolution during the 1970s and 1980s. Many key computer innovations occurred in firms that had absolutely no use for them: the mouse, the windows-style user interface, simple word processing software, and even the personal computer itself were developed and then rejected by the likes of Xerox and Hewlett Packard, which saw no applicability or profit in these innovations.[62]

In response to these persistent market failures, public R&D spending has become a fairly effective way to improve innovation. Of course, channeling tax revenues to solve problems is a simple, classic government solution, one regularly demanded by voters and policymakers alike. It is also a traditional way for elected officials to demonstrate to their constituents that they recognize an issue and are acting on it. Hence, for many observers, spending more R&D money is the natural answer to the innovation problem. Tables 4.1 and 4.2 show the top and bottom government spenders on R&D (as a percentage of gross domestic product [GDP]) within the relatively wealthy Organization for Economic Cooperation and Development (OECD) nations. These data confirm that many

Table 4.1 **Gross Domestic Expenditures on R&D (GERD) as % of GDP, Decadal Averages***

1980s Top R&D Spenders		*1990s Top R&D Spenders*		*2000s Top R&D Spenders*	
United States	2.61%	Sweden	3.23%	Israel	4.50%
Sweden	2.58	Israel†	2.83	Sweden	3.76
Germany	2.56	Japan	2.80	Finland	3.42
Japan	2.48	Switzerland	2.61	Japan	3.23
Switzerland	2.41	United States	2.58	Switzerland	2.72
United Kingdom	2.18	Finland	2.39	Korea	2.67
France	2.11	Germany	2.32	United States	2.65
		France	2.27	Denmark	2.52
		Korea†	2.14	Germany	2.49
				Austria	2.36
				Taiwan	2.32
				Singapore	2.19
				France	2.13

* "Top Spender" defined as spending 2% or more of GDP on R&D
†OECD data collection began for this country during this decade

Source: OECD Main Science and Technology Indicators.

of the world's most innovative nations are those that provide the most public support for research in S&T, while many of the least innovative nations are those whose governments spend the least on R&D.

However, Tables 4.1 and 4.2 also show that some highly innovative countries have suffered *declines* in their relative position even though they *increased* their R&D spending per GDP. Two examples stand out: Sweden and Switzerland have steadily increased their share of R&D spending from 1981 onward but have gotten mixed results. Switzerland's scientific productivity has soared, but this is not translating into better rates of technological invention. Sweden is doing well in technology but slowly losing its lead in science. In contrast, Canada has for decades consistently spent less than 2% of GDP on R&D and yet has remained one of the world's top sources of high technology. Conversely, some of the lowest R&D spenders in the OECD have nonetheless remained midlevel innovators. These include New Zealand (spent less than 1% of GDP on R&D during the 1980s and 1990s, even now only 1.2% of GDP), Ireland (spent less than 1% of GDP between 1981 and 1991 and from 1% to 1.25% between 1992 and

Table 4.2 **Gross Domestic Expenditures on R&D (GERD), Decadal Averages***

1980s Bottom R&D Spenders		*1990s Bottom R&D Spenders*		*2000s Bottom R&D Spenders*	
New Zealand	0.87	New Zealand	1.00	Portugal	0.93
South Africa	0.78	Hungary†	0.87	Hungary	0.93
Ireland	0.74	Spain	0.83	South Africa	0.85
Spain	0.54	Poland†	0.71	Poland	0.58
Portugal	0.36	Romania†	0.70	Greece	0.57
Greece	0.25	South Africa	0.68	Turkey	0.55
		China†	0.67	Slovakia	0.54
		Portugal	0.58	Argentina	0.45
		Greece	0.45	Romania	0.43
		Argentina†	0.43	Mexico	0.38
		Turkey†	0.34		
		Mexico†	0.30		

* "Bottom Spender" defined as spending 1% or less of GDP on R&D
†OECD data collection began for this country during this decade

Source: OECD Main Science and Technology Indicators.

2006), and Spain (spent less than 1% of GDP between 1981 and 2002, only reaching 1.35% in 2008). These three countries spend far less than the world's most innovative nations, yet they have not completely disappeared from the technological frontier.

So what's going on? First, merely increasing R&D expenditures does not necessarily cause high levels of technological change. R&D money is just as easily misspent or misappropriated as any other type of government largess. The US supersonic transport program (SST) serves as an example.[63] Lasting from 1962 until 1971, and costing $920 million, the SST was initially motivated by national security and economic competitiveness concerns. The SST arose largely in reaction to similar supersonic research programs that had been initiated in the Soviet Union, France, and Great Britain during the late 1950s. As early as December 1963, a financial analysis performed for President Johnson recommended that the United States abandon part or all of the SST, describing it as not economically competitive without substantial government support.[64] Seven years later, President Nixon's SST Ad Hoc Review Committee of science and technical advisers likewise recommended discontinuation of the program. However, the SST program had become a source of lucrative R&D contracts, jobs, and other economic stimuli throughout the country. It also had become tightly linked with national security in the public mind. Therefore, Congress and many in the executive branch were loath to cancel the program, which continued through years of cost overruns and scheduling delays. Only after the SST's air pollution problems were denounced, during the fervor of environmental politics in 1970, was the program finally cancelled.[65] Critics have since argued that the space shuttle, synthetic fuels, ethanol, the B-1 bomber, and the Strategic Defense Initiative (SDI) are other examples of major, often multi-billion-dollar, R&D programs that have produced relatively little broadly useful innovation per dollar invested.

Another problem with R&D subsidies is that costs can be purposely inflated by private investors to win support for government funding. For example, skeptics argue that the high estimates for pharmaceutical R&D cited earlier are often based on small, possibly unrepresentative, sets of proprietary industry data. Sometimes these estimates include questionable conjectures about missing data or heroic assumptions about important variables such as the costs of capital, development times, tax savings, and opportunity costs. One critical independent analysis estimated the average costs of R&D for new pharmaceuticals to be as low as only $43.4 million per new drug rather than the $1.8 billion touted by industry.[66]

Moreover, generous R&D subsidies from governments might be creating perverse incentives for innovation. When government involvement in established industries is strong, the taxpayers usually fund basic research with revolutionary potential. This allows private business to focus on developing and marketing minor, less risky innovations. Again, the pharmaceutical sector provides examples. Government now lavishes R&D funding on medical and drug research to the tune of tens of billions of dollars per year. A 2006 study revealed that over 80% of all funds for basic research on new drugs and vaccines come from public sources, an activity on which private firms spend only 1.3% of their own revenues.[67] Meanwhile, the output of new drugs has been questionable. Most drug innovations during the past several decades have consisted of minor variations on existing drugs, thus offering little additional benefit. The 1996 Barral Report, a study of drug development from 1974 to 1994, found that only 11% of internationally marketed new drugs were therapeutically and pharmacologically innovative.[68] Since 2000, independent studies in both the United States and Europe have corroborated this finding, suggesting that roughly 85% to 90% of all new drugs provide little or no medical advantages over existing treatments.[69] Critics argue that some of these new drugs might even be less safe or less effective than existing ones, such as Vioxx (Merck), Avandia (GlaxoSmithKline), Tequin (Kyorin), and Xigris (Eli Lilly).[70]

Of course, pharmaceuticals constitute just one industry, and possibly an outlier at that; so what does the overall picture look like? For that we return to national statistics. Statistical analysis of national patents, STEM publishing activity, and OECD R&D spending data suggest that roughly 52% of the national variation in technological innovation is explained by R&D spending as a percentage of GDP. For scientific progress, only around 35% is explained by R&D spending.[71] Moreover, the explanatory power of R&D spending for technological innovation drops from 58% during the 1980s to 48% during the 1990s, while remaining consistent for scientific progress. That is, there might be diminishing returns over time to national R&D spending.

If we combine IPR protection (Pillar One) with R&D spending (Pillar Two) for the entire 1980–2010 time period, then together they explain 68% of the national differences in technological innovation rates, and 49% in scientific progress. Thus, we have edged closer to a complete explanation for differences in national innovation rates. Yes, R&D spending is still a vitally important policy tool for innovation, but there is a considerable amount of national performance that remains unexplained. For that, we need to look at the third classic pillar of S&T policy: education.

Pillar Three: Education

As early as the 1840s, in his widely read theory of economic nationalism, the German economist Friedrich List identified education as playing a central role in determining the productivity of nations. Specifically, he described education as being intricately bound with science and invention, and hence national economic competitiveness. He therefore scolded Adam Smith posthumously for his reliance on the simple division of labor to increase skills and foster inventions, writing, "[Smith] does not even assign a productive character to the mental labours of those who . . . cultivate and promote instruction, religion, science, and art."[72]

Education fosters innovation in three ways.[73] First, formally trained scientists and engineers are a direct input to innovative activity. Certainly this was not always the case. Skilled workers with little or no formal education often acted as key innovators during the first industrial revolution. These include Richard Arkwright, Samuel Crompton, James Watt, and many other eighteenth-century pioneers of Britain's radical innovations in textiles, steam power, and iron manufacturing, who received much or all of their education outside of any formal school system. However, since the rise of the research university (1810), the industrial laboratory (1870s), and full-time corporate R&D facilities (1900), formally educated STEM workers have gradually become an essential input to national innovative activity.[74] Elsewhere, on the factory floor, skilled workers have been shown to regularly contribute to process innovations and product improvements. These are workers who generally have at least a decade of formal education, followed by extensive in-house training by their employer. Their innovative contributions were an important element of Japan's and Germany's manufacturing "miracles" during the 1970s and 1980s.[75]

Second, even when workers are not responsible for creating new technology, many still require S&T education to perform their jobs. For example, technological change can complement educated workers, with an increase in one driving demand for the other. This is the logical consequence of economist John Hicks's observation that "A change in the relative prices of the factors of production is itself a spur to invention, and to invention of a particular kind—directed to economizing the use of a factor which has become relatively expensive."[76] During the 1700s and 1800s, this generally meant technology replacing expensive skilled labor. During the twentieth century, however, technological change increased the demand for skilled workers to use it. The positive effects of innovation and skilled labor on one another have been documented by economists David Autor, Alan Krueger, and others,[77] and then developed into a theory of "directed" or "biased" technological change by economist Daron Acemoglu.[78] As skilled workers enter the market, they create demand for more and higher levels of technology that they need to perform their labor.[79] Hence, as higher levels of education create more skilled workers, these workers demand more and better technology.

Third, educated consumers tend to promote technological change. For example, Eric Von Hippel has shown that in many fields users, not producers, drive innovation.[80] He documents how, in industries from scientific equipment to software to sporting goods, consumers are responsible for a considerable amount of technological change. Technology enthusiasts in these industries tend to be very adept at recognizing the need for particular improvements in the products they use, sometimes even building prototypes and sharing them with manufacturers. How much is unclear, but studies suggest that from 10% to 40% of users contribute innovations to develop or modify the products they use.[81] Even when they are not innovating, educated consumers tend to demand ever-improving technologies. Often radical innovations succeed in part due to their ability to penetrate highly educated consumer markets. Automobiles, radios, aircraft, televisions, personal computers, and cell phones each made their first appearance as activities for technically savvy hobbyists and next as luxury items for highly educated, wealthy consumers. Finally, schools are often the venue where young consumers are first introduced to new technologies and taught their applications to work and daily life.

What does the data say about the effects of education on S&T performance? The best collected indicator of national education policy is spending data.[82] Tables 4.3 and 4.4 show the top and bottom spenders in education among those

Table 4.3 **Top Education Spending as Percentage of GDP, Decadal Averages*** **(OECD Observed Countries)**

1970s		*1980s*		*1990s*		*2000s*	
Canada	7.83	Israel	8.95	Denmark	7.99	Denmark	8.37
US	7.35	Sweden	7.94	Norway	7.39	Sweden	7.30
Netherlands	7.06	Canada	6.66	Sweden	7.20	Norway	7.10
Sweden	7.04	Netherlands	6.52	Israel	6.97	Israel	6.71
Denmark	6.96	Denmark	6.49	New Zlnd	6.61	New Zlnd	6.56
Israel	6.38	US	6.43	S. Africa	6.21	Finland	6.20
Belgium	6.08	Norway	6.03	Finland	6.16	Belgium	6.04
				Canada	6.03		

*Where "Top Spender" indicates a spending level of 6% of GDP or above.

Source: World Development Indicators, World Bank

Table 4.4 **Lowest Education Spending as Percentage of GDP, Decadal Averages (OECD Observed Countries)**

1970s		*1980s*		*1990s*		*2000s*	
China	1.49	Turkey	2.02	China	2.06	China	2.9*
Argentina	1.67	Argentina	2.02	Greece	2.65	Singapore	2.98
Greece	1.73	Greece	2.10	Turkey	2.65	Greece	3.16
Spain	1.78	China	2.51	Singapore	3.04	Romania	3.32
Portugal	2.29	Spain	2.60	Luxemburg	3.25	Russia	3.48
India	2.39	India	3.03	Romania	3.36	Japan	3.61
S. Korea	2.79	Portugal	3.42	S. Korea	3.50	India	3.67
Singapore	2.91	Singapore	3.56	Japan	3.55	Turkey	3.69

*Estimate.

Source: World Development Indicators, World Bank

countries observed by the OECD. As expected, we find that many top innovators are also top education spenders. However, this correlation is not strong. We also find several midlevel innovators (Denmark, Norway, New Zealand, and Belgium) and some low-level innovators (South Africa) among the top education spenders. For example, Sweden consistently spends more than 7% of GDP on education but has suffered a relative decline in innovation rates during the past several decades. Meanwhile, the United States has entirely dropped off the list of top education spenders since the 1980s but has nonetheless remained at the edge of the technological frontier. Interestingly, South Korea and Japan ranked low on education spending for several decades yet have risen from the technological backwaters to become top innovators. Likewise, China and India have consistently been among the lowest spenders on education and yet are popularly viewed as rising technological threats.

Table 4.5 reveals another interesting trend. Some of the largest decreases in education spending over time not only have occurred in lead innovating nations but also have done so *without* hurting their national S&T competitiveness. Meanwhile, those countries with the greatest percentage increases in education spending have seen little rise in their relative innovation rates.[83]

Table 4.5 **Nations with Largest Percentage Changes in Education Spending (1970–2000)***

Increases		*Decreases*	
Portugal	3.16	Canada	–2.65
Argentina	2.54	Netherlands	–1.94
Spain	2.49	US	–1.69
Mexico	2.38	Japan	–0.98
		UK	–0.79

*As % of GDP, data shown is change in percentage points across decadal averages.

Source: World Development Indicators, World Bank.

Of course, just spending money on schools does not necessarily result in better-educated students; perhaps a more accurate gauge of education is actual student performance. For this data, we turn to the OECD's Programme for International Student Assessment (PISA). PISA is a triennial survey of over 70 countries that attempts to assess national education systems by testing the reading, math, and science capabilities of fifteen-year-old students. Administered since 2000, the PISA test scores show Hong Kong, New Zealand, and Poland regularly ranking among the world's best education systems, with the highest percentage of their students achieving top scores in science and mathematics.[84] Other high-ranking test achievers are Australia and Ireland. Yet none of these countries also rank among the most innovative or rapidly innovative nations. Conversely, we can find three top or rapid innovators (Israel, Sweden, and United States) consistently sitting among PISA's middle ranks of math and science educators. In fact, as Figure 4.3 shows, the correlation between student test score rankings and relative national innovation rates is quite low. All told, test

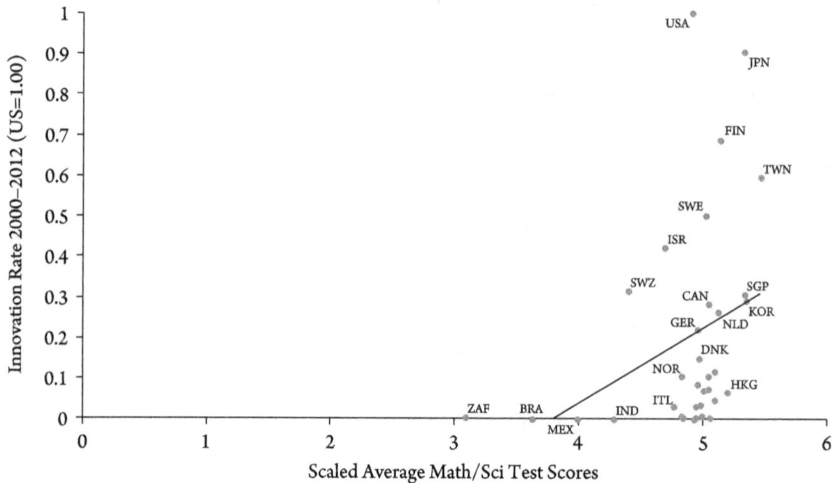

Figure 4.3 Science-math test scores versus national innovation rate (2000–2012). Average test score in math and science, primary through end of secondary school, all years (scaled to PISA scale divided by 100). Top 34 most innovative countries shown. Source: Hanushek and Woessmann (2012).

scores explain only around 10% of the variation in innovation rates among the top thirty-four most innovative countries, those responsible for over 99% of the world's S&T output.

One could argue that primary and secondary education are not the best places to look for correlations with national S&T performance. Evidence for this can be seen even more clearly in Figure 4.4, which plots four bivariate regression equations of average years of schooling versus national S&T performance. It clearly shows that tertiary education has a much greater payoff for innovation than overall education. However, while the effects of tertiary education are relatively large, statistical analysis shows that it still only explains 31% of national differences in technological innovation rates, and 37% of national differences in STEM research output.

Figures 4.5 and 4.6 take the logical next step by plotting college (tertiary) education in STEM against national performance in science and technology. Here the effect of additional STEM students on innovation is large, but it still only explains roughly 8% to 15% of national variation in science and technology performance. While surprising, this finding dovetails with other data. In 1950, only around 0.25% of the US labor force consisted of scientists and engineers engaged in R&D.[85] This number had grown to 1.62% of the workforce by 2008.[86] In other words, while the per capita number of STEM workers active in R&D has grown over sixfold, it still only represents a tiny fraction of US workers. To drive this point home, if calculated as a percentage of total population, all of the fantastic

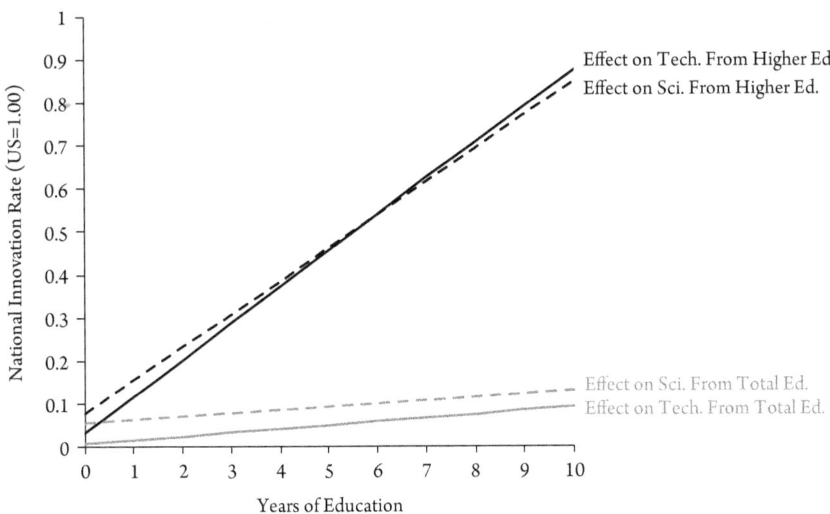

Figure 4.4 National S&T performance versus average schooling years. Plots are estimates, representing four separate regression lines of STEM research publications and technological patents (both per capita, weighted by forward citations) against average schooling years. Sources: Barro and Lee (2010); NBER Patent Dataset; and Thomson-ISI.

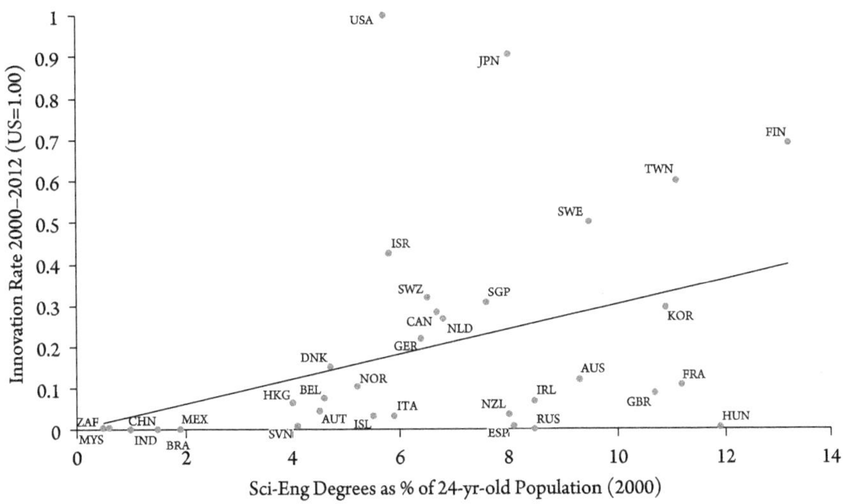

Figure 4.5 STEM undergraduates versus national technology performance.
Source: National Science Foundation (2004). Appendix table 2-33: First university degrees and ratio of first university degrees and S&E degrees to 24-year-old population in selected locations, by region: 2000 or most recent year (revised); NBER Patent Database.

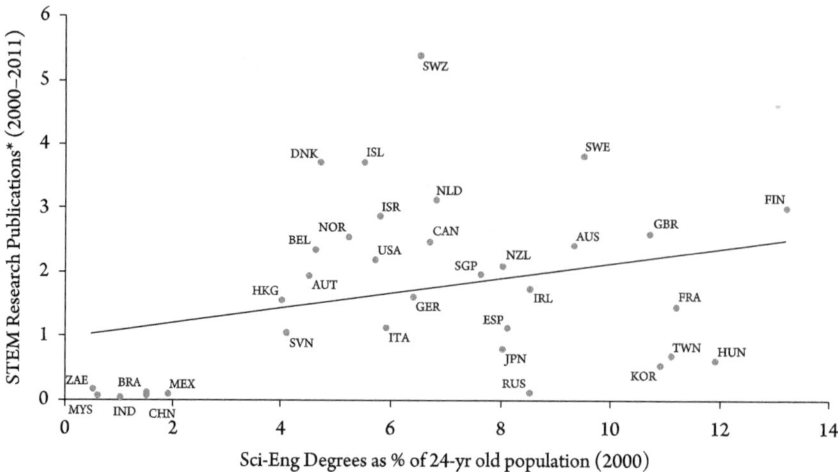

Figure 4.6 STEM undergraduates versus national science performance.
Source: National Science Foundation (2004) Appendix table 2–33: First university degrees and ratio of first university degrees and S&E degrees to 24-year-old population in selected locations, by region: 2000 or most recent year (revised); Thomson-ISI.
*Per capita, weighted by forward citations

advances in US science and technology achieved during the past sixty years have been based on work performed by much fewer than 1% of American citizens.[87]

If we now combine the data on our three pillars (IPR protection, R&D spending, and tertiary STEM education), then together they still explain under 70% of the national differences in technological innovation rates, and roughly 56% of national differences in scientific progress. Hence, we continue to march closer to a complete explanation for differences in national innovation rates, but with diminishing returns. This is partly because of correlations between the three pillars. The three pillars are, at least in part, expressions of similar national phenomena; they represent broadly shared values and goals, and perhaps even conceptions of risk and return. They therefore have overlapping effects. They each appear to matter for national innovation rates, but still there remains a significant chunk of unexplained performance. For that, we need to investigate the role of public research organizations, especially universities.

Pillar Four: Research Universities

Universities, and institutions like them, have acted as bastions of S&T since the first philosophical schools of ancient Greece. However, for much of history, universities were more places of pure theory and the diffusion of existing knowledge than seats of scientific discovery or the creation of new technology. Change came in 1810, when the Prussian government established the first research universities in Berlin.[88] This "Humboldtian" university model, which prioritized scientific investigation over teaching, soon spread across Europe. Thousands of American students who traveled to Germany to complete their education during the 1800s eventually brought this university model back with them to the United States.

The idea of an S&T-oriented research university found fertile ground in the postbellum United States. The Morrill Act of 1862 already provided federal land upon which states were to erect public universities and colleges for the teaching of agricultural science and the mechanical arts. This was followed by federal support for agricultural research at university-based experiment stations around the country (Hatch Act of 1887) and for the diffusion of new scientific knowledge (Smith-Lever Act of 1914). These efforts combined with the Humboldtian movement to produce a revolution in American higher education and scientific research. It began with the founding of Johns Hopkins University in 1876.[89] The first of its kind in the United States, Johns Hopkins provided advanced laboratories and tremendous academic freedom to attract top scientific researchers and those students who wished to train under them. It was so successful that, by 1900, a handful of universities across the country were adopting the John Hopkins approach: Harvard, Columbia, Chicago, Cornell, Stanford, the University of Michigan, and the University of Wisconsin.

During the ensuing decades, the American research university slowly assumed the form we see today, often likened to a nineteenth-century German research university grafted upon a seventeenth-century English gentlemen's college.[90] The rise of racist fascism in Europe during the 1930s drove into American universities a deluge of top scientists and engineers, including such leading lights as Albert Einstein (architect of modern physics), Max Delbruck (father of molecular biology), and Leo Szilard (creator of the electron microscope and cyclotron). Government-subsidized universities then proved themselves invaluable for their contributions of S&T to American efforts in World War II. Afterward, they were enlisted to play an even grander role during the Cold War.[91] In recent decades, massive infusions of federal research dollars and state subsidies have been funneled to US universities to improve national S&T competitiveness, first against a resurgent Japan and Germany, and later against Taiwan, South Korea, China, and India.[92]

Universities aid national S&T competitiveness in several ways. Most obviously, university laboratories are where much scientific research and technological innovation get done. Countless major discoveries and inventions were the direct results of university research, such as the artificial heart, the World Wide Web, DNA sequencing, and nuclear power. Universities also provide training for a nation's STEM workers through degree granting programs, another vital input to innovation. Universities also foster technological change indirectly, via their links with industry and government. For example, a survey of 1,267 corporate R&D managers ranked ten types of linkages by which universities contribute indirectly to industrial innovation:[93] research publications (41% of industry respondents found these important), informal exchanges of information (36%), meetings and conferences (35%), university consulting (32%) and contract research (21%), hiring of graduates (20%), joint R&D projects (18%), the use of university patents (18%) and licenses (9.5%), and mutual exchanges of STEM personnel (5.8%).[94]

For these reasons, governments around the world have supported an expansion of universities. In China, not only are universities proliferating at historic rates but also governments there now seek to rival the best Western research schools at places like Peking University, Tsinghua University, and Fudan University. India has likewise tried to emulate top British and American S&T universities with its fifteen Indian Institutes of Technology, over half of which were established in 2008–2009. Meanwhile, universities in the United States and Europe are putting ever greater emphasis on research, for both faculty and students alike. Even some Middle Eastern countries, such as Dubai and Qatar, now view universities as a bridge from an oil-based economy to a globally competitive high-tech economy.[95]

However, universities only take us so far in explaining national S&T performance. For example, there are relatively few high-ranked universities in Japan, South Korea, and Taiwan, but this has not prevented these countries from producing globally competitive S&T. Meanwhile, Great Britain ranks quite high, second only to the United States, in total number of respected research universities but remains a midlevel innovator by many measures. Perhaps more disappointing, Germany, France, and Italy are replete with institutions of higher education that themselves produce few patents, publications, or STEM prizes. As Figure 4.7 shows, the relationship between research universities and national innovation rates is strong, but far from deterministic. Statistical analysis reveals, for example, that hosting top-ranked universities explains only around 10% of the global variation in national innovation rates.

Certainly California's Silicon Valley and Boston's Route 128 both have several top-ranked research universities in their midst, with regional businesses acting to commercialize the science and technology coming out of academic laboratories. Such university-based commercial regions have been viewed as critical to national S&T competitiveness.[96] Yet, similar university-based high-technology regions failed to appear around top research universities located in Atlanta, New Haven, or Ann Arbor. Nor have attempts to export the Silicon Valley model typically been quite so successful in countries such as Mexico, China, and South Korea.[97] Meanwhile, the history of Silicon Valley reveals that, decades before the integrated circuit boom of the 1960s, it was Stanford University that drew upon

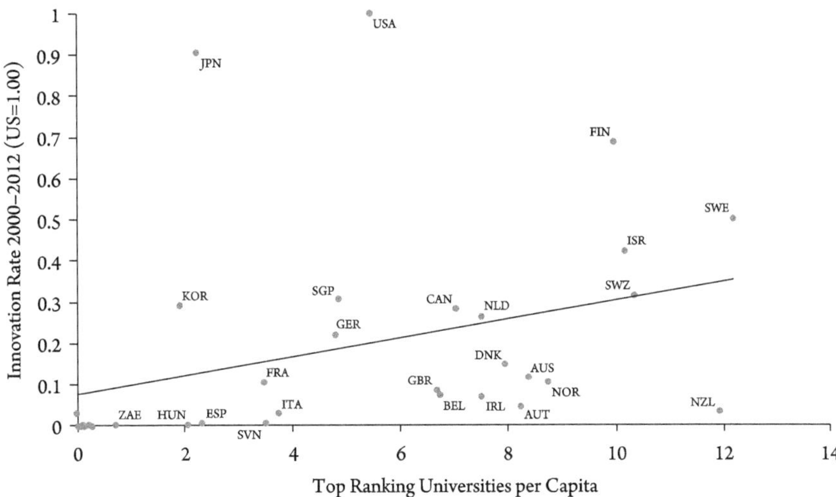

Figure 4.7 Top universities versus national technology performance. Average number of top ranking universities per 10 million people, 2003–2013. Sources: NBER Patent Database; Academic Ranking of World Universities (ARWU) published by the Center for World-Class Universities and the Institute of Higher Education of Shanghai Jiao Tong University.

surrounding electronics firms to build its early research programs, not the other way around.[98]

Problems with the funding and direction of university research have also arisen in recent years. The overall costs of research per faculty member are constantly and rapidly increasing, from an average of $17,000 per tenure-track faculty (1975) to over $250,000 (2010).[99] In some S&T fields, such as engineering, the start-up costs for hiring research faculty can top $1.5 million due to laboratory and equipment requirements.[100] Meanwhile, state support for university R&D has been declining slowly but steadily. In 1975, the federal government paid for just over 67% of all science and engineering R&D performed at research universities, while state governments paid for another 9.7%. In 2010, those figures had fallen to 62% and 6.2%, respectively.[101] While these declines appear small in percentage terms, they constitute hundreds of millions of dollars that must be found elsewhere.

To pay these exorbitant costs, universities have increasingly turned to private industry. As of 2010, private investors funded an average of 5.8% (or $3.1 billion) of all academic research, and up to 25% in some fields, such as biotechnology.[102] But to earn a return on its investment, private industry often requires ownership of the intellectual property rights that come out of it. Private investors also often seek limits on faculty autonomy, seeing them not as free thinkers, but more like contractors hired to solve specific research problems. Some private donors even have intellectual or ideological agendas that can affect the direction or results of university research. Therefore, industry-university ties can conflict with the public, objective, and open traditions of American universities.[103] These problems have become known as the "privatization" of university research.

The Bayh-Dole Act of 1980 is often cited as a key driver of the privatization of university research. Bayh-Dole was the federal government's policy response to widespread complaints that, during the 1970s, university research was producing few practical applications. Bayh-Dole also promised to provide a mechanism by which universities might earn revenues to pay for research. The act allowed those university researchers funded by the federal government to patent their discoveries and inventions, then license out these technologies to private industry for development. As a result, patents awarded to American universities appeared to have increased dramatically, from roughly 300 per year (1975) to 2,818 (2008), and have become the basis for faculty promotion and tenure at many schools.[104] Famous examples of success include Carnegie Mellon's $25 million windfall from its Lycos Internet search engine, and Stanford's $143 million in proceeds from its patent on a new gene-splicing process. However, subsequent studies have shown that most universities have not generated extraordinary revenues from patenting and licensing.[105] Nor has Bayh-Dole significantly affected the commercialization of university research; in most fields, commercialization was occurring anyway and Bayh-Dole did little to accelerate that trend.[106] In fact, in most fields of university research, only a small portion of faculty engage in licensing at all.[107] Many scholars also fear that Bayh-Dole has restricted disclosure and data sharing, lowered research quality, forced the substitution of applied research for basic research, and adversely affected incentives for S&T education.[108]

Yet another problem that has crept into public universities is academic earmarking. This involves the determination of research funding based purely on lobbying and politics rather than on scientific peer review. In the United States during 2010, 875 academic institutions received a total of $1.98 billion in federal earmarks, with the most funding going to universities in those states with high-ranking members of Congress.[109] The problem is that these earmarks tend to fund research that is lower quality and has a lower impact than that paid for by competitive funding, and that universities which receive earmarks do not subsequently improve their research standing. For example, the presence of Senator Thad Cochran (R-MI) on the Senate Appropriations Committee ensured that four Mississippi universities were among the top twenty-five recipients of academic earmarks in 2010, despite the fact that none of these schools broke the top one hundred rankings of research universities. Nearby Auburn University and the University of Alabama joined this list largely thanks to powerful Alabama Senator Richard Shelby.[110] This type of academic earmarking not only funds low-impact research but also crowds out peer-reviewed competitive research grants. Hence, the net effect of academic earmarking is to redirect public R&D dollars away from top research universities and toward those middle- and lower-quality schools that have powerful lobbying offices in Washington.[111]

Pillar Five: Trade Policy

Trade policy extends the previous four pillars into the international economy. Depending on how protectionist it is, a nation's trade policy can create a wall that attempts to lock in positive spillovers, lock out negative spillovers, and prevent foreign monopolies from dominating local markets while still promoting exports. It therefore affects S&T indirectly. That is, trade policy may not immediately jump to mind as a form of innovation policy, but it is. One need only observe that each of the technological leaders across history benefited from being heavily involved in world trade to see this. The ancient Greeks and Romans; the medieval Arabs and Venetians; later the Dutch, British, Americans, Germans, and Japanese; and most recently the Chinese each experienced a correlation between their rise in world trade and a subsequent rise in S&T capabilities.

Trade affects innovation through various mechanisms. Most obviously, trade brings societies into contact with foreign advances in S&T, as well as diverse ideas about S&T applications and businesses for selling them. Americans may have invented the transistor, but the Japanese understood how to make it the basis for new lines of low-cost consumer electronics such as radios, toys, watches, calculators, and computers. Trade also generates competition among businesses and between nations, creating international contests for greater efficiency and new products. Often these contests can only be won through investment in technological change. Trade also allows specialization, and therefore intense economic focus on particular sectors of S&T, such as Taiwan in computer hardware, Singapore's recent focus on biotechnology, and the Nordic specialization in mobile telecommunications.[112] Trade can create the surplus wealth necessary for investment in R&D and new high-tech industries. Often this occurs through the emergence, alongside major trading operations, of a large internationally competitive financial sector. Also, trade creates demand for security, for the physical protection and stability of distant consumer markets, distribution chains, and production facilities. This can translate into military R&D, which results in not only new weapons but also technological spillovers into the civilian sector. Perhaps most important, trade creates economies of scale, making profitable large S&T investments that might not be rewarded in smaller national markets. In sum, to understand all the S&T benefits of trade, one need only ask whether the state of, say, Michigan would be as technologically advanced today if it were not part of a union with forty-nine other states that compose the massive US free trade zone, all of which also trade with the rest of the world.

Ironically, for centuries it was protectionism that was considered essential for technological development. One of the oldest economic justifications for protectionism is the "infant industry" argument. As applied to S&T, the infant industry argument holds that developing economies have a potential comparative advantage in high technology, but high-tech industries are difficult to develop from scratch in developing countries because they cannot initially compete with the existing technology coming out of the advanced innovators. Therefore, developing countries must use tariffs or import quotas to limit foreign competition until domestic industries are strong enough to compete on world technology markets. Otherwise, developing countries will simply be swamped with imports of high technology from the frontier innovators, and therefore will never industrialize or develop. Even in the twenty-first century, this remains one of the more respected arguments against free trade. After all, three of the world's most technologically advanced economies, the United States, Japan, and Germany, each began their paths to national high-technology competitiveness behind substantial trade barriers.

During the 1970s, however, observers realized major problems with infant industry protection, especially where it took the form of import substituting industrialization (ISI). ISI is the strategy whereby a country limits imports of specific technologies that they want to produce domestically. By limiting imports of a technology, the government drives up domestic demand for that technology, and hence also drives up prices and profits, which should draw domestic producers in to fill the gap. ISI was popular with developing countries from the 1930s through the 1970s. But one problem with ISI is that protecting high-technology sectors is only good policy *if* it makes firms in those sectors more competitive, and this does not always happen.

For decades, countries throughout Latin America, as well as India and Pakistan, protected their technologically advanced sectors. In each of these countries, indigenous innovation took hold at first, leading to some initial modernization and industrialization. Many domestic producers then simply hid behind this protection and failed to become more competitive, or they became competitive for reasons that had little to do with protectionism. If taken too far, protectionism can cut an economy off from inflows of capital, know-how, skilled labor, and even new technology itself. Under these conditions, countries must essentially reinvent entire industries from scratch, which is a very risky and costly endeavor. As a result, most of those nations that practiced ISI still had to import sophisticated technological goods such as computers, electronic instruments, and precision tools because they never modernized enough to produce them domestically. ISI can lead to the creation of more domestic manufacturing, but few of the countries that adopted ISI ever showed any signs of catching up with the advanced countries. As a result, many economists now doubt the ability of ISI to modernize nations or to help them develop high-tech industries at all.

After the 1970s, enthusiasm for protectionism was gradually replaced with support for export-led growth strategies. The main idea behind export-led strategies is for a developing country to use its comparative advantage in cheap but well-educated and well-disciplined labor to become a base for manufacturing high-tech goods. This requires that developing nations open their economies to imports of all inputs in which the country does not have a comparative advantage. Then, domestic firms or government can either set up increasingly high-tech industries themselves (e.g., Japan, South Korea, and Taiwan) or allow foreign companies to do so through foreign direct investment (e.g., China and Singapore). These industries usually produce for export to wealthy markets, while providing the host country with factories, more STEM-oriented jobs, higher wages, and massive transfers of technology and know-how. Slowly, host-country workers, managers, and engineers should learn enough from the advanced foreigners to start up their own domestic firms and compete, and thereby move up the value chain.

At first, starting during the 1960s, only a small group of primarily East Asian countries pursued this export-led strategy (e.g., Japan, South Korea, Hong Kong, Taiwan, and Singapore). They have since been joined by China, Chile, Finland, to some degree India, and others. Observers highlight three remarkable characteristics about the countries that pursue export-led strategies: their rapid economic growth, their equally rapid modernization and industrialization, and their relative openness to trade. While each country tends to develop its own variation on the export-led approach, compared to the ISI countries, the export-led countries tend to suffer from much lower and less varied rates of protectionism.

For advanced countries, trade policy fosters innovation by affecting market size, specialization, and competition. First, trade can increase the size of potential consumer markets. Larger markets translate into larger potential profits, thereby incentivizing greater investment in innovation. Technologies that may not be profitable to develop and produce in a small country that is closed to trade may be hugely profitable on world markets. For example, many of the new drugs developed by Switzerland's advanced pharmaceutical industries would not be profitable if they only served the tiny Swiss market, especially for those diseases that strike a small percentage of the population. Only by exporting to the rest of the world have the likes of Novartis, Merck, and La Roche been able to become profitable innovators at the technological frontier. A similar dynamic allows the customization of technologies to particular consumer tastes, leading to an increased variety of automobiles, information and communications technologies, and soon genetic-based medicines.

Second, intraindustry trade between advanced economies motivates their firms to further specialize according to their competitive advantage. This allows nations to focus their investments more efficiently on innovation in those industries and links in the supply chain where they best compete. At first, this specialization was fairly broad, as during the 1980s when Japan specialized in innovations for family cars, and Germany and Italy in sports cars. During the 1990s, national S&T specialties got finer grained: a laptop computer might be designed in Japan but built from Taiwanese components and use software written in the United States, Germany, and Israel. In the twenty-first century, intraindustry trade has transformed into intraproduct trade, leading to even more highly specialized innovation. For example, Boeing's new 787 Dreamliner includes innovations made in the United States (body design), the United Kingdom (engines), France (seating, safety, avionics), Japan (lithium-ion batteries, in-flight entertainment, wing components), Australia (wing components), Italy (fuselage, stabilizers), and several other countries.[113]

Third, trade fosters competition between the advanced nations, forcing them to innovate in existing industries and graduate out of increasingly obsolete ones. During the early twentieth century, foreign competition in textiles, basic metals and chemicals, and light manufacturing helped push the United States into the development of its early automobile and consumer electronics industries. Then again, after the 1960s, Japan's rise in competitiveness in autos, electronics, and computing forced the United States and other lead innovators to not only improve their own S&T competitiveness and production but also put greater emphasis on new technologies such as network computing, software, aeronautics, and telecommunications. Most recently, as China, Taiwan, South Korea, Israel, Ireland, and the Nordic nations advance into these industries, the United States has been forced to become the leader in innovation and in the biotechnology, medical equipment, nanotechnology, and energy sectors.

However, of all the Five Pillars, trade policy seems to have the weakest correlation with any of the innovation measures in any time period (Figure 4.8). Perhaps the strongest relationship between trade and innovation can be found during the early 1970s. Yet, even during this period, statistical analysis reveals that trade openness explains only around 15% of the variation in national innovation rates. Within two decades, the correlation had dropped to under 3%. This is not to say that trade hurts or inhibits innovation, but rather that several countries with relatively low exposure to world trade have innovated quite well, while some countries with large exposures to trade have not. Indeed, it is hard to deny either the great success of China's openness in fostering its export-led push into high technology or Japan's closed strategy of using infant industry protections, legal or otherwise, to grow its way to the high-tech frontier. Either strategy can work.

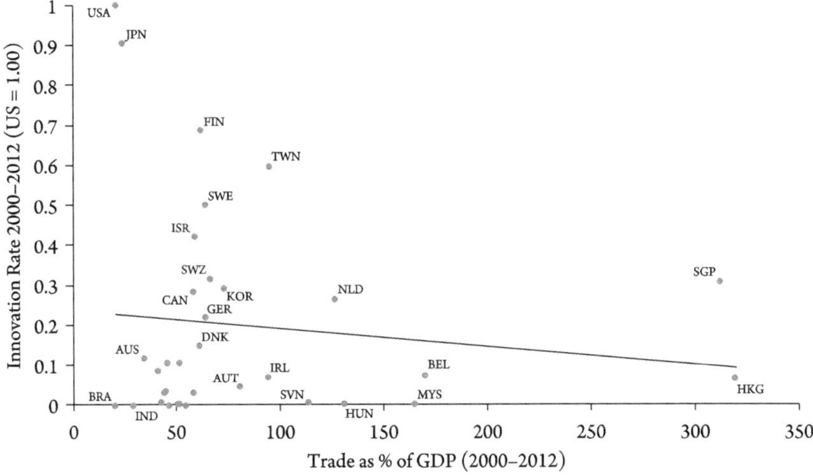

Figure 4.8 Trade and innovation (2000–2012). Sources: World Bank Development Indicators, World Bank; NBER Patent Database.

The Five Pillars Acting as One

The preceding sections revealed that no single one of the Five Pillars alone acts as a silver bullet for fostering S&T competitiveness, so perhaps instead, countries must execute well on each. That is, perhaps the effects of one policy pillar are partly dependent upon the strength of the others. For example, over 55% of US basic research is performed at universities,[114] which are themselves partly incentivized to innovate by the Bayh-Dole Act, which allows them to profit from their IPRs, which are strongly enforced in the United States. However, these correlations appear not to hold overall (Table 4.6). On the one hand, there is a high correlation between R&D spending (per GDP) and the level of intellectual property rights (0.7). On the other hand, there is a somewhat lower correlation between R&D and education spending (0.54), and IPR and top universities (0.44). And correlations between the other pillars are relatively weak. So it is not necessarily true that each of a country's major S&T institutions and policies must be strong to get good results.

Also, the Five Pillars policies can contradict one another. For example, critics of the Bayh-Dole Act argue that the introduction of IPRs into university research has increased secrecy at formerly transparent public institutions. There are reports of university professors withholding data, methods, and findings to protect the business aspects of their research.[115] Meanwhile, increases in spending for STEM higher education are sometimes diverted to fund research or used to fund foreign students who then return home to innovate for our competition.[116]

Table 4.6 **Correlations between the Five Pillars of Innovation Policy**

R&D Spending	1				
Education Spending	0.54	1			
IPRs	0.70	0.25	1		
Top Universities	0.36	0.00	0.44	1	
Trade Openness	0.11	0.28	0.12	−0.37	1
	R&D	Educ.	IPRs	Univ.	Trade

Statistical analysis suggests that collectively, the Five Pillars might explain up to 90% of the differences in national innovation rates.[117] However, there are problems with this finding as well. First, even if taken at face value, there are major violations to the "Five Pillars as One" thesis that demand explanation. For example, no country covered by the OECD's data scores in top or bottom ranks in each of the Five Pillars policy areas (Table 4.7). Also, surprisingly, only a few of the countries observed by the OECD do little right (Turkey and Slovak Republic), while only a few countries rank highly in more than two categories (Canada, the United States, and Japan). In fact, some top innovators ironically appear in the bottom ranks of some categories (Taiwan, the United States, and Japan) or rank highly in only one or none (Israel, Sweden, Finland, Germany, and Switzerland).

There are also important nuances to the design of each of the Five Pillars. For example, R&D spending can be allocated to either basic research, applied research, or development. Education spending can be focused on identifying and equipping the best and the brightest, or it can work to elevate the average student or even the lowest-performing student. Intellectual property rights are rife with important legal differences across countries, including qualifications for filing, time duration of patent rights, and types of inventions patentable. These details may matter for the effectiveness of these institutions in fostering S&T.

There are clearly numerous, significant causal relationships at work between the Five Pillars and a nation's innovation rate, but in the end, there are two important points to take from all the data and case studies. The first is that each of the Five Pillars does matter for improving national innovation rates. Market failures can slow innovation; therefore, there *is* a role for public policy to correct them, and thereby boost S&T performance. However, the second point is that the Five Pillars do *not* explain as much innovation as we might expect. Regardless of which major policy we investigated previously, and even if all five were packaged together, we found that there remained a significant amount of

Table 4.7 **Relative Ranks in the Five Pillars Policy Areas***

	R&D Spending	*IPR Protection*	*Top Universities*	*Higher Ed Years*	*Trade Openness*
Canada	—	Top	Top	Top	—
US	—	Top	Top	Top	Bottom
Japan	Top	Top	Top	—	Bottom
Italy	—	Top	Top	—	—
France	—	Top	Top	—	—
Belgium	—	Top	—	—	Top
Ireland	—	Top	—	—	Top
Israel	Top	—	—	—	—
Sweden	Top	—	—	—	—
Finland	Top	—	—	—	—
Netherlands	—	Top	—	—	—
Denmark	—	Top	—	—	—
Germany	—	—	Top	—	—
UK	—	—	Top	—	—
New Zlnd	—	—	—	Top	—
Singapore	—	—	—	Bottom	Top
Luxmbrg	—	—	Bottom	—	Top
Australia	—	—	—	—	Bottom
South Africa	—	—	—	Bottom	—
Portugal	—	—	—	Bottom	—
Slovenia	—	—	Bottom	—	—
Czech.	—	Bottom	—	—	—
Poland	Bottom	—	—	—	—
Greece	Bottom	—	—	—	—
China	—	Bottom	—	Bottom	—
Taiwan	—	Bottom	Bottom	—	—
Mexico	Bottom	—	—	Bottom	—
Romania	Bottom	—	Bottom	—	—
Argentina	Bottom	—	—	—	Bottom
Slovakia	Bottom	Bottom	Bottom	—	Top
Turkey	Bottom	—	Bottom	Bottom	Bottom

*Not shown are Austria, Brazil, Hong Kong, Hungary, India, Korea, Malaysia, Norway, Russia, Spain, and Switzerland which fail to place in either the top or bottom of any policy category.

unexplained innovation. Also, there are simply too many important cases of innovative nations *not* scoring highly across the Five Pillars yet still producing cutting-edge S&T and S&T-based industries. The experience of several countries reveals that simply increasing R&D spending, protecting IPRs, or setting up schools and universities does not result in innovation at the scientific or technological frontier. So what's going on? A likely answer is that there is more to "good" government action than just the classic Five Pillars. Perhaps we just have not identified the right institutions and policies, or the right combination of them. The next chapter therefore investigates even broader, "macro" institutions and policies that likely determine national innovation rates.

5

"Why Nations Fail"

Capitalism, Democracy, and Decentralization

This book's quest, to discover why some countries are better than others at science and technology (S&T), has taken an interesting turn. Thus far, we have learned from the data that puzzling differences in national innovation rates persist despite globalization. Theory and history suggest that these puzzles should be explained by differences in government institutions and policies. Specifically, markets appear to be excellent drivers of innovation, but markets for S&T also suffer from notorious failures. Therefore, differences in government actions to solve these market failures should explain differences in national innovation rates. This led us to the "Five Pillars" of innovation explored in the previous chapter: intellectual property rights, research subsidies, education, research universities, and trade policy. These are the five most trusted, most widely used institutions and policies for solving the market failures that slow S&T progress. But strangely, the Five Pillars leave a significant amount of unexplained success and failure in S&T. This chapter asks: what accounts for the remaining variation?

Most innovation researchers argue that the answer still lies in institutions and policies. After all, nations have dozens of domestic institutions and policies at all levels of government that can affect national S&T performance. And what about macro institutions like capitalism, democracy, and political decentralization? Certainly they play key roles in allowing innovation to flourish. Selecting only five policies to investigate, as the previous chapter did, seems quite narrow. Clearly we are not looking at enough institutions and policies, or the right combination of them. Wouldn't we gain even more explanatory power if we add more policies and institutions to our list?

Investigating the effects of myriad different national institutions and policies has become the passion of many innovation scholars, including myself, over the past three decades. Our belief is that there exists a complicated "special sauce" of institutions and policies that is the key to explaining why some countries are better at S&T. Our goal is to discover that recipe. To this end, we have examined a multitude of national institutions and policies in countries around the globe. This chapter surveys what we have found. It is the most "wonky" of this book's chapters, but it is also the most important because it dismantles the conventional wisdom that a particular set of institutions or policies causes S&T progress.

Two useful concepts appear in this chapter: *endogenous* and *exogenous*.[1] An *exogenous* factor is something *outside* a system that affects its performance. To take a non-S&T example, my body weight is largely a result of my genes, age, diet, and exercise. I cannot change the first two variables. My genes and age are both given to me by nature; therefore, they would be termed *exogenous* variables. *Exogenous* variables may change, but not because of anything within the model. In fact, it is often the case that one cannot model *exogenous* change but must accept it as given, determined by as yet unexplained or overly complex forces. In contrast, an *endogenous* factor refers to something *within* a system that affects its performance. My body weight is also affected by my diet and exercise. I can change these two variables. Therefore, if I were to devise a scientific theory or economic model of the differences between people's body weights, then diet and exercise would be called *endogenous* variables because they would be "inside" that model, perhaps affected by psychology, wealth, culture, and so on. Also, *endogenous* variables can be affected by other variables within the model (e.g., when some people exogenously grow fatter or older, they begin to diet and exercise more). These two concepts matter for this chapter because scholars who study institutions and policies get into intense arguments about which are exogenous or endogenous; which are fixed and which can be affected by other forces; and, most important, which are variables that societies can do something about.

National Innovation Systems

That multiple national policies and institutions work in concert to foster innovation is the idea behind the National Innovation Systems (NIS) approach to explaining national S&T performance. NIS was perhaps the first systematic cross-national approach to studying innovation rates.[2] It arose in the mid-1980s in response to empirical puzzles posed by radical and unexpected changes in national innovation rates during the preceding decade. At the time, economists were shocked by the apparent decline of established technological leaders such as the United States and Great Britain, Japan's rapid rise to technological power, and then the sudden appearance of Taiwan, South Korea, and other newly industrialized countries at or near the technological frontier. None of these phenomena were easily explained by existing theories of innovation in economics. Moreover, the flurry of anecdote-driven research that did attempt to explain these anomalies created instead a confusing array of conflicting theories and policy prescriptions. In response, political economists in the United States and Europe created NIS.[3] The first NIS scholars wanted to address what they described as the feebleness of general innovation theory and the "hyped and rather haphazard" innovation research and policy of the time.[4] Ironically, NIS went on to create the opposite situation: a library full of excellent empirical case studies of domestic institutions and policies, but no general theory of national innovation rates. Regardless, since its inception, NIS has become one of the dominant paradigms within innovation research.[5]

The NIS approach to explaining national innovation rates starts with the recognition that innovation, be it performed by firms or individuals, occurs within the context of broader political and economic institutions and policies. NIS further posits that these institutions and policies together form a *system* that determines a country's rate and direction of *innovation*. Because these institutions and policies differ from nation to nation, and in fact define *nations* to some extent, they therefore constitute "national innovation systems." Of course, NIS scholars recognized that this view of technological change was not entirely new, but was reminiscent of similar ideas put forward by Alexander Hamilton (1791) and Friedrich List (1841), each of whom had posited his own influential vision of how national economic systems worked.[6]

What *was* new in the NIS research program was the empirical depth and thoroughness with which its proponents approached the subject. Generally using a case study approach, NIS scholars focused their research on identifying and probing the roles of dozens of specific national institutions and policies that affect innovation. Pioneered by economists Christopher Freeman, Bengt-Ake Lundvall, Richard Nelson, and Charles Edquist,[7] NIS scholars examined the interactions and effects on innovation of different educational institutions, science policies, trade regimes, legal frameworks, financial institutions, antitrust laws, and so forth. They also took care to observe these domestic institutions and policies across a wide spectrum of nations, many of which had been little studied in previous research on innovation. For instance, in one seminal study, NIS scholars analyzed large, wealthy, frontier innovators (Japan, the United States, and Germany); small, wealthy, but innovative states (Denmark, Canada, and Sweden); and lesser developed countries, both innovative (Israel and Taiwan) and seemingly stalled (Argentina and Brazil). Since then, other researchers have gone on to apply the NIS methodology to a variety of disparate countries from Finland to China, Slovakia to Algeria, Hungary to India.[8]

However, while the NIS research program has made major empirical contributions to the debate over national innovation rates, a problem with generalizability soon emerged. Taken as a whole, the separate NIS case studies suggest dozens of policies and institutions (Table 5.1), each of which may play a role in technological innovation depending on its configuration vis-à-vis

Table 5.1 **Abbreviated List of NIS Institutions and Policies**

Financial Systems	Antitrust Policy	Govt. Procurement Programs	Science Policy
Defense Policy	Industrial Relations	Environmental Regulations	Labor Policy
Space Policy	Food Policy	Govt. Budget Procedures	Energy Policy
Exchange Rate Regimes	Legal Systems	Health Policy	Lands Management
Zoning Laws	Telecoms Policy	Transportation Policy	Tech Transfer Policy
Agricultural Subsidies	Tax Policy	Safety Regulations	Immigration Policy

each other. Thus, NIS has brought to light the complexity of the innovation process and the diversity of factors involved in it but has failed to produce any general theory.

For example, in the case of the United States, NIS scholars concluded that the key drivers of technological progress since World War II include military procurement programs, timely and strong antitrust actions, small firms, and universities.[9] Yet none of these variables figure significantly in Japan's national innovation system. Rather, Japan's innovative strength during the postwar period emanated from tight government control over trade and investment, cooperative industry-labor relations, and specific corporate management techniques, each of which is missing from the US case.[10] Studies of the United Kingdom, Germany, France, Korea, and Taiwan similarly expanded the list of variables.[11] Each country has its own unique set of institutions and policies that constitute its particular NIS.

Furthermore, since the successful operation of each NIS institution or policy often depends on its relationship with other institutions and policies, NIS scholars found themselves with a rapid proliferation of viable national innovation systems. So while the relatively strong American antitrust regime helps innovation in the United States, it does so in the context of free trade and capital mobility. Conversely, Tokyo's relatively weak antitrust enforcement seems to aid Japanese innovation when configured with Japan's system of industrial policy and captive finance. Hence, in addition to a large number of variables, the NIS approach produces an exponentially greater number of possible combinations of these variables, each of which may promote or hinder innovation. This lack of parsimony poses a problem for both theorizing and testing, especially in cases where the *same* institution or policy is attributed with *different* effects on innovation rates in different countries.[12]

Thus, after almost thirty years of research, NIS scholars have yet to produce any general hypotheses to explain differences in national innovation rates. That is, while they have achieved their empirical goal of increasing the set of data points and potential relationships between them, NIS scholars have yet to fit a theory to them.

In fact, it is now rare for anyone to identify a policy or institution that NIS scholars have not already studied. Certainly, it is still common to hear arguments that policy or institution "X" is essential for nations to become more innovative. Sometimes these claimants are experts in a specific region, country, industry, or time period, and institution "X" may full well seem to explain innovation rates in their particular area of study. But often these claimants are unaware of the NIS literature, which has usually studied their particular "X" in multiple industries, countries, and time periods and failed to find consistent outcomes.

It is possible that additional NIS research may yet identify a particular institution, policy, or combination thereof that *does* provide a generalizable explanation of national innovation rates. But to date, NIS research has been of such high quality and thoroughness that many feel that new approaches should be taken, and new variables considered. Among those who responded to this conundrum were "Varieties of Capitalism" theorists who generated an exciting new line of innovation research, which is the subject of the next section.

Varieties of Capitalism

One prominent school of thought that attempts to explain the failure of NIS is "Varieties of Capitalism" (VoC) theory.[13] VoC theory argues that the behavior of a country's NIS institutions, and even of the Five Pillars discussed in the last chapter, are endogenous to markets.[14] So too are a nation's innovators. In other words, perhaps the S&T goals of NIS institutions and policies, and their efficiency in achieving these goals, are determined by even larger political and economic institutions. In particular, VoC posits that the more a nation allows markets to structure its domestic economic relationships, the more radically innovative its economic actors will be. Conversely, the more a nation chooses to coordinate economic relationships via nonmarket mechanisms, the more slowly and incrementally innovative its economic actors will be. This is admittedly a highly condensed version of a nuanced and sophisticated theory, but it is accurate for our purposes.

This may sound exactly like the market versus state debate that led us to the Five Pillars in the first place, but it is not. The Five Pillars are micro-economic solutions. In designing them, the main concerns are to identify individual market failures and then to solve them. One therefore winds up with policies or institutions that are tightly focused on maximizing efficiency and innovation in particular markets (e.g., education, research, intellectual property). In contrast, VoC takes a macro-economic approach. It is more interested in how to design and maintain an entire market system within the context of various economic actors (firms, unions, the state) who must share the costs, risks, and rewards of that system. The question for these actors is how to divvy up the burden sharing and how much to let the market itself determine it. Since countries have come up with different answers to these questions, we can now find a wide variety of "capitalisms" around the world. VoC theorists use this variation to explain a host of comparative and international political-economic behaviors.

VoC theory is therefore broad and foundational; it touches upon multiple aspects of political and economic life, of which innovation is but one part. Interestingly, VoC theory does not divide the world into "state-owned versus privatized" or "free trade versus protectionist" systems as is traditionally done. Rather, VoC theory places business firms at the focal points of trade and production within a capitalist economy. It therefore takes the firm, not the state or the individual, as the primary unit of analysis. Certainly the firm is not a lone or independent actor in VoC's analysis. Successful operation of the firm depends on its relationships with labor, investors, government, and other firms. It is these crucial relationships that, in turn, explain patterns of economic activity and policymaking. Therefore, the central claims of VoC theory focus on how a nation's macro-institutional environment determines the conduct of these crucial relationships, and thus how economic actors organize to solve the classic coordination problems that afflict such relations.

At its most basic level, VoC is a theory of capitalism by gradation: some countries permit free markets more than others to coordinate economic actors. For example, at one end of the VoC spectrum lie the "Liberal Market Economies" (LMEs), such as Australia, Canada, Great Britain, Ireland, New Zealand, and the United States. In LMEs, business firms tend to coordinate their relations and activities in the manner best described by Nobel Prize–winning economist Oliver Williamson: internally through corporate hierarchies and externally through atomistic competitive market arrangements.[15] Nonmarket collaborations are often barred by law.[16] Free markets reign!

At the other end of the spectrum sit the "Coordinated Market Economies" (CMEs), such as Austria, Belgium, Denmark, Finland, Germany, Japan, the Netherlands, Norway, Sweden, and Switzerland. In CMEs, firms tend to coordinate more like families or friends: via nonmarket relationships, not just with other firms, but often with labor groups and government as well. In CMEs, economic actors depend more on long-term, sometimes informal relationships. Contracts are often incomplete, exchanges of information occur within the context of enduring alliances, and there is a high degree of collaboration instead of fierce competition or outright confrontation.

In between these two ideal types, and of less importance to VoC scholars, sit a handful of hybrids denoted as "Mediterranean Market Economies" (MMEs) which have mixed CME and LME characteristics. These countries include France, Greece, Italy, Portugal, Spain, and Turkey. Countries such as Luxembourg and Iceland are eliminated from the VoC typology due to their small size, while others, such as Mexico, are disqualified because they are developing nations.[17]

The distinctions between LMEs and CMEs have important implications for explaining and predicting national differences in innovation. According to VoC theory, technological innovation comes in two types, radical and incremental, each of which forms the basis for a different mode of production. Radical innovation is that which brings about the development of entirely new goods and services. It thus requires major shifts in product lines or production processes.[18] Radical innovation is therefore vital to production in high-technology sectors that require rapid and significant product changes (e.g., biotechnology, semiconductors, and software) or in the manufacture of complex systems-based products (e.g., telecommunications, defense, and airlines). Incremental innovation, on the other hand, is typified by regular small-scale improvements to existing product lines and production processes.[19] Unlike production based on radical innovation, where speed and flexibility are crucial, production based on incremental innovation prioritizes the maintenance of high quality in established goods. Incremental innovation involves constant improvements in manufacturing processes to bring down costs and prices, but only occasional minor improvements in the product line. Incremental innovation is therefore essential for competitiveness in capital goods production (e.g., machine tools, factory equipment, consumer durables, and engines).

VoC theory predicts that LMEs and CMEs will tend to exert greater effort toward, and be successful in, different types of technological innovation. This does not mean that a given political-economic structure will result in only one kind of innovation, but that different institutions will create different types of comparative advantage for innovators. For example, incremental innovation requires a workforce that is skilled enough to come up with it, is secure enough to risk suggesting it, and has enough autonomy to see innovation as a part of its job. This in turn requires that firms provide workers with secure environments, autonomy in the workplace, opportunities to influence firm decisions, education and training beyond just task-specific skills (preferably industry-specific technical skills), and close interfirm collaboration that encourages clients and suppliers to suggest innovations as well. These are exactly the kinds of apparatuses provided by CME institutions.

In fact, CMEs are *defined* by the very institutions that provide a comparative advantage for incremental innovation. These institutions include highly coordinated industrial relations systems; corporate structures characterized by works councils and consensus-style decision making; a dense network of intercorporate linkages (such as interlocking corporate directorates and cross-shareholding); systems of corporate governance that insulate against hostile takeovers and reduce sensitivity to current profits; and appropriate laws for relationship-based, incomplete contracting between firms. VoC scholars argue that this combination of institutions results in long employment tenures, corporate strategies based on product differentiation rather than intense product competition, and formal training systems for employees that focus on high skills and a mix of company-specific and industry-specific skills—in other words, the very factors that combine to foster incremental innovation.

On the other hand, VoC scholars argue that these same CME institutions that provide comparative advantages for incremental innovation also serve as obstacles to radical innovation. For instance, worker representation in corporate leadership combines with consensus-style decision making to make radical change and reorganization difficult. Also, long employment tenures make acquisition of new skills and rebalancing one's labor mix difficult. Further, dense intercorporate networks make the diffusion of disruptive innovations slow and arduous, and technological acquisition by mergers and acquisitions or takeovers hard. All of these act against, or reduce the potential rewards of, radical innovation.

In LMEs, the situation is reversed. LMEs are defined by institutions that provide a comparative advantage for radical innovation while creating obstacles to incremental innovation. LMEs have flexible labor markets with few restrictions on layoffs, which means that companies can drastically change their product lines and still acquire the proper labor mix. LMEs also support extensive equity markets with dispersed shareholders providing innovators of all sizes with relatively unfettered access to capital. Also, interfirm relations in LMEs allow for a variety of aggressive asset exchanges with few restrictions on mergers and acquisitions, buyouts, personnel poaching, licensing, and so forth, which permits firms to easily acquire scientific expertise and new technology. Concentration of power at the top of LME-based firms augments these institutions, allowing management to quickly force major change on complex organizations. All of these factors combine to create large incentives for, and an environment accommodative to, radical innovation. Conversely, LMEs' capacity for incremental innovation is limited due to financial arrangements that emphasize current profitability, corporate structures that concentrate unilateral control at the top and eliminate workforce security, and antitrust and contract laws that discourage interfirm collaboration in incremental innovation. Meanwhile, fluid labor markets and short job tenures motivate workers to pursue selfish career goals and to acquire mobile general skills rather than firm-specific or industry-specific skills. Hence, in VoC's analysis, neither workers nor firms in LMEs tend to have the incentives or the resources for sustained incremental innovation.

Testing the Varieties of Capitalism Claims

The VoC causal logic outlined previously is theoretically appealing and dovetails with some widely held stereotypes about national differences in innovation. But is there any evidence for it? At first, early studies seemed to support the VoC claims. An analysis of European Patent Office patent data in thirty industries during two separate two-year periods, 1983–1984 and 1993–1994, found that the United States (an archetypal LME) specialized its patenting in industries typified by radical innovation, while Germany (an archetypal CME) specialized its patenting in industries typified by incremental innovation.[20]

Of course, only four years of patent data from only two countries is a thin basis for proving VoC's pervasive claims. Indeed, these findings break down if the dataset is expanded. For example, a subsequent study looked at US and German patenting over seventeen years, 1978–1995, and found a handful of industries that failed to meet VoC predictions. Even more discrepancies arise when the country list is expanded to compare patent specialization across all LME countries versus all CME countries, or over longer periods of time, or when US Patent Office data is used. But the most striking disparity occurs when the United States is excluded from the set of LME countries; under these conditions, VoC theory has only marginally more predictive power than random chance.[21]

Thus, after analyzing two different patent datasets and competing industry classification methods, it appears that the success of VoC theory strongly depends on the inclusion of the United States as an LME.

Figure 5.1 best captures and summarizes the overall picture. The vertical measure is citations-weighted patents per capita for the 1970–2012 period. It serves as a proxy for the entire innovative output for each country over four decades, though smaller time periods produce similar results. For comparison's sake, the plots are split horizontally into three groups (LMEs, CMEs, and other countries). As a group, the LMEs are on average more radically innovative than the CMEs. But this finding depends entirely on the inclusion of the United States as an LME. If the United States is left out of the analysis, as some recent research suggests it should be,[22] then the remaining LMEs appear to be *less* radically innovative than the CMEs. Perhaps the most honest interpretation of Figure 5.1 is

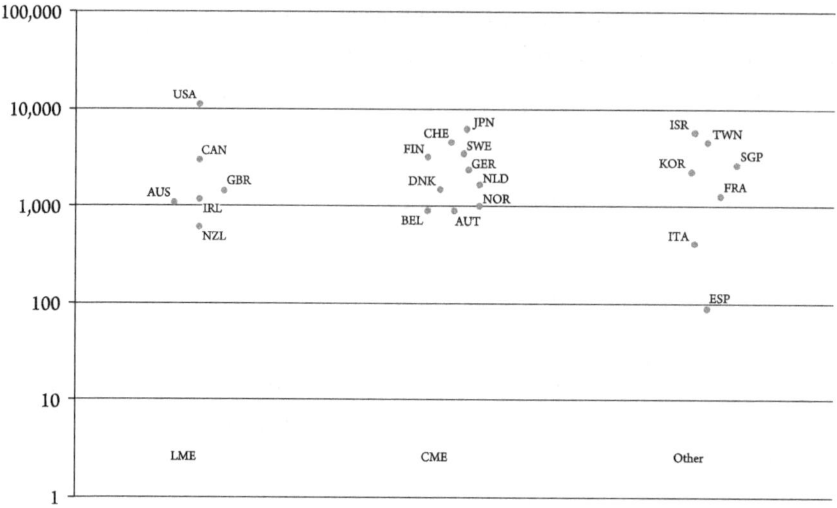

Figure 5.1 Total forward citations, per capita (1970–2012), per 100,000 people (mean population 1970–2012). Sources: World Bank; NBER Patent Dataset (2001, 2006); USPTO.

that there exist no strong general differences in innovation rates between the different VoC country types.[23] Interestingly, Australia, New Zealand, Ireland, and even Great Britain appear to deserve a place among the main body of CMEs, while Japan and Switzerland seem to be among the most radical innovators. While we are not immediately concerned with hybrid MMEs, the three that appear (France, Italy, and Spain) have significant differences between them and do not appear to form a cohesive group. Also, the high placement of Israel (arguably a pre-1970s CME, increasingly MME thereafter) and Taiwan (arguably an MME), not mentioned in VoC theory, further suggests that there may be more to radical innovation than the variables captured by VoC. Finally, the addition of controls for industry category or subcategory (not shown) does not change these results, except for some minor shuffling. Nor is the effect of CMEs or LMEs on the innovation rate conditional on the industry selected.[24]

Science, technology, engineering, and mathematics (STEM) research articles are another useful measure of innovation that reinforces the cross-national findings discussed earlier. VoC theory does not make specific predictions regarding research publication patterns, and indeed its authors may never have intended it to. Nonetheless, we might infer from VoC theory the following hypothesis: that scholarly publications by LME researchers should show specialization in fields associated with revolutionary scientific advances, while CMEs should show specialization in fields associated with incremental scientific advances. Although it is not quite clear what a "radically" versus "incrementally" innovative field might be, one could simply map the typology used by VoC scholars for industrial sectors over to academic sectors. For example, CMEs should excel in publishing in the engineering and technology journals, LMEs in biology, medicine, and physics. A second hypothesis might surmise that researchers in the CMEs should excel in professional journals and applied sciences publications where incremental research is more prominent, while LME researchers should publish heavily in the more academic or theoretical sciences journals where the research tends toward the revolutionary. A third, and less controversial, hypothesis would be that LME publications should simply have higher forward citation averages than CME publications.

Yet, none of the patterns hypothesized can be found in the cross-national publications data. Consider the simple STEM journal publication data compiled in Table 5.2. Compare the world publication rates by field with those of the LMEs and CMEs. As a group, the LMEs tend to consistently specialize in clinical medicine, biology, earth-space, psychology, social science, health, and professional journals; CMEs tend to consistently specialize in clinical medicine, chemistry, and physics. Over time the CMEs have increased their specialization in biomedical research, physics, and earth-space but weakened in clinical medicine, chemistry, and engineering and technology; the LMEs have increased their specialization in biomedical, physics, and earth-space. Using forward citation indices (Table 5.3), we find the LMEs beating CMEs in all fields. When we exclude the United States from the set of LMEs, the LMEs appear to have higher citations than the CMEs in all fields except earth-space, engineering, and physics. Relatively speaking, LMEs are strongest in chemistry, physics, biomedical research, and math. CMEs are strongest in chemistry, engineering, physics, and biology. None of these findings is what we might expect from VoC theory.

Finally, despite problems in measuring pre-1960s innovation and diffusion, history provides researchers with some natural experiments that deserve further investigation. For example, Japan, during its first brush with capitalism (1910s–1930s), was distinctively "LME-ish" but was arguably less innovative than postwar CME Japan. During this earlier period, Japan had a strong and confrontational labor movement upon which business did not hesitate to inflict frequent and severe dislocations for the sake of technological advance. Moreover, the dependence of prewar Japan on external trade and finance exposed even the powerful *zaibatsu* to the vicissitudes of international markets and created many LME-type incentives for economic actors. Yet the Japanese appear to have been consistent incremental innovators during the first third of the twentieth century. On the other hand, the Germans of this time period rivaled the United States in technological advance, producing wave after wave of radical innovation in multiple fields, including the gas-powered automobile, the Zeppelin, the Haber-Bosch process, blood-typing, aspirin, and organic chemicals to name but a few. Yet the Germans had many of the same CME-type institutions and incentives as

Table 5.2 **Specialization in Scholarly Publications (Publications per Field as a Percentage of Total)**

1986	*Clincl Med*	*Bio-Med*	*Bio*	*Chem*	*Phys*	*Earth-Space*	*Eng-Tech*	*Math*	*Psych*	*Soc Sci*	*Health*	*Prof*	*Total*
World	29.8	15.0	7.9	12.5	12.2	4.4	6.7	1.8	2.7	3.7	0.9	2.7	*100%*
LME	31.6	14.6	9.1	7.7	9.1	4.9	6.4	1.8	3.9	5.1	1.4	4.4	*100%*
CME	34.2	15.1	6.8	14.2	12.9	3.0	8.0	1.7	1.4	1.8	0.3	0.6	*100%*
LME (ex-US)	32.7	13.8	12.2	8.6	7.9	5.3	6.3	1.7	3.1	4.8	1.0	2.6	*100%*
1999	*Clincl Med*	*Bio-Med*	*Bio*	*Chem*	*Phys*	*Earth Space*	*Eng-Tech*	*Math*	*Psych*	*Soc Sci*	*Health*	*Prof.*	*Total*
World	29.0	15.0	7.0	12.5	15.0	5.4	6.8	2.0	2.0	2.7	0.9	1.8	*100%*
LME	32.1	16.0	7.3	8.0	10.0	6.2	5.9	1.8	3.3	4.2	1.5	3.3	*100%*
CME	32.7	15.0	6.5	13.5	17.0	4.0	6.2	1.5	1.2	1.3	0.4	0.5	*100%*
LME (ex-US)	32.0	14.4	10.0	8.5	9.4	6.4	6.1	1.7	3.0	4.4	1.6	2.2	*100%*

Source: National Science Board 2002, Appendix Tables 5-43, 5-52.

Table 5.3 **Relative Prominence of Scientific Literature by Country/Economy and Field (1999)**

	All Fields	*Bio*	*Bio-Med*	*Chem*	*Clincl Med*	*Earth-Space*	*Eng-Tech*	*Math*	*Phys*	*Soc Sci*	*Psych*	*Health*	*Prof*
United States	1.35	1.16	1.40	1.50	1.27	1.31	1.20	1.24	1.47	1.28	1.12	1.14	1.16
United Kingdom	1.04	1.25	0.98	1.14	1.00	1.03	0.99	1.23	1.07	1.07	1.16	0.90	0.64
Canada	0.99	1.05	0.91	1.30	1.11	0.89	0.89	0.92	0.99	0.84	1.07	0.87	0.89
Australia	0.87	1.04	0.78	1.05	0.91	0.88	1.05	1.02	0.90	0.65	0.80	0.88	0.84
Ireland	0.82	0.99	0.57	0.98	0.87	0.67	0.85	1.02	0.93	0.56	0.76	0.67	0.47
New Zealand	0.76	0.89	0.57	1.00	0.86	0.71	0.99	0.65	1.07	0.78	1.06	0.97	0.73
LME	**1.235**	**1.136**	**1.264**	**1.381**	**1.188**	**1.190**	**1.123**	**1.193**	**1.340**	**1.167**	**1.104**	**1.055**	**1.069**
LME (ex-US)	**0.986**	**1.104**	**0.918**	**1.160**	**1.007**	**0.944**	**0.966**	**1.082**	**1.027**	**0.932**	**1.066**	**0.889**	**0.729**
Switzerland	1.37	1.41	1.40	1.45	1.08	1.16	1.77	1.07	1.36	0.66	0.59	0.48	0.86
Netherlands	1.12	1.19	0.89	1.41	1.08	1.14	1.24	0.94	1.26	0.87	1.03	1.13	0.86
Sweden	1.07	1.30	0.87	1.33	0.99	0.78	1.11	1.02	1.10	0.86	0.78	0.93	0.53
Denmark	1.04	1.21	0.77	1.20	0.94	0.85	1.34	1.36	1.35	0.55	0.63	0.70	1.17
Finland	1.02	1.17	0.86	0.94	1.03	0.63	0.95	0.92	1.01	0.72	0.89	1.38	0.73
Germany	1.01	1.08	1.00	1.07	0.83	1.11	1.06	1.08	1.27	0.42	0.72	0.48	0.31
Belgium	0.95	1.14	0.80	1.06	0.92	0.75	1.01	1.04	0.96	0.72	0.86	0.34	0.81

(continued)

Table 5.3 **Continued**

	All Fields	*Bio*	*Bio-Med*	*Chem*	*Clincl Med*	*Earth-Space*	*Eng-Tech*	*Math*	*Phys*	*Soc Sci*	*Psych*	*Health*	*Prof*
Austria	0.91	1.04	0.83	0.96	0.81	0.64	1.01	0.64	1.15	0.45	0.65	0.83	0.51
Japan	0.83	0.79	0.78	0.99	0.76	0.83	1.00	0.72	0.87	0.41	0.43	0.53	0.62
Norway	0.82	1.18	0.67	0.80	0.82	0.86	1.04	1.23	0.84	0.76	0.82	0.71	0.58
CME	**0.968**	**1.041**	**0.899**	**1.078**	**0.871**	**0.968**	**1.070**	**0.968**	**1.069**	**0.613**	**0.762**	**0.854**	**0.612**

Each number represents the country's share of cited literature adjusted for its share of published literature. For example, a score of 1.00 would indicate that the country's share of cited literature is equal to the country's world share of scientific literature. A score greater (less) than 1.00 would indicate that the country is cited relatively more (less) than is indicated by the country's share of scientific literature.

Example: $I_{\text{US biology}} = (\#\,US_{\text{biology, cited}} / \#\,World_{\text{biology, cited}}) / (\#\,US_{\text{biology, published}} / \#\,World_{\text{biology, published}})$.

Source: National Science Board (2002), Appendix Tables 5-43, 5-52

we find there today, including a national welfare system, national health care, and large business cartels negotiating with each other, and sometimes with workers, in a fairly CME-like manner.

Of course, capitalism is more than just VoC theory, and it is important to put to rest the widely believed assumption that free market capitalism is *the* explanation for innovative economies. Therefore, Figure 5.2 presents completely different data on the relationship between market freedoms and national innovation rates for fifty countries. On the horizontal scale, the measure of market freedom is the Heritage Foundation's Economic Freedom Index. This measure combines ten dimensions of market freedom, from property rights to regulatory efficiency, to create an overall national average.[25] On the vertical scale, innovation is measured by citations-weighted patents per capita, relative to the United States, though other measures produce similar results. The time period is brief, 1995–2010, because the Economic Freedom Index data only goes back to 1995. Included in Figure 5.2 are countries with the largest changes in economic freedoms, as well as the "most innovative" and "rapid innovators" already identified during this time period. Naturally we should expect countries with more economic freedom to perform better at technological innovation. However, the data

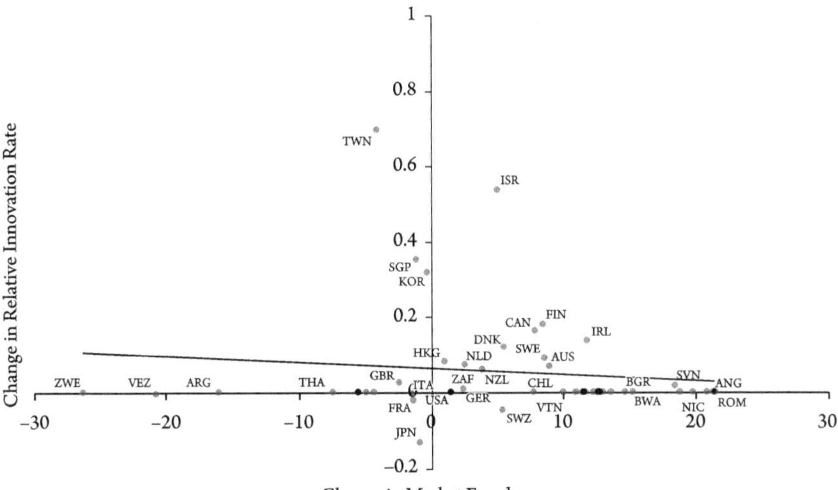

Figure 5.2 Innovation versus free markets in 50 countries (1995–2010). Countries shown: Albania, Angola, Argentina, Australia, Bahrain, Bangladesh, Botswana, Bulgaria, Canada, Chile, Croatia, Denmark, Ecuador, Egypt, Finland, France, Germany, Guinea, Haiti, Hong Kong, Ireland, Israel, Italy, Japan, South Korea, Madagascar, Malta, Moldova, Mongolia, Mozambique, Netherlands, New Zealand, Nicaragua, Peru, Poland, Romania, Singapore, Slovenia, South Africa, Sweden, Switzerland, Taiwan, Thailand, Tunisia, Ukraine, United Kingdom, United States, Venezuela, Vietnam, Zimbabwe. Sources: Index of Economic Freedom (Heritage Foundation), World Bank, NBER Patents Database.

show that countries with the greatest increases in market freedoms enjoyed few improvements in innovation rates (e.g., Romania, Angola, Moldova, Albania, Nicaragua, Slovenia, Botswana, Bulgaria, Peru, and Croatia). One could counterargue that free markets need more time to work their magic; however, some countries have enjoyed free markets for decades, yet still rank only as midlevel innovators or do not innovate much at all (e.g., Australia, New Zealand, the United Kingdom, and Chile). Also, some of the world's most rapid innovators (Taiwan, Singapore, and South Korea) simultaneously saw *decreases* in market freedoms according to Heritage, or *never* ranked highly as "free market." Yet these countries still innovated. Also, at least two of the countries that suffered major declines in market freedoms (Argentina and Thailand) paradoxically enjoyed marginal *increases* in national innovation rates, though too small to be seen on the scale shown in Figure 5.2. Other measures of free markets and innovation corroborate these results.

In sum, free market capitalism does not appear to explain national innovation rates. We find this fact repeated regardless of whether patent or publication data is used, the type of industry classification system, or whether simple counts or forward citations are used. Subsequent studies have confirmed this finding using broader measures of innovation and industry studies,[26] cluster analysis and artificial neural networks,[27] and within-country case studies.[28] We will explore some of these country case studies more deeply in later chapters.

So what is wrong with the free market hypothesis? One obvious problem with free market theory is its heavy focus on corporations. While business firms may be the key actors in capitalist economies, and the primary producers of goods and services, it is difficult to ignore the role of the state in innovation as strongly as free market theorists do. Throughout the world, much useful innovation is the result of state-sponsored and state-managed research and development (R&D). In many countries, an appreciable amount of innovation comes out of the public university system, or from private universities benefiting from significant state support. In still other states, innovation takes the form of incremental improvements on imported technologies, where the government has had a heavy hand in deciding which technologies get imported. Often, government also plays a key role as a market maker for, and main diffuser of, new innovations. However, free market theory tends to dismiss these causal mechanisms entirely.

None of this is meant to argue that free markets do not matter, or never matter, for national S&T performance; rather, the point is that extreme levels of market freedom are neither necessary nor sufficient for a country to become innovative. Something else is going on that determines how innovative a society is.

Democracy

Democracy may offer another institutional route to national S&T competitiveness. In fact, the latest version of the domestic institutions argument holds that democracy is the sine qua non for achieving national power and prosperity. It claims that democracy accounts for why some countries have stronger, more innovative economies than others, while the absence of democracy explains "why nations fail."[29] Democracy may therefore explain the differences in national innovation rates observed in chapter 3. As an extra bonus, the democracy argument can also account for the weak explanatory power of both the NIS and VoC approaches. It holds that both VoC's markets and NIS's long list of institutions and policies are endogenous to a nation's political institutions.

Political institutions, like democratic government, were brought into the modern economic growth debate by Douglass North, for which he won a Nobel Prize in 1993.[30] North used historical analysis to suggest that technological change is endogenous to political institutions. He implied that "good" institutions are necessary for technology-based industrialization, modernization, and economic competitiveness. Similar to the approach taken in chapter 4, the "good" institutions that North focused on were property rights, and efficient markets for trading them, because these are the institutions that motivate the investment and risk taking necessary for innovation.[31] North later recognized that the specification and enforcement of property rights and markets are political issues. Therefore, political institutions need also be efficient and therefore democratic.[32]

Why democratic institutions? To North, the most efficient political institutions are those that enact legislation and policies that grow the economy over time. Such legislation might foster the development of new S&T, the creation of new industries, the opening of new markets, improvements in workers' skills, or the discovery of new natural resources. The problem is that the costs and benefits of economic growth are never equally spread across society. So to win national support for economic growth policies, the "winners" in the economy must compensate the "losers" at a cost low enough to make it worthwhile for everyone. Of course, only well-informed participants are able to calculate all the costs and benefits that they are likely to incur under different policy regimes. This means that, to close complicated national deals over policy, again and again over time, all participants need to be well informed about the policies that affect them (taxes, subsidies, regulations, etc.). These participants must also be able to clearly communicate their policy preferences to legislators, who must then act faithfully according to these wishes. Finally, at the national level, all of these local preferences must be aggregated so that the results can be clearly discerned, national policy decisions made, and the "losers" compensated appropriately.

And this complicated decision-making process must be cheap enough such that the benefits of all the negotiating and communicating outweigh their costs.[33]

North argued that democratic political institutions are the most likely to achieve these goals. Democracies are more efficient than nondemocracies at passing pro-growth legislation because they gather and communicate the most information at the cheapest cost. They aggregate preferences and allocate compensation far more efficiently than nondemocracies. Of course, even the best modern democracy fails to achieve the perfect ideal. Voters are often ill-informed. Legislators act according to their own selfish interests. Economic "losers" are rarely well compensated. Participants are not given equal access to the political process. But even with these flaws, democracies are still better than nondemocracies at making efficient, growth-oriented policy decisions over the long run.

Recently, these arguments have been further developed by growth economists such as Daron Acemoglu, Simon Johnson, and James Robinson.[34] They identify competitive democracy as *the* fundamental institutional requirement for long-run national economic success, including S&T performance. The basic idea here (diagramed in Figure 5.3) is that a nation's economic institutions and policies affect the incentives to invest in S&T, but these economic institutions and policies are determined by a country's political process, which is itself determined by national political institutions. The causal links here are subtle, so let's break this idea down into its component parts.

The first step is that economic institutions, like those identified by NIS and VoC scholars, strongly affect the incentives for members of a society to innovate. Certainly, the best and brightest exist in any society. But in some nations they pursue excellence in S&T, while in others they enter into the military, arts, religion, politics, or organized crime. Economic institutions help to determine these choices. They do so by affecting the incentives, resources, and rewards to become educated in STEM subjects and skills, to save and invest in R&D, to become entrepreneurs and take new technologies to market, to start new industries, and so forth.

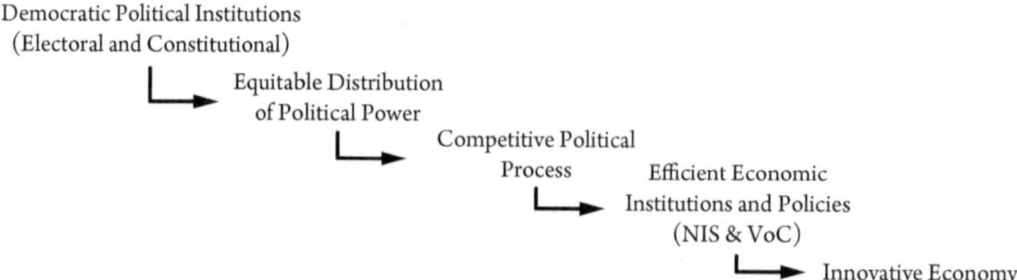

Figure 5.3 How democracy determines national S&T performance.

However, a nation's political process determines which economic institutions and policies it will have and how effective they will be. Patent systems, R&D subsidies, and university systems do not drop magically from the sky; nor are they maintained and operated by benevolent automatons. These economic institutions and policies are established and managed through a political process. In this process, different people with different interests, preferences, hopes, and fears collectively make decisions about which economic institutions will be created and how to run them.

Finally, this political decision-making process and the results it produces are both strongly affected by a nation's political institutions. A nation's political institutions determine who can rule, how these rulers are chosen, and how power is distributed across government. Political institutions therefore determine how political power is distributed across society and the constraints upon that power. Also, the constraints on and balance of political power within society naturally affect the conduct of the decision-making process.

This link between political institutions and economic institutions is vitally important for economic outcomes, such as S&T performance. For example, in a dictatorship or monarchy, political power is narrowly distributed and relatively unrestricted. In such cases, a small ruling class should tend to use its existing power to create economic institutions that will further enrich and empower itself. These institutions will keep out any economic competition and redirect national resources toward the ruling class. These are called "extractive institutions" because they expropriate resources from the rest of society to benefit a few ruling elites.

On the other hand, say political power is constrained and distributed across a broad coalition of groups in society. This is called "pluralism." In pluralism, the combination of shared interests and competition between broad and diverse groups tends to result in Northian economic institutions and policies that enrich society as a whole. These economic institutions include private property, freedom of contracts, a strong and impartial legal system, and the freedom to form new businesses. They are called "inclusive institutions" because they allow and encourage widespread participation in the economy. They therefore foster the investment, mobility, efficiency, and creative destruction necessary for innovation.[35]

Of course, extreme pluralism can be destructive. In countries like Somalia, Iraq, Afghanistan, or Pakistan, political power is so widely distributed across society (clans, tribes, and gangs) and so constrained that chaos rules. Governments there have difficulty establishing any economic institutions and policies, nor can they credibly commit to the maintenance of those institutions and policies that do exist. As a result, the incentives to innovate in extremely pluralist societies are weak.

Democracy is supposedly the most effective form of pluralism. It distributes political power broadly across society, but not so broadly that it turns into anarchy. With its elections and constitutional guarantees, democracy also constrains political power, but not so much that government is shackled into impotence.[36] Democratic countries will therefore have a broadly inclusive political process, generally resulting in inclusive economic institutions. Inventors and entrepreneurs will be given the incentives and freedoms to succeed, while inefficient or obsolete firms and industries will be free to fail.

In undemocratic societies, powerful elites have little incentive to allow new businesses or industries to erode their economic wealth. Nor will they tolerate much taxation to pay for widespread public goods. With little political competition or constraints on their power, they will use political institutions to create economic institutions that defend their wealth. This cannot happen in a democracy, where selfish rulers are constrained from asserting such power while those caught attempting it will be voted out of power.

Democratic innovation theory certainly sounds convincing; but can we find any evidence for it in the innovation data and country histories? To answer this question, Figure 5.4 presents a plot of democratization versus innovation for fifty countries for the 1970–2010 period. It includes the thirty-eight countries with

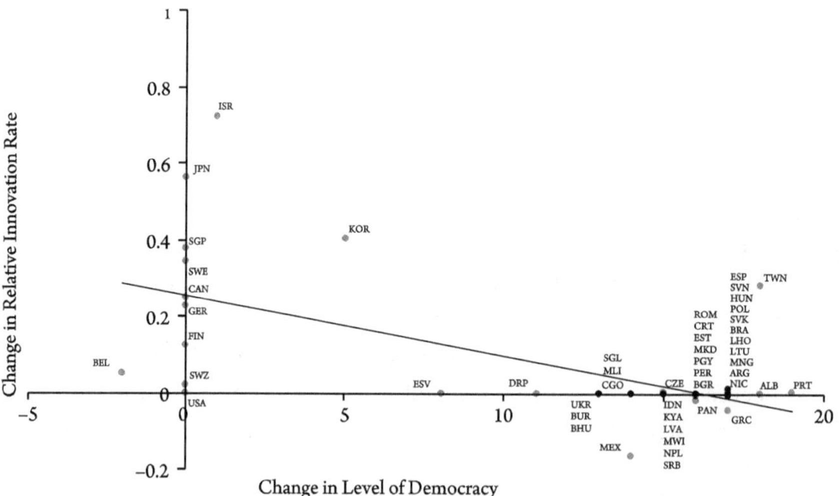

Figure 5.4 Innovation versus democracy in 50 countries (1970–2010). Countries shown: Albania, Argentina, Belgium, Bhutan, Brazil, Bulgaria, Burundi, Canada, Congo (Dem Repub), Croatia, Czech Republic, Dominican Rep, El Salvador, Estonia, Finland, Germany, Greece, Hungary, Indonesia, Israel, Japan, Kenya, South Korea, Latvia, Lesotho, Lithuania, Macedonia, Malawi, Mali, Mexico, Mongolia, Nepal, Nicaragua, Panama, Paraguay, Peru, Poland, Portugal, Romania, Senegal, Serbia, Singapore, Slovakia, Slovenia, Spain, Sweden, Switzerland, Taiwan, Ukraine, United States

the greatest changes in democracy, as well as the twelve countries previously identified as most innovative or rapid innovators during the same time period. The measure of democracy used comes from the Polity IV dataset, which rates national governments on a twenty-one-point scale ranging from −10 (hereditary monarchy) to +10 (consolidated democracy).[37] If democracy has such a strong effect on national innovation rates, then we should see a clear diagonal line of data points stretching from bottom left to upper right. Instead, if we force a regression line onto the data, we find the opposite: democracy appears to hurt S&T production, even over the course of forty years. Yet, given the mostly cross-shaped scatterplot, perhaps the most honest interpretation of the data is that democracy does *not* have a strong relationship with S&T performance.

Of course, this poor result could be due to selection bias, such as wealth or durability. That is, many of the nations that have experienced the greatest surge in democracy over the last generation have either done so very recently (e.g., since the end of the Cold War), been burdened by poverty, or both. Surely a durable democracy will result in a more innovative society over the long run, especially given an economy with sufficient levels of wealth to spend on education and research. But Table 5.4 effectively discredits that hypothesis. It reveals that many of the world's longest-running democracies (e.g., India, Costa Rica, and Jamaica) have not performed well at S&T, even if they are blessed with middle-income or wealthy economies (e.g., Spain, New Zealand, Australia, and Italy). Regression analysis that uses multiple measures of democracy, innovation, and myriad conditional variables corroborates these findings. It is not that democracy does not matter or never matters for S&T, but that democracy is neither necessary nor sufficient to explain why some countries are better at S&T than others.

Political Decentralization

Political decentralization offers another possible route to high innovation rates, one that might explain the weak explanatory power of the democracy hypothesis, as well as the apparent failure of both the NIS and VoC approaches.[38] Political decentralization is different from democracy. Certainly democracies are almost always less politically centralized than countries run by fascist, communist, or autocratic governments. Yet democracies still vary widely along the centralized versus decentralized dimension. Therefore, these differences might explain why some democracies fail to innovate much while others excel at S&T.

Political decentralization is also one of the most popular explanations for national S&T success. Decentralized governments are widely seen as agile, competitive, and well structured to adapt to innovation's gale of creative

Table 5.4 **Strong Durable Democracy—Insufficient to Turn These Twenty Countries into Top S&T Competitors**

Strong Durable Democracy Low-Income Economy but POOR INNOVATOR	*Strong Durable Democracy Middle-Income Economy but POOR INNOVATOR*	*Strong Durable Democracy Wealthy Economy but MIDLEVEL INNOVATOR*
Botswana (1966)	Argentina (1983)	Australia (1901)
Costa Rica (1919)	Brazil (1985)	Austria (1983)
El Salvador (1984)	Cyprus (1974)	Belgium (1944)
India (1950)	Greece (1975)	Italy (1948)
Mauritius (1968)	Jamaica (1963)	New Zealand (1877)
	Portugal (1976)	Norway (1945)[†]
	Spain (1978)	
	Trinidad (1962)	
	Uruguay (1985)	

First year of continuous "strong, durable" democratic period indicated in parentheses. "Strong" is defined as having Polity2 score of 8 or greater; "durable" is defined as lasting for thirty continuous years or more as of 2014. Economic wealth is defined by GDP per capita (in 1984 to allow sufficient time for innovation to occur, constant $US—2005): Low-income is defined as GDP per capita below $3000, Middle-income is defined as GDP per capita of $3000 to $15000; wealthy is defined as GDP per capita of $20,000 or greater. For comparison, US GDP per capita was $28,400; the world average was $8660.

[†]Norway is relatively weak in technology, but strong in science.

Sources: World Bank, Polity IV, NBER.

destruction. Meanwhile, centralized organizations of all sizes, from firms to nation-states, have come to be viewed as rigid and anti-innovation. They are seen as hostile to the risks, costs, and change associated with new S&T. They are criticized for clinging too long to foolhardy or outdated technological projects. These sentiments are so pervasive that they can be found both in the popular press[39] and throughout the academic literature.[40] But are these stereotypes true?

First, let's define political decentralization, which is a relative term. A nation becomes more politically decentralized as it increases the number and equality of centers of political power and policymaking. This can occur in two directions, either vertically or horizontally. Vertical decentralization simply means federalism: political power is shared between the central government and local governments (state, county, and city). Horizontal decentralization means checks and balances between the different branches of government. Here, political power is shared between an executive, a legislature, a judiciary, and in some cases even a strong bureaucracy or autonomous military.[41] Finally, when measuring the degree of decentralization, it is also important to recognize that the distribution of political power can have both formal components (e.g., those expressed in law or constitution) and informal components (e.g., the extent of party alignment across different branches of government, or the extent of preference heterogeneity within each legislative branch).

The United States is an example of a highly decentralized state. Its government formally divides power vertically between the federal, state, county, and municipal governments, and horizontally between the executive, legislative, and judicial branches. At both the federal and subnational levels, substantial checks and balances exist to reinforce the horizontal divisions between the three branches of government. By design, each horizontal branch of government invades the others' jurisdictions. This creates overlapping and competing responsibilities for many policy decisions, personnel appointments, and government functions. Vertically, while important powers are reserved only for the federal government, especially in defense and international relations, the individual US state governments still enjoy residual power over all those responsibilities not expressly given to the federal government in the US Constitution. This includes considerable power to tax, spend, regulate, and even employ limited military and quasi-military force. But it does not end there. Each of the US states further devolves significant political power to county and city governments. Also, across the entire American political system, actions by the federal and local governments are subject to judicial review by a vertically divided and politically independent court system. Rarely does a single party control more than one branch of the US government, and when it does, party members soon start fighting among themselves. Indeed, the major political parties in the United States are fairly heterogeneous, with both Republicans and Democrats displaying wide differences in policy preferences among their own party members.

At the other extreme sits Great Britain during much of the twentieth century, which possessed a highly centralized, unitary government concentrated on a single branch of government. Specifically, the lower house of Parliament (House of Commons), often controlled by a single, relatively cohesive party, held enormous power. Little formal autonomy or significant power to "check" or "balance" it was given to the subnational governments or even the other branches of government. The lower house determined the leadership of the executive branch, and hence the national bureaucracy. The lower house also dictated policy to local and regional governments. Local governments, while popularly elected, had little or no input into policy. Regional issues were handled by the central government in London and quasi-government bodies.

The various subnational governments often merely administered the policies passed down to them from above, their power existing at the whim of the prime minister or Parliament.[42] Nor was the British judiciary formally independent. All judges and important judicial officers were appointed by the prime minister,[43] and senior judicial officials were cabinet ministers, were members of Parliament, or sat in on cabinet meetings.[44] Even today, the British judiciary does not have any substantial power of judicial review. In fact, any legal ruling by a British court can be overturned by an act of Parliament. At best, the judiciary can only question the authority of individual actions and thereby force Parliament to formally clarify its policies.[45]

So how is political decentralization supposed to aid innovation? The first mechanism is simple. Decentralization increases the number of governments and agencies that fund, participate in, and demand innovative activities. This not only multiplies R&D efforts[46] but also should increase their diversity and the amount of information acquired through them.[47] More R&D and more diversity in R&D should result in more innovation overall. For example, the US federal government has its Federally Funded Research and Development Centers (FFRDCs) (e.g., Los Alamos, Jet Propulsion Laboratory, National Center for Atmospheric Research), as well as labs in the executive branch, such as in the Department of Defense, Department of Energy, and Department of Agriculture. The fifty state governments also fund their own research facilities, often within multiple state university systems. Still further, innovators can also receive grants, subsidies, and funding from government departments throughout the American political system.

Second, by increasing the number of political units in an economy, decentralization increases competition between them, thus increasing the incentives and resources for innovation. High-technology firms bring with them high tax revenues, demand for all sorts of supporting businesses, and high-salary employees to whatever cities and states in which they locate. This translates into larger budgets and lower unemployment for those states and cities that can attract them. As a result, independent state and city governments often feel compelled to compete with one another to entice both high-tech business investment and STEM workers. To that end, local governments will constantly improve the legal, tax, and regulatory environments for innovators to lure them away from neighboring states and cities.[48] This has become known as the "Delaware effect," because Delaware has been famously successful at using low taxes and easy regulations to attract business investment, resulting in an outsized number of corporate headquarters located there. In academic circles, this concept has become known as "market-preserving federalism," which holds that the political competition bred by federalism prevents government from acting in a predatory manner toward innovators.[49] This competition, created by federalism, also forces governments to commit to pro-market policies and the provision of S&T-relevant public goods such as education, infrastructure, and R&D subsidies.

Third, political decentralization should also aid innovation through both better policy design and public goods provision at the local level. The idea here is that local policymakers simply have superior information about local conditions than do distant national legislators or bureaucrats. They can therefore customize policy for the local environment.[50] Better policy should in turn mean more efficient allocation of resources toward, and proper incentives for, local innovators and investors. In addition, decentralized local public goods production is often better at reflecting popular preferences than is centralized national public goods production.

Different and independent subnational governments can also provide a menu of different policy environments. This allows different kinds of consumers of public goods to choose the environment that is right for them.[51] These might be innovators consuming scientific knowledge, investors looking for R&D opportunities, high-tech labor seeking employment, and so forth. So, for example, innovators in Massachusetts can use state government funding to pursue stem cell research, while Kansas's more rural and religious taxpayers can instead fund initiatives in agricultural sciences, and California's public universities can focus on alternative energy. In a unitary state, this type of public goods preference matching would not occur as systematically. Some see this as a form of decentralization-driven specialization that makes innovators more productive and efficient.[52] It could alternately be interpreted as precisely the kind of national environment conducive to producing "creative cities."[53]

Fourth, several scholars argue that political decentralization aids national innovation rates by making government policy less vulnerable to capture by status quo interest groups.[54] Put simply, more centralized governments are more vulnerable to interest-group capture because they have fewer decision-making points and veto players to control. Therefore, all else equal, more captureable centralized governments are more likely to make policies that slow technological innovation. And once made, such policies will be imposed across the entire nation due to the centralized nature of government in these states. Conversely, in decentralized states, even if similar policies arise, they can be reversed or overridden by subnational governments. A good example in the United States might be AIDS research during the 1980s. Powerful business and conservative groups opposed spending on AIDS research and exerted their influence on the federal executive branch to withhold support for it. However, the federal legislature and state and city governments were able to override the objections of the executive branch and provide regulatory or budgetary support for research, while the independent courts served as an additional point of entry for supporters of technological progress.[55]

This fourth aspect of political decentralization might also help to explain why NIS and VoC institutional explanations have failed to generalize across different countries and time periods. According to the decentralization argument, progress in S&T poses not just a public goods dilemma; it also suffers from an interest-group capture problem. Status quo interest groups are those whose assets (e.g., skills, capital, and land) are hurt by technological change. To obstruct threatening technological changes, these interest groups will often seek to influence or capture precisely those institutions and policies that NIS scholars use to explain innovation rates. Even the presence of free markets cannot prevent this phenomenon because markets and property rights are just institutions subject to the will of captured state apparatuses.[56] Thus, NIS and VoC explanations may fail to generalize across time and space because the institutions and policies they prescribe are endogenous to government structure. Their technological goals, and their efficiency in achieving these goals, are determined by the ability of the state to resist interest-group capture.

Testing the Political Decentralization Claims

The political decentralization thesis sounds compelling. But is there any evidence for it? To date, just like NIS and VoC theories, popular beliefs about the benefits of political decentralization are much stronger than the actual evidence, which consists mostly of anecdotal observations and stylized case studies. Instead, a rigorous and comprehensive look at the data tells a more equivocal story about the advantages of decentralization for innovators.

Ideally, to test the political decentralization thesis, one would want to perform an experiment, in which changes in government structure can be followed by observations of changes in innovative activity, with all other factors held constant. While no historical situation fits this ideal perfectly, we do have a number of cases in which governments have decentralized over time, and where we can also collect some quantitative data on innovative outputs. These are presented in Figure 5.5. This graph plots changes in decentralization versus changes in relative innovation rate in the twenty countries that underwent the largest changes in government decentralization from 1970 to 2010. In addition, I also plotted the results for the twenty countries with the largest changes in relative innovation rates. The measure of innovation used (vertical axis) is based on citations-weighted patents per capita; similar results can be obtained using STEM publications or other measures of S&T performance.[57]

As the measure of overall decentralization in this graph (horizontal), Figure 5.5 employs the POLCON Index developed by Witold Henisz at Wharton Business School, University of Pennsylvania.[58] The POLCON Index is a measure that takes into account the number of independent branches of government

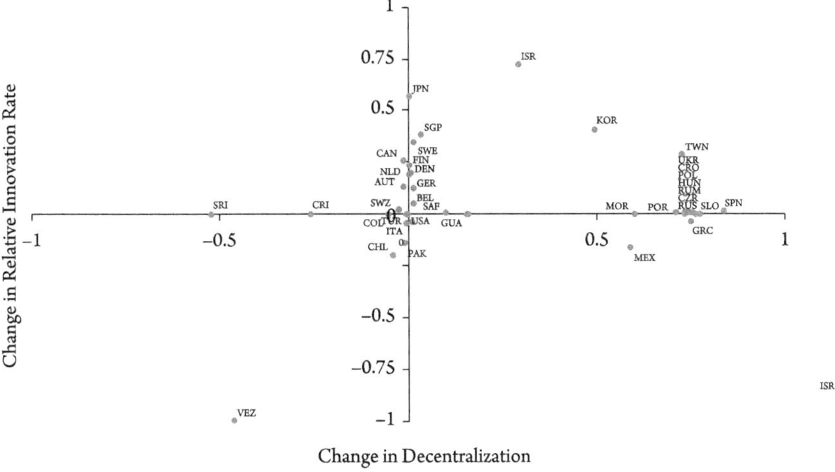

Figure 5.5 Innovation versus decentralization in 40 countries (1970–2010).
Source: United States Patent & Trademark Office, NBER (2006, 2012).

with veto power over policy, modified by the extent of party alignment across branches of government and the extent of preference heterogeneity within each legislative branch.[59] The inclusion of party alignment and legislative preferences means that POLCON allows us to control for states that may be formally decentralized but that may suffer ineffective de facto checks and balances. It also provides a finer gauge than the traditional technique of using a yes-or-no judgment of political decentralization. Moreover, the POLCON index has been shown to be statistically and positively significant in affecting both business investment decisions and technological diffusion in various countries; therefore, it is natural to ask whether it holds similar significance for national innovation rates.[60]

If decentralization is as overwhelming an influence on innovation as is assumed in the literature, then those states that have decentralized the most should enjoy significant improvements in innovation rates. That is, we should see a clear diagonal line of data points stretching upward and to the right across the graph in Figure 5.5. However, the graph reveals that only Israel, Taiwan, and South Korea appear to have experienced significant increases in both variables, while only Venezuela has both centralized drastically and suffered a drop in relative innovation rate. Otherwise, the countries that decentralized the most (Spain, Greece, Portugal, Mexico, and several former Communist bloc countries) experienced little change in innovation rates, while many countries that had major shifts in innovative performance (Japan, Singapore, Sweden, and Finland) underwent little change in government structure. Of course, "decentralization" in some of these countries was more horizontal and informal, and is perhaps better described as a move from autocracy or single-party government toward genuine multiparty democracy. But this is precisely the point: even using the broadest definition and least formal measure of political decentralization, it is difficult to find a correlation with innovation.

Using the same measure of innovation, Figure 5.6 selects out those countries with the largest changes in innovation rates between the period 1970–1975 and 2000–2005 (using different or longer time periods produces results similar to those shown here).[61] It compares each country's percentage of the world's total S&T output for each time period and shows the change in percentage points. The first thing that should strike us here is how little change in relative innovation rates there is at all. Few of the 162 countries sampled registered any significant shift in their relative rankings, and those with less than a 0.05 percentage point change have been left off of the graph altogether.

Second, even a cursory examination of Figure 5.6 reveals that the most decentralized countries (the United States, Germany, Switzerland, Austria, Australia, and Canada) have had little innovative advantage over other countries, regardless of size or wealth. Decentralized Australia and Canada both experienced large relative gains in per capita innovative output; meanwhile, the federalist United States, Germany, and Switzerland suffered significant relative declines. Among the biggest gainers are countries like Japan, Taiwan, Israel, Singapore, and South Korea, all relatively centralized states. Two major innovators (Japan and Canada) even marginally *increased* their political centralization, at least as measured by POLCON. Before we credit centralization with this achievement, we

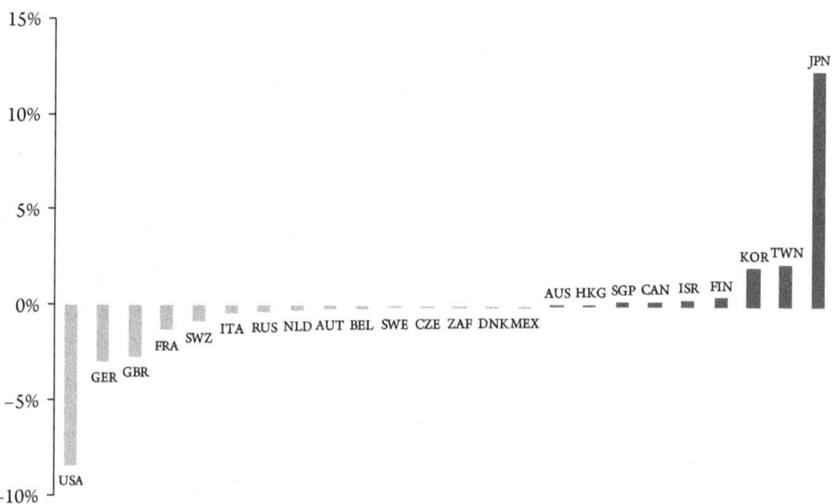

Figure 5.6 Change in citations-weighted patents received (1970–1975 vs. 2000–2005). As percent of world total, change in percent points shown between 1970-1975 and 2000-2005. N=162, countries not shown had a change of less than 0.05 percentage points.
Sources: United States Patent & Trademark Office, NBER (2001, 2006).

must also note that three of the most centralized European states (France, Great Britain, and Sweden) are among the largest decliners in relative innovation rates. Most interesting is the nation that does not appear in Figure 5.6, Spain, which significantly decentralized by almost any measure one can calculate. Spain's positive change in relative innovative performance (a mere –0.014 percentage point) is too small to register on this graph, despite the fact that its government continuously decentralized, both horizontally and vertically, formally and informally, throughout the entire time period sampled. Hence, even if we "cheat" by looking only at cases of success and ignoring the failures (i.e., selecting on the dependent variable), we still cannot substantiate a relationship between political decentralization and innovation!

Of course, these simple statistical tests do not allow us to simultaneously control for important conditional variables that might also affect innovation rates. Certainly when one controls for economic development, democracy, education, and so forth, then shouldn't the causal strengths of political decentralization become apparent? A 2007 study conducted quantitative analyses along precisely these lines.[62] Surprisingly, with but a single exception, no analysis yielded a significant coefficient for any measure of decentralization used in any combination with any of the innovation measures or conditional variables. The results were triangulated using multiple distinct and independent measures of national innovation rates, different measures of political decentralization (both vertical and horizontal), and more than a dozen different control variables (Table 5.5). These control variables were not run together in a "kitchen sink" regression but were modeled according to theory or developed through discussions with policy experts. The lone case in which the null hypothesis could be rejected occurred when countries were subdivided by wealth, but here the effect was fairly small, only applied to the wealthiest subset of nations, and was not consistent across different measures of decentralization. This is not what one would expect from such a well-theorized and widely accepted causal relationship.

Of course, statistical analysis has its weaknesses and limitations; therefore, given the strength of decentralization theory, a subsequent set of comparative case studies was performed to corroborate the previous quantitative analysis.[63] This qualitative approach adds value because it allows us to better (dis)confirm causal mechanisms and expose potential issues with endogeneity, and can reveal model specification errors—omitted variable bias is of particular concern in this case. To that end, the case studies examined innovation in two drastically different technologies and time periods (blood products 1981–1987 and electric power 1879–1914) across five countries (France, Germany, Japan, the United Kingdom, and the United States) for each. The case studies generally corroborated the statistical findings. In neither technology did political decentralization appear to have a significant or systematic effect on innovation rates.

Table 5.5 **Summary of Decentralization-Innovation Regressions**

Different Measures of Decentralization	*Multiple Control Variables*	*Different Measures of Innovation*

• Federalism dummies (Watts)
• Federalism (Lijphart scale)
• Horizontal decentralization (Lijphart scale)
• Veto players (Henitz POLCON)
	• Econ development
	  • Electricity consumption/capita
	  • Gross domestic product (GDP)/capita
	  • Lagged dependent variable
	• Size
	  • Population
	  • GDP
	• Democracy (Polity IV)
	• Trade openness (% of GDP)
	• Military spending (% of GDP)
	• Natural resource curse:
	  • Arable land (% of total)
	  • Fuel exports (% of total)
	  • Metal/ore exports (% of total)
	• Education:
	  • Literacy
	  • Science/eng undergrads
	  • Education spending (% total)
	• R&D spending (% GNP)
	• US dummy
	• OECD member dummy
	• High vs. low GDP/capita dummy
		• Patents (citations weighted, per capita)
		• Science-engineering research STEM publications (citations weighted, per capita)
		• High-tech exports (per GDP)

However, the case studies did find that technologies in both sectors and time periods consistently *diffused* more slowly in the centralized states than in the decentralized states.[64] This might explain the perception that innovation also occurs more rapidly in these countries. That is, since both innovation and diffusion manifest themselves in the appearance of new technology, the two phenomena can be easily mistaken for one another at a superficial level.

Given that much of the existing evidence for a decentralization-innovation thesis involves stylized facts and anecdotal case studies, it is possible that the empirical observations reported in prior research are actually instances of political decentralization aiding diffusion that were misidentified as innovation.

Those Stubborn Rapid Innovators!

Finally, an overwhelming problem with the institutions argument is that many of the world's greatest S&T success stories have not been very free market, democratic, or decentralized. For example, Japan has been a fairly centralized, one-party state, with an economy aggressively managed by government bureaucrats for much of the time since 1955, just three years after the end of the US occupation. In Japan's powerful House of Representatives, the ruling Liberal Democratic Party (LDP) won a plurality of the vote in every election between 1955 and 2008, allowing it to dominate the executive branch and policymaking for more than a half century. LDP domination mattered because, during this time, Japan's strong executive bureaucracy was poorly balanced by a weak judiciary and subnational governments. Rather, Japan's subnational governments were composed of a mix of elected and appointed officials with only a small degree of local autonomy over fiscal and policy matters.[65] At the national level, the Ministry of Trade and Industry[66] and Ministry of Finance famously managed the economy. Nicknamed "Japan Inc.," these LDP-controlled ministries worked together with big business to obstruct free trade, tightly control capital allocation, target investments, select national champions and euthanize obsolete industries, restrict consumer and environmental protections, repress labor unrest, and block unwanted foreign participation in the economy.[67] Yet despite all of these "bad" institutions, Japan rapidly graduated from agriculture and basic industries to become one of the most advanced S&T nations in history.[68]

The institutions for Taiwan, South Korea, and Singapore have arguably been even "worse" than Japan's. After World War II, South Korea was ruled by various autocrats and military dictators until its first democratic elections in 1987. Even then, the military did not relinquish its hold on the Korean presidency until 1993. Like Japan, South Korea's economy is dominated by a powerful executive bureaucracy that works closely with a handful of the country's business conglomerates in a highly interventionist fashion. Taiwan was created in 1949 as a one-party dictatorship, an authoritarian state whose government continues to intervene substantially in the economy. In fact, Taiwan suffered martial law for four decades until 1987, and then endured one-party rule until 1991 when ruling elites gradually liberalized and democratized the system. Singapore is to this day a soft-authoritarian state in which the executive branch dominates policy design and implementation, while the public merely provides feedback. We will examine these cases more deeply in the following chapter, but the point here is that both Taiwan and South Korea democratized *after* their surge in innovation rates had begun, not before, while innovative Singapore remains today only marginally democratic, and each of these governments continues to intervene heavily into markets.

Meanwhile, dozens of countries have enjoyed fully functioning democracies, decentralized polities, and relatively free markets, or have strongly improved in these regards, but *still* failed to achieve anywhere near the hyperbolic S&T success as Japan, Taiwan, South Korea, Singapore, and others. For example, Australia, New Zealand, and the United Kingdom have had decades of "strong" institutions by every measure. Yet they remain midlevel innovators. There are several more countries (e.g., Belgium, Belize, Brazil, Chile, Costa Rica, Greece, India, Italy, Norway, Portugal, and Thailand) that have decades of "good" or vastly improving domestic institutions but little corresponding improvement in national innovation rates. Again, if domestic institutions are so powerful, then how can we explain Spain? Spain has been institutionally transformed since 1975, from a socialist military dictatorship into a market-oriented, competitive, decentralized democracy. Yet, despite this revolution, there has been little relative change in Spain's national innovation rate!

Finally, it is important to recognize that the United States itself violates the democracy and free market thesis. The United States went through its first surge in S&T performance during the mid-nineteenth century through the early twentieth century. Yet, throughout this era, less than half the population was allowed to vote or hold office. Women, African Americans, and many immigrants (an outsized portion of the US population at the time) were legally or de facto barred from participating in elections, holding elected positions, being appointed as government officials, or merely holding jobs as civil service workers. This was also the period when Progressives took control of US government to greatly enlarge federal authority over markets. The Roosevelt and Wilson administrations passed a slew of economy-wide regulations, price controls, and trade protections that increased federal power at the expense of state governments, even nationalizing some industries and curtailing civil rights and liberties during World War I. Yet, it was during this same time period that the US economy advanced from being an S&T backwater, often mocked by Europeans for its technological and scientific vulgarity, to becoming one of the world's S&T leaders. This constitutes a major unexplained outlier for democracy and free market theorists.

Conclusions

So where do we stand? The NIS scholars have found that: pick your favorite policy or midlevel institution (financial system, antitrust regime, education policy, etc.), you can find both highly innovative *and* lowly innovative states that employ it. The innovation devil may yet be in the policy details, but thirty years of research have yet to identify him. VoC scholars attempted to explain this by arguing that both NIS institutions and innovative behavior are endogenous to markets, but the empirical data fails to show any aggregate effect of a nation's "variety of capitalism" on innovation rates. Theories about democracy and political decentralization can then be brought in to argue that both NIS institutions and a nation's variety of capitalism are endogenous to government structure. But decades of technology patents, science-engineering publications, and high-tech export data fail to substantiate any of these hypotheses.

It is important to restate here that I am *not* arguing that democracy, decentralization, and free markets have *no* effect on national innovation rates. Rather, I am contending that theories that put these institutions at their core, as both necessary and sufficient for sustained S&T progress, have been overstated, have been oversimplified, and need to be re-examined. They simply do not have the predictive or explanatory power we assume them to have. Domestic institutions and policies do not determine the rate and direction of national inventive activity. Like a carpenter's tools, institutions and policies do *influence* outcomes, but they are *not* causal forces. Good tools do not make someone an expert carpenter; good institutions and policies do not compel a society to innovate.

What is happening here? I argue in the rest of the book that what's happening is "omitted variable bias." In other words, we are missing something. To find that missing something, we need to abandon our preconceived notions of what makes societies innovate. We need to get beyond the vague platitude that "institutions and policies matter!" Therefore, the next chapter will instead let the data tell us what works, or not, in different countries. We will examine some recent S&T success stories (e.g., Israel and Taiwan) to see what characteristics they shared. We will then compare them against a case of more moderate success (Ireland) and a case of relative failure (Mexico). From this comparison, we can get a better idea of how institutions and policies fit into the innovation equation. We can also identify clearly one activity that more successful S&T nations do that less fruitful societies fail to do: networking.

6

How Nations Succeed

Networks, Clusters, and Standards

We have thus far found that every government policy and institution that one would expect to determine national science and technology (S&T) performance actually has either limited or no predictive power. There are just too many countries with "good" institutions and policies that fail to innovate much, and too many countries with "bad" or missing institutions and policies that innovate quite well. Furthermore, all sorts of data and case studies show that the institutional keys to national success in high technology do *not* lie in different degrees or styles of capitalism, market freedom, democracy, or government structure. Nor can we locate S&T success in further additions to the endless list of "national innovation systems," with its universe full of wildly different policy and institutional constellations.

Perhaps we are being too theoretical. Until now, we have allowed all sorts of abstract assumptions and preconceptions to dictate our thinking about innovation. So instead of letting theory guide our attempt to explain national innovation rates, this chapter begins by letting the data inform us. That is, maybe the best way to figure out why some nations are better at S&T is to investigate recent cases of success and failure. We can then ask what *successful* governments do, or avoid doing, that the cases of *failure* did not? One logical place to start this investigation is in the rapidly innovating nations. These are the countries that recently graduated from agriculture and basic manufacturing to global competitiveness in high technology in the span of a single generation. A better understanding of the government actions, or inactions, that drove these success stories would be a useful improvement over the vague platitude that "institutions and policies matter."

It is worth divulging two surprises that come out of this chapter's comparison of successes versus failures. First, there are still no silver bullets. The successful countries do not appear to share any single "best" institution or policy design. Rather, the key to national success in S&T is not *which* particular institution or policy governments use, but that the market failures get solved. Also, the evidence suggests that many *different* institutions and policy designs can solve the market failures that obstruct innovation. The differences between these various designs may not matter much, or they may matter only at the margins. Governments therefore have considerable freedom to customize national strategies for improving their nation's innovation rate. Put simply, nations have choices. They need not adopt the institutions of past success stories like the United States, Germany, or Japan. Each nation can design its S&T institutions and policies to best fit its own history, politics, and culture.[1]

Second, the national case studies that follow point us toward factors often ignored in the research on national innovation systems: social networks, industrial clusters, and technology standards. The cases consistently reveal that informal social networks, both domestic *and* international, play important roles in determining national S&T achievement. That is, innovation is not just a market failure problem; it is also a network failure problem. Social networks provide vital information that neither markets nor governments easily capture. This includes essential information about science, technology, engineering, and mathematics (STEM) labor; investment opportunities; and markets for highly specialized S&T inputs and outputs. Certainly these kinds of information problems plague all businesses, but they are especially tricky in S&T-based industries. S&T actors are extremely specialized and disparate, while business conditions in these sectors change more rapidly and unexpectedly than others. In capturing and distributing information cheaply, social networks help S&T actors to find one another and to increase their flexibility to rapid change. In so doing, networks drastically reduce the high costs and risks of innovation. Markets and governments simply do not capture this kind of information cheaply or well. Therefore, governments need to be thinking about how to create and maintain active networks for innovation in S&T. Clusters are a particular form of network that reduces costs, creates complementarities, and increases spillovers within a concentrated geographic area. Finally, one condition for building successful networks is standards. Standards help to determine how large a network can get and how well its members can interoperate. Standards also solve several types of market failures that can slow the creation or adoption of new S&T.

Three Stories of Science and Technology Success: Israel, Taiwan, and Ireland

Let's start by examining recent studies of innovation in three nations that have drastically accelerated their climb up the S&T value chain: Israel, Taiwan, and Ireland. The case studies in this section draw partly upon the research of Dan

Breznitz, whose empirical work on innovation in developmental states has changed how many scholars think about rapid innovators.[2] From a political-economic point of view, Israel, Taiwan, and Ireland share many similarities. Each country entered the 1950s with similar demographics in terms of size, population, education levels, and skilled labor (i.e., few STEM workers). All three economies also depended heavily on agriculture. Most important, each of these countries also suffered from classic market failures that discouraged innovation. In Israel, Taiwan, and Ireland, intellectual property rights were then poorly defined and not well enforced, especially when compared with the United States or the most technologically advanced states in Western Europe. Private investment in both research and development (R&D) and STEM education was minimal during the 1950s. Even public goods, such as basic physical infrastructure and national communication systems, were poorly provided or not provided at all. Thus, innovation stagnated.

These conditions continued for decades until Israel, Taiwan, and Ireland each recognized the critical need for the state to intervene to solve the market failures that obstructed innovation in their economies. To that end, each country's government established a variety of institutions and policies to develop indigenous high-tech industries. Certainly, there were similarities in their policy strategies. For example, the governments of Israel, Taiwan, and Ireland each took action to improve the physical infrastructure, telecommunications network, and education systems of their nations. Also, none of them based their development strategy on large national champions, as Korea and Japan did so successfully; instead, they relied on small and medium-size enterprises.

Yet, these three states otherwise selected very different development strategies, which should have led to vastly different outcomes. In Israel, technological leadership was left to private domestic firms, while the government heavily subsidized R&D. The focus here was on the domestic development of new high-tech products, which were financed and marketed via international networks. In Taiwan, the government itself led the R&D effort in the form of public research institutes, the products of which were then diffused to private industry to manufacture and distribute. Moreover, Taiwan sought innovation in intermediate product design and manufacturing, rather than new high-technology end-products for consumers or businesses. Ireland pursued the most free market strategy, one focused on inward foreign direct investment (FDI) from high-tech multinational corporations (MNCs). Here the government's focus was on creating jobs in technology services, but not an indigenous manufacturing or research capability.

Interestingly, despite their different institutions and policy strategies, all three countries generally succeeded in overcoming similar obstacles and becoming globally competitive high-tech producers in a fairly short time span.[3] Let's briefly explore how each nation did it.

Israel: High Success

When Israel was first established as a nation in 1948, it was devoid of cutting-edge S&T. For decades thereafter, Israel remained a highly protectionist, quasi-socialist state that relied on a heavily agrarian economy. Strong labor unions and their powerful representatives in government coexisted in friendly tension with supporters of private markets. The result was a mixed economy where free markets were infused with substantial government intervention.[4] Yet industrial R&D was rare, especially in the private sector. Also, rapid immigration of impoverished Jews from lower-income countries brought down national education and skill levels. "High tech" in Israel then best referred to the domestic textiles industry and perhaps a few subsectors of the defense industries, all government subsidized. Perhaps Israel's only initial strengths in S&T were a few research universities, its many primary and secondary schools, a history of respect for science and education, and a miniscule but growing R&D program within the defense sector heavily focused on niche weapons, nuclear research, and computers.

Israel's technological backwardness changed rapidly during the late 1960s. In 1965, the government created new R&D grant programs for industry. The state soon began to redirect existing government funding and resources toward developing Israel's S&T capabilities. By the end of the decade, science advisers were assigned to the leadership of each of Israel's major government ministries. The Israelis did not limit their research efforts to basic science; they also targeted the development of new technologies and industries based on them. Also, all R&D was recognized to have value, even if success was delayed. A top Israeli S&T policymaker later recalled, "From the national point of view, a failure in a research-and-development project [was] not a loss. . . . This was my sole guiding principle when I gave grants to companies."[5]

At first, Israel's defense research programs led the way. Interestingly, these laboratories were run more like university departments than military units, with much flatter hierarchies and greater openness to experimentation. In information technology, the Israeli army's armaments development program, which had built some of Israel's first indigenous computers during the 1950s, soon emerged as a national S&T incubator during the 1960s. Its employees and intellectual property were encouraged to spill over into other government R&D programs and even into private industry, resulting in a flowering of high-tech start-ups during the 1970s. Ministries across government then began to computerize their operations. In the process, they further subsidized training in, and demand for, computer skills and R&D. Skilled STEM workers began to flow purposely between government and private industry. In one direction, government-trained STEM workers rapidly fed the development of private firms in computers, aeronautics, and telecommunications.[6] In the other direction, industry workers brought back into government their connections and expertise with private markets, which served as a basis for revising and updating national S&T policy.

One idea brought into the Israeli government from private industry was that of state-based venture capital. At the time, precious few Israeli banks were willing to invest in a risky domestic high-tech sector. Therefore, the Israeli government promoted its Office of the Chief Scientist (OCS)[7] to become Israel's primary S&T investment institution. For years, the OCS was the main, and often only, source of financial capital for Israeli high-tech ventures. Yet the Israeli state did not pick winners. Instead, Israel put private firms at the center of its strategy, subsidizing them with public R&D money and skilled STEM labor generously leaked out of military research programs. For example, the first full-time head of the OCS recalled approaching Israel high-tech firms with the following offer: "Bring me one R&D project which you want to conduct and you cannot for lack of capital, and I will declare it a national project and . . . grant you 80 percent of the cost."[8] Aside from subsidizing R&D, the state largely stayed out of private industry's way. Meanwhile, the government sharply reduced funding for public research institutions, except for their joint projects with private firms. The idea here was to reduce, but not eliminate, the costs and risks of private sector innovation.

Another successful idea, this one mainly emanating from the state, was to pressure Israeli companies to form international networks. This meant linkages with foreign, especially American, firms for finance, marketing, and technology transfer.[9] To achieve this, Israeli financiers flew to San Francisco and New York to cultivate ties with, and gather expert advice from, high-level Jewish financiers in Silicon Valley and on Wall Street. Some of these ties led to early US-Israeli joint ventures and, starting in 1972, listings of Israeli firms on American stock exchanges. Then, in 1976, the Israeli government created the Bi-National Industrial Research Foundation (BIRD) within the OCS. The mission of BIRD was to foster networks and joint ventures between Israeli and US firms. By funding up to 50% of joint R&D projects, BIRD became instrumental in attracting US high-technology firms to set up joint research facilities in Israel. R&D facilities were soon being built in Israel by global S&T leaders, such as IBM, Lucent, Digital, Motorola, National Semiconductor, and Intel. Interestingly, BIRD's grants were not government giveaways. Like much of OCS financing, BIRD's investments were to be recouped out of sales. In fact, BIRD's international ventures were so successful that, in some cases, they earned profits for the Israeli government of 50% *over* the original grant repayment, which was then ploughed back into new R&D projects.[10]

As time passed, the Israeli government's approach to S&T networks grew highly sophisticated. For example, the OCS created legal mechanisms through which foreign MNCs could shelter themselves from taxes at home by investing in R&D centers in Israel. Loans and financing were even provided to sweeten the deal. The government also got actively involved in networking Israeli firms and domestic finance together with foreign financial markets. As a result, foreign financial markets soon became major sources of capital for Israeli high-tech firms. Also, a variety of trade policies were designed to help Israeli firms link into American and European markets. These trade relationships addressed two notorious weaknesses of Israeli high tech: a need for major export markets and a lack of foreign supply partnerships for marketing and business development. Finally, another major international network was formed by Jewish immigrants from more advanced S&T countries. Israel's first waves of immigrants had consisted of large numbers of farmers and unskilled labor; now, Israel's rising S&T sectors also attracted Jewish STEM workers from countries with fewer economic and social opportunities for them, especially in Europe and the Communist bloc. For example, the Israeli government played a central role in recruiting the surge of highly educated ex-Soviets who migrated during the 1970s and 1990s. Israel even won financial assistance from the United States to settle them. Thousands of these ex-Soviet Jews entered Israel with extensive STEM backgrounds, making them an important input to the Israeli high-tech sector.[11]

As a result of these institutions, policies, and networks, Israel is today a leader in several S&T sectors. Israel firms now compete globally in computer software, network security, pharmaceuticals, medical devices, communications, and advanced defense technologies. Israel regularly ranks as the country with the most NASDAQ listings after the United States and Canada, with over one hundred high-tech firms sold on American stock exchanges. And while venture capitalists generally expect only 10% of high-tech start-ups to survive more than five years, Israel's five-year success rate is closer to 65%.[12] On a per capita basis, Israeli innovators are now consistently among the top ten most highly patented nationalities and with many of the most highly cited patents. In the sciences and engineering, Israel ranks among the world's top three in per capita research publications. Since 2004, Israeli scientists have won four Nobel Prizes in the sciences and a Fields Medal in mathematics, and they sponsor one of the two dozen remaining teams competing for the Google Lunar X Prize. Also, thanks to Israel's extensive international networks, foreign companies now invest $4 billion to $5 billion annually in Israeli R&D, which equates to almost half of what the Israelis themselves invest (roughly $10 billion) in civilian R&D.[13] In only forty years, Israel has leapt from S&T nonentity to globally respected competitor, a success story par excellence.

But which of Israel's triumphant institutions and policies are shared by other successful S&T nations?

Taiwan: High Success

Taiwan is another recent technological success story, frequently heralded as an "economic miracle" because of its rapid innovation in high-tech industries.[14] Like Israel, Taiwan began as an S&T backwater. For decades after its break with mainland China in 1949, the main exports from Taiwan were natural resources (woods and petroleum), foodstuffs, and basic textiles.[15] Then, during the late 1960s, Taiwan began to shift its resources into S&T. By 1970, television and radio equipment made Taiwan's list of top exports, along with more sophisticated manufactures of clothing and processed foods. A decade later, exports of electrical machinery, telecommunications equipment, and integrated circuits were flowing out of Taiwan. By the mid-1990s, Taiwan was out-producing most Western economies in many S&T products. Since 2000, Taiwan has patented new technologies at a level beaten only consistently by Japan and the United States.[16] In science, Taiwan now matches the research output of several European nations in engineering, clinical medicine, physics, and chemistry.[17] Five of the world's top ten producers of solar cells and thin-film panels are currently Taiwanese.[18] The semiconductor foundry industry in Taiwan is the world's largest, with an output valued at $23 billion in 2013.[19] As a result of all this innovation, for over a decade, Taiwanese firms have been the world's lead manufacturers of computer motherboards, laptops, monitors, and digital cameras.[20]

Taiwan's innovation strategy has been very different than Israel's and employs distinctly different institutions and policies. At home, to deal with the market failures associated with the high risks and costs of domestic innovation, Taiwan set up several high-level public research institutions. Take, for example, the information technology (IT) sector, which quickly became Taiwan's leading S&T industry. In IT, the most prominent Taiwanese public research institutions are the Industrial Technology Research Institution (ITRI) for research in computer hardware, Hsinchu Science-Based Industrial Park for semiconductors, and the Institute for Information Industry (III) for computer software. Domestically, the ITRI, III, and Hsinchu not only funded R&D themselves but also brought together networks of scientists and then connected them with industry. For example, Hsinchu Park was formed in 1979 specifically to knit together networks of researchers from Taiwan's top three engineering schools situated nearby and then feed their research into a nascent domestic semiconductor industry.[21] Together, these government-run research institutions decided which technologies to pursue and then undertook the initial R&D. If successful, the results and prototypes from government labs were disseminated to industry. Taiwan's firms would then develop final products and take them into mass production. Even some Taiwanese companies were state owned or joint ventures with the government. To fund them, the Ministry of Economic Affairs would organize coalitions of investors and corporate partners. So, unlike Israel, where the production of S&T was usually left to universities and private industry, Taiwan has instead followed a strategy of heavy government intervention into the economy, with the state selecting projects, conducting R&D, and actively transferring technology to private industry.

On the other hand, similar to Israel, Taiwan valued the development of social networks, both domestic and international, as an essential component of its S&T approach. For example, Taiwan's initial innovation strategy was to use its low-cost, but well-educated and disciplined, labor force to attract FDI into high-tech sectors. This was not a glitzy marketing campaign or a vague government directive. Instead, policymakers and businessmen in Taiwan actively targeted individual firms and their executives in the United States' and Europe's high-tech sectors, aggressively building personal networks with foreign investors.[22] These networks provided foreigners with information on Taiwan's resources and investment potential that was often difficult to obtain abroad, while simultaneously establishing relationships built on reciprocity and trust. As a result, as early as the 1960s, Taiwan successfully attracted General Instrument, Philips, and dozens of other firms to set up facilities there, resulting in a blooming electronics export industry.[23]

Then, during the 1970s, Taiwan began to reach out to individual engineers and executives at leading American high-tech firms, such as Texas Instruments, RCA, IBM, and others.[24] Often these Americans were Chinese ex-patriots and graduates of top US research universities, who had years of laboratory and management experience in the private sector. Together they formed in the United States a network of Chinese American S&T experts who met regularly to advise Taiwan on establishing domestic R&D laboratories in electronics and semiconductors. Biannual seminars in Taiwan then brought these American experts together with Taiwanese STEM and business elites, creating a regular channel for expertise and relationships.[25]

Even after Taiwan established itself as a competitive high-tech producer during the 1980s, these international networks continued to be instrumental to Taiwan's success in S&T. For example, Taiwan's network of foreign S&T advisers continued to guide Taiwan's investment strategy, for years steering the country clear of the memory chip sector, and instead directing Taiwan into the production of advanced integrated circuits. Taiwan also pursued joint ventures with American firms, often run by Chinese Americans, which then sold their output into Korea and Japan. Also, thousands of Taiwanese scientists and engineers trained in US graduate schools began to return to their ancestral home, bringing with them both the S&T expertise and relationships they had established in the United States. These STEM returnees soon created a revolution in Taiwan's computer hardware industry. Some founded new firms, while others staffed existing ventures desperate for well-trained STEM labor. And the inflows were not limited to human capital. Technology transfer from abroad, often steered by ITRI, provided Taiwanese firms with constant access to cutting-edge technologies coming out of the United States, Japan, and Europe.[26]

International networks have additional importance in the Taiwan case. Unlike Israel, which aims at cutting-edge high-technology product development, Taiwan has sought to become a lead supplier of high-tech components and design services to frontier innovators in the United States, Japan, and Europe.[27] This leaves the riskiest and most costly aspects of new product development to companies in the lead innovating nations. Once these final products have been developed in foreign markets, Taiwan applies its competitive advantage in producing second-generation technologies as inputs to them. Hence, networking into foreign markets is not merely a means to Taiwan's S&T goals, but one of her S&T goals itself.

Ireland: Moderate Success

Over on the Emerald Isle, one can find another case of S&T success, but here the advances were belated and far more moderate than those in either Israel or Taiwan. Ireland made its graduation from an agrarian economy to high-tech competitor more recently, during the late 1980s. Like Israel and Taiwan, Ireland began with an economy based on natural resources, agriculture, and textiles. Ireland's main exports in 1970 were livestock, dairy products, and basic textiles. In 1990, computers and office machines had joined the list, but Ireland's economy was still dismissed by critics as "producing sclerosis," "anti-intellectual," and even "relatively retarded."[28] Nevertheless, before the decade was over, Ireland was being celebrated as a Celtic tiger due to its rapid rise in the production of globally competitive computer software, IT services, chemicals, and pharmaceutical goods.[29] Yet Ireland failed to become a major producer of new science or an inventor of revolutionary new technologies. On many S&T performance measures, the Irish remain to this day midlevel innovators, perhaps even below the Western European average. What did the Irish government do, or fail to do, to explain this good, but muted, outcome?

The Irish state did act successfully to create domestic institutions and policies that solved market failures. From the late 1950s through the mid-1990s, the Industrial Development Authority (IDA) led this effort, acting as Ireland's primary development agency. On the market failure side, the state expanded its education system, with a heavy emphasis on subsidizing a supply of high-quality Irish STEM labor. Ireland also upgraded its physical and communications infrastructures to increase its attractiveness to MNCs seeking bases for export. In both of these endeavors, the IDA played a major part, aggressively reforming the Irish education system and eventually becoming a top owner of Ireland's industrial land.[30] The government also lowered taxes on investment and provided grant incentives. The Irish patent system was another victory. During the 1960s, patent protection in Ireland was dismal, scoring as low as 1.71 on economist Walter G. Park's zero- to five-point scale of national intellectual property rights (IPR) systems.[31] By 2000, that ranking was up to 4.67 and the US State Department applauded it as "one of the most comprehensive systems of IPR protection in Europe."[32] Most recently, Ireland has increased and better targeted its subsidies for R&D. For example, in 2000, Science Foundation Ireland was created with a budget of around $600 million to fund research in niche areas within biotechnology, information and communications technology, and energy.[33]

Yet Ireland's domestic institutions and policy actions were far more limited those in Taiwan or Israel. Irish spending on R&D (per gross domestic product [GDP]) has averaged around half that of Taiwan and as little as a third that of Israel, and consistently trails the Organization for Economic Cooperation and Development (OECD) and EU averages.[34] R&D grants were also harder to get, and funded a smaller portion of expenses, than those in Israel.[35] Another problem was that Irish universities and public research institutions were geared more toward STEM training than indigenous R&D; after decades of neglect, only recently did Irish schools acquire the resources to carry out high-quality research.[36] Also, unlike Israel or Taiwan, little attention was paid to developing indigenous production capabilities in Ireland. The Irish state did not actively support domestic high-tech start-ups via grants, subsidies, or military procurement programs. Only in a few sectors, such as computer software, and only after a few private sector success stories has the Irish state recently begun to change its development strategy toward greater government intervention. Even here, the state often limits its role to that of export promoter, with perhaps small movement toward creating a domestic venture capital sector.[37]

To the extent that Ireland created and maintained the necessary institutions and policies, some marked successes were achieved. For example, a globally competitive Irish software industry arose during the 1990s, with state policy playing a positive role. Dublin distributed grant aid, created soft supports for marketing and management, promoted business associations, and even actively financed some start-ups.[38] However, the software industry's success was tenuous. It suffered greatly in 2001–2003 due to the bursting of the dot.com bubble. Also, Irish firms have generally taken a backseat to foreign S&T ventures. These foreign MNCs often survive economic slumps, while Irish S&T firms either fail or get bought up. Today, Irish innovation has arguably created the foundation for a diversified software and business services sector, but far more investment is needed.[39]

The relative shortcomings of Ireland's domestic S&T institutions and policies stem from Dublin's innovation strategy. State institutions and policies have been effective insofar as they have been established. However, Ireland's approach is based on inward technology transfer from abroad, *not* indigenous state-run laboratories or heavy government intervention. The Irish S&T development strategy has been to attract foreign high-tech MNCs to set up large-scale manufacturing facilities in Ireland, but not necessarily R&D centers. The original plan prioritized exports and used low taxes, grant aid, funding matches, and low-cost STEM labor to attract FDI. Restrictions on foreign ownership were eliminated to lure foreign MNCs to set up production. Meanwhile, the IDA created special economic zones around major transportation points and successfully lobbied to cut export taxes. This was all enormously successful. A flurry of leading US high-tech firms began to set up production in Ireland starting in the 1990s, including Digital Equipment, IBM, Dell, Microsoft, Oracle, Symantec, and Novell. However, few indigenous high-tech firms appeared, and domestic R&D projects did not flourish. Irish S&T firms had trouble competing for sparse investment finance and STEM labor, much of which went instead to foreign MNCs, and Irish universities suffered from a paucity of financial support.[40]

The Irish government has made similarly half-hearted attempts at setting up international networks. At first, Irish networking simply meant establishing free trade relationships with the United Kingdom and the European Union. Then the IDA set up offices in foreign countries to attract high-tech MNCs to Ireland. These activities partly explain the high concentration of American firms in Ireland's high-tech industries. Seeking access to the European market, by 1998, over 60% of electronics plants in Ireland were owned by US firms, and these plants accounted for over 80% of employment in the electronics sector.[41] Often, the Irish government sought networks in a far more superficial and less targeted way than either Taiwan or Israel. For example, because of Ireland's almost singular focus on attracting and maintaining FDI, most Irish S&T firms serve as flexible suppliers to powerful, foreign MNCs. This means that Irish firms participate more in highly ephemeral networks than in stable ones. These are networks characterized by highly fluid relationships, with ever-shifting short-term contracts between participants rather than reliable long-run relationships that foster heavy investment into new R&D.[42]

Ireland's domestic networks have also received far less government support than in Israel or Taiwan. At home, the IDA seems to have restricted its domestic networking to state actors, mostly just coordinating disparate government departments and ministries to support its policies. Programs were established during the 1980s to create working partnerships between the universities, government development agencies, and industry. However, these efforts were modest, and decades later, linkages between training, education, and the labor markets in Ireland remain relatively weak.[43] One common factor with Israel and Taiwan was the creation of S&T information networks that provide low-cost access to detailed technical knowledge as an aid to, and aggregator of, research. During the 1990s, some attempts were made to link together Irish firms in cooperative ventures. These were successful, but the programs were short term and not renewed.[44] As a result, Irish corporate networks now tend to run across industry lines rather than being specialized. This means that Irish S&T firms tend to focus on breadth rather than depth. Thus, there are few Irish national corporations to serve as anchors for smaller firms.[45]

In sum, like Israel and Taiwan, Ireland's successful strategy was to create institutions and networks, both domestic and international, that solved market failures. However, Ireland was the least successful high-tech "miracle" of the three. Arguably, this is because Irish institutions have been less aggressive in attacking S&T market failures *and* because Ireland has done the least to create either domestic or international networks that embed foreign high-tech actors within the Irish political economy. Foreign MNCs therefore view Ireland and its generous supply of STEM labor as an export base, and perhaps increasingly a source of high-tech services. Only in pharmaceuticals has Ireland become an R&D hub, though one dominated by foreign firms.[46] Crucially, if foreign MNCs ever choose to move on in search of cheaper or different types of STEM labor, then Ireland may be left with little indigenous high-tech sector with which to compete.

A Story of Relative Failure: Mexico

One problem with innovation research is that much of it looks only at cases of success but ignores the failures; it can therefore miss important differences between them. In science, this error is known as "selecting on the dependent variable." It can lead researchers to mistake an inconsequential characteristic for a decisive causal difference. That is, we cannot know if a factor is shared in common between success and failure countries if we do not bother to investigate the failures. Even if all the success stories share a common characteristic, if the failures possess it too, then it must not be a determining causal factor.

To contrast the previous cases of S&T success, an insightful example of relative failure can be found in Mexico. Admittedly, Mexico is a very different type of country than Israel, Taiwan, or Ireland, especially in terms of size, natural resources, regime type, culture, history, and geography. But this is precisely the point. If *similar* cause-effect dynamics can be found in such a *different* country, then it strengthens the argument about the roles institutions and networks play in influencing national innovation rates.

By almost any measure, Mexico has long been an S&T nonperformer, especially relative to Israel, Taiwan, and Ireland (Figure 6.1). For decades, Mexico has patented at a fraction of the per capita rate of any of these other nations

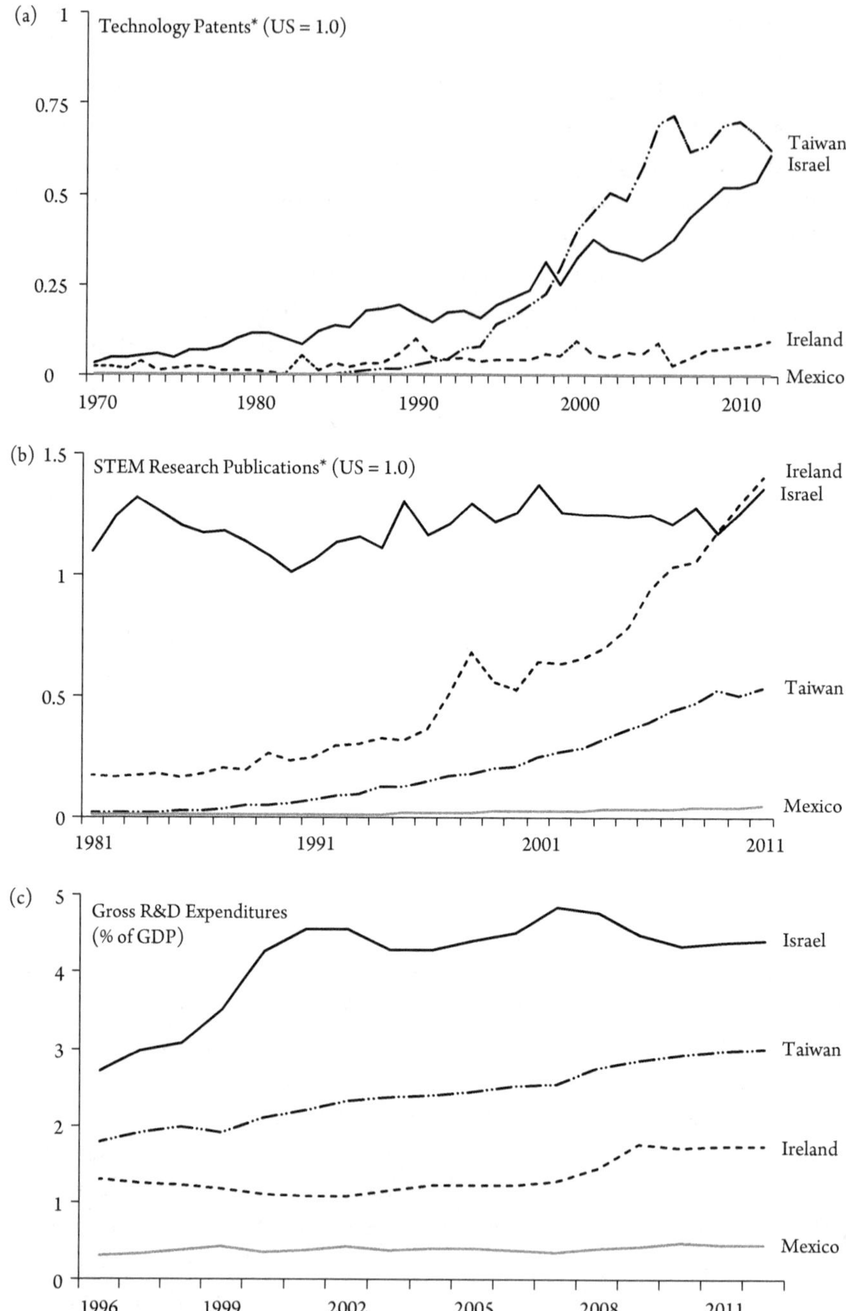

Figure 6.1a–d Selected comparisons of S&T performance..

Sources: NBER Patent Database; Thomson-ISI; OECD; National Science Foundation.

*Per capita, weighted by forward citations

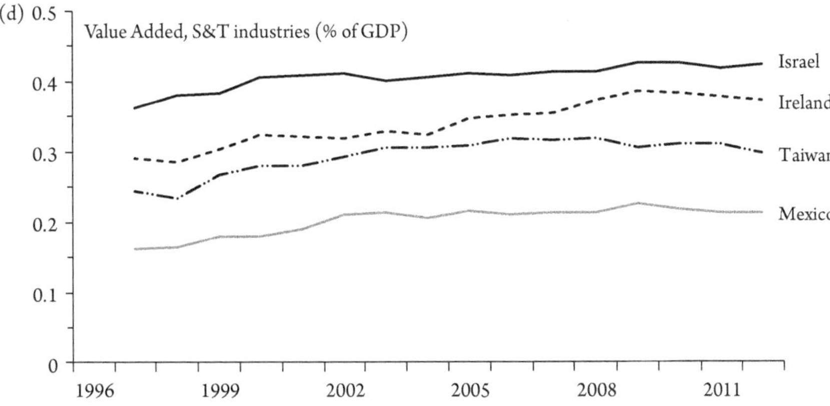

Figure 6.1a–d Continued

(though more so than Taiwan until the mid-1970s). Also, Mexican patents receive, on average, only around half the forward citations of the patents from those other countries.[47] Similarly, Mexico's per capita scientific output is only around 10% that of Taiwan's, 5% of Ireland's, and even less that of Israel's.[48] Mexico has nonetheless managed to build up a strong high-tech export sector, especially in the automotive, electronics, and telecommunications industries. However, the firms in these sectors are almost all *maquiladoras*: foreign-owned and foreign-operated factories that employ low-skilled Mexican labor and use little indigenous technology. If one considers only Mexican firms, then around 90% of them are today focused only on low-tech, local markets in retail, services, and agriculture.[49] There are few Mexican high-tech producers to be found.

What has caused Mexico's weak S&T performance? Certainly Mexico has been a poor country during much of its history, but wealth is not to blame. In fact, Mexico had far greater per capita wealth than Taiwan until the early 1980s.[50] Interestingly, Mexicans also enjoyed greater political rights and civil liberties than the Taiwanese until the early 1990s.[51] If we allow South Korea and Singapore, both rapid innovators, into the comparison, then Mexico looks even better in terms of wealth and democratic institutions for decades after World War II. Rather, the problem was that Mexico invested a far lesser share of her wealth into overcoming the market failures that obstruct innovation. Mexico also failed to create and maintain the networks that promote innovation.

This is most clearly seen in the IT sector, where Mexico did enjoy some brief prosperity. Starting in the 1970s, a relatively successful domestic computer industry grew around Mexico's high-tech self-sufficiency programs. Under the direction of Mexico's National Council on Science and Technology (CONACYT), many of these programs addressed market failures and established international networks in ways similar to those in Taiwan or Israel. Under these programs, foreign firms were invited to invest in Mexican computer production, but only through joint ventures in which local partners got majority ownership. Foreign computer manufacturers were also required to invest in Mexican R&D and STEM training centers. Other policies, such as domestic content requirements, government procurement programs, and tax and financial incentives, rounded out the successful strategy. Hence, Mexico's domestic institutions established networks that embedded foreign high-tech producers within the domestic economy.[52]

While they lasted, CONACYT's programs during the 1970s were fairly successful in their attempts to attract FDI with a large S&T manufacturing component. Over sixty foreign high-tech firms entered into joint production ventures in Mexico, including major computing MNCs such as Hewlett-Packard, IBM, Digital, NCR, Tandem, and Wang. Mexican computer production eventually reached $400 million, split between micro-computers, mini-computers, and peripheral equipment, with half exported to the United States and Canada. The Mexican company Printaform became the top domestic producer of personal computers. Printaform soon manufactured computers of high enough quality that Mexico's top university (UNAM) began to purchase them instead of those made by foreign competitors.[53]

However, starting in the mid-1980s, Mexico altered its policy strategy and dramatically liberalized its economy. This changed the nature of both Mexican domestic institutions and the international networks they promoted. Mexico pursued extreme free market policies by dropping tariffs, lowering licensing requirements, and ultimately joining the North American Free Trade Agreement (NAFTA) in 1994. This new development strategy was intended to attract FDI via almost complete market liberalization and to allow Mexico's advantage in low-wage labor to lure in foreign flagship S&T firms. Once foreign firms set up manufacturing facilities, Mexico's political leadership believed that knowledge spillovers and technology transfer would naturally follow, as the foreign MNCs trained local workers and suppliers in S&T production.[54]

One problem with this strategy was that, as the economy liberalized, foreign computer manufacturers in Mexico began to insist on exemptions from Mexican self-sufficiency requirements. This meant that foreign high-tech firms could remove themselves from local networks. It also meant that former Mexican-foreign partners in innovation now became competitors. The first exemption came in 1985. In exchange for a STEM training center, Mexico allowed IBM to set up a wholly owned production facility in Guadalajara without any local partners. Other foreign firms soon followed suit, often with no stipulations for local development projects extracted in exchange.[55] This had disastrous results when, during the 1990s, the protections afforded by

Mexico's industrial policy gave way to NAFTA and the new free market development strategies. Without anything tying their fate to the local high-tech sector, foreign computer manufacturers located in Mexico simply wiped out their Mexican competition.[56]

Also, unlike the previous national success stories, the Mexican government did not intervene to address the market failures associated with high-tech production. There was little state-led effort to improve STEM education, subsidize R&D centers, or provide finance to domestic high-tech start-ups. Instead, to attract FDI, the state eliminated the protections that functioned with relative success during the 1970s.[57] Nor did the Mexican state invest much in knitting together domestic networks of investors, entrepreneurs, industry, and STEM workers. The state also failed to embed foreign S&T manufacturers within those domestic innovation networks that did exist. For example, instead of developing indigenous R&D capabilities at Mexican universities linked to foreign high-tech ventures, Mexico's colleges were instead tasked by foreign firms to help with quality control and to perfect assembly operations. Instead of drawing upon local manufacturers of components, foreign firms brought in foreign suppliers like Flextronics and Solectron. Soon, the only major input that Mexico provided was low-skilled labor, while neither the government nor the market provided much incentive for foreign S&T manufacturers to transfer knowledge or skills to the local economy.[58]

The final blow came in 2001, when foreign computer manufacturers began to depart Mexico, leaving little domestic computer industry or indigenous STEM labor behind. The accession of China to the World Trade Organization (WTO) provided a powerful source of competition as a destination for high-tech FDI. Mexico might compete well with China on transportation costs, but not in terms of wages, skilled labor, or potential domestic market size.[59] The near-simultaneous collapse of the IT bubble put additional pressure on computer firms throughout the industry, forcing them to reduce their foreign operations, especially in relatively small IT markets like Mexico. The combination of Chinese competition and an IT industry bust thus ended Mexico's flirtation with a globally competitive high-technology sector. Had foreign high-tech investment been embedded in Mexican networks and supported by state policies to solve the S&T market failures that plagued local innovation, then leaving Mexico would have made little sense.[60] The Mexican IT industry would have innovated its way to competitiveness, not failed.

Thus, Mexico achieved some success at developing national S&T capabilities, at least within IT, during the 1970s. At that time, its domestic institutions worked to solve basic market failures associated with innovation. Mexican policy also created international and domestic networks that not only linked STEM labor together with local entrepreneurs and investors but also linked domestic innovators with foreign markets for exports, investment capital, and sources of foreign technical skills and knowledge. However, when Mexico abandoned these types of domestic institutions and international networks, she lost her bid for global high-technology competitiveness.

The point here is not that Mexico is a case of total failure, but that it is a relative one. There have indeed been pockets of innovative activity in Mexico. The city of Monterrey is a respected innovation hub, home to the top engineering school in the country, Instituto Tecnológico y de Estudios Superiores de Monterrey, which graduates a steady stream of well-qualified STEM workers, and a handful of high-tech firms. Also, in the automotive sector, for decades, Mexican firms have served as the base for supply chains that distribute product to advanced auto manufacturers across North America. Nor has Mexico's underperformance in S&T prevented the emergence of several world-class multinational corporations there, such as Cemex, Alfa, and Vitro. Yet despite these achievements, in its overall S&T performance, Mexico continues to trail behind many nations with far fewer resources.[61]

Clues in Success Versus Failure

These four case studies of relative success and failure provide important clues for explaining national innovation rates. First, each national S&T success story appears to be different, but the failures share many similarities. That is, one surprise finding in these case studies is that the common trait between successful S&T countries is their dedication, not to particular institutions or policy designs, but to solving market failures in general. There does not appear to be some "best" institutional or policy design that the world's policymakers need converge upon to achieve national S&T competitiveness. This means that nations have choices. Governments can customize their S&T institutions and policies to fit their society's culture, history, and political-economic situation. The important thing is that the market failures that obstruct innovation get solved.

What were these market failures? In each case, government needed to create a situation in which a large number of informed, rational individuals were involved in the free exchange of S&T-related goods, services, and capital. To achieve this, successful governments created institutions and policies that improved the quality and quantity of information available to market actors. Successful governments stepped in to provide, or subsidize, those goods and services (e.g., R&D and STEM education) that private markets did not provide more efficiently. Positive spillovers were not just compensated for, but encouraged. Where IPRs were weak, government either strengthened them or funded investment itself. The costs of market participation were lowered, with policymakers acting to reduce transaction costs and solve coordination dilemmas. Yet each country solved these market failures using *different* national strategies and policy approaches.

How generalizable is this finding, and how do we know it applies to other countries? That there is no single best institution or policy seems fairly conclusive. The previous chapters surveyed data on the effects of a handful of institutions and policies and cited studies that investigate dozens more. No single institution or policy, or combination of them, has yet been found to be either necessary or sufficient for promoting S&T competitiveness. Each S&T institution and policy has its strengths and weaknesses. Also, there are many highly innovative countries that score low on important institutions and policies, while many countries with healthy institutions do not innovate much at all. In fact, several countries (e.g., Taiwan, South Korea, and Israel) adopted "good" institutions only *after* they had vastly improved their S&T performance. We need more than institutions to explain why nations succeed or fail.

Social Networks

The previous studies also point us to a second, often ignored, finding: social networks make a difference.[62] The cases of Taiwan, Israel, Ireland, and Mexico each suggest that social networks play important roles in determining national S&T competitiveness. Domestic social networks must knit together STEM labor and then link it with local entrepreneurs and investors. International networks must link domestic innovators with foreign markets for exports, investment capital, and sources of technical skills and knowledge. Indeed, the tools of institutions, policies, and networks appear to build upon one another: successful domestic institutions and policies are those that, regardless of design, create and maintain domestic and international networks.[63]

What exactly are social networks doing better than markets or governments? Recently there has been an explosion of research on social networks and their roles in economic activity.[64] One consistent finding of these investigations is that social networks provide vital information that neither markets nor governments easily gather. This means that networks can sometimes bring people and resources together better than markets can. In doing so, social networks build social capital and drastically reduce the costs and risks of innovation. This may seem a bit confusing because, as chapter 4 showed, much S&T information seems almost too easy to acquire. That is, some information, such as scientific discoveries and technical knowledge, can be so inexpensive to copy and share that governments must create institutions and policies (e.g., patents, subsidies, and universities) to incentivize its production. However, the histories of national success and failure in S&T reveal that still other kinds of information are extremely difficult to get, and possessing it can drastically lower the costs and risks of innovation.

Let's illustrate this with a thought experiment. Say you manage a Boston-based firm that needs to hire a biochemical engineer for a research project to develop a new drug. Taking a free market approach, you place job advertisements with the top universities and recruitment websites. You soon receive a hundred resumes that all look amazing. Now, how do you know *which* resumes are really from highly qualified, well-experienced, responsible researchers? After all, some applicants will fib or exaggerate about their backgrounds. Others may have cheated to pass important university classes or been heavily dependent upon smarter classmates to perform their work. Still others may be intellectually qualified but irresponsible, or have a hard time finishing projects, or be psychologically unable to work well in teams. Clearly, hiring a sloppy, lazy, or incompetent engineer will drive up the costs and risks of the research project, while hiring a smart, energetic team player can lower the costs and risks of success. The problem is that none of this information is easily discernible from the resumes, or even job interviews, that typify transactions in the job market. However, this information *is* captured by a person's social network of friends and colleagues. Professors often know which of their students are smart, hard-working, and responsible. Former employers and colleagues can tell you which of their associates are "the real thing" and which are bumblers, malcontents, or frauds. Thus, one approach to hiring a good biochemical engineer is to tap into your network of friends and colleagues in industry and academia who may have personal experience with potential hires.[65] A few inexpensive phone calls and emails can get you valuable information that might be quite costly, or even unavailable, on the free market.

Moreover, networks are even better at providing *distant* information. Continuing with the previous illustration, as a manager who lives and works in Boston, you probably already have access to much information about the local talent pool and how to evaluate it, but relatively little information about more distant cities.[66] That is, you likely already know a lot about which are the best companies to poach from, and the best university laboratories to tap, in the New England region. But you probably know far less about the talent pools around Atlanta, Los Angeles, and Chicago, and have no clue about how to evaluate all those resumes coming from Asia or Europe. Once again, the free market gives you little low-cost help here. However, you likely have old college friends, ex-roommates, and former colleagues who now live in these regions who *will* have much valuable information about it. You can therefore use *your* social network as a means of accessing *their* social network, and thus tapping into all that distant knowledge. From these friends of friends, you might learn that graduates of Professor Roy Anderson's laboratory at Imperial College of London[67] or former employees of Hisamitsu Pharmaceuticals in Japan[68] are far higher quality than those coming from many universities or companies in your own backyard. These extended networks likely contain information about individuals whose reputations are entirely unknown outside their own immediate locale. Through them, you may find skilled researchers eager to move to Boston but who would never have seen your free market job advert.

This type of information problem goes beyond simply hiring good STEM workers. As the brief country studies earlier suggested, networks also contain vital information for matching entrepreneurs and investors with new S&T business opportunities. Networks also help entrepreneurs find business markets for highly specialized S&T products. Networks even aid S&T firms in finding reliable suppliers and distributors of complex products used as inputs to the R&D and production of new technology. These types of information problems plague all businesses but are especially bad in the S&T industries, where actors are so specialized and disparate, and where business conditions change so rapidly. Neither markets nor governments alone solve these kinds of information problems well, but networks can. Since networks can be domestic or international, the next sections look more deeply into how these two types of networks facilitate innovation.

Domestic Networks: Innovative Clusters

Perhaps the best way to understand how domestic networks promote innovation is by focusing on a particular type of network: the industrial or R&D cluster. Many innovation and competitiveness scholars point out that America's most innovative firms frequently cluster together in small, relatively well-defined regions. These highly innovative clusters have included Detroit's collection of carmakers, the aerospace and defense firms concentrated in Southern California, and the research triangle centered in Raleigh–Durham–Chapel Hill. Also, the cluster phenomenon is not unique to the United States. Recent examples of successful foreign clusters include India's high-tech enclave around Bangalore, the Taipei-Hsinchu corridor in Taiwan that once dominated world production of computer components, and the swath of high-performance automobile manufacturers in southern Germany. The questions for us are whether clustering is cause or effect of innovative activity and, if clusters do aid innovation, then what can government do to help create and maintain productive clusters?

Although clusters seem like a recent phenomenon, they are not new. One of the founders of modern economics, Alfred Marshall, observed in 1890 that industries have been clustering for centuries. He noted in England that specialized industries often herded together in particular regions, such as iron making in Wales, pottery in Staffordshire, and cutlery in Sheffield.[69] Marshall ascribed three benefits to clusters. First, he thought that a single location for industry-specific skills helped skilled laborers and their industrial employers to more easily find one another. Second, an industry cluster creates efficient markets for inputs that are specific to that industry. For example, manufacturers of customized auto parts want to be close to as many automakers as possible because, outside of auto production, there is little other demand for their specialized parts. So without clusters, these specialized inputs would be difficult to trade, or even find. Third, technical information about production processes and marketing naturally spill over from one firm to another. That is, clusters produce valuable industrial "gossip" that helps nearby firms to be more competitive and productive, while distant firms either never receive this technical gossip or hear it too late.

One reason clusters seem so novel is that they were generally ignored by economists and policymakers until they were rediscovered with great fanfare during the 1990s. Most prominently, Paul Krugman won a Nobel Prize in part for his 1991 research on the economics of clusters. However, he disagreed with Marshall about how clusters work. Krugman argued that economies of scale were the main benefits from, and drivers of, clusters.[70] When manufacturers locate close to each other, their major customers and suppliers will also gather nearby. This creates something like an industrial-sized bulk shopping mall with all the convenience, choice, competition, and low transportation costs that come with it. If everyone is piled into the same location, then buyers and sellers can trade in all sorts of industry-relevant products and services at the lowest possible prices.

Writing concurrently, Harvard business scholar Michael Porter took clusters to the national level. He argued that the presence of high-tech clusters helps to explain "the competitive advantage of nations."[71] He argued that clusters in the manufacturing and high-tech sectors are the driving force for increasing a country's exports and act like magnets for attracting massive FDI. Porter also observed that globalization allows firms to purchase inputs and to locate their operations wherever it is most cost-effective. Therefore, geography should not matter much for modern business activities. Yet geographic clustering still occurs. Therefore, Porter concluded that much competitive advantage must lie in the cluster rather than in particular firms. He thought that clusters worked because they provided their members with linkages, complementarities, and spillovers in all sorts of valuable assets: technology, information, skills, marketing, and customer needs. In Porter's judgment, the benefit of clusters was that they enhanced competition by creating vigorous local rivalries. That is, by combining cooperation with competition, clusters increase productivity and innovation while stimulating the formation of new businesses.

In 1994, AnnaLee Saxenian threw cold water on the cluster craze. She generally agreed with the potential benefits of clusters, but she showed how clusters can also become stagnant, unproductive, and backward. As an example, Saxenian studied the decline of one high-tech cluster, Route 128 around Boston, and compared its performance against the success of another cluster, Silicon Valley in California.[72] She found that clusters work best when they allow STEM workers to easily move from firm to firm, or even to create spin-offs or start-ups of their own. In the Boston cluster, Digital Equipment Corp (DEC) embodied all the problems of a stagnating cluster. DEC started as an entrepreneurial and innovative firm that rose to become a leading manufacturer of computer systems, software, and peripherals during the 1970s and 1980s. However, along the way, DEC evolved into a vertically integrated and highly centralized behemoth that demanded total loyalty from its workers. This type of behavior was not particular to DEC, but occurred throughout the Boston cluster. With their employees thus paralyzed, many major firms around Route 128 became isolated from one another, highly secretive, inflexible, and self-contained. Ultimately, one by one, the firms in the Boston cluster became technologically uncompetitive and backward. By the 1990s, most of the top IT firms along Route 128 went bankrupt or were forced to seek acquisition. These included industry leaders such as DEC, Wang Laboratories, Data General, Compugraphics, and Prime Computers. Route 128 provides stark evidence that clusters can fail.

The Silicon Valley cluster also experienced a crisis during the 1980s. However, these firms shared information, developed alliances, and even allowed their employees to job-hop or start their own ventures. For decades, employees from different companies across Silicon Valley met regularly to exchange ideas at trade shows, conferences, and even social gatherings. Engineers from competing firms often worked together to solve common technical problems. STEM workers and entrepreneurs throughout the region formed professional friendships based on loyalties to their craft, rather than their company. Job-hopping became commonplace, as did new ventures. One famous regional collaboration was the Homebrew Computer Club founded in 1975 as an informal group of micro-computer enthusiasts. Homebrew quickly became the breeding ground for two dozen computer companies, including Apple Computer, Osborne Computer, and North Star.[73] Thus, when the downturn in semiconductors and mainframes came, the Silicon Valley cluster recovered quickly thanks in part to a surge in start-ups, spin-offs, and collaborative ventures into new IT products and services.[74]

Since these studies were performed during the early 1990s, there has been a proliferation of clusters, as well as a flurry of government activity to promote them. In 2001, the Japanese government created a dual program to build nineteen industrial clusters and eighteen knowledge clusters throughout Japan. The following year, the Canadians launched a national innovation strategy with a goal of creating ten internationally recognized clusters within the decade. In 2004, France established one of the most aggressive cluster programs, seeking to create roughly eighty *poles de competitivite* throughout the country to promote innovation in both traditional and high-tech industries. Add to these, government support for a biotechnology cluster around Vienna in Austria, an engineering cluster around Dunedin in New Zealand, and an international life science cluster in the Medicon Valley in Scandinavia. And the entire city-state of Singapore is attempting to transform itself into a national biotech cluster.[75]

These projects have provided a wealth of data and case studies resulting in a blossoming of new research on clusters. As a result, several regularities in cluster creation and behavior have now been fairly well established. First, an abundant supply of skilled labor matters. Thick local labor markets with strong, dynamic supplies of talented and experienced workers appear to be essential for cluster success; meanwhile, a lack of skilled labor explains many cluster failures. Steady supplies of skilled labor not only attract firms to cluster in a specific region but also can often anchor firms in that region for the long run.

Second, Richard Florida and others have shown that diversity and tolerance matter. Considerable statistical data and case studies show that high concentrations of gays, "bohemians,"[76] and foreign-born residents are leading indicators of a metropolitan area's high-technology success.[77] It is not that biomolecular engineers and software designers are all gay foreign artists, but rather that populations of iconoclasts act as indicators to mobile, high-talent workers. Innovative and creative people break traditions almost by definition. Their job is to create new designs and new combinations of existing ideas. They therefore tend to seek environments where a diversity of people, experiences, and ideas provides them with ample resources to draw upon and be stimulated by. Gays or bohemians act like social "canaries in a coal mine" signaling whether a city's environment is healthy for alternative lifestyles.[78] A city with high levels of tolerance and diversity signals that all kinds of social barriers to entry should be low. All else equal, it should be easier to join networks of all types, rent apartments, buy houses, get loans, feel physically safe, and have overall better social lives; or at least differences in lifestyle and biology will not pose obstacles. The theory here is that tolerant and diverse cities attract the creative class of high-talent workers, who then attract firms, or start them, to form innovative high-technology clusters.

Third, cluster differences matter. Recent histories and case studies reveal that there is no one-size-fits-all type of cluster behavior.[79] The most important differences in clusters appear to be those of sector, size, and age or maturity. For example, younger firms and emerging industries seem to profit more from clusters than do older firms and established industries. Clusters of the former also seem to flourish better in large, economically broad cities, while clusters of more mature and routinized businesses often locate in small, specialized cities.[80] Also, different sectors produce different cluster dynamics. For example, universities and public research institutes are often essential players in biotechnology and life science clusters, but less so in automotive or industrial engineering clusters, where interfirm relationships matter far more.[81] The importance of cluster differences cannot be understated. In fact, cross-national studies of clusters show that heterogeneity across cluster types is decisive and dwarfs other differences across countries.[82]

Beyond these basic findings, innovation researchers are still figuring out why clusters work and what their benefits are. For example, clustering clearly has a strong effect on business formation for start-ups, spin-offs, subsidiaries, and suppliers. However, this could simply be a result of entrepreneurs preferring to do business in their home regions. Also, studies of firms in the new French clusters seem to show Krugman's economies of scale at work. That is, the more workers concentrated in a particular French industry and region, the higher the productivity is of the firms there. Yet the effects are small. Also, some French sectors have even seen their productivity fall as a result of clustering. Other comparisons suggest that high-technology sectors supported by the French government's new cluster policies do not seem to benefit more than other sectors.[83] It is also not yet clear the degree to which cluster benefits are sector specific or general to all clusters. This matters because if benefits are sector specific, then the concentration of firms in a given industry matters most, but if cluster benefits are cross-sectoral, then city size is most important. Perhaps most puzzling is that, as our experience with clusters grows, observers are finding that the cluster story is not all roses. For example, clusters come with considerable costs to their regions: local congestion, overburdened public goods (schools, parks, roads, and hospitals), rising local prices, less green space, and rising income inequality. It may be that when these broader negative effects are included, the benefits of clusters may not be worth the costs. Or the mix of costs and benefits might show a redistribution of wealth between the cluster's locality and the rest of the nation.[84]

The statistics on cluster development are perhaps too new to provide deep insights. Nevertheless, Figure 6.2 presents a best attempt at quantification. The y-axis is our standard measure of innovation (citations-weighted patents per capita) for the 2000–2012 period. The x-axis is a recently created measure of "State of Cluster Development" for 2014, produced by Cornell University, INSEAD, and the World Intellectual Property Organization (an agency of the United Nations) as part of their *Global Innovation Index*. The scatterplot suggests that there may be a strong relationship between clusters and innovation, but only after they are well developed. Of course, Figure 6.2 also suggests a few

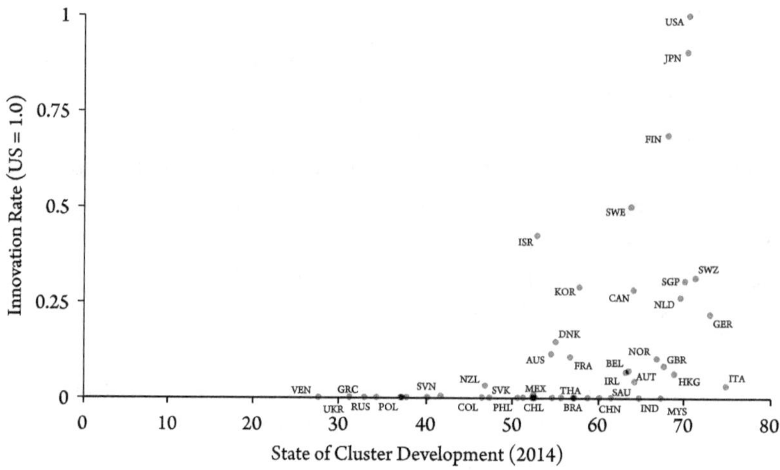

Figure 6.2 Cluster development versus innovation rate. Innovation rate is for 2000–2012. Taiwan excluded for lack of cluster data. Sources: NBER Patent Database; Global Innovation Index.

countries with well-developed clusters but that have yet to see their technology performance pick up (e.g., Italy, Hong Kong, Great Britain, Norway, and Malaysia). This may be a product of the short time span, time period selection bias, or data constraints that put the cause ahead of the effect. Or it may suggest a more nuanced, complicated relationship between clusters and innovation. Clearly additional research is needed.

It is also not yet clear what government can do to create clusters or aid their growth. There is some consensus that government can promote clusters by investing in education and infrastructure, stimulating new business formation, promoting diversity and tolerance, and guaranteeing basic civil rights and civil liberties. Government can also encourage collaborations among existing actors in regions: joint research projects, public research institutes, S&T parks, and knowledge exchange networks. However, cluster scholars also agree that many highly successful clusters are unique. Despite several attempts, Silicon Valley has not been successfully copied elsewhere.[85] Nor should governments attempt to create clusters in regions where a critical mass of infrastructure and skilled labor do not yet exist. In fact, the consensus is that top-down policy interventions are almost always ineffective at successful cluster creation.[86] Rather, the best role for government might be to clear itself, and other obstacles, out of the way of natural cluster formation.[87]

Finally, clusters are just one of many approach toward studying domestic networks and innovation. Another of the more prominent research programs is the Triple Helix theory, which focuses on national differences in the relationships between three specific sets of S&T institutions: universities, industry, and government.[88] Other scholars have used NIS as their jumping-off point, breaking down the "national" innovation system approach into a regional,[89] sectoral,[90] or technological innovation system approach, arguing that these levels of analysis allow more proximate investigation into the domestic networks that drive national S&T performance. Rounding out such a list should include scholarship on the Knowledge-Based Economy,[91] the Information Society,[92] New Production of Knowledge (Mode 1 and Mode 2),[93] and Bengt-Ake Lundvall's recent GLOBELICS (Global/Regional Networks for Economics of Learning, Innovation, and Competence Building Systems) research program.[94] Each of these places emphasis on different aspects of networks for knowledge creation, diffusion, and application.

International Networks

The case studies of Taiwan, Israel, and Ireland also reveal several ways in which international networks can improve national innovation rates. International networks provide information about distant markets for S&T. They help to match entrepreneurs and investors with foreign S&T business opportunities. For example, this is why Israel built networks between Jewish financiers in New York and San Francisco with high-tech start-ups in Tel Aviv. These networks brought into communication sets of investors and entrepreneurs who otherwise would not have found one another or gotten enough information upon which to base substantial investments into Israeli high tech. International networks also help entrepreneurs find business markets for highly specialized S&T products. This occurred, albeit in limited fashion, when Ireland set itself up as an entrepôt between US high-tech manufacturers and EU businesses. Networks even aid S&T firms in finding reliable suppliers and distributors of complex products used as inputs to the R&D and production of new technology. Here Taiwan serves as an example, where both domestic and international networks bring together far-flung, uncoordinated suppliers and distributors of advanced IT products.

But do international networks explain innovation rates in other countries? Showing the generalizability of international networks is complicated because networks are far more difficult to identify, and collect data on, than institutions. Also, recent research on social networks and innovation reveals a vast array of different types of international relationships that countries use to build national S&T competitiveness. Table 6.1 lists just a subset of them. The problem for data jocks is that there exists no single national statistic that captures the myriad international linkages listed in Table 6.1. Also, different countries have different combinations of these international networks depending on their availability, costs, benefits, and historical experience. Once again, each national S&T

Table 6.1 **International Networks Important for National Innovation Rates**

• Overseas training and education in STEM subjects
• Use of foreign consultants and technical assistance
• Overseas plant consults
• Consultations with foreign capital goods and high-technology suppliers/consumers
• Inward FDI in production and R&D facilities from more advanced countries
• Mergers and acquisitions
• Joint R&D projects, marketing agreements, and financing relationships
• Immigration of scientists, engineers, and highly skilled labor
• Establishing R&D facilities in high-tech countries
• Attendance to international expositions, conferences, and lectures
• Technology licensing agreements
• Targeted imports of capital goods and high-technology products

success story appears to be different, even though the failures may all be similar. For example, studies of innovation in Japan have highlighted that country's reliance on the reverse-engineering of imports, technology licenses, and the use of foreign consultants,[95] while the United States once relied on infusions of international capital and the immigration of scientists and high-skilled labor,[96] and many top Finnish S&T firms tapped into American and European research institutes.[97]

While this network diversity handicaps statistical analysis, researchers have looked at some of the most likely, and best-measured, indices of international S&T linkages. These measures include graduate students sent abroad to pursue STEM degrees at top-ranked universities,[98] international flows of STEM labor,[99] trade in capital goods,[100] and FDI flows.[101] Clearly, these measures only capture an imperfect subset of the many international linkages listed in Table 6.1, but the results are strong and robust. The most important finding of these analyses is that international networks strongly affect national innovation rates. Multiple studies have shown significant and positive results, regardless of statistical technique employed, time period considered, or factor controlled for (or omitted). Rough estimates suggest that, on average, international networks explain at least 20% to 30% of cross-country differences in national innovation rates.[102] This is almost exactly the amount of variation left unexplained by the domestic institutions and policies investigated in previous chapters. Studies also show that it is international networks that aid innovation rates, rather than the reverse. The networks come first, and then the innovation follows. Most important, these results hold even when controlling for democracy, free markets, political rights, and civil liberties.[103]

As a first cut, we can see this using the KOF Globalization Index.[104] Published by researchers at the Swiss Federal Institute of Technology, Zurich, the KOF Index captures economic flows, information flows, and personal and political connections between a nation and the outside world.[105] It thus provides a rough, single measure of how networked a country is to the rest of the world. The KOF Index has been calculated on a yearly basis for 207 countries over the period 1970–2010. A plot of the KOF Index against national innovation rates is presented in Figure 6.3

Figure 6.3 reveals that more globally networked countries enjoy higher national innovation rates, and that the effect of globalization appears to become stronger the more networked a country is. For example, African, Latin American, and ex–Communist bloc nations all tend to have relatively low levels of S&T performance. Of course, countries in these regions are typified by "bad" domestic institutions and policies: poorly functioning markets, loosely enforced intellectual property rights, lack of public investment in STEM education and R&D, and high levels of corruption. Hence, domestic institutions and policies seem like the primary source of their low innovation rates. However, these same countries are also typified by fewer and shallower international networks, especially with lead innovators. In contrast, Taiwan and South Korea became rapid innovators during prolonged periods of "poor" domestic institutions: martial law, one-party rule, and military dictatorship. Democratic Israel began its sprint in S&T performance during the 1970s, when its economic market institutions suffered from an increase in government intervention, subsidies, and transfers.

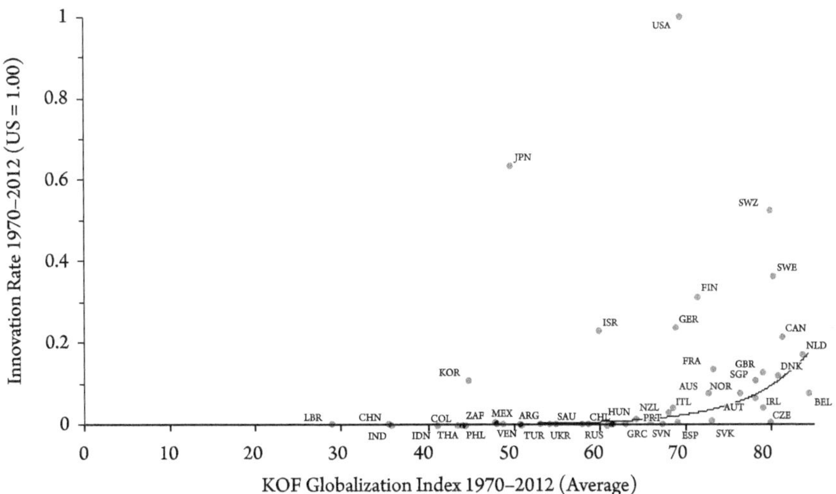

Figure 6.3 Globalization versus national innovation rate (1970–2012). Sources: NBER Patent Database (2001, 2006); USPTO; World Bank; Dreher, Axel. 2013. KOF Globalization Index. Swiss Federal Institute of Technology, Zurich http://globalization.kof.ethz.ch/

Similar histories can be told regarding Japan during the last century and the United States during its initial surge in S&T performance. In each of these countries, poor democratic and market institutions should have been inconsistent with their steadily increasing innovation rates. Yet, each of South Korea, Taiwan, Israel, Japan, and the emerging United States was typified by strong international networks, especially with lead foreign innovators, involving major transfers of scientific and technical knowledge via the types of linkages listed in Table 6.1.

Things get even more interesting when we compare the KOF Index highs and lows against the institutional "goods" and "bads." That is, we have puzzled over the fact that several countries with "good" institutions fail to innovate better than many countries with "bad" or missing institutions. The KOF Index suggests that networks might explain much of this paradox. Take, for example, France and Italy. By most measures, each has quite "good" institutions and policies. Both France and Italy have wealthy, industrialized, democratic societies that once led the world in science and technology. France still boasts at least twenty of the world's best research universities,[106] while Italy spends respectable amounts on R&D.[107] Both states also offer some of the world's strongest intellectual property rights regimes. Yet each is only a midlevel innovator, far outdone by countries with much weaker domestic institutions. Perhaps this is because both France and Italy are each poorly networked relative to most of their cohort, at least according to the KOF Index. Among the twenty-five countries this book identifies as the world's top, rapid, or midlevel innovators, France and Italy rank only twelfth and eighteenth, respectively, in their average KOF Index between 1970 and 2012. Specifically, the KOF Index gives France and Italy only middling scores in networks of trade, investment, labor, and cultural connections with the rest of the world, despite being members of the European Union and World Trade Organization.[108] A similar combination of good institutions but meager national S&T performance can also be found in New Zealand, Hungary, and Slovenia, each of which the KOF Index also ranks as relatively poorly networked.[109]

Singapore

Singapore is an excellent example of the opposite situation. From an institutional perspective, Singapore should be a dreadful environment for innovators. Since its independence in 1965, Singapore has had one of the most centralized political systems in the world, a "soft authoritarianism" in which the prime minister and his cabinet dictate policy, the legislature legitimizes it, and a politically disengaged public merely provides feedback.[110] Although Singapore strongly supports free trade, its domestic economy is far from the free market ideal. For example, the Singapore government intervenes heavily in local markets for labor, finance, education, land, housing, health care, and even entertainment. State-owned or state-linked enterprises pervade the domestic business landscape, responsible for 60% of GDP in some years. The state is especially interventionist in Singapore's aerospace, telecommunications, military, steel, and shipbuilding industries.[111] Singapore does score well on its research universities and STEM education, but critics charge that its students are taught rote memorization, not independent analysis or critical thinking, which are key to innovating.[112] Singapore also gets only middling scores for intellectual property rights protections.[113] Yet, despite these institutional and policy "failures," Singapore is a rapid innovator.

Singapore's success at S&T is largely due to the fact that it is one of the most well-networked societies in the world, both internationally and domestically. For example, the KOF Index has placed Singapore among its top ten most globalized economies almost every year since 1970. A closer look reveals that, in STEM-based industries, Singapore has for decades aggressively recruited prominent high-tech multinationals to set up research and manufacturing centers there. These MNCs include leading S&T firms such as Hewlett-Packard, Hitachi, Siemens, IBM, Infineon, and Flextronics, which have brought an enormous amount of innovative capacity to the city-state. One can also find in Singapore a transnational elite of expatriates who play a vital part in entrepreneurship, R&D, and directing foreign investment into local S&T-based industries.[114] Foreign researchers and instructors saturate Singapore's top universities, which have also developed extensive links with other top research universities around the world.[115] This has vastly improved Singapore's R&D performance, while simultaneously turning the city-state into a regional STEM research and education hub.[116] Singapore has even set up industrial parks in foreign countries.[117] At home, the government of Singapore has been active in linking domestic manufacturers and processors to global production networks in chemicals, electronics, transportation equipment, and most recently biotechnology.[118] In sum, networking has done much good for Singapore's capacity to innovate.[119]

The Two Koreas

Networks also help to explain the "two Koreas" case frequently offered as compelling evidence that "good" domestic institutions determine innovation rates.[120] The standard story goes something like this: after World War II, the once united Korean peninsula split into two countries, each with drastically different institutions and policies that explain their different economic and technological trajectories. On the one hand, South Korea supposedly embraced strong property rights and free markets for trading them. The government in Seoul ruled according to an unbiased set of laws and created a level playing field for business and a competitive environment for free entry and exit. As a result, South Korea has evolved into one of the world's top innovators, with globally competitive S&T industries such as electronics, semiconductor chips, automobiles, cellular phones, and most recently biotechnology.[121] On the other hand, North Korea became a highly centralized, totalitarian state, a modern satrapy based on the ruling Kim family dynasty with few political freedoms, private property rights, or free markets. As a result, according to this argument, North Korea remains today a woefully underdeveloped and technologically backward economy, heavily dependent on China, and suffering from regular famines, anemic industries, and poor living standards.

Of course, the truth is more complicated. First, South Korea became a democracy only very recently. After World War II, South Korea turned into an authoritarian state whose leaders fixed elections and brutally repressed free speech, protests, and political competition until 1987. The military, which seized power in 1961, did not lose its hold on South Korea's presidency until 1993.[122] Opposition parties were not fully integrated into the Korean political system until they were allowed to win the presidency in late 1997.[123] Thus, South Korea democratized long *after* it became wealthy and innovative.

Nor has South Korea ever had a free market economy.[124] As late as the 1990s and 2000s, the Heritage Foundation ranked South Korea's economy as merely "moderately free." This is because the South Korean state has always intervened heavily to direct markets there,[125] with a special emphasis on building massive, state-supported, national champions, known as *chaebol,* which still dominate South Korea's S&T sectors, as well as many basic and intermediate industries. These *chaebol* include such well-known high-tech behemoths as Samsung, LG, and Hyundai.[126] Meanwhile, dozens of government-affiliated research institutes supply industrially oriented, basic R&D to firms throughout the South Korean economy. Even today, South Korea's intellectual property rights protections rank below those of much of Western Europe, the United States, Canada, and Japan.[127] Yes South Korea is innovative, but not as a result of free markets and liberal democracy.

Rather, what the institutionalists ignore is that South Korea and North Korea also differed in their approach toward social networks. South Korea knitted itself deeply into specific foreign trade, financial, and technical networks, first with the United States and then with Japan, which gave it access to vital S&T knowledge, as well as investment capital and access to international markets.[128] South Korea did protect its budding S&T industries from foreign competition and kept out much FDI, but otherwise it built impressive networks both domestically and internationally. It accepted generous amounts of financial aid from the United States and Japan, which Seoul then used to build up new industries and subsidize exporters. For decades, South Korea also massively imported capital goods, technology licenses, and foreign technical assistance, most heavily from Japan. This allowed South Korea to persistently enter ever more advanced S&T-based industries on a regular basis. Also, since the 1960s, thousands of South Korean graduate students have been sent abroad to attend the world's top-ranked S&T research universities, where they earned advanced degrees in STEM subjects before returning home.[129] Domestically, the large, diversified *chaebol* quickly became the focal points of national and international networks, which brought together STEM workers, state and private finance, and local businessmen around the formation of new S&T-based firms and product lines. The *chaebol* also liberally doled out technical advice to their suppliers and circulated STEM personnel, while sending many of their own workers and managers to be trained abroad in advanced S&T countries. It was these networks that were the keys to South Korea's rapid innovation rate.[130]

Conversely, North Korea mostly cut itself off from the world.[131] International trade has always been heavily restricted there, with imports dominated by raw materials, often from China.[132] North Korea's major international industries are smuggling, drug trafficking, counterfeiting, and illicit arms trade. The dictatorship in Pyongyang has effectively sealed the country's borders to international flows of human capital and information. Few, if any, North Koreans received S&T degrees at foreign research universities, joined international research collaborations, or attended international S&T conferences. Little foreign investment or trade was allowed with nations at the S&T frontier. Even foreign books, journals, and magazines on S&T subjects are stopped at the North Korean border or only circulated under tight restrictions. The North Korean economy maintains only tenuous ties with Koreans worldwide and supporters in Beijing, while Pyongyang has bullied South Korea, Japan, Europe, and the United States for aid, and allowed a modicum of technology transfer to pass through its border with China. Otherwise, North Korea is generally considered to be the least networked country in the world.[133]

The "institutions rule!" argument also ignores the two areas where North Korea has excelled in S&T: missile technology and nuclear weapons. These are precisely the fields in which North Korea has aggressively tapped into international networks while simultaneously setting up domestic networks. In most aspects, North Korea is a self-consciously isolated "hermit kingdom," whose political elites see autarky as the key to both their personal power and state security.[134] Yet, to achieve a successful nuclear weapons program, even North Korea had to establish international networks to finance research, transfer skills and technologies, and access technical advice.[135] The Soviets supplied a research reactor and trained North Korean nuclear scientists and engineers, Pakistan transferred enrichment skills and centrifuge technology, China provided further

S&T training, firms in France and Austria supplied nuclear equipment, and North Korea's first "indigenous" success was actually based on British reactor designs.[136]

This does not mean that domestic institutions and policies are irrelevant to the North Korea case, just that they are not sufficient to explain that nation's S&T trajectory. The North Korean government did set up dozens of engineering enterprises, major research centers, and a national academy of science. These institutions solved basic market failures by reducing the transactions costs and spreading the risks of research while providing identifiable focal points of investment in an information-poor, nonmarket society. These STEM workers and business managers were then networked together domestically into a North Korean military-industrial complex.[137] Thus, even in a country where political elites are jealous of competing domestic power centers, leaders were forced to create the institutions *and* networks necessary to acquire the S&T capabilities required for a successful nuclear weapons program.[138]

Together, these stylized observations suggest that to better understand the sources of national competitiveness in S&T, perhaps we should focus less exclusively on comparisons of domestic institutions and policies and examine more deeply the effects of networks. International and domestic networks may affect innovation rates by acting as conduits for valuable scientific and technical knowledge, by allowing the formation of epistemic or business communities, or perhaps via mechanisms not yet identified. This is not to argue that domestic institutions are insignificant, but that failure to consider the scope and depth of a country's networks constitutes a source of omitted variable bias and a competing explanation for innovation rates. Therefore, factors such as those listed in Table 6.1, especially between lead innovators and other countries, should be examined for their effects on innovation. Put simply, social networks play a pivotal role in innovation!

Standards

One cannot discuss networks without also emphasizing the importance of standards. Standards can be loosely defined as well-documented technical specifications for goods, services, and activities. They can be as basic as measurements, weights, or languages; they can also be fairly abstruse, like the number of connector pins on a printer cable or the precise voltage of a transmission line. While all types of standards can be important, technology standards have become a major twenty-first-century policy tool for improving national innovation rates. Research on standards has yet to develop a large body of cross-national case studies or statistical data over time. Consequently, this book does not offer hypotheses on which particular differences in standards affect national innovation rates. However, standards have emerged as a powerful tool used by some actors to affect innovation. Therefore, standards may be the future of innovation research and deserve a basic explanation here.

Standards are the sine qua non for a successful network because they enable communication between network participants, be they individuals, companies, industries, or governments. Without standards, individual actors cannot network properly because they cannot understand one another. They will speak somewhat different languages, and thus end up talking past one another, resulting in failed connections or fruitless debates even where there may be no real disagreement. Standards therefore enable productive coordination and exchange among network participants. Standards also determine how large a network can get and how well its participants can interoperate.

Standards are so pervasive in our everyday lives that we tend to ignore them; but when standards break down, the results can be catastrophic. Such a standards tragedy struck NASA in 1999 when it lost the Mars Climate Orbiter just hours before achieving orbit. Apparently, the spacecraft entered Mars's atmosphere 60 kilometers above the surface instead of the planned 150 kilometers, thereby ruining the mission. A review of the accident found that "one team used English units [inches, feet, and pounds] while the other used metric units for a key spacecraft operation."[139] This simple mismatch in measurement standards resulted in a $94 million disaster and the loss of years of astronomical exploration. Nor are standards a problem reserved for major science and technology projects. Every day individuals encounter standards issues whenever they try to charge an American electric device in a foreign country's socket, attempt to open a new computer file with old software, or want to use mobile phones on different networks.

Standards are particularly vital for innovation because they also solve coordination problems that can cause both networks and markets to fail. These are situations in which everyone can benefit from cooperation, but only if they make mutually consistent decisions over time. Should we use metric or English measurements? Build a 220-volt or 110-volt electrical system? Transmit television signals on the 450- to 460-MHz band or the 470- to 480-MHz band of the frequency spectrum? These are often noncontroversial, but strategic, interactions that must be resolved for producers and consumers of new technology to progress. The coordination problem occurs because there are multiple options, none of which may be any more or less desirable than the other. Society simply needs to agree upon one, a standard, and stick to it.

Standards can also solve information problems. In some cases, innovators will not produce a new technology unless they are confident that it will operate with existing or subsequent technologies. Meanwhile, consumers may hold back from purchasing a new technology if they are unsure of its quality, safety, or ability to work with technologies that they have already purchased. If consumers are reluctant to buy and producers are hesitant to sell, then a classic "market for lemons" failure can develop in which the market shrinks as participants pull out due to uncertainty. By confirming that a new wireless router meets IEEE 802.11, a major printing firm adheres to ISO 14001, or a new electric lathe satisfies NFPA 70E, standards provide vital information that reduces risk, improves trust, and lowers the transaction costs involved in the production and consumption of new technology.

Standards' best function may be in building economies of scale. Imagine a world in which every ten miles the following occurred: subway and railroad tracks changed their gauge, cell phone networks changed their frequencies and encoding rules, DVD players used different formats, and the Internet used different address and routing protocols. The result would be millions of fragmented technology markets, each only ten miles in diameter. In this fragmented world, it would be prohibitively expensive to produce a different train, cell phone, DVD player, or Internet software for each tiny market. Meanwhile, to function, consumers traveling through this splintered land would be forced to switch technologies every ten miles. The whole situation would be ludicrously expensive, difficult to use, and nightmarishly annoying. The use of nationwide or global technology standards avoids this type of problem. When a standard is adopted across a large economic area, then it allows for large economies of scale, and thus lower costs and prices. Meanwhile, the ability to use a single computer laptop, cell phone, or train that operates seamlessly across state lines or national borders increases the usefulness of these technologies, while indirectly driving down costs, for consumers.

Where do standards come from? Technology standards can come from one of three sources. First, the market itself can converge on a standard. After all, given the enormous benefits of standards, it makes good sense for private actors to provide them. The problem here is that first-movers can gain a competitive advantage over their rivals. Because a standard grows more valuable as more producers and consumers adopt it (i.e., due to network effects and economies of scale), if a producer can get the market to converge on its standard first, then that producer can then use its standard to dominate the market. Other competing standards will be driven out simply because they came too late, leaving the victor to charge exorbitant licensing fees and, some argue, little incentive to innovate or improve quality. This is especially true when a firm's patented or proprietary technology is linked to a particular standard, such as the Microsoft operating system, ETSI's GSM cell phone standard, JVC's VHS format for videotapes, or Philips's compact disc format. Each of these firms won highly lucrative "standards wars," and sometimes near monopolies, over their rivals: Apple's

Mac operating system, Qualcomm's CDMA cellular network, Sony's Betamax videocassette, and Sony's digital audio tape.[140]

Perhaps most frustrating is when the private market converges on an inferior standard, which then gets locked in because that standard becomes so widely used that it becomes too costly to switch to a superior standard. The QWERTY keyboard is the classic example. It was purposely designed to slow typewriting speeds because early typewriters jammed easily. Yet, after the jamming issues were resolved, the inefficient QWERTY system stuck because producers and consumers had already invested so much time and money into it. An attempt to diffuse a far more efficient DVORAK keyboard was made during the 1930s and 1940s. Despite the fact that the DVORAK keyboard required less finger motion, increased typing rates, and reduced errors, it failed miserably because the QWERTY keyboard was locked in by decades of popular adoption.[141] Other examples of lock-in include light water nuclear power reactors (whose inefficiencies contributed to the Three Mile Island nuclear disaster), fossil fuels (which dominate global energy markets but pollute the environment while enriching many autocracies and terrorist states), and the widely used Microsoft Windows and Office software (which critics argue offer performance inferior to smaller, niche competitors).

A second source of technology standards is formal standards organizations. These can be national bodies, like France's Association Francaise de Normalisation (AFNOR), or international bodies, the most well known and active of which are the International Organization for Standardization (ISO), the International Association of Electrical and Electronics Engineers (IEEE), and the International Telecommunication Union (ITU).[142] These standards organizations can be quite productive and effective, and are the authors of the lion's share of all standards in existence. For example, since its founding in 1947, the ISO has published over 19,000 international standards covering almost all aspects of technology and business (e.g., food safety, manufacturing, computers, aircraft, agriculture, and health care). These organizations are private; hence, their standards are voluntary. The ISO, IEEE, and ITU and their institutional kin have no enforcement power, though national governments often adopt and reference their standards in state regulations.

In standards organizations, the technical work of designing standards is typically carried out by a large network of hundreds of committees, subcommittees, and working groups. They provide forums for debate and decision making that often include tens of thousands of experts from industry, research institutes, public regulatory agencies, and noncommercial interest groups. For international standards organizations (ISO and ITU), representatives of national standards design organizations are often the main contributors (e.g., ANSI for the United States, DNI for Germany, and BSI for the Great Britain).

The problem with standards organizations is that producers and businesses tend to be well represented within them, consumers not so much. This is because, although consumers of new technology are deeply affected by the outcome of the standardization process, they do not generally participate in the standardization process. For most consumers, the personal costs of participation are simply too high relative to the diffuse benefits received. Also, the technical knowledge required to participate constructively in standards deliberations is often too arcane for the average consumer. Even when consumers are involved, they often have no influence on the outcome of the standardization process. Hence, one problem for policymakers is to ensure that the interests of consumers are better taken into account by standards organizations.

To avoid the monopoly problems of market-driven standards or the producer bias of institution-driven standards, many argue for a third source of standards: government. Part of the justification here is that many standards have a public goods nature. Like new scientific knowledge, standards are often nonrival and nonexcludable; therefore, there is an economic justification for the state to provide them. Alternately, where standards have a private goods nature, government can prevent a single firm from using its proprietary standards to dominate the markets. This is exactly what AT&T did with telephony, and threatened to do with computing, during the first half of the twentieth century. For decades, AT&T used its legal control over its proprietary telecommunications standards to eliminate rivals and prevent new competition from arising, even in minor products like peripheral equipment. Any new technology that interacted with the AT&T network was banned as a violation of its legal monopoly until the government stepped in to demand more open access.[143] Similarly, IBM used its computer hardware and software standards to monopolize business computing during the 1960s and 1970s until government forced the firm to allow competitors to interoperate.[144] The solutions in these examples took the form of antitrust; however, the creation or adoption of public standards may be a more efficient response. Governments may also be best at producing and enforcing those minimum quality standards that ensure the provision of other public goods such as health, safety, security, and environmental protection.

Governments have also used standards to advance national economic agendas. For example, from the 1970s onward, Japan used its national standards to keep out imports of foreign pharmaceuticals, agricultural goods, and even foreign snow skis on the excuse that these products were not compatible with Japanese physiology, nutrition, or snow. Similarly protectionist standards were supported by the governments of European high-tech exporting nations such as France and Germany. In response, the World Trade Organization included standards in its 1995 formative agreements. Member states of the WTO are now required to adopt international standards where they exist and cannot knowingly use standards to discriminate against foreign imports. However, this has not kept governments from using technology standards to advance national agendas.[145]

Currently, the advent of Chinese national technology standards looms as a potential S&T power play.[146] Since the mid-1990s, China has made technology standards part of its national strategy to develop indigenous innovation capabilities free of foreign technology or expertise. China also uses domestic standards to reduce its dependence on, and royalty payments for, foreign standards and to redirect those royalties and sales to Chinese entities. For example, toward these ends, the Chinese government first backed a domestic video compact disc standard called Super Video CD (SVCD). SVCD enjoyed short-run success until it was dislodged by the DVD standard developed by an alliance of Japanese, American, and European companies. Similarly, in 1995, the Chinese government committed itself to developing a national, third-generation (3G) mobile telephony standard, TD-SCDMA. China succeeded in getting the ITU to accept this standard as "international" alongside its European competitors. The Chinese government then invested billions of renminbi to develop TD-SCDMA, while refusing also to permit the rollout of 3G telephony services in China until TD-SCDMA was ready for commercial use.[147] In yet another instance, in 2003, China used standards to improve its firms' position in the wireless LAN sector. Beijing announced a new effort to create a unique, indigenous, and mandatory local wireless Internet protocol standard called WAPI. The technical details of WAPI were then provided exclusively to only eleven Chinese producers. This meant that foreign manufactures seeking to sell wireless network devices on the Chinese market would be forced to make deals with these Chinese firms.

Despite these efforts, the jury is still out on the effects of standards on national innovation rates and the proper role for government. Governments can sometimes act like "blind giants" in standards development, rolling out standards too slowly or designing standards that are inferior. For example, China's TD-SCDMA standard suffered constant development delays, taking nearly fifteen years to publish. Also, because the Chinese government forced all 3G services to wait on TD-SCDMA, it inadvertently slowed Chinese innovation in, and adoption of, mobile telephony throughout the country. Worse yet, by the time the 3G TD-SCDMA standard finally made it to market in 2010, the rest of the world had moved on to a more advanced 4G standard. Nor did China achieve its goals with its WAPI standard. It immediately provoked a trade dispute with the United States, and WAPI was subsequently rejected by the ISO in 2006. While WAPI still exists as a "preference" of the Chinese government, it has failed as a monopolistic domestic standard.[148] Yet, although China's schemes failed to protect domestic markets, their push for indigenous standards did succeed at fostering R&D (perhaps even more effectively than direct R&D subsidies), developing interfirm networks, and forcing foreign owners of proprietary standards to lower their royalty rates for Chinese producers.[149]

Most studies suggest that standards can help innovation, economic growth, and competitiveness in international trade under certain conditions. These conditions are that standards should be widely accessible at all stages of their development and publication, be openly arrived at through a broad consensus of stakeholders, and be applied globally with little or no charge for implementation.[150] Government may have a useful role in creating and mandating minimum health, safety, and environmental quality standards. Government can also keep the standards process open and accessible, perhaps even representing excluded interests at negotiating forums. However, for standards that promote technical compatibility, information provision, or variety reduction, government should likely hold back from design or mandates. Rather, the problem that government must address is that, over time, standards can grow obsolete, not appear when needed, or become so dense that they act like a standards "thicket" that restrains innovation. In these cases, one role for government might be to act like a diligent gardener pruning her trees to maximize their bloom. This means promoting comprehensive coverage of standards, but also encouraging innovation, limiting monopolization, minimizing duplication, and quickly cutting out the dead wood of obsolete standards.[151]

Conclusions

This chapter has revealed that there do exist additional tools, often ignored in the institutions and policy debate, that governments can use to improve S&T competitiveness: networks. Networks help to explain why institutions and policies alone are not sufficient for achieving national success in S&T. That is, success at S&T is not simply a matter of governments solving market failures, but also of dealing with network failures. States that seek innovative economies must first knit together domestic networks of STEM labor with local entrepreneurs and investors. Then, the government must help create several types of international networks, especially linkages between domestic innovators and foreign markets for exports, investment capital, and sources of technical skills and knowledge. Nations must also be strategic about decisions to create and internationalize technology standards, and whether to accept foreign ones. This also explains why a focus on *domestic* factors alone cannot explain national innovation rates. Successful S&T states are typified by *international* networks of trade, finance, production, knowledge, and human capital flows that play important roles in determining national innovation rates.

At last, we now have a better explanation of *how* countries innovate. The most innovative nations are those that design domestic institutions and policies to solve the basic public goods problems that plague S&T progress. Theoretically, this means that successful institutions must lower transaction costs, lower information costs, spread out and reduce risk, and provide those collective public goods not well provided by private markets. In practice, it means that the state must create institutions that help to sustain R&D, the education and training of STEM labor, technology and knowledge transfer, information on consumer markets, and above all inexpensive, patient financial capital. But innovative societies must *also* create and maintain networks, both domestic and international, to store knowledge, transmit information, and build the trust and social capital essential for new S&T ventures. Indeed, these three tools (institutions, policies, and networks) must build upon one another. Specifically, the case studies explored by this chapter clearly showed the importance of domestic institutions and policies that create and maintain both domestic and international networks.

Finally, nations still have choices. As yet, there is no evidence that a specific type of network must be combined with particular institutions or policies to create a "special sauce" for S&T competitiveness. There is no one best type of institution, policy, or network upon which all countries must converge. Nor do networks constitute a "silver bullet." They can just as easily be used for fostering drug trafficking, tourism, or illicit financial transactions as for S&T progress. Like institutions, networks are not causal forces; they are a means to a national technological end. This fact helps to explain the vast differences among the success stories.

Of course, this still leaves us with a major puzzle: *why* do some societies create institutions, policies, and networks to aid innovation, while other states fail to do this? Why don't all governments acquire the necessary tools (institutions, policies, and networks) for innovation, use them properly, and maintain them over time? The answer is that S&T progress has subtle enemies. These enemies are the interest groups that feel threatened by new S&T or by the institutions and policies that aid innovation. They react by resorting to politics. They pressure government to alter national institutions and policies to slow down S&T over the long run. The next chapter introduces us to these enemies and explains what they do to harm national innovation rates, and why. Until we understand the resistance against S&T, we cannot fully explain national innovation rates.

PART THREE

WHY DO NATIONS INNOVATE?

Creative Insecurity

7

Technological Losers and Political Resistance to Innovation

Let's briefly recap where our investigation stands. Most explanations of Cardwell's Law tend to conflate the *how* and *why* of national innovation rates. For example, the last three chapters surveyed the major policy, institutional, and network explanations for Cardwell's Law. We found that, if a nation wants to improve its science and technology (S&T) performance, then its government must act to solve both market failures and network failures. This is the lesson suggested by a vast inventory of case histories, statistical analyses, anecdotal evidence, and even country and industry studies by innovation researchers. It makes good theoretical sense too. But this lesson only tells us half the story. Institutions, policies, and networks explain *how* nations innovate, but not *why*. That is, if the solution to the innovation puzzle is just "fix markets and create networks," then it leaves us asking: why do some governments create and support markets and networks for S&T better than others? Markets and networks just move us down the causal chain. After all, for perhaps hundreds of years, people have advocated for stronger intellectual property rights, research and development (R&D) spending, the establishment of universities, the advancement of education, and strategic trade initiatives to foster national S&T competitiveness. If policymakers and constituents alike already know so well how to improve innovation, then why do so many countries fail to do it well? Why do some countries allocate more resources to implement "good" S&T institutions, policies, and networks, and why are they better at maintaining them, than others? The next three chapters attempt to answer the *why* question.[1] And perhaps the best way to begin is with a tale of technological failure from early nineteenth-century England.

Early Automobiles: The Revolution That Failed

On July 27, 1829, a new technology appeared on the country roads of Great Britain: the first automobile.[2] This test vehicle was a steam-powered coach that, having been developed to "perfection" by its inventor, Dr. Goldsworthy Gurney, proceeded to drive ninety miles from the outskirts of London to Bath. Gurney's steam coach reached speeds of fourteen miles per hour that day, leaving behind the traditional horse-drawn mail carriages and phaetons. After this successful road test, Gurney made arrangements to offer regular passenger service and won the financial backing of engineers, bankers, military men, and a retired East India Company official. His first steam carriage route opened in February 1831 over the bumpy road between Cheltenham and Gloucester. Developing their own technologies, dozens of competing steam carriage lines soon appeared across Great Britain during the 1830s. Meanwhile, Gurney demonstrated his automobiles to the Duke of Wellington and the British army. Soon, investing in steam carriage companies became a popular fad among financial speculators. With additional innovation, steam cars got faster, leading some observers to predict top speeds of fifty miles per hour. The steam carriage also appeared in the United States, where a rudimentary steam car company was founded as early as 1832, and in France, Germany, and Belgium, where auto innovation and entrepreneurialism took somewhat longer to sprout.

Gurney's automobile *should* have changed the world, ushering in a wave of innovation and thereby revolutionizing ground transport. There was certainly a market for this kind of technological change. Steam had been transforming the operation of mines across Europe since the early 1710s, of factories since 1790, and of boats and shipping since 1807.[3] Thus, the application of steam power to land transport was a natural progression. Indeed, after they were introduced by Goldsworthy Gurney, British steam-powered carriages gained in popularity during the early 1830s, selling tens of thousands of passenger miles in a few short years. Steam carriage service was especially valued by the lower classes, who could not afford personal horse carriages, and because riding in a steam carriage was fast and relatively comfortable. It was also economical. A trip on one of Gurney's steam coaches cost only one shilling, while the same trip on a stagecoach with four horses cost two shillings.

However, by the end of 1832, Gurney was out of business, and his fellow competitors gradually followed. By 1841, the British automobile industry was comatose, and automotive innovation slept with it for the next forty years. Automobile ventures in other nations followed suit, virtually killing innovation around the world in the fledgling industry. The automobile became, once again, a pursuit for individual hobbyists or a curiosity occasionally displayed at fairs and exhibitions. It was only when the internal combustion engine appeared, run by petroleum, that sustained interest in automobile innovation took hold again. As a result, most people today identify the inventions of Karl Benz and Gottlieb Daimler in 1885–1886 as holding the title of "first automobiles," while Gurney and his innovations have been forgotten.

What killed Britain's first automobiles? The same force that retards much innovation around the world today: political opposition from the "losers" created by new S&T. As long as Gurney's steam carriage was a personal hobby, it troubled few people. However, as it improved into a viable business, the steam car came to threaten a wide range of interest groups across Britain. Horse-drawn stagecoach proprietors feared for their incomes if steam power were to replace horses. So too did stable-hands and the landlords who sold oats and rented stables to the traditional stagecoach industry. Road trustees, horse owners, and pedestrians, as well as farmers with land adjoining steam carriage routes, became convinced to oppose steam cars on turnpike roads as a nuisance and lethal danger. Yet by far, most damaging to steam carriages was the emerging railroad industry and its beneficiaries, who refused to tolerate any competition for passengers, freight, or investment capital.

To stop their common enemy, these opponents resorted to politics. They put forward a vast arsenal of "objective" arguments for why steam carriages must be heavily taxed and regulated by Parliament. Road trustees complained of damage to the roads and irresponsible business models. The horse industry warned of boiler explosions and accidents from steam carriages. Civic and cultural elites worried that important landmarks and buildings might be damaged. The railroad industry cautioned that steam cars frightened people and horses, thus disrupting work and travel. Certainly, each of these complaints could be leveled equally at the railroads themselves. However, the railroads were much more profitable and benefited far more, and more powerful, interest groups. Therefore, political resistance to the railways was muted. Also, railroad representatives sat on every parliamentary panel related to steam carriages and served as frequent witnesses in investigations. There was plenty of proof and testimony that steam cars made good economic sense and did not scare horses, blow up, or destroy roads. Nonetheless, a parliamentary committee found in 1836 that steam carriages were dangerous and expensive, while railroads faced none of these official criticisms or committees.

In response to this widespread and well-financed political pressure, Parliament and local governments soon placed heavy taxes and regulations on the steam carriage industry. Road trustees charged exorbitant tolls or littered rocks on their roads to obstruct the carriages. On some roads, steam vehicles were required to pay six times the toll levied against horse-drawn carriages. As these tolls sprang up across England, they became a de facto injunction against steam carriage companies and bought the railroad interests valuable time to organize their representatives in Parliament. By the mid-1830s, the British government at all levels was increasingly captured by railroad supporters, who defeated most attempts to repeal the exorbitant tolls on steam cars. Worse yet, new ordinances were enacted to place severe speed limits on steam carriages. They were restricted to ten miles per hour on the country roads, about the same as a horse-drawn carriage, and five miles per hour in the cities, despite the fact that a city horse omnibus went faster, seven miles per hour. In some urban districts, steam carriages were even banned outright as "inconvenient." Perhaps most onerous was the infamous Red Flag Act, which required a man to walk one hundred yards ahead of any steam carriage to warn other traffic of its approach.

These tolls and regulations were both ubiquitous and fatal to automobile innovation. Throughout Great Britain, wherever a new steam carriage line appeared, new tolls were suddenly levied, sometimes after the first run. As the tolls hit and began to force steamline closures, the reality of government opposition began to scare away investors, entrepreneurs, and innovators alike. Railway firms also warned and threatened investors against financing steam cars, while enticing them to put their money into rails. After all, railroads had vastly greater economies of scale, were natural monopolies, and enjoyed ever-growing support in Parliament. Investors and bankers now piled their money into rails instead, producing a sudden acceleration of capital flows into England's railways after 1835. Entrepreneurs and innovators willing to get into railroads could quickly become flush with investment finance. Thereafter, a steady flow of bills from Parliament further favored railways and discriminated against steamcars, forcing the extinction of regular steam carriage service throughout the United Kingdom by 1839.

Experiments with steam carriages outside of Great Britain were similarly cut short by opponents during the early and mid-1800s. France created prohibitive regulations and registration requirements, while also restricting the speed limits of steam carriages so that they could not compete well with horses. In Germany, steam carriages often faced outright bans and drivers were arrested. In the capital-scarce United States, railroads (often funded by British financiers) absorbed all the available capital, leaving little for steam carriage investment, especially since steam cars could not compete over the much longer travel distances there.

The first automobile revolution was thus aborted, shortly after it began. With tolls and regulations eliminating steam carriage profits, both investors and innovators turned their energies elsewhere. They would reappear in strength only after the returns on investment in railroads had slowed to a trickle and interest had formed around a new investment: petroleum.

Innovation and Its Discontents

The Gurney steam carriage is a typical example of how innovation can be waylaid by political forces. Unfortunately, Gurney's steam carriage is just one of thousands, perhaps millions, of innovations that have been slowed or stopped by political opposition from the losers they threatened.[4] Examples of resistance to new technology can be cited at great length. We can find cases of political or economic resistance to innovations across all sectors and countries throughout history, including silk reeling in Meiji Japan,[5] fishing in Sweden,[6] timber processing in Norway,[7] newspaper production in modern Britain,[8] semiconductors in France,[9] HIV-safe blood products around the industrialized world,[10] mechanical lathes in Renaissance Europe,[11] and even freight transport in ancient Rome.[12]

Political resistance to new S&T throws a wrench into traditional theories of national innovation rates, and can wreck the policies and institutions designed to promote innovation. It contradicts popular assumptions about innovation. That is, following the prescriptions of free market economics, and plain common sense, we tend to assume that innovation is neutral:[13] new S&T acts to expand the production and consumption possibilities for the nation; innovation therefore benefits everyone, especially in the long run. According to this assumption, the only opponents to technological progress are either inefficient rent seekers or irrational Luddites.[14] Thus, the primary obstacles to technological progress are the market and network failures discussed thus far.

This chapter shows that this stereotype is incorrect. Scientific progress and technological change are *not* neutral. New S&T helps some, but hurts others. Sometimes those hurt by new S&T are steadily and irrevocably wiped out.[15] For example, new S&T is economically distributive in that it allows people to perform established activities with increased efficiency. It can therefore give its adopters a competitive advantage within the economy by increasing productivity or through factor accumulation. Sociologists and historians have also shown that new science and technology can empower or disadvantage one social group over others by changing the demand for labor, changing the patterns of consumption, or altering access to information.[16] New S&T can also change the nature of human activity in work, communications, war, manufacturing, transportation, and so forth and thereby fundamentally alter the roles or identities of the people performing these activities, and hence their social, economic, or political standing.[17] New S&T can erode the wealth and political power of everyone tied to the old, doomed S&T. So too can new S&T institutions, policies, and networks. They can redistribute wealth, power, and prestige in the same manner as innovation itself. This means that even if people universally support S&T progress, some might oppose the institutions and policies necessary to promote innovation.

It is this aspect of innovation—change that threatens some groups and favors others—that is often ignored in discussions of S&T policies and institutions.[18] Such threats lie at the core of economist Joseph Schumpeter's insights into innovation. He called innovation "creative destruction," the killing off of the old by the new.[19] The destruction element is crucial for Schumpeter as it clears the path for the new. Airlines killed off intercity passenger railroads and cross-ocean liners in the process of improving commercial and recreational travel. The premium that people were willing to pay for faster travel gradually ate away alternative transport as airliner safety and comfort improved. Schumpeter's insight explains the opposition to innovation. The losers see their fate. Innovation may benefit society, but it has its victims, and these victims fight back.

The argument is *not* that these "technological losers" oppose *all* S&T. Only rarely does one find technophobes yearning to live in grass huts or revert society back to preindustrial simplicity. In fact, most "losers" openly admire S&T in general. Rather, their opposition is usually targeted at a particular innovation that threatens *their* personal economic wealth, social rank, political power, or strongly held cultural values. Nor is this opposition uncommon or particularly evil. In fact, most of us are guilty of this kind of opposition to new S&T, at least indirectly. For example, neither gasoline consumers nor the oil industry are fond of paying taxes to support alternative energy research. Labor unions fight technologies that can replace workers. Vacationers and business owners on Cape Cod fiercely obstruct plans to build ugly windmills off their coast. Evangelical Christians do not want their tax dollars spent on stem cell research or new contraception technologies. No one wants a nuclear power plant or waste dump in their neighborhood. We love S&T, just not the particular innovations that threaten our individual interests, and we do not want to personally bear the costs or risks of developing or diffusing new S&T.

The problem is that even small, indirect opposition to bits and pieces of S&T can add up to have large effects. When the "losers" fight a particular technology, they also fight the industry that produces it, and all of the jobs and investors involved. If these status quo groups win, then they can deter future innovators, entrepreneurs, and investors from risking their time, energy, and resources on other new technologies. All of the taxes, regulations, subsidies, and so forth for which the losers fight can add up to slow S&T progress across society. It becomes death by a thousand cuts, stagnation by millions of tiny foot drags—though in some cases, it may only take a few major interest groups to thwart S&T progress.

Note also that political resistance affects innovators, investors, and entrepreneurs alike. It therefore retards every stage of S&T progress: from research to development to mass production. Here we find the messy overlap between diffusion and innovation. These two phenomena are sometimes so interdependent that they are difficult to separate out. This book makes no claim to have solved this perennial problem. However, both theory and history strongly suggest that successfully blocked diffusion results in less innovation. If an innovation cannot be sold widely, then science, technology, engineering, and mathematics (STEM) labor, entrepreneurs, and investors will not get sufficient returns on their investment. Many will therefore turn away from S&T and follow other pursuits. Why assume all the risk, expense, and valuable time to innovate if your invention will never make it out of the laboratory and into general use? Many innovators will instead return to "normal" jobs or direct their creativity and resources toward art, finance, religion, war, or other avenues where they *can* get the rewards they seek.

Revolutionary or Evolutionary . . . It Doesn't Matter!

Opposition to new S&T is particularly fierce when an innovation is revolutionary. For example, when Thomas Edison began to market his new electric power stations during the 1880s, resistance appeared across the economic and political spectrum. The "losers" with respect to electricity included the seventy-year-old gas industry (which had a near monopoly on lighting in most cities and sought to retain it), municipal governments (whose power was threatened by the ever-increasing size and scope of the local electricity monopolies), consumers (who feared exploitation by monopoly pricing and service), and a broad cross-section of people who felt that electrical fires and electrocution posed a serious threat to their lives and property. In almost every country where Edison sought to establish electricity generation, each of these interest groups campaigned for government restrictions on electricity to protect their political or economic assets.

Because electricity is a general-purpose technology, one with applications throughout society, these regulations slowed technological change throughout the economy, by either lowering the incentives to innovate or obstructing it outright. For example, the first central power stations appeared around the same time in the United States (1882), Great Britain (1882), France (1883), and Germany (1884). Each of these countries also experienced political resistance to the innovation and diffusion in electricity. However, in the United States, political resistance was lightest. Electricity providers there could often either bribe city officials or capture state politicians to get their support. As a result, Americans soon led the world in the development and diffusion of incandescent lighting, electric trams, alternating current, and overall electricity generation. In Europe, electrification was far more complicated and costly due to staunch resistance from gas monopolies, city governments, and a range of urban interests. They ensured that, for example, in London, a new electric power station required either an act of Parliament or a provisional order from the president of the Board of Trade.[20] Thus, in Great Britain and France, where opposition was the heaviest, electricity innovation and diffusion lagged tremendously (Table 7.1). Great Britain and France even trailed years behind Germany, despite the fact that incandescent lighting had been independently invented in Britain by Joseph Swan in 1878, while the French had been leaders in electricity research since the 1780s.[21]

Table 7.1 **Appearance and Diffusion of Various Electric Power Technologies**

	First Central Power Station	*Incandescent Lighting, 1887 (US=100)*	*First Electric Tram*	*Miles of Electric Trams, 1900*	*First AC Power**	*Generating Capacity, 1912–1915 (kWh)*
United States	1882	100	1887	20,000	1893	5,165,000 (1912)
Germany	1884	37.5	1890	1,800	1891	2,075,000 (1913)
Great Britain	1882	25	1896	572	1899	1,135,000 (1914)
France	1883	8	1895	292	1895	1,800,000 (1913)

*Modern, 3-phase electric power.

Sources: Hughes (1983); Levy-LeBoyer and Morsel (1994a, 1994b); Millard (1981); Todd (1984).

Incremental innovations often face less opposition than radical ones; however, a new technology need not be a "revolutionary" invention like electricity, automobiles, or the power looms scorned by Ned Ludd to arouse resistance against it. Take, for example, the fluorescent lamp designed in 1934 by the Hygrade Lamp Corporation, a medium-sized producer of lamps.[22] Fluorescent lighting was an incremental invention that had been mostly used for decorative outdoor tint lighting since the 1920s. Hygrade's improvement was to produce an ultra-high-efficiency "white" fluorescent bulb that could be used indoors. Hygrade's lamps were so successful that, by 1939, they threatened to drive the major lamp producers, General Electric (GE) and Westinghouse, out of the still-growing indoor market. Hygrade lamps also used materials and electricity in such a way that they changed the relative market power and profit margins of established players in the indoor electric lighting business. Thus, as consumers began to use Hygrade fluorescent lamps, not only did they constitute a technological challenge to GE, Westinghouse, and the fixtures (sockets, reflectors, switches, etc.) manufacturers linked to them, but also they threatened to cut in half the share of electric lighting profits received by the electric utilities.

In response, GE, Westinghouse, the fixtures manufacturers, and the utilities companies united to defend their markets. Together they designed a heavier, *less efficient* fluorescent lamp that had different material requirements for its production and used far *more electricity* than Hygrade's lamps, but in doing so they redistributed profits back to the established players. To further drive Hygrade out of the market, these firms also formed a certification scheme, which established tests, standards, and guarantees in support of the less efficient lamps but left Hygrade's products "uncertified." When Hygrade refused an offer to become a licensee of GE and thereby accept limits on its market share, GE also initiated a patent infringement lawsuit. Although Hygrade countersued and the Justice Department soon began antitrust actions against GE, World War II had begun. GE was then able to leverage its importance to the war effort to convince the War Department to intercede and have the antitrust investigation suspended. So here we have an incremental technological change that merely chipped away at a submarket of electric power products but that eventually drew in the US Secretary of War to contribute to resistance against it.

Military Resistance to Innovation

Even the military is not immune to technological resistance, despite its urgent and dangerous mission of national defense.[23] In fact, since many military functions are built around particular technologies (guns, artillery, aircraft, ships), resistance to new technologies that might replace them can be quite intense. Innovation is threatening to military personnel because changes to their technology can sometimes demand major changes to long-established strategic doctrines, battlefield tactics, or bureaucratic organizations. Military advancement is built on these things; therefore, soldiers and sailors often resist technological changes that might alter or break their careers. Also, new technologies can create new paths for promotion, often at the expense of, or perceived insult to, more traditional service jobs, prompting additional resistance. Similarly, new military technologies can privilege one branch or mission over another, and thereby trigger interservice or intraservice rivalries. Alternately, by altering or reducing the dangers of combat, new technology can affect the prestige of particular assignments. All soldiers value their lives, but many in the most dangerous jobs also savor the respect and exhilaration that come with the peril. Therefore, some may actually resist innovations that could reduce their jeopardy or create career tracks for more risk-averse colleagues.

Civilians can also slow military innovation. For example, party politics can come into play when an innovation supported by one political party or faction prompts opposition from another. Sometimes, the president may champion a particular military technology, giving legislators a political opportunity to bash him or a lever by which to assert their own preferences on foreign policy. Finally, as always, fights over money are a common source of technological resistance. Budgets allocated toward the development of a new military innovation usually mean either higher taxes or spending cuts on other items and missions.

The introduction of radio communications into the US Navy in 1899 serves as a typical example.[24] Innovation in radio surged soon after Guglielmo Marconi successfully demonstrated his wireless telegraph in 1896. Within four years, the White Star and Cunard ship lines had installed the new technology on their ocean liners, while trans-Atlantic wireless service was serving businesses, such as *The New York Times*, by 1907. Yet it took roughly fifteen years to fully integrate the radio into US naval operations, lagging far behind the British and German navies. This is because myriad organizational and political forces in the United States resisted the new technology. Isolationist congressmen who opposed Roosevelt's imperialism fought against budget appropriations for the radio, while conservatives tried to block his naval reforms. For their part, naval bureaucrats felt they had higher priorities, such as ship construction or munitions acquisition, and therefore often neglected the innovation. Nor did radios offer clear paths to promotion for officers or bureaucrats on land or sea, so wireless communication received little attention from either. Most important, senior naval officers saw the radio as a direct threat to their authority onboard ships. Once out of port, ship captains and fleet commanders were autonomous, often acting like independent executives over their own forces. Radio communication would eliminate that independence. It would subordinate sea-going officers to their land-based rivals and to military bureaucrats back in Washington, who could command them at whim from any distance. Naval radio sets were therefore left in gangways, given over to enlisted men who used them mostly for personal communications, or prohibited entirely. When, in 1912, a senior officer position was finally created for the entire fleet to promote radio communication, the admiral in command burdened the appointee with supervising boat races and boxing matches to undermine his job and deflate the prestige of his position. Resistance at the top was perhaps best exemplified by the commander-in-chief of the Atlantic Fleet, Rear Admiral Hugo Osterhaus, who in 1913 refused to allow his ships to be deployed by radio and permitted only communications by flags and pennants. It would take World War I, combined with several acts of Congress and executive orders by President Wilson, to finally force the shift to a radio navy.

A more recent example can be found in cruise missiles. The Tomahawk cruise missile has been one of the cornerstones of American defense since its deadly accuracy was demonstrated in the 1991 Gulf War.[25] However, the development of the cruise missile took over thirty years and was cancelled or delayed on several occasions by its opponents within the military and government.[26] The first major cruise missile R&D program was the 1953 Regulus. It was scuttled in 1958 because it took funding away from Admiral Rickover's beloved Polaris ballistic missile submarine. Interest in cruise missiles was not revived until a decade later, in response to the sinking of an Israeli destroyer by an Egyptian antiship missile in 1967. The secretary of the navy then advocated for a cruise missile research program to come up with a similar weapon for the US arsenal. However, the aircraft community within the navy furiously objected to any long-range, ship-to-ship or ship-to-surface weapon that might compete with their raison d'être. They argued that manned aircraft already fulfilled these missions, and did so far more efficiently. The pilots saw to it that the final product, the 1977 Harpoon antiship missile, possessed limited range and had to be launched from navy patrol planes.

During the early 1970s, interest arose in developing a submarine-launched, nuclear-armed cruise missile that might have antiship capabilities as an additional capability. This time resistance from the naval aircraft carrier community was joined by opposition from the US Air Force. Both services perceived long-range cruise missiles as a threat to their primary missions. Bomber pilots were especially enraged when an air force variant was proposed, to be carried by a wide-bodied cruise missile carrier—a jumbo jet loaded with cruise missiles that might eventually replace manned penetrating bombers.[27] Instead, the air force called for the navy's cruise missile budget to be reallocated to R&D for the new B-1 bomber. Furthermore, each of these military R&D programs was opposed by arms-control proponents in government who sought to quash any new weapons systems that might endanger negotiations with the Soviets.[28] They were eventually joined by antiwar liberals who argued that cruise missiles were either too offensive (and therefore an inducement to war) or bound to malfunction (and therefore a waste of taxpayer money better spent on social programs).[29]

Ironically, it was arms control that saved the Tomahawk. The landmark SALT I agreements, reached in 1972, restricted ballistic missiles systems but placed no limitations on cruise missiles. This provided hawks in Congress a loophole through which to improve the US nuclear posture. Thus disguised by its strategic nuclear mission, the long-range antiship and land-attack Tomahawk programs finally snuck through Congress during the mid-1970s. The Tomahawks' survival was further aided by Watergate, combined with turnover in senior Pentagon personnel, which distracted both civilian and military attentions. Yet, even after the Tomahawk's introduction in 1983, naval commanders continued to resist the weapon's installation. They feared the lack of control that came with the new over-the-horizon missile, which could neither be recalled nor targeted by sight. If a Tomahawk malfunctioned and hit a neutral or friendly ship, then the senior officer would likely lose his command and possibly be court martialed. Even when properly targeted at the enemy, Tomahawks still relied on a range of new, complex systems of questionable reliability. Traditional manned air and gun assaults were seen as far more trustworthy. As a result, the antiship version of the Tomahawk was never used in combat and was withdrawn from service by the early 1990s, while the land-attack Tomahawk sat unused until the massive mission requirements of Desert Storm forced it into combat.[30]

The list of similar cases is long and spans across military history. Armored knights opposed the advent of longbows because archery brought common farmers onto the battlefield and gave them terrific advantage over mounted nobility.[31] Similarly, elites attempted to restrict firearms in early Ming China, Ottoman Turkey, and Japan's Tokugawa shogunate to maintain their control over warfare and national politics.[32] Egypt's Mamluk warriors were famously resistant to guns, in part because their political legitimacy was heavily based on their supremacy in mounted archery.[33] During the nineteenth century, elements of navies around the world fought against the adoption of steam engines and steel hulls because of the drastic changes in skills, equipment, and war-fighting tactics that the new technologies demanded. Between the two world wars, battleship admirals fiercely opposed the advent of carrier strike aviation that might render them obsolete.[34] On the eve of World War II, the British government had to order the Royal Air Force to build a modern air defense system against the airmen's insistence on a doctrine of strategic bombing.[35] During the 1950s, the commandant of the US Marine Corps argued that the helicopter was essential to his service's future relevance. He was resisted by his own fixed-wing aircraft community (who feared that helicopters would divert resources away from their primary missions), his infantry (who worried about disruptions to their tactics and strategies), and his artillery regiments (which suspected that the armed helicopters would eliminate their mission).[36]

Nor is feared loss of power or budgets the sole reason for military resistance to innovation; prestige, honor, and culture can also produce staunch opposition to new technologies. For example, the head of the US Strategic Air Command (SAC), General Curtis E. LeMay, was famously reluctant to support the development of intercontinental ballistic missile (ICBM) technologies. He insisted that, while they might gain strategic value some day in the far future, ICBMs mostly served as just "political and psychological weapons" or "penetration aids" for manned bombers. LeMay long believed that airplanes operated by trained pilots were the proper technology for the air force's bombing mission. He and other pilots at SAC therefore dragged their feet on ICBMs throughout the 1950s, fearing that the new missiles would transform their command into "the silent silo-sitters of the sixties."[37] Twenty-first-century military pilots are no different, as they fight to find a place for themselves in an age when drones may replace manned aircraft.[38]

Who Loses and Why?

Exactly who are these "losers" created by new S&T, and why do they oppose innovation? Broadly speaking, there are four sets of losers: economic, social, cultural, and political (Table 7.2).

Table 7.2 **Major Losers Created by New S&T**

Type of S&T Loser	*Description*	*Generally Includes*
Economic	Holders of assets whose value is decreased by new S&T	Labor, land owners, environmentalists, consumers/producers of status quo S&T, investors in status quo S&T
Social	The subset of people for whom an innovation will alter their ability to access or control an existing technology or will negatively affect the costs, risks, or benefits of an existing technology	Minorities of all types
Cultural	Individuals or groups who object to S&T progress that conflicts with strongly held ethical or normative values	Religious or other cultural groups
Political	Individuals or groups whose political power or legitimacy is threatened by S&T progress	Elected officials, political parties, bureaucrats, military, interest groups

These represent ideal-types for descriptive purposes. Historically, the economic, social, cultural, and political objections to innovation are combined in fights against S&T.

Economic Losers

Economically, technological losers are the holders of assets whose value is decreased by scientific progress or technological change. Economic losers can be producers of competing technologies who seek to retain market share and profitability; consumers with large-sunk costs in existing technologies; owners of land (or environmentalists) who seek to prevent its destruction or degradation; or even investors in stocks, bonds, or physical capital who seek to maximize their return on investment. Regardless of their individual characteristics, economic losers are generally holders of assets (skills, capital, land, resources, etc.) whose value will be hurt due to the effects of technological change on supply-and-demand conditions. And the more they are tied down by an asset threatened by innovation, the greater their motivation is to resist new S&T that competes with it.[39]

The classic economic "loser" created by innovation is labor. Take, for example, the modern, standardized shipping container.[40] Seemingly simple metal boxes, shipping containers are actually a complex mixture of advanced transportation technologies and computer software. The advent of shipping containers during the 1960s drastically changed the demand for dock labor.[41] Before containerization, the relatively short time that a ship spent at dock might account for fully three-quarters of its voyage costs, with dockworker wages accounting for half of all maritime shipping costs.[42] Longshoremen understood these costs and recognized their vulnerability to shipper innovations to reduce them. They therefore tended to strike against any technological change that might reduce dock work, even at the margins. Containerization at new or union-weak port facilities would eventually create competition, drawing work away from heavily unionized ports such as New York City and forcing compromises between container shippers and labor unions. However, labor resistance against containers led to years of strikes and negotiations, eventually involving the Kennedy and Johnson administrations, as well as Congress. This discouraged many shippers and ports from experimenting with containers and bankrupted a few that did. Thus, in some ports, labor opposition prevented containerization for years.

Furthermore, not only were dock unions powerful, but also the major ports they dominated were a vital source of jobs for local economies and hence political support for state- and city-level politicians. For example, during the early 1950s, on the eve of modern containerization, the ports of New York City (NYC) handled roughly one-third of American ocean-going trade in manufactures. This translated into roughly 114,000 jobs directly involved in NYC's seaborne freight. Another 100,000 in manufacturing jobs were located in the factories and processing plants that lined the waterfront, adding value to the goods coming through the NYC ports. Additional jobs in marine construction, ship repair, banking, law, insurance, and other port-related service brought the total to an estimated 400,000 to 500,000 jobs out of citywide employment of roughly three million at the time.[43] NYC politicians therefore had little incentive to tinker with the status quo. As a result, any proposals to introduce containerization into NYC ports were solidly rejected by the unions, city transport departments, and city and borough politicians. Even as modern containerization facilities sprouted up across the harbor in New Jersey during the 1950s and 1960s, NYC merely repaired or increased capacity at existing docks rather than adopting the new container technology.

Hence, the speed of innovation and diffusion of container shipping depended, in part, on political considerations. Around the world, those national and local governments able to compensate or coerce the losers saw their ports and transportation firms become global leaders in modern container-based shipping. Examples of these innovative organizations include the ports of Singapore, Shanghai, Los Angeles, Newark, and Tilbury (UK) and the corporations Sea-Land, Evergreen, and Maersk. However, governments unable to resolve political resistance to containers saw their ports shrink and corporations fall. These failures include the once-dominant, but now virtually extinct, ports of London, Liverpool, and New York, as well as the shipping industry leader, Grace Company.

Social Losers

A second set of losers are those who fight against S&T that might privilege one social group over another. This often means opposition to those innovations that alter the access to, control over, risks of, capabilities of, or distributive effects of existing technology. Resistance by social losers may be purely political in nature, but it can drastically affect the physical form and technical operation of new technology, what capabilities a technology will have, and how the technology is to be physically used and controlled.[44] For example, Robert Moses, the designer of New York's expressways and state parks, deliberately used bridge, road, and even pool design to restrict their usage by poor and lower-middle class families, especially African Americans. Bridges were intentionally designed to prevent cheap mass transit from passing underneath, roads were built to limit bus access, public pools were kept at low temperatures under the assumption that "Negroes did not like cold water," and buses (the most affordable transport technology for the lower classes) were required to have permits on certain roads.[45] Perhaps more infamously, the perceived cultural and "eugenic" impurity of Jews during the 1930s prompted their evisceration from the rosters of German scientists, resulting in severe setbacks in German chemistry, atomic physics, and medicine, and perhaps costing Hitler the discovery of the atomic bomb.[46]

Cultural Losers

Cultural losers constitute a third set. These are people who object to S&T progress that conflicts with strongly held ethical or normative values. An illustration of this type of resistance is the near-century-long federal ban on the sale and public discussion of contraceptives in the United States, initiated in 1873. Contraceptives were seen by many resistors as immoral, an encouragement to recreational, unmarried sex. The federal ban discouraged investment and entrepreneurship in contraception R&D. As a result, innovations such as the birth control pill were greatly delayed in the United States and had to be developed either out of country or in relative secrecy.[47] On a far larger scale, some argue that the costly "not invented here" syndrome, which prejudices in-house science and technology over technology transfer from outside, is a form of resistance born out of cultural insecurity.[48] Recently, cultural arguments have been made to restrict evolutionary biology, stem-cell research, robotics, and genetically modified organisms (GMOs).[49]

Political Losers

The political losers created by innovation are individuals or groups whose political power or legitimacy is threatened by S&T progress. Politicians and policymakers generally seek re-election or reappointment, and therefore desire both votes and money to achieve those ends. Even in nondemocratic societies, political elites do not last long in power if they fail to win the support of important interest groups. Political elites are also the only actors able to enact fiscal and regulatory policies that can support or obstruct technological change. Of course, the power of a political position may be proportional to the economic, social, or cultural power of attendant technologies or groups (e.g., automobile regulators are far more powerful than today's horse-and-buggy regulators). These facts link together political losers with economic, social, and cultural losers. For example, many of the New York politicians who opposed modern shipping containers could not have held office long if they had *not* acted against the new logistics technology. The political power of General Curtis E. LeMay's position would have been greatly deflated had his bomber pilots been rapidly replaced with computerized ICBMs. Hitler's anti-Semitic policy agenda would have been severely compromised if his top scientists were Jews. And the staunchest opponents of climate change R&D have been political elites from coal and petroleum regions.

The Chorus of Losers

Usually the economic, social, cultural, and political objections to innovation are mixed together in fights against S&T. Take, for example, the fight against contraceptives innovation. Cultural opponents view contraception as immoral, a sin against God, and conducive to wicked behavior. Social opponents have attacked contraception as a threat to the traditional role of women and a form of "race suicide." Early on, the economic "losers" created by innovations in birth control technologies were physicians who sought to prevent nonprofessional medical providers from entering their markets. So while the physicians alone could possibly have obstructed these innovations, their political resistance was considerably strengthened by alliances with religious and other groups that felt culturally and socially threatened by contraception.[50]

The distributive aspects of innovation also help to explain why revolutionary S&T can be fought so successfully for so long, while some incremental innovations are able to proceed more rapidly. Whereas incremental innovation may threaten only a single firm's product line, and thus decrease its profits, revolutionary innovation threatens entire industries, their workers, and hence the economic vitality of the regions in which they are located. Therefore, in instances of revolutionary technological change, political elites are pressured by much larger interest groups seeking protection (entire industries, unions, consumer groups, etc.) often in command of far greater resources. Since the revolutionary technologies they resist are not firm specific, these interest groups can seek relatively simple policy solutions: general taxes, regulations, the removal of government support for the revolutionary technology, or increases in the procurement and protections for the status quo technology. Many of these interest groups (industries, unions) are geographically concentrated in specific electoral districts. Therefore, they may also represent a large share of their political representative's constituency. So if key or large interest groups in a region opt to resist a new technology, then their political elites should act to structure tax, regulatory, pork, and procurement legislation that will tend to favor the status quo technology and raise the costs of (or obstruct) innovation and diffusion of the revolutionary technology. Thus, if the losers choose to resist, then their political elites should tend to support them. In comparison, a revolutionary innovation will have few supporters. That is, from the politician's perspective, a new technology has yet to build a constituency of voters. Hence, there is much less "fight" coming from pro-S&T interests. This often leaves status quo interests as the key determinants of political action.

Several economists have further argued that the degree of resistance to pieces of new S&T should be directly linked to the costs of abandoning the old technology it threatens to replace.[51] The lower the costs of moving one's assets out of a particular existing technology, the less resistant and more supportive one will be to technological changes that threaten it. Conversely, the higher the costs of discarding an existing technology, the more resistant and less supportive one will be to innovations that threaten it. For example, the skills of a nuclear engineer are far more tightly linked to the technology of nuclear power than, say, a Duke Energy Corporation[52] bond held by an investor. Hence, that investor might support new clean fuel innovation (such as windmills, tidal generators, and solar power) since he or she can easily sell the bond and reinvest in the new technologies, while the engineer should be more likely to resist these technologies and to favor politicians and policies that support nuclear power since his or her skills are tied to the fate of that technology. The most mobile assets are those that are either highly liquid (e.g., stocks and bonds), generally unaffected by technological change (e.g., accounting skills, a physics degree), or uncommitted (e.g., cash, college entrants). Owners of these highly mobile assets should seek out the highest return on investment with the lowest risk and should support technologies that offer these characteristics. Owners of immobile assets should fight like hell against new S&T that threatens their value.

Opposition to Science

While much of this chapter has focused on political resistance to technological change, interest groups have also used politics to obstruct progress on the "science" side of S&T. The motivations here are similar to those behind technological resistance. The economic, social, cultural, and political losers created by science use their political clout to hamper research that they perceive as hurting their interests. Some resistors oppose lines of scientific research that appear to be threats in and of themselves (e.g., genetically modified organisms, stem cells, and nuclear power). In other cases, opponents fear the policy implications of scientific research rather than the science itself, yet they must attack the latter to prevent the former. For example, research on phenomena such as climate change, antiballistic missile systems, and agricultural pesticides proceeded for years without arousing much opposition. It was only when these research programs built up enough evidence to have serious implications for public policy, and thereby create winners and losers, that political resistance kicked in.

Political resistance to scientific progress often results in actions different than those used against technological change. For example, only in the most extreme cases is science funding cut or research prohibited. The quintessential illustration of this occurred in 2001, when George W. Bush used a presidential directive to severely curtail research on stem cells in response to pressure from religious conservatives. Decades earlier, federal research on the supersonic transport plane ended similarly, partly due to pressure from civic groups concerned about sonic booms and air pollution.

A far more common form of resistance is to have scientists silenced, dismissed, or pressured out of R&D. Almost since they first entered government, federal scientists have been dismissed from departments such as the Fish and Wildlife Service, the Environmental Protection Agency, Health and Human Services, and various scientific advisory councils for presenting findings that conflicted with administration policies on health or the environment.[53] Others have left of their own accord. For example, during the 2000s, dozens of scientists quit the Centers for Disease Control and Prevention (CDC) after years of pressure by the Bush administration to abandon scientific solutions to sexually transmitted diseases and unwanted pregnancy and instead support abstinence-only programs.[54] In another example, in 2000, US Department of Agriculture (USDA) microbiologist James Zahn began to study antibiotic-resistant bacteria emerging on American hog farms. Concerned about the farm vote, his political superiors ordered him not to present or publish his findings, then pressured him to end his research altogether. Zahn soon quit his research and left the USDA.[55]

Another form of resistance is for the losers to repress, alter, dilute, or censor scientific findings to advance or defend their interests. For example, in 2003, factsheets produced by the National Cancer Institute were altered by conservatives to indicate that abortion raises the incidence of breast cancer in women.[56] In another example, from 2001 to 2005, a lawyer for the oil industry systematically censored US government reports on climate change. He was put in charge of the White House Council for Environmental Quality, where he regularly deleted findings, altered evidence, and distorted analysis to suggest that the science behind climate change was murky and its effects mild.[57] Meanwhile, political appointees at the Fish and Wildlife Service have occasionally inflated estimates of animal populations to keep them off the endangered species list.[58]

A particularly subtle form of resistance is to create opposing pseudo-science in the name of "honest scientific debate" to cloud the minds of policymakers and the public. This technique was perhaps developed most by the tobacco industry, which spent decades and tens of millions of dollars on "research" to muddy the consensus that cigarette smoking caused lung cancer and heart disease. A now-infamous 1969 industry memo explained: "Doubt is our product. . . . It is the best means of competing with the 'body of fact' that exists in the mind of the general public. It is also the means of establishing a controversy."[59] This strategy of creating doubt has been used far more successfully by opponents to climate change science. Despite the near certainty, since at least 1995, of the science behind anthropogenic global warming,[60] climate change opponents have established a false impression among the public and many policymakers that "the science [of climate change] is not settled."[61] To accomplish this, with considerable funding from the oil industry and libertarian groups, climate change opponents founded their own scientific journals, think tanks, and studies that have systematically misrepresented legitimate science, willfully misinterpreted data, and misreported findings. Political allies then drew upon this pseudo-science to cloud debate and delay action.[62]

It is important to recognize that *both* conservatives and liberals have anti-science resistors in their midst.[63] Conservatives tend to oppose science that is inimical to big business (climate change) or religion (evolutionary biology) or viewed as a threat to individual freedoms and self-determination (social science). They regularly blast federal civilian research for its waste and frivolity, arguing for major spending cuts at the National Science Foundation, while accusing it of billions of dollars of fraud, duplication, junk science, and mismanagement.[64] Liberals launch almost identical critiques of military research.[65] Resistors within the political left also routinely fight against scientific research that they fear will adversely affect health (e.g., chemical pesticides, bovine growth hormones, and X-ray scanners in airports), the environment (e.g., supersonic transport, wind power, and nuclear energy), and animal rights (e.g., medical research using animal subjects). Sometimes these objections have little or no basis in fact. Take, for example, the fight against cell phones and electric power lines because they supposedly cause cancer, the idea that vaccines cause autism, or the completely unsubstantiated claim that GMOs are harmful to human health. Ironically, these baseless attacks often have their worst effects on the poor and vulnerable populations who benefit most from scientific progress and the technology upon which it is based.[66]

Finally, there are even internecine fights within science that can retard progress. Physicists have long battled with biologists for control over federal research funding, with the former stressing national security or energy policy and the latter citing its medical and health benefits. During the Cold War, the physicists consistently won these fights for funding; more recently, health scientists have instead emerged victorious. Even within fields of research, there are distributive fights over resources. In physics, proponents of string theory have captured an enormous fraction of available research funding and journal coverage at the expense of competing theoretical and experimental avenues. In medicine, Judah Folkman, the surgeon who revolutionized cancer research during the 1960s with his theory of angiogenesis, had his research funding cut by traditional cancer researchers because "we don't want Folkman to build an empire" and because they resented a clinical doctor trespassing on their scientific turf. In doing so, they delayed cancer research and treatments for decades.[67]

On a broader scale, university laboratories compete with military laboratories and private research institutes for government largess. Research projects are doled out, or eliminated, like any other pork barrel project meted out by members of Congress eager to please their constituents, who are themselves caught between their conflicting desires for more federal spending in their districts and greater tax cuts overall.[68] Therefore, it is no coincidence that Lyndon B. Johnson saw to it that NASA's facilities were based in his home state of Texas, nor that House Speaker Newt Gingrich got so much military research funneled to his district of Marietta, Georgia, while still arguing for massive tax cuts.

The sum of all these pressures can severely injure the scientific enterprise. Political resistance can result in limits, formal or informal, on what research questions scientists are allowed to ask. It can constrain the methods that STEM workers use to conduct R&D. Political opponents can restrict selection of who is permitted to ask scientific questions, propose or execute research projects, or even merely provide scientific advice. Even in democracies, opponents can suppress the reporting of scientific findings that conflict with the interests of powerful interest groups. Political resistance can even result in the de facto sanctioning of misleading or unjustified scientific claims. All told, this means diminished rewards, even punishments, for the most talented scientists. These hindrances combine to create disincentives for innovators, entrepreneurs, and investors to bear the risk and expense of R&D.

Resistance to Institutions and Policies

It is not S&T alone that creates winners and losers; so too do S&T institutions and policies. The most obvious of these are government subsidies, R&D funding, and procurement programs. Each of these policies explicitly tasks the government with picking winners and losers. Winners are then funded through tax revenues, in a classic form of redistribution. For example, economists argue that the most efficient way to fund research in alternative energy is to tax fossil fuels, then use the revenues to support R&D in wind, solar, tidal, and other noncarbon power sources.[69] This redistributes wealth from petroleum firms and gasoline consumers to producers and consumers of alternative energy. In fact, any public R&D subsidy acts to redistribute wealth away from taxpayers and into new S&T. Push-back from antitax conservatives can thus slow S&T progress, especially when it comes from taxpayers who believe that they are funding R&D that will hurt their jobs or other assets.

Intellectual property rights are another S&T institution that creates winners and losers. A stark example here is Myriad Genetics, which for years held patents on naturally occurring BRCA genes.[70] When mutations of BRCA genes were found to severely increase the risk of breast and ovarian cancer in women, Myriad's patents gave it a monopoly on tests for BRCA genes. Myriad's patents also potentially restricted who could legally conduct research on BRCA genes. Theoretically, these patents implied that people do not own their own genes. Practically speaking, this meant that any corporation could patent a human gene and then use the patent to control that gene's study and use. This created a glaring set of winners and losers. Proponents argued that the patents protected Myriad from intellectual poachers and free-riders, and that they were necessary to motivate investment in the R&D. Yet, gene patent holders could monopolize the R&D and treatment of any disease related to the gene specified in their patent. They could drive up prices, even delay progress, at the expense of competitors, consumers, scientists, and disease sufferers.

The point is that, while the general public broadly supported new S&T to identify and treat breast and ovarian cancer, different interest groups fought bitterly over the patent rights to it. The American press generally blasted the idea of gene patents, except in Utah, which housed Myriad's corporate headquarters.[71] In England, when Myriad attempted to enforce its patents, the British perceived it as a foreign, corporate threat to their public health and national sovereignty. British opposition quickly mobilized against the patenting of genes in general.

They convinced Parliament to create a government-run, national BRCA testing service, open to all. Back in the United States, a coalition of scientists, physicians, and patients, represented by the American Civil Liberties Union, brought suit against Myriad. In June 2013, the US Supreme Court invalidated patents on naturally occurring genes.[72]

Technology standards are yet another S&T institution that can create winners and losers. For example, the efficiency gains from modern shipping containers would have been limited if one firm's containers could not fit another firm's infrastructure (e.g., cranes, ship cells, truckbeds, railcars, etc.). However, whoever controlled the standard would have a competitive advantage in the marketplace. Several interest groups therefore competed over different standards and technical specifications for containers. In 1958, the US Maritime Administration (MARAD), supported by the US Navy and with an obligation to maintain a logistical fleet vital for defense, moved first. It formed two expert committees to determine optimum container dimensions and weight for use on American ships. This aroused opposition from the American Standards Association (ASA), which was dominated by the trucking and rail industry. The ASA formed its own standards committee and demanded that MARAD disband its standardization program. Meanwhile, the National Defense Transportation Association, made up of civilian suppliers of both commercial and military transportation and logistical services, formed yet another standardization effort that rushed to beat MARAD and ASA. Finally, the International Standards Organization (ISO), with its thirty-seven member nations, entered the picture with a completely different approach to standardization. The ISO was concerned with performance rather than size, and therefore emphasized standards in container construction materials more than dimensions or weight.

The different standardization programs, each representing different constituencies, fought over every aspect of the container's technical specifications. Even the political battles over the mere dimensions and fittings of the container were surprisingly Byzantine and had severe distributional implications. Each player had a reason for favoring its own design because different sizes would distribute profits to different players. Different container lengths also made economic sense for different cargoes and routes. Changes in heights might affect East versus West Coast truckers who faced different traffic rules in their respective states, while shorter containers would reduce cargo volume and thus hurt the profits of maritime shippers. Smaller containers might help truckers, but also meant more time loading trains and ships. Fights over construction and fittings standards compounded the politics. Railroads wanted heavier end walls (for strength against the frequent shifts incurred on the rails), while ocean shippers opposed them as adding more useless weight. Europeans fought for the smaller, steel containers used there, while Americans pressed for their larger, aluminum containers. Meanwhile, patents and patent disputes prevented the adoption of lifting and locking device standards, while everyone fought over different corner fittings. Even these minute technical aspects affected profits. Every second added to grabbing and lifting a container was estimated to cost thousands of dollars per ship per year. Simply replacing corner fittings on a firm's existing containers and crane frames might cost upward of $1 million. Hence, many older container shippers, who did not depend on government subsidies, would have to write off millions of dollars of recent investments in their existing containers and support technologies. Therefore, late-comers to containerization, many of whom were subsidized, tried to use standards to benefit at the expense of established players.

The Blood Holocaust

If there is one example that ties all these strands together in a striking way, it is innovation in blood S&T during the early AIDS crisis.[73] Some of the most shocking examples of resistance to S&T can be found in the battles against the technologies devised to protect the world's blood supply against contamination by HIV, the virus that causes AIDS. The crisis began during the winter of 1980–1981, when doctors in New York and San Francisco began to notice curious lesions and pneumonia among previously healthy male patients. Soon, health experts in Paris, London, and Berlin began to report similar afflictions in their populations. No one knew what caused the new disease or how it was being transmitted. Over the next thirty years, it would kill some thirty-five million people and infect another thirty-five million worldwide.[74] In the United States, experts eventually realized that HIV had first entered the American blood supply in 1977 and had been infecting people there ever since. Thus, AIDS posed a deadly threat to all transfusion recipients, especially the hundreds of thousands of hemophiliacs whose lives depended on sometimes weekly transfusions of blood derivatives.[75] So thorough was the devastation among hemophiliacs that the 1977–1985 period has become known as a "holocaust" during which AIDS killed 40% of that population.[76]

The technological solutions to this transfusion problem ultimately consisted of two innovations. The first was a blood test: an enzyme-linked immunosorbent assay (ELISA) adapted to identify the presence of HIV in the blood. The second fix was a heat treatment process designed to kill HIV in transfused blood and blood products.[77] These innovations were elusive, but not difficult. Most, if not all, of the component technologies that formed the foundations of the HIV ELISA test and heat treatment process had existed for at least a decade.

What is so striking is how long technological change took. The first HIV ELISA tests were developed and applied in French research laboratories in

July–August 1983, and the first successful heat treatment process was licensed to its German industrial developer, Behringwerke A.G., in 1981.[78] These innovations then took years, until 1985–1986, to diffuse into usage wide enough to affect a solution to the problem posed by HIV. In the meantime, tens of thousands of people contracted transfusion AIDS and died, sometimes not before unknowingly passing the virus on to others. Given the widespread and lethal nature of the threat and the relative simplicity of the technological fixes, it is puzzling that the technological solutions took so long in coming, and that months, if not years, passed between the lead and late adopters.

Resistance

What delayed technological innovation and diffusion? Opposition! All fronts of society resisted allocating political or economic resources to the S&T response to AIDS. The most obvious opposition was cultural. AIDS was often perceived as a homosexual affliction at a time when popular attitudes toward gays were generally hostile. The "immoral" gay victims were blamed for their fate and anyone supporting AIDS research, especially politicians who called for more funding, made themselves vulnerable to being tarred with election-losing criticism.[79] Intravenous drug users constituted another large segment of AIDS victims, one which attracted even less sympathy from voters or politicians. In Japan, hemophiliac sufferers far outnumbered either gay or intravenous drug-related victims of AIDS, making it less of a moral issue.[80] But Japanese culture places high value on physical cleanliness. Hence, for many Japanese, the impurity of an AIDS patient's blood was more taboo than the homosexual connotations of the disease. Again, AIDS sufferers were social outcasts to be cursed and avoided, not aided.

Governments around the world also delayed action on AIDS research for budget reasons. Why did action by the state matter? One major reason was simply funding. Responding to AIDS with S&T, rather than with quarantines or repressive social regulation, was hugely expensive. The discovery of HIV and its means of transmission required highly trained scientists and technicians, advanced equipment, the construction of specialized facilities, and sometimes massive epidemiological studies.[81] The costs of these resources were far beyond the budgets of most private research institutions. The costs were even difficult to fit into existing public research budgets. Moreover, during the early stages of the disease, there was no clear profit for private industry. This left new government spending as the main source of scientific research on AIDS.

No country's government responded to the advent of AIDS with significant budget outlays for scientific or technological research. Their reactions were typified by that of the United States. There the appearance of AIDS as a public health issue coincided with the presidency of Ronald Reagan. The Reagan administration had been elected on a platform of fiscal restraint, smaller government, lower taxes, deregulation, and a strong military. It therefore prioritized deep budget cuts across almost all nonmilitary functions of government, which included the budgets of both the CDC and the National Institutes of Health (NIH), the primary research institutes for US health problems. Reagan continued these policies even after AIDS had been declared an epidemic. Where federal spending on AIDS was permitted at all, the Reagan administration insisted that government resources be redirected toward AIDS from existing projects, rather than spending any new money on the disease.[82]

The Thatcher government in the United Kingdom had similar priorities, and AIDS research was considered "very small fry" there throughout the early 1980s.[83] Medical research in the United Kingdom was controlled by the Medical Research Council (MRC), a government agency funded entirely by the Department of Education and Science, which also controlled funding for the top universities.[84] Until 1987, the MRC allocated less than a million pounds annually toward AIDS research, often splitting tiny sums between multiple projects that were heavily weighted toward information gathering rather than research.[85] Attempts to introduce policy change were limited. They consisted mostly of questions in parliamentary session about the safety of the blood supply and public criticism of Britain's lack of research. None of these moved the Thatcher government to take substantive action.[86]

Even in France, which was then headed by a socialist prime minister, the government's interest in AIDS research was all but nonexistent. In France, national public health coverage meant that wholesale testing and heat treatment for HIV would entail significant public expenditure and therefore required cabinet-wide approval.[87] However, the French executive branch, like that of the United States, preferred to spend its money on other priorities. France's Ministry of Research and Higher Education (MRES) controlled the research funding for most public research institutes and all of the universities, which meant that most of the top schools and research centers essentially ignored AIDS until the MRES changed its agenda.[88] And since France had a large state-run business sector, even industrial research was affected by the government's funding decisions. Within the French pharmaceuticals industry, comparatively little spending was dedicated to addressing the AIDS threat. The end result was that the entire French public research establishment remained relatively detached from AIDS research until roughly 1989.[89]

The Robert Gallo Incident

Yet another drag on innovation was the hoarding of resources within the scientific community itself, best illustrated by the infamous Robert Gallo incident.

Dr. Robert Gallo was one of the top researchers at the US NIH's National Cancer Institute (NCI). As part of the "war on cancer," Gallo had gained global recognition in 1980 by proving that a certain kind of virus, a retrovirus, caused a leukemia common in Japan. In mid-1982, he developed a side interest in AIDS research.[90] Gallo felt that AIDS was similarly caused and saw it as an opportunity to further develop his own line of research on retroviruses. However, Gallo's interest in AIDS was, like the NCI's, only a sideline and progress was slow.

Suddenly, in April 1983, Gallo's AIDS research was made an institute priority. By then, AIDS was afflicting thousands of Americans, and the NCI was embarrassed by its lack of effort. So powerful was Gallo's reputation that the majority of US federal support for AIDS research was soon directed to him, while other AIDS research labs at the NIH foundered for lack of resources.[91] Gallo's lab became the best-supported research team in the entire US federal system, which meant that the Reagan administration, now heavily criticized for its lack of action, had a considerable stake in Gallo's research. The problem was that Gallo's research was headed down the wrong track! Gallo mistakenly believed that AIDS was caused by a virus similar to his leukemia retrovirus.

Meanwhile, the real scientific discoveries were being made by a small, underfunded lab in France.[92] The leading French AIDS researcher, Luc Montagnier, entered the field in autumn of 1982 at the request of the Pasteur Institute's industrial subsidiary, Pasteur Institute of Production (IPP). IPP wanted to investigate the possibility of AIDS transmission via blood plasma imported from the United States. Working on a shoestring budget, Montagnier's team succeeded in isolating the AIDS virus in January 1983.[93] However, Montagnier's discovery was of a *lentivirus*, a special type of retrovirus that destroyed T cells en masse, rather than infecting them and multiplying as Gallo's leukemia virus did.

In the course of their research, the Pasteur Institute went on to invent many of the first working HIV antibody tests. In March 1983, Montagnier used a radioactive assay developed the previous month to become the first scientist to identify HIV.[94] By July–August 1983, his laboratory had perfected a simpler ELISA test for HIV antibodies and submitted patent applications for the assay in Europe in early September and to the US Patent Office in early December. Using these tests, the Pasteur Institute confirmed the presence of HIV in French blood supplies in August 1983 and immediately informed the French government.

Back in the United States, Gallo turned out to be a determined competitor within the US research establishment. He not only absorbed valuable funds, equipment, and personnel at time when such resources were scarce but also used his considerable clout to *oppose* the funding, pursuit, and scientific acceptance of competing lines of research by other laboratories, including Montagnier's.[95] Since Gallo's line of research was ultimately wrongheaded, this postponed the US discovery of the AIDS virus and the development of commercial HIV tests for as long as a year. For years after, the combination of Gallo's prestige, NIH's reputation, and the fact that both the NIH and the Reagan administration had invested substantial political capital in an American solution combined to cloud and limit recognition of Montagnier's 1983 discovery.[96]

Even after Montagnier's work gained global recognition, the Reagan administration still insisted on backing Gallo, even giving him credit for the discovery of HIV. In April 1984, Secretary of Health and Human Services Margaret Heckler proclaimed side by side with Gallo that the United States and the Reagan administration had "discovered" the AIDS virus, and that an HIV blood test would soon follow, despite the fact that a patent application for Montagnier's HIV test had *already* been submitted to the US Patent and Trademark Office in December 1983. In a final twist, on closer inspection it was later found that Gallo's 1984 AIDS virus was actually the lentivirus originally discovered by Montagnier! Somehow, it had come into Gallo's possession either by accidental cross-contamination or outright theft.[97] Ultimately, a treaty was needed to resolve the patent and the lawsuits that resulted.[98]

Industry Capture

In some countries, the greatest delays in technological progress occurred because of highly effective industry capture. For example, in France, thousands of victims contracted transfusion HIV because French bureaucrats and the blood industry *blocked* imports of foreign ELISA tests. In 1985, after over a year of dithering, the French government finally admitted that the national blood supply was infected and ordered mandatory testing. But, in spite of the Pasteur Institute's rapid advances in the laboratory, the production runs of the French ELISA test were not ready in time to compete with the first American exports. Created by Abbot Laboratories, the American ELISA had received its US licenses in March 1985 and was available commercially within a month at half the cost of the Pasteur test. Anticipating opportunities in the large European market, Abbot Labs had applied for a French license for its ELISA test in mid-February 1985. However, the French government delayed for months the approval of Abbot's ELISA to buy time for Diagnostics Pasteur (formerly IPP) to perfect its HIV antibody test. Pasteur's ELISA test eventually received its license in late June, with plenty of time to ramp up production for compulsory national blood testing, which was also delayed (until August 1) to accommodate Pasteur's production schedule. As for Abbot Labs, they finally received their import license on July 25, less than a week before mandatory testing was to begin in France.[99]

The creation of a French heat treatment process also dragged years behind innovation in America and Germany. Prior to the AIDS crisis, the French government had pumped money into a National Blood Transfusion Center to eliminate imports. But it took years, until autumn 1985, for that facility to perfect its heat treatment technology. Meanwhile, cheap imports of safe, heat-treated blood became available in March 1983. Yet, the government refused to allow imports of safe blood products because they would divert profits from domestic industry and signal a failed industrial policy. So French officials insisted on continuing to distribute domestic blood despite near certainty of infection.[100]

In Japan, hemophiliacs responded quickly to the first US reports of transfusion AIDS (July 1982) by demanding that their government ban imports of US blood products.[101] As they feared, the first recorded AIDS death in Japan was that of a hemophiliac in July 1983.[102] This meant that Japanese blood inventories were almost certainly contaminated. Yet, despite a positive diagnosis by visiting CDC researchers and warnings about the existence of transfusion AIDS, the Ministry of Health and Welfare (MWH) refused to report the 1983 AIDS case.[103] Instead, the first "official" Japanese AIDS victim was not reported by Tokyo until March 1985, the case of an artist returning from an extended stay in the United States. This 1985 victim was more culturally acceptable to the Japanese because he was by profession and locale a social outlier.[104] It was not until 1987, after the death of a Kobe prostitute, that a national policy debate was sparked within Japan. Prior to this, AIDS was popularly dismissed as a foreign problem.

More important, unlike the earlier hemophiliac deaths, the 1985 AIDS case did not pose a threat to Japan's domestic blood supply and hence to Japan's blood industry, which had strong ties with the MHW. The MHW relied heavily on advisory committees consisting largely of people who had a financial stake in MHW regulatory decisions. Also, top MHW officials were regularly rewarded for their government service with lucrative jobs in the pharmaceutical industry that they regulated.[105] Thus, market share was often an overt consideration in MHW regulatory decisions.[106] Also, cheap foreign imports were an important source of profits for Japanese physicians and hospitals, who were reimbursed by the government at more expensive domestic price levels.[107] Hence, the MHW, which had regulatory jurisdiction over pharmaceutical imports and was advised by members of the medical community who profited from them, did nothing.[108] Indeed, it was not until the second half of 1985 that the Japanese government terminated distribution of unheated blood products, and blood testing was not introduced until November 1986.[109]

Perhaps most egregious was resistance by Japan's largest pharmaceuticals firm, Green Cross.[110] Founded in 1950 as a commercial blood bank, Green Cross controlled half of the Japanese market in blood derivatives by the 1980s.[111] Its main foreign competitor was the United States' Baxter Healthcare, which had perfected its blood heat treatment process in 1983 and quickly applied to the MHW for permission to sell its products in Japan. At the time, Baxter had less than 20% of the Japanese market and saw the absence of a Japanese competitor in heat-treated blood derivatives as an opportunity to expand.[112] However, despite the fact that *un*heated Baxter products were sold widely in Japan, the MHW refused to license any of its heated blood derivatives.[113] Government identification of a hemophiliac AIDS victim would have compounded the situation and posed a significant threat to the livelihood of Green Cross, which did not produce heated product and held vast unsold inventories of unheated blood. This fact is important because the Japanese pharmaceuticals industry, and Green Cross in particular, were heavily represented in the MHW's 1983 AIDS Task Force, which made the policy and reporting decisions regarding the HIV threat. The chairman of the 1983 AIDS Task Force was later found to have accepted money from Green Cross and to have demanded payment from Green Cross's rivals in exchange for backing clinical testing of their heated blood products.[114] Other members of the AIDS Task Force and their superiors at the MHW received powerful or lucrative jobs in either government or the pharmaceuticals industry, including senior positions at Green Cross and its affiliates.[115]

Delays due to industry capture also plagued technological progress in the United States. During the 1980s, responsibility for regulating the safety of the blood supply fell under the jurisdiction of the Blood Products Advisory Committee (BPAC) within the US Food and Drug Administration (FDA). While BPAC had no direct policymaking power, it did advise the FDA on blood regulation when granting licenses and approvals for new blood products.[116] At the time of the AIDS crisis, BPAC was chaired by Dr. Joseph Bove, who simultaneously led the American Association of Blood Banks, the same industry the FDA was supposed to regulate. Bove, and the industry he represented, consistently denied the existence of transfusion AIDS until 1984–1985, and Bove used his position at the FDA to downplay the threat of AIDS and argue against regulations that might drive up the costs of production, including testing and heat treatment. For example, immediately after the December 1982 announcement of the hemophiliac AIDS cases, Bove went on network television to declare that there was no evidence that transfusions spread AIDS.[117] When the CDC called a meeting with the blood industry the following January to warn against the dangers of transfusion AIDS, Bove cautioned against overreacting just because "one baby got AIDS got from transfusion."[118] In August 1983, Bove continued this argument in testimony before Congress, mocking "the element of hysteria that surrounds the disease."[119]

. . . And Everyone Else

Ironically, even those interest groups most affected by the AIDS threat (blood banks, gays, hemophiliacs) also sought to impede the S&T solutions to AIDS. For example, many politically active gays perceived blood testing as a tool for discrimination, a step toward quarantines, or the equivalent of assigning them a biological "pink triangle" reminiscent of the Nazis. [120] Other gays feared that a focus on testing would shift priorities away from finding a cure, which would also stymie the sex lives of those testing positive. For all these reasons, many gays stridently opposed the development of an AIDS test.

Blood collectors and blood banks, like the Red Cross, saw HIV tests and heat treatment as technologies with questionable effectiveness, but certain to drive up the costs of doing business. They also feared that HIV tests would drive away gay blood donors, highly valued in some regions, while attracting potential AIDS sufferers seeking free and anonymous diagnoses. And since heat treatment increased the price of blood products by upward of 60%, the blood banks, their customers, and the medical insurers were not enthusiastic about the effect on their bottom lines, especially since the etiology of the disease was open to debate.[121] It did not matter how either the whole blood market or blood plasma collection was organized. Both private and public, profit and nonprofit actors attempted to slow innovation.

Even hemophiliacs were initially wary of any technological changes. Hemophiliacs depended on sometimes weekly transfusions of blood or blood derivatives. They had only recently been granted "normal lives" by the invention of frozen, and then powdered, antihemophilic factor (AHF) during the 1960s.[122] The new AHF products eliminated the need for expensive storage facilities and enabled injection by nonmedical personnel. They also ended the need for frequent hospital visits for most hemophiliacs. However, AHF was still made from donated blood, and hence was a potential vector for the HIV virus. Nonetheless, when the AIDS threat first surfaced, the hemophiliac community was strongly opposed to any technological changes that might affect the quality, availability, or cost of their precious AHF.

For years, each of these groups took advantage of the uncertainty about the science of AIDS, and the uncertainties surrounding the HIV antibody tests and the heat treatment process, to defend their political and economic interests by slowing technological change. They pushed their politicians and government bureaucracies to alter budgets and regulations in ways that slowed innovation. Yes, S&T did eventually move forward, and sometimes the delays only lasted a matter of months. But S&T could have moved much faster, and thereby saved countless lives. In some instances, life-saving S&T was resisted for years with disastrous results.

Conclusion

This chapter has offered three important observations. First, S&T progress creates winners and losers, and the losers can resort to politics to obstruct innovations that threaten their interests. The overall picture is perhaps best described by historian of technology Cyril Smith, who observed that "every innovation is born into an uncongenial society, has few friends and many enemies, and only the hardiest and luckiest survive," and a substantial amount of case history appears to back up this assertion.[123]

Second, government is rarely a neutral observer in these upheavals but, rather, is pursued by both sides in the hope of gaining policy advantages in their mortal conflict.[124] These politics are often neglected by innovation researchers, who tend to assume widespread support for progress in science and technology and then ask which types of policies will achieve the best results. Yet political resistance to technological change can obstruct or warp otherwise "good" S&T policy. Time and again, the losing interest groups created by scientific progress or technological change have been able to convince politicians to block, slow, or alter government support for scientific and technological progress. They support taxes, regulations, subsidies, procurement policies, spending, and so forth that obstruct progress in new S&T, and favor the status quo S&T. The losers and their political representatives have interfered with markets, public institutions and policies, and even the scientific debate itself—whatever they can to protect their interests.

Third, political opposition to the "creative destruction" aspects of innovation helps to explain why some countries are better at S&T than others. Political opposition lowers the incentives to innovate. It drives away innovators, investors, and entrepreneurs. It is not yet clear what happens to this disgruntled creative class. They may apply their talents to other pursuits within their society, such as religion, art, war, or crime. Or they may move to other countries where they can more fully capture the benefits of their S&T activities. Regardless, when political opposition slows innovation in one country, it provides an opportunity for other countries to surpass it.

Of course, resistance does not tell the whole story. Innovation creates losers in all nations. This means that all countries have status quo interest groups that will oppose innovation. Therefore, innovators should encounter resistance wherever they go. Over the long run, S&T should progress with equal speed in all societies. But this is not what we see in the data. So if political resistance by technological losers is a force opposing innovation, then there *must* be some force supporting innovation. After all, Gurney's automobile may have been defeated, thereby setting back auto innovation for over a generation, but railroads and rail innovation took off. Electricity innovation was successfully obstructed by opponents in France and Great Britain, but opponents were far less able to do so in the United States, where electricity S&T surged ahead. The cruise missile did eventually get made and was successfully put into combat, despite widespread opposition, even from many of its own commanders. Despite opposition from all sides, even from their beneficiaries, HIV tests and blood treatments are now advanced technologies that keep the world's blood supply safe, efficiently and inexpensively. What, then, is the counteracting force that pushes innovation forward, over the opposition of the losers?

The next chapter argues that a nation's external threats act as that opposing force. It contends that threats of economic or military competition from abroad can overcome domestic political opposition to new S&T. The theory is that when a nation's interest groups and political elites feel more threatened by external hazards than by domestic rivals, they enter into a state of *creative insecurity*. Creative insecurity generally motivates broad and sustained support for S&T. The greater the creative insecurity and the longer a nation is faced with it, the more its people are willing to bear the costs and risks of rapid S&T progress.

8

Creative Insecurity

Olson's Nemesis

The previous chapter revealed that progress in science and technology (S&T) is political. Innovation does not just happen naturally; it comes about only after a substantial investment of human capital, material and financial resources, and time.[1] These resources must be allocated *toward* innovative activity, often at considerable risk, and *away* from activities such as welfare programs or personal consumption. Therefore, at the national level, the decision to innovate is a political decision. It is political because it prioritizes certain national goals (S&T) at the expense of others (everything else). It also demands that government create and maintain costly institutions, policies, and networks to support innovation. But, as with all political decisions, different interest groups fight over the costs, benefits, and distributional aspects of scientific progress and technological change. Too often the losers created by new S&T are able to block or manipulate institutions and policies to slow or obstruct those innovations that threaten their interests. The implication is that these attacks can sum up over time to discourage innovators, entrepreneurs, and investors, and thereby slow national innovation rates overall.

However, if the political opposition to innovation described in the previous chapter was the entire story, then no nation would last long at the technological frontier. The United Kingdom would now be in torpor. The United States would have hit a plateau a few S&T revolutions ago. The Japanese technological juggernaut should have been felled during its never-ending recession. As all sectors of society seek to use politics to defend themselves against the costs, risks, and distributive effects of technological change, they should slow it down into stagnation. Status quo lobbies should accumulate over time to block S&T progress in these countries. Taxes, regulations, subsidies, and government spending should clog the system. Market failures should go unfixed, and networks never built. But we know that this has not been the case. Why not?

This chapter argues that external economic and military threats constitute a force that can counteract the domestic distributional politics that cause S&T stagnation.[2] It posits that, when a nation enjoys a state of creative insecurity, its rate of innovation will tend to accelerate. Creative insecurity is the condition of perceiving more threats from external hazards than from domestic rivals. *It is the positive difference between the threats of economic or military competition from abroad and the dangers of political-economic rivalries at home.* Put more simply, people tend to stop fighting over how to share their pie when the pie itself is threatened by others. And under particular threats, the best way to defend the pie is through S&T progress.

I use the term *creative insecurity* in direct contrast to Joseph Schumpeter's *creative destruction*. Schumpeter argued that innovation is a "perennial gale" that constantly transforms a nation's economy from within by sweeping away old industries and creating new ones again and again.[3] Thus, innovation was an entirely domestic affair for Schumpeter, driven by either a nation's entrepreneurs or its firms. I argue that domestic and external forces interact to affect national innovation rates. A nation's entrepreneurs or firms may be important actors, but they act in response to larger national and international forces.

One major implication of the evidence presented in this chapter and the next is that creative insecurity can generally motivate broad and sustained support for S&T. The greater the creative insecurity and the longer a nation is faced with it, the more its people seem willing to risk their political capital and economic resources on rapid S&T progress. This relationship appears to hold true regardless of a nation's institutions or policies. The bottom line is that *countries for which external threats are relatively greater than domestic rivalries should have higher national innovation rates than countries for which domestic rivalries outweigh external threats.*

Let's start with a brief illustration of this dynamic found in the battles over S&T, and the institutions and policies that support innovation, which occurred among the Founding Fathers of the United States.

Creative Insecurity and Innovation in Early America

Immediately following the Revolutionary War, Americans split into two camps regarding S&T progress and its supporting institutions.[4] Especially divisive was the technological change then driving forward textiles manufacturing and other basic industries. On one side were the proto-industrialists, championed by visionaries such as Alexander Hamilton and Tench Coxe. They explicitly prescribed S&T-based industrialization as the solution to the external threats faced by the young United States.[5] George Washington himself argued that the security, prosperity, and liberty of Americans "require that they should promote such manufactories as tend to render them independent of others for essential, particularly military, supplies."[6] The proto-industrialists also saw valuable roles for S&T to play in their new country beyond industrialization: as a domestic source of weapons and military supplies; for accurate charting of the coastline for commercial shipping and defense purposes; and for the engineering of advanced roads, ports, bridges, and canals to foster domestic commerce and aid defense.[7]

However, many of these projects were beyond the means, the interests, and sometimes even the imagination of the independent farmers and small businessmen who dominated the early American economy. Recognizing this, many pro-industrialists cohered into the Federalist Party (most active from 1792 to 1816) to advance their agenda at the national level.[8] While others favored stimulating innovation with less invasive methods, such as one-time government rewards or prizes, the Federalists pushed for a more comprehensive, government-led approach to increase national S&T capabilities. This included a national patent system; protective tariffs; import restrictions; financial inducements; a centralized banking system for investment finance; the training of a domestic science, technology, engineering, and mathematics (STEM) labor force (and incentives for the immigration of skilled foreigners) as inputs to these and other technical projects; and a range of other federal institutions and resources to foster and support domestic innovation.[9]

In the opposite camp were the early American losers created by S&T progress and by the institutions and policies proposed by the Federalists. These were equally visionary men whose de facto leader was Thomas Jefferson.[10] They adhered to a "pastoralist" vision for the United States, which called for an economy based on the virtues of self-sufficient agriculture, evolving into a republic of small independent farmers. Jefferson and his supporters were greatly disturbed by the mechanization occurring in England. They pointed out that the advance of manufacturing in Britain had brought with it industrial slavery, reckless urbanization, environmental degradation, and moral decay (e.g., prostitution, alcoholism, urban crime). In other words, they viewed the invention of spinning jennies, power looms, and cotton gins not only as a source of destructive domestic social and economic tensions but also as constituting an internal cultural threat to the young United States.

To the pastoralists, manufacturing technologies also threatened liberty and democracy. A factory worker had no land to farm. Men without land could not feed themselves and were forever dependent on others. Such dependents could never vote freely or be truly free. Rather, independent farming alone, complemented by free trade, and defended from foreign threats by putative economic sanctions, could preserve the United States.[11] As early as 1782, Jefferson even went so far as to advise that the United States forgo industrialization altogether: "let our workshops remain in Europe. . . . The loss by transportation of commodities across the Atlantic will be made up in happiness and permanence of Government."[12]

Jefferson and other early American pastoralists also generally feared a federal government replete with powerful institutions and policies that could subsidize, tax, and regulate American citizens. They suspected that such authority would be used to enrich and empower already wealthy financial and commercial interests, and would eventually threaten American liberty and democracy itself. Jefferson made such an argument to President Washington, warning in 1792 that the Federalist system "flowed from principles adverse to liberty, and was calculated to undermine and demolish the republic."[13] James Madison similarly blasted the proto-industrialists. He wrote of Hamilton's proto-industrialist manifesto, the *Report on Manufactures* (1791), "the parchment had better be thrown into the fire at once."[14] These pastoralists especially feared the establishment of European-style aristocracy in the United States, enforced by an invasive central government and backed by a well-armed, standing military. For example, in 1790, Senator William Maclay (PA) attacked the Federalist plan for a central bank as "an Aristocratic engine . . . a Machine for the Mischievous purposes of bad Ministers."[15] In a worst-case scenario, the pastoralists worried that the Federalists' proposed institutions and policies might be manipulated to lead the newly created United States back into Britain's sphere of influence.[16]

Jefferson and his followers therefore virulently opposed the entire Federalist agenda, including many S&T institutions and policies.[17] For example, they disagreed with the private goods aspects of innovation and fought against the establishment of a national patent system.[18] Rather, like Benjamin Franklin, they saw technology as the property of the community, and technological change as being subject to communal values and social welfare. Many pastoralists, including Jefferson himself, were also regularly indebted plantation farmers, who harbored a passionate hatred of the banking system, and even paper money.[19] Especially distrusted was the aforementioned national Bank of the United States, founded in part to provide investment finance to new industries.[20] Such banks favored wealthy urban creditors at the expense of poor rural debtors, encouraged reckless speculation, and violated the sovereignty of the state governments. The pastoralists similarly distrusted the federal incorporation of businesses, which explicitly put government on the side of already wealthy and well-connected businessmen. As farmers, they also stood to lose from protectionist tariffs, which threatened the free trade upon which many of the wealthiest farmers depended.

Free trade also formed the basis of Jeffersonian foreign policy; trade sanctions were supposed to be enacted to coerce foreign imperialists, not to advance domestic interests.[21]

At first, due to the continued threat of debt-driven economic instability at home and foreign invasion from abroad, the Federalists won some of their early policy battles. A national patent office was created, with relatively simple requirements for submission (1790). A central bank was established in the form of the Bank of the United States (1791). Federal armories were built for the domestic manufacture of military weapons (1794). Even some mild import tariffs were enacted (1792).[22] In perhaps his most subtle victory, Hamilton, again aided by Coxe, even established a government-sponsored Society for Establishing Useful Manufactures (SEUM) in 1791 to promote innovation. The SEUM was granted a rare charter to appropriate property for the construction of experimental manufacturing facilities based on new industrial technologies. These projects were not only exempted from taxation but also granted pecuniary inducements by the government.[23]

Soon, however, the balance of military and economic threats faced by the United States changed to favor the Jeffersonian pastoralists. Britain, France, and Spain still menaced the United States after 1792, but they gradually became more distracted by domestic upheavals at home, or in making war upon each other. Both resulted in increased exports for Americans, and thus a return to economic growth and fiscal solvency for the United States. As the foreign threats became less existential, early Americans began to subscribe in ever greater numbers to Jeffersonian fears about a powerful, corrupt federal government. These concerns were exacerbated by the heavy-handed administration of President Adams (1797–1801), with its repression of the opposition press, military build-up, and reputed admiration for monarchy. Soon domestic rivalries between interest groups and their leaders within the United States began to outweigh fears of external threats.[24]

As a result, Jefferson was elected to the US presidency in 1800, and his fellow pastoralists swept into Congress in the form of the Democratic-Republican party. In line with their shared perceptions of the domestic threats to US security, Jefferson's first presidential administration worked with Congress to attack many of the S&T institutions and polices favored by the Federalists. They virtually eliminated federal taxes and dramatically shrank the federal government and civil service. Jefferson also severely reduced the federal military, halving its budget and placing the defense burden on state militia and river and coastal defense, rather than a modern army and navy. Hence, demand for advanced wartime technologies disappeared. Jefferson even attacked the federal judiciary, which had been loaded with Federalists intent on protecting private property and contracts. The succeeding Madison administration (1809–1817), also

Democratic-Republican, continued these policies, allowing Hamilton's financial brainchild, the Bank of the United States, to expire.

Jefferson was not opposed to all S&T; indeed, he and many of his fellow pastoralists were themselves scientists and inventors. In fact, Jefferson *supported* those S&T institutions and policies that addressed specific domestic threats that he believed endangered the young United States. For example, he called for publically funded education to gird average Americans against wild demagoguery and superstition. He supported exploratory expeditions to discover and survey new lands for yeoman farmers. He called for a national weather bureau to create meteorological forecasts for use in farming and trade. Jefferson had been instrumental in designing the United States' first standards of weights and measures, also essential for land development and free trade. He also supported paleontology in hopes of discrediting a popular theory about the natural inferiority of American plants, animals, and indigenous peoples. He even created a pro-science federal military academy at West Point to better ingrain America's officer corps with the values of Democratic Republicanism.[25]

Yet, many items on President Jefferson's limited list of S&T institutions and policies continued to be rejected by his own pastoralist allies. Why? These men sought to protect from the federal grasp their personal wealth and power, which were often based on lucrative exports of plantation agriculture. They likewise defended the power of their state governments against federal encroachment, partly because they had considerably more influence over the former than the latter. Also, they saw little reason to pay for S&T projects, policies, and institutions that would benefit Americans in rival states, industries, or economic classes, and over which they would have little control. And even the most altruistic, patriotic resistors continued to fear empowering the federal government in ways that might spiral into tyranny.

The Democratic-Republicans therefore repeatedly voted down plans for a national S&T university, funding for overseas exploration, domestic scientific research, costly engineering projects, procurement of military hardware, and even public education. In one of his few S&T victories as president, Jefferson created the Corps of Discovery (1804–1806). This was the expedition led by Lewis and Clark to explore and map the newly acquired Louisiana territory. However, Jefferson was only able to fund the expedition by proposing it to Congress in secret, and by emphasizing its economic and security benefits. For its part, Congress was only able to approve the expedition by militarizing it (by using army funds and personnel) and insisting that it was a one-time affair, thus creating no lasting federal institutions or polices.[26]

However, during Jefferson's presidency, Europe slid into a continental war that would eventually cut off the United States from European trade. Since this war was fought by the leading scientific and technological countries, France and

Great Britain, it increasingly deprived the United States of both manufactured goods and access to the technical knowledge that produced them. While the United States would not face direct military attack until the 1810s, the blockades of European trade from 1806 onward threatened to cut off vital inputs to the fragile American economy. Thus, the external threat to US security was perceived to outweigh the potential ills of domestic industrialization. By 1809, this led Jefferson to reverse his views on technology-based industrialization,[27] and he would eventually insist:

> to be independent for the comforts of life we must fabricate them ourselves. We must now place the manufacturer by the side of the agriculturist. . . . Shall we make our own comforts or go without them, at the will of a foreign nation? He, therefore, who is now against domestic manufacture, must be for reducing us either to dependence on that foreign nation, or to be clothed in skins, and to live like wild beasts. . . . Experience has taught me that manufactures are now as necessary to our independence as to our comfort.[28]

As the external military and economic threats to the United States grew, eventually drawing America into war (1812–1815), even many pastoralists radically changed their views on S&T. They came to support state and federal universities, and rapidly transformed West Point into the nation's leading science-engineering school. They supported tariffs and trade embargos on European-manufactured goods, partly to force peaceful negotiations, but partly as an aid to domestic manufactures.[29] Jefferson himself had observed in France the use of advanced manufacturing techniques for the production of weapons; now he called for the expansion of federal weapons factories and increased arms funding. Advanced ships were built for the US Navy. The federal government was directed to fund and direct massive engineering project improvements to bolster the physical infrastructure and transportation. By 1816, a Congress loaded with now-hawkish Democratic-Republicans even rechartered the dreaded Bank of the United States to better coordinate and direct investment finance at the national level. Ultimately, many leading Democratic-Republicans came out in support of a plan for an "American System," which adopted wholesale much of the proto-industrialist S&T agenda.[30]

After the war ended, the external threats to the United States gradually subsided, once again eroding the political support for S&T and its institutions. France was irrevocably weakened by its defeat. Spain was all but ejected from the Americas. Russia was a potential rival, but only in the Northern Pacific. Only Great Britain remained as a significant military threat. But, having formally settled its territorial and border disputes with the United States, Great Britain now discovered its self-interest in enforcing America's Monroe Doctrine and generally respecting US sovereignty.[31] The British found that they could get much of what they wanted from the United States through trade and investment rather than by conquest. Thus, after 1816, foreign military threats to the United States dwindled until they were almost nonexistent; even warlike Native American tribes became only a minor irritant.

External economic threats also subsided. The US economy initially boomed from supplying war-torn Europe. A sharp postwar recession hit in 1819–1822, but thereafter the development of new farmland, especially southern slavery-based cotton plantations, became the engine of remarkable economic growth in the United States. There were few strategic agricultural goods or natural resources that could not be produced domestically. Basic industries in shipping, textiles, farm implements, and weapons had also formed. Certainly much advanced technology and manufactured goods were still imported from abroad. But these were amply paid for by American exports, or by moderate import tariffs and sales of federal lands, which provided a seemingly endless source of revenue for the government. Hence, the federal debt steadily dwindled out of existence, while trade deficits ceased to be a financial concern.

As their foreign threats faded, wartime spending ended, and the economy restored, Americans soon fell into squabbling among themselves; S&T became a victim of these rivalries. In politics, the Democratic-Republicans split into several factions that fought over the direction of the US government and policy. Some supported the pro-S&T American System. Others called for a return to Jefferson's pastoralism. A large group of populists backed new, Western candidates to clean up corruption and open up government to average Americans and new men, which meant decreasing the relative power of banking and industry. Still others formed a coalition of plantation farmers and financial interests. The domestic political fight over the distribution of America's resources, and her institutions, was on.

In 1824, the initial victor of this squabbling was John Quincy Adams. As a newly elected president, he proposed a bold new economic program that he outlined in his first state of the union address.[32] His would be the first administration to throw its entire weight behind S&T. He would support a national university, scientific research expeditions, a naval academy heavy with STEM instruction, major engineering projects of all sorts (harbors, ports, bridges, dams, roads, and river transport improvements), and a host of other pro-S&T projects.[33] Such policies, he argued, were essential for the glory, responsibilities, and prosperity of a great nation.

However, Adams's S&T program posed too many threats to too many domestic interest groups. Old fears of corrupt federal government and American aristocracy re-emerged. After reading the drafts, Adams's cabinet members advised him urgently against the proposal. "It is excessively bold . . . ," warned his attorney general. "It would give strong hold to the [opposition] party in Virginia, who represent you as grasping for power. . . . [It] would be cried down as a partiality for monarchies."[34] The president's advisers further predicted a withering fight to get the plan past a hostile Congress.[35]

As foreseen by his advisers, the Adams proclamation backfired. The federal government was supposed to be small, weak, and limited. Adams's program would empower it to initiate all sorts of intrusive actions not specified in the Constitution. His rival, wartime hero General Andrew Jackson, who in the next election would defeat Adams in a landslide, howled that the president's new plan "must end in consolidation, & then in despotism."[36] Worse yet, Adams's plan threatened to spend precious tax and tariff dollars on projects that would most directly benefit already wealthy, powerful citizens and corporations (e.g., industry, commerce, and banking). In the process, Adams seemed also to place the financial burden of these projects upon the 80% of Americans who worked in agriculture, often at near-subsistence levels. Many interpreted this as a blatant corruption of government for private purposes. To others, the Adams S&T program read like a flight of fancy, government aid for philosophers and their frivolous scientific amusements. The entire program was blasted in the press as the "wildest construction" ever seen.[37] Although Adams's vision for American S&T might seem commonsensical to us in the twenty-first century, it was then lambasted as too expensive, too undemocratic, and simply too absurd for serious voters and politicians to support.

Little of Adams's S&T program ever made it through Congress. Political resistance by the losers created by S&T and its supporting institutions would afflict and obstruct Adams's entire presidency, and haunt American science and technology for decades thereafter. Wealthy southerners came to especially hate protectionist tariffs, which raised prices on industrial goods (which they did not produce) and triggered reciprocal tariffs against agricultural exports (which they did). Southerners also feared that any further empowerment of the federal government, or any deviation from a strict interpretation of the Constitution to create national S&T institutions, could be used as justification to eliminate slavery. Even when money was freely donated to fund federal science and technology, the politics of resistance could ruin the day. In one instance, an enormous trust fund bequeathed to create America's first federal science research institution, the Smithsonian Institute, was held up by congressional objections for a decade. Meanwhile, the telegraph, railroads, mechanized printing, modern physics and chemistry, and other advanced S&T would want for overt federal support until the next economic depression or war erupted. Soon, land grants and sales became the most popular, and sometimes only, form of federal innovation policy for years to come.

Creative Insecurity: A Theory of National Innovation Rates

This abridged history illustrates how creative insecurity works. Creative insecurity theory posits two opposing dynamics that affect national innovation rates: domestic rivalries versus external threats (Figure 8.1). S&T progress creates winners and losers, and the losers resort to politics to slow innovation. However, external threats increase political support for S&T and thereby counteract domestic political resistance to innovation. Indeed, as the threat balance shifts more and more toward the external, even many domestic losers may recognize that their interests are better served by accepting the costs of technological change, and government actions that support it. Thus, a nation's elites, and the people they represent, often must enter into a state of creative insecurity before they are willing to accept the risks, costs, and distributional[38] consequences of S&T. They must feel enough military and economic threats from external sources to overcome their domestic fears and jealousies.

Viewed another way, innovation is a function of competition. In a world of limited resources, and where human behavior is typified by social competition, all individuals, interest groups, and organizations must regularly defend their assets, values, and interests against rivals. Which rivals? At the macro level, the solidification of the nation-state as a defining social unit has brought into resolution two specific classes of rivals: domestic and foreign.

My domestic rivals are those who seek to increase their wealth, power, security, and prestige *relative* to mine. Not all of my countrymen may seek to do this, but enough do. Some innovations, institutions, or policies will help my domestic rivals to succeed in their efforts, thereby creating relative winners (my rivals) and losers (myself) within my society. I should therefore tend to oppose those particular innovations, institutions, and policies that threaten to place me in a position of relative loss. Also, the more threatened I feel by my domestic rivals (i.e., the more I have to lose, if they win), the more I should act to oppose the

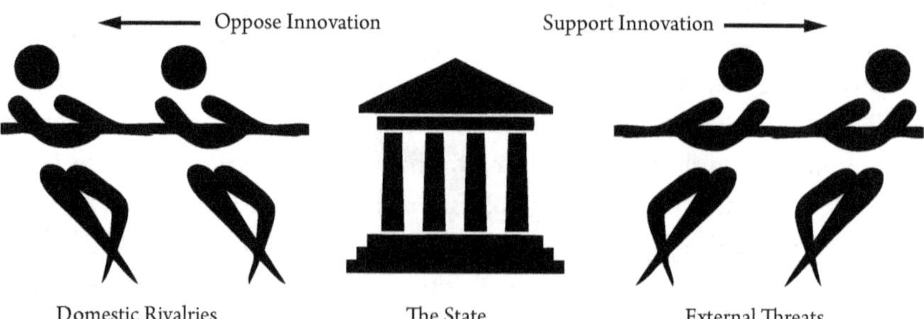

Figure 8.1 Creative insecurity theory.

innovations, institutions, and policies that might hurt my relative status. This was precisely the logic of Jefferson's pastoralists and John Quincy Adams's opponents. If enough other people behave similarly, then a choir of disparate voices throughout my society (some weak, others powerful, but all competing), each resisting a particular S&T or institution that threatens them, will harmonize into a chorus of anti-innovation overall. However unintentionally, this chorus will wind up damaging, warping, or neglecting the institutions and policies necessary to promote S&T nationwide.

Foreign rivals also seek to increase their position relative to mine. Yet in doing so, they put me in good company, because foreign rivals seek to increase their relative wealth, power, security, and prestige at the expense of that of my entire nation. My nation's choir of competing individuals and groups must therefore now cooperate to defend against the designs of common rivals abroad. Yes, there will be relative winners and losers within my society as a result. But many of these losers will reason that it is better to accept a smaller portion of their nation's wealth and power than to shrink or lose the nation itself. Others may feel that their social, cultural, ideological, or historical bonds with their own countrymen outweigh any personal economic or political losses. Certainly some percentage at the extremes will either altruistically accept the long-term costs of innovation or selfishly fight them to the bitter end. The latter may have to be forced to capitulate. Regardless, the domestic losers must be convinced, compensated, or coerced to accept their fate.

Of course, innovation is only one of many strategies a nation can use to defend its interests against external threats. For example, like the early American pastoralists, a nation might instead import its S&T, but only if it can earn the foreign exchange to pay for these imports, perhaps through exports of agricultural goods or natural resources. Or, like Fidel Castro's Cuba, clever leaders might be able to play foreign allies and enemies off each other to win both military security and economic subsidies.[39] However, innovation is often the *best* strategy for a society to use against particular external threats. These include the threats of military conquest, severe cuts to strategic imports (due to either military action nearby or abroad, or failure to earn sufficient foreign exchange to pay for these imports),[40] or massive flights of capital abroad.[41] When these particular types of external threats loom large enough to outweigh those posed by domestic rivals, then both popular and elite support should shift in favor of S&T.

Therefore, creative insecurity theory asserts that the key to explaining national innovation rates is not asking *which* institutions or policies a country should use, but what are the politics *behind* a country's pursuit of innovation. What conditions motivate politicians, and the interest groups that support them, to encourage innovation versus defending the status quo? The next two sections explain how this works.

Distributional Politics: The Enemy of Science and Technology

The previous chapter illustrated how the domestic distributional politics of S&T act to *slow* innovation. Progress in S&T may increase the wealth and capabilities of society as a whole, but it is distributive within society. Put simply, innovation creates winners and losers. So too do the institutions and policies that foster innovation. These losers are varied and myriad across society. They are created when, as a result of S&T progress or its supporting institutions, some economic assets lose their relative value, some individuals or groups see their relative political power or legitimacy decline, some strongly held ethical or normative values are compromised, or some social groups get privileged over others. These losers recognize that they are innovation's victims and they seek to defy their fate. They resist the S&T progress and institutions that threaten their relative status and values. To this end, they use politics to attack or capture the institutions and policies necessary for solving the market failures and network failures that slow innovation.

These distributional politics impede national innovation rates via several mechanisms. First are the political fights over the *inputs* to S&T progress. Innovation is very expensive. Also, every dollar that government allocates toward S&T progress is a dollar not available for welfare provision, natural resource development, consumption, or the lining of elite pockets. Nor do status quo interest groups want to see their taxes raised, or subsidies lowered, to fund rival S&T. As with any other activity, supporters of scientific and technological change must compete politically for power and resources against actors with other priorities. If the resistors of S&T win these fights, then innovation slows.

A second way that domestic distributional politics act to slow innovation is through the battles over the *effects* of S&T progress. Partly, this is just the downside of Schumpeter's creative destruction. Innovation creates new industries while destroying existing ones. In doing so, it creates jobs for some workers while eliminating others. Exciting new start-up firms make headlines, right next to stories announcing bankruptcies or buyouts of firms that could not keep pace. Even innovative firms that satisfy the market's most sophisticated consumers can be usurped by "disruptive innovations" that appeal to the general public.[42] New S&T can also create pollution, waste, new diseases, and even public dangers that externalize innovation's costs and risks onto people without their consent. New S&T can also lower relative information, communication, and other organizational costs, thereby allowing lower social castes to rise in status or heterodox cultural values to spread. Those people most likely to suffer negatively from these types of S&T effects often take political action to obstruct it.

Finally, even when people support S&T, domestic political resistance can arise to oppose S&T institutions and policies. Not only is technological innovation very expensive, but also, as the previous chapters have shown, it suffers from exceptionally high risk, uncertainty, and a variety of market and network failures. But the solutions to these obstacles may take the form of government institutions or policies that can be more threatening than the S&T itself. For example, patents help established innovators to defend their S&T advantage, but they simultaneously put rivals and new innovators at a disadvantage. Infant industry protections help new high-tech sectors, but only at the expense of consumers. National programs that support R&D can threaten the power base of local governments and offend believers in federalism and states' rights. Hence, even if everyone celebrates S&T progress, interest groups may still fight against the institutions and policies that foster it.

The problem is that these attacks add up. Promoting S&T is not an obvious choice for political elites to make, nor for their constituencies to support.[43] Almost any significant innovation or institution will threaten or tax some group somewhere. Hence, the pressures for political resistance to S&T are broad. They can be especially powerful when the distributive effects of innovation overlap long-standing conflicts within society, for example, between rival geographic regions, different ethnic groups, or opposing cultural groups, or across economic classes. Also, the more revolutionary the new S&T, the greater the redistributive threat is. To make matters worse, when opponents fight against a particular technology (or against an S&T institution or policy), they implicitly attack the budding industries that produce it or use it, and all of the jobs and investors involved. So when status quo groups win their fights against S&T, they deter future investors from risking their resources on other new innovations. And since new S&T often has unexpected applications, these benefits are killed too.

The summary point is that S&T progress, and the institutions and policies that support it, can trigger defensive political reactions. Losing interest groups will pressure government to take actions to slow particular innovations or to spike specific institutions and policies. Governments should tend to respond sympathetically to these requests. Some political elites will do so to quiet domestic tensions. Others will represent resistor interests. Even politicians who merely seek to win their next election, or despots who want to maintain stability or retain the loyalty of important domestic supporters, should also tend to restrain changes that might upset the status quo. Each of these should tend to show limited policy support for S&T progress, and perhaps even oppose it. The net effect is that a nation's domestic rivalries tend to act as a force that diminishes support for S&T and its supporting institutions.

Security Politics: The Ally of Science and Technology

The second type of politics that affects national innovation rates is the politics of security, which act to *accelerate* S&T progress. The general principle here is that S&T enhances a nation's ability to provide security for itself. While S&T can sometimes be imported from abroad, certain types of external threats are best addressed by improving a country's domestic S&T capabilities. These sorts of security threats, described next, therefore tend to increase and broaden political support for S&T and its supporting institutions and polices.

It is important to specify that "security" in this formulation is defined as having both military and economic dimensions. The military dimension of security refers to the ability of a nation to defend its territory at home and its interests abroad. Such capabilities are obviously enhanced by S&T.[44] This often entails the acquisition of advanced weapons technologies, as well as state-of-the-art capabilities in communications, transportation, and information processing. Of course, mere possession of advanced S&T is not enough. A society must also possess the skills necessary to use these technologies effectively and to maintain and repair them over time. Therefore, the possession of a well-trained STEM workforce can also be an important component.

This is not to argue that technology is deterministic for achieving military dominance. Technology does *not* govern one's security. It rarely dictates when or how a military conflict will be conducted or end.[45] However, it can increase the odds of victory. That is, possessing more advanced S&T does not guarantee triumph in conflict,[46] but it can certainly help.[47]

The economic dimension of national security is less widely discussed, and therefore needs some clarification. Economic performance matters for national security because an uncompetitive economy may not earn the foreign exchange necessary to purchase strategic imports. These strategic imports can include food, energy, raw materials, or capital goods. They may also include the weaponry and other technologies necessary for military security discussed previously. Also, over the long run, a stagnant economy can lead to increasingly obsolete domestic production. An obsolete industrial sector means that society is supplied with increasingly inferior domestic technologies at relatively higher prices than those obtained by competing economies or militaries. Such an economy may also become dependent on high-cost imports of foreign technology, which again requires a country to earn the foreign exchange to pay for them. Without globally competitive sectors, investment capital may flee overseas and domestic jobs can evaporate, forcing a nation's skilled labor or youths to emigrate abroad, leaving behind an uncompetitive workforce burdened by an aging population.

How do these types of external threats create incentives to support innovation? External threats to a nation's military or economic security increase the relative benefits of technological change, while raising the relative costs of technological stagnation. First, innovation can create a more competitive economy on international markets. As a result, innovation can boost exports, thus earning the foreign exchange necessary to purchase strategic imports. Second, a globally competitive high-technology sector can provide the foundation for a domestic defense industry. This can ease a nation's reliance on foreign weaponry. Finally, in civilian sectors, the development of indigenous S&T capabilities can enable domestic industry to produce those strategic goods that either are expensive to purchase abroad, have unreliable foreign suppliers, or are vulnerable to hostile interdiction. Competitive S&T-based industries can also generate capital by satisfying investors at home and luring investment from abroad. They can also provide jobs to skilled workers and a career path for youths, while arguably pulling up the aggregate skill level.[48]

In sum, S&T progress can best solve certain types of external threats. This creates pressure on the losers, as well as on political-economic elites, to reverse their calculus regarding the relative costs and risks of technological change. The net effect is that external threats to a nation's military or economic security tend to act as a force that increases support for innovation and its supporting institutions.

Mancur Olson and All That

Critics may be tempted to dismiss creative insecurity as merely a restatement of Mancur Olson's classic theory about the rise and decline of nations.[49] As an economist interested in politics, Olson wondered why small interest groups win their policy battles so often, even to the detriment of the popular majority. After all, democracy is supposed to be vulnerable to tyrannies of the majority, not the minority. The source of minority power, Olson reasoned, is that collective action to affect policy is itself a public goods problem. The few people who participate in collective action (e.g., protests, lobbying, and campaigns) must bear all of the costs and risks of their activism. But if these few activists are successful, then *everyone* may benefit from their hard work. As Olson brilliantly put it:

> . . .those who contribute nothing to the effort will get just as much as those who made a contribution. It pays to "let George do it" but George has little or no incentive to do anything in the group interest either, so. . .[under these conditions] there will be little, if any, group action. The paradox, then, is that . . . large groups, at least if they are composed of rational individuals, will *not* act in their group interest.[50]

However, small groups are less costly to organize than large ones. Also, if the benefits of collective action can be restricted to participants (a.k.a. "selective incentives"), then free-riders are eliminated. Thus, smaller groups, and those that have access to selective incentives, will be more likely to cooperate to obtain collective goods, and win, than larger groups or those who do not have selective incentives.[51] Under these conditions, participants may even get a substantial return on an investment in collective action.

Olson's theory of collective action would appear to describe well political resistance by technological losers. It is easy to imagine that organizing, say, six major oil firms to lobby against new technologies in alternative energy is a relatively easy task because the costs of coordinating a small number of preexisting corporations are low. Also, each firm stands to gain one-sixth of any mutual gains. The six firms can even design government subsidies, tax breaks, and regulations such that only *they* gain from the redistribution that follows. In contrast, organizing one hundred million consumers to support innovations in solar, wind, or tidal power is a far more expensive and difficult task. Also, not only will each individual consumer receive little in personal reward, but also each individual can free-ride on the efforts of the others. There is no way to limit the gains of political action to just the participants. This means that narrowly defined, self-serving interest groups that defend the status quo have an inherent advantage over broad groups that support technological change to help society as a whole. Writ large, this means that status quo lobbies tend to accumulate over time to block S&T progress.

Since Olson applied this logic to economic stagnation in 1982, a handful of other scholars have also observed that S&T progress creates winners and losers, and that the losers will resort to political resistance. Major contributions include those made by economists such as Joel Mokyr,[52] Daron Acemoglu and James Robinson,[53] and others.[54] In political science, similar important arguments have been made by Etel Solingen,[55] Stephan Haggard,[56] Daniel Drezner,[57] Richard Doner et al.,[58] and others.[59]

However, creative insecurity theory is distinctly different from any of these other arguments about the political-economic power of status quo interest groups. First, I point out that it is often S&T that is in the political minority, not the status quo forces. By definition, new S&T does not yet exist; therefore, its constituency is mostly potential and theoretical. Its existing interest group is often restricted to the innovators, entrepreneurs, employees, and others directly invested in the new S&T. Experience also tells us that many of these people allocate little time to, or interest in, political action. They are often far more absorbed by the science, technology, and business aspects of their innovations. Meanwhile, the status quo technologies often have large, well-established sets of interest groups who benefit from the existing S&T, enough of whom *do* recognize the importance of politics to defend their interests. This is the reverse of Olson's logic.

Second, some of the Olsonian scholars listed previously are primarily concerned with explaining economic growth or development in general; they therefore either ignore S&T progress in particular or refer to it only peripherally. In these theories, S&T often gets lost among a number of other causal factors that contribute to economic growth or development. Alternately, some of these scholars explicitly focus on explaining the diffusion or adoption of new S&T rather than innovation itself. In contrast, this book recognizes that innovation and diffusion can overlap, interact, and be difficult to distinguish from one another or from economic growth and development. Yet, where possible, creative insecurity theory attempts to focus narrowly on S&T progress in particular; most other theories do not.

Worse yet, some Olsonian theories lump institutions and policies together with S&T in their hypotheses. All are treated as causal variables to explain overall economic performance. To the contrary, creative insecurity separates them out: institutions and policies are treated as causes, and national S&T performance is the effect. Creative insecurity then argues that institutions and policies affect, but do not determine, national innovation rates, and that institutions and policies are better thought of as tools rather than causal forces.

Third, and most strikingly, almost all scholars who recognize the distributive aspects of S&T also universally prescribe "good" institutions and policies as their solutions. For some, the argument is that the less an economy is controlled by government, the less vulnerable it will be to capture by status quo interest groups. This ignores the fact that progress in S&T suffers from a variety of major market failures and network failures and therefore often *requires* government intervention. Previous chapters have established this very firmly. Therefore, others argue that we simply need the right institutions and policies. These usually take the form of property rights, free markets, and decentralized democracy. However, as we have already seen, this overlooks the massive evidence that shows that even solidly democratic and capitalist institutions and policies are *themselves* vulnerable to capture by status quo interest groups. Many of these highly recommended institutions and polices were tested in the previous chapters, with disappointing results. Again, there are simply too many countries with "good" institutions that fail to innovate much, and too many with "bad" or missing institutions that innovate surprisingly well. For any institution, policy, or combination, there are significant outliers, failures, or leftover unexplained variation. And even if we still buy the "institutions rule!" argument, this just brings us back to the following question: why do some countries create and maintain with better institutions and policies than others? I argue that the answer is creative insecurity.

What about Mancur Olson himself? He made several predictions about the conditions under which a nation should suffer stagnation due to build-ups of status quo interest groups.[60] First, he argued that stable societies with unchanged boundaries should tend to build up these anti-innovation groups over time, resulting in relative economic decline. He further contended that large, diverse nations would suffer less resistance to change than would smaller, homogeneous societies, because collective action by status quo interests is easier in the latter. Olson also concluded that only a major shake-up, or violent catastrophe, that sweeps away the cobwebs of cartels and old institutions can renew a country's technological vitality. He identified World War II as just such a deck-clearing event for Japan and Germany, thereby explaining their technological performance during the decades immediately after.

However, the innovation data and case histories fail to support Olson's hypotheses well. For example, Figure 8.2a presents data on regime stability and innovation. Here a stable regime is defined as one that changes little over time, with no drastic shifts in its type of government. The x-axis indicates the number of years (going back to the year 1800) since the most recent regime change as of 2012.[61] The y-axis shows our usual national innovation measure (citations-weighted patents per capita, US = 1.00) during the past forty-two-year block. If Olson is correct, then older, and hence more stable, regimes should be less innovative due to the accumulation of status quo interest groups there. Yet the scatterplot reveals that stable societies have a *positive* relationship with national innovation rates, rather than the negative relationship suggested by Olson.

As for size, recall that in a previous chapter we found that the size of a country's economy or population does not correlate well with innovation rates. Olson specifically refers to the costs of collective action; therefore, population size is of particular interest here. Figure 8.2b reminds us that there may be a moderate relationship between population size and innovation on average, but that this average is often violated. Once again, we can see that there are many large countries that fail to innovate much (e.g., China, India, Indonesia, Brazil, Russia, Mexico, and the Philippines) and many small countries that innovate quite well (e.g., Singapore, Ireland, Finland, Israel, Denmark, Switzerland, and Sweden).

As for diversity, Figures 8.2c–e suggest little strong relationship on any measure. The diversity data shown here is for various types of fractionalization. Fractionalization is the probability that two individuals chosen randomly from a society belong to different groups. The data reveal that religious fractionalization may aid national innovation rates slightly, while ethnic fractionalization appears to have a somewhat negative correlation, and fractionalization by linguistic group seems to have little relationship at all. Use of data on polarization, instead of fractionalization, produces very similar results.[62] So both fractionalization and polarization cut all ways: some types help, other types hurt, and still others have

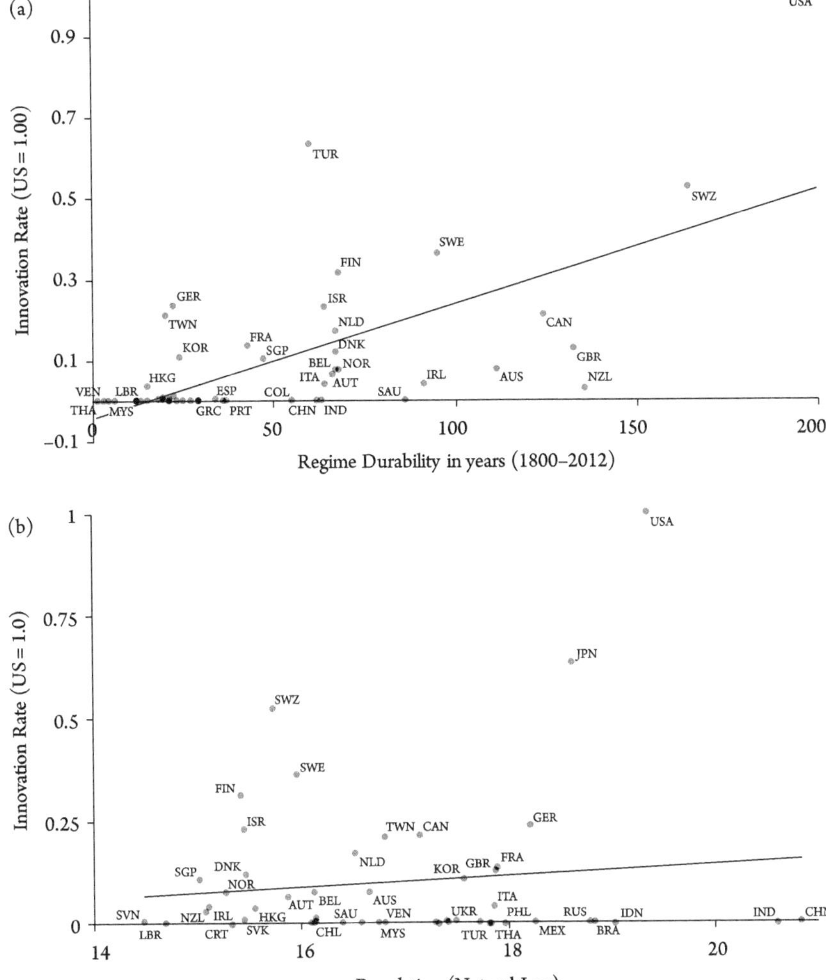

Figure 8.2 Testing Mancur Olson. a. Innovation versus regime durability. b. Innovation versus population. c. Innovation versus religious fractionalization. d. Innovation versus ethnic fractionalization. e. Innovation versus linguistic fractionalization. f. Innovation versus combined Olson variables.

no effect. In no case is the relationship between any type of fractionalization (or polarization) and innovation very strong or rigorous. There are many nations placed far away from the regression line and on either side of it. To further corroborate this nonfinding, multiple studies of fractionalization and polarization also contradict Olson's hypothesis about their positive effects on economic growth and development.[63]

If we combine all of Olson's causal variables into a single statistical regression (Figure 8.2f), then we get a similarly dissatisfying outcome. In the results of such

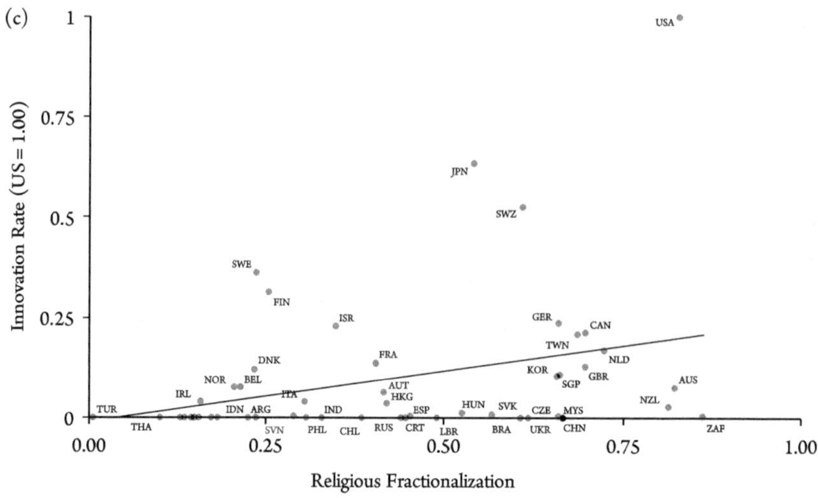

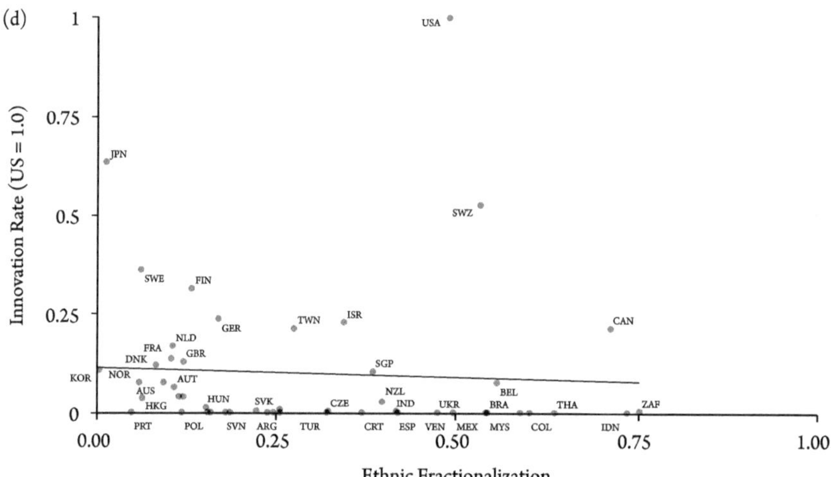

Figure 8.2 Continued

a regression, only regime durability is statistically significant, the signs on the coefficients generally point the wrong way, and the entire set of Olson's variables explain only around 40% of the variation.

Even if we look at only the most likely cases, we still cannot find confirmation of Olson's thesis. Within our sample, the four most homogenous, small, and stable states in the world are Portugal, Norway, Ireland, and Greece.[64] Each of these nations also enjoys relatively stable societies and borders, at least by Olson's definition. There have been no recent civil wars, regime changes, and so forth. Therefore, these societies should be mired in Olsonian stagnation, as status quo interest groups build up like muck to gum up the works of the economy, thereby preventing innovation. Certainly this description might fit Portugal or

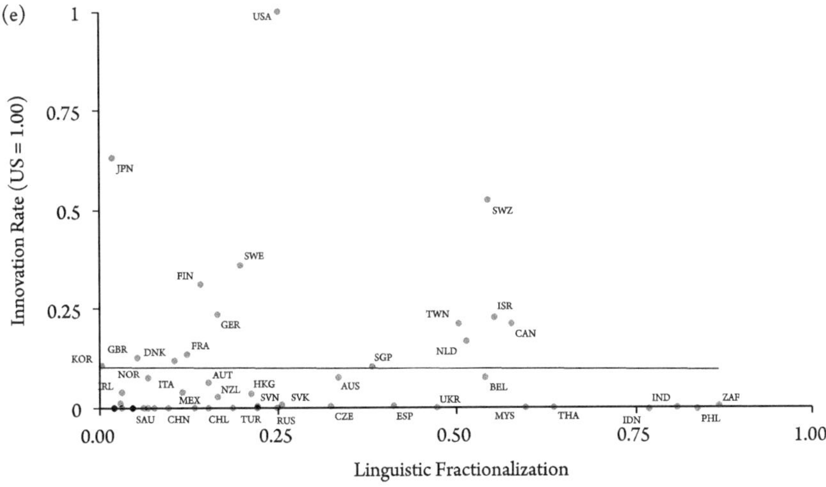

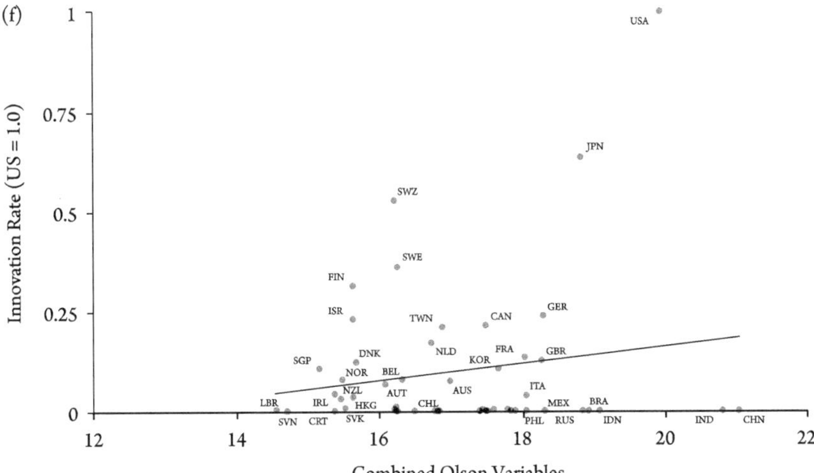

Figure 8.2 Continued

Greece; however, we have already shown that Ireland became a rapid innovator, and Norway is a midlevel innovator. At the other extreme, the two largest and most diverse states in the sample are Indonesia and the United States. The US has become the world's leader in innovation (predicted by Olson's theory), but Indonesia is a relative non-performer (contradicts Olson).

Finally, Olson believed that great crises wiped out status quo interest groups, thus releasing the forces of innovation. While the next chapter will investigate several cases in greater depth, we can here quickly observe that many rapid innovators suffered no such crises. In fact, Olson wrote his masterpiece primarily to explain the apparent stagnation that had arrested the United States throughout the 1970s. Since then, there has been no massive crisis that forced a revolutionary shakeup of American society, yet innovation there has flourished.[65] Nor have there been any radical house cleanings in Singapore, Israel, Sweden, Finland, or Canada to explain the timing or extent of their high S&T productivity.

On the other hand, many countries hit by Olsonian catastrophes *failed* to become innovative. For example, the 1997 economic crisis in Indonesia was precisely the kind of violent catastrophe that Olson said *should* wipe out status quo interest groups and free the country to shift into high technology. Even more profound crises and revolutions swept through Eastern Europe during the early 1990s. Yet, twenty years later, none of these countries has innovated nearly as well as Japan or Germany did at the same point in their histories after World War II. Consider also the following major regime changes since 1970: Thatcher's political-economic revolution in Britain; France's abandonment of extreme dirigisme; the regular, peaceful regime shake-ups in Thailand; the Chavez revolution in Venezuela; the post-Franco transformation of Spain; the establishment of Portugal's Third Republic; and the end of apartheid in South Africa. Each of these would fit Olson's criterion for "countries whose distributional coalitions have been emasculated or abolished";[66] yet not one of these crises has yet borne much fruit in terms of major changes to national innovation rates.

To sum up, Olson was correct when he claimed that status quo interest groups will resort to politics to block changes that threaten their interests, but his other theses are not well supported, at least not as they apply to innovation. Perhaps these contradictions are why, toward the end of his career, Olson also embraced the "institutions rule!" thesis. In Olson's final years, he concluded that decentralized government and "good governance" were the best solutions to the stagnation problem.[67] But the previous chapters have already described the dead ends to which these arguments lead us.

Statistical Evidence for Creative Insecurity

Does any evidence exist for creative insecurity? The remainder of this chapter uses statistical data to perform some basic plausibility tests of the theory; the next chapter goes deeper by investigating several case studies. This combination of different methodologies and data types provides a powerful tool with which to assay creative insecurity theory. The statistics assess the fundamental credibility of creative insecurity: do cross-national time-series data show supporting correlations, and in the predicted directions, overall? Statistical analysis also allows us to examine a large number of nations across several decades, and thereby judge how universally creative insecurity theory applies (i.e., do most countries adhere close to the average or are there many outliers?). The next chapter's case studies will allow us to investigate whether creative insecurity focuses on the correct variables and causal mechanisms. That is, statistics can show correlation, but only case studies can show causation. Case studies can also reveal endogeneity (i.e., does creative insecurity cause innovation or vice versa?). Finally, quantitative measures of both creative insecurity and innovation are vulnerable to criticism; therefore, case studies provide us with independent qualitative data with which to confirm the statistics. In sum, statistics allow us to look at the overall "big picture," but these data are often noisy. Case studies get us past this noise by examining the country-specific details, but these individual country studies do not provide the "big picture." Only when they are used together can we acquire a balanced inventory of empirical evidence.

Statistical tests bring up the issue of measuring creative insecurity. The major problem here is that domestic rivalries and external threats have subjective components. Just like innovation, rivalry and threat measurement can be based on perception, based on psychology, or even socially constructed. However, if creative insecurity theory has any explanatory power, then it should be confirmable in simple cross-national correlations of some relatively noncontroversial data. While there are no established measures for "relative threat balance," we can look at a combination of common-sense proxies such as domestic political violence, external wars, and strategic imports.

For example, countries typified by intense domestic rivalries tend to suffer frequent strikes, protests, and high levels of economic inequality. Governments there may even use force to redistribute wealth away from, or to severely regulate, innovative activity to ameliorate status quo interests and deaden the gale of creative destruction. In extreme cases, antagonistic societies may experience bouts of civil war. We can therefore use these types of data to construct a rough measure of a nation's domestic rivalries.

External threats, as defined by creative insecurity, are slightly easier to observe. Countries facing considerable external military threat are often characterized by histories of frequent international conflict. As for external economic threats, these are defined as a heavy reliance on imports for strategic inputs, such as food and energy. These data can be used to build a measure of a nation's external hazards.

Figures 8.3a–c attempt to test the basic plausibility of creative insecurity by looking at different statistical proxies for domestic rivalries and external threats. In each scatterplot, the y-axis is our standard national innovation measure (citations-weighted patents per capita, US = 1.00) during the 1970–2012 period. Figure 8.3a attempts to gauge the relationship between domestic rivalries and innovation by using the Political Terror Scale created by Reed Wood and Mark Gibney while at the University of North Carolina at Asheville.[68] High scores for political terror correspond with the greater use by elites of imprisonment, threats, violence, and executions against political opposition groups.

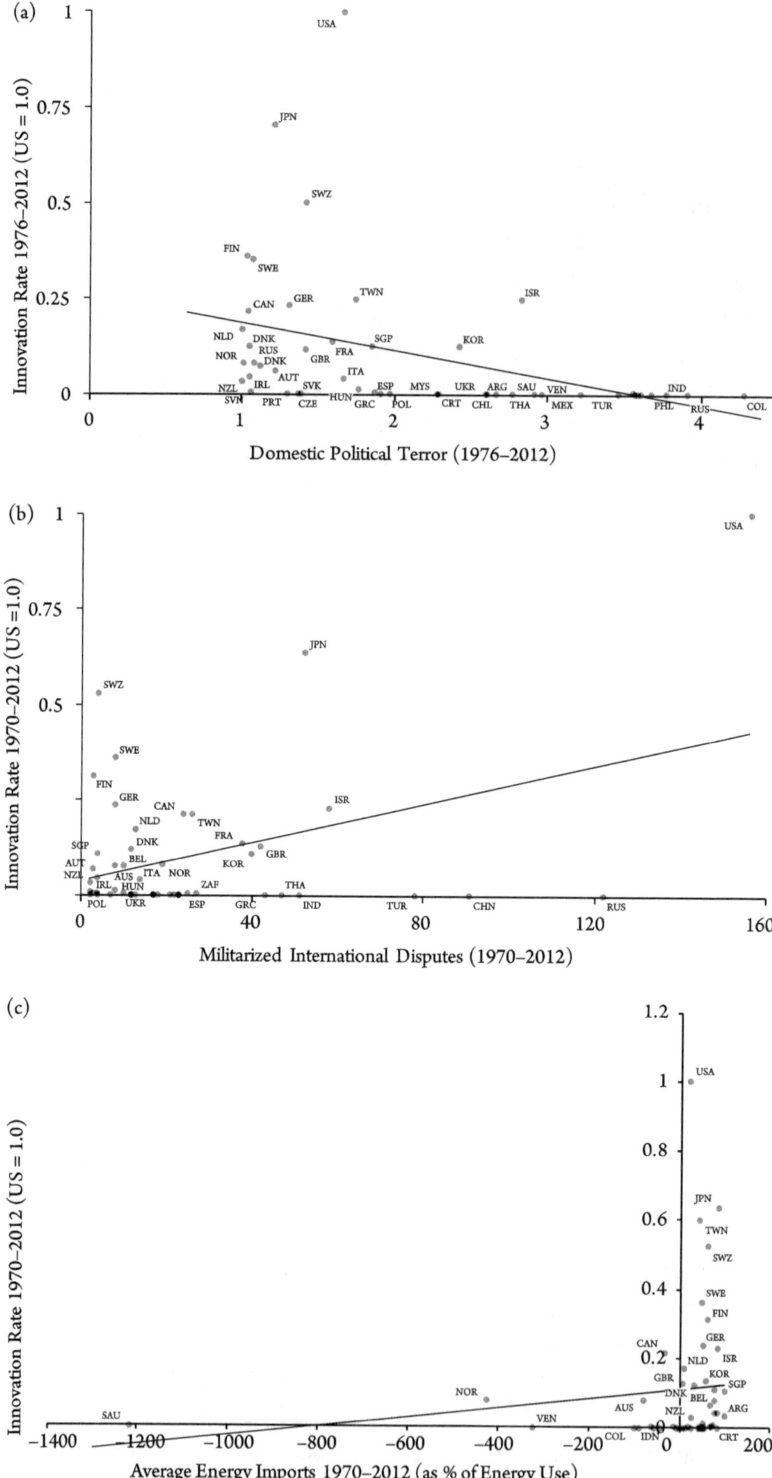

Figure 8.3 Innovation, domestic tensions, and external threats. a. Innovation versus domestic political terror. b Innovation versus militarized international disputes. c Innovation versus energy imports.

The assumption here is that, as domestic rivalries increase in scope and intensity, opposing domestic groups will increasingly use force to defend their interests. The scatterplot suggests an overall negative relationship between domestic rivalries and innovation, as predicted by creative insecurity. On average, as countries experience more domestic political terror, they tend to innovate less.

Figure 8.3b attempts to gauge external military threats by using data on the number of militarized interstate disputes (MIDs) experienced by a country during the 1970–2012 time period. MIDs are defined as

> cases of conflict in which the threat, display or use of military force short of war by one member state is explicitly directed towards the government, official representatives, official forces, property, or territory of another state. . . . [MIDs] range in intensity from threats to use force to actual combat short of war.[69]

MIDs are used instead of full-scale wars because the latter (defined as 1,000 or morebattle deaths) constitute a very small sample (less than two dozen) and omit much important external threat. The underlying premise here is that a greater number of MIDs indicates a greater external threat. These data suggest that the more often countries must threaten or use armed force against a foreign enemy, the greater their innovation rate, also as predicted by creative insecurity.

Figure 8.3c looks at the economic component of external threats through the lens of energy imports. Even though this measures the vulnerability of just one strategic import, the results here are fairly striking. For all countries, there is an average positive relationship, as predicted by creative insecurity. Interestingly, the relationship is markedly stronger for net energy importers than for net energy exporters. That is, as countries grow more dependent on imports for energy, their innovative rate accelerates.

Of course, creative insecurity requires us to combine these two forces, domestic rivalries and external threats, into a single measure of "relative threat balance." Table 8.1 presents an elementary, but straightforward, attempt to do this. It combines measures of several different types of security concerns. Nations are judged to have *relatively* greater domestic tensions than external threats if they experience relatively more labor strikes, greater economic inequality, less reliance on imports of food and energy, or fewer years of external conflict. Conversely, nations are judged to have relatively greater external threats than domestic tensions if they have *relatively* fewer labor strikes, less economic inequality, higher reliance on imports of food and energy, or more years of external conflict. Finally, countries that have recently suffered a civil war or a military dictatorship that actively redistributes wealth away from S&T sectors and

Table 8.1 **Indicators of a Country's Relative Balance of Security Concerns**

External Threats > Domestic Rivalries	*Domestic Tensions > External Rivalries*
• Fewer labor strikes	• More labor strikes
• Lower economic inequality	• Greater economic inequality
• Higher imports of food and energy as percentage of total consumed	• Lower imports of food and energy as percentage of total consumed
• Longer recent history of external conflicts	• Shorter recent history of external conflicts
• No recent civil war	• Recent civil war
	• Anti-S&T, pro–status quo military dictatorship

Sources: National strike data is taken from the International Labor Organization's *Yearbook of Labour Statistics.* Economic inequality data comes from the University of Texas Inequality Project. Energy and food import dependency data is taken from the World Bank Development Indicators (energy imports as percentage of total energy used, agricultural land as percent of total land area). Conflict data comes from the Correlates of War (external conflict duration) and the University of Texas Political Regime Dataset (years civil war). Regime data comes from the University of Texas Political Regime Dataset (years military dictatorship). See Galbraith (2009) and http://utip.govs.utexas.edu/data.html.

entrepreneurs (and toward status quo actors, labor, welfare, agriculture, or natural resource sectors) are considered to have a *relatively* greater concern with domestic rivalries.[70]

To create a single indicator, the data are treated as follows. For each category in Table 8.1 (strikes, inequality, etc.), the data are averaged across all countries. Then, within each category, nations above the mathematical average are assigned +1 (for more external), and nations below the average are assigned –1 (for more domestic). Each country's scores are then summed across categories for a rough approximation of its overall relative balance of security concerns. Countries are then further categorized into five levels of relative threat balance, from strongly external to neutral to strongly domestic. These levels are then tested against our data on national innovation rates. While this test is admittedly simplistic, it provides prima facie evidence in support of creative insecurity theory.

Figure 8.4 shows the results of this simple test for the 1970–2010 period. The relative balance of security concerns is indicated along the x-axis. Countries for which threat balance is strongly domestic are found toward the left, countries with a neutral balance are in the center, and countries with a relatively greater external threat balance are placed toward the right. The y-axis indicates the national innovation rate using our standard measure (technology patents

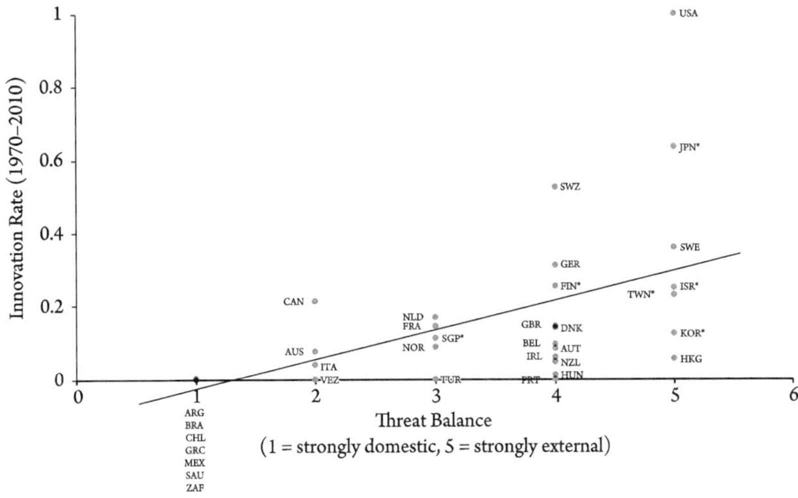

Figure 8.4 Relative balance of security concerns versus national innovation rates (1970–2010). *Rapid innovators: nations with largest and most rapid improvements in innovation rates between 1970 and 2010.

per capita, weighted by forward citations, granted during the time period, with US = 1.0).

The results presented in Figure 8.4 generally support the creative insecurity theory. Every nation in the category of strongly domestic threat balance also has very poor S&T performance. As the threat balance shifts toward the external, we find more innovative nations. At the extreme right, *all* of the nations with the largest and most rapid improvements in annual innovation rates during the past several decades (Finland, Ireland, Israel, Japan, South Korea, and Taiwan) can be found among the states with the strongest external threat balance. While each of these highly innovative countries was certainly troubled by domestic rivalries, these internal tensions were outweighed by external threats. It is also worth noting that the favorable regression line shown in Figure 8.4 is biased *against* confirming creative insecurity theory. How? Recall that this scatterplot uses national S&T outputs *averaged* over forty years. Hence, the poor performance of rapid innovators (like Japan, Israel, Taiwan, South Korea, and Finland) during the 1970s drags these countries down and flattens the regression line. It downplays the swift, dramatic improvements in these nations' S&T performance.

What about outliers? Overall, Canada is the only major outlier in Figure 8.4. Canada has long been one of the world's most innovative countries, yet it falls in to the category of moderately domestic in its relative threat balance. Perhaps one might explain away Canada as an extension or beneficiary of US demand for innovation. Clearly more research is needed here. Less easy to explain away are Austria and Italy, though they are also less strikingly deviant. They each have moderately domestic threat balances, but also only rank as midlevel innovators. A fourth curious case is Portugal, which is not much of an innovator, but it falls into the moderately external category for its relative threat balance. Otherwise, countries generally fall where creative insecurity theory would predict.

Independent statistical confirmation can be found in preliminary research by Joseph M. Grieco at Duke University.[71] In a recent study, Grieco et al. looked at the patenting behavior of 104 countries between 1984 and 2012. To control for the role of domestic conflict in economic transactions, they used a measure of domestic conflict developed by Arthur Banks (2012), which incorporates data on assassinations, general strikes, guerrilla warfare, government crises, purges, riots, revolutions, and antigovernment demonstrations. For their measure of external threats, they looked only at militarized interstate disputes, not economic dependency. Yet, they found that even after controlling for a range of domestic economic, scientific, and political conditions, nations that experience more military conflicts tend to achieve higher national innovation rates. Specifically, their statistical analysis suggests that, on average, every additional external military conflict is associated with at least a 6% increase in patenting, and possibly as high as 40%. They further corroborated these results using two independent sources of patent data, as well as data on high-tech exports.

Of course, in each scatterplot in Figures 8.3 and 8.4, the spread of data points around the trend lines is wide; therefore, the statistical relationships are admittedly loose. There is much noise in these data. Nevertheless, each relationship is statistically significant and slopes in the direction predicted by creative insecurity theory. Also recall that the purpose of this data is not to prove beyond reproach that creative security theory works, but to test its basic plausibility. If the statistics had showed no relationship or relationships opposite of those predicted, then we might easily dismiss creative security as not plausible or generalizable. Instead, the statistical data do generally corroborate the creative insecurity theory. Having passed these simple smell tests, the next step is stricter analyses. We must go beyond correlation and get at causal mechanisms. We need to corroborate these statistics and flesh out the details of cause and effect. For this purpose, the next chapter delves deeper into the experiences of a few countries. Because we already have some knowledge of Israel, Taiwan, Ireland, and Mexico from chapter 6, we return to these nations. What were the politics behind their relative success or failure in S&T? How well does creative insecurity explain this set of very diverse cases?

9

Critical Cases of Creative Insecurity

Thus far, this book has argued that none of the conventional wisdom fully explains or predicts national innovation rates well. There appear to be no institutional or policy "silver bullets," no competitive advantages to be gained from size or history. Even democracy and capitalism explain little. There are simply too many violations and outliers, too many most likely cases that fail, and too many least likely cases that succeed. The cases and data do not support any of the most popular explanations either in the aggregate or over time. At best, institutions, policies, and networks help us to explain *how* nations innovate, but not *why* they do so. A new, better theory is needed.

The previous two chapters then argued that the fundamental drivers of national innovation rates are society-wide, political calculations over the costs and benefits of science and technology (S&T). Innovation creates winners and losers. These two forces battle it out, via politics, over resources and regulations. Certain conditions favor S&T as the victor, while other conditions favor status quo interest groups. Creative insecurity theory posits that the pivotal factor is security. Specifically, all societies confront a combination of domestic rivalries and external threats. Where external military and economic threats outweigh domestic rivalries, increasing the production of S&T is often the best strategy for a country to pursue. Under these conditions, the losers created by S&T or its institutions will tend to be convinced, compensated, or coerced into supporting innovation. Therefore, countries whose external threats dominate over domestic rivalries should tend to innovate more than countries whose domestic rivalries outweigh external threats.

Does creative insecurity theory perform any better than its rivals? The last chapter offered an opening salvo of statistics. These data support the plausibility of creative insecurity, but statistics can only take us so far. Some important measures can only be approximated, some data are admittedly rough, and even flawless statistical analysis can show only correlation, not causation. Rather, in a perfect world, one would perform in-depth, individual case studies of every country over the past seventy years to verify the causal mechanisms and relationships posited in the previous chapters. Future volumes should certainly endeavor to undertake this mighty task, but we need to be more circumspect here.

This chapter therefore revisits the cases of Israel, Taiwan, Ireland, and Mexico. These countries were not cherry-picked a priori because they confirm creative insecurity. Rather, they are useful for several reasons. First, they steer us away from the already well-known and well-documented cases of the United States, Japan, and South Korea, each of which tends to confirm creative insecurity.[1] This chapter recognizes that the innovation debate can gain far more from investigations of nations that are less well studied. Second, readers should now be somewhat familiar with Israel, Taiwan, Ireland, and Mexico from chapter 6, which investigated how and when each country recently succeeded or failed at innovation. This chapter builds upon this knowledge base. It explores the constellations of changing threats faced by each of these societies and links them to changes in political support for S&T. Third, these four countries represent starkly different regions, cultures, histories, and sizes, as well as drastically different types of government, institutions, policies, and networks. This is important because, if creative insecurity is so powerful an explanation, then it should work regardless of these other national characteristics. Fourth, these four countries allow us to compare various degrees of success and failure, rather than looking only at cases of high success, as is often done with other theories. We should find that, regardless of the differences between them, each nation's balance of security challenges should generally match its innovation rate. Also, this relationship should hold both across countries and within the same country over time. That is, as each nation's balance of security threats shifts between external and domestic, we should see similar shifts in support for S&T policies, institutions, and networks, and then the resulting changes in S&T performance.

As the cases in this chapter reveal, a combination of military and economic security concerns *do* appear to trigger demands for policy change. Success in addressing security concerns often requires that elites increase national S&T capabilities. It is partly due to their ability to solve the market failures and network failures that obstruct innovation, and to reduce the costs of S&T development, that elites fully implement some of the institutions and policies examined in the previous chapters. Let's examine how this works.

Israel Revisited: War, Recession, Integration, and Science and Technology in the Jewish State

Israel's experience fits the "creative insecurity" explanation fairly well.[2] For twenty years after its founding in 1948, Israel was mired in technological backwardness. It was disadvantaged by a heavily agricultural economy, little industry, and even less public support for S&T or the institutions that foster innovation. The Israelis did not hate or fear S&T; they simply had higher priorities. Specifically, they allocated their resources toward defeating the centrifugal forces that threatened to undermine their new nation, for Israel was then in chaos. It was a society bursting with immigrants from dozens of nations and cultures, constantly in political-economic disputes with one another, all crammed into a tiny, resource-poor country. Externally, Israel's hostile neighbors were relatively less threatening. The Arab states were then too divided, disorganized, and poorly equipped to invade or besiege Israel.

This situation drastically changed during the late 1960s and early 1970s. Israel's domestic concerns faded as a generation of political compromise forged both a cohesive Israeli identity and a strong social contract. However, the external threats to Israel's military and economic security soared. Regional politics combined with Cold War conflicts to forge a stronger, more united Arab opposition, while creating distance between Israel and its most important allies. Meanwhile, years of government spending and economic inefficiency brought Israel into a decade of inflation, slow growth, and balance-of-payments difficulties. This new combination of threats prompted widespread calls within Israel for an indigenous S&T capability to counter them, while lowering political opposition to the costs and redistribution that such innovation might bring. These pressures soon created strong political support for changes to Israeli S&T institutions, policies, and networking, which increased the incentives and rewards for innovation. In fact, the shift was so drastic and sustained that Israel quickly became a global competitor in S&T and high-technology industries. Israel became innovative because it found itself in a state of creative insecurity that remains to this day. Let's unpack this story to see how creative insecurity worked there.

From 1948 to 1967, Israel's primary national problems were all related to resolving the fierce domestic tensions that threatened its very existence. Israel was then plagued by a highly fragmented and divided polity. Disparate interest groups fought constantly over economic resources, political power, and policy control. Perhaps the driving centrifugal force was immigration. After years of relatively slow population growth, in 1948, hundreds of thousands of immigrants rushed into the small state of less than a million people.[3] Over the next three years, Israel experienced a sudden 60% expansion of its population, which was already packed into only eight thousand square miles of mostly desert.[4] Thereafter, per capita immigration rates remained high for years as Israel was infused with waves of immigrants from around Europe, the Middle East, and Africa.[5] Settlement of these newcomers put enormous pressure on Israel's frail institutions and sparse resources. Soon tensions developed between the new immigrants and older residents, while immigrant diversity only intensified these conflicts. These new "Israelis" spoke myriad languages, came from different cultures, and brought with them personal beliefs and experiences derived from disparate social, political, and economic systems.[6]

A three-sided political contest soon emerged within Israel over economic resources and state policies. On one side were the more educated, skilled, secular, white Ashkenazi Jews from Europe. These Israelis tended to support social welfare programs at home and a peaceful foreign policy abroad. A second front consisted of more religious, less educated or skilled Sephardic Jews from the Middle East and North Africa. These groups favored more spending on, and protections for, agriculture and labor. Both these groups competed with a third, ultra-orthodox Jewish minority who questioned the very legitimacy of a pre-messianic Israeli state and Jews' obligations to it. These splits regularly manifested themselves in fierce debates over economic, defense, and social policies and spending.[7] None of these groups prioritized S&T.

As a result of these divisions, social cohesion among Israelis was weak to the point of threatening the nation itself. Each faction had radically different interests in, and ideas for, the Israeli state and their own role within it. Prime Minister Golda Meir later described Israel during this time as a "rather claustrophobic community, coping—not always well—with all sorts of economic, political, and social discontents."[8] Even military security was at risk because the Israeli armed forces became incoherent. The Israel Defense Force (IDF), created by a wartime executive order, was formed quickly out of an underground resistance movement.[9] Yet for months thereafter, both leftist and rightist political groups in Israel tried to maintain independent armies, each under its own command and frequently in disagreement over territory and tactics.[10] Even within the IDF, military units tended to self-segregate, with soldiers defending only the settlements from which they were recruited. Then, after independence, huge numbers of experienced native soldiers quit the IDF, leaving the Israeli military saturated with fresh immigrants who spoke neither Hebrew nor each other's native languages.[11] It was a perfect Babel.

With its society so divided, Israel's top priority was to forge a more durable, united polity. Without such unity, the new state might not survive long, much less prosper. To this end, Israeli elites and interest groups quickly created a highly interventionist state. The government's primary goal was to absorb Israel's disparate groups and knit them together into a strong, cohesive Jewish society that could defend itself against Arab incursions.[12] S&T was simply not perceived as a means to this end. If anything, heavy investments in S&T and its institutions would likely exacerbate tensions by creating economic winners and losers among the already divisive factions.

Instead, to erode Israel's divisions and forge a strong Jewish national identity, Israel adopted a low-tech, quasi-socialist approach toward its economy. All Israelis were to share in the nation's resources and in the benefits and costs of economic development. The government therefore created institutions and policies that favored agriculture and basic industries, but that also benefited labor, religious groups, and the lower classes. For example, one major development institution was collectivist farming. Backed by the state, these *kibbutz* and *Moshav* settlements came to account for 15% of gross domestic product (GDP) and 30% of exports.[13] Outside of the agricultural sector, the labor unions (*Histadrut*) dominated economic life. They brought together the interests of diverse groups of unskilled and semiskilled immigrants. The *Histadrut* owned large-scale industrial enterprises, the major health service, pension funds, and an array of other economic concerns. A third pier of Israel's development plan was the state itself, which also played a prominent role in the economy. The state owned the vast majority of Israeli land, rigidly controlled all foreign exchange and all import and export licenses, directed virtually all financial capital, and owned most physical and technological infrastructure (e.g., electricity, ports, telecommunications, the major airline), and state-owned enterprises made up a large portion of the national economy. Coordinating it all, the Labor Party, backed and staffed by the *Histadrut* and its allies, became the strongest political force in Israel and primary determinant of national policy. Hence, all of the state's and labor's efforts were directed toward forging a strong Jewish national identity, with a bias toward the middle and lower classes.[14]

With the entire Israeli nation absorbed in forging unity through religion, agriculture, military service, basic industry, and social welfare, relatively few assets were left for science and technology. In fact, prior to the late 1960s, neither Israeli society nor the state put much priority on S&T or the development of high-tech industries. Perhaps the only major exception was Israel's nuclear program, which provided few spillovers to other sectors due to its secrecy.[15] Otherwise, Israel's domestic institutions and policies were *not* directed toward promoting S&T. The patent system was weak, little support was given to research and development (R&D), education spending was low, and Israeli trade policy was geared toward promoting imports of foreign technology, especially weapons. Even within defense, there was relatively little focus on high technology other than atomic weapons. Overall R&D spending was lower than any Organization for Economic Cooperation and Development (OECD) country except Italy, and Israel employed less than half the proportion of science, technology, engineering, and mathematics (STEM) labor as frontier innovators like United States and Sweden.[16] In fact, until the early 1970s, only a single Israeli university offered engineering degrees.[17] Israelis may have awarded S&T high rhetoric, but they did not give it many resources.

In some quarters of Israeli society, historical traditions of science and intellectualism were then even identified with weakness. For example, one scholar-journalist writes that, during this time, Israel's labor and Zionist groups "saw in

Jewish bookishness a distorted personality and general unhealthiness. They held that excessive intellectualism was bad . . . a form of escapism."[18] As a result, scholastic excellence and entrepreneurialism were de-emphasized in some schools, while teamwork, strength, and bravery were prioritized.[19] Teaching these latter values to Israeli youths was the solution to Israel's most pressing problems (i.e., domestic tensions and social cohesion), not laboratory research or STEM courses.

It helped that, before the mid-1960s, Israel's external threats were relatively less existential. Although menaced on all sides by hostile Arab states, Israel's adversaries were in fact weak and constantly infighting. The Arabs scowled and blustered. But they also suffered from fractious interstate rivalries that rendered them unable to form a viable military coalition to invade Israel.[20] In fact, Israel even maintained an informal strategic alliance with neighboring Jordan, which partly insulated Israel against Arab machinations. Despite occasional clashes, Jordanian artifice made possible Israel's victory in its War of Independence in 1948 and then prevented the emergence of an independent Palestine.[21] Arab militaries were also weak, poorly trained, and often suffered a numerical disadvantage to Israel's forces.[22] Finally, Israel's ruling Labor Party was relatively more dovish on security issues and a strong advocate for peace. As a result, Israel suffered only one major military conflict in the eighteen years after its independence. This occurred in 1956 and lasted for just two weeks, during which Israel acted as part of an overwhelming coalition with France and the United Kingdom against Egypt's nationalization of the Suez Canal.[23]

Then, during the late 1960s, Israel's balance of domestic tensions versus external threats radically reversed itself. Military and terror incidents near the borders with Syria and Jordan increased, eventually escalating into major armed confrontations. As a result, the delicate trust between Israel and Jordan broke down. Jordan soon signed a joint defense pact with Egypt, which was already allied with Syria. More ominously, the USSR emerged as an ally of the Arabs, providing them with military intelligence and political support, and even arming Egypt with ever more sophisticated weaponry.[24] This new collusion pit Israel against a technological superpower. In 1967, war finally broke out; Israel now finally faced an existential threat from its neighbors. Egypt, Jordan, and Syria at last cooperated to organize hundreds of thousands of troops along Israel's borders. Eight other Arab states and the Palestine Liberation Organization contributed various forms of support for the Six Day War that followed.[25] The military threats to Israel only grew larger thereafter. Repeated skirmishes erupted with Egypt (1969–1970), Arab terror attacks rose, and Israel suffered the surprise attacks of the Yom Kippur War (1973). Thereafter, Palestinian groups initiated a routine of chronic terrorist attacks against Israel. Although US support for Israel was increasing, it was then new, of questionable reliability, and never entirely trusted by Israelis.[26] Israel's fragile external security had broken down.

In prior crises, Israel could reliably depend on foreign imports for much of its energy, manufactured goods, and military hardware. In particular, France was its primary supplier of weapons and technological assistance, including tanks, aircraft, missile technology, and even atomic research. However, on the eve of the 1967 war, France suddenly cut off Israel from its weapons exports but continued to ship arms to Israel's enemies.[27] This left the Jewish state strategically vulnerable to its predatory neighbors.

Simultaneously, Israel was also hit by repeated and prolonged economic crises. Its first economic recession struck in 1965–1967, the result of years of heavy government spending, protectionism, and growing inefficiencies in agriculture and industry.[28] The recession exacerbated Israel's security situation by creating a prolonged surge in unemployment, while also eating into the foreign reserves needed to pay for strategic imports. Starting in 1973, the threat to Israel's foreign exchange reserves mounted further as Israel fell into a twelve-year economic slump. Economic growth slowed from 9%–10% to 3% per year, foreign debts and inflation skyrocketed, and the Israeli banking system collapsed.[29] There were few domestic sources of timber, minerals, or energy that Israel could fall back on to either use at home or export for foreign exchange.

In contrast, on the domestic front, Israel's internal divisions had ratcheted down. After decades of unification policies, the political, economic, and cultural differences between different Jewish groups had become far less severe. Also, by the late 1960s, immigration as a percentage of the total population had eased such that major sections of Israeli society were no longer being transformed on a regular basis. The major left-wing political parties, which had dominated Israeli politics since statehood, began to share power, however reluctantly, with the Right.[30] By the mid-1970s, a viable multiparty democracy had emerged in Israel supported by an admittedly argumentative but strongly cohesive society. Thus, after 1967, Israel's balance of security concerns consistently shifted away from domestic tensions and toward external threats.

This is when Israel's S&T revolution began (described in chapter 6). The external threats, both military and economic, combined with a decrease in domestic tensions to create a widespread surge in Israeli support for S&T and high-tech industries. Having forged a strong national identity, and with major interest groups willing to compromise with one another on economic policy, Israel's main priority now became to earn foreign exchange and reduce dependence on foreign technology. Israel's major actors and interest groups recognized that the creation of indigenous high-technology industries would do both. A phalanx of globally competitive, R&D-based, private industries would allow Israel to earn the dollars, francs, and pounds necessary for strategic imports. They would also provide indigenous capability in military technologies, thus reducing the Israeli military's reliance on foreign imports. A surge in high-tech industries could additionally create high-wage jobs and reduce unemployment. S&T therefore quickly graduated from near irrelevance to the primary solution to Israel's military and economic problems.

Israel now redirected its institutions and policies to foster S&T. Parties on the Right and Left came together to support major fiscal reforms, which lowered taxation on business and investment while eliminating copious exemptions for special interest groups.[31] Patent laws were strengthened. R&D spending quadrupled. New universities were founded and existing STEM training programs strengthened. S&T advisers were elevated across government. By the early 1970s, government, military, labor, and business groups had united to support a broad reform of Israeli political-economic institutions and networks favoring greater investment in science and technology, such as those documented in chapter 6. The Israeli innovation miracle was underway.

Taiwan Revisited: Science and Technology in the Battle for Chinese Sovereignty

Taiwan's rapid turnaround in S&T was triggered by very similar external crises in military and economic security. Like Israel, Taiwan mostly ignored S&T while it was wrestling with national identity and state formation issues. But when existential threats from abroad loomed, resources were redirected into S&T and institutions that foster innovation. In particular, this political story of Taiwan's pursuit of S&T is deeply interwoven with that of the Chinese Nationalist Party (KMT). The KMT first established the Republic of China (RoC) on mainland China in 1927. Ever since, the KMT has struggled for power and security against domestic rivals and foreign invaders. These KMT struggles have had a direct effect on the S&T trajectory of Taiwan, which lies just over a hundred miles off the shores of China.

The island of Taiwan entered the twentieth century firmly under Japanese rule. Taiwan had been ceded by Beijing to Tokyo in 1895 after Imperial China lost the First Sino-Japanese War. Because Japan was then in a process of rapid industrialization and modernization, Taiwan soon became more technologically advanced than mainland China. To transform Taiwan into a fully functioning part of their empire, the Japanese expanded and modernized Taiwan's roads, harbors, rails, electricity, and health care infrastructure. They also built hundreds of schools and established a university.[32] STEM education was especially emphasized, in part as an alternative to the social sciences and humanities, which might serve as the basis for Taiwanese or Chinese nationalism.[33] After the mid-1930s, the Japanese also built up heavily S&T-based industries on Taiwan to support their war effort. While local resistance to the Japanese was never-ending, and often violent, it was far from universal. Taiwan had long been ethnically divided between a handful of Chinese immigrant populations and indigenous tribes, not always living at ease with one another. These diverse Taiwanese populations also divided along economic, geographic, and political lines. Some of these groups flourished under Japanese rule, while others suffered, resulting in fierce domestic rivalries. Japan's concerns over empire outweighed these domestic tensions, and S&T progress was imposed through a combination of brute force, compromise, and compensation.

In 1945, after the Japanese surrender, KMT troops from the mainland stormed in to retake control of Taiwan. The poor, barely educated Chinese soldiers viewed the local Taiwanese as traitors, collaborators, and corrupted by fifty years of Japanese rule. They detested Taiwan's S&T institutions and polices as the devices of a foreign enemy. The KMT therefore proceeded to systematically loot and strip Taiwan of its S&T infrastructure, factories, and financial capital for shipment back to mainland China to be used in reconstruction there. Meanwhile, corruption and organized crime, often ethnically based, became rampant among the local population.

The plunder of Taiwan ended soon after fighting broke out back on mainland China between the KMT nationalists and Mao Zedong's communists. As the KMT rapidly lost land and power to the communists, the island of Taiwan was identified as a safe haven. In 1948, when the nationalist evacuation of the mainland became inevitable, the KMT leadership halted the transfer of resources out of Taiwan. Within a year, roughly two million nationalist mainlanders fled China to the island of Taiwan, including some six hundred thousand KMT soldiers.[34] As a final act, the KMT transferred their government to Taiwan's capital, Taipei. They declared martial law in Taiwan and blasted Mao's new People's Republic of China (PRC) as heretical, perverse, and fleeting. Instead, the KMT proclaimed that their new government in Taiwan represented all of China.

Domestic tensions on Taiwan soared. The island was immediately militarized, and Taiwanese society became severely divided along economic, political, and ethnic lines. The exiled mainlanders owned no land or assets in Taiwan. Hence, their status and income in Taiwan derived entirely from the KMT's lock on power there. Meanwhile, the local Taiwanese were perceived by the KMT as poor allies, dismissed as "Japanized," and therefore seen as badly in need of tutelage. [35] Ethnic divides among the Taiwanese further exacerbated domestic relations. Even KMT unity was threatened by the fragmented groups of mainlanders who had relocated to the island from disparate provinces in China. So to put down local resistance and dissent, the KMT initiated a prolonged terror campaign, which included mass arrests of Taiwanese intellectuals and social elites.

The KMT now became obsessed with the domestic threats to their power, with terrible consequences for S&T. Back on mainland China, the KMT had been strong supporters of S&T institutions and STEM education programs since the 1920s.[36] S&T was then both a symbol of modernity and a medium for providing security for post–Imperial China. S&T was also a means by which the KMT had legitimized their early rule as being modern, smart, and forward. The acquisition of domestic S&T capabilities was a way to demonstrate to domestic and international audiences alike that China had "arrived" in the twentieth century, and had been led there by the KMT. Government encouragement of S&T also won support from Chinese intellectuals who might otherwise criticize or oppose the KMT, while simultaneously producing domestic experts for nation building. Thus, the old KMT had promulgated and funded a handful of S&T institutions and STEM education programs.[37]

However, once on Taiwan, the KMT mostly lost interest in S&T and even high-tech industrialization. From 1949 until the 1970s, their top three goals became ensuring the Republic of China's survival on Taiwan, enforcing KMT leadership of the RoC, and retaking the mainland. To these ends, the KMT government in Taipei supported research only in agriculture, medicine, and nuclear weapons, with some additional funding for transportation infrastructure and essential industries.[38] In other words, the government supported only those S&T sectors that were deemed fundamental to the security and survival of the KMT and RoC, in part because they helped to make Taiwan self-sufficient. But the KMT did not replicate on Taiwan the scientific institutions or policies that it had so strongly supported during its contested reign over mainland China.[39] To invest in scientific facilities, institutions, and STEM education in Taiwan would have represented a costly, *permanent* commitment to an explicitly *temporary* hideout.

As a result, political support for STEM training dwindled on Taiwan. Instead of S&T, the KMT redirected Taiwan's education resources toward the humanities and social sciences. The goal here was to strengthen the pretense that the KMT was the guardian and patron of Chinese culture and history, and that Taiwan was the "true" China. The universities were therefore tightly regulated and manipulated to discourage opposition. Even language became a domestic battleground, as the KMT made Mandarin the official idiom of Taiwan and fined schools that allowed the use of local dialects.[40] Such strong emphasis on Chinese humanities and social science was also intended to attract to Taiwan, and to the KMT, the allegiance of Chinese everywhere: within Taiwan, within mainland China, and among Chinese ex-pats abroad. By comparison, the supply of STEM graduates in Taiwan was paltry. A 1950 survey of Taiwan's government institutions and state-owned enterprises revealed only 464 scientists working in twenty-nine factories and twenty-one laboratories, some of these overlapping.

Meanwhile, throughout Taiwan's university system, faculty complained of low pay, poor facilities, and lack of equipment and materials.[41]

Ironically, the outbreak of the Korean War (1950–1953) further lowered interest in S&T because it prompted foreign guarantees of Taiwan's defense. Within days of North Korea's invasion of South Korea, the Truman administration sailed the US Navy's Seventh Fleet into the Taiwan Strait to prevent any attack on the island by Mao's communist forces. The PRC's poorly equipped navy had no chance of successfully invading Taiwan against such an advanced defense force. US financial aid also began to pour into Taiwan at the rate of around $100 million per year for the next fifteen years.

The Eisenhower administration (1953–1961) proved even more pro-Taiwan, sending military aid and advanced weapons and threatening to "unleash" Chiang Kai-shek against the mainland. At the time, the United States had no major military allies in East Asia (Japan had not yet rearmed) against the rising communist tide there. Hence, the KMT was only game in town for a United States suddenly confronted with a global cold war.[42] Such was the urgency felt in Washington that, before the end of the 1950s, American nuclear weapons were being deployed near Taiwan.[43] Meanwhile, after achieving only minor success in conquering some contested offshore islands during the First and Second Taiwan Straits Crises (1953–1955 and 1958), the PRC got distracted from any serious machinations against Taiwan. The Chinese economy had been incapacitated by Mao's disastrous "Great Leap Forward" (1958) and the resulting Great Chinese Famine (1958–1962). Finally, a breakdown in both Sino-Soviet and Sino-Indian relations served to preoccupy mainland China's military for years.[44]

With its external security now guaranteed by the United States, both militarily and financially, and mainland China weak and distracted, the KMT government felt no pressure to pursue the risks and costs of indigenous S&T. In economic policy, it instead initiated an import substitution strategy.[45] This approach is often used by policymakers as a form of infant industry protection to aid domestic high-tech industries. However, in Taiwan, the focus was instead on labor-intensive industries, such as textiles, paper, rubber products, basic chemicals, and plastics. These sectors required little high technology, scientific skills, or start-up capital.[46] Yet, Taiwan's economy still flourished. Its GDP grew more than 4% per year during the 1950s, and then rose to 12% through the mid-1960s, all while inflation remained below 5%.[47] Crucial measures of social welfare and public health also rose. As a result, domestic support for S&T in Taiwan continued to languish. There was simply little demand for indigenous S&T capabilities. Only scientists and the intellectual community within Taiwan, and US foreign aid groups, pushed Taiwan to innovate. As a result, S&T efforts made by the KMT government were superficial, done mostly to attract US funding, and achieved little. Good scholars left Taiwan; the state's STEM books were stored in garages, not libraries; and laboratories and research facilities were simplistic. As late as the mid-1960s, foreign scientists were still referring to Taiwan as a "scientific desert."[48]

After late 1964, Taiwan's security situation rapidly changed. In a shocking series of reversals, Mao successfully tested an atomic fission bomb that October, followed in 1966 by successful demonstrations of a Chinese hydrogen fusion bomb and guided missile technology. These rendered hopeless any Taiwanese attack on the mainland, while threatening the annihilation of the KMT in Taiwan.[49] China's accomplishments in military hardware also spotlighted S&T as newly contested ground in the ongoing competition between the PRC and RoC. The KMT leadership wanted Taiwan to win this new battleground. The shock in Taiwan was akin to that felt in the United States after the Soviet launch of Sputnik. So the KMT leadership denounced PRC science as the stuff of weapons, militarism, and the destruction of Chinese culture, while Taiwan's science was to be celebrated as peaceful, supportive of social development, economic modernization, and the protection of Chinese culture.[50]

In another blow to Taiwan's external security, in 1965, a deficit-wary US Congress ended its financial aid to the RoC, cutting off vital flows of foreign exchange. Since 1950, American foreign aid had been essential to Taiwan's economic well-being. US nonmilitary aid alone totaled $1.46 billion, or roughly 6.4% of Taiwan's gross national product (GNP) from 1950 to 1965.[51] Expertly invested by US and Taiwanese administrators, the aid had more than doubled Taiwan's annual rate of economic growth, quadrupled per capita wealth, and arguably cut three decades off the time necessary for Taiwan to attain its 1964 living standards.[52] Now this money was gone. Taiwan suddenly had to earn its own foreign exchange through exports. But Taiwan's agriculture- and natural resource–based economy was not profitable enough to suffice.

In response to Taiwan's new military and financial situation, the KMT government immediately raised the priority of S&T. The government convened the nation's First Science Meeting (1965), which was a joint ministerial conference on reforming Taiwan's S&T policy and institutions. There, Taiwan's president and premier each gave speeches explicitly linking domestic S&T to military and economic security.[53] The KMT also created Taiwan's first serious, state-run research institute, the Chungshan Institute of Science and Technology (1965). This was a "research institute for national defense," specifically tasked to advance Taiwan's capabilities in nuclear physics, rockets, missiles, and applied electronics.[54] Then, in 1967, Taiwan kicked off a two-year program to overhaul its S&T institutions and policies. This included the creation of a new science and technology National Security Council funded with a generous budget.[55]

KMT government technocrats now became more proactive regarding the economic aspects of domestic S&T.[56] Previously Taiwan's exports had been economic surplus, leftovers from domestic production. They mostly consisted of foodstuffs, wood products, basic textiles, and natural resource derivatives.[57] Taiwan now needed higher-value exports and foreign direct investment (FDI) as sources of foreign exchange and investment capital. To attract FDI, the government realized that Taiwan needed cheap STEM labor. Hence, the Ministry of Economic Affairs began to actively encourage government to improve STEM education, R&D, and their links to S&T-based industrialization. By the early 1970s, major strides had been made. Taiwan had more engineers per capita engaged in manufacturing than all other developing countries for which data is available, with the possible exception of Singapore.[58] The Taiwanese government also invited foreign S&T experts to advise on national institutions and strategy, including a high-level team from the United States sent by President Johnson. Their recommendations provided a new vision for the role of S&T in Taiwan's economic security, which was studied closely by the top-ranking officials in the KMT government.[59]

During the early 1970s, Taiwan's external threats rose further. Mao's PRC not only began to normalize its relations with Western nations but also did so at the expense of their formal recognition of Taiwan. Within a few years, over one hundred countries had established diplomatic ties with mainland China, while forty nations had *de*-recognized Taiwan.[60] In July 1971, the United States further imperiled Taiwan with Kissinger's secret mission to Beijing, after which a follow-up visit by President Nixon was announced. By the year's end, Taiwan was stripped of its membership in the United Nations, replaced there by the PRC. It was now increasingly clear that the RoC would not retake mainland China, and that Taiwan's most powerful ally, the United States, was warming to the PRC. To add injury to insult, the United States also canceled its sales of offensive military weapons to Taiwan, instead adopting a policy of supplying only defensive weapons. By 1974, US nukes were being removed from Taiwan.[61] On the economic side, the 1973 oil crisis and global recession cut Taiwan's economic growth rate by over two-thirds.[62] Taiwan's external troubles were mounting higher.

Meanwhile, domestic tensions within Taiwan had eased.[63] By the late 1960s, the KMT reigned supreme in Taiwanese politics and public policy. It now possessed more domestic control and less opposition than many explicit dictatorships. Taiwan had also become a more cohesive society. Decades of intermarriage have decreased ethnic tensions between mainlanders and the Taiwanese. And having grown up on Taiwan, younger KMT members were also far less committed to retaking China and more interested in investing in Taiwan. Local Taiwanese were by now fully integrated into the RoC business community and increasingly into the KMT itself, and hence positions within government, through President Chiang Ching-kuo's explicit policy of "Taiwanization."[64] Finally, the government had scored a major policy success with its wealth redistribution programs. A key part of this redistribution was extensive land reforms. Since neither the KMT nor the mainlanders had a stake in existing land holdings in Taiwan, they felt no qualms about forcefully breaking up concentrations of agricultural land.[65] Together with welfare, education, and other domestic programs, these reforms steadily reduced the wealth gap in Taiwan. As a result, by the 1980s, Taiwan enjoyed one of the lowest levels of economic inequality in the world.[66]

S&T was now seen within Taiwan as the best solution to the new combination of security threats. A strong domestic S&T capability could serve as the basis for a modern defense industry, replace high-tech imports, and bring Taiwan badly need foreign exchange. Also, the high costs, risks, and disruptions of S&T were no longer threats to the domestic order. Therefore, the state began to pursue S&T even more aggressively during the early 1970s.[67] In 1973, the government undertook its Ten Major Construction Projects, which represented a massive investment by the KMT in Taiwan's technical infrastructure. They consisted of six transportation system projects, three industrial ventures, and one power generation project, totaling roughly US $8 billion.[68] The same year, the government built the Industrial Technology Research Institution (ITRI) for research in computer hardware. Well-funded and expertly staffed, the ITRI would soon become a primary source of Taiwanese S&T, forming a linchpin in the national drive for global competitiveness in semiconductors that the National Science Council implemented the following year.[69]

Perhaps the most extreme security pressures came in 1978–1979, when Taiwan's external threats hit crisis levels. In 1978, President Carter announced that the United States would de-recognize Taiwan. He then blocked sales of the most advanced US defense weaponry to Taiwan, a policy continued by the Reagan administration (1981–1989). This was also the time of the second oil crisis (1979), which drove up the costs of Taiwan's energy imports and presaged a sharp downturn in growth rates. Now Taiwan's political leaders got fully behind S&T as the primary means of Taiwan's economic development. President Chiang Ching-kuo and his premier, an engineer, became major proponents of domestic S&T programs, such as the Hsinchu Science Park (built 1979), a senior-level Science and Technology Advisory Group to which all ministries would eventually become accountable (created 1979), and the active courting of foreign S&T firms to advise and invest in Taiwan.[70]

International S&T relationships were now also prioritized. On a political level, international S&T linkages were seen as a primary means of maintaining relations with foreign states and experts in the wake of the de-recognitions of the RoC. With only twenty-four minor nations left maintaining diplomatic ties, Taiwan was now politically isolated.[71] S&T exports and joint ventures were seen as strategic means of integrating Taiwan back into the global economy and in an indispensable way. Taiwan therefore sought to embed itself economically in the global system by becoming a major supplier of essential electronics and computing components to the United States, Europe, and Japan. Competitiveness in these industries would also earn Taiwan the foreign exchange necessary to import vital supplies of energy, natural resources, and advanced weaponry. Hence, the Taiwanese state rapidly expanded its role in R&D and actively linked S&T outputs to industrial production (described in chapter 6). Taiwan's authoritarian leadership now unequivocally tied S&T-based economic development to Taiwan's political survival and hence their own. By 1982, Taiwan had created the institutions and policies necessary to foster a globally competitive S&T sector. Within the decade, Taiwan's output of science and technology was headed rapidly upward; soon Taiwan would join the elite club of the world's most innovative nations.

Ireland Revisited: Middle Success in the Isle of Discontent

Creative insecurity also explains cases of midlevel success, like Ireland. Recall from chapter 6 that Ireland has become a moderate achiever in S&T, but not a major producer of new science or inventor of revolutionary new technologies. This is partly because Irish institutions have been less aggressive at creating markets for S&T progress or in attacking the market failures that obstruct it. Nor has Ireland's policy been to develop rich networks that embed high-tech actors deeply within Ireland's political-economic system. Ireland has never pursued these costly, risky, and highly disruptive S&T strategies because the payoffs have only occasionally seemed worth it. Instead, Ireland's combative economic and religious groups have demanded that their government focus its resources elsewhere. After all, the Irish have no need for a strong modern military, suffer only intermittent balance-of-payments crises, and possess a highly competitive agricultural sector. So why gamble heavily on S&T? Only during wartime or when hit with overwhelming economic crises have the Irish invested in S&T and supporting institutions with any enthusiasm. Otherwise, non-S&T strategies have been less costly, less risky, and less disruptive solutions to the particular problems that confront the Irish, problems that are often created by conflicting domestic interest groups.

Ireland has never had an external military threat like those faced by Israel or Taiwan. The Republic of Ireland[72] broke away from the United Kingdom soon after World War I. But compared to the creation of Israel or Taiwan, the partition of Ireland was a far less contested event. Irish independence was certainly not a mass revolution against a dedicated external enemy. Rather, it emerged gradually through years of political protest and low-level violence, during which the majority Catholic counties in the south established a fully independent Republic of Ireland. Neither Britain nor Northern Ireland sought to combat the new Irish Republic. Most British had long accepted Irish independence as inevitable. When the Irish War of Independence finally came in 1919–1921, it was a bloody but limited affair.[73]

Within Ireland, a year-long civil war erupted (1922–1923) over the terms of independence.[74] This was almost entirely a domestic conflict. There were only isolated incidents of violence against British agents and troops, which were countered in a tit-for-tat manner, but there was no massing of the British military on Ireland's shores nor any attempt by London at reconquest. Indeed, most British were glad to be rid of the "Irish problem." Hence, neither the United Kingdom nor its military played much role in Ireland's new troubles. Even large parts of Ireland itself were left untouched by the hostilities.[75]

Nor did the newly independent Irish turn bellicose against Britain. There was no Irish military build-up, no invasion scares, not even a radical restructuring of Irish domestic life. Schemes to weaken the new partition of Ireland were quietly but sternly dismissed by governments on either side of border. The republic even continued most of the British economic and political institutions it had inherited, including free elections, parliamentary democracy, free trade, and low levels of government intervention in the economy.[76]

Rather, the primary threats to the new Republic of Ireland were domestic. Irish society was menaced by fierce divides across class, religion, and urban-rural demographics that frequently blossomed into tense political-economic fights and even violence. Hence, the top priority of the Irish Republic was to consolidate the revolution and stabilize the new state. Their strategy was to forge unity via the creation of a common Irish Catholic identity.[77] To this end, education was dominated by Catholic theology and Irish humanities. Few STEM subjects were taught and few students pursued these fields of study beyond high school, especially since most Irish youths left school by their early teens.[78]

In fact, S&T was seen as entirely tangential, if not detrimental, to the new republic's goals. Ireland's economy was then very low technology, almost wholly based on agriculture, with little manufacturing or S&T-based sectors.[79] In such a backward economy and fragile polity, the redistribution of scant resources toward major government investments in S&T would have been highly disruptive. No Irish elites, interest groups, or political party of any size or power demanded such policies. Also, the minority Protestants who dominated Ireland's small business sector had lost considerable influence over policy. Exports of farm goods sufficed to earn the foreign exchange needed to pay for imports. And with no serious military threat, there was little demand for an expensive defense industry. Instead, the republic's leadership was preoccupied with courting opposing factions and political parties to enter the new political system, and with preventing the emergence of a radical anti-Republic opposition. This meant reducing as much economic pain and upheaval as possible. Massive S&T spending, or even industrialization, would have stymied these efforts. Instead, the new government placed its economic bets on Ireland's low-tech agriculture, which had already demonstrated a comparative advantage in livestock and dairy production.[80]

Ireland's new government also enforced strict fiscal discipline to minimize its debt burden, especially debt owed to foreign (i.e., mostly British) creditors. Welfare programs were reduced, as were taxes. Hence, there was little state funding available for investment in costly R&D. Where domestic actors pressured for more spending, it was for welfare or subsidies, not R&D. As a result, during the 1920s, the Republic's "high-tech" industries were no more advanced than basic food processing: brewing, distilling, milling, baking, curing, and sugar production.[81] With little investment or government support, economic growth flattened and income inequality increased. The poor economy led to high outflows of emigrants. These emigrants were often poor, uneducated, and low skilled; they also sent back massive remittances (fully 3.4% of the Republic's GDP during the 1920s) from their new jobs in labor-scarce Britain.[82] Hence, emigration acted as a social safety valve and source of foreign exchange for the new Republic. Once again, the political and economic impulses for S&T were weak.

The Great Depression forced a shift in the Irish Republic's technological trajectory. By the 1930s, dependence on the British economy had become so heavy that it was deemed by many Irish as a threat to their newly won sovereignty. Britain was also widely blamed as the primary cause of inequality and economic stagnation at home.[83] Therefore, in 1932, a leftist and more stridently nationalist regime, *Fianna Fail*, was swept into power by Irish voters. *Fianna Fail* was more willing to use the state to pursue economic development. An "Irish Ireland" was their cultural goal; self-sufficiency was their economic objective.[84] The new government immediately confronted Great Britain over historic land annuities and naval stations, resulting in a tense Anglo-Irish trade war. Meanwhile, to ameliorate domestic inequality, the new Irish government initiated a major homebuilding program, expanded welfare programs, redistributed farmland, and increased pension allowances. Each of these policy shifts was broadly, albeit not universally, supported by Ireland's voters and interest groups.

With domestic tensions eased somewhat and external threats now moderately raised, it made sense for the Irish Republic to make small investments in S&T. A stronger domestic S&T capability could reduce technological dependency on Britain. Meanwhile, the new government's social spending helped mollify domestic opposition to any redistribution that new S&T policy might entail. But the foreign threats were not severe enough, and domestic tranquility was still too fragile. So Ireland's investments in S&T were moderate. Instead of bold new S&T institutions, Ireland used far less costly and controversial tools such as trade and investment policy. Tariffs were raised to lock out foreign competition and spur domestic industry. Two Control of Manufactures Acts (1932 and 1934) were passed, which required all new firms to be majority Irish owned to ensure protection of the domestic industrial base.[85] Conspicuously, these measures had the ring of nationalism to them, which further sterilized potential critics within Ireland.

Import substitution and industrial policy now combined to gradually force a wide range of technological upgrades in Irish industry and agriculture. Peat farmers switched from hand cultivation to mechanized turf harvesting. New advances were made in sugar processing and automobile assembly. The domestic production of textiles, shoes, and hosiery was improved and expanded. But since the institutions and investments in S&T were limited, so too were the results. Often Ireland's advances remained dependent on imports of foreign machinery.[86] Also, once Irish industry captured the small domestic market, the technological and economic advances tended to slow dramatically. This even applied to scientific endeavors. In 1940, the Dublin Institute for Advanced Studies was created for all types of academic research. However, its scholarship in S&T fields was mostly theoretical and cosmic, not practical or applied.[87] With neither foreign competition nor serious external threats as justification, larger investments in S&T were seen by most Irish as unnecessary, too costly, and too risky.

World War II did not much alter Ireland's poor S&T trajectory. All agreed that to take sides in the conflict would likely ignite a civil war in Ireland; therefore, the path to the Republic's security lay through neutrality. Sitting comfortably behind the front lines, the Republic suffered little violence during the war.[88] Most important, any military threat to Ireland was a de facto threat to the United Kingdom. Therefore, the Republic could rely on the British Royal Navy and Air Force to defend it against invasion. As result, there was little military pressure to innovate. Ireland's armed forces remained small and poorly equipped, even getting weaker during the 1940s.[89] Because its resources were not diverted to the war effort, the Irish enjoyed less debt and rationing than the combatants. The government even brought back unemployment benefits, increased old-age pensions, and introduced income allowances to families with more than three children.[90] The Republic also became a key source of food and labor for the United Kingdom. Hence, Irish farmers became richer, while unhappy youths and the unemployed kept emigrating to Britain or Northern Ireland in large numbers, sending back regular remittances. Domestic manufacturers continued to enjoy captive domestic markets and the increased profits that came with them. But without competition from foreign imports, there remained little pressure on Irish firms to invest in R&D or even new equipment.

However, the war *did* pose an external threat to the Irish Republic's imports of energy and strategic commodities, which prompted mild S&T investments in these sectors. Ireland's economy depended heavily on foreign transport ships and on raw materials imports, especially coal, which were increasingly commandeered by the combatants in Europe. In response, Ireland's defense minister created an Emergency Scientific Research Bureau during the 1940s to conduct research on those commodities deemed essential to national survival.[91] Examples of its R&D projects included the conversion of phosphate deposits into fertilizer, the development of peat-based gasoline and charcoals, the extraction of pesticides from tobacco dust, and an attempt to develop flour out of potato starch.[92] Still, opponents repeatedly blasted the bureau as too costly or mocked it in the *Irish Times* and *Dublin Opinion* for pursuing scientific flights of fancy.[93] As for the ships, the government simply bought them rather than assume the risk and cost of developing a domestic shipping industry.[94]

After World War II, pressure again slackened on the Republic to innovate or invest in S&T.[95] It was far from the front lines of the Cold War, in which Ireland remained unaligned, and enjoyed the de facto military protection of NATO. Meanwhile, the Marshall Plan provided Ireland with an easy $145 million in foreign exchange, or nearly half of all government investment from 1948 to 1952.[96] So rather than S&T, the state chose to spend its money on social aims: public housing, hospitals, roads, river drainage, and natural resource development.[97] Attempts to strengthen STEM education, or even expand vocational schools, were handicapped by lack of political support for funding increases. The Catholic majority continued to fight against STEM education because too much emphasis on these subjects might secularize Ireland. As a result, school curricula throughout the Republic remained centered on humanities-based subjects, such as Greek, Latin, and religion, at the expense of science. At one point, a Council of Education was created to consider reforms, but it strongly rejected the need for any significant modernization of the curriculum and actually opposed the expansion of high school.[98]

When the Marshall Plan ended and Europe recovered during the 1950s, Ireland's economy fell into a prolonged recession. Still, the pain was not enough to force much investment in S&T. Rather, Ireland addressed its economic problems by increasing income taxes and indirect revenues, while removing subsidies on basic foodstuffs.[99] However, emigration out of Ireland soon rose to its highest levels in the twentieth century, with over 10% of the total population leaving during the decade after 1950.[100] This problem grew acute enough that Dublin created emergency committees to address the situation, while some observers doubted whether Ireland could survive as an independent state.[101]

The persistence of these twin economic shocks, recession and emigration, eventually discredited decades of Irish protectionism and import substitution industrialization.[102] Labor groups now joined together with business and government to form a consensus on economic reforms.[103] They resolved, after 1958, to shift the Republic's economic strategy toward free trade, foreign direct investment, and a reorientation to export-led growth.[104] The Republic therefore steadily reduced tariffs on imports, cut restrictions on foreign ownership of Irish businesses, and eased requirements on foreign firms to use local inputs.[105] The Republic also redirected spending away from social welfare toward productive investment. But the emphasis of all these programs remained on agriculture rather than S&T-based industries. The external threats to Ireland were still not high enough to justify the costs and risks of massive investments in indigenous S&T.

The economic crises of the 1950s did, however, prompt two significant changes in Ireland's S&T institutions. One was the gradual elevation of the Industrial Development Agency (IDA), which would eventually take over Irish industrial policy. During these early years, it simply began to make industrial grants (1956) and aggressively seek out high-tech FDI.[106] Another major change occurred in education policy. As late as the mid-1960s, half of Ireland's children left school by age thirteen because further schooling was too costly.[107] The Republic now began to offer students scholarships (1961), capital grants (1964), and finally free secondary education and school transportation (1966–1967).[108] Also, tertiary education was tripled and vocational education expanded, and, in 1969, the Republic created five Regional Technical Colleges.[109] Previously the state had helped finance but did not control education. Rather, the Catholic Church held sway, in part because it owned many of the school buildings, facilities, and institutional infrastructure.[110] Now the state took over education reform, with a newly founded National Institutes of Higher Education pushing for more training in STEM and less in humanities and culture.[111] Interestingly, the catalyst for these measures was often pressure from *foreign* sources of finance, such the OECD and World Bank, not domestic demand from powerful blocs of Irish voters or interest groups.[112]

Ireland's shift toward free trade and FDI kicked off a twenty-year golden age in the Irish economy, though not in domestic S&T. The boom started around 1960 and was extended by the Republic's entry into the European Economic Community (EEC) in 1973. The EEC rewarded Ireland with enormous subsidies, grants, and development funds, mostly directed toward Ireland's farm sector. Europe's agricultural price supports further increased the real incomes of farmers, while severely reducing their burden on Ireland's budget.[113] Foreign exchange reserves soon recovered, partly due to massive remittances from the prior decade's emigrants, and job creation eventually reversed Irish emigration.[114] This took further pressure off Ireland to invest in R&D or strengthen its S&T institutions. Instead, Ireland chose to pursue a far less risky and less expensive economic strategy. It sought to become a low-cost, low-tax export hub for American multinational firms seeking to sell into the European market. This only required some technological upgrades to attract foreign firms, specifically investments in roads and telecommunications infrastructure, which Ireland dutifully performed. This strategy worked well, luring massive FDI in the production of integrated circuits, minicomputers, disc drives, and software.[115] But with so much technology now coming from abroad, there was little need for Ireland to invest in domestic S&T capabilities. Hence, the few domestic S&T policy improvements that occurred were often at the insistence of European, American, or international organizations.[116]

By 1979, Ireland's economic boom was faltering. The second global oil crisis hit Ireland hard, in part because increased reliance on imports had been combined with several decades of fiscal profligacy. Ireland's national debt soon hit 120% of GDP, while its foreign exchange imbalances were matched only by Greece, Portugal, and Spain.[117] Worse yet, a major 1982 industrial survey found that few of the foreign firms investing in Ireland had set up any R&D facilities there;[118] meanwhile, neither Irish firms nor universities were doing much R&D of their own. To deal with its debt problem, the government increased taxes and cut spending, especially in health care and public investment. Consumption soon flattened and unemployment climbed annually, surpassing 21% of the labor force in early 1993.[119] The result was another tidal wave of emigration, which began as early as 1981 and peaked around 1990. In 1989 alone, 1.1% of the population left Ireland to search for employment abroad.[120] This time, those leaving Ireland were far better educated than their predecessors, with a high proportion of professional and managerial workers and a low proportion of agricultural and unskilled labor. Most emigrants were therefore from Ireland's cities and had at least some high school education; many had tertiary education.[121] This catastrophe was unique in Irish history. It constituted a massive, expensive brain drain of Ireland's scarce human capital.

With twin economic crises underway in balance of payments and human capital, warnings of economic collapse reached apocalyptic levels.[122] Ireland's bitterly divided political-economic actors temporarily suspended their quarrels and finally agreed to support the promotion of S&T-based industries, both to create jobs and to improve the trade balance.[123] Once again, however, emphasis was put on attracting foreign high-tech businesses, not massive investments in indigenous S&T. The domestic part of Ireland's plan was to create a highly educated STEM labor force with which to lure foreign high-tech employers. As a result, during the 1980s, there came a renewed push for more engineering and computer science education, with funding earmarked specifically for those disciplines. In 1995, university fees were abolished to expand college education.

Within a generation, Ireland's younger workers had become among Europe's most educated.[124]

This time, Ireland more seriously reformed its existing S&T institutions and created new ones.[125] Moderate spending on R&D in computing was prioritized (1991). The IDA was restructured to focus on domestic high-tech industries (1994). An Irish Council for Science, Technology, and Innovation was established (1997). A Program for Research in Third Level Institutions (1998) was created to strengthen Irish R&D capabilities. And to subsidize domestic R&D, Science Foundation Ireland was created (2000).

Despite these initiatives, Ireland's efforts to build its indigenous S&T capabilities remain moderate. The education and skill levels of returning migrants and new immigrants to Ireland during the 1993–2003 period were *higher* than those of the native population.[126] Still today, only around one-third of Irish natives have graduated college, compared to over half of the Europeans who have immigrated to Ireland.[127] R&D funding as a share of Ireland's GDP peaked in 1996, did not recover until 2008, and has consistently sat below the EU average.[128] Even Ireland's famed high-tech "Celtic tiger" period (1996–2003)[129] was dominated by foreign firms. For example, Dell and Microsoft became Ireland's biggest exporters, together responsible for around 10% of GDP in 2003, but neither company performed R&D or product design there.[130] All told, during the 1990s, foreign firms accounted for over 70% of private sector R&D.[131] Ireland did make significant investments in pharmaceutical R&D, which persists as an indigenous S&T strength today.[132] Yet many of Ireland's own S&T programs were actually financed not by Ireland, but by European Structural Funds as a prelude to the formation of the European Union. Nor were skills in the performance of R&D a significant aspect of Ireland's STEM education push. Therefore, as early as 1998, foreign high-tech firms began to leave Ireland for the cheaper labor available in East Asia and Eastern Europe.[133]

Ireland has clearly improved its S&T capabilities over the decades, but only moderately, and usually in response to equally moderate external economic crises. There has never been a serious enough military threat to Ireland to overcome domestic aversions to the costs, risks, and distributional effects of S&T. A century of history has proven to Ireland that it enjoys the de facto protection of its neighbors and their allies, as it sits comfortably behind the front lines of global conflicts. The only exception was a brief security threat to Ireland's imports of commodities and energy during World War II. To this, Ireland responded by setting up indigenous R&D in these areas. These S&T efforts evaporated once the external threat was over. Thereafter, Ireland's contending domestic interest groups only supported investment in S&T when balance-of-payment crises struck or when emigration hit such extreme levels that it seemed to threaten Ireland's viability as a state. Even in these instances, Ireland's S&T investments and institutional reforms were mild, often not sustained, and heavily focused on attracting foreign S&T rather than building up capabilities at home. Ireland's support for R&D funding and S&T institutions is tepid because S&T is not broadly seen as the best solution for any dire problem afflicting Ireland.

Mexico Revisited: A History of Science and Technology Failure

By almost any measure, Mexico is a drastically different type of country than either Israel, Taiwan, or Ireland, yet creative insecurity theory still explains it relatively well. Most prominently, Mexico has served as a case of relative S&T failure for hundreds of years. While it is tempting to blame the nation's history of poverty, Mexico was wealthier than Taiwan until the 1980s, and only somewhat poorer than either Israel or Ireland during much of the twentieth century.[134] Rather, the fault appears to lie in Mexico's enduring domestic rivalries. Compared to the more successful S&T countries, Mexico has been more stubbornly preoccupied by violent divisions across class, religion, region, and economic sector.[135] As a result of these divides, investment in domestic S&T has been too costly, too risky, and with too little benefit to Mexicans *relative* to other options. Instead, it has been more logical for Mexicans to allocate their resources toward agriculture, natural resources, welfare programs, black markets, and fighting civil conflicts. Meanwhile, Mexico's vast holdings of precious metals, agricultural lands, and most recently oil have provided domestic supplies of strategic goods and an occasional financial cushion against recurring balance-of-payments crises. Only twice in its history have Mexico's external threats moderately outweighed its domestic tensions for a prolonged period of time, in 1876–1910 and 1940–1982. In both these periods, investment in innovation made sense and Mexico enjoyed a burst of technology-based industrialization and a strengthening of its S&T institutions. Yet, in neither period was the threat imbalance strong enough to motivate the massive risk taking and investment in domestic S&T that was undertaken in either Israel or Taiwan, or even the more moderate investments made in Ireland. As a result, to this day much of Mexico's S&T has been imported. Let's explore this history.

Mexico declared its independence from Spain (1821) after years of rebellion. But rather than usher in a period of stability, Mexican independence kicked off over five decades of recurrent civil war.[136] The new country's domestic conflicts were legion: conservative monarchists clashed with liberal republicans, ethnic Europeans strove to marginalize the masses of mixed-blood Mexicans, indigenous tribes battled for local autonomy, and secular liberals fought for control over Mexico's institutions against the powerful Catholic Church and its devout followers. And, as in all heavily unequal societies, a minority of wealthy elites violently clung to political and economic power against the poor multitudes striving for greater resources.[137]

As a result of these domestic divides, between 1821 and 1876, Mexico suffered a chaotic succession of roughly seventy-five dictators, generals, and elected presidents.[138] Almost all of these governments were violently contested by domestic opponents, sometimes resulting in simultaneous rule by contending political factions. Once in office, national leaders habitually raided state coffers for personal consumption, lavish celebrations, ceremonial buildings, and patronage expenditures on their networks of friends and allies. Local leaders became warlords who imposed internal tariffs on commerce, thus fragmenting the national economy for personal gain. Meanwhile, a bloated military demanded high pay for its loyalty, often acting like a Praetorian guard available to the highest bidder. The central government became unable even to provide internal security. At times, banditry and brigandage became so widespread that the Mexican Congress could not meet due to the dangers of travel to the capital.[139]

Under these conditions, there were neither the resources nor the political support available for Mexican S&T institutions or programs. Even as S&T was first being embraced as a policy goal in the United States and Europe, much of Mexico's preexisting S&T and supporting institutions were being destroyed in the chaos. Colonial Mexico's mining technologies had been among the most advanced in the world, while its textiles industry was competitive with many of those in Europe.[140] However, after 1821, Mexico's mines, machinery, factories, and even basic infrastructure were demolished in civil conflicts or rendered useless from decades of neglect. As a result of its technological backwardness, the Mexican economy actually *declined* throughout much of the mid-1800s.[141] Colonial Mexico had also been home to the hemisphere's first universities and technical schools, some of which were established during the sixteenth century.[142] But after independence, major Mexican universities were shuttered by republican radicals who perceived them as the malevolent instruments of European monarchs and the Catholic Church. General literacy dropped to 10% of the population, while what little formal education remained was centered on religion.[143] In an instance that epitomizes this period, one of Mexico's more enlightened rulers ordered the destruction of the Chapultepec Astronomical Observatory (1864) so that he might better landscape his castle.[144]

Two external threats during this era could have galvanized the collective action necessary to support S&T progress in Mexico but failed to. First, although the loss of Texas in 1836 might be interpreted as a product of civil war,[145] the 1846–1848 war fought by Mexico against the United States would seem to pose a clear external threat. In this later confrontation, President James K. Polk used a combination of intimidation and diplomacy against Mexico in an attempt to coerce the sale of its territories north of the Rio Grande. When these negotiations broke down, Polk placed American troops in harm's way and then forced Congress to accept war when they were attacked in the disputed border region. In the subsequent conflict, Mexico suffered a humiliating military loss, one that has insulted Mexican national pride ever since. Yet this bruising contest with a more powerful, northern neighbor failed to result in much S&T progress in Mexico. This would seem to violate creative insecurity theory.

The main counterargument is that the actual danger to Mexico posed by the Mexican-American War was far from existential. The conflict was mainly fought over vast undeveloped, peripheral territories to the far north. These were lands over which the Mexican government had never fully established control.[146] Also, only 2% of Mexico's population lived there, mostly mixed-blood peasants living in impoverished towns settled amidst bands of predatory Native American tribes.[147] Thus, instead of defending them from conquest by the United States, Mexico's rival generals just as often led their troops south to Mexico City to seize national power for themselves.

Certainly the external threat increased dramatically when, during 1847, US military forces penetrated deep into the Mexican heartland. In March, the US Navy occupied the major port of Veracruz, providing a base from which the army could march inland. And over the following months, US soldiers proceeded to seize city after city, eventually occupying the capital itself. This would seem to constitute a clear, existential threat to Mexico. However, Mexico failed to respond by setting up S&T institutions, policies, or networks.

Therefore, it also may be that the duration of the external threat was too brief. The war was over by February 1848, after which the US military retreated back over the Rio Grande, and the Mexicans returned to their usual infighting. The threat of conquest was essentially over because, during and after the 1840s, most Americans strongly *opposed* the US acquisition of Mexico for a variety of reasons. Some argued that military conquest contradicted American ideals. Others feared absorbing Mexico's alien people, culture, and values, especially Mexico's majority Catholic, nonwhite population. Abolitionists and free labor advocates were stridently against the war, worried that the seizure of Mexico might provide opportunities for the expansion of slave-based plantation agriculture. Meanwhile, southerners were unenthusiastic about Mexico's history of strident antislavery laws. Hence, the US Congress and President Polk vocally rejected proposals for absorbing all of Mexico into the United States. Only rarely were such expansionist ideas supported in the United States.[148]

Rather, the dangers posed by domestic rivalries within Mexico continued to eclipse the external threats. Even during the invasion by the United States, many Mexicans feared their own military more than they did the Americans. For example, the inhabitants of the northern territories conquered by the United States were not hauled off in chains, but were offered American citizenship and security against Indian raids.[149] Meanwhile, the Mexican Army consisted mostly of peasant soldiers whose loyalties to their local village far outweighed their fealty to the generals who had forcibly drafted them into service. Also, once conscripted, these peasant soldiers were poorly equipped, badly fed, barely trained, and viciously treated by their superiors. As a result, high rates of dissertation plagued the Mexican military throughout the conflict, often with soldiers fleeing just before battle. The Mexican peasantry simply had far more to lose from their own army officers than from the invading American forces.

Apparently, many of Mexico's military and local leaders felt no differently. Even during the depths of occupation, they often preferred to guard their local powerbases rather than risk precious troops or resources in defense of distant lands for which they cared less. Mexico's strategic imports and territories were not threatened with elimination, while the wealth and power of most Mexican elites were far more endangered by domestic foes than by American troops. Therefore, there arose no widespread calls for costly and risky investments in domestic S&T to defend or reconquer the territories lost to the United States.

The second major external threat during this period was that of foreign invasion by a European great power. In 1861, troops from France, England, and Spain jointly occupied the port of Veracruz. Once again the invaders sought not to conquer Mexico nor interfere with the Mexican government. Their mission was only to seize the customs house to appropriate repayment on defaulted loans. Also, their presence came partly at the urging of conservative, white Mexican elites who were then being overpowered by their mixed-blood, secular, liberal countrymen.[150] In early 1862, at the invitation of these Mexican conservatives and the Catholic Church, the French military contingent marched inland from Veracruz; but troops from the other nations withdrew back to Europe. The French soon poured tens of thousands of soldiers into Mexico to re-establish monarchical rule over parts of Mexico by 1864. Yet again, the French were not unwelcome conquerors. They received continuous aid and support from wealthy white Mexicans and Mexican Catholics who sought to drive their republican rivals out of power, and even participated in the selection of their new emperor. Nor did the French occupation last long. The new emperor backed many of the same social and economic policies as did Mexico's liberal republicans, which dulled his support among Mexican monarchists. Meanwhile, England and Spain increased pressure on France to withdraw.[151] The end finally came in 1866–1867 when a postbellum United States could again credibly enforce its Monroe Doctrine. The French withdrew, the emperor was executed, and Mexico fell back into its cycle of civil war and warlordism for another decade.[152] In sum, the external threat was not existential and enjoyed the complicity of Mexico's elites in pursuit of their own self-interest. Hence, investment in S&T to repel the French invasion was not a widely supported strategy.

From 1876 to 1910, the balance of threats to Mexico reversed itself enough to produce widespread and sustained support for modernization and industrialization. On the external threat side, the United States and the European great powers had entered their imperialist phase. The Germans, British, and French revealed their growing interests in the region for markets, natural resources, and military bases.[153] However, the Americans were by far the greatest danger. The United States initiated a major build-up and modernization of its navy (1882), which had already been used aggressively to force access to Hawaii (1842), China (1844), Japan (1853), Korea (1867), and several Pacific islands.[154] With American trade and migration burgeoning, the United States now also sought to secure a canal across Latin America and to increase its influence in the region. American imperialism climaxed with the Spanish-American War (1898), in which Cuba and the Philippines were seized. President Theodore Roosevelt then declared that mere "chronic wrongdoing" or "impotence" would justify future US military intervention in the Western Hemisphere (1904).[155] American troops and ships were now regularly inserted into Latin America, sometimes in response to minor insults.[156] The United States was simultaneously developing its southern borderlands, which implicitly gave Americans an interest in the Mexican north, just when trouble with Guatemala threatened to distract Mexico on its southern border.[157]

Meanwhile, Mexico's domestic tensions had eased considerably. The catalyst was the liberal dictator Porfirio Diaz, whose thirty-four-year rule was a time of domestic peace and rapid industrialization. Diaz and his supporters recognized that Mexico's domestic chaos had been the root cause of its poverty and insecurity. They also believed that the application of S&T to government and the economy was the key to Mexico's future.[158] After his election in 1876, the Diaz administration used a combination of patronage, bayonets, and compromise to force obedience from Mexico's regional warlords and powerful Catholics.[159] Diaz also brought into government cadres of technocrat *cientificos* to help modernize the country. They eliminated Mexico's internal tariffs to create a national market, and moved to link the Mexican economy to the world economy. Diaz then used Mexico's vast wealth in metals and minerals to attract investment from the United States and Europe. Rather than consumption, these investments were directed toward developing networks of modern roads, railroads, telegraphs, and telephone systems. Old mines were upgraded and new ones developed, as were smelting and processing operations. Modern port facilities were built, agriculture was modernized, and a quasi-national bank was created (1884) to stabilize Mexico's finances and to provide domestic investment capital. Mexico soon developed significant manufacturing capacity in steel, cement, textiles, processed foods, paper, and cigarettes.[160] Diaz even re-established the National Astronomical Observatory (1878).

However, the Porfirian S&T strategy was almost entirely based on imports of foreign science and technology.[161] Mexico was so backward in S&T that the high costs and risks of developing domestic capabilities could not be justified. Imported S&T was far less costly and risky. After all, exports of natural resources could keep Mexico's economy solvent. The vague threat posed by the United States' capricious imperialism was balanced by Americans' far more well-defined and self-interested role as the primary foreign investors in Mexico. Also, given their recent history, Mexicans widely feared their military as a rival power center and a threat to stability. This meant that there was little interest within the Diaz administration, or among its supporters, in creating a well-equipped military or modern defense industry—not that a strong military was needed to defend Mexico because, ironically, a jealous United States served as a reliable protector of Mexico against the European great powers. Diaz therefore decided that he could more cheaply defend against America's haphazard imperialism by establishing better relations with his northern neighbor. To this end, Diaz reopened formal diplomatic relations, toured the United States, and even married the daughter of a US Army general.[162] All told, it did not make political or economic sense to make massive investments in domestic S&T capabilities.

As a result, the main beneficiary of Mexican S&T policy was education, especially in STEM subjects. State funding for primary schools soared and compulsory education was finally established (1892). But even this simple policy had domestic opponents. The Catholic Church and indigenous peoples fiercely fought against secular state schools and protested loudly whenever science education contradicted religious or traditional beliefs.[163] Perhaps as a result, spending on higher education, predominately in medicine, engineering, law, and business, was increased even more, up to seventeen times that spent on primary education.[164] Given the priority of metals and minerals in the Porfirian economy, Mexico soon developed an intense specialty in geology, civil, and mining engineering, even playing host to international engineering conferences. However, there was little or no R&D spending by either the private or public sector. Thus, Mexican STEM labor continued to be almost entirely imported, even after domestic technical education was producing engineers of equal quality.[165]

By 1910, Mexico had become increasingly corrupt and unequal under an aging Diaz, who had largely abandoned popular democracy.[166] A financial crisis in the United States had thrown the Mexican economy into depression and hardened Diaz's opposition. Political rivals, disillusioned supporters, economic "losers" (labor, farmers), ardent traditionalists, and antiscience Catholics now rose up to redress their grievances, while attacking Diaz for "selling out" Mexico to foreign investors. The result was a swift and surprising armed rebellion, which drove the dictator into exile. With no clear successor, there ensued thirty years of violent civil conflict across Mexico. During this time, there re-emerged the familiar cavalcade of warlords, military leaders, charismatic rebels, and indigenous revolts.[167]

Due to this renewed domestic chaos between 1910 and 1940, neither much thought nor many resources were given to Mexican S&T or its institutions. In the minds of many Mexicans, S&T and its supporters were heavily associated with the Diaz dictatorship and its *cientificos*. Therefore, S&T institutions and policies, even modernization itself, were perceived as either threat or disappointment by large segments of the Mexican population. Once again, the best achievements in Mexican S&T during this time were in basic STEM education. Although they disagreed on other policies, most Mexican leaders during this period invested heavily in widespread literacy programs, including science and technical subjects, as well as massive school and library construction. Yet again, even this was violently resisted by the Catholic Church and superstitious peasant farmers who often abused, assaulted, and even lynched the "heretical" government teachers sent into their midst.[168] Perhaps the only silver lining to the cloud of political unrest was that large parts of Mexico's technological assets remained untouched, for they were recognized as too valuable to destroy by combatants eager for resources. However, prior to the mid-1930s, only modest technical upgrades and investments in new technology were attempted.[169]

By 1940, Mexico's external versus internal threats had rebalanced. Internally, Mexico had been pacified and stabilized through a combination of violent repression, political compromise, wealth redistribution, and welfare programs.[170] The major interest groups and political factions were herded together into a single political party, which dominated Mexican politics for the next sixty years. On the other hand, new external threats rose to endanger Mexico: a combination of balance-of-payment crises, the Great Depression, and the outbreak of war in Europe. Initially neutral in the war, Mexican shipping soon suffered Nazi attacks, while Axis spy networks threatened to infiltrate the country.[171] Similar threats would loom during the subsequent Cold War. However, while external threats now outweighed domestic tensions, the imbalance was only moderate.[172] Mexico still enjoyed the de facto protection of the United States against invasion or major attack by a rival power. The United States itself had ceased being a military threat during the 1920s and instead pursued increasingly cordial relations with Mexico.[173] Economically, Mexico now enjoyed near-constant demand for its exports of oil, industrial raw materials, precious metals, and food, a demand that surged whenever the United States went to war or its economy boomed.

As a result, from 1940 to 1982, once again Mexico experienced a burst of S&T progress. At first, World War II forced import substitution on the country, which Mexico then augmented with its own development policies: government loans, tax breaks, local content requirements, import tariffs, and foreign ownership caps.[174] American investors flocked to establish a manufacturing presence in Mexico, bringing their S&T with them, including Coca-Cola, Ford, Dow Chemical, John Deere, and General Motors. Where private businesses failed to invest in S&T, state-owned enterprises did. Mexican industry soon came to include textiles, food processing, electricity, petroleum, fertilizer, cement, and steel.[175] Agriculture was modernized with advanced irrigation, farm equipment, and fertilizer technologies.[176] Massive public works and infrastructure projects were undertaken.[177] Mexican firms began producing radios, televisions, and other consumer electronics in the 1940s and 1950s, eventually moving into computer manufacturing during the 1970s.[178]

However, Mexico did not experience the same major leaps in S&T as those achieved by Israel or Taiwan. With no serious military threats and easy access to imported weapons, there was little support for defense R&D. In fact, Mexico consistently reduced its defense budget during the Cold War until it ranked among the lowest in the Western Hemisphere.[179] The money was instead diverted to welfare programs to address persistent economic inequality. Whenever domestic inequality surged, the Mexican government further redirected resources away from S&T-related activities (modernization, industrialization) and toward welfare, housing, health care, and land redistribution.[180] The only constant was strong and sustained support for primary and secondary education. However, support for tertiary education programs was inconsistent. New universities were constructed, but with few facilities or funding for R&D, and at times, not even the university libraries were stocked.[181]

Suddenly, during the 1980s and 1990s, external threats to Mexico's economy increased dramatically. Due to recurring balance-of-payments and currency crises, Mexico became heavily indebted to foreign banks and governments. This was widely seen not only as humiliating to Mexico but also as a threat to its policy independence and therefore an affront to Mexican sovereignty.[182] In response, the Mexican state's primary goal became to increase foreign exchange earnings and thereby restore macro-economic stability. Only then could Mexico escape the dictates of foreign creditors.

At first, Mexico's response to this increase in external threat was increased support for S&T-based innovation via domestic institutions. Trade, investment, and procurement policies were developed or changed to foster innovation in the automotive, pharmaceutical, microcomputer, and capital goods sectors. Taxes on business were reduced, and innovators and businesspeople were given more freedom to increase their income earned through their industries.[183]

Unfortunately, the economic shocks hit Mexico faster than these policies could counter.[184] Real wages plummeted, urban unemployment skyrocketed, and inflation rose sharply throughout much of the 1980s. Mexico's wealthy shielded themselves by shifting their assets abroad, leaving the middle and lower classes, especially the peasant farmers, to bear the burden of the economic crises. Hence, as inequality grew, domestic tensions began to rise. Robberies in the capital went up by 250%, major strikes and protests reached new highs, and millions of desperate workers risked physical harm and incarceration to cross illegally into the United States; meanwhile, corruption plagued federal and local government.[185] The incompetence of the government's response to the 1985 earthquake, which devastated parts of Mexico City, killing up to forty thousand people and leaving over one hundred thousand homeless, served to further catalyze domestic unrest. By the 1990s, domestic tensions had turned violent. An armed uprising of Zapatista rebels appeared in Chiapas. The ruling party's handpicked candidate for president was assassinated. Police had begun to massacre agricultural protesters. A Maoist guerrilla movement, the Popular Revolutionary Army, rose up in Guerreo and soon initiated attacks on army, police, and government targets.[186]

In response, the Mexican government has since been forced to repeatedly rebalance its resources back to the provision of basic welfare, health, and education for the poor.[187] As a percentage of GDP, general spending on R&D activities was cut by over 50% during the mid-1980s, never to recover.[188] Social spending was also cut, but not by nearly so much.[189] For example, spending on education (mostly primary and secondary) was cut by 30%, while health spending fell by only 23%.[190] Yet these two categories remained the lion's share of social spending. Taken together, they bottomed at 5.3% of GDP during the mid-1980s, but have since risen sharply to 8.2%.[191] Meanwhile, higher education in twenty-first-century Mexico remains flat and does not necessarily entail STEM training. For example, the public universities are seen more as a venue for students to start political careers, not to enter the sciences or engineering.[192] Even within STEM, the same fraction of Mexico's college-educated researchers are employed in the social sciences and humanities (27% of total) as in the natural sciences (27%), and almost twice those in engineering and technology (15%).[193] As for S&T policies, after its 1994 financial crisis, Mexico sought to avoid frightening off potential foreign investors. The government therefore weakened requirements for local ownership, joint ventures, and technology transfer.[194] Hence, Mexico's largest export remains petroleum, while in S&T-based industries, Mexico can compete only in low-skill assembly and production operations in automobiles and electronics, and mostly in exports to the United States, which are protected from Chinese competition by the North American Free Trade Agreement (NAFTA).[195]

Today, Mexico is not a total failure, but a relative one. There do exist a few hubs of innovative activity in Mexico, such as in the city of Monterrey or within the automotive inputs sector. Nor has Mexico's underperformance in S&T

prevented the emergence of several world-class multinational corporations there. But overall, Mexico's political leadership is mostly content to wait and hope for knowledge spillovers and technology transfer to happen naturally, from foreign firms training local workers and suppliers in their technology production chains.[196] Major investments, such as those made by Taiwan or Israel, in creating markets and networks for S&T progress, or in addressing the market and network failures that obstruct it, are not made by Mexico. S&T progress there has simply not yet garnered enough political support from Mexico's rivalrous interest groups. That is, Mexico has generally failed to enter a state of creative insecurity.

10

Conclusion

Creative Insecurity and Its Implications

At its core, the argument of this book is simple: competition causes innovation, not institutions or policies, and the most compelling form of competition is that which takes place between states in the international arena. Without international competition in the form of external threats to a society's economic and military security, then national innovation rates tend to slow. External threats matter because they counter the domestic political fights over distribution that kill off the incentives and rewards for innovation. Absent an economic or military imperative to innovation, domestic institutions will not be created, used, or maintained properly to improve national innovation rates. Instead, they will be neglected or directed toward other ends, often redistributive or ideological. Thus, it is the balance between domestic rivalries and external threats that ultimately drives national science and technology (S&T) performance by influencing the effectiveness of institutions and policies.

This final chapter provides some important conclusions. It reviews this book's major findings and discusses the limitations of creative insecurity theory. It then employs creative insecurity theory to make some unexpected predictions about national innovation rates during the next twenty years. It also explains the implications of this book's findings for policymakers, innovation researchers, and voters, while offering additional advice and warnings. It ends with suggestions for future study and an explanation of why everyone should care about the future of innovation research.

Seven Findings from the Cases and Statistics

Seven findings are firmly substantiated by the evidence presented in this book. First, the data and case studies suggest that Cardwell's Law still holds strong. Despite globalization and the now widely recognized importance of S&T, there remains significant variation in national S&T outputs across time and country. Even recently, during the past seventy years, a handful of nations have experienced dramatic improvements in their S&T capabilities, such as Japan, Finland, Israel, Taiwan, Korea, and Singapore. Also, among the top innovators, we can find substantial variation in S&T outputs. For example, the United States, Switzerland, Germany, and Sweden have been strong, stable, leading S&T nations for decades. A dozen other nations have remained equally reliable mid-level innovators (e.g., the Netherlands, France, Italy, and Spain), and there are a large number of low-level innovators (e.g., Hungary, Malaysia, Portugal, South Africa, Turkey, and Argentina). This divergence remains despite the seemingly clear policy and fiscal requirements for promoting innovative behavior. Even among the wealthy industrialized democracies, some countries are consistently more successful than others at innovation.

Second, the data and case studies do not support the most popular explanations for why nations innovate. Differences in national innovation rates are not well explained by random chance, country size, economy size, military spending, first-mover advantages, or late industrialization. The point here is not to argue that none of these causal factors has any effect on national innovation rates, but rather to defuse some older, unsubstantiated generalizations about the sources of relative technological power. These explanations are sometimes presented as "accepted wisdom" during discussions of national innovation rates. Certainly some of them might make sense when used to explain a particular country's innovation rate at a specific point in time. Yet on closer consideration, not one of these popular theories can be consistently applied across time and space to explain the world's most (or least) innovative countries. Statistical analysis tends to confirm these nonfindings.

Third, when they function properly, markets appear to be excellent producers of innovation. However, market failures can slow innovation; therefore, there *is* a role for public policy to correct them, and thereby boost S&T performance. This book focused first on a handful of classic state actions, nicknamed the "Five Pillars" of innovation: intellectual property rights, research subsidies, education, research universities, and trade policy. The data suggest that each of the Five Pillars does matter for improving national innovation rates. However, the Five Pillars do *not* explain as much innovation as we might expect. Regardless of which major policy we investigated, and even if all five were packaged together, we found that there remained a significant amount of unexplained innovation. Also, there are simply too many important cases of innovative nations *not* scoring highly across the Five Pillars yet still producing cutting-edge S&T and S&T-based industries. The experience of several countries reveals that simply increasing research and development (R&D) spending, protecting intellectual property rights (IPRs), or setting up schools and universities does not necessarily result in innovation at the scientific or technological frontier.

Fourth, the evidence failed to identify any "best" institution or policy, or combination thereof, that the world's policymakers must converge upon to achieve national S&T competitiveness. Rather, in a reversal of Anna Karenina's dictum, each national S&T success story appears to be different, but the failures may all be the same.[1] That is, one surprise finding in the data and case studies is that the common trait between successful S&T countries is their dedication, not to particular institutions or policy designs, but to solving market failures and network failures in general. There is no particular national innovation system, type of government, or variety of capitalism that strongly correlates with successful innovation.

It is important to restate here that I am *not* arguing that particular institutions and policies (including capitalism, democracy, and decentralization) have *no* effect on national innovation rates. Rather, I am contending that theories that put these institutions at their core, as both necessary and sufficient for sustained S&T progress, have been overstated and oversimplified, and need to be re-examined. They simply do not have the predictive or explanatory power we assume them to have. Domestic institutions and policies do not determine the rate and direction of national inventive activity. Like a carpenter's tools, institutions and policies do *influence* outcomes, but they are *not* causal forces. Good tools do not make someone an expert carpenter; good institutions and policies do not compel a society to innovate. At best, they help us to understand *how* nations innovate, but not *why*.

Fifth, the data and case studies point us toward factors often ignored in the research on national innovation systems: social networks, industrial clusters, and technology standards. The cases consistently reveal that informal social networks, both domestic *and* international, play important roles in determining national S&T achievement. That is, innovation is not just a market failure problem; it is also a network failure problem. Social networks provide vital information that neither markets nor governments easily capture. This includes essential information about science, technology, engineering, and mathematics (STEM) labor; investment opportunities; and markets for highly specialized S&T inputs and outputs. Certainly these kinds of information problems plague all businesses, but they are especially tricky in S&T-based industries. S&T actors are extremely specialized and disparate. Also, the business conditions in S&T-based sectors change more rapidly and unexpectedly than others. In capturing and distributing information cheaply, social networks help S&T actors to find one another and to increase their flexibility to rapid change. In so doing, networks drastically reduce the high costs and risks of innovation. One condition for building physical networks, and hence the social networks upon which they are based, is standards. Technology standards help to determine how large a network can get and how well its members can interoperate. Standards are especially important for S&T because they can solve several types of market failures that can slow the creation or adoption of innovations. Yet, like institutions and policies, networks are tools, not causes; they do not explain *why* nations innovate, but *how* they might do so.

Sixth, innovation creates winners and losers, and the losers often resort to politics to obstruct S&T progress that threatens their interests. Even when there is broad support for new S&T, losers can be created by the institutions, policies, and networks used to foster innovation. Government is rarely a neutral observer in these upheavals, but rather is pursued by both sides in the hope of gaining policy advantages in their mortal conflict. This political resistance to technological change can obstruct or warp otherwise "good" S&T policy. Time and again, the losing interest groups created by scientific progress or technological change have been able to convince politicians to block, slow, or alter government support for scientific and technological progress. They support taxes, regulations, subsidies, procurement policies, spending, and so forth that obstruct progress in new S&T and favor the status quo S&T. History confirms that technological losers and their political representatives have interfered with markets, public institutions and policies, and even the scientific debate itself to protect their interests. Political resistance by technological losers therefore acts as a force *opposing* innovation, helping to explain *why* some countries are better at S&T than others.

Seventh, a nation's external threats (both military and economic) appear to act as a counteracting force that *supports* innovation. Innovation is often the best strategy for a society to use against particular external threats. These include the threats of military conquest, severe cuts to strategic imports, or massive flights of capital abroad. When these particular types of external threats loom large enough to outweigh those posed by domestic rivals, both popular and elite support tend to shift in favor of S&T and its supporting institutions and policies.

To successfully innovate at the national level, and over the long run, a country's interest groups must cooperate to accept the high risk and high costs of innovation, which may include major institutional changes and the restructuring of the entire economy. In other words, innovation causes pain. Countries must therefore face a penalty for not innovating. The pain of innovation must be outweighed by the pain of *not* innovating. Thus, creative insecurity theory asserts that the key to explaining national innovation rates is not asking *which* institutions or policies a country should use, but focusing attention on the politics *behind* a country's pursuit of innovation.

This book's solution to the innovation puzzle has been new in several respects. Foremost, it has challenged the prevailing sentiment that "institutions rule!"—that there is a deterministic relationship between domestic institutions and innovation that, despite its problems, remains little critiqued.[2] Importantly, this book has examined several causal factors that are either omitted in prior research or are not simultaneously controlled for in comparative tests. Additionally, the theory and evidence presented in the book are more generalizable than much prior research. The investigations reported here used cross-national datasets and country histories covering several decades, rather than just single-country or single-industry studies or brief time periods. One problem with the conventional wisdom is that many of its supporting studies look only at cases of success, and only during the time during which these nations improved and maintained their innovation rate. They do not study cases of failure. They do not follow successful countries as they decline and after they decline, nor do they examine them long before they improved. This book has addressed these problems by using a far more extensive set of data and cases. Finally, this book has suggested a new approach to innovation theory, one in which national institutions and policies are redefined as tools rather than causal forces. It argues that our primary question should be why some nations elect to pursue innovation and to employ and maintain these costly tools, rather than whether a "best" tool exists. That is, "politics rule!"

For those readers not yet convinced by creative insecurity, this book still offers solid evidence of the need for new explanations of national innovation rates. It also establishes enough empirical ground for the development of new theory. Specifically, if the statistics and case studies herein do not provide exhaustive tests of creative insecurity, they at least demonstrate its plausibility. This book therefore lays a strong empirical foundation upon which additional research can be built.

Caveats, Conditions, and Context

Creative insecurity theory does not claim to be a universal theory of everything. It has several limitations that must be taken seriously if the theory's full potential is to be realized.

First, the hypotheses posited in this book are meant to be probabilistic, not determinist. As Mancur Olson himself put it: "Although we should not be satisfied with any theory that fails to explain a lot with a little, we need not of course expect any one theory to explain everything or even the most important thing."[3] Creative insecurity explains and predicts much of the variation in national innovation rates over time, but it does not claim to explain each and every case throughout history. Rather, this book's claim is that creative insecurity provides us with a *better* explanation for national innovation rates. It better fits the data, explains more of the data, and explains many outliers and unexpected results that other theories fail to account for.

Second, as corollary to the previous limitation, this theory does not rule out other important causal factors.[4] That is, innovation has many powerful driving forces; I claim that, at the level of the nation-state, creative insecurity is one of them, but not necessarily the only one. Personally, I speculate that culture, ideology, individual leadership, climate, and perhaps even social psychology may also play important causal roles in explaining differences in national innovation rates. Each of these factors is understudied and deserves more attention from innovation scholars. However, no single book can tackle all of these rich dynamics and interactions. Investigation of these other causal variables, and how they interact with creative insecurity, must therefore be left for future research.

Third, creative insecurity theory expects lags across time and within society. That is, it does not predict an instantaneous change in support for S&T in response to a change in a nation's balance of external threats versus domestic rivalries. Nor does it predict complete society-wide agreement on supporting or opposing S&T. Some individuals and interest groups will change their minds faster than others. Some will not change their minds at all. A few may even support or oppose S&T out of habit or ideology, or in allegiance with their social network. But creative insecurity does predict that, on average, changes in the balance of domestic rivalries versus external threats will trigger changes in the political support for S&T over time, and thereby affect national innovation rates.

It is also important to emphasize what creative insecurity is *not* arguing. It is not arguing that nations only innovate when threatened with invasion.[5] If this were the case, then Belgium, the Balkan states, Iraq, and Afghanistan would currently rank among the most innovative countries on earth, while the United States should be stuck in the preindustrial era. Nor does creative insecurity argue that defense spending and military procurement are necessary for technological development.[6] Clearly, important outliers such as Japan, Germany, and Switzerland (each notoriously low military spenders) and Saudi Arabia (one of the world's top military spenders) make hash of this assertion. Creative insecurity does not contend that a nation's "systemic vulnerabilities" increase leaders' support for technological upgrading, while decreasing the number of "veto players" in a political system.[7] It does not argue that innovation occurs when natural resource constraints force particular choices on political actors fighting for their political survival during economic crises.[8] It does not claim that inherited organizational structures determine the ability of political-economic actors to get their way, or that external shocks or pressures force specific policy choices on interest groups.[9] Some of these arguments may sound similar to creative insecurity, but they are distinctly different.[10]

Predictions

Winston Churchill once quipped, "I always avoid prophesying beforehand because it is much better policy to prophesy after the event has already taken place."[11] We social scientists have turned this witticism into an art form. We eagerly explain the past, but most of us tend to pathologically avoid making predictions about the future. Perhaps this is wise. However, good theories should be able to both explain and predict, perhaps not perfectly but with some reliability. This is what we have come to expect from theories in physics and chemistry. We should expect no less from political science and economics. Also, predictions about future performance will provide additional evidence with which to confirm, discredit, or revise creative insecurity theory.

I therefore offer my predictions of national S&T performance over the next twenty years. These predictions are generated using recent data on economic inequality, domestic political terror, militarized disputes, and imports of food and energy. The results are presented in Table 10.1. The leftmost column reveals that each of the top or rapid innovators identified back in chapter 3 continues to enjoy the conditions ripe for creative insecurity. The "Potential Surprises" column lists states that are most likely to exceed past performance or to outperform current expectations, perhaps even dramatically, during the next twenty years. "Potential Disappointments" lists states that should underperform expectations. The final column lists countries that we should monitor closely. For nations in this column, the forces of creative insecurity are potentially quite strong for either outperformance or underperformance during the next twenty years. However, due to rapidly and frequently changing conditions in these countries, these "Close Call" predictions are made with somewhat less confidence than those listed in the other columns.

While this brief chapter is not the place for a case-by-case analysis of the roughly sixty countries listed in Table 10.1, we nonetheless should note some interesting predictions contained therein. First, all of the countries that are currently the world's leading innovators are expected to remain so for at least another decade or two. We should see no major setbacks, even in the United States. Second, some current low and midlevel innovators may make unexpected advances toward the technological frontier, such as Spain, Croatia, and Slovenia. These are countries where the domestic tensions left over from the Cold War have calmed dramatically relative to the external economic and military threats. Hence, their innovation rates should begin to accelerate. This contradicts today's conventional wisdom, which views many of the countries in this column as being perennially stuck in lesser states of development, even judged by some observers as economic basket cases. Conversely, many of the nations listed as "Potential

Table 10.1 **Predictions of Future S&T Performance**

Continued Leadership	*Potential Surprises (+)*	*Potential Disappointments (–)*	*Close Calls**
Canada	Australia	Bahrain	China (–)
Finland	Austria	Belarus	Cyprus (+)
France	Belgium	Brazil	Greece (+)
Germany	Bulgaria	Chile	Ireland (–)
Israel	Croatia	Egypt	Latvia (+)
Japan	Czech Republic	India	Philippines (+)
South Korea	Estonia	Indonesia	Romania (+)
Sweden	Hungary	Iran	Singapore (–)
Switzerland	Italy	Kuwait	Thailand (+)
Taiwan	Lithuania	Mexico	Turkey (+)
United States	Netherlands	Nigeria	Ukraine (+)
	Norway	Qatar	Vietnam (–)
	Panama	Russia	
	Poland	Saudi Arabia	
	Portugal	South Africa	
	Slovak Rep	Sri Lanka	
	Slovenia		
	Spain		
	UK		

*(+) indicates likely surprise, (-) indicates likely disappointment.

Disappointments" are currently trumpeted by the media as the world's next big innovators. This list of predicted future disappointments include many of the "Breakout Nations," BRICS, and MINT countries now widely touted as looming twenty-first-century S&T success stories.[12] However, each of these countries suffers from fairly high levels of domestic inequality, political unrest, and civil strife, while their borders and strategic imports are either relatively secure or at least more secure than the domestic situation. Therefore, creative insecurity expects that the contending domestic interest groups and elites in these countries will likely fail to cooperate to accept the risks, costs, and redistributive aspects of rapid S&T progress. This includes China and India, both of which lead popular expectations of S&T performance over the next few decades. However, I predict that unless they encounter some new existential threat outside their borders, the domestic rivalries among different regions, ethnic groups, and economic classes will hobble attempts at making good S&T policy and institutions in these countries.

The Major Implications of Creative Insecurity

If we accept creative insecurity as a powerful force that motivates nations to innovate, then what are the implications for policymakers, politicians, and voters? The case histories and statistical evidence presented in this book strongly suggest two policy implications: customization and activism.

First, there is no magic bullet institution or secret sauce of policies for achieving national S&T competitiveness. Where the conventional wisdom predicts uniformity, the research on innovation finds that there is no one structural form, no one timeline, for successful development of S&T capabilities. This corroborates findings by scholars in other fields.[13] Globalization is *not* forcing nations to converge on a specific set of institutions or policies, as was suggested last century by the "Gerschenkron school"[14] and many observers of Germany's and Japan's economic miracles. The best S&T success stories include countries that followed radically *different* development paths to achieve competitiveness in S&T. This means that nations have choices. Governments can customize their tools (i.e., S&T institutions and policies) to fit their society's culture, history, and political-economic situation. Institutions and policies can take myriad forms to achieve national S&T goals, with vastly different types and degrees of government intervention into private markets.

Second, governments must be proactive in fostering science and technology. Perhaps the quote that most accurately captures this point comes from a top globalization scholar who writes, "Since national economic backwardness equals powerlessness in the international arena, states do not, and should not, wait idly hoping that the miraculous power of the market will throw some economic growth their way."[15] The enormous weight of cross-national evidence and experience shows that the same can be said of innovation.

Specifically, if a nation wants to improve its S&T performance, then its government must act to solve both market failures *and* network failures. The market failure aspect of innovation is well understood. Research and development are fraught with high risks, high costs, and considerable uncertainty. Property rights are unclear. Externalities are rife. Stagnant technological monopolies are frequent occurrences. Essential information and skill sets are often fragmented and dispersed. So if ever there was a clear and compelling justification for the state to intervene in the economy, then these problems posed by innovation provide it. There is a role for the policies and institutions reviewed in this book *if* there is a strong enough national political consensus in support of S&T progress as a national priority. If enough popular will exists, then government's tools (i.e., S&T institutions and policies) can be used well.

Yet, solving market failures is only half a strategy; governments must act also to address network failure.[16] The policy recommendations here are more novel. Scholars and policymakers are only beginning to discover what works and what does not. Some emphasize the organic, grassroots nature of networks, which implies that government should enable networks and then get out of the way. This might mean building the kinds of comprehensive, high-quality, physical infrastructure upon which social networks are based, especially transportation and communication networks.[17] It might also entail not only creating universities but also better linking them together with one another and to the business community. Others point to a more proactive role for government to facilitate, if not manage, innovation networks. These might take the form of joint R&D projects, research symposia, industrial clusters, or government-business consortia, perhaps focused on finding S&T solutions to specific policy problems. Still others argue that government should be actively creating innovation clusters, like those described in chapter 6, or circulating innovators through government-run national innovation programs.[18]

Veto Players

For scholars and theorists, one major theoretical implication of creative insecurity is that institutions are endogenous. Take, for example, veto players.[19] As applied to innovation, veto-players theory suggests that states with *fewer* veto players can act more decisively, because fewer interests need to be negotiated. These states can therefore better overcome domestic resistance to technological change and innovate more rapidly. States with a large number of veto players have the opposite characteristics. It is harder to generate consensus among numerous veto players; therefore, these governments are less able to execute decisively to support S&T progress. However, chapter 5 presented evidence that the number of veto players, at least as captured by democracy or political decentralization, does not affect national innovation rates in any systematic manner.

Creative insecurity provides an explanation for this: decisiveness does not determine action. Although the number of veto players may affect how adroitly a state can act, it does not determine the direction in which states do act. A dictator can just as easily support modernization and technological change (e.g., Peter the Great, Lee Kuan Yew, Adolf Hitler) as oppose it (e.g., the Tokugawa Shogunate, Tsar Nicholas I, Robert Mugabe). Similarly, a state with many veto players (e.g., a highly decentralized democracy) can commit equally to rapid

S&T progress (e.g., the United States) or not (e.g., Spain). There is no a priori reason that the number of veto players should determine overall support for innovation. Regardless of their total numbers, each individual veto player must consider the mix of external threats and domestic rivals that he or she, his or her interest group, or her nation faces, which should then affect her political support for new S&T. The pivotal question becomes: from whence does each veto player draw his or her sense of security or threat?

This further implies that, instead of determining actions, the number of veto players may instead determine which causal forces are most relevant. At the individual level, a veto player's support for S&T may have as much to do with objective calculations of political-economic self-interest as with personal ideas, experience, and psychology. Where these individualistic factors are not shared among veto players, they should act like random noise and therefore get cancelled out in states with large numbers of veto players. Therefore, in states with large numbers of veto players, policy agendas may be determined more by systematic calculations of national political-economic interest. But as the number of veto players in a state decreases, these individual, random characteristics (personal preferences, ideas, and psychology) may grow in importance.[20] This potential interaction between creative insecurity and veto players is clearly an avenue for future research.

Selectorate Theory

Creative insecurity theory offers a similar response to "selectorate theory."[21] Selectorate theory holds that two institutional factors primarily determine leadership tenure and behavior: the number of individuals who have the right to select a nation's leadership (selectorate size), and the number of people whose approval is necessary for the leader to claim office (winning coalition size), where the winning coalition is usually a subset of the total selectorate. Selectorate theory's primary causal variable, therefore, is the size of the winning coalition relative to the total selectorate. In any polity, leaders must reward their winning coalition enough to prevent them from defecting to support a challenger. Where the winning coalition size is relatively large (e.g., democracy), leaders are motivated to provide lots of diffuse public goods to build up the requisite number of supporters needed to claim office. But where the winning coalition is small (e.g., monarchy), leaders are motivated to provide concentrated private goods (e.g., bribes, subsidies, government contracts, economic protectionism, and bureaucratic fiefdoms) to those few supporters who will help them stay in power. The implication is that societies that require large winning coalitions (e.g., presidential democracies) will tend to enjoy lots of public goods but little inefficient corruption or protectionism, while societies that require small winning coalitions (e.g., monarchies and military juntas) will suffer from few public goods and high levels of corruption, crime, and economic inefficiency.

Again, creative insecurity theory would argue that there is no a priori reason that winning coalition size should determine government support for S&T. While the size of a winning coalition may affect the *amount* of public goods or government favoritism, it does not necessarily determine their *form* or *goal*. Public goods can just as easily support S&T (e.g., STEM education, research subsidies, universities, and science conferences) as divert resources away from it (e.g., welfare programs, physical infrastructure, environmental improvement, and culture and the arts). Private goods, even when provided by corrupt dictatorships, are similarly ambivalent. Certainly private goods might take the form of specialized kickbacks, protectionism, and government largess. But, as Linda Cohen and Roger Noll have demonstrated, government support can just as easily take the form of a "technology pork barrel."[22] Governments can direct to their particular supporters subsidies for R&D laboratories, research universities, procurement programs for new technological systems, and protection for infant industries.

This brings us back to creative insecurity. Winning coalitions, regardless of their relative size, should tend to demand support for S&T progress when they perceive external threats as being relatively greater than domestic rivalries. That is, a winning coalition of wealthy farmers or industrial labor workers will likely demand very different rewards than a coalition of military leaders or heads of multinational corporations. But more urgently, if the winning coalition benefits from new S&T, then leaders should provide support for it. Again, the important question becomes: from whence do winning coalition members draw their sense of security or threat?

Advice

I further argue that the theory and evidence offered in this book, combined with the general findings of innovation scholars and policymakers over the past twenty years, offer ground for three additional pieces of advice that merit strong consideration.

Think Training, Not Welfare

Good innovation policies can appear to critics as a form charity or welfare; this is the wrong model. To create a more innovative economy, government actions should instead be patterned on the methods used to train elite athletes or warriors. In this model, government plays the role of coach or trainer, not philanthropist.

Coaches and trainers provide the best resources to the finest men and women whom they can recruit. Yet these athletes and warriors must still prove themselves on the competitive playing field or battleground. They are not protected from failure but are taught to grow stronger from it. Applied to innovation, this means that government *should* subsidize STEM education, and probably also education in business, management, and entrepreneurship. Government must also ensure that capital markets are trustworthy and flush with finance for investment in new S&T. In the most risky or long-run S&T projects, government should act as a funder and risk taker of last resort. For entirely new industries, government must act like a market maker. This means that the state must subsidize both supply *and* demand, not supply *or* demand. This implies a valuable role for government procurement programs in creating and improving markets for S&T.[23] At the extremes, government may even want to increase the overall provision of basic human necessities like food, shelter, clothing, health care, transportation, information, and communication. After all, the best and brightest of the twenty-first century should be worried about beating their competition, not where their next meal, safe home, or necessary medicines are coming from.

The difference between welfare and training is that the subsidized individuals and businesses must be made to compete. Good innovation policy should enrich the environment to create better competitors, but it should neither eliminate competition nor decide who wins it. Competition can even be incorporated selectively and delicately into the subsidies for education, research funding, and business finance. Some critics may prefer to diminish the role of competition. However, without competition, there can be no sense of creative insecurity.[24] It is not only our desire for recognition, respect, wealth, and power that motivate us to innovate but also the insecurity of losing these things to peers or rivals.

Furthermore, the mistakes and failures realized through competition are necessary learning tools.[25] They contain valuable information and lessons about our weaknesses, bad habits, and poor practices. Competition prevents an "everybody gets a prize" approach to subsidizing S&T, which might instead create a culture in which mistakes and failures are judged as embarrassing foibles that cannot be openly named or discussed. The freedom to fail is an essential external threat that drives individuals, organizations, and nations to innovate and grow stronger.[26] Thus, *provisions of state support must not eliminate competition, self-reliance, or personal responsibility, but elevate them to a higher level.*

Optimize Competition, Don't Maximize It

Yet competition should not be an all-out Hobbesian war of all against all. Considerable research, experience, and history tell us that when the competitive stakes are too high, it becomes a better strategy for people to lie, cheat, steal, sabotage, violently protest, or rebel rather than take the risks and costs of innovation.[27] Therefore, the policy prescription should not be to increase competition everywhere and always. Rather, scholars and policymakers must study and experiment to discover the most productive levels of competition for different actors and environments. Some individuals will innovate no matter what. These are those few happy innovators who find the pursuit of S&T, and its commercialization, to be interesting, enjoyable, and compelling in its own right.[28] However, much of the R&D that results in improvements at the national level (in productivity, new industries, and new weapons) comes from far less altruistic groups working together in concert. They include not only STEM labor and entrepreneurs but also experts in finance, marketing, and distribution, as well as taxpayers, consumers, military officials, and government bureaucrats. If there is too little competition, or competition with stakes that are too low, then few of these actors will be motivated to innovate. If there is too much competition, or competition with stakes that are too high, then the fear and greed can become so pervasive that some competitors will instead resort to unproductive behavior. Hence, an important corollary to “competition not charity” is: *competition should be optimized, not maximized.*

Balance Competition with Economies of Scale

If getting competition right is the Scylla of good innovation policy, then optimizing firm size and economies of scale is its Charybdis.[29] This is because, sometimes, only large organizations can martial enough resources to develop and profit from major new S&T projects; yet pro-competition policy often requires antitrust actions to break up large firms. That is, some technologies require economies of scale to succeed. They demand massive investments, the management of large-scale R&D and commercialization projects, and access to consumers worldwide. Examples might include new pharmaceuticals, medical equipment, biotechnologies, and advanced telecommunications and transportation systems. This often results in a few very large corporations that necessarily dominate their markets, such as Boeing, Microsoft, Pfizer, Apple, and Intel.

However, the standard critique of large firms is that they reduce competition, either by driving competitors out of business or by acquiring them. Regardless, as competition declines, the remaining large S&T firms can often charge higher-than-market prices, thus absorbing consumer resources away from other investments. Worse yet, with less competition, large firms have less incentive to innovate. They can even use their market and political power to block rival innovations, such as was described in chapter 7. Anticompetitive actions by

AT&T and IBM during the mid-twentieth century serve as classic examples. Therefore, from this perspective, policymakers who seek to foster innovation should actively regulate or break up large corporations.

This tension between the benefits of competition and economies of scale is as old as Joseph Schumpeter (1883–1950), who pointed out, to a prewar America obsessed with antitrust, the advantages for innovation gained by large firms. Nor is this merely an academic debate. Some economic historians blame the retreat of the United Kingdom from global technological leadership after 1870 on Britain's highly atomistic form of market competition.[30] According to this thesis, British firms never became large enough to generate the Schumpeterian innovation enjoyed by their massive German and American competitors. However, others argue that monopolies have held back the ability of some nations to innovate, such as Mexico,[31] Italy,[32] and France.[33]

Perhaps the solution to this dilemma is *not* to split up monopolies and oligopolies into small firms or fragmented markets, but for policymakers to force competition through other means. For example, when S&T firms acquire a large fraction of market share, government might instead fund or subsidize new competitors through loans, procurement programs, and grants. Alternately, government might experiment with regulating innovation, delaying antitrust in return for regular improvements in the technical, productivity, and performance aspects of the goods and services produced by large S&T firms. Government could even enter into competition itself, by performing competitive R&D in government labs that is then spun off to create new firms in the private sector. Regardless, the idea here is not to produce "big government" but to create and improve competition without destroying economies of scale in the private sector.

In many cases, governments might also require "modularity" as a basis for competition in S&T. The problem is that firms of all sizes can use anticompetitive practices to prevent outsiders from interfering with (read: innovating upon) their technological systems. Therefore, innovators should be given free rein to advance technologies that link into termination points of competing systems, provided that they do no harm to it. That is, innovators large and small must remain free to design and manage their own technologies as they see fit. However, they should be required to retain standard interfaces, such that new technologies can always "plug in" to one another like modules or Lego blocks.[34] This allows innovators to retain control over their own S&T but stops them from preventing others from innovating upon those systems. It is precisely this type of environment (i.e., modularity-enabled competition in S&T) that energized the late twentieth-century revolution in Internet, computing, and telecommunications, which continues to this day.[35]

Make Life, Not War

Make war! This is perhaps the most dangerous and wrongheaded lesson one could take from creative insecurity theory. This cynical interpretation holds that politicians and policymakers must forever generate external threats, real or perceived, to motivate innovation, for if the balance of security threats determines national innovation rates, then governments should do whatever possible to tweak security threats to increase political support for new S&T. In practice, this would require that the state regularly pick fights or invite attacks from foreign powers. And if there are no real external threats to be had, then the state must create widespread belief in imaginary ones.

Over time, this strategy tends toward the gradual militarization of a nation's entire S&T complex. S&T would become both a vital component of and a powerful justification for a garrison state. In a vicious spiral, investment in new S&T would be justified in terms of external threat, and ever greater national security functions of the state would then be justified in terms of the advancement of S&T. The twisted logic may even evolve that we need S&T to provide security, and therefore a massive security apparatus is necessary to invest in S&T.

This dynamic appears to describe the US case all too well.[36] In the decades following Pearl Harbor, US government investment in S&T was mostly restricted to defense contracts for advanced military systems, which then grew ever larger over time. These investments were enormously successful. They generated many of the major US computing, telecommunications, and aerospace innovations during the Cold War. These innovations then spilled over into the private sector, laying the foundation for economy-wide technological progress. After the shock of Sputnik, national security–related investments in S&T were expanded to include large subsidies for STEM education and universities. The argument here was that the United States was falling behind the Soviets in S&T because America was not producing enough STEM workers. Aerospace, satellites, and physics R&D were also major beneficiaries. Then, after the rise of Japan and Western Europe, industrial policy was folded into the national security apparatus. This meant more taxpayer money for commercially relevant government R&D, spin-offs, technology transfer, and procurement programs. Energy R&D entered the defense mix early, mostly restricted to nuclear projects at first. Then energy R&D spending spiked, during the early 1970s through the mid-1980s, in response to the oil embargoes, with funds going toward new S&T in fusion, renewables, fossil fuels, and conservation. Then, after years of quiescence, energy R&D rose again after 9/11. The dual motivations here have been to increase American security by decreasing reliance on fuel imports and to cut flows of oil money to foreign enemies of the United States. Most recently, health care is now slowly being absorbed into the security complex, with the Pentagon demanding better battlefield medicines, medical technologies, and postcombat rehabilitation treatments. Much like earlier defense innovations, it is expected that medical S&T developed for military purposes can spill over into the private sector. Interestingly, even federal research in the social sciences is now being justified in terms of external military or economic threats.[37] In sum, in an environment where any spending *not* linked to military or economic security is gridlocked in Congress or obstructed by state governments, there are few areas of American S&T that have not yet been framed in terms of external threats to win bipartisan support.

My argument here is not that framing S&T in security terms is foolish; it is that we must be wary of abuses. Many of the external threats faced by the United States during the past seventy years have been quite real. Much of the money was well spent. However, there is a tendency for the security-S&T loop to be reinforcing. It can become difficult for those benefiting from massive defense spending on S&T to separate their personal or corporate interests from the national interests. It is all too tempting for these beneficiaries to trump up threats of foreign enemies, to encourage a path toward international conflicts, or at least not to object to such a trajectory, rather than to argue for more peaceful resolutions. Perhaps we are already seeing this in US-China relations, in which both sides seem ready to stoke general fears or inflate minor security threats into national priorities with S&T solutions.[38] And what better way to distract attention away from problems at home. After all, the exploitation of external threats to counteract domestic tensions, or distract from them, is a long-practiced political strategy. Creative insecurity would now seem to legitimize it.

However, this is a losing policy in the long run. In a world increasingly typified by freedom of information and debate, this innovation strategy is wasteful and self-defeating. In open societies, false alarms about manufactured enemies soon become transparent. This can delegitimize political support for S&T. Also, without a real competitive threat, S&T institutions and policies become corrupt and mismanaged.[39] Worse yet, in nations typified by restricted information and debate, such a strategy is highly destructive. Imaginary enemies can become real ones, risking unnecessary and destructive conflicts. In either case, it leads to a bloated defense sector and a militarized society in which any government funding must be justified by its relevance to national security.

Furthermore, to maximize the returns on investment in new S&T, nations must increasingly solve market failures and network failures at the global level. If *national* markets and networks reduce the costs, risks, and uncertainties of innovation, then *global* markets and networks can do so better by leveraging exponentially more people and resources. In fact, global cooperation may be the only way to tackle important mega-science projects such as nuclear fusion power plants, ocean and air purification, space exploration, and the eradication of common deadly or debilitating diseases. Yes, nations still matter, and likely will continue to matter for the foreseeable future. So too will cities and provinces. However, the region and globe will need to take higher priority in twenty-first-century innovation policy. Internationally, this will likely require deepening and broadening the types of networking activities discussed in chapter 6. Regardless, a global approach to markets and networks will require us to go beyond the prejudices of techno-nationalism and antiquated, parochial conceptions of the nation-state. Clearly an innovation policy based on forever manufacturing external threats does not jibe well with the demands of global cooperation, especially if one's most valuable partners are also those that pose the most credible external threats.

Thankfully, conflict-driven innovation policy need not be the case. Modern society has shown that it can evolve beyond a fixation on violence as a motivating force. A hopeful example might be found in Japan during the Cold War. After 1868, Japan innovated in exactly the martial way described by creative insecurity theory. National investments in S&T were driven by a deeply felt desire to "enrich the country, strengthen the army", reverse the humiliations forced upon Japan by the West, and rise to great power status. This culminated during the 1930s and 1940s in the technologically advanced Japanese empire, an expansionist regime run by a military dictatorship with widespread public support. However, Japan's total defeat in 1945 and subsequent occupation by a foreign power delegitimized the Japanese military. Defense spending and industries were virtually eliminated. Even when faced with a heavily armed and aggressive USSR and China, the military remained wildly unpopular in Japan. Rearmament was done quietly, with defense innovation typified more by spin-on than spin-off. The Japanese instead plunged into civilian innovation with now-famous results. Former military enemies became relatively close S&T partners with Japan; even China, as it has risen, continues to have deep trade and investment relationships with Japan in S&T-related industries. While there has clearly been a strong nationalist component of Japanese innovation, this nationalism has not prevented valuable international cooperation, nor led to a remilitarization of the Japanese S&T establishment.

Rather than manufacture false security concerns, I argue that we should instead broaden our concept of security. Policymakers and politicians should focus on the very real, nonstate, external threats their citizens face. For example, climate change poses a catastrophic risk for all Americans everywhere. The already-present danger of droughts, floods, rising sea levels, and major weather events should scare us enough to motivate massive investment in innovations in fusion, solar, wind, and other noncarbon energy sources. A recent conservative estimate put the *annual* costs of damage due to climate change at around 1% to 2% of global gross domestic product. In the United States alone, this equates to around $150 billion to $300 billion every year, or roughly $500 to $1,000 per man, woman, and child.[40] However, the federal government spends little on S&T to address the causes of climate change. During the entire decade from 2003 to 2012, the United States spent only around $13 billion on renewable fuels and energy efficiency, which lie at the heart of all serious climate change solutions, or less than $4.35 per American per year.[41]

Even if one does not fear the risks of climate change, then the economic and military hazards imposed by carbon-based energy should still motivate support for R&D in conservation and alternative fuel sources. Take, for example, America's massive imports of foreign oil. In the past decade alone, the United States has imported over 7.6 billion barrels of oil from the Persian Gulf, and another 8.9 billion from Russia, Venezuela, and Nigeria.[42] This amounts to vast exports of American wealth to declared rivals of the United States, funders of terrorism, and sources of regional and global instability. Worse yet, petroleum is a finite energy source that will ultimately face escalating production costs and inevitable depletion, thus putting much of our transportation and electric infrastructure at risk. One could further add the billions of dollars of loss, cleanup costs, and damage done to coastlines, fisheries, and ocean habitats created by regular oil spills, such as Deepwater Horizon (2010). Meanwhile, pollution from petroleum use has had costly and devastating effects on health and living standards in American cities, such as Los Angeles, Atlanta, Chicago, San Francisco, Phoenix, and Pittsburgh. Nor is coal a better alternative, as demonstrated by the choking gray smog that frequently envelops Beijing, Mexico City, Santiago, and New Deli. Thus, even at their best, carbon fuels represent a pollutive, finite resource that is hoarded and exploited by some of America's worst enemies.

Aging and disease constitute two other "external" terrors faced by all people. They are often the greatest threat to that demographic of older, wealthy voters who form the most politically active voting block in many democracies. Heart disease, cancer, diabetes, and Alzheimer's disease eventually point the cold finger of death at us all. Together with cerebrovascular and lung disease, these major ailments are responsible for 60% of all Americans' deaths every year.[43] Meanwhile, some combination of hypertension, macular degeneration, arthritis, back pain, hearing loss, declining energy, and decreased libido haunts the remaining years of all Americans over age forty. For younger Americans, drug and alcohol addiction, bronchiolitis, croup, impetigo, meningitis, asthma, autism, Lyme disease, and a long list of childhood diseases and birth defects threaten to cut short young lives or dim their futures. Also, every year, mental illness turns responsible, legal gun owners into domestic terrorists who threaten the schools, churches, and government buildings used by every day Americans, while simultaneously threatening our constitutional rights to gun ownership. Yet despite the pervasive and dire nature of these threats, the federal government spends only around $40 per person on medical R&D annually.[44]

These types of threats should be the nightmares trotted out by politicians and policymakers to motivate support for S&T. They are all the more nightmarish because these threats are clear, present, and *real*. We do not need fabricated enemies abroad to generate a widespread and constructive sense of creative insecurity.

What Next?

This book is meant to start discussions about innovation, not to end them. Along these lines, I enthusiastically encourage my fellow researchers to conduct more case studies and additional statistical analyses to confirm, or revise, the theory and findings in this book. Of particular interest would be empirical studies of seemingly unthreatened yet innovative countries, such as Canada, Denmark, Finland, and Switzerland. Alternately, a creative insecurity dynamic may explain yet other types of state action, such as regulatory or development policy.[45] Future innovation research should also attempt to separate out science from technology, innovation from diffusion, and perhaps even break down innovation into its component steps of innovation (e.g., research, invention, development, mass production, and improvement). Also, this book has argued that institutions are endogenous to domestic rivalries and external threats, and provides some evidence for it. But more work needs to be done to better specify the causal mechanisms. This book also did not delve much into antitrust policy. If competition is key, then perhaps getting the nuances of antitrust right could be an important part of the policy solution. I might also suggest that we need more psychology and brain science research to better explain risk taking and innovation at the individual level. Understanding what drives individuals to innovate can aid policymakers in designing institutions at the national level. Finally, recent innovation research has mostly looked at S&T as the effect or "dependent variable"; it is high time for scholars to revisit the role of scientific progress and technological change as independent variables that cause particular types of change in domestic and international politics. In sum, there is much work for innovation scholars to do.

I would also urge that political scientists play a greater role in future research on how S&T progresses. This book has shown that innovation is inherently political in that it involves highly contested decisions over the allocation of resources, institution and policy design, contested value systems, and the formation and maintenance of domestic and international political-economic networks. Therefore, the study of innovation should not be left to economists, business scholars, and sociologists who tend to ignore or dismiss politics in their research. Political scientists have competitive advantage here and should assert themselves in the innovation debate. Likewise, innovation scholars from other fields should take notice of the pivotal role of politics in affecting S&T progress, as well as the institutions and policies that affect it.

Political scientists themselves should want greater participation because the paucity of research on the politics of S&T is holding back progress in several major debates within the field. Science and technology play important causal roles in questions of cooperation and conflict, systemic governance, systemic change, the evolution of institutions, and the developmental state, to name but a few. Technology changes the interests of states and the role of government by reconcentrating power, allowing new activities, and producing new market failures. Yet we still have only a limited understanding of the political causality surrounding S&T, either as an independent or a dependent variable. Science, technology, and innovation, therefore, appear to constitute a "reverse salient" in the study of international politics. Furthermore, studies of economic growth, comparative advantage, production theory, and even some aspects of finance theory hinge on technological change as an independent variable. This implies that, until we can explain technological change as a dependent variable, these lines of research will likewise suffer. Therefore, the conception of a political theory of technological change has greater stakes than simply satisfying the intellectual curiosity of a handful of S&T scholars. It will have a major impact on scholarship across political science, economics, and business. It should therefore be made a greater priority for political research. A better understanding of science, technology, and innovation will help political scientists in all subfields better solve *their* problems and answer *their* major questions. It is therefore time for this debate to enter the political science mainstream.

Why Should We Care?

A senior scholar once quipped that he wished that every essay would end by answering the question: "whose mind do you expect to change about what?" This book hopes to change all those minds that ignore the powerful politics that determine the rate and direction of scientific progress and technological change. If we continue to ignore these politics, then we will never adequately explain, predict, or affect national S&T performance. Policymakers will continue to see their "good" institutions and policies misfire. Many scientists and engineers will find their work and careers tossed about by seemingly inexplicable storms and tides. Businesses managers will waste investments in projects that struggle blindly against hostile political-economic environments, while ignoring friendly ones. Worst of all, voters and interest groups will fail to recognize their own culpability in affecting American economic competitiveness and military prowess.

The theoretical and policy implications of this book's findings are enormous. Current theory prioritizes the role of domestic institutions and policies in fostering national innovation rates. Most observers argue that institutions determine national S&T performance by creating the incentives and rewards for innovation at the level of the firm and the individual. The theoretical shorthand for this is that "good" institutions and policies cause innovation. Hence, failure is caused by "bad" or missing institutions or policies.[46] However, such a narrow focus ignores the fact that all domestic institutions and policies operate within a broader context of national and international politics. Institutions are not an end in themselves. Nor are they a causal force. Rather, institutions are a means to an end. Institutions are tools that interest groups, elites, and policymakers can use to affect social conditions such as economic growth, national security, income distribution, and S&T progress.

One key distinction made in this book is that most studies of innovation take support for science and technology as given. They then wonder which institutions or policies can best achieve the nation's science and technology goals. In contrast, this book shows that widespread support for S&T cannot be taken for granted. History shows that the losers will fight to obstruct, co-opt, or alter otherwise practical policies that promote science, technology, and innovation. Thus, understanding how and why these fights evolve is essential for understanding why some countries are better at science and technological change than others.

Put differently, what this book contributes, that previous work has not, is a better understanding of how and why political resistance to technological change arises, and the conditions under which it can affect S&T institutions, policies, and outcomes. Without this change in perspective, we may blame bad S&T outcomes on innocent policy designs or institutions. Alternately, we may expend considerable resources to install institutions into societies or circumstances where they may not function properly.

Creative insecurity therefore helps to explain why otherwise "good" policies and institutions fail to deliver scientific and technological progress. It informs the innovation debates taking place within a variety of disciplines, such as economics, political science, business, and industry studies. Scholars in each of these fields often omit analysis of the distributive politics behind innovation policies and institutions. They lack a general model of these politics. This forces them on their inconclusive and never-ending search for the right institutions and policies.

This book also informs the policy process. It identifies the conditions under which domestic institutions and policies might be more or less likely to be passed by legislatures and properly implemented by executives. This can aid strategies for achieving more widespread political support for S&T institutions and policies, and their proper implementation, and thereby help policymakers deliver more effective solutions.

Most important, this book has revealed that a diverse set of approaches can improve our understanding of the innovation process. In many ways, innovation scholars in different fields resemble the proverbial blind men who examine different limbs of an elephant and then disagree upon what animal it is. In fact, despite similar findings on questions of common interest, few disparate innovation scholars cite one another, and many seem generally unaware of the contributions each may have for the other. This book seeks to demonstrate the value of bringing together diverse theories, methods, and data for explaining national S&T competitiveness, and for developing new policy implications. Hence, this book can be interpreted as an appeal for greater integration of politics into the study of innovation. It also begs innovation researchers to combine disbursed problem-specific and country-specific approaches into a more generalizable theoretical and policy-relevant cross-field debate. Thus, this book is a call for greater cooperation and common focus among fragmented S&T scholars not just within political science, but across the social sciences.

APPENDICES

DEFINITIONS, MEASUREMENT, AND DATA

Appendix 1

THE GREAT DEFINITIONS (NON)DEBATE

The science and technology (S&T) definitions used in this book may sound simple, straightforward, and noncontroversial, but they are nothing of the sort. It is important to recognize that definitions of these key terms have radically changed over time and across different fields of study. Strangely, these conflicts are rarely addressed in innovation research. Therefore, one author's *technology* can be misunderstood as another author's *ideas* or still another's *innovation*. Unfortunately, few participants acknowledge this Babylon. This appendix therefore presents a short historical survey of the definitional twists and turns. One of its goals is to get all readers onto the same page in terms of vocabulary. Another is to clarify where this book falls within the innovation debate.

Let's start with the words *science, technology*, and *innovation*. They seem to us like old words for timeworn concepts, but that is not accurate. Each of these words has a relatively new meaning, which was established only within our lifetime. For example, before the nineteenth century, *science* was more about data collection and taxonomy than about formulating and testing causal hypotheses. In fact, until the late 1800s, scientific theories and hypotheses were often ridiculed as speculation because they were impossible to test or prove.[1] Also, what we currently think of as core science subjects (e.g., physics, chemistry, biology, geology) were for centuries lumped together under the term *natural philosophy*. It was not until the mid-1800s that schools of "physics" or "chemistry" first appeared on university campuses, splitting off from natural philosophy schools. But, even as late as the 1890s, top universities and scientists in the lead scientific country, Great Britain, still published treatises and textbooks on "natural philosophy," by which was meant "the investigation of laws in the material world, and the deduction of results not directly observed."[2]

Similarly, no man was called a *scientist* until the 1830s, and certainly not to his face.[3] The term was first suggested as a whimsical nickname, but it had an unseemly ring to it. The world-famous biologist Thomas Huxley, speaking for many of his contemporaries, lambasted the term in 1894 as an insult to his profession, undignified, and improper.[4] In fact, until the spread of the industrial laboratory during the early 1900s, the practice of science offered neither careers nor even full-time jobs, except maybe to a few university professors who spent most of their time teaching, not doing research.[5] Scientific research was then a hobby, often affordable only to wealthy men, usually European aristocrats.[6] It was not until the 1910s that both terms, *science* and *scientist,* attained their modern meanings and widespread acceptance.

The word *technology* was not popularized until the 1930s. Before then, economists, historians, and policymakers instead spoke in terms of *the useful arts, applied science, invention, manufactories, industry,* and *machines*. To them, *technology* was not even a thing. It instead defined a field of study, specifically the study of machines or *mechanical arts*. Hence, when the Massachusetts Institute of Technology (MIT) was founded in 1861, its name suggested a school of higher education in the principles of machinery. Among academics and intellectuals, the word *technology* began to attain its current meaning around 1900. At that time, the economist Thorstein Veblen and historian Charles Beard sought to show that material progress in the *useful arts,* especially that embodied in industrial machines and practices, was drastically reshaping modern society. That is pretty close to the modern definition of technology, and to these men, technological change *was* progress. Specifically, Veblen's work imported the meaning of the German word *technik* from German social science and transferred its definition to the English word *technology*. Then Beard and other scholars began to mix Veblen's *technology* interchangeably with older terms. Finally, during the 1930s, popular writers, newspapers, and other media escorted the new word out of the ivory tower and into popular parlance.[7]

Innovation was for centuries a very bad thing. It meant heterodoxy, or more likely heresy, in religion, politics, business, or the arts. An innovator was a pushy malcontent whose personal ambition sought to upend tradition or the divine order for personal gain. Innovation therefore implied cheating, revolution, and chaos! And it had nothing to do with progress in S&T, which instead was referred to as *novelty* or *invention*. It was only during the social foment of the 1750–1850 period that European philosophers and political activists began to associate innovation with progress. In the wake of their political revolution, French thinkers began to describe innovation as a positive, even superlative activity. The postrevolutionary French also began to use innovation to describe advances in S&T. At first, the term described only the introduction of scientific methods to the useful arts. But as the nineteenth century closed, social scientists had begun to use *innovation* to describe creativity when they theorized about the origins of genius, invention, or productive imagination.[8] It was only during the 1920s and 1930s that American sociologists finally began to apply the terms *innovation* and *innovator* to progress in S&T.[9]

Hence, only by the 1940s had the terms *science, technology,* and *innovation* entered general usage with meanings very similar to how we understand these words today. They were vaguely understood to have something to do with one another, though not always, and the boundaries were unclear. And this problem was exacerbated when mainstream economics "discovered" innovation during the 1950s.

Political Economists and Innovation

Throughout most of history, S&T progress had been either peripheral to or implicit in the study of economics, so there was little pressure to define terms. A few economists[10] recognized that technological progress was dreadfully important for nations, but they rarely defined it. Like Justice Potter Stewart's famous definition of pornography, they assumed that people knew technology or innovation when they saw it. In books, letters, and speeches by economists during the two centuries preceding 1950, one instead finds phrases such as "adequate protection of industry," "improvements and the perfection of machinery," "the manufacturing arts," and "progress of industry." These writings include works by then-famous theorists and policymakers such as Alexander Hamilton, Daniel Raymond, Henry Carey, Henry Clay, Francis Wayland, Frederich List, Karl Marx, and Thorsten Veblen.

As for theories of innovation, most of these classical thinkers simply accepted Adam Smith's (1776) brief explanation of innovation: technological change was the natural result of either the division of labor or scientifically inclined individuals. As an aside, most classical economists had little love for free trade when it came to technological progress, for while free trade was highly desirable to them for a host of other reasons, they realized it was not always good for innovation. Hence, one can find in classical economics many iterations of the "infant industry" argument for protecting a nation's budding high-tech sectors.

Rather than its causes, classical economists and policymakers were far more concerned with the effects of technological change. Most agreed that while technological progress was good for national might, it could be bad for the individual laborer. A few even saw technology as altogether evil. Yet, even Karl Marx, who wrote volumes about the effects of technological change, offered little in the way of explanation for what drove it, nor precise definitions of it.[11]

Schumpeter

One major exception was Joseph Alois Schumpeter (1883–1950). Schumpeter was one of the first modern economists to put innovation at the center of his economic theories.[12] This was an incredible break with the mainstream practice of his day. Both the older *classical* and emerging *marginalist* strains of economics tended to ignore technological change. Schumpeter found these approaches to be too static. They focused on how markets reach equilibrium; therefore, they failed to explain change, because once a market equilibrium was reached, then it needed some random, external shock to set change in motion, which just resulted in a new equilibrium. Schumpeter believed that the economy was not typified by equilibriums but by constant change. And it was technological competition, rather than price competition, that was the real driver of capitalism according to Schumpeter. He was also among the first economists to define innovation, describing it as "new combinations": a new or improved product, process, or method of production; a new market; a new form of industrial organization; even the "conquest of a new source of raw materials."[13] Of course, this is a very broad definition! He also defined *entrepreneurs* as the actors who performed this "combinatory" activity. He explained that entrepreneurs innovate because they are motivated by a desire for things like money, power, social rank, or prestige; ego; or the simple joys of getting things done and exercising one's own energy and ingenuity. To accomplish their new combinations, entrepreneurs needed access to two things, technical knowledge and credit.[14]

Interestingly, Schumpeter distinguished *innovation* from *invention*, treating them separately. At first, he argued that invention was something determined by noneconomic forces that could not be modeled by economists.[15] But later, Schumpeter argued that technological change was determined by forces within the firm, especially large firms.[16] Here again he broke with popular beliefs, which held monopolies in suspicion of being stagnant actors that fought against innovation. Instead, he argued that large firms have access to greater financial resources, better human capital, and superior methods than small firms. Thus, large monopolies could innovate better than small firms. He also suggested that the free entry aspect of perfect competition would make technological innovation impossible because it eliminated the enormous profits that encourage innovation. That is, small firms in free markets tend to compete away each other's profits. But monopolies can have the entire market to themselves, and therefore have a large profit incentive to introduce new products. Schumpeter also predicted that innovation would slowly be routinized; it was doomed to be taken over by a managerial bureaucracy that would destroy its spirit and end in socialism.[17]

But Schumpeter was an anomaly; during the first half of the twentieth century, most economists instead focused on working out the kinks of microeconomic theory. They fought over the assumptions of competitive markets. They debated whether free markets could be perfected or if monopolies could be competitive. They refined and clarified the roles of marginal prices, costs, and revenues. After 1929, explaining the Great Depression dominated economic theory, which demanded new studies of unemployment, inflation, and business cycles.[18] Science and technology were sideshows, afterthoughts, or assumed to be "black boxes" proceeding according to their own internal processes largely independent of political or economic forces.[19]

The Economists' Turn

Then suddenly, during the 1950s, economists took up the innovation debate, which previously had been only peripheral or episodic in their studies. As a result, *science, technology,* and *innovation* permanently entered mainstream economics, and eventually political science as well. There were three major strands of debate, each driven in part by World War II, the Cold War, and the economic "miracles" occurring in Japan and Western Europe. One of these debates sought to find the sources of economic growth. The second tried to explain the economics of science. A third tried to describe the history of economic development. Each of these separate strands later converged to form the foundations of the twenty-first-century debate over national innovation rates.

The growth economists moved first.[20] Observing the rapid recovery of postwar Europe, and especially the Soviet Union, many argued that the key to economic growth was heavy investment in industry and capital infrastructure, and that therefore, the United States should adopt a strong industrial policy. Others disagreed, arguing that there was only so much capital that labor could absorb. They argued that Europe's seemingly miraculous recovery was merely due to the fact that so much of its capital had been destroyed during the war. In this view, improving labor productivity was the main driver of economic growth because it allowed labor to use more and more advanced physical capital.

The predominant growth theory at the time, the Harrod-Domar model, was of little help. It had been designed in the wake of the Great Depression to analyze the business cycle.[21] It was therefore of limited use in resolving the postwar growth debate. It assumed that labor and capital could not be substituted for one another; hence, a nation's economic growth was purely a function of its level of savings and the productivity of capital. Economists now sought to model economic growth in a way that avoided this implausible assumption. In doing so, they were forced to make *technology* an explicit causal variable, whereas it had been implicit in Harrod-Domar. Concurrently, some growth economists sought to estimate just how much land, labor, and capital separately contributed to economic growth. Others wanted to figure out exactly how much economic output was gained from each unit of input.[22]

What their research discovered was shocking. In a famous paper, Moses Abramovitz (1956) showed that something akin to 50% of economic growth and 80% to 90% of labor productivity improvement in the United States during the previous eighty years could *not* be accounted for by mere additions of labor or capital.[23] Other studies generally confirmed these findings.[24] Something else was causing all that growth. Abramovitz assumed it was technological progress. Robert Solow's (1957) solution was to create a new mathematical model that dealt explicitly with technology while bringing together the previously separate fields of growth economics and growth accounting. [25] The Solow model established a whole new way of thinking about economic growth, winning him a Nobel Prize in the process.[26]

But neither Abramovitz nor Solow ever defined *technology* or *innovation*. Technology was the "residual," the amount of economic growth that could *not* be attributed to increases in labor or capital. Everyone agreed that it had something to do with knowledge, research, education, and applying all of that to economic production. But beyond this, they were none too specific. Abramovitz famously described the residual as a "sort of measure of our ignorance."[27] Growth economist Daron Acemoglu later quipped that "it was the residual that we could not explain and we decided to call it 'technology.' "[28] But explaining that darned residual now became a major problem in economics. Was it "learning by doing"?[29] Was it modern transportation networks?[30] Was it formal education?[31]

Meanwhile, economists of science and technology continued with their own investigations, only rarely citing the growth economists. These men were concerned with the surprising advances in S&T achieved by the USSR, especially after Sputnik. How could communists outperform capitalists? What were free markets doing wrong? In an attempt to answer these questions, Zvi Griliches wrote seminal articles on the rates of return to research and development (R&D) (1957), as well as the costs of research, finding that R&D created enormous gains in productivity (1958).[32] But to Griliches, *innovation* was an undefined mix of invention and technological diffusion, usually more of the latter.

Richard R. Nelson and Kenneth Arrow are more often credited with founding the economics of science. But they did not agree on definitions either. Nelson (1959) defined *science* as the advancement of knowledge, *invention* as the "creation of new and improved practical products and processes."[33] My definitions are almost identical. In contrast, Kenneth Arrow (1962) broadly interpreted *invention* as the production of knowledge or information. But Arrow used *invent* and *innovate* interchangeably, while using *inventive activities* and *research activities* separately. He also used *innovation* to refer to both outputs (new technology) and the process of inventing and developing them.[34] And in yet another seminal piece, Arrow wrote that "At any moment of new time, the new capital goods incorporate all the knowledge then available. . ." [35] The debate was getting more confusing, not less! It did not help that neither Nelson nor Arrow ever defined *innovation.*[36] Sometimes it was treated more like technology, other times like invention, and still other times like entrepreneurialism.[37]

Then came the economic development debate, which mixed *development, industrialization,* and *modernization* into the innovation melting pot. This debate began during the 1950s and 1960s, when both scholars and the media routinely observed that "economic miracles" were underway in Germany,[38] Italy,[39] Japan,[40] and even Spain,[41] where the emergence of S&T-based industries had resulted in spectacular growth. Obviously, replicating these incredible performances was highly desirable. But what was causing them? Economic historians thought they had the answers. Albert O. Hirschman (1958) argued that economic imbalances explained rapid development. Successful economies were those whose governments invested heavily in a few key industries with strong linkages throughout the rest of the economy.[42] W. W. Rostow (1960) used the analogy of an airplane building up speed to take off, describing five distinct stages of economic growth that societies historically pass through, with ever-increasing technology and wealth.[43] Alexander Gerschenkron (1962) thought that stages like Rostow's were too one size fits all. History tells us, he argued, that more industrially "backward" countries have very different development paths than less backward countries.[44] Yet few of these economic development scholars clearly defined or distinguished their terms. Science, technology, and innovation were almost indistinguishably mixed into discussions of modernization, industrialization, economic growth, upgrading, productivity, standards of living, and competitive advantage.[45]

A common conclusion of each of these three debates was that government could play a major role in explaining national innovation rates. This brought political scientists into the innovation debate. With their expertise in the politics and policies of individual developing countries, they all but took over the development debate during 1980s, producing a rich body of research on the "developmental state."[46] Also, since innovation clearly played a pivotal role in war, military alliances, and international conflict, political scholars of national security entered the fray. To them, *innovation* included advances in military doctrine, strategy, and organizations.[47] This further expanded the scope of definitions used in the innovation debate. Meanwhile, a handful of historians and sociologists began to split off to form their own subfields with journals, conferences, and university departments that focused solely on science and technology. Each brought its own combination of terms, definitions, overlaps, and omissions to the innovation debate.

The emphasis on government also brought economists onto the turf of political science. From the 1970s onward, Douglass North, Robert Thomas, Nathan Rosenberg, and other economic historians argued that innovation was aided by specific government institutions and policies. They consistently put the highest priority on private property, patent systems, free markets, and democracy. These revelations among economists, who had generally preferred to dismiss government as an irrelevant obstacle to free markets, were aided by Paul Romer. In two papers, Romer succeeded in formally "endogenizing" technological change within models of economic growth theory.[48] That is, Romer solved a problem left over by Solow, who had never explained where technological change came from. In Solow's 1957 model, *technological change* occurred randomly, falling like "manna from heaven."[49] It was "exogenous," unexplained, something that occurred outside of Solow's model. Romer brought technological change into growth theory and described how it occurred. He posited that the production of new knowledge depended on human capital to produce it. Therefore, economic growth and technological innovation should be a function of the number of trained scientists, engineers, and inventors. But Romer's definition of *technology* was inconsistent. He alternately described it as either a *recipe*, a *set of instructions*, an *idea*, or a *design*. The differences between them seem subtle, but they have major implications for specifying theory or designing policy.[50]

Regardless, subsequent growth theorists then argued that domestic institutions and policies determine a country's investment in its human capital, and thereby determine innovation rates.[51] This new emphasis on the role of government prompted still other economists to take inventory, country by country, of all the major institutions and policies that seemed to aid innovation. The idea here was that government institutions and policies fit together to form a "national innovation system" that could be studied and typologized.[52]

Meanwhile, the study of *innovation* exploded in business and management schools during the early 1990s, further multiplying terms and definitions. This was prompted in part by the concurrent Internet boom, which defied traditional patterns of R&D and production. It was also a response to the realization that firms, not governments, were increasingly the source of cutting-edge S&T around the world. Hence, these studies focused on figuring out the best corporate practices and business strategies, as well as the role of industrial organization and government-business relations.[53]

After 2000, innovation research skyrocketed in nearly every field of research, now including research in psychology, anthropology, geography, and urban studies, just to name a few. It seems that almost everyone now wants to measure, explain, predict, and control S&T progress. Innovation research has even spawned entirely new fields, such as *industry studies* and *the science of science policy*. This proliferation of research defies a brief summary. If my attempt to abridge over a hundred years of innovation research prior to the twenty-first century in just the few previous paragraphs was a misdemeanor of scholarship, then it would be a capital crime to do so for these latest developments. For example, a cursory search of the research literature over the past thirteen years reveals the publication of just under 20,000 research articles on technological innovation in over one hundred different categories of social science research. Compare this to the preceding fifty years, which saw publication of only around 4,800 articles on technological innovation, and over 80% of those were printed recently, during the 1990s. Yet despite all of this study and debate, there still remains no consensus on the precise definition of *innovation* or *technology*.

Appendix 2

A BRIEF HISTORY OF INNOVATION MEASUREMENT

Why is it so difficult to measure a nation's innovation rate? Once again, a brief history lesson is useful here. It shows how political and contested this seemingly simple task has been. The first attempts were made by polymath Francis Galton, and they were a product of his research on heredity and eugenics during the 1860s to 1870s.[1] In Galton's day, it was widely accepted that civilization was propelled forward by extraordinary individuals.[2] But it was feared that the number of these great men was in steep decline throughout Great Britain. Hence, British culture and power were sure to follow. Galton, who was also the founder of modern statistics, sought to quantify the number of great minds in British society to demonstrate this decline. Galton believed that greatness, especially intellectual genius, was an inherited trait, and therefore, eminent families must breed more.[3] Galton became especially concerned with the presence of these eminent men in British science, which was then falling behind Germany in the second industrial revolution. He therefore conducted surveys of British scientists and published his analyses, which were the first quantitative estimates of a nation's science and technology (S&T) capabilities.[4]

Galton's work was eagerly read in the United States by James McKeen Cattell, the research psychologist who owned and edited the magazine *Science*.[5] Cattell was a deep believer in eugenics and heredity, and he became an acolyte of Galton's analysis, which he sought to replicate in the United States. But whereas Galton's surveys provided snapshots of British S&T capabilities at particular points in time, Cattell produced a continuous time series of data. Working under contract from the newly founded Carnegie Institution, Cattell collected thousands of biographical summaries of American scientists, which he then published in a directory, *American Men of Science*. It was first printed in 1906 and has remained in annual publication until the present day.[6] This was the first sustained, systematic effort to quantify scientific research at the national level. And Cattell's analysis went further than Galton's. He tabulated not only the number of scientists but also their geographic concentration within the United States (e.g., he noted a high proportion around Boston, but a "lamentable . . . stagnation" throughout the South) and their relative performance rankings.[7] He even used his data to produce the first university rankings in S&T (Harvard, Columbia, and the University of Chicago topped this first rankings list).

Around the same time, the systematic use of *bibliometrics* also emerged out of the field of psychology. Bibliometrics is the analysis of research publication data to measure S&T performance. Once again, politics was the driving force for this advance, though this time it was the politics of science. During the late 1800s, "professional" scientists in psychology were attempting to separate themselves from men they deemed to be charlatans and quacks. To this end, research publications and conference papers were being made requirements for membership in the top psychology professional associations. Psychologists then began to use their publications to establish that what they did as individuals, and as a field, was "real" science. Bibliometrics was born in 1892, when S. W. Fernberger at the University of Pennsylvania began tabulating psychology conference papers and used his data to create a performance ranking of universities. In 1917, he included data on foreign publications in his analysis for cross-national comparisons (he found that Germany led the world, England was trending upward, and France was in decline). That same year, S. I. Franz, a former psychology student of Cattell's, while working at the Government Hospital for the Insane in Washington, DC, began to use publication data to show that psychology was rapidly advancing as a science and deserved equal recognition with the physical sciences.[8]

During the 1910s, governments first got into the business of S&T data gathering. They were led by the United States, where Progressives sought to inventory and manage America's S&T capabilities for the purposes of war and economic growth. In 1916, President Wilson issued an executive order to create the National Research Council (NRC) within the National Academy of Sciences. The NRC was to be a wartime science advisory board to the US government. It immediately began to measure science activities in the United States, then mostly embodied in American industrial laboratories but also scattered among a handful of universities and embryonic government science programs. The NRC also formed a Research Information Service to track exchanges of scientific information among the US allies. After World War I ended, the Research Information Service became a national information clearinghouse on US research activities.[9]

American scientists, and their political representatives, became enthusiastic supporters of the government's S&T data gathering efforts when they discovered that NRC data could be used to lobby for more public funding of research. As a result, by 1920, the NRC was regularly publishing directories of American S&T

capabilities. These NRC publications attempted to inventory all US research laboratories; ongoing research programs; science, technology, engineering, and mathematics (STEM) personnel; S&T societies; research universities; funding sources; and S&T information sources. Over time, America's closest trade and military partners adopted the US model of tracking national performance in S&T. For example, Canada initiated its own S&T data gathering efforts during in the 1930s, and the United Kingdom followed during the 1940s. Even at this early stage, elementary estimates of national research expenditures were emerging as the most widely used measure of national S&T performance.[10]

The 1930s and 1940s revolutionized how S&T data were gathered and interpreted. First, the Great Depression ushered in the field of macro-economics, which changed how people thought about the national economy. Previously, economists and policymakers had focused on *micro*-economic behavior, that of individuals and firms. Since these actors were the principal producers and consumers of goods and services, they had been the focus of economic analysis since the days of Adam Smith. If an economist or policymaker wanted to understand the national economy, then he logically aggregated the behavior of all these individual actors. But the Depression revealed that a nation must be studied as a distinct economic unit to explain the booms and busts of the modern business cycle. That is, economists realized that a country operates as a whole differently than just adding up its constituent parts. This *macro*-economic approach required a different kind of data gathering and analysis. Therefore, national income accounting emerged as a priority statistical task. Its goal was to tabulate the economic behavior of the entire nation, resulting in the now familiar gross national product (GNP) measure.[11]

As described in appendix 1, the emerging focus on all things *macro* kicked off a race among growth economists to formulate new mathematical models that could best describe national economic growth. Soon the 1950s findings of Abramovitz, Solow, and other economists revealed that technological change could account for much of the differences in national productivity and economic growth rates during the preceding decades.[12] However, explaining technological change itself was problematic. And if economists were going to explain what caused the rate of technological change, then they needed to measure it.

A second catalyst for change was World War II. More than any conflict before it, this was a war won by technology and industrial might. The victors on the battlefield often relied on either superior weaponry or the ability to mass-produce and distribute war materiel. Combatants were also aided by revolutionary innovations in fighter aircraft, submarines, penicillin, synthetic materials, radar, food processing, targeting computers, and atomic weaponry. The repeated wartime successes of government research and development (R&D) programs in the United States, Great Britain, Germany, and Japan convinced economists and policymakers that science drives much innovation, and that government has a productive role to play in the innovation process. This point was formalized in 1945 by Vannevar Bush, science adviser to President Roosevelt. His now famous testament, *Science: The Endless Frontier*, helped to bring about a new interventionist approach to S&T policy in the United States.[13] And the demand for the federal government to intervene to improve national S&T capabilities only grew stronger as the Cold War loomed and the Soviets appeared to beat America in bomber aircraft, ballistic missiles, and eventually satellites and manned space travel.

These two impulses came together to forge a new S&T data paradigm. If the US government was going to play a strong, permanent role in improving national innovation rates, then it needed data upon which to base policy decisions and gauge success. Therefore, in 1947, President Truman requested regular estimations of national R&D funding and a detailed analysis of the US research system.[14] Various attempts were then made within the White House and by Congress to inventory the nation's S&T capability. Importantly, many of these exercises adopted the new national accounting frameworks then coming out of macro-economics.[15] Worth noting is the extensive attempt performed within the Office of the Secretary of Defense (OSD). The OSD's tabulation created new categories of R&D expenditure and performance, distinguishing between those who spent the money and those who did the work, and indicating the relationships between them.[16]

This new data paradigm became the National Science Foundation's (NSF) framework for categorizing S&T data when it took over measurement of US S&T in 1953. Created by an act of Congress in 1950, the NSF got its data facilities as a result of politics. Naturally, the NSF wanted autonomy in judging scientific merit and awarding its research grants. But budget hawks throughout government feared that the newly empowered NSF would be fiscally irresponsible. They joked that its pursuit of the "endless frontier" would soon become an "endless expenditure."[17] As a check against budgetary excess, the NSF was instructed to measure and evaluate scientific research throughout the federal system. It was also required to "provide a central clearinghouse for information covering all scientific and technical personnel in the United States."[18] As a result, the NSF got a mandate, and therefore a de facto monopoly, within the federal government over the official measurement of national S&T capabilities. Hence, the NSF's definitions and methods of S&T measurement soon became the US standard.

The NSF's approach towards measuring national S&T performance eventually went international. At first, few countries other than Canada and the United Kingdom actively tracked or studied their own S&T performance. But by the late 1950s, the postwar recovery was well underway in Western Europe and Japan.

In many of these countries, S&T-based industries were clearly driving economic growth and creating trade surpluses. Hence, governments in the countries finally became interested in cataloging their nations' S&T capabilities. But they wanted a uniform, standardized methodology that would allow for cross-national comparisons that might inform policymakers. To this end, data experts from the newly created Organization for Economic Cooperation and Development (OECD) gathered in Frascati, Italy, to debate a common standard, ultimately adopting much of the NSF methodology. The resulting *Frascati Manual*, now in its sixth edition, has become the OECD's operating statistical manual for R&D data collection and is a global standard.[19]

The *Frascati Manual* was first prepared in 1963 by British economist Christopher Freeman, in which he advanced three sets of guidelines. First, the manual defined science and distinguished research from other types of scientific activities (e.g., teaching, conferences, and industrial production). Second, it provided a classification system that distinguished research by sector (e.g., government, university, industry, and nonprofit), character (e.g., basic, applied, and product/process development), and academic discipline. Third, it advanced *gross expenditures on R&D* (GERD) as a basic cross-national measure for policy purposes.

At roughly the same time, the United Nations Educational, Scientific and Cultural Organization (UNESCO) initiated its own grand attempt at cross-national S&T data collection. After years of haphazard data gathering, UNESCO established in 1965 a section on Science Statistics that conducted worldwide surveys of national S&T data. However, politics doomed them to failure. UNESCO's efforts were plagued with definitional and methodological disputes, budgetary issues, and a lack of cooperation from the OECD. Many countries had no use for the data that UNESCO sought to collect. Poorer countries lacked the infrastructure with which to collect it. Hobbled by these difficulties, UNESCO's survey efforts dwindled during the 1970s. In 1984, they were terminated altogether when the conservative Reagan administration, frustrated by the organization's apparent leftward drift and fiscal profligacy, withdrew US membership in UNESCO, depriving it of a major source of funding.[20]

Meanwhile, individual economists and sociologists began to delve ever deeper into national patent data as indices of inventiveness. Patent statistics had been used sporadically by scholars as rough measures of national innovation rates since at least the 1920s.[21] This practice became more common, and was made more rigorous, as a result of academic research done during the 1950s. Among the most influential were statistician Barkev Sanders and his team, who used patents to identify new trends in technological progress and its effects on the economy.[22] Over in economics, F. M. Scherer and Jacob Schmookler pioneered the use of patents in advancing new theories of innovation.[23] And in sociology, A. B. Stafford used patents to decry a sudden decline in American inventiveness.[24] During the 1960s, they were joined by Derek deSolla Price and later Zvi Griliches, who became intellectual giants in both the economics of innovation and the uses of patent data as an S&T measure.[25] However, there was not yet any easily accessible, systematic repository or reporting system for patent data.

In 1968, Congress put additional pressure on the NSF's measurement mandate, forcing it to advance from aggregating data to constructing S&T indicators. Previously, the NSF had collected and disseminated raw S&T spending and STEM personnel data. But it had generally avoided making policy recommendations or adding analysis to the data it collected. Now Congress directed it to annually "appraise the impact of research upon industrial development and upon the general welfare . . . and to provide a source of information for policy formulation."[26] This meant the construction of S&T indicators, which might consist of multiple statistics and be based on a theoretical model. After much study, and perhaps some foot dragging, the NSF finally put out *Science Indicators* in 1973, with just under one hundred pages of indicators and analysis. The premier edition of *Science Indicators* proclaimed itself as the "first effort to develop indicators of the state of the science enterprise in the United States,"[27] though it built upon similar policy-driven measurement exercises in Europe.[28] Currently entering its fourth decade of publication, the NSF's annual indicator exercise has evolved into the now familiar *Science and Engineering Indicators.*

The NSF's new approach toward S&T measurement was then formally adopted by the OECD in 1984, which began publication of its own annual series of indicators, today known as *Main Science and Technology Indicators.*[29] Also, by the 1980s, various S&T data reporting systems were in place in the more advanced Western European countries, though most of them were not comparable to one another. Some of these reports were published only occasionally with varying types of data and inconsistent formats, many of which were only available in local languages. In Japan, major English-language S&T reports began appearing in 1988. Eastern European and Latin American countries only began to regularly report S&T data during the 1990s.

Starting in the late 1980s, advances in both theory and measurement ushered in a wave of new research on "national innovation systems."[30] Described in chapter 5, this new movement was led by Christopher Freeman, Richard R. Nelson, Bengt-Ake Lundvall, and Charles Edquist. One of their central ideas was that *innovation* was a phenomenon distinct from *scientific research,* and therefore required a new set of data and indicators.[31] This resulted, in 1992, in a new OECD methodology known as the *Oslo Manual.*[32] It established definitions and methods for data gathering in technological product and process innovation in manufacturing, and has since been expanded to cover innovation in the services sector, as well as marketing and organizational innovation. And since human STEM labor is a key input to science, technology, and innovation, the OECD also developed the *Canberra Manual* in 1995 "to provide guidelines for the measurement of Human Resources devoted to Science and Technology and the analysis of such data."[33]

Since the 1990s, there have proliferated a number of innovation data sets, indicators, scoreboards, surveys, and indices. The first EU collective effort at S&T data gathering appeared in 1994, followed by a second in 1997, and a third in 2003.[34] The European Union has also now begun to produce a biannual Community Innovation Survey, which regularly asks firms across Europe what new products and processes they have introduced. In the United States, the National Bureau of Economic Research (NBER) published its US Patent Citations Data File in 2001, and then updated it in 2010, with data on 3.3 million patents to innovators worldwide by the US Patent and Trademark Office, including basic citation information. Thomson Reuters offers its Web of Science database, which covers global STEM research publications in over 12,000 peer-review journals, as well as over 150,000 research conference proceedings, with some coverage going back over a century.[35] Most recently, a new StarMetrics project, a multiagency venture within the US executive branch, attempts to document the outcomes of science investments to the public with data on federal research grants, awardees, and costs.[36]

At this point, a full compendium of the universe of S&T and innovation measures, as well as their possibilities and pitfalls, would take up a small bookshelf and can be found elsewhere.[37] Table A2.1 provides an abbreviated list of the most often used American and cross-national reports and data sets. Many of these

Table A2.1 **Major US and Cross-National S&T Reports and Data Sets (by Source)**

Source	*Data Set*
Cengage	*American Men and Women of Science*
European Patent Office	*Worldwide Patent Statistical Database*
European Union	*Community Innovation Survey*
National Science Foundation	*Science and Engineering Indicators*
National Opinion Research Center	*Survey of Earned Doctorates*
Organization for Economic Cooperation and Development	*Main Science and Technology Indicators*
Thomson-ISI	*Web of Knowledge Database*
US Patent and Trademark Office	*NBER Patents Database*

data are used in this book, or in the work upon which this book draws or challenges. The strengths and weaknesses of these data are examined in appendix 3.

Recommended Reading

- Godin, Benoit. 2005. *Measurement and Statistics on Science and Technology: 1920 to the Present.* New York City: Routledge.

Appendix 3

TOUR OF INNOVATION MEASURES, DATA, AND SOURCES

To understand innovation measures and indicators, one simply needs to recall the "black box" problem from chapter 2. It states that innovation is hard for policymakers to observe; and even when observed, innovation is hard to recognize; and even when recognized, it is not obvious how to quantify it. Once we realize that observation, recognition, and measurement are major problems, that we have this unobservable black box called innovation, then all the measures and indices of innovation become much clearer. In fact, Figure 2.1 (reprinted here as Figure A3.1) illustrates both the problem and the attempts at solutions.

To simplify, there are four major types of innovation measures to consider. First, science and technology (S&T) *input measures* attempt to gauge innovation by quantifying the resources dedicated to producing scientific progress and technological change. Usually this involves measuring proximate inputs to the research and development (R&D) process such as spending; science, technology, engineering, and mathematics (STEM) labor; and different types of research equipment or facilities. Second, S&T *output measures* track the products of the R&D process, ranging from proximate measures (technology patents, research publications, and new products and processes) to more distant calculations (the performance of high-tech corporations or of the general economy). Third, *surveys* ask the judgment of experts, businesses, or scientists regarding the value and sophistication of science and technology in their sector or country. Finally, innovation *indices* aggregate input and output measures into a single figure using some sort of weighted average decided upon by the index author(s). Many indices also often include survey data and measures of political-economic institutions (e.g., property rights, education systems, and financial institutions) and technological diffusion.

In this volume, output measures are often preferred over input measures for four reasons. First, inputs do not necessarily lead to high-quality or high-quantity

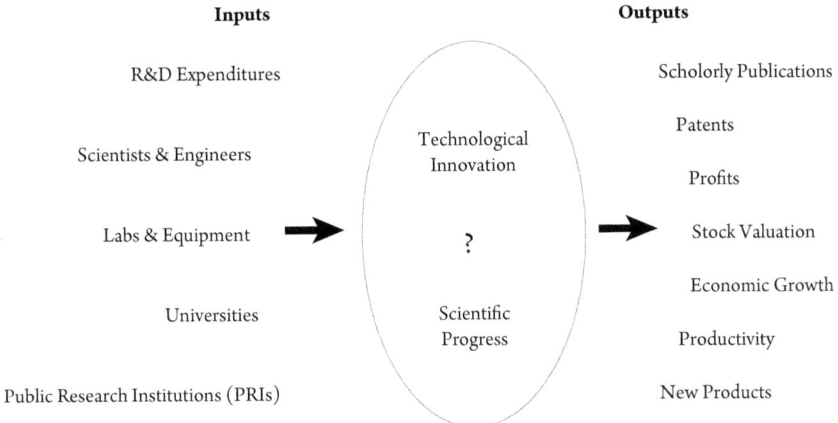

Figure A3.1 The black box of innovation (reprint of Figure 2.1).

outputs. R&D monies can be misspent or misappropriated. STEM workers may not be used for much R&D or may not be well qualified. Equipment may sit unused for lack of properly trained personnel, because it is not suited to the necessary R&D task, or because it is obsolete or dysfunctional. Second, the effectiveness of S&T inputs on innovation often depends on the sector or industry in which they are employed. For example, R&D spending is heaviest in manufacturing industries; therefore, countries with large service sectors would see their innovation rate underreported relative to countries with large indigenous manufacturing sectors. Third, there is often a time lag between the application of inputs to R&D activity and the delivery of new science or technology, often stretching across several years. Hence, it is sometimes not clear how to match the dates of the inputs with the resulting innovations. Fourth, and perhaps most important, this book seeks to test the effects of different institutions and policies on national innovation rates. They are inputs too. So it would be tautological to use both input measures of innovation *and* data on institutions and policies in the same test. For example, if government creates a policy to increase R&D spending (a policy variable), then obviously we expect that R&D will rise (an input measure of innovation). But to claim this as proof that policy increases innovation is dishonest. It shows a tautology, not causality. It makes little sense to use inputs as measures of the very outputs we seek to explain. In sum, this book does use some input measures where appropriate, but it prefers output measures where possible.

Finally, it is important to recognize that comprehensive cross-national data sets on S&T performance are rare. Most innovation data is for individual countries, and even this data can be difficult to find or be measured in incommensurable ways across different countries. Hence, even the aggregation of national statistics can be problematic. The usual producers or aggregators of cross-national data include the Organization for Economic Cooperation and Development (OECD), the European Union, Thomson-ISI, and the US government, and there are a handful of data sets created by independent scholars, think tanks, and research groups. But even where they exist, cross-national data sets may cover only a few years, usually recent ones. One solution to these problems is to triangulate wherever possible. This means using multiple, independent data sets of the same phenomenon, perhaps together with case studies, to test a theory. The idea here is that the random noise in any single data set gets cancelled out by randomness in others, allowing the common signal to come through. Also, if different measures each produce the same result, then we can be more confident of the result than when using a single data set. A complementary solution is to remind ourselves that all data have errors, noise, and perhaps bias. The more statistically minded readers will note that, as long as the measurement error is random and uncorrelated with the explanatory variables, statistical regressions should produce unbiased estimates of the coefficients (and generally with inflated standard errors).

Even in physics, chemistry, and engineering, the problems of measure error, noise, and bias arise. In fact, in the physical sciences, many important properties could not be well measured for decades, including velocity, heat, pressure, brightness, and magnetism. Yet these fields still progressed, providing us with a steady stream of valuable insights along the way. *So we should not let our quest for "perfect" innovation data prevent us from using much "good" data that we have available. We just need to beware of their limitations.*

Input Measures

R&D expenditure data are among the oldest and most frequently used input measures. The unofficial gold standard is *gross domestic expenditure on R&D* (GERD), often expressed as a percentage of gross domestic product (GDP).[1] Spending data are so popular because they are self-explanatory, relatively easily measured, and widely understood and reported, and they represent a universally necessary input to the innovation process. After all, innovators need to spend money regardless of time, country, or sector. Also, more revolutionary research often requires massive spending on expensive equipment, lab space, and STEM labor. However, further analysis has shown that R&D expenditures are much lower for research than for development.[2] Also, historically, R&D spending in manufacturing is better reported than that in services. So a country's GERD data will be affected by the balance of these two sectors in its economy. And of course, given the risky nature of innovation, not all R&D

expenditure leads to successful innovation. In fact, a large R&D budget could indicate a massive failure in innovation, as stubborn investors throw good money after bad. The poster child here is the biotechnology industry in East Asia, which has continued to receive billions of dollars in R&D over the past two decades, with little to show for it.[3] Or large R&D expenditures simply may implicate "turf": a politically well-connected research unit that can bring in funding despite a lack of output. Examples of this include the US military's infamously wasteful but well-funded B-1 bomber, the Crusader cannon, and the Comanche helicopter programs. In addition, there can be a long time lag between R&D expenditures and the appearance of a commercially viable technology, especially in sectors with strict health and safety requirements, such as those for new pharmaceuticals.

The highest-quality, cross-national R&D spending data is found in the *OECD Main Science Indicators*.[4] It covers OECD member countries and seven nonmember economies (Argentina, China, Romania, Russia, Singapore, South Africa, and Taiwan) from 1981 onward. However, the OECD database has several problems. It is full of missing cells in years for which data is not available, often creating breaks in a country's time series. In some cases, the OECD secretariat provides estimates or projections based on national sources, and in other cases the OECD adjusts the national data. In some cases defense R&D is excluded, and in others it is not. In some cases, R&D spending includes research in the social sciences and humanities. In some cases, capital expenditures are excluded. Other cells are footnoted as "provisional" or "underestimated." Hence, apples-to-apples comparisons are difficult. Due to its flaws, it may be better at tracking innovation that occurs in the laboratory than that which occurs on the factory floor, design center, or programmer's suite. It also tends to omit innovation performed by small firms without R&D labs. Yet, all other R&D spending data sets either offer still lower-quality data or are country specific (and therefore do not allow the cross-national comparisons that we require here).

The second most important input to the innovation process is the highly skilled labor that makes S&T progress happen. These highly skilled workers are currently grouped together in STEM. STEM labor can be tracked through various national measures, but they are often incommensurate across different countries. The OECD's *Frascati Manual* addresses some of these problems. Adopted in 1963 and revised in 2002, it identifies three categories of R&D personnel: researchers, technicians, and supporting staff. The *Canberra Manual*, first published in 1995, goes further. It covers all human resources actually or potentially devoted to the creation and diffusion of S&T knowledge (including educators), or who are employed in S&T activities, or who have received STEM qualifications. Once again, cross-national STEM labor data can be found in the *OECD Main Science Indicators*, as well as publications by the United Nations, the

National Science Foundation (NSF), and the University of Chicago's National Opinion Research Center (NORC).[5]

Much scientific progress and technological innovation occurs in, or is kicked off at, universities; therefore, cross-national university rankings are an interesting measure of national S&T capability. Examples of prominent rankings systems include *The Times Higher Education World University Rankings* based out of Great Britain, the *Academic Ranking of World Universities* (ARWU) maintained by the Center for World-Class Universities at Shanghai Jiao Tong University, and the *QS World University Rankings* created by Quacquarelli Symonds Limited. Of course, all such ranking systems are potentially flawed because they are based on subjective decisions about which measures to include, how to weight these measures, and which formula is used to compute the ranking.[6] Also, no comparable data or rankings are available for public research institutes (e.g., Los Alamos in the United States or the Industrial Technology Research Institute of Taiwan), which are cutting-edge innovators in many countries.

Data on numbers of new firms, entrepreneurs, or new products or processes could be very useful for comparing national innovation rates. However, as of this printing, there are few good cross-national compilations of data on this. What data does exist is either national or falls under the category of survey, index, or scoreboard, which are discussed later. For example, attempts to measure cross-national entrepreneurialism have been made at the OECD, but these are just compilations of different data sets, often based on a preset theoretical model.[7] Also, data gathering on entrepreneurs is a recent effort; therefore, these data sets do not provide the time duration we need for longer-run comparisons.

Similarly, data on research laboratories and equipment would be useful. Ideally this could be done either by quantity (square footage, dollars invested, and numbers of labs or pieces of equipment) or quality (are a country's labs using equipment that is more or less advanced than its competitors?). Certainly each approach has its strengths and weaknesses. For example, we have yet to figure out how to control for quality, productivity, efficiency of laboratories, or equipment usage. However, the overarching problem is that this data is currently not collected cross-nationally, in a standardized manner, or regularly across time.

Output Measures

Patents

This book uses one of the most frequently employed output measures of innovation: patents. The debate over the proper use of patent data has proceeded vigorously and with increasing sophistication over the past several decades. The current consensus holds that patent data are better measures of innovation when used in the aggregate (e.g., as a rough measure of national levels of innovation across long periods of time) but are less appropriate when used as a measure of micro-level innovation (to compare the innovativeness of individual firms or specific industries from year to year). And while this debate is ongoing and more thoroughly recounted elsewhere,[8] this section will address some of the more pressing issues surrounding patent measures and their use in testing explanations of national innovation rates.

Strictly speaking, a patent is a temporary legal monopoly granted by the government to an inventor for the commercial use of his or her invention, where the invention can take the form of a process, machine, article of manufacture, or composition of matters, or any new useful improvement thereof.[9] A patent is a specific property right that is granted only after formal examination of the invention has revealed it to be nontrivial (i.e., it would not appear obvious to a skilled user of the relevant technology), useful (i.e., it has potential commercial value), and novel (i.e., it is significantly different than existing technology). As such, patents have characteristics that make them a potentially useful tool for the quantification of inventive activity. First, patents are by definition related to innovation, each representing a "quantum of invention" that has passed the scrutiny of a trained specialist. Second, patents represent technological advances that have gained the support of investors and researchers who must dedicate time, effort, and often significant resources for its physical development and subsequent legal protection. Third, patent data are widely available and are perhaps the only observable result of inventive activity that covers almost every field of invention in most developed countries over long periods of time. Fourth, the granting of patents is based on relatively objective and slowly changing standards. Finally, the US Patent and Trademark Office and the European Patent Office provide researchers with centralized patenting institutions for the two largest markets for new technology. In practical terms, this allows researchers to get around the issue of national differences in patenting laws, as well as providing two separate and fairly independent data pools.

Given these qualities, patents have been used as a basis for the economic analysis of innovative activity for almost a century. Current practice began with the pioneering work of Frederic Scherer and Jacob Schmookler, who used patent statistics to investigate the demand-side determinants of innovation during the 1960s.[10] However, the labor-intensive nature of patent analysis, which used to involve the manual location and coding of thousands of patent documents, severely limited the extent (or at least the appeal) of their use in political and economic research. These limitations were eased somewhat during the 1970s when the advent of machine-readable patent data sparked a wave of econometric analysis.[11] In the late 1980s, the use of patent data was further facilitated by computerization, which increased the practical size of patent data sets into millions of observations. Recently, economists at the National Bureau of Economic Research (NBER) have compiled a statistical database of several million patents complete with geographic, industry, and citation information.[12] This book uses the NBER patent data to test various claims about national innovation rates.

However, patents do have significant drawbacks, which somewhat restrict, but by no means eliminate, their usage as an index of innovation. First, there is the classification problem, in that it is difficult to assign a particular industry to a patent, especially since the industry of invention may not be the industry of eventual production or the industry of use or benefit. This problem applies to analysis of innovation at the level of the industry, firm, or individual. In those cases, it can be addressed by using multiple, independent patent data sets with assorted systems and levels of patent classification. And when answering some research questions, classification of patents may not be something we care about. In particular, this book deals with innovation at the national level. In this case, where all innovation is aggregated across all the industries in a country, the classification issue does not pose a measurement problem.

Second, some critics point out that patents vary widely in their technical and economic significance: most are for minor inventions, while a few represent extremely valuable and far-reaching innovations. Moreover, it has been found that simple patent counts do *not* provide a good measure of the radicalness, importance, or "size" of an innovation. Simple patents counts correlate well with innovation inputs such as R&D outlays, but they are too noisy to serve as anything but a very rough measure of innovation output.[13] Therefore, where possible, this book uses patent counts that have been weighted by forward citations, per capita. Forward citations on patents have been found to be a good indicator of the importance or value of an innovation, just as scholarly journal articles are often valuated by the number of times they are cited. The idea here is that minor or incremental innovations receive few if any citations, and revolutionary innovations receive tens or hundreds. There is also a monetary incentive for inventors and corporations to get citations right. Too many citations reduce the scope of the monopoly granted by the patent; too few citations increase the risk of litigation. Empirical support for this interpretation has arisen in various quarters: citations-weighted patents have been found to correlate well with market value of the corporate patent holder, the likelihood of patent renewal and litigation, inventor perception of value, and other measures of innovation outputs.[14]

Finally, it is not yet clear what fraction of a nation's innovation is represented by patents. After all, not all inventions are patentable, and not all patentable inventions are patented. It is also not clear how much selection bias exists in any given set of patent data. These problems are exacerbated when attempting comparative research since different industries and different countries may differ significantly in their propensity to patent. *Yet, at the national level, patent measures have been found to correlate highly with other phenomena that we generally associate with aggregate innovation rates, including GDP growth, manufacturing growth, exports of capital goods, R&D spending, capital formation, and Nobel Prize winners.*[15] As a reality check, we can also ask whether there exists a technologically innovative country that is *not* relatively well represented by its aggregate patent data. Historically, we find that even the USSR and communist China regularly applied for foreign patents during the Cold War and innovated at roughly the rate and quality represented by their citations-weighted patents per capita. Also, there is no counterfactual. That is, there is no spacecraft industry in Paraguay or advanced medical research sector in Moldova whose innovation is somehow not being captured by those nations' foreign patents.

The ultimate sources for patent information are each country's national patent office. The data from these offices are then aggregated into databases by third parties. This book uses data from the NBER's US Patent Citations Data File, the European Patent Office, and the OECD's PAT-STAT database.

Publications

Science and engineering research articles are another useful measure of innovation. Research publications offer advantages similar to those of patents, with each journal article representing a quantum of research innovation that must pass independent review and that tends to be cited in proportion to its innovative impact. More important, scholarly publications data are completely independent of patents. They are generally produced by a different set of innovators, affected by different incentives, and judged according to different institutional standards.[16] Of course, journal articles also suffer many of the same shortcomings as patents, including difficulties in classification, problems with valuation, and uncertainty regarding to what degree journals represent the universe of innovation.[17] These difficulties are further complicated by changing journal sets, the lack of a single standardized referee process, and the relative importance of prestige and popularity in the publication process. However, just as with patents, information science scholars have found legitimate and rigorous applications for publications data in measuring innovative output. While this debate is better summarized elsewhere, the current consensus is that there is a reasonable basis for using journal articles as a window on innovative activity in the aggregate.[18] This book uses a data set of just over thirty million STEM research articles published between 1981 and 2011 by researchers in over two hundred countries tracked by Thomson Reuters (Scientific).

Technology Balance of Payments

This measure tracks commercial transactions related to international transfers of technology and technical knowledge. Technology balance of payments (TBP) is an accounting of international payments and receipts for the use of licenses, patents, unpatented knowledge, patterns, trademarks, designs, models, technical services and assistance, and industrial R&D carried out in foreign territory. The lion's share of these exchanges consists of transactions between parent companies and their affiliates. Therefore, TBP data should be considered as only partial measures of international technology flows. Critics further argue that coverage of TBP data can vary from country to country, and that the data are statistically not very accurate, have time-reporting issues, and can miss informal transfers of innovation. Also, although the TBP indicates a nation's ability to use foreign technologies and to export its own S&T abroad, a TBP deficit does not necessarily signal a poor competitor. It could indicate S&T specialization, the use of affiliates for tax purposes, or a home bias for some R&D. For sources of this data, the OECD tracks TBP as one of its *Main Science and Technology Indicators*.[19]

High-Technology Exports

Often expressed as a share of GDP, high-tech exports are another popular proxy for national innovation rates. Exports allow us to better capture undocumented innovation, while further stressing a country's capacity for economically valuable innovation. Of course, some high-technology exports can represent purely locational moves by high-technology firms into low-cost labor countries. For example, Japan has many factories in low-cost labor countries like Malaysia, Thailand, and Indonesia, which produce high-tech products that then get exported to the rest of the world. But researchers who have visited these factories have shown that quality of labor is fairly high, and that these factories can and do rapidly start moving up the value chain. Also, a corporate decision to locate factories is partly based on the technical capabilities of the indigenous workforce. In sum, for high-technology exports to constitute a significant share of a nation's GDP over several decades, the exporting country must have a meaningful and rapidly improving technological capability.[20]

High-technology exports data can be found in the United Nations *Comtrade* database. It consists of trade data on total exports in those industry classes defined by the OECD as "high technology." This OECD definition of "high-technology industries" is based on R&D intensity and has been used widely by academic researchers and major government institutions for almost two decades.[21] Its sectors include aircraft, spacecraft, pharmaceuticals, office machinery (including accounting and computing), telecommunications equipment (including radio and television), and medical and scientific instruments.[22]

Total Factor Productivity and Gross Domestic Product Growth

These are two additional popular proxies for national innovation rates. Productivity implies output per unit of input. Labor and capital are the most common inputs studied by economists. Hence, labor productivity and capital productivity data are most commonly reported by governments. But we know that labor and capital only tell part of the story. Total factor productivity (TFP), sometimes referred to as *multifactor productivity*, therefore invokes Solow's definition of technology as the residual leftover after accounting for labor and capital.[23] Hence, TFP growth is the growth in output *not* due to increases in either labor or capital. The problem with TFP is that it can suffer from time lags, or it can be attributable to increases in skills, education, or organizational improvements. TFP increases can even result from better institutions and policies, which are precisely the inputs we want to study. Cross-national data on TFP is regularly reported by the OECD, as well as the Conference Board's Total Economy Database.[24]

GDP growth, especially per capita, is an obvious outcome of a strong national innovation rate. New technologies mean greater competitiveness on global markets, hence stronger exports. Technological change can also result in new industries and greater efficiency in existing sectors. All of these can dramatically increase the size of an economy. However, GDP growth is a fairly rough measure of innovation. It is also caused by discoveries of natural resources, an expansion of free trade (hence increased specialization and division of labor), more efficient domestic institutions and policies, greater investments in capital stock, and access to larger or new markets. GDP data are widely available, including the Penn World Tables and the World Bank Development Indicators database.

Surveys

During the 1980s, interest grew in measuring innovation more directly; one response was innovation surveys. These surveys either ask firms about their activities or ask S&T experts to identify major innovations. The advantage of such surveys is that they focus specifically on technology. In particular, expert surveys can provide a form of external assessment or, depending on how they are worded, a historical perspective on innovation. These valuable, qualitative evaluations arguably go beyond what can ascertained through raw output data. But surveys have their weaknesses too. Routine innovations can go underreported by experts, while more obvious or striking innovations tend to get overemphasized. Perhaps most important, most innovation surveys are limited to single countries, sometimes just individual industries or sectors.[25]

The European Community Innovation Survey (CIS) is perhaps the only cross-national survey carried out with any regularity for more than a decade. This survey takes place every two years in EU member states and a number of neighboring countries. The CIS now queries roughly 220,000 firms about their activity during the previous two years. Questions are often of the yes-no or high-medium-low variety, including queries such as "Did your enterprise introduce new or significantly improved goods?" and "Did your enterprise engage in in-house R&D?" However, the question set has changed over the years. When the survey was begun in 1992, it asked only about products and processes that were new to the firm, but not necessarily new to the market as a whole. Because this allowed firms to report newly adopted technologies, the survey mixed innovation with diffusion. More recent editions of the survey have added questions to resolve this issue. Most criticisms of the CIS now focus on its potentially restrictive definitions and on whether its approach, originally developed for manufacturing, is applicable to service industries. Also, while individual countries outside of Europe, such as Japan and South Korea, have initiated copies of the CIS, there is as yet no broader cross-national survey.[26] Thus, for our purposes, the CIS's limitation to Europe similarly limits its applicability for testing the ideas discussed in this book.

Innovation Indices and Scoreboards

Innovation indices and scoreboards have become an increasingly popular way of measuring national innovation rates. Their strengths are that they combine different kinds of data to overcome the biases and weaknesses of any single data type. For example, an innovation index might include a mix of data on patents, STEM labor, universities, survey data, intellectual property rights, R&D spending, and so forth. Some indices are the products of statistical regressions, and are therefore based on an underlying theoretical model.[27] Others use factor analysis, which tests correlations between different measures to find hidden commonalties between them.[28] Still other indices simply select a handful of measures, assign different weights to them, and then add or average them together.

Perhaps due to their ability to grab headlines, the number of innovation indices and scoreboards is constantly growing (Table A3.1). The European Union has regularly published an innovation scoreboard since 2000.[29] Global

Table A3.1 **Major Innovation Scoreboards and Indicators (by Source)**

Source	*Scoreboard or Indicator*
European Union	*Europe 2020 Competitiveness Report*
European Union	*European Competitiveness Report*
European Union	*European Report on Science & Technology Indicators*
European Union	*Innovation Union Competitiveness Report*
European Union	*Innovation Union Scoreboard* (previously the *European Innovation Scoreboard*)
Information Technology and Innovation Foundation (ITIF)	*Atlantic Century*
INSEAD Business School	*Global Innovation Index**
Organization for Economic Cooperation and Development	*Science, Technology and Industry Outlook*
Organization for Economic Cooperation and Development	*Science, Technology and Industry Scoreboard*
World Economic Forum	*Global Competitiveness Report*

*Now copublished by Cornell University, INSEAD, and the World Intellectual Property Organization (an agency of the United Nations).

innovation indices have also been developed by organizations such as the World Economic Forum, the INSEAD Business School, and the Information Technology and Innovation Foundation (ITIF). The OECD publishes its STAN Indicators, which has nation-level data on production, investment, and business R&D since 1970.[30] A cadre of innovation scholars have advanced a Triple Helix model of innovation, with measures that attempt to synthesize the interactions between, and outputs of, universities, business, and government.[31] Creativity expert Richard Florida publishes a *Global Creativity Index* out of his Martin Prosperity Institute at the University of Toronto. Now even consulting firms and business magazines and newspapers have gotten into the act, publishing their own national innovation indices and scoreboards.[32]

The problem with these indices and scoreboards is that they are highly subjective and inconsistent. There is no objective rule for which measures to include/exclude or how to weight them. Many innovation measures overlap, covering the same input or output but from different angles. So there is a certain amount of double counting (or more) in many indices. It is also not clear how to address the problem of different units. How does one combine a patent, an R&D dollar, a STEM worker, and so forth into a meaningful composite? Finally, scores and ranks can vary considerably. One can get wildly different country rankings depending on how one applies alternative aggregation procedures, different weights, or different sets of input measures. Any parent or student who has wrestled with the oddities of university rankings should understand these conundrums.[33]

In sum, innovation measures are often imprecise, indirect, and fraught with errors and potential biases. This might sound like a damning set of problems, but it just makes them like any other measure in economics or politics, and even many in the physical sciences. All empirical measures come with flaws. The solution is *not* to dismiss these data out of hand. It would be unscientific to discard valuable statistical information together with the randomness and errors that come with it. Rather, good scientists take the best data they can get. They then try to extract the signal from the noise by using multiple independent data sets and methodologies. This is the strategy used in this book. But innovation scholars and policymakers also need to be honest and explicit about the potential problems with the data. Too many theories and policies are sold to the public without much discussion of how messy the data might be. If the arguments made in this book stand the test of time, it is because they have been based on the most honest and scientific assessments of as much data as possible.

Recommended Reading

- Fagerberg, Jan, David C. Mowery, and Richard R. Nelson, eds. 2004. *The Oxford Handbook of Innovation*. New York, Oxford University Press.
- Fealing, Kaye Husbands, Julia I. Lane, John H. Marburger III, and Stephanie S. Shipp, eds. 2011. *The Science of Science Policy: A Handbook*. Stanford, CA: Stanford University Press.
- Gault, Fred, ed. 2013. *Handbook of Innovation Indicators and Measurement*. Cheltenham, UK: Edward Elgar Publishing.
- Greenhalgh, Christine, and Mark Rogers. 2010. *Innovation, Intellectual Property, and Economic Growth*. Princeton, NJ: Princeton University Press.
- National Research Council (US). 2012. *Improving Measures of Science, Technology, and Innovation*. Washington, DC: National Academies Press.

NOTES

Chapter 1

1. Cardwell (1972). Admittedly, Cardwell was not the first to notice the incessant shifts in national leadership in S&T. Over two centuries previously, Scottish philosopher David Hume (1742) also recognized that "when the arts and sciences come to perfection in any state, from that moment they naturally, or rather necessarily decline, and seldom or never revive in that nation, where they formerly flourished." Hume believed that free government was required for the arts and sciences to rise and flourish. In particular, a republic was most favorable to science, while a civilized monarch was more favorable to the arts. More recently, throughout the twentieth century, many eminent historians and social scientists also observed something like Cardwell's Law in action, including E. H. Carr (1961), Robert Gilpin (1981), Mancur Olson (1982), and Paul Kennedy (1987). Nevertheless, Cardwell's Law was only recently canonized and made popular by economist Joel Mokyr in a series of historical analyses written during the 1990s. See Mokyr (1990, 1992, 1994, 1998).
2. Historically, most societies ignored, even eschewed, advanced S&T until recently, including the Americans, Japanese, and Chinese. They often saw technological change as unnecessary, effete, and even dangerous to society. Most governments also then believed they could do little to support S&T, instead perceiving discovery and invention as random acts. Also, the connection between science and technology was not widely recognized until the mid- to late 1800s. Rather, before 1900, science was more often viewed as a quirky hobby for wealthy individuals than a useful, respected profession, or as an input into the development of new technology. See Chapter 2 and Appendix 1 for more.
3. Although the Usa anecdote is generally regarded as apocryphal, it captures real beliefs and practices of the time. For example, as late as 1969, most American consumers believed that Sony was a US company. Sony so feared a loss of consumer and investor confidence if it were discovered to be Japanese that it actively fed this misconception, even to the point of placing the "Made in Japan" label on its products in the least conspicuous position and in the smallest possible size. See Nathan (1999).
4. Ozawa (1974).
5. At the time, the top ten producers of cutting-edge memory chips (1k DRAMs) were all American firms. See Kodama (1991).
6. Kodama (1991).
7. Kodama (1991).
8. The rapid and drastic change is even captured in cultural references of the time, such as the *Back to the Future* film trilogy. When the fictional Dr. Emmett Brown explains in 1955, "No wonder this circuit failed. It says 'Made in Japan,' " his time-travelling protégé from 1985, Marty McFly, replies, "What do you mean, Doc? All the best stuff is made in Japan." Doc exclaims, "Unbelievable!"

9. Taylor (1995).
10. Hitchcock (1998); Hogan (1987); Wexler (1983).
11. Botelho (1995).
12. The Finns might beg to differ with this generalization. However, their most distinctive characteristic is perhaps the Finnish language, which is not related to the languages in the other Nordic countries. Finnish is a member of the Finnic group of the Uralic family of languages, and is therefore closer to Estonian or Hungarian. In contrast, Swedish, Danish, and Norwegian are closely related members of the North Germanic family of languages. Yet Swedish is spoken by 5% of Finns, mostly among populations living along the western and southern coasts of Finland (Statistics Finland, 2013). Language has sometimes been used as a proxy for ethnic differences in Finland; however, ethnicities vary as much within Finland as across Scandinavia. For an insightful take on the Finnish identity and its history, see Broberg and Roll-Hansen (1996).
13. Ornston (2014).
14. During the third quarter of the twentieth century, Sweden suddenly suffered several decades of relative S&T decline, only to recover during the last decade of the twentieth century. But even during this time period, Sweden remained among the world's top S&T producing nations, though dropping in relative rank. See Schön (2012); Ahlström (1996); Magnusson (2000).
15. Similar descriptions might be made of other steady, midlevel innovators, such as the wealthy, industrialized democracies of Austria, Italy, the Netherlands, Belgium, Spain, Australia, and New Zealand, whose relative innovation rate has changed little over the past half century.
16. Norway does rank high in total factor productivity (TFP) due to its capital-intensive energy industry. Several small oil states likewise show similarly disproportional TFPs, yet have relatively little innovative output or indigenous S&T capabilities (e.g., Qatar, Brunei, Kuwait, and United Arab Emirates). See Espinoza (2012).
17. *The Independent* (2011).
18. Graham (1993).
19. Dupree (1964).
20. Letter from Joseph Henry to Alexander Dallas Bache, sent from Princeton, NJ, on August 9, 1838.
21. De Tocqueville (1840).
22. *New York Times* (1860).
23. Nordhasus (1972); Nussbaum (1980); Womack (1981).
24. Tyson and Zysman, (1983); Cohen and Zysman (1987); Ferguson (1987); Tyson (1992).
25. National Center for Education Statistics (n.d.); Mooney (2005); Berezow and Campbell (2012).
26. Griliches (1989); Office of the United States Trade Representative (1994).
27. Reich (2010); Atkinson and Ezell (2012); Marsh (2012a); Pisano and Shih (2012).
28. National Research Council (2005).
29. National Research Council (2010).
30. National Research Council (2010).
31. National Intelligence Council (2012).
32. Acemoglu and Robinson (2012).
33. Much prior work in this area has mostly focused on US science policy; see, for example, the excellent scholarship by Guston (2000) and Sarewitz (1996).
34. I use the term *creative insecurity* in direct contrast to Joseph Schumpeter's *creative destruction.* For more explanation, see Chapter 8 and Appendix 1. See also Taylor (2012).
35. Olson (1982).
36. Sapolsky and Taylor (2011).
37. Mokyr (1992); Parente and Prescott (1994); Krusell and Ríos-Rull (1996); Comin and Hobijn (2009); Acemoglu and Robinson (2000).
38. Bauer (1995); Cohen and Noll (1991).
39. Rogers and Kingsley (2007); Duffy (1997).
40. Banchoff (2005).
41. Hahn and Cecot (2009); Gamboa and Munda (2007).

42. Epstein (1996); Taylor (2009a).
43. Sweezy and Long (2005).
44. The effects of S&T progress on skills and the labor market is a subject of rich and hotly contested debate among economists. See Acemoglu and Autor (2012); Goldin and Katz (2008); Autor, Levy, and Murnane (2003); Acemoglu (2002b); Card and DiNardo (2002).
45. The header refers to Cleese, John and Graham Chapman. 1972. "Argument Clinic" in *The Money Programme*. Monty Python's Flying Circus.
46. Olson (1982); Doner (2009); Haggard (1990); Haggard and Kaufman (1992); Solingen (2007a, 2007b); Ruttan (2006).
47. Perhaps the most well known and influential include Olson (1982), Mokyr (1990, 1998), Acemoglu and Robinson (2012), Acemoglu (2009), Parente and Prescott (1994), Krusell and Ríos-Rull (1996), and Comin and Hobijn (2009). In political science, we can find similar arguments being made by Drezner (2001); Doner (2009); Doner, Hicken, and Ritchie (2009); Doner, Ritchie, and Slater (2005); and Henisz (2002a). Admittedly, some of these scholars are more concerned with economic growth in general, or technological diffusion in particular; they therefore either ignore S&T progress or refer to it only peripherally. Others add important conditional variables, like country size, age, stability, or expandable borders.
48. See Doner, Ritchie, and Slater (2005); Doner (2009); and Doner, Hicken, and Ritchie (2009).
49. Taylor and Wilson (2012); Friedel (2007); White and Wright (2002); Hargadon (2003).
50. Winner (1977); Barnes (1982).
51. Mahoney and Thelen (2010).
52. Weiss (2014).

Chapter 2

1. Levinson (2006).
2. However, Donald Cardwell himself may have quibbled with such a narrow interpretation of his remark, or with the term *national innovation rates*. Taken literally, Cardwell's observation was about global leadership in "creativity." My more narrow interpretation, which restricts the application of Cardwell's Law to science and technology, was first and best made by economic historian Joel Mokyr (1990, 1994).
3. See appendix 2. Progress is being made here by economic historians such as Zorina Khan, Ryan Lamp, Petra Moser, Alessandro Nuvolari, James Sumner, and others.
4. This book is especially concerned with the roughly sixty-five countries with economies larger than $50 billion US in annual gross domestic product (roughly the same gross domestic product as New Hampshire). This may sound restrictive, but it actually creates a fairly large and representative sample of states, with ample variation that can be leveraged for theory generation and hypothesis testing. Every region, culture, wealth level, and type of economy is represented. No significant innovators are left out. Many failures and mediocre innovators are included. But by eliminating small nations, we also eliminate many distractions. That is, we are not much concerned with countries that clearly lack the resources, scale, or scope to build globally competitive S&T capabilities. We are far more concerned with nations that could and should innovate but do not. These are countries that have plenty of resources for innovation but fail to produce much S&T. We need to understand why.
5. Roughly the same gross domestic product as the city of Amarillo, Texas.
6. These definitions are *not* posited as a universally agreed upon vocabulary to be thrust upon all participants in all books and papers everywhere. Their purpose here is purely pragmatic: to get the author and readers on the same page, rather than talk past each other in the chapters that follow. Some of these definitions were developed in Taylor (2012), which can be referenced at http://www.tandfonline.com/.
7. This includes computer software, which, though invisible to the naked eye, is still a physical product (i.e., ordered electrons).
8. These conflicts are sometimes referred to as the "politics of science": debates within a field over proper theories, data, methods, research questions, data analysis, and interpretations. See Kuhn (1962) and Lakatos (1976).
9. Utterback (1996).

10. Alac (2002).
11. North (1990, 3).
12. Wilson (2008).
13. See Streeck and Thelen (2005); Moran, Rein, and Goodin (2008); Morgan, Campbell, Crouch, Pedersen, and Whitley (2010).
14. For an excellent summary, see Godin (2015).
15. Abramovitz (1956, 11).
16. Nelson (1959).
17. Arrow (1962a).
18. For example, economist W. W. Rostow never defined *technology, modernization,* and *innovation,* which were so vital to his famous theory of economic "take-off." And yet, in his discussion of the stages of economic growth, he distinguishes between *applied* and *unapplied* technology, *invention* and *innovation,* and *vertical* and *lateral* innovation. See Rostow (1960).
19. For a fascinating historical survey, see Godin (2005).
20. Whitley (1972); Rosenberg (1982).
21. The amplification of electric currents is useful for processing and transmitting information; electric switches are the basic building blocks of the logic circuits used in modern computers.
22. *New York Times* (1948).
23. Riordan and Hoddeson (1997).
24. Shockley was actually trying to beat his collaborators to the patent office because he felt that his work on the transistor was being ignored. But to his great chagrin, Shockley instead found that key parts of his research had already been performed.
25. Riordan and Hoddeson (1997, 169).
26. It was the three-inch by five-inch Regency TR-1 transistor radio that is generally considered to be the first revolutionary application of the transistor. It went on market in 1954 and used four transistors. After its success, transistor applications soared.
27. Because forward citations allow us to distinguish more revolutionary innovations from insignificant or incremental innovations.
28. Because a large population means more inventors and entrepreneurs, and hence more patents; therefore, to compare large and small countries, we need to look at *per capita* citations-weighted patents.

Chapter 3

1. Excellent survey histories include Mokyr (1990), Cardwell (2001), Pacey (1990), and McClellan and Dorn (1999).
2. The term *nation* is used loosely here to include city-states, monarchies, empires, republics, and so forth. It implies a geographically limited unit of society unified by common obedience to a single sovereign, institutionalized in a government and recognized by foreign actors. Of course, nations have changed over the centuries. Older nations had physical boundaries that were often only vaguely defined; terms of citizenship and institutions of political power could also be poorly defined or inconsistently applied. In contrast, the modern *nation-state,* with its relatively fixed and widely recognized boundaries, formal terms of citizenship, and extensively codified political institutions, appeared continuously only after the mid-sixteenth century.
3. To further blunt any Euro-centrism, we should also recognize that significant S&T achievements were accomplished independently by czarist Russia, India during its Gupta Empire, and the medieval civilizations of Central and South America.
4. Morrell and Thackray (1981); Mowery and Rosenberg (1998); Reich (1985).
5. It was only during the 1910s, after the rise of industrial laboratories, that scientists became widely respected professionals. See Reich (1985), Mowery and Rosenberg (1998), and Edgerton and Horrocks (1994).
6. Marx (1964); Wendling (2009); Mokyr (1990).
7. This evolution is summarized by appendix 1.
8. See appendix 1.
9. Cordesman and Al-Rodhan (2007); Cordesman (2003).

10. In descending order of high-tech exports per GDP, the top ten are Romania, Lithuania, Poland, the Czech Republic, Latvia, the Slovak Republic, Estonia, Bulgaria, Hungary, and Slovenia. Source: World Bank (2014).
11. Lengyel and Leydesdorff (2011); World Bank (2008); Piech and Radosevic (2006).
12. Some data-gathering organizations (e.g., United Nations, World Bank, International Monetary Fund, World Intellectual Property Organization) recognize as many as two dozen.
13. Weighted by forward citations. Hall, Jaffe, and Trajtenberg (2001); Thomson-ISI (2013).
14. The term *midlevel* is a relative one. It recognizes that these countries innovate better than approximately one hundred nations that produced little or no patented innovation during the 1970–2012 period (i.e., averaging a single patent or less per year) and the slightly more innovative twenty-five countries that averaged fewer than ten patents annually.
15. Amsden and Mourshed (1997).
16. The composite score awards ten points to each ranking of 1, nine points to each ranking of 2, and so forth, then sums the awarded points.
17. Scott (2010).
18. Marsh (2012b); Kohut (2013).
19. Utility model patents, often nicknamed "petty patents," are granted for minor technical innovations that relate only to shapes or structures. These applications are generally subject only to a basic novelty assessment and a formality examination. In contrast, applications for patents on new products or processes, also called "invention patents," are subject to much broader search, novelty, and examination requirements.
20. National Science Foundation (2012b).
21. Gereff, Wadhwa, Rissing, and Ong (2008); Farrell, Laboissière, Rosenfeld, Stürze, and Umezawa (2005); Patel (2010).
22. Organization for Economic Cooperation and Development (2012c).
23. Carnoy et al. (2013).
24. Breznitz and Murphree (2011).
25. Autor, Dorn, and Hanson (2013); Scott (2011); Xing and Detert (2010).
26. Kraemer, Linden, and Dedrick (2011).
27. Teardown.com (2014).
28. Branstetter and Lardy (2008); Man, Wang, and Zhu (2013); Koopman and Wang (2008).
29. World Bank (2014).
30. Smith (1985); Leslie (1994); Edwards (1996); Parker (1996); Ruttan (2006).
31. Weiss (2014).
32. Samuels (1994).
33. Stockholm International Peace Research Institute (Multiple years).
34. Needham (1954); Mokyr (1990).
35. Gerschenkron (1962).
36. One could argue that the Japanese made this decision decades earlier, but still later than the United States and many European nations.
37. See Dore (1987); Greif (1994); Temin (1997); Landes (1998); Harrison and Huntington (2000); Hofstede (1980, 2001); Florida (2002); House, Hanges, Javidan, Dorfman, and Gupta (2004).
38. Harrison and Huntington (2000).
39. Guiso, Sapienza, and Zingales (2006).
40. Mokyr (2002, 18).
41. Though recent research suggests that individualism and certain types of collectivism correlate highly with national innovation rates. Cerne, Jaklic, and Skerlavaj (2013); Taylor and Wilson (2012); Yao, Wang, Dang, and Wang (2012); Shane (1993).

Chapter 4

1. Barnett (2009).
2. Hanson (2003); Easterly and Fischer (1995); Suny (2010).
3. The data in this paragraph are taken from contemporary reports and surveys performed by *The Economist* (1988, 1989a, 1989b, 1990a, 1990b).

4. *The Economist* (1990a, 6).
5. *The Economist* (1989a, 70).
6. Technically, efficiency is defined as that state of an economy such that no one can be made better off without somebody else being made worse off. That is, given many possible sets of resource allocations and a group of individuals, a movement from one allocation set to another that can make at least one individual better off without making anyone else worse off is called a "Pareto" improvement. If resources are allocated such that Pareto improvements are no longer possible, then economists call that allocation set "Pareto efficient" or "Pareto optimal." See Hall and Lieberman (2013).
7. New technology often precedes the scientific knowledge that explains it. Indeed, this was the rule rather than the exception up until the end of the nineteenth century. The shift occurred when modern industrial and government laboratories began to systematically pursue scientific discovery as the basis for new products and production techniques. It occurred earlier in Western Europe, later in the United States. See Fox and Guagnini (1999), Reich (1985), and Rosenberg (1982).
8. To address this type of market failure, the Federal Deposit Insurance Corporation was created in 1933, which today protects up to $250,000 per depositor, per insured bank.
9. The definition of markets also suggests that, at least for the goal of efficiency, governments also need to regulate the behavior of clearly irrational actors (e.g., children, addicts, people with severe mental disabilities). It is not clear that this is directly necessary for the goal of innovation.
10. Service (2009).
11. For a well-written, popular account of these perceptions, see Wolfe (1979).
12. Herken (1985).
13. Ivan Bunin won the 1933 Nobel Prize in Literature while in exile in Paris. Three Russians won Nobel Prizes for science during the early 1900s, prior to the Russian Revolution.
14. Graham (1993); Birstein (2002).
15. Stearns (1970); Greene (1984); Daniels (1968); Timmons (2005).
16. Though historically the causal arrow from science to technology generally ran in the *opposite* direction and sometimes still does today. See Nelson (1959) and Rosenberg (1982).
17. Arrow (1962a).
18. Prior to the European Patent Convention of 1973, patent durations varied by nation. For example, the United Kingdom awarded fourteen years, while France and Germany offered fifteen years. In the United States, patents came with a seventeen-year monopoly until 1995, when adherence to the international Agreement on Trade Related Aspects of Intellectual Property Rights (TRIPS) created a general twenty-year patent duration for members of the World Trade Organization, with some exceptions for developing countries. See Dutfield and Suthersanen (2008).
19. In Europe, specification of patented knowledge was historically the exception rather than the rule. Disclosure emerged there as an irregular practice during the early 1800s but was not mandated by law until much later. For example, while available to the English since 1624, patents there were often monopolies on production granted by the monarch to his or her domestic allies in return for political or financial support rather than instruments of early S&T policy. Patents awarded in the United Kingdom did not legally require specification until the 1883 Patents Act. See May and Sell (2006).
20. Certainly critics of the system have existed since its inception. For example, Eli Whitney, inventor of the 1793 cotton gin, was famously unable to enforce his patent on it and lost millions of dollars in unclaimed revenues. In Europe, so bad were the abuses and inefficiencies of the centuries-old Dutch patent system that they voted to abolish it in 1869 for forty years. Meanwhile Switzerland had no patent system until 1907. See Basall (1988).
21. Hall and Harhoff (2012).
22. Jaffe and Lerner (2004).
23. US Patent No. 6,004,596. Smucker's lawsuits were eventually rejected by a federal appeals court, but only after over four years of litigation. See Bertin (2001) and Munoz (2005).
24. *Wall Street Journal* (1999); Kaufman (1999).
25. Lewis (1998); *New York Times* (1999); Foreshew (2001).

26. Marsden (2011); Dredge and Arthur (2011).
27. Lee (2011).
28. The Supreme Court later ruled that Prometheus's methodology was not patentable in *Mayo v. Prometheus* (March 2012). However, the Court issued a narrow opinion applying to Prometheus's particular technology but refused to establish a definitive standard or test for patent eligibility across all technologies more generally. Hence, the patentability of "indicate a need" technologies remains contested.
29. Bessen and Meurer (2008).
30. US Patent No. 5,930,474.
31. Frank (2007).
32. Cumulative knowledge is defined as that which forms the basis for subsequent discoveries and innovations.
33. Steven Jobs speaking at Macworld 2007 (Jan. 9, 2007).
34. Gilroy and D'Amato (2009).
35. Boldrin and Levine (2008).
36. Goodman and Myers (2005).
37. Bessen and Meurer (2009).
38. Grossman and Lai (2004).
39. Ginarte and Park (1997).
40. Deere-Birkbeck (2009); Chaudhry (2013).
41. Park (2008).
42. Most recently, in June 2014, the US Supreme Court held that an analytical method implemented by a computer or Internet link is not eligible for patent protection. *Alice Corporation Pty. Ltd. v. CLS Bank International* (2014).
43. *Talk of the Nation* (2011); Bessen (2012).
44. Bessen and Meurer (2008); Boldrin and Levine (2008); Jaffe and Lerner (2004); Raustiala and Sprigman (2012).
45. Using simple bivariate regressions.
46. Landes, Mokyr, and Baumol (2010); Greene (2000).
47. McClellan and Dorn (2006).
48. McClellan and Dorn (2006).
49. Arrow (1962a).
50. Basic research is defined here as research activities aimed at deriving fundamental knowledge (i.e., discovery). Applied research is aimed at using fundamental S&T knowledge to create new technology or improve existing technology (i.e., invention, prototypes). Development is defined as those S&T activities required to bring products and processes into commercial usage (i.e., marketable products and services).
51. Kaiser (2002).
52. Antony and Grebel (2012).
53. Bednyagin and Gnansounou (2012).
54. Kafouros, Buckley, and Clegg (2012); Keller (2002).
55. Congressional Budget Office (2006).
56. In 2010 dollars; the original figure was $231 million (in 1987 dollars); the analysis involved ninety-three randomly selected new drugs produced by twelve pharmaceutical firms. See DiMasi, Hansen, Grabowski, and Lasagna (1991).
57. In 2010 dollars; the original figure is $800 million (in 2000 dollars). See DiMasi, Hansen, and Grabowski (2003).
58. Paul et al. (2010); Goozner (2004).
59. The strongest counterargument comes from Donald Light (University of Pennsylvania), who holds that these spillovers are vastly overstated, while R&D subsidies and IPRs incentivize companies to develop increasing numbers of new drugs that have few clinical advantages over existing medicines. See Light (2007) and Light and Lexchin (2012).
60. Reiffen and Ward (2005).
61. Congressional Budget Office (2006)
62. Smith (1988); Freiberger and Swaine (2000).
63. Edelman (1991).

64. Black and Osborne (1963).
65. Edelman (1992).
66. Light and Warburton (2011). A systematic review of twenty years of cost studies provided a range of $161 million to $1.8 billion. It found that "Differences in methods, data sources, and time periods explain some of the variation in estimates. Lack of transparency limits many studies. Confidential information provided by unnamed companies about unspecified products forms all or part of the data underlying [over 75% of the studies included]." Morgan, Grootendorst, Lexchine, Cunningham, and Greyson (2011).
67. Light and Lexchin (2005); Burke (2006).
68. Barral (1996).
69. Hunt, Kotis, and Chockley (2000); Angell (2004); Morgan et al. (2005); Motola et al. (2006); Van Luijn, Gribnau, and Leufkens (2010).
70. Each of these drugs has been either recalled or restricted due to safety or performance issues. Light and Lexchin (2012).
71. Using bivariate regression analysis.
72. List (1916, 111).
73. Varsakelis (2006).
74. The dates indicate first appearances rather than general diffusion. Humboldt University (1810) in Berlin is considered to be the first university to prioritize scientific research rather than the application of existing knowledge. The first industrial laboratories were established in Germany to develop products based on breakthroughs in organic chemistry, as well as Edison's "invention factory" in the United States (1876). The competing claims to the first full-time corporate R&D facility include GE's (1900), Dow's (1901), and DuPont's (1902). See Carlsson, Acs, Audretsch, and Braunerhjelm (2009) and Maurer and Scotchmer (2004).
75. Dore and Sako (1989); Shapira (1995); Kenney and Florida (1993); Funk (1992); Japan Management Association (1989).
76. Hicks (1932, 124-125).
77. Autor, Levy, and Murnane (2003); Autor, Katz, and Krueger (1998).
78. Acemoglu (2002a, 2002b).
79. Powell and Snellman (2004); Bresnahan, Brynjolfsson, and Hitt (2002).
80. Von Hippel (1988).
81. Von Hippel (2005).
82. National Center for Education Statistics (n.d.). See also the Organization for Economic Cooperation and Development (2014c); Ripley (2013).
83. Certainly some of these changes in per GDP spending over time can be explained by the aging demographics of developing and developed countries. Throughout much of the world, and especially in East Asia, fewer youths has translated into lower education spending. While the 2008 OECD observed average for children aged zero to fourteen is 18.6% of the population, it is now far lower in Japan (13%), Germany (14%), and Italy (14%) than in China (21%), Mexico (29%), and India (32%).
84. Percentage of all students scoring at Level Five or Six. Organization for Economic Cooperation and Development (2013b).
85. 158,000 out of 63,858,000 (1950), US Department of Commerce (1975).
86. 2,507,000 out of 154,287,000 (2008), where the active STEM R&D workers are defined as S&E occupations with R&D as their major work activity minus social scientists. National Science Foundation (2012a); Bureau of Labor Statistics (2008).
87. Merely 0.10% of the US population was STEM workers in 1950, and still only 0.82% in 2008. National Science Foundation (2012a); Bureau of Labor Statistics (2008).
88. Clark (2006); Ruegg (2004).
89. Cole (2009); Geiger (1995); Veysey (1964).
90. Rudolph (1962).
91. Lowen (1997); Bush (1945).
92. Cole (2009); Vest (2007).
93. Percentage of respondents rating a particular link as "very important" or "moderately important" for industrial R&D shown in parentheses.
94. Cohen, Nelson, and Walsh (2002).

95. Davidson (2009).
96. Porter (1998).
97. Breznitz and Murphree (2011); Gallagher and Zarsky (2007); Sohn and Kenney (2007).
98. Lecuyer (2006).
99. Data from NSF Survey of Research and Development Expenditures at Universities and Colleges/Higher Education Research and Development Survey; IPEDS Salaries, Tenure, and Fringe Benefits Survey. Found via WebCASPAR.
100. Ehrenberg, Rizzo, and Jakubson (2007).
101. Nation Science Foundation (2012c).
102. Nation Science Foundation (2012a); Kleinman (2010).
103. Vest (2007).
104. Mowery et al. (2004); Nation Science Foundation (2012a).
105. Liberwitz (2007).
106. Mowery et al. (2004).
107. Thursby and Thursby (2007).
108. Baldini (2008). However, the data do suggest that Bayh-Dole may have helped to improve the rate and productivity of high-tech spin-offs from universities. See also Aldridge and Audretsch (2011) and Kenney and Patton (2011).
109. Lederman (2010); de Figueiredo and Silverman (2006).
110. Lederman (2010).
111. De Figueiredo and Silverman (2007).
112. Wong (2011); Breznitz (2007).
113. Plumer (2013).
114. $42.4 billion out of $76.0 billion total (2009), National Science Foundation (2012a).
115. Radder (2010).
116. Ehrenberg et al. (2007).
117. Using multiple regression analysis.

Chapter 5

1. The terms *exogenous* and *endogenous* come to innovation research from modern economic growth theory, which also has much to say about national innovation rates (see appendix 2). Specifically, economic growth theory initially assumed that new S&T was created randomly. S&T progress was therefore described as an *exogenous* variable because it could not be modeled. Innovation just happened. Later, economists realized that societies can take actions to increase S&T production, and thereby affect rates of economic growth. This meant that science and technology were *endogenous* variables, and the new growth model became known as *endogenous growth theory*. Thus, the language used in the debate over national innovation rates has become infused with terms and concepts from the economic growth debate; recognizing this is vital for the innovation debate to proceed constructively (see appendix 1).
2. The seminal works in NIS are Nelson (1993), Lundvall (1992), and Edquist (1997).
3. Lundvall (2004); Freeman (1987). For an alternate and more far-reaching history, see Godin (2009a).
4. Nelson (1993).
5. Naubahar (2006).
6. Lundvall (1992); Freeman (1995).
7. Nelson (1993); Lundvall (1992); Edquist (1997).
8. Sharma, Nookala, and Sharma (2012). See also Oinas (2005), Sun (2002), Balaz (2005), Saad and Zawdie (2005), De Tournemine and Muller (1996), and Correa (1998).
9. Mowrey and Rosenberg (1993).
10. Odagiri and Goto (1993).
11. Nelson (1993); see also Kim and Nelson (2000).
12. While I critique NIS here for its lack of strong theoretical foundations, it is important to note that its atheoretical approach was a strategic choice by some of its founders, not a product of bad research design. For example, the 1993 case studies coordinated by NIS pioneer Richard Nelson were written in direct response to the inability of innovation theory

to predict empirical reality. While endogenous growth theorists had made enormous contributions to economists' understanding of innovation, Nelson critiqued them for neglecting or mis-specifying many important independent variables and causal relationships. He recommended that empirical research, in the form of in-depth qualitative case studies, was necessary to capture the causal factors missed by grand theory (Nelson 1997). However, much of the existing empirical research of the sort suggested by Nelson was based on just a single country (often Japan). Hence, one idea behind the NIS movement was to increase "the number of 'points' that a causal theory had to 'fit'" (Nelson 1993, 4).

13. Parts of this section were published previously by the author in the journal *International Organization*; they are republished here by permission of the copyright holder, Cambridge University Press. See Taylor (2004).
14. This section is specifically concerned with those aspects of VoC theory formulated by Hall and Soskice (2001).
15. Williamson (1975, 1985).
16. For example, the $325 million fine levied in 2014 against Apple, Google, Adobe, and Intel for agreeing not to poach employees from one another.
17. A recent attempt to incorporate developing economies into VoC theory can be found in Nölke and Vliegenthart (2009).
18. Hall and Soskice (2001).
19. Hall and Soskice (2001).
20. Hall and Soskice (2001).
21. For example, using the US Patent and Trademark Office data, VoC's predictions are borne out relatively well, approximately 70% to 80% of the time, when applied to only the United States and Germany. However, when all LME and CME countries are included, VoC theory loses a considerable amount of its predictive power, with a 72% success rate in 1983–1984, but only 50% in 1993–1994, and 56% over the entire 1963–1999 period. Omitting the United States from the set of LMEs results in further deterioration, with VoC's success rate ranging from 44% to 56%, about the same as a coin flip.
22. Weiss (2014).
23. Even when the United States is included, the innovative difference between LMEs and CMEs is smaller than a single citation per patent. Although this may be a statistically significant amount, it is far smaller than the innovative difference between the most and the least innovative industries and does not suggest a large innovation gap.
24. For an alternative analysis, which argues that VoC does hold true for some industries, see Akkermans, Castaldi, and Los (2009).
25. For its Economic Freedom Index, Heritage measures ten quantitative and qualitative aspects of economic freedom, grouped into four broad categories: Rule of Law (property rights, freedom from corruption), Limited Government (fiscal freedom, government spending), Regulatory Efficiency (business freedom, labor freedom, monetary freedom), and Open Markets (trade freedom, investment freedom, financial freedom). Each of these ten economic aspects is graded on a scale of 0 to 100. A country's overall score is derived by averaging these ten economic freedoms, with equal weight being given to each. http://www.heritage.org/index/
26. Akkermans, Castaldi, and Los (2009).
27. Balaz (2011).
28. Rafiqui (2010).
29. Acemoglu and Robinson (2012).
30. North (1981, 1990).
31. North and Thomas (1973).
32. North (1990).
33. North (1990).
34. Acemoglu, Johnson, and Robinson (2005); Acemoglu and Robinson (2000, 2006); Acemoglu (2003).
35. Acemoglu and Robinson (2012).
36. Though elections alone are not enough. Plenty of nondemocratic states hold elections, including the Soviet Union, Iraq under Saddam Hussein, and Iran under its Ayatollahs. To

create democracy, elections must be free, fair, competitive, and held at regular, frequent intervals. Only then can groups and individuals compete for power, resources, and public goods without fear of destruction or retaliation. Constitutional guarantees of the freedom of speech, organization, and so forth can further enhance pluralism. See Held (2006) and Dahl (1998).

37. The Polity IV dataset brings together six different measures of executive recruitment, constraints on executive authority, and political competition. It also includes changes in ruling institutions. The Polity data focuses on the institutions of central government and on political groups acting within the scope of their authority. It does not consider groups or territories that are removed from the authority of the central government, such as separatists or insurgencies, or populations that have not been effectively assimilated into the national political process. Marshall, Gurr, and Jaggers (2014).
38. Parts of this section were published previously by the author in the journal *Review of Policy Research*; they are republished here by permission of the copyright holder, John Wiley & Sons. See Taylor (2007).
39. Surowiecki (2004).
40. Rosenberg and Birdzell (1985); Mokyr (1990, 2002); Drezner (2001); Acemoglu, Aghion, Lelarge, Van Reenen, and Zilibotti (2007).
41. In practice, many states decentralize further, with power formally divided between different houses of the legislature, competing bureaucracies, or branches of the armed forces.
42. Since 1997, a significant degree of political power has been "devolved" to regional and local governments within the United Kingdom. See Norton (2010).
43. Technically, judges are nominated by the British monarch on the advice of the prime minister.
44. The Constitutional Reform Act 2005 has since increased the independence of the British judiciary.
45. Norton (2010).
46. Drezner (2001); Mokyr (1990, 2002); Weingast (1995); Nelson (2005); Acemoglu, Johnson, and Robinson (2005).
47. Drezner (2001); Mokyr (1990, 2002); Rosenberg and Birdzell (1985); Suroweicki (2004); Acemoglu et al. (2005).
48. Cary (1974); Oates (1972).
49. Weingast (1995); Qian and Weingast (1997).
50. Hayek (1945).
51. Tiebout (1956).
52. Surowecki (2004).
53. Florida (2002).
54. Drezner (2001); Mokyr (1990, 2002); Rosenberg and Birdzell (1985); Weingast (1995); Acemoglu et al. (2005)
55. Shilts (1987).
56. Acemoglu et al. (2005); Drezner (2001).
57. In Figure 5.5, the vertical axis indicates the shift in innovation rate relative to the United States.
58. Henisz (2000).
59. The variable "polconv" is used here: 1970: Max (0.88), Mean (0.23), Min (0), Standard Deviation (0.32), Obs (133); 2010: Max (0.89), Mean (0.43), Min (0), Standard Deviation (0.31), Obs (133); change in value 1975–2010: Max (0.84), Mean (0.20), Min (–0.72), Standard Deviation (0.32).
60. Delios and Henisz (2000); Henisz (2002b); Henisz and Zelner (2001).
61. The 2000–2005 period is chosen as the end point to address suspicions of selection bias that might come from the global financial crisis from 2007 onward. However, analysis of data for the 2007–2012 produces almost identical results.
62. Taylor (2007).
63. Taylor (2009).
64. This is not a new or original finding, but merely confirms a prediction made in prior research. See Rogers (1995); Walker (1969).

65. Kingston (2013); Hayes (2009).
66. Since 2001 reorganized into the Ministry of Economy, Trade, and Industry (METI).
67. Johnson (1982); Taylor (1995).
68. In fact, a similar story of "bad" or inconsistent institutions could be told regarding Japan in the ninety years prior to 1955, during which time both democratic and market institutions gyrated drastically against a backdrop of steadily increasing innovation. See Duus (1998), Morris-Suzuki (1994), and Sims (2001).

Chapter 6

1. See also Rodrik (2007).
2. Breznitz (2007); Breznitz and Ornston (2013); Breznitz (2012). Breznitz builds upon Evans (1995), Ansell (2000), and O'Riain (2004).
3. However, only Israel managed to create strong sustainable domestic hardware and software industries. Taiwan succeeded only in hardware, while Ireland succeeded only in software. See Breznitz (2007).
4. Razin and Sadka (1993).
5. Quoting Itzhak Yaakov, Breznitz (2007, 56).
6. Trajtenberg (2001).
7. A preexisting agency within the Ministry of Trade and Industry.
8. Quoting Itzhak Yaakov, Breznitz (2007, 55).
9. Mayer, Schoors, and Yafeh (2005).
10. Bi-National Industrial Research Foundation (2012).
11. Toren (1994); *Research & Development* (1989); Gandal, Hanson, and Slaughter (2004).
12. Central Bureau of Statistics, Israel (2012).
13. Central Bureau of Statistics, Israel (2012).
14. Taiwan is a case of being more successful at producing new high technology than cutting-edge science. See Gold (1986), Simon and Kau (1997), and Goldstein (1997).
15. NBER-UN World Trade Data from Feenstra et. al. (2005).
16. Per capita and weighted by forward citations. In some individual years, Taiwan was also beaten by Sweden (2000, 2002, and 2003) and Finland (2000, 2002–2012). National Bureau of Economic Research (2011). The years 2007–2012 are estimates.
17. Thomson-ISI (2013).
18. Colville (2012).
19. Chai (2012).
20. In recent years, much of Taiwan's IT hardware production and assembly work has been moved to mainland China; however, most of the innovative research, design, and development activities have remained in Taiwan.
21. Breznitz (2007).
22. Breznitz (2007).
23. Amsden and Chu (2003).
24. Greene (2008).
25. Rowen, Hancock, and Miller (2007).
26. Breznitz (2007).
27. Feenstra and Hamilton (2006).
28. Guiomard (1995, 222); Lee (1989, 545, 635).
29. NBER-UN Trade Data from Feenstra et. al. (2005); O'Hearn (1998); Sweeney (1998).
30. ÓRiain (2004).
31. Park (2008).
32. Put another way, Ireland's IPR system strengthened from 35th out of 113 countries (1960) to 3rd strongest out of 122 countries (2000 onward). See Park (2008) and http://nw08.american.edu/~wgp/. The quote comes from US Department of State (2001, 8).
33. http://www.sfi.ie
34. Organization for Economic Cooperation and Development (2012c).
35. Frenkel, Shefer, and Roper (2003).
36. Organization for Economic Cooperation and Development (2006).

37. O'Riain (2014); Groh, von Liechtenstein, and Lieser (2010).
38. ÓRiain (2004).
39. O'Riain (2014); Groh, von Liechtenstein, and Lieser (2010).
40. Breznitz (2012); Lin, Chang, and Shen (2010); Edquist and Hommen (2008).
41. Roper and Frenkel (2000).
42. Villa and Antonelli (2009).
43. Smyth and Hannan (2000).
44. O'Malley, Hewitt-Dundas, and Roper (2008).
45. Villa and Antonelli (2009).
46. Lin, Chang, and Shen (2010).
47. National Bureau of Economic Research (2011).
48. Thomson-ISI Dataset (2013).
49. Organization for Economic Cooperation and Development (2009b).
50. In 1965, Mexico enjoyed over twice the per capita GDP of Taiwan. This ratio declined only slowly over time, but Mexican per capita GDP remained over 120% that of Taiwan's in 1980. By comparison, during this entire time period, Mexico's GDP per capita was consistently around half that of Israel's, and two-thirds that of Ireland's. Data from Feenstra et al. (2015).
51. According to the Polity IV dataset and Freedom House's *Freedom in the World* index. Marshall, Gurr, and Jaggers (2014)
52. Cimoli (2000); Blomstrom and Wolff (1994).
53. Gallagher and Zarsky (2007).
54. Lustig (1998).
55. Gallagher and Zarsky (2007).
56. Botzman (1999).
57. Organization for Economic Cooperation and Development (2009b); Kuznetsov and Dahlman (2008).
58. Gallagher and Zarsky (2007).
59. Gordon (2010).
60. Gallagher and Zarsky (2007); Cimoli (2000).
61. Solleiro and Gaona (2012); Solleiro and Castanon (2005).
62. Important exceptions in the political economy of development literature include Evans (1995), Ansell (2000), O'Riain (2004), and Breznitz (2007).
63. For additional perspectives, see Whitford and Shrank (forthcoming), Whitford (2005), and Block and Keller (2011).
64. For recent surveys of research on social networks, see Knoke (2013), Kadushin (2012), Jackson (2008), and Goyal (2007).
65. Granovetter (1995).
66. Granovetter (1973).
67. Sir Roy Anderson is a top British researcher in public health and disease control, and creator of path-breaking mathematical models of the epidemiology of infectious diseases, such as AIDS and schistosomiasis.
68. Hisamitsu is a leading innovator in external pain-relieving medicines and transdermal drug delivery technologies.
69. Marshall (1890).
70. Krugman (1991).
71. Porter (1990); Porter (1998b).
72. Saxenian (1994).
73. Freiberger and Swaine (2000); Markoff (2005).
74. Saxenian (1994).
75. Potter and Miranda (2009); Wong (2011).
76. Bohemians are generally defined as workers in cultural industries, such as writers, designers, musicians, actors, directors, dancers, photographers, and artists.
77. Florida (2012); Bieri (2010); Florida (2005).
78. Lang and Danielsen (2005).
79. Duranton, Martin, Mayer, and Mayneris (2010).
80. Frenken, Cefis, and Stam (2011).

81. Wolfe (2009).
82. Eisingerich, Falck, Heblich, and Kretschmer (2012).
83. Duranton, Martin, Mayer, and Mayneris (2010).
84. Potter and Miranda (2009).
85. Casper (2007).
86. Breschi and Malerba (2005).
87. In practice, this implies means eliminating obstacles to labor and firm mobility, as well as reducing the costs of congestion.
88. Etzkowitz and Leydesdorff (1998, 2000).
89. Cooke, Heidenreich, and Braczyk (2004); Maskell and Malmberg (1999).
90. Malerba (2002).
91. Godin (2006b).
92. Godin (2008d).
93. Gibbons (1994).
94. http://www.globelics.org
95. Morris-Suzuki (1994).
96. Toren (1994); Gandal, Hanson, and Slaughter (2004). See Ruiz (2014) for an analysis of recent immigration.
97. Admittedly, Finland is an outlier in that it is one of the less networked stories of S&T success. Specifically, Finnish society is hypernetworked at the domestic level, but not as well integrated internationally. Discussions with Darius Ornston; Steinbock (2001); Ornston (2012).
98. Clotfelter (2010); Solimano (2008).
99. Boeri, Brücker, Docquier, and Rapoport (2012); West (2010).
100. Herrerias and Orts (2013); Kim and Nelson (2000).
101. Keller (2010); Martin and Salomon (2003); Blind and Jungmittag (2004).
102. Taylor (2009b).
103. Taylor (2009b).
104. Dreher (2013).
105. Examples include data on trade, FDI, foreign portfolio investment, income payments to foreign nationals, international telephone and mail traffic, foreign population, media penetration, data on the presence of a few MNCs, and participation in international treaties and organizations.
106. According to Center for World-Class Universities and the Institute of Higher Education of Shanghai Jiao Tong University (2014).
107. Organization for Economic Cooperation and Development (2012c).
108. Italy also suffers from well-known problems with domestic networks, which tend to form around subregions rather than nationally. See Locke (1995) and Putnam (1993).
109. New Zealand, Hungary, and Slovenia each possess relatively strong domestic institutions, yet they innovate relatively poorly. Admittedly, these economies are less developed and industrialized than those in Western Europe, and they cannot draw upon significant histories of performance at the S&T frontier. However, each of these three nations boasts excellent levels of democracy and has embraced free markets. In fact, New Zealand has for years ranked as one of the top five most capitalist economies in the world, according to the Heritage Foundation's Index of Economic Freedom, while Slovenia and Hungary have freed their economies enormously over the past two decades, beating that index's world average during most of these years. Each of these countries has also built at least one world-class research university (New Zealand has five). Also, Slovenia has increased its R&D spending dramatically, while high percentages of students in both Hungary and New Zealand consistently receive among the world's top scores in math and science. Yet New Zealand is only a midlevel innovator, while Hungary and Slovenia are each still "emerging," with better S&T performance than any African, Latin American, or Middle Eastern state, but still far below most of Western Europe. Therefore, the problem may be that New Zealand, Hungary, and Slovenia remain poorly networked relative to their peers in terms of economic and political ties, especially in S&T-relevant sectors. Certainly it may be tempting to blame size, because each of these three states is among the smallest in our sample. But as shown in chapter 3, size

has a limited role in determining S&T performance. For example, midlevel innovator New Zealand has roughly the same population as the much stronger innovators Finland, Ireland, Singapore, and Norway.

110. Leong (2003).
111. Peebles (2002).
112. Hampden-Turner (2009).
113. Park (2008). Updated through 2010 at http://nw08.american.edu/~wgp/
114. Beaverstock (2002).
115. Gopinathan (2007); Wong, Ho, and Singh (2007).
116. Sidhu, Ho, and Yeoh (2011); Olds (2007).
117. Phelps and Wu (2009); Pereira (2007); Yeoh, How, and Leong (2005).
118. Wong (2011).
119. Singapore is still a very insular society in many ways. See Thompson (2014), Rajah (2012), and Tan (2007).
120. Acemoglu and Robinson (2012).
121. Organization for Economic Cooperation and Development (2009a); Wong (2011).
122. Kim (2011); Ringen et al. (2011).
123. Kihl (2005).
124. Amsden (1989).
125. Amsden (1989); Eichengreen, Perkins, and Shin (2012).
126. Recently the South Korean government has intervened to increase the footprint of small and medium-sized enterprises in R&D and S&T industries. See Organization for Economic Cooperation and Development (2009a).
127. Park (2008). Updated through 2010 at http://nw08.american.edu/~wgp/
128. Amsden (1989); Eichengreen, Perkins, and Shin (2012).
129. Institute of International Education (2015); UNESCO Institute for Statistics.
130. Though recently, South Korea's international networking may have suffered relative declines. A recent OECD review of South Korea's innovation policy warns of "weak international linkages," citing too little foreign participation in Korea's domestic STEM and R&D networks. This may explain why South Korea trails behind far better networks of rapid innovators such as Finland, Taiwan, Israel, and Singapore. Organization for Economic Cooperation and Development (2009a).
131. Kim (2008).
132. Noland (2001).
133. Choi, Kim, and Merrill (2003).
134. Armstrong (2013); Lankov (2013).
135. Kim (2008).
136. Pinkston (2008); Pritchard (2007).
137. Pinkston (2008); Pritchard (2007).
138. Solingen (2007a).
139. Wired News Report (1999).
140. Greenstein and Stango (2006).
141. However, some researchers argue that "lock-in" is a rational choice, not an unforeseen and regretted outcome. See Hossain and Morgan (2009), Liebowitz (2002), and Liebowitz and Margolis (1990).
142. The American National Standards Institute (ANSI) is not listed here because its function is to approve standards designed by others, but it does not itself create them.
143. Sterling, Bernt, and Weiss (2006); Spar (2001); Carlson (2001).
144. *U.S. v IBM Corp.*, Civil Action No. 72- 344; Grad (2002).
145. Crane (1979); US Congress (1992); Krislov (1997); Milner and Austin (2001).
146. Ezell (2011); Suttmeier, Yao, and Tan (2006).
147. Marukawa (2010).
148. Lee and Oh (2008).
149. Murphree (2014).
150. DeNardis (2011).
151. Swann (2000, 2010).

Chapter 7

1. Parts of this chapter were published previously by the author and are republished here by permission of the copyright holder, Stanford University Press. See Sapolsky and Taylor (2011).
2. This section draws from Beasley (1988), Beasley (1997), and Porter (1998c).
3. The first successful modern steam engine was the Newcomen engine installed in a coalmine at Dudley Castle in Staffordshire in 1712 and used to pump water out during recurring floods. Steam engines were first used in factories in 1790, when Richard Arkwright introduced a Watt steam engine to produce textiles in Nottingham, England. When synthesized together with a flurry of other mechanical inventions, steam engines allowed Arkwright to mechanize the entire process of cotton thread production. See Rosen (2010).
4. Seminal theoretical works that have attempted to formalize this dynamic include Mokyr (1992), Parente and Prescott (1994), Krusell, and Ríos-Rull (1996), Comin and Hobijn (2009), and Acemoglu and Robinson (2000).
5. McCallion (1983).
6. Bruland (1995).
7. Bruland (1995).
8. Martin (1995).
9. Botelho (1995).
10. Feldman and Bayer (1999); Shilts (1987).
11. Mokyr (1992).
12. Tranquillus (100 AD).
13. Sometimes formalized as "Hicks-neutral" technological change in which a new technology does not alter the marginal rate of substitution between a pair of inputs; see Hicks (1932). Although economic growth theorists do distinguish between Harrod-neutral (labor-augmenting) and Solow-neutral (capital-augmenting) technological change, this practice has been slow to diffuse into other subfields.
14. Luddites are those opposed to technology, named after a British labor movement led by Ned Lud, who between 1811 and 1816 rioted and destroyed labor-saving textile mills and machinery in the belief that such technology would diminish employment. Historians have since argued that the Luddite movement was only partially, or indirectly, a reaction to technological change. See Thompson (1964).
15. This insight is ancient. In Imperial Rome, perhaps the first society to conduct mechanized mass production, Emperor Vespasian is said to have forbade the use of some labor-saving mechanical inventions to "ensure . . . that the working classes earn enough money to buy themselves food." In a similar vein, Pliny recounts the story of a Roman inventor of a pliable glass, whose workshop was destroyed because his innovation threatened not only established glass blowers but also the value of ornamental gold, silver, and copper and hence their entire industries as well. See also Hodge (1990).
16. See, for example, Gainous and Wagner (2014); Weiss, Franklin, and Marianne (2013); Mele (2013); Jundt (2014); Boot (2006); Piore and Sabel (1984); and Taylor (1951).
17. Drucker (2014); Poletti and Rak (2014); O'Riordan (2010); Harrison and Johnson (2009); Hecht (2009); Braman (2005); Cowan (1983).
18. Sapolsky and Taylor (2011).
19. Schumpeter (1942, 81).
20. Hughes (1983).
21. Including advanced research by the physicists Charles-Augustin de Coulomb and André-Marie Ampère, and the codevelopment and usage of arc light during the early 1860s. See also Gorman (1977).
22. Bijker (1995).
23. Students of military innovation should observe that, for the purposes of this book, *innovation* is limited to improvements in technology; it does *not* include changes or improvements in doctrines, organizations, policies, or institutions.
24. Douglas (1985).
25. The Tomahawk long-range, land-attack cruise missile first entered service in 1983 but was not used in combat until 1991, where it achieved a greater than 80% success rate, which was increased above 90% in subsequent uses. See Friedman (1991).

26. te Kulve, and Smit (2010); Long and Sweezey (2005); Pierce (2004); Engel (1994). Also interviews with Austin Long.
27. Betts (1981).
28. Although Kissinger and his team believed that cruise missiles might serve as bargaining chips in arms control negotiations. See, for example, US State Department (1976).
29. Engel (1994). Also interviews with Austin Long.
30. Long (2010).
31. The costs and time required for longbow training also served as a major barrier. See Keegan (1993) and Jones (1987).
32. In each case, the restrictions were of questionable effectiveness, were often short-lived, and applied more to the peasantry than to the gentry. See Chase (2003).
33. Ayalon (1979).
34. Murray and Millett (1996).
35. Posen (1984).
36. Pierce (2004).
37. Builder (1994, 200); Neufeld (1990).
38. Blair (2012); Dombrowski and Gholz (2006).
39. Mokyr (1992).
40. Levinson (2006); Gibson and Donovan (2001); Cudahy (2006).
41. Levinson (2006).
42. Levinson (2006).
43. Levinson (2006).
44. Bijker, Hughes, and Pinch (1989); Bijker (1995).
45. Caro (1974, 319). The battles over birth control technologies might also be appropriate here.
46. Szöllösi-Janze (2001); Medawar and Pyke (2001).
47. Gordon (1976, 1990); Cowan (1997).
48. Katz and Allen (1982).
49. Monroe, Miller, and Tobis (2008); Berkman (2010); Paarlberg (2009); Lin, Abney, and Bekey (2012).
50. Gordon (1976, 1990).
51. Mokyr (1992); Parente and Prescott (1994); Krusell and Ríos-Rull (1996); Comin and Hobijn (2009); Acemoglu and Robinson (2000).
52. Duke Energy is a North Carolina–based firm involved in electric-power production, which owned seven nuclear power plants and stations as of 2015.
53. Perhaps the earliest example is President Taft's dismissal of the first chief of the US Forest Service, Gifford Pinchot, in 1910 for the latter's insubordinate advocacy of scientific forestry and conservation. See Miller (2001).
54. Shulman (2006).
55. Shulman (2006).
56. Shulman (2006).
57. Shulman (2006).
58. Shulman (2006).
59. Brown and Williamson internal document (1969).
60. Intergovernmental Panel on Climate Change (1995). Though scientists have been warning politicians about the threat of climate change since the mid-1960s. See Fleming (1998).
61. Congressman Lamar Smith (R-Texas), Chairman of the House Committee on Science, Space, and Technology, opening remarks at a full committee hearing on Examining the UN Intergovernmental Panel on Climate Change Process (2014).
62. Oreskes and Conway (2010).
63. Mooney (2005); Shulman (2006); Berezow and Campbell (2012).
64. Exemplified by Senator Tom Coburn's (R-Oklahoma) infamous attacks on "shrimp on a treadmill" and laundry-folding robots research. See Coburn (2011).
65. Hartung (2011); Wirls (2010); Eisendrath, Goodman, and Marsh (2001).
66. Paarlberg (2009).
67. Mukunda (2012, 215).
68. Cohen and Noll (1991).

69. Mankiw (2006, 2009); Hoel and Kverndokk (1996); Farzin (1996); Bergstrom (1982).
70. Parthasarathy (2007).
71. Caulfield, Bubela, and Murdoch (2007).
72. *Association for Molecular Pathology v. Myriad Genetics*, 569 U.S. 12-398 (2013).
73. Parts of this section were published previously by the author in the *Journal of Health Politics, Policy and Law*; they are republished here by permission of the copyright holder, Duke University Press. See Taylor (2009a).
74. World Health Organization (2015).
75. Specifically antihemophilic factor.
76. Within the United States. See White (2010).
77. Petricciani, McDougal, and Evatt (1985); Rouzioux et al. (1985).
78. Montagnier (2000); Institute of Medicine (1995).
79. Yet, this was not universal. For example, the French scientific establishment tended to see sexuality as incidental to AIDS and generally avoided this red herring that for years dogged American researchers, who at first perceived of AIDS as a strictly "gay disease." See Shilts (1987).
80. Feldman and Yonemoto (1992).
81. Grmek (1990); Epstein (1996); Mann and Tarantola (1996); Shilts (1987).
82. Shilts (1987).
83. Berridge (1996, 33).
84. Smith, Teeling, and Taylor (1984).
85. Street and Weale (1992).
86. Berridge (1996).
87. Hayward (1973).
88. Kellerman (1988).
89. Steffan (1992).
90. Gallo (1991); Shilts (1987).
91. Shilts (1987).
92. British researchers were also able to make some notable achievements, despite lack of government support and a widely held perception in the British scientific community that French and American AIDS research could not well be competed against. For example, as early as December 1983, Cambridge virologist Abraham Karpas published an electron micrograph of what turned out be the HIV virus months before its identification by Robert Gallo in the U.S. (Berridge 1996). And like Gallo, a British leukemia researcher diverted funds from his cancer research to help to lay the foundations for the first commercial British HIV-antibody test. The laboratory versions of the British test were developed in autumn 1984 by another researcher, Richard Tedder, and were used to conduct viral research and epidemiological studies, including analysis of sera from hemophilia centers (Berridge 1996). However, as in France, the transition from the laboratory to the production line was not as timely.
93. Montagnier (2000).
94. Which had been isolated by Montagnier two months before.
95. Shilts (1987); Epstein (1996); Montagnier (2000).
96. Shilts (1987); Epstein (1996).
97. Crewsdon (2002); Epstein (1996).
98. Crewsdon (2002); Epstein (1996).
99. Feldman (2000); Steffan (1992, 1999).
100. Steffen (1999).
101. Feldman and Yonemoto (1992).
102. Isomure and Mizogami (1992); Swinbanks (1985); Feldman (1999).
103. Swinbanks (1988, 1996).
104. Feldman (1999).
105. A practice known as *amakudari*.
106. Johnson (1982); Suleiman (1978); Feldman (1999).
107. Feldman (1999).
108. Feldman and Yonemoto (1992).

109. Swinbanks (1986); Feldman (1999).
110. Feldman (1999).
111. Starr (1998).
112. Feldman (1999).
113. Agress (1983); Feldman (1999).
114. Dearing (1992). See also Swinbanks (1988).
115. Feldman (1999).
116. Feldman (2000).
117. Shilts (1987).
118. Shilts (1987, 221)
119. Feldman (1999, 26); Bove ultimately changed course in 1984 after mounting evidence; see Shilts (1987).
120. Shilts (1987).
121. Office of Technology Assessment (1995).
122. Transfusion of blood factor is required in hemophiliacs anywhere from once every six months in mild cases to two to three times per week in more severe cases. Phone interview with Nava Rahmanim, Information Specialist, National Hemophilia Foundation (2002). These advances in AHF are credited with adding decades to the average life expectancy of hemophiliacs. See Starr (2000).
123. Smith (1970), quoted in White (1984, 470).
124. Sapolsky and Taylor (2011).

Chapter 8

1. Even random discoveries must be recognized by their inventors and developed at considerable expense.
2. Some material in this chapter is taken from Taylor (2012), which can be referenced at http://www.tandfonline.com/.
3. Writing in the early 1940s, Schumpeter sought to describe the evolutionary character of capitalism. He argued that then-mainstream (classical) economics' single-minded focus on price competition and achieving equilibriums was too static. It gave an incomplete description of the capitalist economy. Instead, Schumpeter argued that what we today call "innovation" drives capitalism forward by means of "creative destruction." He wrote, "This process of Creative Destruction is the essential fact about capitalism . . . the fundamental impulse that sets and keeps the capitalist engine in motion." However, Schumpeter would have used a much broader definition of innovation than I accept in this book, including in it "new consumers' goods, the new methods of production or transportation, the new markets, the new forms of industrial organization that capitalist enterprise creates . . . the new commodity, the new technology, the new source of supply, the new type of organization." See appendix 1 and Schumpeter (1942, 83-84).
4. This section benefited from discussions with the historians Ron Hatzenbuehler, Claudio Katz, Mary Krall, and Barbara Oberg.
5. Hamilton (1791); Cole (1928); Nelson (1979).
6. Washington (1790).
7. Ben-Atar and Oberg (1998); Elkins and McKitrick (1993).
8. Political parties were widely considered anathema at the time; hence, the Federalists generally denied that they were creating one. Also, the proximate trigger for partisanship during this period was an intense debate over US foreign policy: the Federalists were feared as too supportive of Great Britain, while the Democratic-Republicans were seen as dangerously sympathetic to France.
9. Meye (2003); Irwin (2004); Nelson (1987); Wood (2009).
10. Irwin and Sylla (2011); McCoy (1980).
11. Wood (2009); Herring (2008).
12. Jefferson (1782).
13. Jefferson (1792, 353).
14. Madison (1792, 180).

15. Maclay (1790, 15).
16. Wood (2009); Herring (2008).
17. Wood (2009); McCoy (1980).
18. And although the Jeffersonians could not defeat the establishment of a US patent office, they ensured that US patents had the novel feature of requiring full disclosure of their technical specifications. See Cowan (1997) and Walterscheid (1998).
19. Swanson (1993).
20. Sherid (1992).
21. Cogliano (2014); Herring (2008).
22. Tariff acts were passed by Congress in 1789, 1790, 1792, 1794, 1795, and 1796, but not again until 1816. The first two tariff regimes were arguably for revenue only. However, the 1792 Tariff Act incorporated many of the protectionist levies proposed by Hamilton in his *Report on Manufacturers*. See Irwin (2004).
23. Cooke (1975a, 1975b).
24. Some of these domestic tensions were explicitly linked to external threats. Each side of the early American political divide perceived the other as favoring a foreign superpower. See Wood (2009) and Herring (2008).
25. Crackel (1987, 2002).
26. Dupree (1986).
27. However, Jefferson and many pastoralists strongly preferred that American manufacturing be based in private homes as much as possible, rather than in factories. They also held that the evils of manufacturing could be minimalized while the vast vacant land available in the western states and territories could act as a safety valve, allowing laborers to escape attempts "by the other classes to reduce them to the minimum subsistence." See Jefferson (1805). See also Jefferson (1812, 1816).
28. Jefferson (1816). Stronger still is a letter written in autumn 1811 in which Jefferson pleads, "I formerly believed it was best for every country to make what it could make to best advantage, and to exchange it with others for those articles which it could not so well make. I did not then suppose that a whole quarter of the globe could within the short space of a dozen years, from being the most civilized, become the most savage portion of the human race. I am come over therefore to your opinion that, abandoning to a certain degree those agricultural pursuits, which best suited our situation, we must endeavor to make every thing we want within ourselves, and have as little intercourse as possible with Europe in it's present demoralised state." Jefferson (1811). See also Jefferson (1809a, 1809b, 1816).
29. Herring (2008); Wood (2009).
30. Ha (2009).
31. Sexton (2011).
32. Adams (1825).
33. Also suggested were an engineering academy for naval officers, uniform standards of weights and measures, and reforms to the patent office.
34. Adams (1875, 64-65).
35. Remini (2002).
36. Jackson (1826).
37. Ritchie (1825).
38. "Distributional" here recognizes that these political fights are not limited to economic (re) distribution; they are also over the (re)distribution of political, social, and cultural power and assets.
39. I would argue that Finland during the Cold War also fits this description.
40. Taylor (2012).
41. Human and capital flight are classified here as "external" threats because, if there were no foreign nations to flee to, then flight could not occur. While this classification may offend some readers as blurring the dictionary definition of "external," it is nonetheless used here to simplify discussion.
42. Christensen (1997).
43. Olson (1965).
44. Markowitz and Fariss (2013); Lake (2009); Prior (2001); Dudley (1991).

45. Raudzens (1990).
46. Especially when it is on the offensive side or attempting an occupation (e.g., Hitler's campaign into the Soviet Union, the US Vietnam War, the Soviet–Afghan war, the recent US occupations of Iraq and Afghanistan).
47. See Parker (1988), Cipolla (1965), Kennedy (1987), and McNeill (1982).
48. The effects of S&T progress on skills and the labor market is a subject of rich and hotly contested debate among economists. See Acemoglu and Autor (2012); Goldin and Katz (2008); Autor, Levy, and Murnane (2003); Acemoglu (2002); and Card and DiNardo (2002).
49. Olson (1965, 1982).
50. Olson (1982, 18).
51. Some scholars have argued that Olson is only partly correct. Large diffuse interest groups can and do organize, often surprisingly easily. In these cases, the obstacles to organizing broad but shallow interests are real, but the incentives to overcome these obstacles are even greater. See Trumball (2012).
52. Mokyr (1990, 1998).
53. Acemoglu and Robinson (2012); Acemoglu (2009).
54. Parente and Prescott (1994); Krusell and Rios-Rull (1996); Comin and Hobijn (2009).
55. Solingen (2007a, 2007b).
56. Haggard (1990); Haggard and Kaufman (1992).
57. Drezner (2001).
58. Doner (2009); Doner, Hicken, and Ritchie (2009); Doner, Ritchie, and Slater (2005).
59. Henisz (2002a).
60. Olson (1965, 1982).
61. Where "regime change" is defined as a three-point change in a nation's POLITY score over a period of three years or less, or the end of transition period defined by the lack of stable political institutions. The actual US value is 203. See Marshall, Gurr, and Jaggers (2014).
62. Polarization attempts to sum the interpersonal antagonisms between different groups. Antagonism is produced by the interaction of group size, group identification, and the sense of alienation between different groups (intergroup distance). For example, a population with equal parts left-handed and right-handed people would be very fractionalized but not very polarized, while a society with a large Shia majority and a small Sunni minority would be less factionalized but highly polarized. When measured using a statistical index, a value of zero corresponds to a perfectly homogenous society according to either fractionalization or polarization. A fractionalization index approaches "1" as the number of different groups in the society increases. The polarization index approaches "1" as the groups' size differences and antagonisms grow. See Montalvoa and Reynal-Querol (2005) and Alesina, Devleeschauwer, Easterly, Kurlat, and Wacziarg (2003).
63. Papyrakis and Mo (2014); Goeren (2014); Ager and Bruckner (2013); Montalvo and Reynal-Querol (2005); Alesina, Devleeschauwer, Easterly, Kurlat, and Wacziarg (2003).
64. Portugal and Norway rate as highly homogenous across every measure available: ethnic, linguistic, and religious. Both Ireland and Greece are rated as highly homogenous along linguistic and religious lines, but are relatively more heterogenous along ethnic lines, yet still less diverse than the world average. See Alesina, Devleeschauwer, Easterly, Kurlat, and Wacziarg (2003).
65. Conversely, the dual crises of the Great Depression and World War II led to a marked increase in politically active interest groups in the United States, but America still enjoyed a sustained increase in its innovation rate.
66. Olson (1982, 75).
67. Olson, Sarna, and Swamy (2000); Olson (1996).
68. The Political Terror Scale is a five-level index of relative political violence. The data used in compiling this terror scale is derived from the annual US State Department Country Reports on Human Rights Practices, as well as yearly Amnesty International country reports. See http://www.politicalterrorscale.org/ and Wood and Gibney (2010).
69. Jones, Bremer, and Singer (1996, 163).
70. This describes the countries of Argentina, Brazil, Chile, Greece, El Salvador, Panama, Peru, Spain, Turkey, and Uruguay. Certainly pro-S&T military dictatorships can exist in the short

run—South Korea and Taiwan arguably once fit this description—but over time they tend toward stagnation. I therefore make no special classification for them in this test. This is because military dictatorships that are pro-S&T in their initial years tend to become staunch defenders of status quo interests, as industry innovators evolve into established players tied to the regime, and both subsequently attempt to prevent the creative destruction that might spell their replacement. Therefore, its overall effect on national innovation rate is indeterminate and likely dependent on the time frame analyzed. See Acemoglu and Robinson (2005).

71. Grieco, Cheng, and Guzman (2014).

Chapter 9

1. Weiss (2014); Ruttan (2006); Samuels (1994, 2007); Keller and Samuels (2003); Heo and Roehrig (2014).
2. This section benefited from the advice of Jeremy Pressman and Lawrence Rubin.
3. Estimates during the mid-1940s are problematic due to shifting political boundaries and massive migrations. The 1947 population estimates of Palestine are 1.845 million. However, due to war and regime change, the area suffered contested boundaries and an exodus of over seven hundred thousand Palestinians. See United Nations General Assembly (1951) and Shaw (1946).
4. Central Bureau of Statistics, Israel.
5. Israeli immigration rates averaged 1.5% to 2.0% of the population until 1974. Central Bureau of Statistics, Israel.
6. Segev (1993).
7. Sachar (1976).
8. Meir (1975, 346).
9. Ben-Meir (1995).
10. Handel (1973).
11. As many as 40% of Israeli soldiers were new immigrants. See Handel (1973).
12. Horowitz and Lissak (1989).
13. Abramitzky (2011); Halevi and Klinov-Malul (1968); Patinkin (1967).
14. Even the private sector shared in Israel's unity-driven development strategy. To maintain private sector support, the Israeli government gave choice plums to the major business associations such as special investment subsidies, protectionist measures, and other forms of state support. See Aharoni (1998), Hanieh (2003), Arian (1985), and Bruno (1992).
15. Cohen (1998).
16. Breznitz (2007).
17. Alpert (1982).
18. Garfinkle (2000, 121-124). See also Hilberg (2003).
19. Segev (1993).
20. Desch (2008).
21. Flapan (1987); Schlaim (2001); Thomas (1999).
22. Desch (2008); Pollack (2002).
23. Desch (2008).
24. DeRouen (2000).
25. Louis and Shlaim (2012).
26. Arian (1995). See also Desch (2008) and Pressman (2008).
27. Crosbie (1974).
28. Aharoni (1998).
29. Bruno (1992).
30. Arian (1985).
31. Benporath (1977).
32. Huiyu (2009).
33. Tsurumi (1977).
34. Lower estimates put the number at 1.5 million Chinese ex-patriots. Regardless, the migration forced a sudden increase in Taiwan's population of around 13%.
35. Roy (2003).

36. Buck (1970).
37. In practice, early twentieth-century Chinese S&T was mostly basic research, not applied. Little effort was made to connect it to national economic needs. This would change only after the 1937 invasion by Japan, when KMT support for S&T intensified. During the 1930s and 1940s, China's S&T institutions became more comprehensive, with research driven by war needs and results tied directly to economic and military demand. See Bowers (1988).
38. Yager (1988); Solingen (2007a); Chung (1993).
39. Greene (2008).
40. Manthrope (2005).
41. Greene (2008).
42. Garver (1997).
43. Van Staaveren (1962); US Strategic Air Command (1959).
44. Roy (1998).
45. Gold (1986).
46. Baldwin, Chen, and Nelson (1995).
47. National Statistics Bureau, Republic of China (Taiwan).
48. Greene (2008, 47).
49. Garver (1997).
50. Greene (2008).
51. US military aid to Taiwan during this period totaled $2.2 billion. See Wei (2012).
52. Jacoby (1966).
53. Greene (2008).
54. Chung-Shan Institute of Science and Technology.
55. Greene (2008).
56. Gold (1986).
57. Feenstra et al. (2005).
58. Greene (2008).
59. Greene (2008).
60. Roy (2003).
61. Commander in Chief, US Pacific Command (CINCPAC) (1975).
62. National Statistics Bureau, Republic of China (Taiwan).
63. Roy (2003).
64. Jacobs (2005).
65. Yang (1970); Aprthorpe (1979).
66. Ranis (1978).
67. Aberbach, Dollar, and Sokoloff (1994).
68. NT $300 billion at a 1973 exchange rate of $38 New Taiwan dollars per $1 US. See Rubinstein (1999).
69. Hong (1997).
70. Breznitz (2007).
71. Roy (2003).
72. Officially called the "Irish Free State" until 1937, then "Eire" until 1949. From 1949 onward the formal name has been the "Republic of Ireland."
73. Bew (2007).
74. The Anglo-Irish Treaty (1921) created a self-governing, sovereign Irish state with its own army and police. However, Ireland would technically remain an autonomous dominion of the United Kingdom, with the British monarch as its formal head of state (similar to Canada or Australia). Members of the new Irish parliament were also required to take an "oath of allegiance." Britain retained control over several strategic ports in Ireland. Militant republicans in Ireland believed that the treaty failed to deliver full Irish independence (or were furious at not being included in the negotiations), while treaty supporters felt it was the best deal possible at the time.
75. It was a fairly low-level conflict, concentrated in a few major cities, resulting in only around a thousand causalities, who were mostly civilians and police rather than military. See Boyce (1988).
76. Bartlett (2010).

77. Divorce was banned, contraception was outlawed, and censorship was initiated against lewd books and Hollywood movies, resulting in bans on huge numbers of titles. See Bartlett (2010), Graham (2001), and Chriost (2012).
78. O'Buachalla (1988).
79. The tiny sliver of domestic industry that did exist there was chiefly composed of brewing, food processing, and basic textiles. The rest was mostly subsidiary plants of British manufacturers of high-volume, low-value, low-tech goods, such as animal feed, mineral water, or furniture. See Bielenberg (2009).
80. O'Grada (1997).
81. Bielenberg (2009).
82. Bielenberg and Ryan (2013).
83. McCarthy and Keogh (2005).
84. Bew (2007).
85. Daly (1984).
86. Neary and Ograda (1991).
87. Bartlett (2010).
88. Throughout the war, the Irish Republic only suffered a handful of minor, sometimes accidental, air raids, for which Germany sometimes apologized and even paid reparations. See McMahon (2009).
89. Bartlett (2010).
90. Bartlett (2010).
91. Wills (2007).
92. O'Grada (1997).
93. See, for example, *Dublin Opinion* (1941).
94. O'Grada (1997).
95. The republic's continued import protectionism was not a total loss. Its final decade saw moderate technological progress in glass making, chemicals, engineering, plastics, and cement, but most S&T advances remained in food processing. See Bielenberg and Ryan (2013) and O'Grada (1997).
96. O'Grada (1997).
97. O'Grada (1997).
98. O'Buachalla (1988).
99. Whitaker (1958).
100. Based on Bartlett (2010) and Bielenberg and Ryan (2013).
101. Daly (2006); O'Brien (1953).
102. Honohan and O'Grada (1998).
103. O'Grada (1997).
104. O'Grada (1997).
105. Breznitz (2007).
106. O'Riain (2004).
107. Bielenberg and Ryan (2013).
108. Bielenberg and Ryan (2013).
109. O'Riain (2004); Breen et al. (1990); Bielenberg and Ryan (2013).
110. O'Riain (2004); Breen et al. (1990).
111. O'Riain (2004).
112. Bielenberg and Ryan (2013).
113. Grimes (1992); O'Connor (2003).
114. Daly (2006); O'Brien (1953).
115. Munley, Thornton, and Aronson (2002); Mac Sharry, White, and O'Malley (2000).
116. Bielenberg and Ryan (2013).
117. Bartlett (2010); O'Grada (1997).
118. Telesis Consulting Group (1982).
119. Bielenberg and Ryan (2013).
120. Walsh (1999).
121. National Economic and Social Council (NESC) (1991).
122. Crotty (1986); Wiles and Finnegan (1993).

123. Also referred to as "the Tallaght Strategy." See Ornston (2012) and Sinnott (1995).
124. Bielenberg and Ryan (2013).
125. Mac Sharry, White, and O'Malley (2010); Breznitz (2007).
126. During this time period, 40.2% of returnees had a college degree compared with only 16.7% of Ireland's general population. See Barret, Bergin, and Duffy (2006).
127. Bielenberg and Ryan (2013).
128. Organization for Economic Cooperation and Development (2012a).
129. Scholars vary on dating the "Celtic tiger" period. For example, O'Hearn starts it as early as 1994 after an optimistic economic analysis by Morgan Stanley; Breznitz argues that it ended soon after 2000, when initial public offerings (IPOs) of new Irish high-tech firms ceased appearing on the NASDAQ and Ireland's primary domestic economic engine switched to real estate.
130. Breznitz (2007).
131. Bielenberg and Ryan (2013).
132. van Egeraat and Barry (2009); van Egeraat (2010).
133. O'Hearn (1998).
134. For example, in GDP per capita terms, Mexican wealth rose to over twice that of Taiwan (1950–1965) and averaged two-thirds the national wealth of either Ireland (1921–1991) or Israel (1950–1970) for large parts of the twentieth century. See Bolt and van Zanden (2013).
135. Servín, Reina, and Tutino (2007).
136. Henderson (2009).
137. Meyer and Beezley (2000).
138. Only one-quarter of these leaders were fully constitutional, only eight survived in office longer than two years, and the longest lasted just over six years The longest included Guadalupe Victoria (1824–1829), Anastasio Bustamante (1839–1841), José Joaquín de Herrera (1848–1851), Antonio López de Santa Anna (1853–1855), Ignacio Comonfort (1855–1858), Benito Juárez (1858–1864, 1867–1872), and Sebastián Lerdo de Tejada (1872–1876).
139. Meyer, Sherman, and Deeds (1999).
140. Lorey (1993).
141. By 1860, Mexico's per capita economic output had fallen *below* the levels achieved in 1800; sometime during the 1860s, the economy began to recover, but did not surpass its prior peak until the 1880s. See Bolt and van Zanden (2013).
142. Bleichmar (2009); Fortes and Lomnitz (1994).
143. Foster (2007).
144. Fortes and Lomnitz (1994).
145. The argument here is as follows: as recently as 1820, Texas was a poorly inhabited, undeveloped borderland contested by Spain, the United States, and various Indian tribes. After Mexico won independence in 1821, its new federal government opened Texas, over which it had little military control, to American settlers. Since few Mexicans lived in Texas, or sought to, the idea was to create a buffer region of American settlers against the warlike Comanche tribes that constantly raided southward. To entice settlement, the Mexican Constitution of 1824 and other laws gave settlers considerable political autonomy and generous economic benefits. In response, several thousand American settlers immigrated. As a result, by the mid-1830s, the vast majority of the Texas population consisted of white, Protestant Americans. Certainly these new Texans were viewed with suspicion by many within Mexico. At best, their loyalty and obedience to Mexican law were questioned (especially to Mexican prohibitions on slavery); at worst, the settlers were seen as surrogates for US power. Nevertheless, Texan settler elites repeatedly proved willing to resolve conflicts within the context of Mexican institutions. Meanwhile, most Mexicans faced far greater threats from within, for Mexico then remained vexed with violent domestic conflicts and political instability. Between 1833 and 1855, the Mexican presidency changed hands at least thirty-six times. In May 1834, Santa Ana seized power in Mexico, backed by the conservative Mexican clergy and the army, both of which felt threatened by liberal reformers in the Mexican government. Santa Ana dissolved Congress and the state governments, abolished the constitution, and

declared himself dictator. Texas and a handful of other Mexican states then rebelled. But the United States remained distant and neutral. In fact, at first, the Texans fought to restore the liberal Mexican Constitution of 1824, and to establish themselves as a new state within the Mexican federation (Texas had hitherto been merely a *departamento* of the recently created Mexican state of Coahuila y Texas). Even after the conflict evolved into a war for secession, many Mexican-born Hispanics fought on the side of Texan independence, not against it. Also, although US private citizens flocked to take part in the revolution, the US government provided little aid to the rebels. Furthermore, after Texas won independence in 1836, the Jackson administration refused to recognize the new nation for almost a year. Certainly, the Mexican government sent a substantial army, led by Santa Ana himself, to put down the rebellion and prevent Texan secession. But in the end, this was not an American invasion or proxy war. Antislavery and antiexpansionist forces within the United States were too powerful to permit this. Rather, the secession of Texas was the result of a civil war fought for domestic power, over lands that few Mexicans cared about, to solidify the dictatorship of Santa Ana. See Calvert, De Leon, and Cantrell (2013); Howe (2007); and Herring (2008).
146. Merry (2009); Henderson (2007).
147. Foster (2007).
148. Greenberg (2012); Howe (2009).
149. Though both of these promises would be poorly fulfilled by the United States. Howe (2009); Henderson (2007).
150. Meyer, Sherman, and Deeds (1999).
151. Ridley (2001).
152. Meyer, Sherman, and Deeds (1999).
153. Bethell (1986); Herring (2008).
154. Herring (2008).
155. Nicknamed the “Roosevelt Corollary” to the Monroe Doctrine. Roosevelt (1904).
156. Herring (2008).
157. Schoultz (1998); Herring (2008); Buchenau (1996).
158. Beatty (2001).
159. Razo (2008).
160. Beatty (2001); Moreno-Brid and Ros (2009).
161. Moreno-Brid and Ros (2009).
162. Garner (2001); Vazquez and Meyer (1985).
163. Garner (2001).
164. Lorey (1993).
165. Lorey (1993).
166. Gonzales (2002).
167. Meyer, Sherman, and Deeds (1999); Camin and Mayer (1993).
168. Foster (2007); Gonzales (2002).
169. Sustained and widespread new investment in manufacturing technologies began to take hold in 1935. See Haber (1989).
170. Haber (1989); Gonzales (2002); Camin and Mayer (1993).
171. Schuler (1998).
172. Niblo (1995).
173. Even Mexico’s abrupt nationalization of its oil industry (1938) did not derail its relations with the United States, though it did result in a four-year diplomatic break with Great Britain. The Mexican oil industry was an almost entirely foreign-owned (and heavily American) sector. Hence, nationalization resulted in substantial losses for foreign investors. However, the Roosevelt administration insisted only on financial compensation and would neither threaten nor permit a military response. See Vazquez and Meyer (1985) and Knight (1987).
174. King (1970); Hansen (1971).
175. Moreno-Brid and Ros (2009).
176. Sanderson (1986).
177. Moreno-Brid and Ros (2009); Sanderson (1986).
178. Gallagher and Zarsky (2007).
179. Bagley and Quezada (1993).

180. A severe balance-of-payments crisis hit in 1976, which might have triggered more substantial investments in S&T; however, Mexico's discovery of major petroleum deposits, and hence expectations of massive exports, quickly alleviated these pressures. See Moreno-Brid and Ros (2009).
181. Lorey (1993).
182. Lustig (1998).
183. Cimoli (2000).
184. Schlefer (2008).
185. Lustig (1998).
186. Schlefer (2008).
187. Botzman (1999).
188. Mexico's expenditures on R&D peaked in 1981 at 0.45% of GDP and have since hovered at or below that level. See Organization for Economic Cooperation and Development (2012c, 2012d).
189. Organization for Economic Cooperation and Development (2009b).
190. Lustig (1998).
191. 2009 data; World Bank (2014); Organization for Economic Cooperation and Development (2014a).
192. Lorey (1993).
193. Alcorta (1998).
194. Botzman (1999).
195. Organization for Economic Cooperation and Development (2009b).
196. Gallagher and Zarsky (2007); Organization for Economic Cooperation and Development (2009b).

Conclusion

1. *Anna Karenina* is the celebrated classic by Russian novelist Leo Tolstoy, published during the mid-1870s, which begins with the now-famous observation that: "Happy families are all alike; every unhappy family is unhappy in its own way."
2. Important exceptions include Przeworski (2004).
3. Olson (1982, 14).
4. Here again we can quote Mancur Olson: "Absolutely nothing in all of epistemology suggests that valid explanations should be monocausal. An explanation may be entirely valid, yet explain only a part . . . of the variation at issue." Olson (1982, 4).
5. Acemoglu and Robinson (2006).
6. Ruttan (2006).
7. Doner (2009).
8. Solingen (2007b).
9. Haggard (1990).
10. Perhaps the argument most similar to creative insecurity is the "techno-nationalism" description of Japan, which holds that a persistent "cult of vulnerability" there has been a motivating force behind Japanese innovation and industrialization. More recently, it has likewise been argued that the secret to American innovation is the Cold War "national security state," which changes in response to shifts in perceived geopolitical threats and to changes in popular anti-statist sentiments. See Samuels (1994) and Weiss (2014). Other scholars reverse the causal arrow by positing S&T as a primary independent variable in international politics. See Skolnikoff (1993) and Herrera (2006).
11. February 1943 comments to the press, quoted in Churchill (1954, 34).
12. O'Neill (2001, 2013); Sharma (2012).
13. Rodrik (2007).
14. Gerschenkron's model of economic development and modernization prescribes relatively specific institutions and policies that governments must create and describes the conditions under which they must be created. In particular, Gerschenkron argues that less developed countries must converge upon more government intervention and of relatively specific types, while more developed countries require less government intervention. In contrast,

the evidence presented in this book suggests vastly more freedom of choice. I argue that all governments need to take action, but that policymakers can customize their institutions and policies. See Gerschenkron (1962).

15. Breznitz (2007, 6).
16. How is "networking" different from the "coordination" described by Varieties of Capitalism scholars in chapter 5? I would argue that *networking* requires that government provide the infrastructure, opportunity, resources, and perhaps focal reasoning or goals for forming relationships and exchanging information. *Networking* is about bringing actors together, or at least lowering the costs for them to do so themselves. Government here should have a strong, but general, goal for society: "Innovate!" or "Solve Problem X!" Policymakers should then act to improve the environment for networks to form and grow. *Coordination* is more about making, even forcing, political deals, perhaps with government as a party with its own parochial interests and goals. It is about actively picking winners and losers, or ameliorating specific ones. Put another way, if *networking* is about improving the soil, temperature, and water in the garden, then *coordination* is about sowing certain plants while pruning others and weeding out undesirables. This book advocates the former, not the latter.
17. Reich (2010); Wagner (2008).
18. Fuchs (2010).
19. Tsebelis (2002); Henisz (2002a); Doner, Hicken, and Ritchie (2009).
20. Alternately, Richard Doner has argued that "systemic vulnerability" determines the number of veto players, which then affects the speed of economic "upgrading" (i.e., moving up the value chain, producing at high levels of efficiency, and doing so with local inputs). Systemic vulnerability is defined as the sum of three separate pressures on political elites: external security threats, domestic popular discontent, and economic resource constraints. The basic line of causality is that an increase in systemic vulnerability causes an increase in elite interest in economic growth. Increased systemic vulnerability also causes a decrease in the effective number of veto players. And the number of veto players determines the ability of the state to decide and commit to upgrading. However, the relationship is not linear. There exists a "sweet spot" where too few veto players will allow the state to suddenly abandon upgrading when the systemic vulnerability pressures on them to do so are lifted, while too many veto players may prevent elites from forming a consensus to pursue upgrading in the first place. In his research, Doner's focus is more on the diffusion of new science and technology than its discovery, invention, or initial development. See Doner (2009) and Doner, Hicken, and Ritchie (2009).
21. Bueno de Mesquita, Smith, Siverson, and Morrow (2003).
22. Cohen and Noll (1991).
23. Ruttan (2006).
24. Henrekson (2005); Holmes and Schmitz (2001).
25. McArdle (2014).
26. Lewis (2014).
27. Bates, Greif, and Singh (2002); Baumol (1990).
28. Stern (2004).
29. Scylla and Charybdis are legendary sea monsters, described in ancient Greek mythology, who sat on opposite sides of the Straits of Messina. They posed hazards so near to each other that sailors who wished to survive had to carefully navigate a middle passage between them.
30. Elbaum and Lazonick (1986).
31. Organization for Economic Cooperation and Development (2013c).
32. Organization for Economic Cooperation and Development (2012b).
33. Tylecote and Visintin (2008).
34. Cowhey, Aronson, and Richards (2009).
35. Cowhey. Aronson, and Richards (2009).
36. Weiss (2014); Ruttan (2006).
37. Noah (2013); Nelson (2013).
38. Cheung (2013).
39. Cohen and Noll (1991).
40. Nordhaus (2013).

41. Sissine (2012).
42. US Energy Information Agency (2015).
43. Centers for Disease Control and Prevention (2014).
44. Nation Science Foundation (2012a).
45. See new research on "perceived strategic value" by Hsueh (2012, forthcoming).
46. Acemoglu and Robinson (2012).

Appendix 1

1. Dear (2001); Martin (1992); Yeo (1993).
2. Kelvin and Tait (1890, v).
3. Ross (1962); Yeo (1993).
4. These objections came mostly from British scientists, who often preferred to be called "men of science," "naturalists," or "natural philosophers" until World War I. However, in the United States, the term *scientist* was adopted enthusiastically during the 1850s to 1860s, which might partially explain British antipathy to it. See White (2003) and Morrell and Thackray (1981).
5. This occurred earlier in Germany than in the rest of the world. During the 1870s, German firms created the world's first formally organized industrial research laboratories. Their goal was to transform recent discoveries in organic chemistry into commercialized products. The Americans and British followed decades later, with the General Electric Research Laboratory (1900) in Schenectady, New York, and the National Physical Laboratory (1902) in London (earlier British labs were arguably more analytic or trial and error than committed to original scientific research). By comparison, Edison's Menlo Park (1876) was more of a personally led, ad hoc invention shop than a formal industrial research laboratory. See Reich (1985), Mowery and Rosenberg (1998), and Edgerton and Horrocks (1994).
6. Reich (1985).
7. Marx (2010); Schatzberg (2006); Oldenziel (1999).
8. Engell (1981).
9. Godin (2008a).
10. Prior to the 1880s, economists referred to their field as *political economy* and themselves as *political economists.*
11. In Marx's theories, technology replaced labor. It arose from the desire of the owners of capital to maximize surplus value. For an alternative view of Marx, see Bimber (1994).
12. W. Rupert Maclaurin might be added. He developed many of Schumpeter's ideas during the 1940s and influenced many now-famous economists during the 1950s and 1960s. See Godin (2008b).
13. Schumpeter (1911, 66).
14. Schumpeter also questioned the rationality assumptions of neoclassical economists. He thought that entrepreneurs were special individuals, less risk averse than others. They drove economic growth in capitalism by acting as the agents of innovation and invention. Schumpeter had a Says Law or "supply push" model of innovation, in which entrepreneurs shaped consumer tastes by offering new products and services. Thus, the death of the entrepreneurial spirit through routinization would bring the death of capitalism and the triumph of socialism. Also, invention required adequate bank credit. Thus, when credit disappears, firms go bankrupt and innovations start to pile up. When credit returns, they are liberated to trigger a new cycle of rapid growth. He also was among the first economists to note the inertia, or "resistance to new ways," that entrepreneurs had to fight (sometimes against the force of their own habits).
15. Schumpeter (1911).
16. Schumpeter (1942).
17. Schumpeter (1942).
18. Samuels, Biddle, and Davis (2003). Also, Schumpeter (in his two-volume *Business Cycles*) was one of the first economists to study business cycles. He named long-run "Kondratieff waves" after Russian economist Nikolai Kondratieff, who, during the 1920s, had identified forty-five- to sixty-year cycles of economic boom and bust that he could not explain. Schumpeter argued that these were driven by invention and innovation. New inventions and innovation would

accumulate, undeveloped and undiffused, during times of slow economic growth. Then, this stockpile of discoveries would be employed in the production process, kicking off a period of rapid economic growth such as the first and second industrial revolutions, as well as the railroad boom of the mid-1800s. Schumpeter (1939).

19. Rosenberg (1976).
20. See Crafts (2009).
21. Harrod (1939); Domar (1946, 1947).
22. Tinbergen (1942); Leontief (1936).
23. Abramowitz (1956).
24. The pioneering work here is actually Tinbergen (1942). Similar claims had also originated in research done by the National Bureau of Economic Research (NBER), summarized by Fabricant (1954). These were later confirmed by John Kendrick (1961), who concluded that 80% and 88.5% of the growth in labor productivity between 1869 and 1953 and between 1909 and 1948, respectively, was due to total factor productivity. See Kendrick (1961), Denison (1962), Denison (1967), and Griliches (1996).
25. Solow (1957).
26. The 1987 Sveriges Riksbank Prize in Economic Sciences in Memory of Alfred Nobel.
27. Abramovitz (1956, 11)
28. Acemoglu (2009, 89).
29. Arrow (1962b).
30. Fogel (1964).
31. Mankiw, Romer, and Weil (1992).
32. Griliches (1957); Griliches (1958, 1960).
33. Nelson (1959, 299).
34. Arrow (1962a).
35. Arrow (1962b, 157).
36. At one point Nelson described innovation as what producers and consumers did to get economic change out of an invention (Nelson 1959).
37. Writing alongside Nelson and Arrow, Simon Kuznets (1962) did define *innovation.* To him, an *innovation* was an applied invention, one that had left the laboratory and been put into practice in the economy. However, Kuznets often straddled the "growth" and "science" camps, and some of his definitions are similar to those used in this volume. See Kuznets (1962, 1966).
38. *The Economist* (1952, 1966); Struve (1963).
39. Ornati (1963).
40. Hunck (1965); Stone (1969).
41. Holbik (1967).
42. According to Hirschman, this created a disequilibrium, which drove modernization in those industries. Government then moved its investments to other sectors to create new imbalances, correct the original disequilibrium, and thereby spread development throughout the economy. And since many of these countries are poor, foreign capital is sometimes required to take the first "unbalancing steps." See Hirschman (1958).
43. Rostow (1960).
44. Specifically, the more technologically backward a country is, the more it needed stronger and more pervasive government intervention to do the heavy lifting of mass industrialization. This was especially true when making up for scarce supplies of skilled labor or investment capital. See Gerschenkron (1962).
45. For example, Rostow never defined *technology, modernization,* or *innovation,* which were so vital to his theory of economic "take-off." And yet, in his discussion of the stages of economic growth, he distinguishes between *applied* and *unapplied* technology, *invention* and *innovation,* and *vertical* and *lateral* innovation. See Rostow (1960).
46. Major scholars here include Chalmers Johnson, Alice Amsden, Robert Wade, Peter Evans, Stephan Haggard, T. J. Pempel, Meredith Woo-Cummings, Richard Doner, and most recently Fred Block, Dan Breznitz, Joe Wong, Adrian Leftwhich, Sean O'Riain, Henry Yeung, Richard Grabowski, and Meghan Greene.
47. Posen (1984); Rosen (1991).
48. Romer (1986, 1990).

49. Schultz (1958, 925).
50. Explaining the causes of innovation, and prescribing a proper role for government, depends heavily on how easy to copy, share, read, and interpret one defines *technology* to be. Put another way, two sets of factors in one's definition of *technology* and *innovation* are enormously important. The first is the degree of rivalry and excludability (e.g., the degree to which *technology* is a public good or private good). The second, related factor is the degree to which *innovation* depends on knowledge and skills that are tacit versus codified. This book deals implicitly with these issues in chapters 3 through 6.
51. Hall and Jones (1999); Aghion and Howitt (1998).
52. Freeman (1987); Lundvall (1992); Nelson (1993); Edquist (1997).
53. Prime movers were *Research Policy, Journal of Product Innovation Management, R&D Management, Technological Forecasting and Social Change, Harvard Business Review, International Journal of Technology Management,* and *Journal of Business Venturing.*

Appendix 2

1. Godin (2007b).
2. MacLeod (2007); Bowler (1989).
3. Galton (1869).
4. Galton (1874).
5. *Science* was established in 1883 as a weekly journal by Alexander Graham Bell and Gardiner Hubbard. However, the journal gradually ran into financial difficulties. Cattell acquired the journal in 1895, rescuing it from insolvency. He then continued as its editor until his death in 1944. In 1900, it was made the official journal of the American Association for the Advancement of Science (AAAS).
6. Renamed in 1971 as *American Men and Women of Science,* it is a biographical reference on leading scientists in the United States (and now Canada), currently published by Cengage Learning.
7. Godin (2009b, 10); Cattell (1903).
8. Godin (2007b).
9. Cochrane (1978).
10. Godin (2009b).
11. Beginning in the 1980s, GDP began to replace gross national product (GNP) as the standard measure of national economic performance. The former sums all economic activity within a nation's borders, regardless of who performs it. The latter sums all economic activity by a nation's individuals and firms, regardless of where they are located. Historically, the two measures correlate very closely.
12. Solow (1956, 1957); Abramowitz (1956).
13. Bush (1945).
14. Steelman (1947).
15. Blanpied (1999).
16. Department of Defense (1953); Godin (2008c).
17. Godin (2007a, 9).
18. US Congress (1950).
19. Organization for Economic Cooperation and Development (2002).
20. See Godin (2005).
21. Kuznets (1930).
22. Rossman and Sanders (1957); Sanders, Rossman, and Harris (1958).
23. Scherer et al. (1959); Schmookler (1951); Schmookler, (1954).
24. Paying little mind to S. C. Gilfillan, who used patent data to make a similar claim twenty years prior. See Stafford (1952) and Gilfillan (1935).
25. Price (1963).
26. US Congress (1968).
27. National Science Board (1973, iii).
28. Freeman and Young (1965); OECD (1968, 1971).
29. Originally entitled *Science and Technology Indicators,* it was replaced by the *Main Science and Technology Indicators* in 1998.

30. The first explicit use of the term *national innovation system* in modern political economy appears in Freeman (1987). However, Freeman later credited scholar Bengt-Ake Lundvall with coining the term *national innovation system*. See Freeman (1995).
31. Nelson (1993); Lundvall (1992); Edquist (1997).
32. Organization for Economic Cooperation and Development (1992).
33. Organization for Economic Cooperation and Development (1995, 2).
34. European Commission (1994, 1997, 2003).
35. http://thomsonreuters.com/web-of-science/.
36. Largent and Lane (2012); https://www.starmetrics.nih.gov/.
37. Gault (2013); National Research Council (US) (2012); Fealing, Lane, Marburger, and Shipp (2011); Greenhalgh and Rogers (2010); Smith (2004); Geisler (2002).

Appendix 3

1. Many countries have set a spending goal of 3% GERD per GDP, but critics dismiss this number as arbitrary.
2. Nation Science Foundation (2012a).
3. Wong (2011).
4. This database tracks R&D expenditures, as well as STEM researchers, higher education expenditures, and international trade in R&D-intensive industries. Organization for Economic Cooperation and Development (2014b) http://www.oecd.org/science/inno/msti.htm.
5. http://www.oecd.org/science/inno/msti.htm. Organization for Economic Cooperation and Development (2014b)
6. See the excellent piece on problems with rankings by Gladwell (2011).
7. For example, Organization for Economic Cooperation and Development (2013a, 2014d)
8. For a review of the debate, see Jaffe and Trajtenberg (2002); Griliches (1990); Trajtenberg (1990); Archibugi and Pianta (1996); Harhoff, Narin, Scherer, and Vopel (1999); Eaton and Kortum (1999); Jaffe, Trajtenberg, and Fogarty (2000); Hall, Jaffe, and Trajtenberg (2000); and Hall, Jaffe, and Trajtenberg (2001).
9. US Patent and Trademark Office. Designs and plant life can also be patented; however, most econometric analysis of patent data is confined to utility patents granted for inventions such as those listed earlier. For a fuller description of patents and patent laws, classifications, and the application process, see http://www.uspto.gov/main/patents.htm.
10. Scherer (1965); Schmookler (1966).
11. Summaries of which can be found in Griliches (1984); Pakes (1986); and Griliches, Hall, and Pakes (1987).
12. Hall, Jaffe, and Trajtenberg (2001).
13. Griliches (1984).
14. Trajtenberg (1990); Hall, Jaffe, and Trajtenberg (2000); Lanjouw and Shankerman (1997); Lanjouw and Shankerman (1999); Jaffe, Trajtenberg, and Fogarty (2000).
15. Amsden and Mourshed (1997).
16. McMillan and Hamilton (2000).
17. The innovative "representativeness" of journal articles is more of a problem in the social sciences, and less so in the physical sciences; see Hicks (1999).
18. Glanzel and Moed (2002); Bourke and Butler (1996); Garfield (1972).
19. Sirilli (1991); Organization for Economic Cooperation and Development (1999).
20. Yamashita (1991); Blomstrom and Wolff (1994); United Nations Conference on Trade and Development (2003).
21. See OECD (1986, 2003).
22. Specifically, Standard International Trade Classification (rev. 2) codes 54, 75, 76, 77, 87, and 792.
23. Solow (1956, 1957). For deeper discussion, see Lipsey and Carlaw (2004).
24. The Total Economy Database (TED) contains annual data for GDP, population, employment, labor productivity, total factor productivity, hours worked, labor quality, and capital services for roughly 123 countries. It was developed by the Groningen Growth and Development Centre at the University of Groningen.

25. There have been multiple attempts at regional surveys in Europe, for example, Denmark's PatVal project surveyed in Denmark, France, Germany, Great Britain, Hungary, Italy, the Netherlands, Spain, and Sweden. Its primary goal was to measure the economic value of patents across Western Europe. See Giuria et al. (2007).
26. In the United States, the NSF's Business R&D and Innovation Survey (BIRDIS) has some overlap with the CIS. See http://www.nsf.gov/statistics/srvyindustry/about/brdis/start.cfm
27. Furman, Porter, and Stern (2002).
28. Chen (2008); Zeng, Xie, and Tam (2010).
29. European Commission (2015).
30. These indicators draw from the OECD Structural Analysis Database (STAN) and use data from other existing OECD databases. STAN Indicators consist of twenty-nine measures related to international trade, industrial composition, business enterprise R&D, employment, and productivity; they highlight trends in industrial structure and performance for OECD countries and various country groups.
31. Leydesdorff and Strand (2013); Etzkowitz and Leydesdorff (2000); Etzkowitz and Leydesdorff (1997).
32. Examples include Bloomberg's *Global Innovation Index* and Booz & Company's *Global Innovation 1000* study.
33. Gladwell (2011).

REFERENCES

Aberbach, Joel D., David Dollar, and Kenneth L. Sokoloff, eds. 1994. *The Role of the State in Taiwan's Development. Armonk.* New York: ME Sharpe.

Abramitzky, Ran. 2011. "Lessons from the Kibbutz on the Equality-Incentives Trade-Off." *Journal of Economic Perspectives* 25 (1): 185–208.

Abramowitz, Moses. 1956. "Resource and Output Trends in the United States Since 1870." *American Economic Review Papers and Proceedings* 46: 5–23.

Acemoglu, Daron. 2002a. "Directed Technical Change." *Review of Economic Studies* 69: 781–809.

Acemoglu, Daron. 2002b. "Technical Change, Inequality and the Labor Market." *Journal of Economic Literature* 40 (1): 7–72.

Acemoglu, Daron. 2003. "Why Not a Political Coase Theorem? Social Conflict, Commitment, and Politics." *Journal of Comparative Economics* 31 (4): 620–652.

Acemoglu, Daron. 2009. *Introduction to Modern Economic Growth.* Princeton, NJ: Princeton University Press.

Acemoglu, Daron, Philippe Aghion, Claire Lelarge, John Van Reenen, and Fabrizio Zilibotti. 2007. "Technology, Information, and the Decentralization of the Firm." *Quarterly Journal of Economics* 122 (4): 1759–1799.

Acemoglu, Daron, and David Autor. 2012. "What Does Human Capital Do? A Review of Goldin and Katz's the Race Between Education and Technology." *Journal of Economic Literature* 50 (2): 426–463.

Acemoglu, Daron, Simon Johnson, and James Robinson. 2005. "Institutions as the Fundamental Cause of Long-Run Growth." In *The Handbook of Economic Growth*, ed. Philippe Aghion and Steve Durlauf, 365–472. Amsterdam: Elsevier.

Acemoglu, Daron, and James A. Robinson. 2000. "Political Losers as a Barrier to Economic Development." *American Economic Review* 90 (2): 126–130.

Acemoglu, Daron, and James A. Robinson. 2006. "Economic Backwardness in Political Perspective." *American Political Science Review* 100 (1): 115–131.

Acemoglu, Daron, and James A. Robinson. 2012. *Why Nations Fail: The Origins of Power, Prosperity and Poverty.* New York: Crown Publishers.

Adams, John Quincy. 1825. *First Annual Message to Congress on 6 December 1825.*

Adams, John Quincy. 1875. *Memoirs of John Quincy Adams Volume 7*, ed. Charles Francis Adams, 64–65. Philadelphia: J.B. Lippincott & Co.

Ager, Philipp, and Markus Bruckner. 2013. "Cultural Diversity and Economic Growth: Evidence from the US during the Age of Mass Migration." *European Economic Review* 64: 76–97.

Aghion, Philippe, and Peter Howitt. 1998. *Endogenous Growth Theory.* Cambridge, MA: MIT Press.

Agress, Philip. 1983. "Problems Encountered in Marketing US Medical Devices in Japan: Discussions Between Two Governments Aimed at Easing Difficulties." *Food, Drug, Cosmetic Law Journal* 38: 43–47.

Aharoni, Yair. 1998. "The Changing Political Economy of Israel." *Annals of the American Academy of Political and Social Science* 555: 127–147.

Ahlström, Göran. 1996. *Technological Development and Industrial Exhibitions, 1850-1914: Sweden in an International Perspective.* Bromley, UK: Chartwell-Bratt.

Akkermans, Dirk, Carolina Castaldi, and Bart Los. 2009. "Do 'Liberal Market Economies' Really Innovate More Radically Than 'Coordinated Market Economies'? Hall and Soskice Reconsidered." *Research Policy* 38 (1): 181–191.

Alac, Patrik. 2002. *The Bikini: A Cultural History.* New York: Parkstone Press.

Alcorta, L., and W. Peres. 1998. "Innovation Systems and Technological Specialization in Latin America and the Caribbean." *Research Policy* 26 (7–8): 857–881.

Aldridge, T. Taylor, and David Audretsch. 2011. "The Bayh-Dole Act and Scientist Entrepreneurship." *Research Policy* 40 (8): SI 1058–1067.

Alesina, Alberto, Arnaud Devleeschauwer, William Easterly, Sergio Kurlat, and Romain Wacziarg. 2003. "Fractionalization." *Journal of Economic Growth* 8: 155–194.

Alice Corporation Pty. Ltd. v. CLS Bank International, 573 US Supreme Court 2014. 13–298.

Alpert, Carl. 1982. *Technion: The Story of Israel's Institute of Technology.* New York: American Technion Society.

Amsden, Alice H. 1989. *Asia's Next Giant: South Korea and Late Industrialization.* New York: Oxford University Press.

Amsden, Alice, and Wan-wen Chu. 2003. *Beyond Late Development: Taiwan's Upgrading Policies.* Cambridge, MA: MIT Press.

Amsden, Alice H., and Mona Mourshed. 1997. "Scientific Publications, Patents and Technological Capabilities in Late Industrializing Countries." *Technology Analysis and Strategic Management* 9 (3): 343–360.

Angell, Marcia. 2004. *The Truth About the Drug Companies: How They Deceive Us and What To Do About It.* New York: Random.

Ansell, C. K. 2000. "The Networked Polity: Regional Development in Western Europe." *Governance* 13: 279–291.

Antony, Jurgen, and Thomas Grebel. 2012. "Technology Flows Between Sectors and Their Impact on Large-scale Firms." *Applied Economics* 44 (20): 2637–2651.

Aprthorpe, Raymond. 1979. "Burden of Land-Reform in Taiwan-Asian Model of Land-Reform Re-Analyzed." *World Development* 7 (4–5): 519–530.

Archibugi, Daniele, and Mario Pianta. 1996. "Measuring Technological Change Through Patents and Innovation Surveys." *Technovation* 16 (9): 451–468.

Arian, Asher. 1985. *Politics in Israel: The Second Generation.* Chatham, NJ: Chatham House.

Arian, Asher. 1995. *Security Threatened: Surveying Israeli Opinion on Peace and War.* Cambridge: Cambridge University Press.

Armstrong, Charles K. 2013. *Tyranny of the Weak: North Korea and the World, 1950-1992.* Ithaca, NY: Cornell University Press.

Arrow, Kenneth J. 1962a. "Economic Welfare and the Allocation of Resources for Invention." In *The Rate and Direction of Inventive Activity: Economic and Social Factors*, ed. Richard R. Nelson, 609–626. Princeton, NJ: Princeton University Press.

Arrow, Kenneth J. 1962b. "The Economic Implications of Learning by Doing." *Review of Economic Studies* 29 (3): 155–173.

Association for Molecular Pathology v. Myriad Genetics, 569 US Supreme Court 2013. 12–398.

Atkinson, Robert D., and Stephen J. Ezell. 2012. *Innovation Economics: The Race for Global Advantage.* New Haven, CT: Yale University Press.

Autor, David, David Dorn, and Gordon Hanson. 2013. "The China Syndrome: Local Labor Market Effects of Import Competition in the United States." *American Economic Review* 103(6): 2121–2168.

Autor, David H., Lawrence F. Katz, and Alan B. Krueger. 1998. "Computing Inequality: Have Computers Changed the Labor Market?" *Quarterly Journal of Economics* 113 (4): 1169–1213.
Autor, David H., Frank Levy, and Richard J. Murnane. 2003. "The Skill Content of Recent Technological Change: An Empirical Exploration." *Quarterly Journal of Economics* 118 (4): 1279–1333.
Ayalon, David. 1979. *Gunpowder and Firearms in the Mamluk Kingdom: A Challenge to Medieval Society*. New York: Routledge.
Bagley, Bruce Michael, and Sergio Aguayo Quezada, eds. 1993. *Mexico in Search of Security*. Coral Gables, FL: University of Miami.
Balaz, Vladimir. 2005. "Innovation Policy in the Slovak Republic." *Politicka Ekonomie* 53 (4): 513–526.
Balaz, Vladimir. 2011. "Structural Dependencies of the National Innovation Systems: Modelling Non-Linear Dynamics of Institutions with Neural Network." *Ekonomicky Casopis* 59 (1): 3–28.
Baldini, Nicola. 2008. "Negative Effects of University Patenting: Myths and Grounded Evidence." *Scientometrics* 75 (2): 289–311.
Baldwin, Robert E., Tain-Jy Chen, and Douglas Nelson. 1995. *Political Economy of U.S.-Taiwan Trade*. Ann Arbor: University of Michigan Press.
Banchoff, Thomas. 2005. "Path Dependence and Value-Driven Issues: The Comparative Politics of Stem Cell Research." *World Politics* 57: 200–230.
Barnes, Barry. 1982. "The Science-Technology Relationship: A Model and a Query." *Social Studies of Science* 12 (1): 166–172.
Barnett, Vincent. 2009. *A History of Russian Economic Thought*. New York: Routledge.
Barral, P. Etienne. 1996. *20 Years of Pharmaceutical Research Results Throughout the World: 1975–94*. Paris: Foundation Rhone-Poulenc Sante.
Barret, Alan, Adele Bergin, and David Duffy. 2006. "The Labour Market Characteristics and Labor Market Impacts of Immigrants in Ireland." *Economic and Social Review* 37 (1): 1–26.
Barro, Robert J., and Jong Wha Lee. 2010. "A New Data Set of Educational Attainment in the World, 1950–2010." NBER Working Paper, 15902. Cambridge, MA: National Bureau of Economic Research.
Bartlett, Thomas. 2010. *Ireland: A History*. Cambridge: Cambridge University Press.
Basall, George. 1988. *The Evolution of Technology*. New York: Cambridge University Press.
Bates, Robert, Avner Greif, and Smita Singh. 2002. "Organizing Violence." *Journal of Conflict Resolution* 46 (5): 599–628.
Bauer, Martin W., eds. 1995. *Resistance to New Technology: Nuclear Power, Information Technology and Biotechnology*. Cambridge: Cambridge University Press.
Baumol, William J. 1990. "Entrepreneurship: Productive, Unproductive, and Destructive." *Journal of Political Economy* 98 (5): 893–921.
Beasley, David R. 1988. *The Suppression of the Automobile: Skullduggery at the Crossroads*. New York: Greenwood Press.
Beasley, David R. 1997. *Who Really Invented the Automobile*? Buffalo, NY: Davus Publishers.
Beatty, Edward. 2001. *Institutions and Investment: The Political Basis of Industrialization in Mexico before 1911*. Stanford, CA: Stanford University Press.
Beaverstock, Jonathan V. 2002. "Transnational Elites in Global Cities: British Expatriates in Singapore's Financial District." *GeoForum* 33 (4): 525–538.
Bednyagin, Denis, and Edgard Gnansounou. 2012. "Estimating Spillover Benefits of Large R&D Projects: Application of Real Options Modelling Approach to the Case of Thermonuclear Fusion R&D Programme." *Energy Policy* 41: 269–279.
Ben-Atar, Doron, and Barbara B. Oberg, eds. 1998. *Federalists Reconsidered*. Charlottesville: University Press of Virginia.
Ben-Meir, Yehuda. 1995. *Civil-Military Relations in Israel*. New York: Columbia University Press.
Benporath, Bruno M. 1977. "Political-Economy of a Tax Reform: Israel 1975." *Journal of Public Economics* 7 (3): 285–307.

Berezow, Alex B., and Hank Campbell. 2012. *Science Left Behind: Feel-Good Fallacies and the Rise of the Anti-Scientific Left.* New York: Public Affairs.

Bergstrom, Theodore C. 1982. "On Capturing Oil Rents with a National Excise Tax." *American Economic Review* 72 (1): 194–201.

Berkman, Michael B. 2010. *Evolution, Creationism, and the Battle to Control America's Classrooms.* New York: Cambridge University Press.

Berridge, Virginia. 1996. *AIDS in the UK: The Making of Policy, 1981-1994.* New York: Oxford University Press.

Bertin, Oliver. 2001. "J.M. Smucker Gets Crusty Over Rights to Sandwich." *Globe and Mail (Canada)*, January 26, Business sec., B1.

Bessen, James. 2012. "Patent Wars Abuse the System." *The Hill—Congress Blog*, May 12. http://thehill.com/blogs/congress-blog/technology/227525-patent-wars-abuse-the-system.

Bessen, James, and Michael J. Meurer. 2008. *Patent Failure: How Judges, Bureaucrats, and Lawyers Put Innovators at Risk.* Princeton, NJ: Princeton University Press.

Bethell, Leslie. 1986. *The Cambridge History of Latin America*, Vol. 4: *c. 1870 to 1930.* New York: Cambridge University Press.

Betts, Richard K., ed. 1981. *Cruise Missiles: Technology, Strategy, Politics.* Washington, DC: Brookings Institution Press.

Bew, Paul. 2007. *Ireland: The Politics of Enmity 1789-2006.* New York: Oxford University Press.

Bielenberg, Andy. 2009. *Ireland and the Industrial Revolution: The Impact of the Industrial Revolution on Irish Industry, 1801-1922.* New York: Routledge.

Bielenberg, Andy, and Raymond Ryan. 2013. *An Economic History of Ireland Since Independence.* London: Routledge.

Bieri, David S. 2010. "Booming Bohemia? Evidence from the US High-Technology Industry." *Industry & Innovation* 17 (1): 23–49.

Bijker, Wiebe E. 1995. *Of Bicycles, Bakelites, and Bulbs: Toward a Theory of Sociotechnical Change.* Cambridge, MA: MIT Press.

Bijker, Wiebe E., Thomas P. Hughes, and Trevor Pinch. 1989. *The Social Construction of Technological Systems.* Cambridge, MA: MIT Press.

Bimber, Bruce. 1994. "Three Faces of Technological Determinism." In *Does Technology Drive History: The Dilemma of Technological Determinism*, ed. Merritt Roe Smith and Leo Marx, 79–100. Cambridge, MA: MIT Press.

Bi-National Industrial Research Foundation. 2012. "The Bird Model." http://www.birdf.com/

Birstein, Vadim J. 2002. *The Perversion of Knowledge: The True Story of Soviet Science.* Cambridge, MA: Westview Press Books.

Black, Eugene Robert, and Stanley de J. Osborne. 1963. *Report on the Supersonic Transport Program.* Washington, D.C.: US Federal Aviation Agency.

Blair, Dave (Major USAF). 2012. "Ten Thousand Feet and Ten Thousand Miles: Reconciling Our Air Force Culture to Remotely Piloted Aircraft and the New Nature of Aerial Combat." *Air & Space Power Journal*, May–June: 61–69.

Blanpied, William A. 1999. "Science and Public Policy: The Steelman Report and the Politics of Post-World War II Science Policy." In *AAAS Science and Technology Policy Yearbook*, 305–320. Washington, DC: AAAS.

Bleichmar, Daniela, ed. 2009. *Science in the Spanish and Portuguese Empires, 1500-1800.* Stanford, CA: Stanford University Press.

Blind, Knut, and Andre Jungmittag. 2004. "Foreign Direct Investment, Imports and Innovations in the Service Industry." *Review of Industrial Organization* 25 (2): 205–227.

Block, Fred, and Matthew R. Keller, eds. 2011. *State of Innovation: The U.S. Government's Role in Technology Development.* Boulder, CO: Paradigm Publishers.

Blomstrom, Magnus, and Edward N. Wolff. 1994. "Multinational Corporations and Productivity Convergence in Mexico." In *Convergence of Productivity: Cross-National Studies and Historical Evidence*, ed. William Baumol, Richard Nelson, and Ed Wolff, 263–284. New York: Oxford University Press.

Boeri, Tito, Herbert Brücker, Frédéric Docquier, and Hillel Rapoport, eds. 2012. *Brain Drain and Brain Gain: The Global Competition to Attract High-Skilled Migrants.* New York: Oxford University Press.

Boldrin, Michele, and David K. Levine. 2008. *Against Intellectual Monopoly.* New York: Cambridge University Press.

Bolt, Jutta, and Jan Luiten van Zanden. 2013. "The First Update of the Maddison Project: Re-Estimating Growth Before 1820." Maddison Project Working Paper, 4. Groningen, Netherlands: Gronigen Growth and Development Centre, University of Groningen.

Boot, Max. 2006. *War Made New: Technology, Warfare, and the Course of History, 1500 to Today.* New York: Gotham Books.

Botelho, Antonio J. J. 1995. "The Politics of Resistance to New Technology: Semiconductor Diffusion in France and Japan until 1965." In *Resistance to New Technology: Nuclear Power, Information Technology and Biotechnology,* ed. Martin Bauer, 227–254. New York: Cambridge University Press.

Botzman, Thomas J. 1999. *Technology and Competitiveness in Mexico: An Industrial Perspective.* New York: University Press of America.

Bourke, P., and Linda Butler. 1996. "Publication Types, Citation Rates, and Evaluation." *Scientometrics* 37 (3): 473–494.

Bowers, John Z., eds. 1988. *Science and Medicine in Twentieth-Century China: Research and Education.* Ann Arbor: University of Michigan Press.

Bowler, Peter J. 1989. *The Invention of Progress: The Victorians and the Past.* Cambridge, MA: B. Blackwell.

Boyce, David G. 1988. *The Revolution in Ireland, 1879-1923.* New York: Palgrave Macmillan.

Braman, Sandra. 2005. *Information Technology, National Identity and Social Cohesion: A Report of the Project on Technology Futures and Global Power, Wealth, and Conflict.* Washington, DC: CSIS Press.

Branstetter, Lee, and Nicolas Lardy. 2008. "China's Embrace of Globalization." In *China's Economic Transformation: Origins, Mechanisms, and Consequences,* ed. Loren Brandt and Thomas Rawski, 633–682. New York: Cambridge University Press.

Breen, Richard, et al. 1990. *Understanding Contemporary Ireland.* London: Macmillian.

Breschi, Stefano, and Franco Malerba, eds. 2005. *Clusters, Networks, and Innovation.* New York: Oxford University Press.

Bresnahan, Timothy, Erik Brynjolfsson, and Lorin M. Hitt. 2002. "Information Technology, Workplace Organization, and the Demand for Skilled Labor: Firm-level Evidence." *Quarterly Journal of Economics* 117 (1): 339–376.

Breznitz, Dan. 2007. *Innovation and the State: Political Choice and Strategies for Growth in Israel, Taiwan, and Ireland.* New Haven, CT: Yale University Press.

Breznitz, Dan. 2012. "Ideas, Structure, State Action and Economic Growth: Rethinking the Irish Miracle." *Review of International Political Economy* 19 (1): 87–113.

Breznitz, Dan, and Michael Murphree. 2011. *Run of the Red Queen: Government, Innovation, Globalization and Economic Growth in China.* New Haven, CT: Yale University Press.

Breznitz, Dan, and Darius Ornston. 2013. "The Revolutionary Power of Peripheral Agencies: Explaining Radical Policy Innovation in Finland and Israel." *Comparative Political Studies* 46 (10): 1219–1245.

Broberg, Gunnar, and Nils Roll-Hansen, eds. 1996. *Eugenics and the Welfare State: Sterilization Policy in Denmark, Sweden, Norway, and Finland.* East Lansing: Michigan State University Press.

Bruland, Kristine. 1995. "Patterns of Resistance to New Technologies in Scandinavia: An Historical Perspective." In *Resistance to New Technology,* ed. Martin Bauer, 125–145. New York: Cambridge University Press.

Bruno, Michael. 1992. "From Sharp Stabilization to Growth: On the Political Economy of Israel's Transition." *European Economic Review* 36 (2/3): 310–319.

Buchenau, Jürgen. 1996. *In the Shadow of the Giant: The Making of Mexico's Central America Policy, 1876-1930.* Tuscaloosa: University of Alabama Press.

Buck, Peter. 1970. *American Science and Modern China, 1876-1936*. New York: Cambridge University Press.

Bueno de Mesquita, Bruce, Alastair Smith, Randolph M. Siverson, and James D. Morrow. 2003. *The Logic of Political Survival*. Cambridge, MA: MIT Press.

Builder, Carl H. 1994. *The Icarus Syndrome: The Role of Air Power Theory in the Evolution and Fate of the U.S. Air Force*. New Brunswick, NJ: Transaction Publishers.

Bureau of Labor Statistics. 2008. *Employment Status of the Civilian Noninstitutional Population, 1940 to Date*, p. 207 (Table 586). Current Population Survey. Washington D.C.: Bureau of Census.

Burke, M. A., ed. 2006. *Monitoring the Financial Flows for Health Research 2005: Behind the Global Numbers*. Geneva, Switzerland, Global Forum for Health Research, 27–43.

Bush, Vannevar. 1945. *Science: The Endless Frontier. A Report to the President by Director of the Office of Scientific Research and Development*. Washington, DC: US Government Printing Office.

Calvert, Robert A., Arnoldo De Leon, and Gregg Cantrell. 2014. *History of Texas*. 5th ed. West Sussex, UK: John Wiley & Sons.

Camin, Hector Aguilar, and Lorenzo Mayer. 1993. *The Shadow of the Mexican Revolution: Contemporary Mexican History, 1910-1989*. Austin: University of Texas Press.

Card, David, and John E. DiNardo. 2002. "Skill-Biased Technological Change and Rising Wage Inequality: Some Problems and Puzzles." *Journal of Labor Economics* 20 (4): 733–783.

Cardwell, Donald S. L. 1972. *Turning Points in Western Technology: A Study of Technology, Science, and History*. New York: Science History Publications.

Cardwell, Donald S. L. 2001. *Wheels, Clocks, and Rockets: A History of Technology*. New York: W. W. Norton.

Carlson, W. Bernard. 2001. "The Telephone as Political Instrument: Gardiner Hubbard and the Formation of the Middle-Class in America 1875-1880." In *Technologies of Power*, ed. Michael Thad Allen and Gabrielle Hecht, 25–56. Cambridge, MA: MIT Press.

Carlsson, Bo, Zoltan J. Acs, David B. Audretsch, and Pontus Braunerhjelm. 2009. "Knowledge Creation, Entrepreneurship, and Economic Growth: A Historical Review." *Industrial and Corporate Change* 18 (6): 1193–1229.

Carnoy, Martin, Prashant Loyalka, Maria Dobryakova, Rafiq Dossani, Isak Froumin, Katherine Kuhns, Jandhyala Tilak, and Rong Wang. 2013. *University Expansion in a Changing Global Economy: Triumph of the BRICs?* Stanford, CA: Stanford University Press.

Caro, Robert A. 1974. *The Power Broker: Robert Moses and the Fall of New York*. New York: Vintage Press.

Carr, Edward Hallett. 1961. *What Is History?* New York: Vintage Press.

Cary, William L. 1974. "Federalism and Corporate Law: Reflections upon Delaware." *Yale Law Journal* 83 (4): 663–705.

Casper, Steven. 2007. *Creating Silicon Valley in Europe: Public Policy Towards New Technology Industries*. New York: Oxford University Press.

Cattell, McKeen J. 1903. "A Statistical Study of Eminent Men." *Popular Science Monthly* 62: 359–377.

Caulfield, Timothy, Tania Bubela, and C. J. Murdoch. 2007. "Myriad and the Mass Media: The Covering of a Gene Patent Controversy." *Genetics in Medicine* 9 (12): 850–855.

Center for World-Class Universities and the Institute of Higher Education of Shanghai Jiao Tong University. 2014. *Academic Ranking of World Universities Dataset*. Shanghai, China: ShanghaiRanking Consultancy.

Centers for Disease Control and Prevention. 2014. Deaths: Final Data for 2011. *National Vital Statistics Report* 63: 3.

Cerne, Matej, Marko Jaklic, and Miha Skerlavaj. 2013. "Decoupling Management and Technological Innovations: Resolving the Individualism-Collectivism Controversy." *Journal of International Management* 19 (2): 103–117.

Central Bureau of Statistics, Israel. http://www.cbs.gov.il/engindex.htm

Chai, Nobunaga. 2012 "Taiwan Foundry Growth to Reach 6.2% in 2013." *DIGITIMES Research*, October 16. http://www.digitimes.com/Reports/Report.asp.

Chase, Kenneth. 2003. *Firearms: A Global History to 1700*. New York: Cambridge University Press.

Chaudhry, Peggy. 2013. *Protecting Your Intellectual Property Rights: Understanding the Role of Management, Governments, Consumers and Pirates*. New York: Springer.

Chen, Chih-Kai. 2008. "Construct Model of the Knowledge-Based Economy Indicators." *Transformations in Business and Economics* 7 (2): 21–31.

Cheung, Tai Ming, ed. 2013. *China's Emergence as a Defense Technological Power*. London: Routledge.

Choi, E. Kwan, E. Han Kim, and Ye Sook Merrill, eds. 2003. *North Korea in the World Economy*. New York: RoutledgeCurzon.

Chriost, Diarmait Mac Giolla. 2012. "A Question of National Identity or Minority Rights? The Changing Status of the Irish Language in Ireland Since 1922." *Nations and Nationalism* 18 (3): 398–416.

Christensen, Clayton M. 1997. *The Innovator's Dilemma: When New Technologies Cause Great Firms to Fail*. Boston: Harvard Business School Press.

Chung, Chen. 1993. "Nuclear-Science Education in Taiwan, 1956-1992." *Journal of Radioanalytical and Nuclear Chemistry* 171 (1): 23–32.

Chung-Shan Institute of Science and Technology. n.d. http://www.csistdup.org.tw

Churchill, Winston. 1954. *Sir Winston Churchill: A Self-Portrait*. London: Eyre & Spottiswoode.

Cimoli, Mario, eds. 2000. *Developing Innovation Systems: Mexico in a Global Context*. New York: Continuum.

Cipolla, Carlo. 1965. *Guns and Sails in the Early Phase of European Expansion, 1400–1700*. London: Collins.

Clark, William. 2006. *Academic Charisma and the Origins of the Research University*. Chicago: University of Chicago Press.

Clotfelter, Charles T., ed. 2010. *American Universities in a Global Market*. Chicago: University of Chicago Press.

Coburn, Tom A. 2011. *The National Science Foundation: Under the Microscope*. Washington, DC: Office of Senator Tom Coburn.

Cochrane, Rexmond C. 1978. *The National Academy of Sciences: The First Hundred Years 1863-1963*. Washington, DC: National Academy of Sciences.

Cogliano, Francis D. 2014. *Emperor of Liberty: Thomas Jefferson's Foreign Policy*. New Haven, CT: Yale University Press.

Cohen, Avner. 1998. *Israel and the Bomb*. New York: Columbia University Press.

Cohen, Linda R., and Roger G. Noll. 1991. *The Technology Pork Barrel*. Washington, DC: Brookings Institution.

Cohen, Stephen S., and John Zysman. 1987. *Manufacturing Matters: The Myth of the Post-Industrial Economy*. New York: Basic Books.

Cohen, Wesley M., Richard R. Nelson, and John P. Walsh. 2002. "Links and Impacts: The Influence of Public Research on Industrial R&D." *Management Science* 48 (1): 1–23.

Cole, Arthur H., ed. 1928. *Industrial and Commercial Correspondence of Alexander Hamilton, Anticipating his Report on Manufactures*. Chicago: A. W. Shaw.

Cole, Jonathan R. 2009. *The Great American University: Its Rise to Preeminence, Its Indispensable National Role, and Why It Must Be Protected*. New York: Public Affairs.

Colville, Finlay. 2012. "NPD Solarbuss: Top-10 PV Cell Producers in 2011." *PVTECH*, January 23. www.pv-tech.org/guest_blog/npd_solarbuzz_top_10_pv_cell_producers_in_2011.

Comin, Diego, and Bart Hobijn. 2009. "Lobbies and Technology Diffusion." *Review of Economics and Statistics* 91 (2): 229–244.

Commander in Chief, U.S. Pacific Command (CINCPAC). 1975. "CINCPAC Command History for 1974." September 25, 1975, Vol. I, 163–164. Washington, DC: Department of Defense.

Congressional Budget Office. 2006. *Research and Development in the Pharmaceutical Industry*. Washington, DC: Congressional Budget Office.

Cooke, Jacob E. 1975a. "Tench Coxe, Alexander Hamilton, and the Encouragement of American Manufactures." *William and Mary Quarterly, Third Series* 32 (3): 369–392.

Cooke, Jacob E. 1975b. *Tench Coxe, American Economist: The Limitations of Economic Thought in the Early Nationalist Era*. Mansfield, PA: Pennsylvania Historical Association.

Cooke, Philip, Martin Heidenreich, and Hans-Joachim Braczyk, eds. 2004. *Regional Innovation Systems: The Role of Governance in a Globalized World*. New York: Routledge.

Cordesman, Anthony H. 2003. *Saudi Arabia Enters the Twenty-First Century: The Military and International Security Dimensions*. Westport, CT: Praeger.

Cordesman, Anthony H., and Khalid R. Al-Rodhan. 2007. *Gulf Military Forces in an Era of Asymmetric Wars*. Washington D.C.: Center for Strategic and International Studies.

Correa, Carlos M. 1998. "Argentina's National Innovation System." *International Journal of Technology Management* 15 (6–7): 721–760.

Cowan, Ruth Schwartz. 1983. *More Work for Mother: The Ironies of Household Technology from the Open Hearth to the Microwave*. New York: Basic Books.

Cowan, Ruth Schwartz. 1997. *A Social History of American Technology*. New York: Oxford University Press.

Cowhey, Peter F., Jonathan D. Aronson, and John S. Richards. 2009. "Shaping the Architecture of the US Information and Communication Technology Architecture: A Political Economic Analysis." *Review of Policy Research* 26 (1–2): 105–125.

Crackel, Theodore J. 1987. *Mr. Jefferson's Army: Political and Social Reform of the Military Establishment, 1801-1809*. New York: New York University Press.

Crackel, Theodore J. 2002. *West Point: A Bicentennial History*. Lawrence: University of Kansas Press.

Crafts, Nicholas. 2009. "Solow and Growth Accounting: A Perspective from Quantitative Economic History." *History of Political Economy* 41 (1): 200–220.

Crane, R. J. 1979. *The Politics of International Standards: France and the Color TV War*. Norwood, NJ: Alex Publishing.

Crewsdon, John. 2002. *Science Fictions: A Scientific Mystery, a Massive Coverup, and the Dark Legacy of Robert Gallo*. New York: Little, Brown, and Company.

Crosbie, Sylvia K. 1974. *A Tacit Alliance: France and Israel from Suez to the Six-Day War*. Princeton, NJ: Princeton University Press.

Crotty, Raymond D. 1986. *Ireland in Crisis*. Dover, NH: Brandon.

Cudahy, Brian J. 2006. *Box Boats: How Container Ships Changed the World*. New York: Fordham University Press.

Dahl, Robert A. 1998. *On Democracy*. New Haven, CT: Yale University Press.

Daly, Mary E. 1984. "An Irish-Ireland for Business—The Control of Manufactures Acts, 1932 and 1934." *Irish Historical Studies* 24 (94): 246–272.

Daly, Mary E. 2006. *The Slow Failure: Population Decline and Independent Ireland: 1922-1973*. Madison: University of Wisconsin Press.

Daniels, George H. 1968. *American Science in the Age of Jackson*. New York: Columbia University Press.

Davidson, Christopher. 2009. *Dubai: The Vulnerability of Success*. New York: Oxford University Press.

De Figueiredo, John M., and Brian S. Silverman. 2006. "Academic Earmarks and the Returns to Lobbying." *Journal of Law and Economics* 49 (2): 597–625.

De Figueiredo, John M., and Brian S. Silverman. 2007. "How Does the Government (Want to) Fund Science?: Politics, Lobbying, and Academic Earmarks." In *Science and the University*, ed. Paula E. Stephan and Ronald G. Ehrenberg, 36–54. Madison: University of Wisconsin Press.

De Tocqueville, Alexis. 1840. *Democracy in America*. Vol. 2, chap. IX. Paris: Librairie de Charles Gosselin.

De Tournemine, Larue R., and Emmanuel Muller. 1996. "Transition and Development of Innovation Capacities in Hungary." *R & D Management* 26 (2): 101–114.

Dear, Peter. 2001. *Revolutionizing the Sciences: European Knowledge and Its Ambitions, 1500-1700*. Princeton, NJ: Princeton University Press.

Dearing, James W. 1992. "Foreign Blood and Domestic Politics: The Issue of AIDS in Japan." In *AIDS: The Making of a Chronic Disease*, ed. E. Fee and D. M. Fox, 326–345. Berkeley: University of California Press.

Deere-Birkbeck, Carolyn. 2009. *The Implementation Game: The TRIPS Agreement and the Global Politics of Intellectual Property Reform in Developing Countries*. New York: Oxford University Press.

Delios, Andrew, and Witold J. Henisz. 2000. "Japanese Firms' Investment Strategies in Emerging Economies." *Academy of Management Journal* 43 (3): 305–323.

DeNardis, Laura, ed. 2011. *Opening Standards: The Global Politics of Interoperability*. Cambridge, MA: MIT Press.

Denison, Edward F. 1962. *The Sources of Economic Growth in the United States and the Alternatives Before Us*. New York: Committee for Economic Development.

Denison, Edward F. 1967. *Why Growth Rates Differ*. Washington, DC: Brookings Institution.

Department of Defense, Office of the Secretary of Defense (R&D). 1953. *The Growth of Scientific R&D*. RDB 114/34, Washington, DC.

DeRouen, Karl Jr. 2000. "The Guns-Growth Relationship in Israel." *Journal of Peace Research* 37 (1): 69–83.

Desch, Michael C. 2008. *Power and Military Effectiveness: The Fallacy of Democratic Triumphalism*. Baltimore: Johns Hopkins University Press.

DiMasi, Joseph A., Ronald W. Hansen, and Henry G. Grabowski. 2003. "The Price of Innovation: New Estimates of Drug Development Costs." *Journal of Health Economics* 22: 151–185.

DiMasi, Joseph A., Ronald Hansen, Henry Grabowski, and Louis Lasagna. 1991. "Cost of Innovation in the Pharmaceutical Industry." *Journal of Health Economics* 10: 107–142.

Domar, Evsey. 1946. "Capital Expansion, Rate of Growth, and Employment." *Econometrica* 14 (2): 137–147.

Domar, Evsey. 1947. "Expansion and Employment." *American Economic Review* 37: 34–55.

Dombrowski, Peter, and Eugene Gholz. 2006. *Buying Military Transformation: Technological Innovation and the Defense Industry*. New York: Columbia University Press.

Doner, Richard F. 2009. *The Politics of Uneven Development*. New York: Cambridge University Press.

Doner, Richard F., Allen Hicken, and Bryan K. Ritchie. 2009. "Political Challenges of Innovation in the Developing World." *Review of Policy Research* 26 (1–2): 151–171.

Doner, Richard F., Bryan K. Ritchie, and Dan Slater. 2005. "Systemic Vulnerability and the Origins of Developmental States: Northeast and Southeast Asia in Comparative Perspective." *International Organization* 59 (2): 327–361.

Dore, Ronald. 1987 *Taking Japan Seriously: A Confucian Perspective on Leading Economic Issues*. Stanford, CA: Stanford University Press.

Dore, Ronald Philip, and Mari Sako. 1989. *How the Japanese Learn to Work*. New York: Routledge.

Douglas, S. J. 1985. "Technological Innovation and Organizational Change: The Navy's Adoption of Radio, 1899-1919." In *Military Enterprise and Technological Change*, ed. M. R. Smith, 117–173. Cambridge, MA: MIT Press.

Dredge, Stuart, and Charles Arthur. 2011. "Angry Birds Maker Rovio Sued by Lodsys as US Software Patents Multiply." *The Guardian*, July 22.

Dreher, Axel. 2013. *KOF Globalization Index*. Zurich, Switzerland: Swiss Federal Institute of Technology. http://globalization.kof.ethz.ch/.

Drezner, Daniel. 2001. "State Structure, Technological Leadership and the Maintenance of Hegemony." *Review of International Studies* 27 (1): 3–25.

Drucker, Donna J. 2014. *The Machines of Sex Research: Technology and the Politics of Identity, 1945-1985*. New York: Springer.

Dublin Opinion. 1941. "The Substitutes Research Branch of the Department of Supplies." Reprinted in *The Building of the State: Science and Engineering with Government on Merrion Street*, 2011, ed. Clara Cullen and Orla Freely, 32. Dublin, Ireland: University College Dublin.

Dudley, Leonard M. 1991. *The Word and the Sword: How Techniques of Information and Violence Have Shaped Our World.* Cambridge, MA: Blackwell.

Duffy, Robert. J. 1997. *Nuclear Politics in America: A History and Theory of Government Regulation.* Lawrence: University Press of Kansas.

Dupree, A. Hunter. 1964. *Science in the Federal Government: A History of Policies and Activities to 1940.* Baltimore: Johns Hopkins University Press.

Duranton, Gilles, Philippe Martin, Thierry Mayer, and Florian Mayneris. 2010. *The Economics of Clusters: Lessons from the French Experience.* New York: Oxford University Press.

Dutfield, Graham, and Uma Suthersanen. 2008. *Global Intellectual Property Law.* Northampton, MA: Edward Elgar Publishing.

Duus, Peter. 1998. *Modern Japan.* Boston: Houghton Mifflin.

Easterly, William, and Fischer, Stanley, 1995. "The Soviet Economic Decline." *World Bank Economic Review* 9 (3): 341–371.

Eaton, Jonathan, and Samuel Kortum. 1999. "International Technology Diffusion: Theory and Measurement." *International Economic Review* 40 (3): 537–570.

The Economist. 1952. "The Germany Economy—Divided It Stands." October 18.

The Economist. 1966. "The German Lesson." October 15.

The Economist. 1988. "The Soviet Economy: Survey." April 9.

The Economist. 1989a. "Hard at Work." March 18.

The Economist. 1989b. "The Soviet Economy: The Hard Road to Capitalism." November 18.

The Economist. 1990a. "Survey: Perestroika." April 28.

The Economist. 1990b. "The Soviet Union: Survey." October 20.

Edelman, Susan A. 1991. "The American Supersonic Transport." In *The Technology Pork Barrel,* ed. Linda R. Cohen and Roger G. Noll, 97–148. Washington, DC: Brookings.

Edgerton, D. E. H., and S. M. Horrocks. 1994. "British Industrial Research and Development Before 1945." *Economic History Review* 47 (2): 213–238.

Edquist, Charles. 1997. *Systems of Innovation: Technologies, Institutions and Organizations.* London: Pinter.

Edquist, Charles, and Leif Hommen. 2008. *Small Country Innovation Systems—Globalization, Change and Policy in Asia and Europe.* Northampton, MA: Edward Elgar.

Edwards, Paul. 1996. *The Closed World: Computers and the Politics of Discourse in Cold War America.* Cambridge, MA: MIT Press.

Ehrenberg, Ronald G., et al. 2007. "Who Bears the Growing Cost of Science at Universities?" In *Science and the University,* ed. Paula E. Stephan and Ronald G. Ehrenberg, 19–35. Madison: University of Wisconsin Press.

Eichengreen, Barry, Dwight H. Perkins, and Kwanho Shin. 2012. *From Miracle to Maturity: The Growth of the Korean Economy.* Cambridge, MA: Harvard University Press.

Eisendrath, Craig R., Melvin Allan Goodman, and Gerald E. Marsh. 2001. *The Phantom Defense: America's Pursuit of the Star Wars Illusion.* Westport, CT: Praeger.

Eisingerich, Andreas, Oliver Falck, Stephan Heblich, and Tobias Kretschmer. 2012. "Firm Innovativeness Across Cluster Types." *Industry and Innovation* 19 (3): SI 233–248.

Elbaum, Bernard, and William Lazonick, eds. 1986. *The Decline of the British Economy.* Oxford, UK: Clarendon Press.

Elkins, Stanley, and Eric McKitrick. 1993. *The Age of Federalism: The Early American Republic, 1788-1800.* New York: Oxford University Press.

Engel, Gregory A. 1994. "Cruise Missiles and the Tomahawk." In *The Politics of Naval Innovation,* ed. Bradd C. Hayes and Douglas V. Smith, 16–39. Newport, RI: US Naval War College.

Engell, James. 1981. *The Creative Imagination: Enlightenment to Romanticism.* Cambridge, MA: Harvard University Press.

Epstein, Steven. 1996. *Impure Science: AIDS, Activism, and the Politics of Knowledge.* Berkeley: University of California Press.

Espinoza, Raphael. 2012. *Factor Accumulation and the Determinants of TFP in the GCC.* Oxford, UK: University of Oxford, Oxford Centre for the Analysis of Resource Rich Economies.

Espoirs et Conquetes 1881-1918. Paris, France: l'Association pour l'histoire de l'electricite en France.

Etzkowitz, Henry, and Loet Leydesdorff. 1997. *Universities and the Global Knowledge Economy: A Triple Helix of University-Industry-Government Relations*. New York: Pinter.

Etzkowitz, Henry, and Loet Leydesdorff. 1998. "The Endless Transition: A 'Triple Helix' of University-Industry-Government." *Minerva* 36: 203–208.

Etzkowitz, Henry, and Loet Leydesdorff. 2000. "The Dynamics of Innovation: From National Systems and 'Mode 2' to a Triple Helix of University-Industry-Government Relations." *Research Policy* 29 (2): 109–123.

European Commission. 1994. *First European Report on Science & Technology Indicators 1994*. Brussels, Belgium: European Commission.

European Commission. 1997. *Second European Report on Science & Technology Indicators 1997*. Brussels, Belgium: European Commission

European Commission. 2003. *Third European Report on Science & Technology Indicators 2003*. Brussels, Belgium: European Commission

European Commission. 2015. *Innovation Union Scoreboard*. Brussels, Belgium: European Commission

Evans, Peter. 1995. *Embedded Autonomy: States and Industrial Transformation*. Princeton, NJ: Princeton University Press.

Ezell, Stephen. 2011. "Fighting Innovation Mercantilism." *Issues in Science and Technology*, 27 (2): 83–90.

Fabricant, Solomon. 1954. *Economic Progress and Economic Change, NBER 34th Annual Report*. New York: National Bureau of Economic Research.

Farrell, Diana, Martha Laboissière, Jaeson Rosenfeld, Sascha Stürze, and Fusayo Umezawa. 2005. *The Emerging Global Labor Market: Part II—The Supply of Offshore Talent in Services*. New York: McKinsey Global Institute.

Farzin, Yeganeh Hossein. 1996. "Optimal Pricing of Environmental and Natural Resource Use with Stock Externalities." *Journal of Public Economics* 62 (1–2): 31–57.

Fealing, Kaye Husbands, Julia I. Lane, John H. Marburger III, and Stephanie S. Shipp, eds. 2011. *The Science of Science Policy: A Handbook*. Stanford, CA: Stanford University Press.

Feenstra, Robert C., and Gary G. Hamilton. 2006. *Emergent Economies, Divergent Paths: Economic Organization and International Trade in South Korea and Taiwan*. New York: Cambridge University Press.

Feenstra, Robert C., Robert Inklaar, and Marcel P. Timmer. 2015. "The Next Generation of the Penn World Table." *American Economic Review* 105 (10): 3150–3182.

Feenstra, Robert C., Robert E. Lipsey, Haiyan Deng, Alyson C. Ma, and Hengyong Mo. 2005. "World Trade Flows: 1962-2000." Working Paper, 11040. Cambridge, MA: National Bureau of Economic Research.

Feldman, E. A. 1999. "HIV and Blood in Japan: Transforming Private Conflict." In *Blood Feuds: AIDS, Blood, and the Politics of Medical Disaster*, ed. E. A. Feldman and R. Bayer, 59–94. New York: Oxford University Press.

Feldman, E. A. 2000. "Blood Justice: Courts, Conflict, and Compensation in Japan, France, and the United States." *Law and Society Review* 34: 651–701.

Feldman, E. A., and R. Bayer, eds. 1999. *Blood Feuds: AIDS, Blood, and the Politics of Medical Disaster*. New York: Oxford University Press.

Feldman, E. A., and S. Yonemoto. 1992. "Japan: AIDS as a 'Non-Issue.'" In *AIDS in the Industrialized Democracies. Passions, Politics and Policies*, ed. D. L. Kirp and R. Bayer, 339–360. New Brunswick, NJ: Rutgers University Press.

Feldman, Eric A., and Ronald Bayer, eds. 1995. *Blood Feuds: AIDS, Blood, and the Politics of Medical Disaster*. New York: Oxford University Press.

Ferguson, Charles H. 1987. *The Competitive Decline of the U.S. Semiconductor Industry*. Cambridge, MA: Microsystems Research Center, Massachusetts Institute of Technology.

Flapan, Simha. 1987. *The Birth of Israel: Myths and Realities*. New York: Pantheon Books.

Fleming, James R. 1998. *Historical Perspectives on Climate Change*. New York: Oxford University Press.

Florida, Richard. 2002. *The Rise of the Creative Class: And How It's Transforming Work, Leisure, Community and Everyday Life.* New York: Basic Books.

Florida, Richard L. 2005. *Cities and the Creative Class.* New York: Routledge.

Florida, Richard L. 2012. *The Rise of the Creative Class—Revisited.* New York: Basic Books.

Fogel, Robert W. 1964. *Railroads and American Economic Growth: Essays in Economic History.* Baltimore: Johns Hopkins University Press.

Foreshew, Jennifer. 2001. "Fight over Priceline Patent." *The Australian,* September 11, Features section.

Fortes, Jacqueline, and Larissa Adler Lomnitz. 1994. *Becoming a Scientist in Mexico.* University Park: Pennsylvania State University Press.

Foster, Lynn V. 2007. *Mexico: A Brief History.* New York: Checkmark Books.

Fox, Robert, and Anna Guagnini. 1999. *Laboratories, Workshops, and Sites: Concepts and Practices of Research in Industrial Europe, 1800-1914.* Berkeley: University of California, Berkeley Press.

Frank, Hayes. 2007. "Grokking SCO's Demise." *Computerworld* 41 (34): 56.

Franklin, Marianne. 2013. *Digital Dilemmas: Power, Resistance, and the Internet.* New York: Oxford University Press.

Freedom House. 2014. *Freedom in the World Index.* Washington, DC: Freedom House.

Freeman, Christopher. 1987. *Technology Policy and Economic Performance: Lessons from Japan.* London: Pinter.

Freeman, Christopher. 1995. "The 'National System of Innovation' in Historical Perspective." *Cambridge Journal of Economics* 19: 5–24.

Freeman, Christopher, and A. Young. 1965. *The Research and Development Effort in Western Europe, North America and the Soviet Union—An Experimental International Comparison of Research Expenditures and Manpower in 1962.* Paris: OECD.

Freiberger, Paul, and Michael Swaine. 2000. *Fire in the Valley: The Making of the Personal Computer.* New York: McGraw-Hill.

Frenkel, Amnon, Daniel Shefer, and Stephen Roper. 2003. "Public Policy, Locational Choice and the Innovation Capability of High-Tech Firms: A Comparison Between Israel and Ireland." *Papers in Regional Science* 82: 203–221.

Frenken, Koen, Elena Cefis, and Erik Stam. 2011. "Industrial Dynamics and Economic Geography: A Survey." Working Paper no. 11.07. Eindhoven, Netherlands: Eindhoven Centre for Innovation Studies, Eindhoven University of Technology.

Friedel, Robert D. 2007. *A Culture of Improvement: Technology and the Western Millennium.* Cambridge, MA: MIT Press.

Friedman, Norman. 1991. *Desert Victory—The War for Kuwait.* Annapolis, MD: Naval Institute Press.

Fuchs, Erica. 2010. "Rethinking the Role of the State in Technology Development: DARPA and the Case for Embedded Network Governance." *Research Policy* 39: 1133–1147.

Funk, Jeffrey L. 1992. *The Teamwork Advantage: An Inside Look at Japanese Product and Technology Development.* Cambridge, MA: Productivity Press.

Furman, Jeffrey L., Michael E. Porter, and Scott Stern. 2002. "The Determinants of National Innovative Capacity." *Research Policy* 31 (6): 899–933.

Gainous, Jason, and Kevin M. Wagner. 2014. *Tweeting to Power: The Social Media Revolution in American Politics.* New York: Oxford University Press.

Galbraith, James K. 2009. "Inequality, Unemployment and Growth: New Measures for Old Controversies." *Journal of Economic Inequality* 7: 189–206.

Gallagher, Kevin, and Lyuba Zarsky. 2007. *The Enclave Economy: Foreign Investment and Sustainable Development in Mexico's Silicon Valley.* Cambridge, MA: MIT Press.

Gallo, Robert C. 1991. *Virus Hunting: AIDS, Cancer, and the Human Retrovirus: A Story of Scientific Discovery.* New York: Basic Books.

Galton, Francis. 1869. *Hereditary Genius: An Inquiry into Its Laws and Consequences.* London: Macmillan.

Galton, Francis. 1874. *English Men of Science: Their Nature and Nurture.* London: Macmillan.

Gamboa, Gonzalo, and Giuseppe Munda. 2007. "The Problem of Windfarm Location: A Social Multi-criteria Evaluation Framework." *Energy Policy* 35: 1564–1583.

Gandal, Neil, Gordon H. Hanson, and Matthew J. Slaughter. 2004. "Technology, Trade, and Adjustment to Immigration in Israel." *European Economic Review* 48 (2): 403–428.

Garfield, Eugene. 1972. *Citation Indexing: Its Theory and Application in Science, Technology, and Humanities*. New York: John Wiley & Sons.

Garfinkle, Adam. 2000. *Politics and Society in Modern Israel*. Armonk, NY: M. E. Sharpe.

Garner, Paul. 2001. *Porfirio Diaz*. New York: Longman Press.

Garver, John W. 1997. *The Sino-American Alliance: Nationalist China and American Cold War Strategy in Asia*. Armonk, NY: M. E. Sharpe.

Gault, Fred, ed. 2013. *Handbook of Innovation Indicators and Measurement*. Cheltenham, UK: Edward Elgar Publishing.

Geiger, Roger L. 1995. *To Advance Knowledge: The Growth of American Research Universities, 1900-1940*. New York: Oxford University Press.

Geisler, Eliezer. 2002. "The Metrics of Technology Evaluation: Where We Stand and Where We Should Go From Here." *International Journal of Technology Management* 24 (4): 341–374.

Gereff, Gary, Vivek Wadhwa, Ben Rissing, and Ryan Ong. 2008. "Getting the Numbers Right: International Engineering Education in the United States, China, and India." *Journal of Engineering Education* 97 (1): 13–25.

Gerschenkron, Alexander. 1962. *Economic Backwardness in Historical Perspective: A Book of Essays*. Cambridge, MA: Belknap Press of Harvard University Press.

Gibbons, Michael. 1994. *The New Production of Knowledge: The Dynamics of Science and Research in Contemporary Societies*. Thousand Oaks, CA: Sage.

Gibson, Andrew, and Arthur Donovan. 2001. *The Abandoned Ocean: A History of United States Maritime Policy*. Columbia: University of South Carolina Press.

Gilfillan, S. C. 1935. "The Decline of the Patenting Rate, and Recommendations." *Journal of the Patent Office Society* 17: 216–227.

Gilpin, Robert. 1981. *War and Change in World Politics*. New York: Cambridge University Press.

Gilroy, Lindsey, and Tammy D'Amato. 2009. "How Many Patents Does It Take to Build an iPhone?" *Intellectual Property Today*. http://www.iptoday.com/issues/2009/11/articles/how-many-patents-take-build-iPhone.asp.

Ginarte, Juan C., and Walter G. Park. 1997. "Determinants of Patent Rights: A Cross-National Study." *Research Policy* 26 (3): 283–301.

Giuria, Paola, et al. 2007. "Inventors and Invention Processes in Europe: Results from the PatVal-EU survey." *Research Policy* 36 (8): 1107–1127.

Gladwell, Malcolm. 2011. "The Order of Things: What College Rankings Really Tell Us." *The New Yorker*, February 14. http://www.newyorker.com/reporting/2011/02/14/110214fa_fact_gladwell.

Glanzel, Wolfgang, and Henk Moed. 2002. "State-of-the-Art Report: Journal Impact Measures in Bibiliometric Research." *Scientometrics* 53 (2): 171–193.

Godin, Benoit. 2005. *Measurement and Statistics on Science and Technology: 1920 to the Present*. New York: Routledge.

Godin, Benoit. 2006a. "On the Origins of Bibliometrics." *Scientometrics* 68(1): 109–133.

Godin, Benoit. 2006b. "The Knowledge Based Economy: Conceptual Framework or Buzzword?" *Journal of Technology Transfer* 31 (1): 17–30.

Godin, Benoit. 2007a. "What Is Science? Defining Science by the Numbers 1920–2000." Working Paper, 35. Project on the History of Sociology of S&T Statistics. Montreal, Canada.

Godin, Benoit. 2007b. "From Eugenics to Scientometrics: Galton, Cattell and Men of Science." *Social Studies of Science* 37 (5): 691–728.

Godin, Benoit. 2008a. "Innovation: The History of a Category." Working Paper, 1. Project on the Intellectual History of Innovation. Montreal, Canada: INRS.

Godin, Benoit. 2008b. "In the Shadow of Schumpeter: W. Rupert Maclaurin and the Study of Technological Innovation." *Minerva* 46 (3): 343–360.

Godin, Benoit. 2008c. “The Making of Statistical Standards: The OECD and the Frascati Manual, 1962–2002.” Working Paper, 39. Project on the History and Sociology of STI Statistics. Montreal, Canada.

Godin, Benoit. 2008d. “The Information Economy: The History of a Concept Through Its Measurement, 1949–2005.” *History and Technology* 24 (3): 255–287.

Godin, Benoit. 2009a. “National Innovation System: The System Approach.” *Historical Perspective, Science, Technology and Human Values* 34 (4): 476–501.

Godin, Benoit. 2009b. “The Culture of Numbers: The Origins and Development of Statistics on Science.” Working Paper, 40. Project on the History and Sociology of STI Statistics. Montreal, Canada.

Godin, Benoit. 2015. *Innovation Contested—The Idea of Innovation Over the Centuries.* London: Routledge.

Goeren, Erkan. 2014. “How Ethnic Diversity Affects Economic Growth.” *World Development* 59: 275–297.

Gold, Thomas B. 1986. *State and Society in the Taiwan Miracle.* Armonk, NY: M. E. Sharpe.

Goldin, Claudia Dale, and Lawrence F. Katz. 2008. *The Race Between Education and Technology.* Cambridge, MA: Belknap Press of Harvard University Press.

Goldstein, Steven M. 1997. *Taiwan Faces the Twenty-First Century: Continuing the “Miracle.”* New York: Foreign Policy Association.

Gonzales, Michael J. 2002. *The Mexican Revolution 1910-1940.* Albuquerque: University of New Mexico.

Goodman, David J., and Robert A. Myers. 2005. “3G Cellular Standards and Patents.” *IEEE WirelessCom*, June 13. http://eeweb.poly.edu/dgoodman/wirelesscom2005.pdf.

Goozner, Merill. 2004. *The $800 Million Pill: The Truth Behind the Cost of New Drugs.* Berkeley: University of California Press.

Gopinathan, S. 2007. “Globalisation, the Singapore Developmental State, and Education Policy: A Thesis Revisited.” *Globalisation, Societies and Education* 5 (1): 53–70.

Gordon, H. Hanson. 2010. “Why Isn’t Mexico Rich?” *Journal of Economic Literature* 48 (4): 987–1004.

Gordon, Linda. 1976, 1990. *Woman’s Body, Woman’s Right: A Social History of Birth Control in America.* London: Penguin Press.

Gorman, Mel. 1977. “Electric Illumination in Franco-Prussian War.” *Social Studies of Science* 7 (4): 525–529.

Goyal, Sanjeev. 2007. *Connections: An Introduction to the Economics of Networks.* Princeton, NJ: Princeton University Press.

Grad, Burton. 2002. “A Personal Recollection: IBM’s Unbundling of Software and Services.” *IEEE Annals of the History of Computing* 24 (1): 64–71.

Graham, Colin. 2001. *Deconstructing Ireland: Identity, Theory, Culture.* Edinburgh: Edinburgh University Press.

Graham, Loren R. 1993. *Science in Russia and the Soviet Union: A Short History.* New York: Cambridge University Press.

Granovetter, Mark S. 1973. “The Strength of Weak Ties.” *American Journal of Sociology* 78: 1360–1380.

Granovetter, Mark S. 1995. *Getting a Job: A Study of Contacts and Careers.* Chicago: University of Chicago Press.

Greenberg, Amy S. 2012. *A Wicked War: Polk, Clay, Lincoln, and the 1846 U.S. Invasion of Mexico.* New York: Alfred A. Knopf.

Greene, J. Megan. 2008. *The Origins of the Developmental State in Taiwan: Science Policy and the Quest for Modernization.* Cambridge, MA: Harvard University Press.

Greene, John C. 1984. *American Science in the Age of Jefferson.* Ames: Iowa State University Press.

Greene, Kevin. 2000. “Technological Innovation and Economic Progress in the Ancient World: M.I. Finely Re-Considered.” *Economic History Review* 53 (1): 29–59.

Greenhalgh, Christine, and Mark Rogers. 2010. *Innovation, Intellectual Property, and Economic Growth.* Princeton, NJ: Princeton University Press.

Greenstein, Shane, and Victor Stango, eds. 2006. *Standards and Public Policy.* Cambridge, MA: Cambridge University Press.

Greif, Avner. 1994. "Cultural Beliefs and the Organization of Society—A Historical and Theoretical Reflection on Collectivist and Individualist Societies." *Journal of Political Economy* 102 (5): 912–950.

Grieco, Joseph, Cindy Cheng, and Ana Guzman. 2014. "International Conflict and National Technological Innovation." Paper presented at the Annual Meeting of the International Studies Association, March 26. Toronto, Canada.

Griliches, Zvi. 1957. "Hybrid Corn: An Exploration in the Economics of Technological Change." *Econometrica* 25 (4): 501–522.

Griliches, Zvi. 1958. "Research Costs and Social Returns: Hybrid Corn and Related Innovations." *Journal of Political Economy* 66 (5): 419–431.

Griliches, Zvi. 1960. "Hybrid Corn and the Economics of Innovation." *Science* 132 (3422): 275–280.

Griliches, Zvi, ed. 1984. *R&D, Patents, and Productivity*. Chicago: University of Chicago Press.

Griliches, Zvi. 1989. "Patents: Recent Trends and Puzzles." *Brookings Papers on Economic Activity* SI 291–330.

Griliches, Zvi. 1990. "Patents Statistics as Economic Indicators: A Survey." *Journal of Economic Literature* 28 (4): 1661–1707.

Griliches, Zvi. 1996. "The Discovery of the Residual: A Historical Note." *Journal of Economic Literature* 34: 1324–1330.

Griliches, Zvi, Bronwyn H. Hall, and Ariel Pakes. 1987. "The Value of Patents as Indicators of Inventive Activity." In *Economic Policy and Technological Performance,* ed. Partha Dasgupta and Paul Stoneman, 68–103. New York: Cambridge University Press.

Grimes, Seamus. 1992. "Ireland: The Challenge of Development in the European Periphery." *Geography* 77 (334): 22–32.

Grmek, Mirko D. 1990. *History of AIDS: Emergence and Origin of a Modern Pandemic.* Princeton, NJ: Princeton University Press.

Groh, Peter, Heinrich von Liechtenstein, and Karsten Lieser. 2010. "The European Venture Capital and Private Equity Country Attractiveness Indices." *Journal of Corporate Finance* 16 (2): 205–224.

Grossman, Gene A., and Edwin L. C. Lai. 2004. "International Protection of Intellectual Property." *American Economic Review* 94 (5): 1635–1653.

Guiomard, Cathal. 1995. *The Irish Disease and How to Cure It: Common-Sense Economics for a Competitive World.* Dublin: Oak Tree.

Guiso, Luigi, Paola Sapienza, and Luigi Zingales. 2006. "Does Culture Affect Economic Outcomes?" *Journal of Economic Perspectives* 20 (2): 23–48.

Guston, David H. 2000. *Between Politics and Science: Assuring the Integrity and Productivity of Research.* New York: Cambridge University Press.

Ha, Songho. 2009. *The Rise and Fall of the American System: Nationalism and the Development of the American Economy, 1790-1837.* London: Pickering & Chatto.

Haber, Stephen H. 1989. *Industry and Underdevelopment: The Industrialization of Mexico 1890-1940.* Stanford, CA: Stanford University Press.

Haggard, Stephan. 1990. *Pathways from the Periphery: The Politics of Growth in the Newly Industrializing Countries.* Ithaca, NY: Cornell University Press.

Haggard, Stephan, and Robert R. Kaufman, eds. 1992. *The Politics of Economic Adjustment: International Constraints, Distributive Conflicts, and the State.* Princeton, NJ: Princeton University Press.

Hahn, Robert, and Caroline Cecot. 2009. "The Benefits and Costs of Ethanol: An Evaluation of the Government's Analysis." *Journal of Regulatory Economics* 35: 275–295.

Halevi, Nadav, and Ruth Klinov-Malul. 1968. *The Economic Development of Israel.* New York: Praeger.

Hall, Bronwyn H., and Dietmar Harhoff. 2012. "Recent Research on the Economics of Patents." *Annual Review of Economics* 4 (1): 541–565.

Hall, Bronwyn H., Adam Jaffe, and Manuel Trajtenberg. 2000. "Market Value and Patent Citations: A First Look." Working Paper, 7741. Cambridge, MA: National Bureau of Economic Research.

Hall, Bronwyn H., Adam Jaffe, and Manuel Trajtenberg. 2001. "The NBER Patent Citations Data File: Lessons, Insights, and Methodological Tools." Working Paper, 8498. Cambridge, MA: National Bureau of Economic Research.

Hall, Peter A., and David Soskice. 2001. *Varieties of Capitalism: The Institutional Foundations of Comparative Advantage.* New York: Oxford University Press.

Hall, Robert E., and Charles I. Jones. 1999. "Why Do Some Countries Produce So Much More Output Per Worker Than Others?" *Quarterly Journal of Economics* 114 (1): 83–116.

Hall, Robert E., and Marc Lieberman. 2013. *Economics: Principles & Applications.* Mason, OH: South-Western, Cengage Learning.

Hamilton, Alexander. 1791. *Report of the Secretary of the Treasury [Alexander Hamilton] of the United States on the Subject of Manufactures Presented to the House of Representatives December 5, 1791.*

Hampden-Turner, Charles. 2009. *Teaching Innovation and Entrepreneurship: Building on the Singapore Experiment.* New York: Cambridge University Press.

Handel, Michael I. 1973. "Israel's Political-Military Doctrine." Occasional Papers in International Affairs, 30. Cambridge, MA: Harvard University Center for International Affairs.

Hanieh, Adam 2003. "From State-Led Growth to Globalization: The Evolution of Israeli Capitalism." *Journal of Palestine Studies* 32 (4): 5–21.

Hansen, Roger. 1971. *The Politics of Mexican Development.* Baltimore: John Hopkins University Press.

Hanson, Philip. 2003. *The Rise and Fall of the Soviet Economy: An Economic History of the USSR from 1945.* New York: Longman.

Hanushek, Eric A., and Ludger Woessmann. 2012. "Do Better Schools Lead to More Growth? Cognitive Skills, Economic Outcomes, and Causation." *Journal of Economic Growth* 17: 267–321.

Hargadon, Andrew. 2003. *How Breakthroughs Happen: The Surprising Truth About How Companies Innovate.* Cambridge, MA: Harvard Business Review Press.

Harhoff, Dietmar, Francis Narin, F. M. Scherer, and Katrin Vopel. 1999. "Citation Frequency and the Value of Patented Inventories." *Review of Economics and Statistics* 81 (3): 511–515.

Harrison, Carol E., and Ann Johnson, eds. 2009. *National Identity: The Role of Science and Technology.* Chicago: University of Chicago Press.

Harrison, Lawrence, and S. P. Huntington, eds. 2000. *Culture Matters: How Values Shape Human Progress.* New York: Basic Books.

Harrod, Roy F. 1939. "An Essay in Dynamic Theory." *Economic Journal* 49 (193): 14–33.

Hartung, William. 2011. *Prophets of War: Lockheed Martin and the Making of the Military-Industrial Complex.* Philadelphia: Nation Books.

Hayek, Friedrich A. 1945. "The Use of Knowledge in Society." *American Economic Review* 35 (4): 519–530.

Hayes, Louis D. 2009. *Introduction to Japanese Politics.* Armonk, NY: M. E. Sharpe.

Hayward, J. 1973. *The One and Indivisible French Republic.* New York: W. W. Norton.

Hecht, Gabrielle. 2009. *The Radiance of France: Nuclear Power and National Identity After World War II.* Cambridge, MA: MIT Press.

Held, David. 2006. *Models of Democracy*. Stanford, CA: Stanford University Press.

Henderson, Timothy J. 2007. *A Glorious Defeat: Mexico and Its War with the United States.* New York: Hill and Wang.

Henderson, Timothy J. 2009. *The Mexican Wars for Independence.* New York: Hill and Wang.

Henisz, Witold J. 2000. "The Institutional Environment for Economic Growth." *Economics and Politics* 12 (1): 1–31.

Henisz, Witold J. 2002a. *Politics and International Investment: Measuring Risks and Protecting Profits.* Northampton, MA: Edward Elgar.

Henisz, Witold J. 2002b. "The Institutional Environment for Infrastructure Investment." *Industrial and Corporate Change* 11 (2): 355–389.

Henisz, Witold J., and Bennet A. Zelner. 2001. "The Institutional Environment for Telecommunications Investment." *Journal of Economics and Management Strategy* 10 (1): 123–147.

Henrekson, M. 2005. "Entrepreneurship: A Weak Link in the Welfare State?" *Industrial and Corporate Change* 14 (3): 437–467.

Henry, Joseph. 1838. "Letter to Alexander Dallas Bache," sent from Princeton, NJ, on August 9.

Heo, Uk, and Terence Roehrig. 2014. *South Korea's Rise: Economic Development, Power, and Foreign Relations.* Cambridge: Cambridge University Press.

Herken, Gregg. 1985. *Counsels of War.* New York: Oxford University Press.

Herrera, Geoffrey L. 2006. *Technology and International Transformation: The Railroad, the Atom Bomb, and the Politics of Technological Change.* Albany: State University of New York Press.

Herrerias, M. J., and Vincente Orts. 2013. "Capital Goods Imports and Long-Run Growth: Is the Chinese Experience Relevant to Developing Countries?" *Journal of Policy Modeling* 35 (5): 781–797.

Herring, George C. 2008. *From Colony to Superpower: U.S. Foreign Relations Since 1776.* New York: Oxford University Press.

Hicks, Dana. 1999. "The Difficulty of Achieving Full Coverage of International Social Science Literature and the Bibliometric Consequences." *Scientometrics* 44 (2): 193–215

Hicks, John R. 1932. *The Theory of Wages.* London: Macmillan.

Hilberg, Raul. 2003. *The Destruction of the European Jews.* New Haven, CT: Yale University Press.

Hirschman, Albert O. 1958. *The Strategy of Economic Development.* New Haven, CT: Yale University Press.

Hitchcock, William I. 1998. *France Restored: Cold War Diplomacy and the Quest for Leadership in Europe, 1944-1954.* Chapel Hill: University of North Carolina Press.

Hodge, Trevor. 1990. "A Roman Factory." *Scientific American* 263 (5): 106–111.

Hoel, Michael, and Snorre Kverndokk. 1996. "Depletion of Fossil Fuels and the Impacts of Global Warming." *Resource and Energy Economics* 18 (2): 115–136.

Hofstede, Geert. 1980, 2001. *Culture's Consequences: Comparing Values, Behaviors, Institutions, and Organizations Across Nations.* Thousand Oaks, CA: Sage Publications.

Hogan, Michael J. 1987. *The Marshall Plan: America, Britain, and the Reconstruction of Western Europe, 1947–1952.* New York: Cambridge University Press.

Holbik, Karel. 1967. "Analysis of the Spanish Economic Miracle." *Quarterly Review of Economics and Business* 7 (4): 45–57.

Holmes, Thomas J., and James A. Schmitz. 2001. "A Gain from Trade: From Unproductive to Productive Entrepreneurship." *Journal of Monetary Economics* 47 (2): 417–446.

Hong, Sung Gul. 1997. *The Political Economy of Industrial Policy in East Asia: The Semiconductor Industry in Taiwan and South Korea.* Northampton, MA: Edward Elgar.

Honohan, Patrick, and Cormac O'Grada. 1998. "The Irish Macroeconomic Crisis of 1955–56: How Much Was Due to Monetary Policy." *Irish Economic and Social History* 24: 52–80.

Horowitz, Dan, and Moshe Lissak. 1989. *Trouble in Utopia: The Overburdened Polity of Israel.* Albany, NY: SUNY Press.

Hossain, Tanjim, and John Morgan. 2009. "The Quest for QWERTY." *American Economic Review* 99 (2): 435–440.

House, Robert J., Paul J. Hanges, Mansour Javidan, Peter W. Dorfman, and Vipin Gupta, eds. 2004. *Culture, Leadership and Organizations: The GLOBE Study of 62 Societies.* Thousand Oaks, CA: Sage.

Howe, Daniel Walker. 2009. *What Hath God Wrought: The Transformation of America, 1815–1848.* New York: Oxford University Press.

Hsueh, Roselyn. 2012. "China and India in the Age of Globalization: Sectoral Variation in Postliberalization Reregulation." *Comparative Political Studies* 45 (1): 32–61.

Hsueh, Roselyn. 2015. "State Capitalism, Chinese-Style: Strategic Value of Sectors, Sectoral Characteristics, and Globalization." *Governance* (forthcoming) doi:10.1111/gove.12139

Hughes, Thomas P. 1983. *Networks of Power: Electrification in Western Society 1880-1930.* Baltimore: John Hopkins University Press.

Huiyu, Caroline Tsai. 2009. *Taiwan in Japan's Empire Building: An Institutional Approach to Colonial Engineering.* New York: Routledge.

Hume, David. 1742. "On the Rise and Progress of the Arts and Sciences." In *Essays, Moral and Political,* Vol. 1, Part 1, Essay 14.

Hunck, J. M. 1965. "Problems of the Economic Miracle in Japan." *Aussen Politik* 16 (6): 424–436.

Hunt, Michie I., Linda Kotis, and Nancy Chockley. 2000. "Prescription Drugs and Intellectual Property Protection." Issue Brief. Washington D.C.:National Institute for Health Care Management.

The Independent. 2011. "Britain Finishes Last in League of World's Most Innovative Firms." November 15.

Institute of International Education. 2015. *Open Doors.* New York: Institute of International Education.

Institute of International Education. *Open Doors Database.* New York: Institute of International Education.

Institute of Medicine. 1995. *HIV and the Blood Supply: An Analysis of Crisis Decisionmaking.* Washington, DC: National Academy Press.

Intergovernmental Panel on Climate Change. 1995. *Climate Change 1995: The Science of Climate Change.* Geneva, Switzerland: United Nations.

Irwin, Douglas A. 2004. "The Aftermath of Hamilton's Report on Manufactures." *Journal of Economic History* 64 (3): 800–821.

Irwin, Douglas A., and Richard Sylla, eds. 2011. *Founding Choices: American Economic Policy in the 1790s.* Chicago: University of Chicago Press.

Isomura, S., and M. Mizogami. 1992. "The Low Rate of HIV Infection in Japanese Homosexual and Bisexual Men." *AIDS* 6 (5): 501–503.

Israel-U.S. Binational Industrial Research and Development Foundation. 2015. "The Bird Model." http://www.birdf.com.

Jackson, Andrew. 1826, 2002. "March 3, 1826. Letter to John Branch." In *The Papers of Andrew Jackson,* Vol. VI: *1825–1828,* ed. Sam B. Smith and Harriet Chappell Owsley. Knoxville, TN: University of Tennessee Press,141–143.

Jackson, Matthew O. 2008. *Social and Economic Networks.* Princeton, NJ: Princeton University Press.

Jacobs, J. Bruce. 2005. "'Taiwanization' in Taiwan's Politics." In *Cultural, Ethnic, and Political Nationalism in Contemporary Taiwan: Bentuhua,* ed. John Makeham and A-chin Hsiau, 17–54. New York: Palgrave Macmillan.

Jacoby, Neil H. 1966. *U.S. Aid to Taiwan: A Study of Foreign Aid, Self-Help, and Development.* New York: Praeger.

Jaffe, Adam B., and Josh Lerner. 2004. *Innovation and Its Discontents: How Our Broken Patent System Is Endangering Innovation and Progress, and What to Do About It.* Princeton, NJ: Princeton University Press.

Jaffe, Adam B., and Manuel Trajtenberg. 2002. *Patents, Citations, and Innovations: A Window on the Knowledge Economy Cambridge.* Cambridge, MA: MIT Press.

Jaffe, Adam, Manuel Trajtenberg, and Michael Fogarty, 2000. "The Meaning of Patent Citations: Report of the NBER/Case Western Reserve Survey of Patentees." Working Paper, 7631. Cambridge, MA: National Bureau of Economic Research.

Japan Management Association. 1989. *Kanban, Just-in-Time at Toyota: Management Begins at the Workplace.* Cambridge, MA: Productivity Press.

Jefferson, Thomas. 1782. Query 19: "Manufactures." Notes on the State of Virginia.

Jefferson, Thomas 1792. Papers of Thomas Jefferson, Vol. 24 (9 September 1792): 353.

Jefferson, Thomas. January 4, 1805. Letter to Mr. Lithson.

Jefferson, Thomas. January 20, 1809a. Letter to David Humphreys.

Jefferson, Thomas. June 28, 1809b. Letter to P. S. Dupont de Nemours.

Jefferson, Thomas. October 1, 1811. Letter to John Dortie.

Jefferson, Thomas. June 28, 1812. Letter to General Thaddeus Kosciusko.

Jefferson, Thomas. May 8, 1816. Letter to Charles Willson Peale.

Johnson, Chalmers. 1982. *MITI and the Japanese Miracle: The Growth of Industrial Policy, 1925–1975*. Stanford, CA: Stanford University Press.

Jones, Archer. 1987. *The Art of War in the Western World*. Champaign, IL: University of Illinois Press.

Jones, Daniel M., Stuart A. Bremer, and J. David Singer. 1996. "Militarized Interstate Disputes 1816-1992: Rationale, Coding Rules and Empirical Patterns." *Conflict Management and Peace Science* 15 (2): 163–215.

Jundt, Thomas. 2014. *Greening the Red, White, and Blue: The Bomb, Big Business, and Consumer Resistance in Postwar America*. New York: Oxford University Press.

Kadushin, Charles. 2012. *Understanding Social Networks: Theories, Concepts, and Findings*. New York: Oxford University Press.

Kafouros, Mario I., Peter J. Buckley, and Jeremy Clegg. 2012. "The Effects of Global Knowledge Reservoirs on the Productivity of Multinational Enterprises: The Role of International Depth and Breadth." *Research Policy* 41(5): 848–861.

Kaiser, Ulrich. 2002. "Measuring Knowledge Spillovers in Manufacturing and Services: An Empirical Assessment of Alternative Approaches." *Research Policy* 31 (1): 125–144.

Katz, Ralph and Thomas J. Allen. 1982. "Investigating the Not Invented Here (NIH) Syndrome: A Look at the Performance, Tenure and Communication Patterns of 50 R&D Project Groups." *R&D Management* 12: 7–19.

Kaufman, Leslie.1999. "Amazon Sues Big Bookseller over System for Shopping." *New York Times*, October 23, sec. C.

Keegan, John. 1993. *A History of Warfare*. New York: Vintage Books.

Keller, William W., and Richard J. Samuels, eds. 2003. *Crisis and Innovation in Asian Technology*. New York: Cambridge University Press.

Keller, Wolfgang. 2002. "Geographic Localization of International Technology Diffusion." *American Economic Review* 92 (1): 120–142.

Keller, Wolfgang, 2010. "International Trade, Foreign Direct Investment, and Technology Spillovers." In *Handbook of the Economics of Innovation*, ed. Bronwyn Hall and Nathan Rosenberg, 793–829. Amsterdam: Elsevier North-Holland.

Kellerman, E. W. 1988. *Science and Technology in France and Belgium*. New York: Longman.

Kelvin, Baron William Thomson, and Peter Guthrie Tait. 1890. *Treatise on Natural Philosophy*. London: Cambridge University Press.

Kendrick, John W. 1961. *Productivity Trends in the United States*. Princeton, NJ: Princeton University Press.

Kennedy, Paul. 1987. *The Rise and Fall of the Great Powers: Economic Change and Military Conflict from 1500 to 2000*. New York: Random House.

Kenney, Martin, and Richard Florida. 1993. *Beyond Mass Production: The Japanese System and its Transfer to the U.S.* New York: Oxford University Press.

Kenney, Martin, and Donald Patton. 2011. "Does Inventor Ownership Encourage University Research-Derived Entrepreneurship? A Six University Comparison." *Research Policy* 40 (8): SI 1100–1112.

Kihl, Young Whan. 2005. *Transforming Korean Politics: Democracy, Reform, and Culture*. Armonk, NY: M. E. Sharpe.

Kim, Linsu, and Richard R. Nelson, eds. 2000. "Technology, Learning and Innovation: Experiences of Newly Industrializing Economies." Cambridge and New York: Cambridge University Press.

Kim, Hee-Min. 2011. *Korean Democracy in Transition: A Rational Blueprint for Developing Societies*. Lexington: University Press of Kentucky.

Kim, Kyuryoon, ed. 2008. *North Korea's External Economic Relations*. Seoul: Korea Institute for National Unification.

Kim, Linsu, and Richard R. Nelson. 2000. *Technology, Learning and Innovation: Experiences of Newly Industrializing Economies*. New York: Cambridge University Press.

King, Timothy. 1970. *Mexico: Industrialization and Trade Policies Since 1940*. New York: Oxford University Press.

Kingston, Jeff. 2013. *Contemporary Japan: History, Politics, and Social Change Since the 1980s*. Malden, MA: Wiley-Blackwell.

Kleinman, Daniel Lee. 2010. "The Commercialization of Academic Culture and the Future of the University." In *The Commodification of Academic Research: Science and the Modern University*, ed. Hans Radder, 24–43. Pittsburgh, PA: University of Pittsburgh Press.

Knight, Alan. 1987. *US-Mexican Relations 1910-1940*. San Diego: Center for US-Mexican Studies, University of California.

Knoke, David. 2013. *Economic Networks*. Cambridge, UK: Polity Press.

Kodama, Fumio. 1991. *Analyzing Japanese High Technologies*. London: Pinter Publishers.

Kohut, Andrew. 2013. *America's Global Image Remains More Positive Than China's: But Many See China Becoming World's Leading Power*. Pew Global Attitudes Project. Washington, DC: Pew Research Center.

Koopman, Robert, and Zhi Wang. 2008. "How Much of Chinese Exports Is Really Made in China?: Assessing Foreign and Domestic Value-Added in Gross Exports." Working Paper, 2008-03-B. Washington, DC: Office of Economics, US International Trade Commission.

Kraemer, Kenneth L., Greg Linden, and Jason Dedrick. 2011. "Capturing Value in Global Networks: Apple's iPad and iPhone." Irvine: Personal Computing Industry Center, University of California-Irvine. http://pcic.merage.uci.edu/index.htm.

Krislov, Samuel. 1997. *How Nations Choose Product Standards and Standards Change Nations*. Pittsburgh, PA: University of Pittsburgh Press.

Krugman, Paul. 1991. "Increasing Returns and Economic Geography." *Journal of Political Economy* 99 (3): 483–499.

Krusell, Per, and Jose-Victor Ríos-Rull. 1996. "Vested Interests in a Positive Theory of Stagnation and Growth." *Review of Economic Studies* 63 (2): 301–329.

Kuhn, Thomas S. 1962. *The Structure of Scientific Revolutions*. Chicago: University of Chicago Press.

Kulve, Haico te, and Wim A. Smit. 2010. "Novel Naval Technologies: Sustaining or Disrupting Naval Doctrine." *Technological Forecasting & Social Change* 77: 999–1013.

Kuznets, Simon. 1930. *Secular Movements in Production and Prices*. Boston: Houghton Mifflin.

Kuznets, Simon. 1962. "Inventive Activity: Problems of Definition and Measurement." In *The Rate and Direction of Inventive Activity: Economic and Social Factors*, 19–52. New York: National Bureau for Economic Research.

Kuznets, Simon. 1966. *Modern Economic Growth: Rate Structure, and Spread*. New Haven, CT: Yale University Press.

Kuznetsov, Yevgeny N., and Carl J. Dahlman. 2008. *Mexico's Transition to a Knowledge-Based Economy: Challenges and Opportunities*. Washington, DC: World Bank.

Lakatos, Imre. 1976. *Proofs and Refutations*. Cambridge: Cambridge University Press.

Lake, David A. 2009. *Hierarchy in International Relations*. Ithaca, NY: Cornell University Press.

Landes, D. 1998. *The Wealth and Poverty of Nations*. New York: Norton & Company.

Landes, David, S. Joel Mokyr, and William J. Baumol, eds. 2010. *The Invention of Enterprise: Entrepreneurship from Ancient Mesopotamia to Modern Times*. Princeton, NJ: Princeton University Press.

Lang, R., and K. Danielsen. 2005. "Review Roundtable on Cities and the Creative Class." *Journal of the American Planning Association* 71 (2): 203–220.

Lanjouw, Jean O., and Mark Schankerman. 1997. "Stylized Facts of Patent Litigation: Value, Scope, and Ownership." Working Paper, 6297. Cambridge, MA: National Bureau of Economic Research.

Lanjouw, Jean O., and Mark Schankerman. 1999. "The Quality of Ideas: Measuring Innovation with Multiple Indicators." Working Paper, 7345. Cambridge, MA: National Bureau of Economic Research.

Lankov, Andrei. 2013. *The Real North Korea: Life and Politics in the Failed Stalinist Utopia.* New York: Oxford University Press.

Largent, Mark A., and Julia I. Lane. 2012. "STAR METRICS and the Science of Science Policy." *Review of Policy Research* 29(3): 431–438.

Lecuyer, Christophe. 2006. *Making Silicon Valley: Innovation and the Growth of High Tech, 1930-1970.* Cambridge, MA: MIT Press.

Lederman, Doug. 2010. "The Academic Pork Barrel." *Inside Higher Ed.,* April 29.

Lee, Heejin, and Sangjo Oh. 2008. "The Political Economy of Standards Setting by Newcomers: China's WAPI and South Korea's WIPI." *Telecommunications Policy* 32: 662–671.

Lee, Joseph. 1989. *Ireland, 1912-1985: Politics and Society.* New York: Cambridge University Press

Lee, Timothy. 2011. "Medical Mind Control: A New Breed of Patent May Determine How Your Doctor Makes Decisions." *Slate,* December 15.

Lengyel, Balázs, and Loet Leydesdorff. 2011. "Regional Innovation Systems in Hungary: The Failing Synergy at the National Level." *Regional Studies* 45 (5): 677–693.

Leong, Ho Khai. 2003. *Shared Responsibilities, Unshared Power: The Politics of Policy-Making in Singapore.* Singapore: Eastern Universities Press.

Leontief, Wassily. 1936. "Quantitative Input and Output Relations in the Economic System of the United States" *Review of Economics and Statistics* 18(3): 105–125.

Leslie, Stuart W. 1994. *The Cold War and American Science.* New York: Columbia University Press.

Levinson, Marc. 2006. *The Box: How the Shipping Container Made the World Smaller and the World Economy Bigger.* Princeton, NJ: Princeton University Press.

Levy-LeBoyer, Maurice, and Henri Morsel. 1994a. *Histoire Generale de L'Electricite en France,* Vol I: *Espoirs et Conquetes 1881-1918.* Paris, l'Association pour l'histoire de l'electricite en France.

Levy-LeBoyer, Maurice, and Henri Morsel. 1994b. *Histoire Generale de L'Electricite en France,* Vol II: *L'Interconnexion et le Marche 1919-1946.* Paris: l'Association pour l'histoire de l'electricite en France.

Lewis, Peter H. 1998. "Web Concern Gets Patent for Its Model of Business." *New York Times,* August 10, section D.

Lewis, Sarah. 2014. *The Rise: Creativity, the Gift of Failure, and the Search for Mastery.* New York: Simon & Schuster.

Leydesdorff, Loet, and Øivind Strand. 2013. "The Swedish System of Innovation: Regional Synergies in a Knowledge-Based Economy." *Journal of the American Society for Information Science and Technology* 64 (9): 1890–1902.

Liberwitz, Risa L. 2007. "University Science Research Funding: Privatizing Policy and Practice." In *Science and the University,* ed. Paula E. Stephan and Ronald G. Ehrenberg, 55–76. Madison: University of Wisconsin Press.

Liebowitz, Stan J., and Stephen E. Margolis. 1990. "The Fable of the Keys." *Journal of Law & Economics* 33 (1): 1–25.

Liebowitz, Stephen G. 2002. *Rethinking the Networked Economy: The True Forces Driving the Digital Marketplace.* New York: AMACOM.

Light, Donald W. 2007. "Misleading Congress About Drug Development." *Journal of Health Politics, Policy and Law* 32 (5): 895–913.

Light, Donald W., and Joel Lexchin. 2005. "Foreign Free Riders and the High Price of US Medicines." *British Medical Journal* 331: 958–960.

Light, Donald W., and Joel R. Lexchin. 2012. "Pharmaceutical Research and Development: What Do We Get for All That Money?" *British Medical Journal* 345: e4348.

Light, Donald W., and Rebecca Warburton. 2011. "Demythologizing the High Costs of Pharmaceutical Research." *Biosocieties* 6 (1): 34–50.

Lin, Grace Tyng-Ruu, Yo-Hsing Chang, and Yung-Chi Shen. 2010. "Innovation Policy Analysis and Learning: Comparing Ireland and Taiwan." *Entrepreneurship & Regional Development* 22 (7–8): 731–762.

Lin, Patrick, Keith Abney, and George A. Bekey, eds. 2012. *Robot Ethics: The Ethical and Social Implications of Robotics.* Cambridge, MA: MIT Press.

Lipsey, Richard G., and Kenneth I. Carlaw. 2004. "Total Factor Productivity and the Measurement of Technological Change." *Canadian Journal of Economics* 37 (4): 1118–1150.

List, Friedrich. 1841, 1916. *The National System of Political Economy*. Translated by Lloyd S. Sampson. New York: Longmans, Green, and Co.

Locke, Richard M. 1995. *Remaking the Italian Economy.* Ithaca, NY: Cornell University Press.

Long, Austin G. 2010. *First War Syndrome: Military Culture, Professionalization, and Counterinsurgency Doctrine*. Doctoral thesis, Department of Political Science, Massachusetts Institute of Technology.

Long, Austin, and Jodie Sweezey. 2005. *From Concept to Combat: Tomahawk Cruise Missile Program History and Reference Guide, 1972-2004.* Patuxent River, MD: Naval Air Systems Command.

Lorey, David E. 1993. *The University System and Economic Development in Mexico Since 1929.* Stanford, CA: Stanford University Press.

Louis, Roger Wm., and Avi Shlaim. 2012. *The 1967 Arab-Israeli War: Origins and Consequences.* New York: Cambridge University Press.

Lowen, Rebecca S. 1997. *Creating the Cold War University: The Transformation of Stanford.* Berkeley, CA: University of California Press.

Lundvall, Bengt-Ake. 1992. *National Innovation Systems: Towards a Theory of Innovation and Interactive Learning.* London: Pinter.

Lundvall, Bengt-Ake. 2004. "Introduction to 'Technological Infrastructure and International Competitiveness' by Christopher Freeman." *Industrial and Corporate Change* 13 (3): 531–539.

Lustig, Nora. 1998. *Mexico: The Remaking of an Economy.* 2nd ed. Washington, DC: Brookings Institution Press.

Mac Sharry, Ray, Padraic A. White, and Joseph O'Malley. 2000. *The Making of the Celtic Tiger: The Inside Story of Ireland's Boom Economy.* Cork, Ireland: Mercier Press.

MacLay, William. *Journal of William Maclay: United States Senator from Pennsylvania, 1789-1791.* (24 December 1790 entry).

MacLeod, Christine. 2007. *Heroes of Invention: Technology, Liberalism and British Identity, 1750-1914.* New York: Cambridge University Press.

Madison, James. 1792. *Papers of James Madison*. Vol. 14 (1 January 1792): 180.

Magnusson, Lars. 2000. *An Economic History of Sweden*. New York: Routledge.

Mahoney, James, and Kathleen Thelen. 2010. *Explaining Institutional Change: Ambiguity, Agency, and Power.* New York: Cambridge University Press.

Malerba, Franco. 2002. "Sectoral Systems of Innovation and Production." *Research Policy* 31: 247–264.

Man, Hong, Zhi Wang, and Kunfu Zhu. 2013. "Domestic Value-Added in China's Exports and Its Distribution by Firm Ownership. Office of Economics." Working Paper, 2013-05A. Washington, D.C.: US International Trade Commission.

Mankiw, Gregory N. 2006. "Raise the Gas Tax." *Wall Street Journal*, October 20.

Mankiw, Gregory N. 2009. "Smart Taxes: An Open Invitation to Join the Pigou Club." *Eastern Economic Journal* 35: 14–23.

Mankiw, Gregory N., David Romer, and David N. Weil. 1992. "A Contribution to the Empirics of Economic Growth." *Quarterly Journal of Economics* 107 (2): 407–437.

Mann, Jonathan M., and D. J. M. Tarantola, eds. 1996. *AIDS in the World II: Global Dimensions, Social Roots, and Responses.* New York: Oxford University Press.

Manthrope, Jonathan. 2005. *A Forbidden Nation: A History of Taiwan.* New York: Palgrave MacMillan.

Markevich, Andrei, and Mark Harrison. 2011. "Great War, Civil War, and Recovery: Russia's National Income, 1913 to 1928." *Journal of Economic History* 71 (3): 672–703.

Markoff, John. 2005. *What the Dormouse Said: How the Sixties Counterculture Shaped the Personal Computer Industry.* New York: Viking Penguin.

Marsden, Rhodri. 2011. "Are There Now So Many Patents in Silicon Valley That It's Impossible to Innovate?" *The Independent,* August 12. http://www.independent.co.uk

Marsh, Peter. 2012a. *The New Industrial Revolution: Consumers, Globalization and the End of Mass Production.* New Haven, CT: Yale University Press.

Marsh, Peter. 2012b. "China to Rival US Tech Knowhow, Say Execs." *Financial Times Online,* June 27.

Marshall, Alfred. 1890. *Principles of Economics.* Book IV, chap. X. London: Macmillan and Co.

Marshall, Monty G., Ted Robert Gurr, and Keith Jaggers. 2014. *Polity IV Project: Political Regime Characteristics and Transitions, 1800-2013.* Vienna, VA: Center for Systemic Peace.

Martin, Roderick. 1995. "New Technology in Fleet Street, 1975-1980." In *Resistance to New Technology,* ed. Martin Bauer, 189–206. New York: Cambridge University Press.

Martin, Xavier, and Robert Salomon. 2003. "Tacitness, Learning, and International Expansion: A Study of Foreign Direct Investment in a Knowledge-Intensive Industry." *Organization Science* 14 (3): 297–311.

Marukawa, Tomoo. 2010. *Chinese Innovations in Mobile Telecommunications: Third Generation vs. "Guerrilla Handsets."* La Jolla, CA: Conference on Chinese Approaches to National Innovation.

Marx, Leo. 1964. *The Machine in the Garden: Technology and the Pastoral Ideal in America.* New York: Oxford University Press.

Marx, Leo. 2010. "Technology: The Emergence of a Hazardous Concept." *Technology and Culture* 51 (3): 561–577.

Maskell, P., and A. Malmberg. 1999. "Localized Learning and Industrial Competitiveness." *Cambridge Journal of Economics* 23: 167–185.

Maurer, Stephen M., and Suzanne Scotchmer. 2004. "Institutions: A Brief Excursion Through History." In *Innovation and Incentives,* ed. Suzanne Scotchmer, 1–30. Cambridge, MA: MIT Press.

May, Christopher, and Susan Sell. 2006. *Intellectual Property Rights: A Critical History.* Boulder, CO: Lynne Rienner Publishers.

Mayer, Colin P., Koen Schoors, and Yishay Yafeh. 2005. "Sources of Funds and Investment Strategies of Venture Capital Funds: Evidence from Germany, Israel, Japan and the UK." *Journal of Corporate Finance* 11 (3): 586–608.

Mayo Collaborative Services v. Prometheus Laboratories, Inc., 566 US Supreme Court 2012. 10–1150.

McArdle, Megan. 2014. *The Up Side of Down: Why Failing Well Is the Key to Success.* New York: Viking Press.

McCallion, Stephen W. 1983. "Silk Reeling in Meiji Japan: The Limits to Change." PhD dissertation, Ohio State University.

McCarthy, Andrew, and Dermot Keogh. 2005. *Twentieth-Century Ireland: Revolution and State Building.* Dublin: Gill & MacMillan.

McClellan, James E., and Harold Dorn. 1999. *Science and Technology in World History: An Introduction.* Baltimore: Johns Hopkins University Press.

McClellan, James E., and Harold Dorn. 2006. *Science and Technology in World History.* Baltimore: Johns Hopkins University Press.

McCoy, Drew R. 1980. *The Elusive Republic: Political-Economy in Jeffersonian America.* Chapel Hill: University of North Carolina Press.

McMahon, Sean. 2009. *Bombs over Dublin.* Dublin: Currach Press.

McMillan, G. Steven, and Robert D. Hamilton. 2000. "Using Bibliometrics to Measure Firm Knowledge: An Analysis of the US Pharmaceutical Industry." *Technology Analysis & Strategic Management* 12 (4): 465–475.

McNeill, William H. 1982. *The Pursuit of Power: Technology, Armed Forces, and Society Since A.D. 1000.* Chicago: University of Chicago Press.

Medawar, Jean S., and David Pyke. 2001. *Hitler's Gift: The True Story of the Scientists Expelled by the Nazi Regime.* New York: Arcade Publishers.

Meir, Golda. 1975. *My Life*. New York: Dell Publishing.

Mele, Nicco. 2013. *The End of Big: How the Internet Makes David the New Goliath*. New York: St. Martin's Press.

Merry, Robert W. 2009. *A Country of Vast Designs: James K. Polk, the Mexican War, and the Conquest of the American Continent*. New York: Simon & Schuster.

Meyer, David R. 2003. *The Roots of American Industrialization*. Baltimore: Johns Hopkins University Press.

Meyer, Michael C., and William H. Beezley, eds. 2000. *The Oxford History of Mexico*. New York: Oxford University Press.

Meyer, Michael C., William L. Sherman, and Susan M. Deeds. 1999. *The Course of Mexican History*. New York: Oxford University Press.

Millard, Andre. 1981. "The Diffusion of Electric Power Technology in England, 1880-1914." PhD dissertation, Emory University.

Miller, Char. 2001. *Gifford Pinchot and the Making of Modern Environmentalism*. Washington, DC: Island Press.

Milner, H. V., and M. Austin. 2001. "Product Standards and International and Regional Competition." *Journal of European Public Policy* 8 (3): 411–431.

Mokyr, Joel. 1990. *The Lever of Riches: Technological Creativity and Economic Progress*. New York: Oxford Univ. Press.

Mokyr, Joel. 1992. "Technological Inertia in Economic History." *Journal of Economic History* 52 (2): 325–338.

Mokyr, Joel. 1994. "Cardwell's Law and the Political Economy of Technological Progress." *Research Policy* 23: 561–574.

Mokyr, Joel. 1998. "The Political Economy of Technological Change: Resistance and Innovation in Economic History." In *Technological Revolutions in Europe*, ed. Maxine Bergand and Kristin Bruland, 39–64. Cheltenham: Edward Elgar Publishers.

Mokyr, Joel. 2002. *The Gifts of Athena: Historical Origins of the Knowledge Economy*. Princeton, NJ: Princeton University Press.

Monroe, Kristen Renwick, Ronald B. Miller, and Jerome Tobis. 2008. *Fundamentals of the Stem Cell Debate: The Scientific, Religious, Ethnical, and Political Issues*. Berkeley: University of California Press.

Montagnier, Luc. 2000. *Virus: The Co-Discoverer of HIV Tracks Its Rampage and Charts the Future*. New York: W. W. Norton

Montalvo, Jose G., and Marta Reynal-Querol. 2005. "Ethnic Diversity and Economic Development." *Journal of Development Economics* 76 (2): 293–323.

Mooney, Chris C. 2005. *The Republican War on Science*. New York: Basic Books.

Moran Michael, Martin Rein, and Robert E. Goodin. 2008. *The Oxford Handbook of Public Policy*. New York: Oxford University Press.

Moreno-Brid, Juan Carlos, and Jaime Ros. 2009. *Development and Growth in the Mexican Economy: A Historical Perspective*. New York: Oxford University Press.

Morgan, Glenn, John Campbell, Colin Crouch, Ove Kaj Pedersen, and Richard Whitley, eds. 2010. *The Oxford Handbook of Comparative Institutional Analysis*. New York: Oxford University Press.

Morgan, Steven G., Keneth L. Bassett, James M. Wright, Robert Evans, Morris Barer, Patricia Caetano, et al. 2005. "'Breakthrough' Drugs and Growth in Expenditure on Prescription Drugs in Canada." *British Medical Journal* 331: 815–816.

Morgana, Steve, Paul Grootendorst, Joel Lexchine, Colleen Cunningham, and Devon Greyson. 2011. "The Cost of Drug Development: A Systematic Review." *Health Policy* 100: 4–17.

Morrell, Jack, and Arnold Thackray. 1981. *Gentlemen of Science: Early Years of the British Association for the Advancement of Science*. New York: Oxford University Press.

Morris-Suzuki, Tessa. 1994. *The Technological Transformation of Japan: From the Seventeenth to the Twenty-First Century*. New York: Cambridge Press.

Motola, D., F. DePonti, E. Poluzzi, N. Martini, P. Rossi, M. C. Silvani, et al. 2006. "An Update on the First Decade of the European Centralized Procedure: How Many Innovative Drugs?" *British Journal of Clinical Pharmacology* 62: 610–616.

Mowery, David, and Nathan Rosenberg. 1993. "The U.S. National Innovation System." In *National Innovation Systems: A Comparative Study*, ed. R. R. Nelson. New York: Oxford University Press 29–75.

Mowery, David, and Nathan Rosenberg. 1998. *Paths of Innovation: Technological Change in 20th-Century America.* New York: Cambridge University Press.

Mowery, David C., et al. 2004. *Ivory Tower and Industrial Innovation: University-Industry Technology Transfer Before and After the Bayh-Dole Act in the United States.* Stanford, CA: Stanford University Press.

Mukunda, Gautam. 2012. *Indispensable: When Leaders Really Matter.* Cambridge, MA: Harvard Business Review Press.

Munley, Vincent G., Robert J. Thornton, and J. Richard Aronson, eds. 2002. *The Irish Economy in Transition: Successes, Problems, and Prospects.* Boston: Elsevier.

Munoz, Sara Schaefer. 2005. "Court Denies Smucker Patent Bid." *Wall Street Journal*, April 11, sec. B.

Murnane, R. J. 2003. "The Skill Content of Recent Technological Change: An Empirical Exploration." *Quarterly Journal of Economics* 118 (4): 1279–1333.

Murphree, Michael. 2014. "The Political Economy of Standardization: The Chains of Structure and Choice." PhD dissertation in Science, Technology and International Affairs, Georgia Institute of Technology.

Murray, Williamson, and Allan R. Millett, eds. 1996. *Military Innovation in the Interwar Period.* New York: Cambridge University Press.

Nathan, John. 1999. *Sony: A Private Life.* New York: Houghton Mifflin.

National Bureau of Economic Research. 2011. "Patent Dataset." Cambridge, MA: National Bureau of Economic Research. http://www.nber.org/patents/.

National Center for Education Statistics. n.d. Washington, DC: US Department of Education. http://nces.ed.gov/surveys/international.

National Economic and Social Council. 1991. *The Economic and Social Implications of Emigration.* Dublin: NESC.

National Intelligence Council. 2012. *Global Trends 2030: Alternative Worlds.* Washington, DC: Office of the Director of National Intelligence.

National Research Council. 2005. *Rising Above the Gathering Storm: Energizing and Employing America for a Brighter Economic Future.* Washington, DC: National Academies Press.

National Research Council. 2010. *Rising Above the Gathering Storm, Revisited: Rapidly Approaching Category 5.* Washington, DC: National Academies Press.

National Research Council. 2012. *Improving Measures of Science, Technology, and Innovation.* Washington, DC: National Academies Press.

National Science Board. 1973. *Science Indicators 1972.* Washington, DC: National Science Foundation.

National Science Board. 2002. *Science Indicators 2002.* Washington, DC: National Science Foundation.

Nation Science Foundation. 2004. *Science and Engineering Indicators 2004.* Washington, DC: National Science Foundation.

Nation Science Foundation. 2012a. *Science and Engineering Indicators 2012.* Washington, DC: National Science Foundation.

National Science Foundation. 2012b. "Chapter 6: Industry, Technology, and the Global Marketplace." In *Science and Engineering Indicators 2012.* Washington, DC: National Science Foundation.

National Science Foundation. 2012c. *Higher Education Research and Development: Fiscal Year 2010.* Washington, DC: National Science Board.

National Statistics Bureau. "Republic of China (Taiwan)." Taipei, Taiwan: National Statistics Bureau.

Naubahar Sharif. 2006. "Emergence and Development of the National Innovation Systems Concept." *Research Policy* 35 (5): 745–766.

Neary, Peter J., and Cormac Ograda. 1991. "Protection, Economic War and Structural-Change—The 1930s in Ireland." *Irish Historical Studies* 27 (107): 250–266.

Needham, Joseph. 1954. *Science and Civilisation in China*. New York: Cambridge University Press.

Nelson, John R. Jr. 1979. "Alexander Hamilton and American Manufacturing: A Reexamination." *Journal of American History* 65: 971–995.

Nelson, John R. Jr. 1987. *Liberty and Property: Political Economy and Policymaking in the New Nation, 1789-1812*. Baltimore: Johns Hopkins University Press.

Nelson, Libby A. 2013. "Money for Military, Not Poli Sci." *Inside Higer Ed.*, March 21.

Nelson, Richard R. 1959. "The Simple Economics of Basic Scientific Research." *Journal of Political Economy* 67 (3): 297–306.

Nelson, Richard R., ed. 1993. *National Innovation Systems: A Comparative Analysis*. New York: Oxford University Press.

Nelson, Richard R. 1997. "How New Is New Growth Theory." *Challenge* 40 (5): 29–58.

Nelson, Richard R. 2005. *Technology, Institutions, and Economic Growth*. Cambridge, MA: Harvard Press.

Neufeld, Jacob. 1990. *The Development of Ballistic Missiles in the United States Air Force 1945–1960*. Washington, DC: Office of Air Force History, United States Air Force.

New York Times. 1860. "Scientific Progress and Prospects of Science in America." August 25.

New York Times. 1948. "The News of Radio." July 1.

New York Times. 1999. "Microsoft Sued By Priceline." October 14.

Niblo, Stephen R. 1995. *War, Diplomacy, and Development: The United States and Mexico 1938-1954*. Wilmington, DE: SR Books.

Noah, Timothy. 2013. "Political Science in the Crosshairs." *New Republic*, March 22.

Noland, Marcus. 2001. "North Korea's External Economic Relations." In *North Korea and Northeast Asia: New Patterns of Conflict and Cooperation*, ed. Samuel S. Kim and Tai Hwan Lee, 165–194. Lanham, MD: Rowan & Littlefield.

Nölke, Andreas, and Arjan Vliegenthart. 2009. "Enlarging the Varieties of Capitalism: The Emergence of Dependent Market Economies in East Central Europe." *World Politics* 61 (4): 670–702.

Nordhasus, William. 1972. "The Recent Productivity Slowdown." *Brookings Papers on Economic Activity* 3: 493–536.

Nordhaus, William D. 2013. *The Climate Casino: Risk, Uncertainty, and Economics for a Warming World*. New Haven, CT: Yale University Press.

North, Douglass. 1981. *Structure and Change in Economic History*. New York: Cambridge University Press.

North, Douglass. 1990. *Institutions, Institutional Change and Economic Performance*. New York, NY: Cambridge University Press.

North, Douglass, and Robert P. Thomas. 1973. *The Rise of the Western World: A New Economic History*. New York: Cambridge University Press.

Norton, Philip. 2010. *The British Polity*. 5th ed. New York: Longman Press.

Nussbaum, Bruce. 1980. *The Decline of U.S. power (And What We Can Do About It)*. Boston: Houghton Mifflin.

Oates, Wallace. 1972. *Fiscal Federalism*. New York: Harcourt Brace Jovanovich.

O'Brien, John Anthony. 1953. *The Vanishing Irish: The Enigma of the Modern World*. New York: McGraw-Hill.

O'Buachalla, Seamas. 1988. *Education Policy in Twentieth Century Ireland*. Dublin: Wolfhound Press.

O'Connor, Julia S. 2003. "Welfare State Development in the Context of European Integration and Economic Convergence: Situating Ireland within the European Union Context." *Policy and Politics* 31 (3): 387–404.

Odagiri, Hirioyuki, and Akira Goto. 1993. "The Japanese System of Innovation: Past, Present and Future." In *National Innovation Systems: A Comparative Study*, ed. R. R. Nelson. New York: Oxford University Press.

Office of the United States Trade Representative. 1994. *Foreign Trade Barriers*. Washington, DC: USTR.

O'Grada, Cormac. 1997. *A Rocky Road: The Irish Economy Since the 1920s*. Manchester, UK: Manchester University Press.

O'Hearn, Denis. 1998. *Inside the Celtic Tiger: The Irish Economy and the Asian Model*. Sterling, VA: Pluto Press.

Oinas, Paivi. 2005. "Finland: A Success Story?" *European Planning Studies* 13 (8): 1227–1244.

Oldenziel, Ruth. 1999. *Making Technology Masculine: Men, Women, and Modern Machines in America, 1870-1945*. Amsterdam: Amsterdam University Press.

Olds, Kris. 2007. "Global Assemblage: Singapore, Foreign Universities, and the Construction of a Global Education Hub." *World Development* 35 (6): 959–975.

Olson, Mancur. 1965. *The Logic of Collective Action: Public Goods and the Theory of Groups*. Cambridge, MA: Harvard University Press.

Olson, Mancur. 1982. *The Rise and Decline of Nations: Economic Growth, Stagflation, and Social Rigidities*. New Haven, CT: Yale University Press.

Olson, Mancur. 1996. "Distinguished Lecture on Economics in Government—Big Bills Left on the Sidewalk: Why Some Nations Are Rich, and Others Poor." *Journal of Economic Perspectives* 10 (2): 3–24.

Olson, Mancur, N. Sarna, and A. V. Swamy. 2000. "Governance and Growth: A Simple Hypothesis Explaining Cross-Country Differences in Productivity Growth." *Public Choice* 102 (3–4): 341–364.

O'Malley, Eoin, Nola Hewitt-Dundas, and Stephen Roper. 2008. "High Growth and Innovation with Low R&D: Ireland." In *Small Country Innovation Systems: Globalization, Change and Policy in Asia and Europe*, ed. Charles Edquist and Leif Hommen, 156–193. Northampton, MA: Edward Elgar Publishing.

O'Neill, Jim. 2001. "Building Better Global Economic BRICs." Global Economics Paper, 66 (66). New York: Goldman Sachs & Co.

O'Neill, Jim. 2013. "Who You Calling a BRIC?" *Bloomberg View*, November 12.

Oreskes, Naomi, and Erik M. Conway. 2010. *Merchants of Doubt: How a Handful of Scientists Obscured the Truth on Issues from Tobacco Smoke to Global Warming*. New York: Bloomsbury Press.

Organization for Economic Cooperation and Development. 1968. *Gaps in Technology: General Report*. Paris: OECD.

Organization for Economic Cooperation and Development. 1971. *The Conditions for Success in Technological Innovation*. Paris: OECD.

Organization for Economic Cooperation and Development. 1986. *Science and Technology Indicators*. Paris: OECD.

Organization for Economic Cooperation and Development. 1992. *Oslo Manual: Guidelines for Collecting and Interpreting Innovation Data*. Paris: OECD.

Organization for Economic Cooperation and Development. 1995. *Manual on the Measurement of Human Resources Devoted to S&T—Canberra Manual*. Paris: OECD.

Organization for Economic Cooperation and Development. 1999. "Technology Balance of Payments." In *STI Scoreboard of Indicators*, 96, chap. 11.5. Paris: OECD.

Organization for Economic Cooperation and Development. 2002. *Frascati Manual: Proposed Standard Practice for Surveys on Research and Experimental Development*. Paris: OECD.

Organization for Economic Cooperation and Development. 2003. *Science, Technology and Industry Scoreboard 2003-Towards a Knowledge-Based Economy*. Paris: OECD.

Organization for Economic Cooperation and Development. 2006. *OECD Economic Surveys: Ireland*. Paris: OECD.

Organization for Economic Cooperation and Development. 2009a. *OECD Reviews of Innovation Policy: Korea*. Paris: OECD.

Organization for Economic Cooperation and Development. 2009b. *OECD Reviews of Innovation Policy: Mexico*. Paris: OECD

Organization for Economic Cooperation and Development. 2012a. *Gross Domestic Expenditure on R&D, Science and Technology: Key Tables from OECD. No. 1*. Paris: OECD.

Organization for Economic Cooperation and Development. 2012b. *Italy: Reviving Growth and Productivity*. Paris: OECD.

Organization for Economic Cooperation and Development. 2012c. *Main Science and Technology Indicators*. Paris: OECD.

Organization for Economic Cooperation and Development. 2012d. *Mexico in OECD Science, Technology and Industry Outlook*. Paris: OECD.

Organization for Economic Cooperation and Development. 2013a. *Financing SMEs and Entrepreneurs 2013: An OECD Scoreboard*. Paris: OECD.

Organization for Economic Cooperation and Development. 2013b. *PISA 2012 Results: What Students Know and Can Do*. Vol. I. Paris: OECD.

Organization for Economic Cooperation and Development. 2013c. *Getting It Right: Strategic Agenda for Reforms in Mexico*. Paris: OECD.

Organization for Economic Cooperation and Development. 2014a. *OECD Factbook*. Paris: OECD.

Organization for Economic Cooperation and Development. 2014b. *OECD Main Science and Technology Indicators*. Paris: OECD

Organization for Economic Cooperation and Development. 2014c. *Education GPS Dataset*. Paris: OECD.

Organization for Economic Cooperation and Development. 2014d. *OECD-Eurostat Entrepreneurship Indicators Programme*. Paris: OECD.

O'Riain, Sean. 2004. *The Politics of High-Tech Growth: Developmental Network States in the Global Economy*. New York: Cambridge University Press.

O'Riain, Sean. 2014. *The Rise and Fall of Ireland's Celtic Tiger*. Cambridge: Cambridge University Press.

O'Riordan, Kate. 2010. *The Genome Incorporated: Constructing Biodigital Identity*. Burlington, VT: Ashgate.

Ornati, Oscar. 1963. "The Italian Economic Miracle and Organized Labor." *Social Research* 30 (4): 519–526.

Ornston, Darius. 2012. *When Small States Make Big Leaps: Institutional Innovation and High-Tech Competition in Western Europe*. Ithaca, NY: Cornell University Press.

Ornston, Darius. 2014. *Good Governance Gone Bad: Why Successful Societies Fail*. Unpublished manuscript.

Ozawa, Terutomo. 1974. *Japan's Technological Challenge to the West, 1950-1974: Motivation and Accomplishment*. Cambridge, MA: MIT Press.

Paarlberg, Robert. 2009. *Starved for Science: How Biotechnology Is Being Kept Out of Africa*. Cambridge, MA: Harvard University Press.

Pacey, Arnold. 1990. *Technology in World Civilization: A Thousand-Year History*. Cambridge, MA: MIT Press.

Pakes, Ariel. 1986. "Patents as Options: Some Estimates of the Value of Holding European Patent Stocks." *Econometrica* 54 (4): 755–784.

Papyrakis, Elissaios, and Pak Hung Mo. 2014. "Fractionalization, Polarization, and Economic Growth: Identifying the Transmission Channels." *Economic Inquiry* 52 (3): 1204–1218.

Parente, Stephen L., and Edward C. Prescott. 1994. "Barriers to Technology Adoption and Development." *Journal of Political Economy* 102 (2): 298–321.

Park, Walter G. 2008. "International Patent Protection: 1960–2005." *Research Policy* 37: 761–766.

Parker, Geoffrey. 1996. *The Military Revolution: Military Innovation and the Rise of the West, 1500-1800*. New York: Cambridge University Press.

Parthasarathy, Shobita. 2007. *Building Genetic Medicine: Breast Cancer, Technology, and the Comparative Politics of Health Care*. Cambridge, MA: MIT Press.

Patel, Prachi. 2010. "Outsourcing's Education Gap." *IEEE Spectrum*, September 1. http://spectrum.ieee.org/at-work/tech-careers/outsourcings-education-gap.

Patinkin, Don. 1967. *The Israel Economy: The First Decade*. Jerusalem: Maurice Falk Institute for Economic Research.

Paul, S. M., D. S. Mytelka, C. T. Dunwiddie, C. C. Persinger, B. H. Munos, S. R. Lindborg, et al. 2010. "How to Improve R&D Productivity: The Pharmaceutical Industry's Grand Challenge." *Nature Reviews Drug Discovery* 9: 203–214.

Peebles, Gavin. 2002. *Economic Growth and Development in Singapore: Past and Future*. Northampton, MA: Edward Elgar.

Pereira, Alexius A. 2007. "Transnational State Entrepreneurship? Assessing Singapore's Suzhou Industrial Park Project (1994–2004)." *Asia Pacific Viewpoint* 48 (3): 287–298.

Petricciani, J. C., J. S. McDougal, and B. L. Evatt. 1985. "Case for Concluding That Heat-Treated, Licensed Anti-Haemophilic Factor Is Free From HTLV-III." *Lancet* 2: 890–891.

Phelps, N. A., and F. Wu. 2009. "Capital's Search for Order: Foreign Direct Investment in Singapore's Overseas Parks in Southeast and East Asia." *Political Geography* 28 (1): 44–54.

Piech, Krzysztof, and Slavo Radosevic, eds. 2006. *The Knowledge-Based Economy in Central and Eastern Europe: Countries and Industries in a Process of Change*. New York: Palgrave Macmillan.

Pierce, Terry C. 2004. *Warfighting and Disruptive Technologies: Disguising Innovation*. New York: Frank Cass.

Pinkston, Daniel A. 2008. *The North Korean Ballistic Missile Program*. Carlisle Barracks, PA: Strategic Studies Institute, US Army War College.

Piore, Michael J., and Charles F. Sabel. 1984. *The Second Industrial Divide: Possibilities for Prosperity*. New York: Basic Books.

Pisano, Gary P., and Willy C. Shih. 2012. *Producing Prosperity: Why America Needs a Manufacturing Renaissance*. Boston, MA: Harvard Business Review Press.

Pliny. 77. *Natural History* 36.56.195. Loeb Classical Library, Cambridge, MA: Harvard University Press.

Plumer, Brad. 2013. "Is Outsourcing to Blame for Boeing's 787 Dreamliner Woes?" *Washington Post*, January 18, Wonk blog.

Poletti, Anna, and Julie Rak, eds. 2014. *Identity Technologies: Constructing the Self Online*. Madison, WI: University of Wisconsin Press.

Pollack, Kenneth. 2002. *Arabs at War: Military Effectiveness*. Lincoln: University of Nebraska Press.

Posen, Barry. 1984. *The Sources of Military Doctrine: France, Britain, and Germany between the World Wars*. Ithaca, NY: Cornell University Press.

Porter, Michael E. 1990. *The Competitive Advantage of Nations*. New York: Free Press.

Porter, Michael E. 1998a. "Clusters and the New Economics of Competition." *Harvard Business Review* 76 (6): 77–90.

Porter, Michael E. 1998b. *On Competition*. Boston: Harvard Business School Press.

Porter, Dale H. 1998c. *The Life and Times of Sir Goldsworthy Gurney: Gentleman Scientist and Inventor 1793-1875*. Cranbury, NJ: Associated University Presses.

Posen, Barry. 1984. *The Sources of Military Doctrine: France, Britain and Germany Between the World Wars*. Ithaca, NY: Cornell University Press.

Potter, Jonathan, and Gabriela Miranda. 2009. *Clusters, Innovation and Entrepreneurship*. Paris: OECD.

Powell, Walter W., and Kaisa Snellman. 2004. "The Knowledge Economy." *Annual Review of Sociology* 30: 199–220.

Pressman, Jeremy. 2008. *Warring Friends: Alliance Restraint in International Politics*. Ithaca, NY: Cornell University Press.

Price, Derek de Solla. 1963. *Little Science, Big Science*. New York: Columbia University Press.

Prior, Robin. 2001. "Conflict, Technology, and the Impact of Industrialization: The Great War 1914-18." *Journal of Strategic Studies* 24 (3): 128–157.

Pritchard, Charles L. 2007. *Failed Diplomacy: The Tragic Story of How North Korea Got the Bomb*. Washington, DC: Brookings Institution Press.

Przeworski, Adam. 2004. "Institutions Matter?" *Government and Opposition* 39 (4): 527–540.

Putnam, Robert D. 1993. *Making Democracy Work: Civic Traditions in Modern Italy*. Princeton, NJ: Princeton University Press.

Qian, Yingyi, and Barry R. Weingast. 1997. "Federalism as a Commitment to Preserving Market Incentives." *Journal of Economic Perspectives* 11 (4): 83–92.

R&D Magazine. 2014. "The Battelle Report." 2014 Global R&D Funding Forecast.

Radder, Hans. 2010. *The Commodification of Academic Research: Science and the Modern University*. Pittsburgh, PA: University of Pittsburgh Press.

Rafiqui, Pernilla S. 2010. "Varieties of Capitalism and Local Outcomes: A Swedish Case study." *European Urban and Regional Studies* 17 (3): 309–329.

Rajah, Jothie. 2012. *Authoritarian Rule of Law: Legislation, Discourse and Legitimacy in Singapore*. New York: Cambridge University Press.

Ranis, Gustav. 1978. "Equity with Growth in Taiwan: How 'Special' is the 'Special Case'?" *World Development* 6 (3): 397–409.

Raudzens, George. 1990. "War-Winning Weapons: The Measurement of Technological Determinism in Military History." *Journal of Military History* 54 (4): 403–434.

Raustiala, Kal, and Christopher Sprigman. 2012. *The Knockoff Economy: How Imitation Sparks Innovation*. New York: Oxford University Press.

Razin, Assaf, and Efraim Sadka. 1993. *The Economy of Modern Israel: Malaise and Promise*. Chicago: University of Chicago Press.

Razo, Armando. 2008. *Social Foundations of Limited Dictatorship: Networks and Private Protection During Mexico's Early Industrialization*. Stanford, CA: Stanford University Press.

Reich, Leonard S. 1985. *The Making of American Industrial Research: Science and Business at GE and Bell, 1876-1926*. New York: Cambridge University Press.

Reich, Robert B. 2010. *Aftershock: The Next Economy and America's Future*. New York: Alfred A. Knopf.

Reiffen, David, and Michael R. Ward. 2005. "Generic Drug Industry Dynamics." *Review of Economics and Statistics* 87 (1): 37–49.

Remini, Robert V. 2002. *John Quincy Adams*. New York: Times Books, Henry Holt and Company.

Research and Development. 1989. "Immigrant Scientists Get Help in Israel." 31 (7): 24. (Anonymous author)

Ridley, Jasper. 2001. *Maximilian and Juarez*. Phoenix, AZ: Phoenix Press.

Ringen, Seth, et al. 2011. *The Korean State and Social Policy: How South Korea Lifted Itself From Poverty and Dictatorship to Affluence and Democracy*. New York: Oxford University Press.

Riordan, Michael, and Lillian Hoddeson. 1997. *Crystal Fire: The Birth of the Information Age*. New York: Norton.

Ripley, Amanda. 2013. *The Smartest Kids in the World: And How They Got That Way*. New York: Simon & Schuster.

Ritchie, Thomas. 1825. "The President's Message. Splendid Government!" *Enquirer* (Richmond). December 10, 13.

Rodrik, Dani. 2007. *One Economics, Many Recipes: Globalization, Institutions, and Economic Growth*. Princeton, NJ: Princeton University Press.

Rogers, Everett. 1995. *Diffusion of Innovations*. New York: Free Press.

Rogers, Kenneth A., and Marvin G. Kingsley. 2007. *Calculated Risks: Highly Radioactive Waste and Homeland Security*. Burlington, VT: Ashgate Publishing.

Romer, Paul M. 1986. "Increasing Returns and Long-Run Growth." *Journal of Political Economy* 94 (5): 1002–1037.

Romer, Romer M. 1990. "Endogenous Technological Change." *Journal of Political Economy* 98 (5): S71–S102.

Roosevelt, Theodore. 1904. *Fourth Annual Message to Congress on 6 December 1904*.

Roper, Stephen, and Amnon Frenkel. 2000. "Different Paths to Success of the Growth of the Electronics Sector in Ireland and Israel." *Environment and Planning C: Government and Policy* 18: 651–665.

Rosen, Stephen Peter. 1991. *Winning the Next War*. Ithaca, NY: Cornell University Press.

Rosen, William. 2010. *The Most Powerful Idea in the World: A Story of Steam, Industry, and Invention*. New York: Random House.

Rosenberg, Nathan. 1976. *Perspectives on Technology*. New York: Cambridge University Press.

Rosenberg, Nathan. 1982. *Inside the Black Box: Technology and Economics*. New York: Cambridge University Press.

Rosenberg, Nathan, and L. E. Birdzell. 1985. *How the West Grew Rich: The Economic Transformation of the Industrial World*. New York: Basic Books.

Ross, Sydney B. 1962. "Scientist: The Story of a Word." *Annals of Science* 18 (2): 65–85.

Rossman, Joseph, and Barkev S. Sanders, 1957. "The Patent Utilization Study." *Patent, Trademark, and Copyright Journal* 1 (1): 74–111.

Rostow, Walt. W. 1960. *The Stages of Economic Growth: A Non-Communist Manifesto*. New York: Cambridge University Press.

Rouzioux, C., S. Chamaret, L. Montagnier, et al. 1985. "Absence of Antibodies to AIDS Virus in Haemophiliacs Treated with Heat-treated Factor VIII Concentrate." *Lancet* 1: 271–272.

Rowen, Henry S., Marguerite Gong Hancock, and William F. Miller. 2007. *Making IT: The Rise of Asia in High Tech*. Stanford, CA: Stanford University Press.

Roy, Denny. 1998. *China's Foreign Relations*. Lanham, MD: Rowman & Littlefield.

Roy, Denny. 2003. *Taiwan: A Political History*. Ithaca, NY: Cornell University Press.

Rubinstein, Murray A. 1999. *Taiwan: A New History*. Armonk, NY: M. E. Sharpe.

Rudolph, Frederick. 1962. *The American College and University: A History*. New Haven, CT: Yale University Press.

Ruegg, Walter, ed. 2004. *A History of the University in Europe*. Cambridge: Cambridge University Press.

Ruiz, Neil G. 2014. *The Geography of Foreign Students in U.S. Higher Education: Origins and Destinations*. Washington, DC: Brookings Institution.

Ruttan, Vernon W. 2006. *Is War Necessary for Economic Growth?: Military Procurement and Technology Development*. New York: Oxford University Press.

Saad, M., and G. Zawdie. 2005. "From Technology Transfer to the Emergence of a Triple Helix Culture: The Experience of Algeria in Innovation and Technological Capability Development." *Technology Analysis & Strategic Management* 17 (1): 89–103.

Sachar, Howard M. 1976. *A History of Israel: From the Rise of Zionism to Our Time*. New York: Alfred A. Knopf.

Samuels, Richard J. 1994. *"Rich Nation, Strong Army": National Security and the Technological Transformation of Japan*. Ithaca, NY: Cornell University Press.

Samuels, Richard J. 2007. *Securing Japan: Tokyo's Grand Strategy and the Future of East Asia*. Ithaca, NY: Cornell University Press.

Samuels, Warren J., Jeff E. Biddle, and John B. Davis, eds. 2003. *A Companion to the History of Economic Thought*. Malden, MA: Blackwell Publishing.

Sanders, Barkev S., J. Rossman, and L. J. Harris. 1958. "The Economic Impact of Patents." *Patent, Trademark, and Copyright Journal* 2 (2): 340–362.

Sanderson, Steven E. 1986. *The Transformation of Mexican Agriculture*. Princeton, NJ: Princeton University Press.

Sapolsky, Harvey, and Mark Z. Taylor. 2011. "Politics and the Science of Science Policy." In *Handbook of Science of Science Policy*, ed. John H. Marburger III, Kaye Husbands Fealing, Julia Lane, Bill Valdez, and Stephanie Shipp, 31–55. Stanford, CA: Stanford University Press.

Sarewitz, Daniel R. 1996. *Frontiers of Illusion: Science, Technology, and the Politics of Progress*. Philadelphia: Temple University Press.

Saxenian, AnnaLee. 1994. *Regional Advantage: Culture and Competition in Silicon Valley and Route 128*. Cambridge, MA: Harvard University Press.

Schatzberg, Eric. 2006. "'Technik' Comes to America: Changing Meanings of 'Technology' Before 1930." *Technology and Culture* 47 (3): 486–512.

Scherer, Frederic M. 1965. "Firm Size, Market Structure, Opportunity, and the Output of Patented Innovations." *American Economic Review* 55 (5): 1097–1125.

Scherer, Frederic M., et al. 1959. *Patents and the Corporation*. Boston: James Galvin & Assoc.

Schlaim, Avi. 2001. *The Iron Wall: Israel and the Arab World*. New York: W. W. Norton.

Schlefer, Jonathan. 2008. *Palace Politics: How the Ruling Party Brought Crisis to Mexico*. Austin: University of Texas Press.

Schmookler, Jacob. 1951. "Invention and Economic Development." PhD dissertation, University of Pennsylvania.

Schmookler, Jacob. 1954. "The Level of Inventive Activity." *Review of Economic Statistics* 36 (2): 183–190.

Schmookler, Jacob. 1966. *Invention and Economic Growth*. Cambridge, MA: Harvard University Press.

Schön, Lennart. 2012. *An Economic History of Modern Sweden*. New York: Routledge.

Schoultz, Lars. 1998. *Beneath the United States: A History of U.S. Policy Toward Latin America*. Cambridge, MA: Harvard University Press.

Schuler, Friedrich E. 1998. *Mexico Between Hitler and Roosevelt: Mexican Foreign Relations in the Age of Lázaro Cárdenas, 1934-1940*. Albuquerque, NM: University of New Mexico Press.

Schultz, T. W. 1958. "Output-Input Relationships Revisited." *Journal of Farm Economics* 40 (4): 924–932.

Schumpeter, Joseph A. 1911. *The Theory of Economic Development*. Piscataway, NJ: Transaction Publishers.

Schumpeter, Joseph A. 1939. *Business Cycles: A Theoretical, Historical and Statistical Analysis of the Capitalist Process*. New York: McGraw-Hill Book Company.

Schumpeter, Joseph A. 1942. *Capitalism, Socialism and Democracy*. New York: Harper.

Scott, Robert E. 2010. "Unfair China Trade Costs Local Jobs." EPI Briefing Paper, 260. Washington, DC: Economic Policy Institute.

Scott, Robert. 2011. "Growing U.S. Trade Deficit with China Cost 2.8 Million Jobs Between 2001 and 2010." Briefing Paper, 323. Washington, DC: Economic Policy Institute.

Segev, Tom. 1993. *The Seventh Million: The Israelis and the Holocaust*. New York: Hill and Wang.

Service, Robert. 2009. *A History of Modern Russia: From Tsarism to the Twenty-First Century*. Cambridge, MA: Harvard University Press.

Servín, Elisa, Leticia Reina, and John Tutino, eds. 2007. *Cycles of Conflict, Centuries of Change: Crisis, Reform, and Revolution in Mexico*. Durham, NC: Duke University Press.

Sexton, Jay. 2011. *The Monroe Doctrine: Empire and Nation in Nineteenth-Century America*. New York: Hill and Wang.

Shane, Scott. 1993. "Cultural Influences on National Rates of Innovation." *Journal of Business Venturing* 8 (1): 59–73.

Shapira, Philip. 1995. *The R&D Workers: Managing Innovation in Britain, Germany, Japan, and the United States*. Westport, CT: International Research Group on R&D Management, Quorum Books.

Sharma, Pankaj, B. S. Srinivasa Nookala, and Anubhav Sharma. 2012. "India's National and Regional Innovation Systems: Challenges, Opportunities and Recommendations for Policy Makers." *Industry and Innovation* 19 (6): 517–537.

Sharma, Ruchir. 2012. *Breakout Nations: In Pursuit of the Next Economic Miracles*. New York: W. W. Norton.

Shaw, J. V. W, ed. 1946. *A Survey of Palestine (December, 1945- January, 1946) Prepared for the Information of the Anglo-American Committee of Inquiry*. Beirut, Lebanon: Institute for Palestine Studies.

Sherid, Eugene R. 1992. "Thomas Jefferson and the Giles Resolutions." *William & Mary Quarterly* 49 (4): 589–609.

Shilts, Randy. 1987. *And the Band Played On: Politics, People, and the AIDS Epidemic*. New York: St. Martin's Press.

Shulman, Seth. 2006. *Undermining Science: Suppression and Distortion in the Bush Administration.* Berkeley: University of California Press.

Sidhu, Ravinder, K. C. Ho, and Brenda Yeoh. 2011. "Emerging Education Hubs: The Case of Singapore." *Higher Education* 61 (1): 23–40.

Simon, Denis Fred, and Michael Y. M. Kau. 1997. *Taiwan: Beyond the Economic Miracle.* Armonk, NY: M. E. Sharpe.

Sims, Richard L. 2001. *Japanese Political History Since the Meiji Renovation, 1868-2000.* New York: Palgrave.

Sinnott, Richard. 1995. *Irish Voters Decide: Voting Behaviour in the Republic of Ireland Since 1918.* Manchester, UK: Manchester University Press.

Sirilli, Giorgio. 1991. "The Technological Balance of Payments as an Indicator of Technology Transfer in OECD Countries. The Case of Italy." *Technovation* 11 (1): 3–25.

Sissine, Fred. 2012. *Renewable Energy R&D Funding History: A Comparison with Funding for Nuclear Energy, Fossil Energy, and Energy Efficiency R&D.* Washington, D.C.: Congressional Research Service.

Skolnikoff, Eugene B. 1993. *The Elusive Transformation: Science, Technology, and the Evolution of International Politics.* Princeton, NJ: Princeton University Press.

Smith, C. S. 1970. Quoted in White, K. D. 1984. *Greek and Roman Technology,* p. 27. Ithaca, NY: Cornell University Press. Cited as "Technology in History," *Minerva* 8: 470 [erratum].

Smith, Douglas K. 1988. *Fumbling the Future: How Xerox Invented, Then Ignored, the First Personal Computer.* New York: W. Morrow.

Smith, Keith. 2004. "Measuring Innovation." In *The Oxford Handbook of Innovation,* ed. Jan Fagerberg, David C. Mowery, and Richard R. Nelson, 148–178. New York: Oxford University Press.

Smith, Merritt Roe, ed. 1985. *Military Enterprise and Technological Change: Perspectives on the American Experience.* Cambridge, MA: MIT Press.

Smith, G. Teeling, and D. Taylor. 1984. "Health Services." In *UK Science Policy: A Critical Review of Policies for Publicly Funded Research,* ed. Maurice Goldsmith. New York: Longman Press.

Smyth, E., and D. Hannan. 2000. "Education and Inequality." In *Bust to Boom? The Irish Experience of Growth and Inequality,* ed. Brian Noland, Philip O'Connell, and Christopher Whelan, 109–126. Dublin: IPE.

Sohn, Dong-Won, and Martin M. Kenney. 2007. "Universities, Clusters, and Innovation Systems: The Case of Seoul, Korea." *World Development* 35 (6): 991–1004.

Solimano, Andrés, ed. 2008. *The International Mobility of Talent: Types, Causes, and Development Impact.* New York: Oxford University Press.

Solingen, Etel. 2007a. *Nuclear Logics: Contrasting Paths in East Asia and the Middle East.* Princeton, NJ: Princeton University Press.

Solingen, Etel. 2007b. "Pax Asiastica Versus Bella Levantina: The Foundations of War and Peace in East Asia and the Middle East." *American Political Science Review* 101 (4): 757–780.

Solleiro, Jose Luis, and R. Castanon. 2005. "Competitiveness and Innovation Systems: The Challenges for Mexico's Insertion in the Global Context." *Technovation* 25 (9): 1059–1070.

Solleiro, Jose Luis, and Claudia Gaona. 2012. "Promotion of a Regional Innovation System: The Case of the State of Mexico." *Procedia: Social & Behavioral Sciences* 52: 110–119.

Solow, Robert M. 1956. "A Contribution to the Theory of Economic Growth." *Quarterly Journal of Economics* 70 (1): 65–94.

Solow, Robert M. 1957. "Technical Change and the Aggregate Production Function." *Review of Economics and Statistics* 39 (3): 312–320.

Spar, Deborah. 2001. *Ruling the Waves: From the Compass to the Internet, a History of Business and Politics Along the Technological Frontier.* New York: Harcourt Brace.

Stafford, A. B. 1952. "Is the Rate of Invention Declining?" *American Journal of Sociology* 57 (6): 539–545.

Starr, Douglas. 1998. *Blood: An Epic History of Medicine and Commerce.* New York: Knopf.

Statistics Finland. 2013. "Demographic Statistics." Helsinki: Statistics Finland. https://www.stat.fi/org.

Stearns, Raymond. 1970. *Science in the British Colonies of America*. Urbana: University of Illinois Press.

Steelman, John R. 1947. *Science and Public Policy*. Washington, DC: Government Printing Office.

Steffen, Monika. 1992. "France: Social Solidarity and Scientific Expertise." In *AIDS Is the Industrialized Democracies. Passions, Politics and Policies*, ed. D. L. Kirp and R. Bayer, 221–251. New Brunswick, NJ: Rutgers University Press.

Steffen, Monika. 1999. "The Nation's Blood: Medicine, Justice, and the State in France." In *Blood Feuds: AIDS, Blood, and the Politics of Medical Disaster*, ed. Eric Feldman and Ronald Bayer, 95–126. New York: Oxford University Press.

Steinbock, Dan. 2001. *The Nokia Revolution: The Story of an Extraordinary Company That Transformed an Industry*. New York: AMACOM.

Sterling, Christopher H., Phyllis W. Bernt, and Martin B. H. Weiss. 2006. *Shaping American Telecommunications: A History of Technology, Policy, and Economics*. Mahway, NJ: Lawrence Erlbaum Associates Publishers.

Stern, Scott. 2004. "Do Scientists Pay to Be Scientists?" *Management Science* 50 (6): 835–853.

Stockholm International Peace Research Institute. Multiple years. *SPIRI Yearbook*. Stockholm, Sweden: Stockholm International Peace Research Institute.

Stone, Peter B. 1969. *Japan Surges Ahead: The Story of an Economic Miracle*. New York: Praeger.

Streeck, Wolfgang, and Kathleen Thelen, eds. 2005. *Beyond Continuity: Institutional Change in Advanced Political Economies*. New York: Oxford University Press.

Street, John, and Albert Weale. 1992. "Britain: Policy-Making in a Hermetically Sealed System." In *AIDS Is the Industrialized Democracies: Passions, Politics and Policies*, ed. D. L. Kirp and R. Bayer, 185–220. New Brunswick, NJ: Rutgers University Press.

Struve, Walter. 1963. "West Germany's Economic Miracle." *Current History* 44 (260): 231.

Suleiman, Ezra N. 1978. *Elites in French Society*. Princeton, NJ: Princeton University Press.

Sun, Yifei. 2002. "China's National Innovation System in Transition." *Eurasian Geography and Economics* 43 (6): 476–492.

Suny, Ronald. 2010. *The Soviet Experiment: Russia, the USSR, and the Successor States*. New York: Oxford University Press.

Surowiecki, James. 2004. *The Wisdom of Crowds: Why the Many Are Smarter Than the Few and How Collective Wisdom Shapes Business, Economies, Societies, and Nations*. New York: Doubleday.

Suttmeier, Richard P., Xiangkui Yao, and Alex Zixiang Tan. 2006. *Standards of Power? Technology, Institutions, and Politics in the Development of China's National Standards Strategy*. Seattle: National Bureau of Asian Research.

Swann, Peter G. M. 2000. *The Economics of Standardization: Final Report for Standards and Technical Regulations Directorate*. Manchester, UK: Department of Trade and Industry, Manchester Business School, University of Manchester.

Swann, Peter G. M. 2010. *The Economics of Standardization: An Update. Report for the UK Department of Business, Innovation and Skills (BIS)*. London: Innovative Economics Limited.

Swanson, Donald F. 1993. "Bank-Note Will Be but as Oak Leaves: Thomas Jefferson on Paper Money." *Virginia Magazine of History & Biography* 101 (1): 37–52.

Sweeney, Paul. 1998. *The Celtic Tiger: Ireland's Economic Miracle Explained*. Dublin: Oak Tree Press.

Sweezy, J., and Austin Long. 2005. *From Concept to Combat: Tomahawk Cruise Missile Program History and Reference Guide, 1972–2004*. Patuxent River, MD: Naval Air Systems Command.

Swinbanks, David. 1985. "AIDS: Undesirable Import to Japan." *Nature* 315: 8.

Swinbanks, David. 1986. "AIDS in Japan: Test Kit Market Opens Up." *Nature* 323: 384.

Swinbanks, David. 1988. "Japanese AIDS Scandal over Trials and Marketing of Coagulents." *Nature* 331: 552.

Swinbanks, David. 1996. "AIDS Researcher Hid Hemophiliac's Death." *Japan Times*, February 26.

Szöllösi-Janze, Margit. 2001. *Science in the Third Reich*. Oxford: Berg Press.

Talk of the Nation. 2011. "Will Patent Reform Bill Help or Hurt Inventors?" September 12, interview with James Bessen on National Public Radio.

Tan, Kenneth Paul. 2007. *Renaissance Singapore? Economy, Culture and Politics*. Singapore: National University of Singapore Press.

Taylor, George R. 1951. *The Transportation Revolution, 1815–1860*. New York: Rinehart.

Taylor, Mark Z. 1995. "Dominance Through Technology." *Foreign Affairs* 74 (6): 14–20.

Taylor, Mark Z. 2004. "Empirical Evidence Against Varieties of Capitalism's Theory of Technological Innovation." *International Organization* 58 (3): 601–631.

Taylor, Mark Z. 2007. "Political Decentralization and Technological Innovation: Testing the Innovative Advantages of Decentralized States." *Review of Policy Research* 24 (3): 231–257.

Taylor, Mark Z. 2009a. "Federalism and Technological Change in Blood Products." *Journal of Health Politics Policy and Law* 34: 863–898.

Taylor, Mark Z. 2009b. "International Linkages and National Innovation Rates: An Exploratory Probe." *Review of Policy Research* 26 (1–2): 127–149.

Taylor, Mark Z. 2012. "Toward an International Relations Theory of National Innovation Rates" *Security Studies* 21 (1): 113–151.

Taylor, Mark Z., and Sean P. Wilson. 2012. "Does Culture Still Matter?: The Effects of Individualism on National Innovation Rates." *Journal of Business Venturing* 27: 234–247.

Teardown.com. 2014. "Analysis: The Apple iPhone 6 & 6 Plus." Ottawa, Canada. http://www.techinsights.com/teardown.com/apple-iphone-6/.

Telesis Consulting Group. 1982. *A Review of Industrial Policy*. Dublin: National Economic and Social Council.

Temin, Peter. 1997. "Is It Kosher to Talk About Culture?" *Journal of Economic History* 57 (2): 267–287.

Thomas, Baylis. 1999. *How Israel Was Won: A Concise History of the Arab-Israeli Conflict*. Lanham, MD: Lexington Books.

Thompson, Edward P. 1964. *The Making of the English Working Class*. New York: Pantheon.

Thompson, Eric C. 2014. "Immigration, Society and Modalities of Citizenship in Singapore." *Citizenship Studies* 18 (3–4): 315–331.

Thomson-ISI. 2013. *STEM Publications Data*.

Thursby, Jerry G., and Marie C. Thursby. 2007. "Patterns of Research and Licensing Activity of Science and Engineering Faculty." In *Science and the University*, ed. Paula E. Stephan and Ronald G. Ehrenberg, 77–93. Madison: University of Wisconsin Press.

Tiebout, Charles. 1956. "A Pure Theory of Local Expenditures." *Journal of Political Economy* 64 (5): 416–424.

Timmons, Todd. 2005. *Science and Technology in Nineteenth-Century America*. Westport, CT: Greenwood Press.

Tinbergen, J. 1942. "Zur Theorie der Langfirstigen Wirtschaftsentwicklung." *Weltwirtschaftliches Archiv* 55: 511–549.

Todd, Edmund Neville III. 1984. "Technology and Interest Group Politics: Electrification of the Ruhr, 1886-1930." PhD dissertation, University of Pennsylvania.

Toren, Nina. 1994. "Professional-Support and Intellectual-Influence Networks of Russian Immigrant Scientists in Israel." *Social Studies of Science* 24 (4): 725–743.

Trajtenberg, Manuel. 1990. "A Penny for Your Quotes: Patent Citations and the Value of Innovations." *RAND Journal of Economics* 21 (1): 172–187.

Trajtenberg, Manuel. 2001. "Innovation In Israel 1968-1997: A Comparative Analysis Using Patent Data." *Research Policy* 30: 363–389.

Tranquillus, Gaius Suetonius. c. 100 AD. "The Life of Vespasian." In *The Lives of the Twelve Caesers*.

Trumball, Gunnar. 2012. *Strength in Numbers: The Political Power of Weak Interests*. Cambridge, MA: Harvard University Press.

Tsebelis, George. 2002. *Veto Players: How Political Institutions Work*. Princeton, NJ: Princeton University Press.

Tsurumi, E. Patricia. 1977. *Japanese Colonial Education in Taiwan, 1895-1945*. Cambridge, MA: Harvard University Press.

Tylecote, Andrew, and Francesca Visintin. 2008. *Corporate Governance, Finance and the Technological Advantage of Nations*. New York: Routledge.

Tyson, Laura D'Andrea. 1992. *Who's Bashing Whom: Trade Conflicts in High-Technology Industries*. Washington, DC: Institute for International Economics.

Tyson, Laura D'Andrea, and John Zysman, eds. 1983. *American Industry in International Competition: Political and Economic Perspectives*. Ithaca, NY: Cornell University Press

US Congress. 1950. Public Law 81–507.

US Congress. 1968. Public Law 90–407.

US Congress. 1992. Office of Technology Assessment. *Global Standards: Building Blocks for the Future*. Washington, DC: US Government Printing Office.

US Department of Commerce, Bureau of the Census. 1975. Historical Statistics of the United States, Colonial Times to 1970, Part II. Upp. 127, 967.

US Department of Education, Institute of Education Sciences, National Center for Education Statistics. Washington, D.C.

US Department of State. 1976. *Foreign Relations of the United States, 1969-1976*. Vol. XXXIII, SALT II, 1972–1980, Document 137. Paper prepared by the National Security Council Staff. Washington, July 15, 1975. Ford Library, National Security Adviser, Kissinger-Scowcroft West Wing Office Files, Box 33, USSR, Gromyko File, October 1, 1976.

US Department of State. 2001. *2000 Country Reports on Economic Policy and Trade Practices: Ireland*. Washington DC: Bureau of Economic and Business Affairs, US State Department.

US Energy Information Agency. 2015. *U.S. Imports by Country of Origin (Total Crude Oil and Products)*. Washington, D.C.: U.S. Department of Energy.

US Strategic Air Command. 1959. "History of the Strategic Air Command: 1 January 1958–30 June 1958." *Historical Study Number* 73 (1): 88–90.

United Nations. 2015. UNESCO Institute for Statistics. New York.

United Nations Conference on Trade and Development. 2003. *Investment and Technology Policies for Competitiveness: Review of Successful Country Experiences*. New York: United Nations.

United Nations General Assembly. 1951. *General Progress Report and Supplementary Report of the United Nations Conciliation Commission for Palestine*. New York: United Nations.

United States of America v. International Business Machines Corporations, 1956 Civil Action No. 72-344. United States District Court for the Southern District of New York.

Utterback, James M. 1996. *Mastering the Dynamics of Innovation*. Boston: Harvard Business School Press.

Van Egeraat, Chris. 2010. "The Scale and Scope of Process R&D in the Irish Pharmaceutical Industry." *Irish Geography* 43 (1): 35–58.

Van Egeraata, Chris, and Frank Barry. 2009. "The Irish Pharmaceutical Industry over the Boom Period and Beyond." *Irish Geography* 42 (1): 23–44.

Van Luijn, Johan, Frank Gribnau, and Hubert G. M. Leufkens. 2010. "Superior Efficacy of New Medicines?" *European Journal of Clinical Pharmacology* 66: 445–448.

Van Staaveren, Jacob. 1962. *Air Operations in the Taiwan Crisis of 1958*. Washington, DC: Air Force Historical Division Liaison Office.

Varsakelis, Nikos C. 2006. "Education, Political Institutions and Innovative Activity: A Cross-Country Empirical Investigation." *Research Policy* 35 (7): 1083–1090.

Vazquez, Josefina Zoraida, and Lorenzo Meyer. 1985. *The United States and Mexico*. Chicago: University of Chicago Press.

Vest, Charles M. 2007. *The American Research University from World War II to World Wide Web*. Berkeley: University of California Press.

Veysey, Laurence R. 1964. *The Emergence of the American University*. Chicago: University of Chicago Press.

Villa, Agostino, and Dario Antonelli. 2009. *A Road Map to the Development of European SME Networks: Towards Collaborative Innovation*. London: Springer.

Von Hippel, Eric. 1988. *The Sources of Innovation.* New York: Oxford University Press

Von Hippel, Eric. 2005. *Democratizing Innovation.* Cambridge, MA: MIT Press.

Wagner, Caroline S. 2008. *The New Invisible College: Science for Development.* Washington, DC: Brookings Institution Press.

Walker, Jack L. 1969. "The Diffusion of Innovations Among the Various States." *American Political Science Review* 63 (3): 880–899.

Wall Street Journal. 1999. "Amazon.com Is Awarded Patent." October 13, section C.

Walsh, Brendan. 1999. "The Persistence of High Unemployment in a Small Open Labor Market: The Irish Case." In *Understanding Ireland's Economic Growth,* ed. F. Barry, 193–226. London: Macmillan.

Walterscheid, Edward C. 1998. "Thomas Jefferson and the Patent Act of 1793." In *Essays in History,* 40. Charlottesville, VA: Corcoran Department of History at the University of Virginia.

Washington, George. 1790. *First Annual Message to Congress on 8 January 1790.*

Wei, George C. X. 2012. *China-Taiwan Relations in a Global Context: Taiwan's Foreign Policy and Relations.* New York: Routledge.

Weingast, Barry R. 1995. "The Economic Role of Political Institutions: Market-Preserving Federalism and Economic Development." *Journal of Law, Economics, and Organization* 11 (1): 1–31.

Franklin, Marianne. 2013. *Digital Dilemmas: Power, Resistance, and the Internet.* New York: Oxford University Press.

Weiss, Linda. 2014. *America Inc?: Innovation and Enterprise in the National Security State.* Cornell, NY: Cornell University Press.

Wendling, Amy E. 2009. *Karl Marx on Technology and Alienation.* New York: Palgrave Macmillan

West, Darrell M. 2010. *Brain Gain: Rethinking U.S. Immigration Policy.* Washington, DC: Brookings Institution Press.

Wexler, Imanuel. 1983. *The Marshall Plan Revisited: The European Recovery Program in Economic Perspective.* Westport, CT: Greenwood Press.

Whitaker, Ken T. 1958. *Economic Development.* Dublin: Department of Finance.

White, Gilbert C. 2010. "Hemophilia: An Amazing 35-Year Journey from the Depths of HIV to the Threshold of Cure." *Transactions of the American Clinical and Climatological Association* 121: 61–75.

White, Paul. 2003. *Thomas Huxley: Making the "Man of Science."* New York: Cambridge University Press.

White, Shira P., and G. Patton Wright. 2002. *New Ideas About New Ideas: Insights on Creativity from the World's Leading Innovators.* Cambridge, MA: Perseus Pub.

Whitford, Josh. 2005. *The New Old Economy: Networks, Institutions, and the Organizational Transformation of American Manufacturing.* New York: Oxford University Press.

Whitford, Josh, and Andrew Shrank. Forthcoming. *When Networks Fail.* Princeton, NJ: Princeton University Press.

Whitley, Richard. 1972. "Black Boxism and the Sociology of Science: A Discussion of the Major Developments in the Field." *Sociological Review Monograph: The Sociology of Science* 18: 61–92.

Wiles, James L., and Richard D. Finnegan. 1993. *Aspirations and Realities: A Documentary History of Economic Development Policy in Ireland Since 1922.* Westport, CT: Greenwood Press

Williamson, Oliver. 1975. *Markets and Hierarchies.* New York: Free Press.

Williamson, Oliver. 1985. *The Economic Institutions of Capitalism: Firms, Markets, Relational Contracting.* New York: Free Press.

Wills, Clair. 2007. *That Neutral Island: A Cultural History of Ireland During the Second World War.* London: Faber and Faber.

Wilson, Richard. 2008. "Policy Analysis as Policy Advice." In *The Oxford Handbook of Public Policy,* ed. Michael Moran, Martin Rein, and Robert E. Goodin, 152–168. New York: Oxford University Press.

Winner, Langdon. 1977. *Autonomous Technology: Technics-Out-of-Control as a Theme in Political Thought.* Cambridge, MA: MIT Press.

Wired News Report. 1999. "Mars Mission's Metric Mixup." September 30.

Wirls, Daniel. 2010. *Irrational Security: The Politics of Defense from Reagan to Obama.* Baltimore: Johns Hopkins University Press.

Wolfe, David A. 2009. Special Issue on Embedded Clusters in the Global Economy. *European Planning Studies* 17 (2): 179–343.

Wolfe, Tom. 1979. *The Right Stuff.* New York: Bantam Books.

Womack, James P. 1981. *The Decline of the American Auto Industry and the Search for Industrial Policy.* Cambridge, MA: Future of the Automobile Program.

Wong, Joseph. 2011. *Betting on Biotech: Innovation and the Limits of Asia's Developmental State.* Ithaca, NY: Cornell University Press.

Wong, Poh-Kam, Yuen-Ping Ho, and Annette Singh. 2007. "Towards an 'Entrepreneurial University' Model to Support Knowledge-Based Economic Development: The Case of the National University of Singapore." *World Development* 35 (6): 941–958.

Wood, Gordon S. 2009. *Empire of Liberty: A History of the Early Republic, 1789-1815.* New York: Oxford University Press.

Wood, Reed M., and Mark Gibney. 2010. "The Political Terror Scale (PTS): A Re-Introduction and a Comparison to CIRI." *Human Rights Quarterly* 32: 367–400.

World Bank. 2008. *Unleashing Prosperity: Productivity Growth in Eastern Europe and the Former Soviet Union.* Washington, DC: World Bank.

World Bank. 2014. *World Development Indicators.* Washington, DC: World Bank.

World Health Organization. 2015. *Global Health Observatory.* New York: United Nations.

World Trade Organization. *Overview: The TRIPS Agreement.* Geneva, Switzerland: WTO.

Xing, Yuqing, and Neal Detert. 2010. "How the iPhone Widens the United States Trade Deficit with the People's Republic of China." ADBI Working Paper Series, 257. Tokyo: Asian Development Bank Institute.

Yager, Joseph A. 1988. *Transforming Agriculture in Taiwan.* Ithaca, NY: Cornell University Press.

Yamashita, Shoichi, ed. 1991. *Transfer of Japanese Technology and Management to the ASEAN Countries.* Tokyo: University of Tokyo Press.

Yang, Maochun. 1970. *Socio-Economic Results of Land Reform in Taiwan.* Honolulu, HI: East-West Center Press.

Yao, Xiang, Shuhong Wang, Junhua Dang, and Lei Wang. 2012. "The Role of Individualism-Collectivism in the Individual Creative Process." *Creativity Research Journal* 24 (4): 296–303.

Yeo, Richard. 1993. *Defining Science: William Whewell, Natural Knowledge, and Public Debate in Early Victorian Britain.* Cambridge: Cambridge University Press.

Yeoh, C., W. P. N. How, and A. L. Leong. 2005. "Creative Enclaves for Enterprise: An Empirical Study of Singapore's Industrial Parks in Indonesia, Vietnam and China." *Entrepreneurship and Regional Development* 17 (6): 479–499.

Zeng, Saixing, Xuemei Xie, and Chimign Tam. 2010. "Evaluation Innovation Capabilities for Science Parks: A System Model." *Technological and Economic Development of Economy* 16 (3): 397–413.

INDEX

CPSIA information can be obtained
at www.ICGtesting.com
Printed in the USA
BVHW042250130619
550986BV00003B/6/P